On Real Relation

(Disputatio Metaphysica XLVII)

Francisco Suárez, S.J.

On Real Relation
(Disputatio Metaphysica XLVII)

A Translation from the Latin, with an Introduction and Notes

by

John P. Doyle
Professor of Philosophy
St. Louis University

MARQUETTE
UNIVERSITY

PRESS

Library of Congress Cataloging-in-Publication Data

Suárez, Francisco, 1548-1617.
  [Disputationes metaphysicae. 47. English & Latin]
  On real relation = (Disputatio metaphysica XLVII) / Francisco Suárez ; a translation from
the Latin, with an introduction and notes, by John P. Doyle.
      p. cm. — (Medieval philosophical texts in translation ; no. 42)
  Includes bibliographical references (p.   ) and indexes.
  ISBN-13: 978-0-87462-245-4 (pbk. : alk. paper)
  ISBN-10: 0-87462-245-X (pbk. : alk. paper)
  1. Relation (Philosophy) 2. Ontology. 3. Transcendentals. I. Doyle, John P., 1930- II.
Title. III. Mediaeval philosophical texts in translation ; no. 42.
  B785.S823D5713 2006
  111—dc22
                                                                          2006003693

⊗The paper used in this publication meets the minimum requirements of the
American National Standard for Information Sciences—
Permanence of Paper for Printed Library Materials, ANSI Z39.48-1992.

MARQUETTE UNIVERSITY PRESS
MILWAUKEE

The Association of Jesuit University Presses

To Mary Gale
My Devoted Wife of Forty-Three Years,
the Loving Mother of Our Children
and Dear Grandmother of Their Children,
with Affection & Gratitude.

Contents

I. INTRODUCTION:

A. Suárez, the Man, his Work, and his Place in the
History of Philosophy 9

B. Suárez as a Disciple of Aristotle. 16

C. Relation in Aristotelian Philosophy 19

  1. Principal Places in which Aristotle treats the Category of Relation:
Categories, c. 7 and *Metaphysics* V, c. 15. 19

  2. A Wider Overview 19

  3. Some Connected Issues. 21

    (a) The Aristotelian Division of Being 22

    (b) The Nature of the Categories 22

    (c) Relation and the Last Six Categories. 24

D. Suárez on Relation

  1. Two chief places in the *Disputationes metaphysicae*: 26
Disputation 47 and Disputation 54, Section 6. The Dividing Line
between Real Being in the Categories and Being of Reason 26

  2. Some other places in the *Disputationes*. 26

  3. Some Theological Concerns—Christian Dimensions both in Suárez's
sources and in his own Doctrine—especially Trinity and Incarnation 27

E. Summaries of the Sections of Disputation 47. 28

II. Translator's Notes

The Terminology of Relation 33

III. DISPUTATION FORTY-SEVEN: "About Created Real Relations"— ..
English Translation 37

Section I. Whether Relation Is a True Category of Real Being,
Different from Other Categories? 40

Section II. Whether a Categorical Relation Is Actually and Really
Distinguished from All Absolute Beings? 57

Section III. How Many Kinds of Relation Exist?
And Which Is Truly Categorical? 79

Section IV. How Does a Categorical Relation Differ from a
Transcendental One? 91

Section V. What Is the Essential Definition of a Categorical Relation? . 107

Section VI. About the Subject of a Categorical Relation 117

Section VII. About the Foundation of a Categorical Relation and
about the Reason for That Foundation 123

Section VIII. About the Terminus of a Categorical Relation 133

Section IX. What Distinction Must There Be between the Foundation and the Terminus of a Relation?... 143
Section X. Whether Three Kinds of Relatives Were Correctly Divided on a Threefold Basis by Aristotle? 149
Section XI. About the First Kind of Relations, Based on Number or Unity.. 163
Section XII. About the Second Kind of Relations, Based on Potency or Action 177
Section XIII. About the Third Kind of Relations, Based on the Character of Measure... 185
Section XIV. Is the Mentioned Division Sufficient, and Does It Comprehend All Relations? 191
Section XV. Whether All the Relations of the Third Kind, and Only These, Are Non-Mutual?—Where We Discuss the Relations of God to Creatures.. 197
Section XVI. Is the Formal Terminus of a Relation Another Relation or Some Absolute Character?—Where Incidentally Various Questions Are Also Explained 219
Section XVII. In What Way the Category "Toward Something" Can Be Ordered under One Supreme Genus.—Where We Also Discuss the Individual Distinction of Relations 245
Section XVIII. What Are the Properties of a Relation?.......................... 263
IV. DISPUTATION FORTY-SEVEN: "De Relationibus Realibus Creatis" —A Latin Transcription 267
V. Persons Mentioned by Suárez in the Forty-Seventh Disputation......... 407
VI. Bibliography.. 411
VII. Index of Names.. 419
VIII. Subject Index... 423

Introduction

A. Suárez, the Man, His Work, and His Place in the History of Philosophy.[1]

Although this is ground well traveled, both by others and by me in earlier publications, it is I think useful to travel it once more for readers who are comparatively unaquainted with Suárez and his work.

Francisco Suárez was born at Granada in Spain on January 5, 1548. In 1561, he enrolled at the University of Salamanca, where he began his study of Law, an interest he would have for the rest of his life. In 1564 he entered the Jesuits, i.e., the Society of Jesus, which had been founded thirty years before by St. Ignatius of Loyola (1491-1556). In October 1566, following two years of philosophical education, he began to study theology, still at Salamanca. In this study, the best known and most important of his teachers was the Dominican, Juan Mancio (1497-1576), who was, fourth in succession after the famous Francisco de Vitoria (1492/3-1546), holding Salamanca's principal chair (*Cátedra de Prima*) of theology.

In 1570 Suárez started to teach philosophy, first at Salamanca and then at Segovia. He was ordained a priest in March 1572, and he continued to lecture in philosophy until, in September 1574, at the Jesuit College, Valladolid, he began what would be his life's work as a theology teacher for the Society. In time after, he taught theology at Avila (1575), Segovia (1575), Valladolid again (1576), Rome (1580), Alcalá (1585), and Salamanca (1593). In 1597, at the request of King Philip II, he accepted the principal chair of theology at the University of Coimbra, where in 1612 he published the distillate of his legal teaching in his treatise, "On Laws," (*De legibus*). He remained at Coimbra until his retirement in 1615. On 25 September 1617, he died in Lisbon.

---

1 For details of Suárez's life, see Raoul De Scorraille, S.J., *François Suarez de la Compagnie de Jésus*, 2 vols., Paris, 1911-13. In English see Joseph Fichter, *Man of Spain, Francis Suarez*, New York, 1940. For a shorter but yet reliable source, cf. P. Monnot, "Suarez, François. I. Vie et oeuvres," in *Dictionnaire de Théologie Catholique*, XIV, 2₀ partie (Paris, 1941) cols. 2638-2649. For more recent presentations, cf. Jorge J.E. Gracia, "Francisco Suárez: The Man in History," *The American Catholic Philosophical Quarterly*, LXV (1991), pp. 259-266; Carlos Noreña, "Suárez and the Jesuits," ibid., pp. 267-286, and John P. Doyle, "Suárez, Francisco," *Routledge Encyclopedia of Philosophy* (London/New York: Routledge, 1998), vol. 9, pp. 189-196. Also see Jacob Schmutz: "Francisco Suárez, S.J." at http://www.ulb.ac.be/philo/scholasticon/nomenS.htm#suarez.

Beyond his teaching, Suárez engaged in theological and political debates. the most famous of these was the controversy *De auxiliis* ("On the Helps [for Salvation]"). Between Jesuits and Dominicans, debate here centered on God's foreknowledge and causality, grace and human freedom. Suárez, with his fellow Jesuits, St. Robert Bellarmine (1542-1621) and Luis Molina (1535-1600), allowed for divine prerogatives but also championed human free will. Less metaphysical was the dispute between the Republic of Venice and the papacy about the limits of papal jurisdiction. In the course of this dispute Suárez in 1607 composed (but did not publish) a pro-papal treatise entitled, "On Ecclesiastical Immunity Violated by the Venetians."[2] Praising his effort, Pope Paul V [Camillo Borghese (1552-1621), pope (1605-1621)], in the year of its composition, said that the work showed its author to be "an outstanding and pious doctor" (*Doctor eximius ac pius*). From this came the honorific title Suárez has received in the history of Scholasticism—"*Doctor eximius*," "the Outstanding Doctor."

Suárez's published writings, which fill 26 volumes in their most accessible edition,[3] were mainly theological and normally corresponded to some area of the *Summa Theologiae* of St. Thomas Aquinas (1225-1274). Outside this Thomistic framework are the two volumes of the *Disputationes metaphysicae* ("Metaphysical Disputations"), which were published at Salamanca in 1597. Suárez's most important and most influential work, the volumes rehearse his own and other Scholastics' thought on myriad questions, arranged systematically in the form of fifty-four "Disputations," which deal with topics in metaphysics.

Any reader will be struck by the work's phenomenal display of learning. In the just mentioned edition, it contains almost 2000 quarto pages, which, from a word count of a sample page, I estimate to contain more than 1.4 million words. After stating each problem, Suárez searched the history of philosophy and theology for solutions that had been offered to it. With as many as twenty-two opinions listed in connection with a single question, almost every available Greek, Arabic, Patristic, and especially Scholastic writer has been cited, often many times. As a rule, these citations are from original sources and exact references are given. One historian has counted 7709 citations, referring to 245

---

2 The work was finally published by Mgr. J.-B. Malou, bishop of Bruges, as the 4th Treatise in a volume entitled: *R.P. Francisci Suarezii, Opuscula sex inedita*, Paris/ Bruxelles: P. Gueau, 1859.

3 *Opera Omnia*, Paris: L. Vivès, 1856-1866; plus two volumes (27 and 28) of indices, 1878.

different authors.[4] Not surprising in a work on metaphysics, Aristotle (384-322 BC) was most mentioned, a total of 1735 times, while St. Thomas Aquinas was next, cited 1008 times.[5] However, Suárez does not just recite opinions; he is always an independent thinker who faithfully reports as many positions as he can and gives fair treatment both to those he accepts and to those he rejects.[6]

In the first Disputation (*Opera omnia*, Paris: Vivès [1856]: vol. 25, pp. 1-64), he tells us that the object of metaphysics is "being insofar as it is real being." Sharpening this, he follows Aristotle[7] to exclude from that object both being of reason and incidental being (i.e. *ens per accidens*). In a way then that reflects Avicenna's (980-1037) understanding of Aristotelian metaphysics, the precise object of metaphysics abstracts from existence and transcends all categories, genera, species and differences to embrace everything real, which is to say mind-independent.

The second part and second volume of the *Disputationes* goes on in Disputation 28 (Vivès: vol. 26, pp. 1-21) to divide being between infinite and finite. In Disputation 29 (pp. 21-60), Suárez demonstrates the existence of God in a quasi-deductive manner from the common concept of being. After an inves- tigation of the divine nature in Disputation 30 (pp. 60-224), Disputation 31 (pp. 224-312) begins treatment of finite being with a denial of the Thomistic real distinction of essence and existence in creatures. In Disputation 32 (pp. 312-329), substance and accidents are considered in a general way and over the next four Disputations (pp. 329-491) substance is treated in detail while the various categories of accident are treated in Disputations 37 to 53 (pp. 491-1014). Real relation is the subject matter of the forty-seventh Disputation, which is our concern now.

The whole of the *Disputationes* concludes in Disputation 54 (pp. 1014-1041) with a systematic discussion of "beings of reason" (*entia rationis*), which are divided into negations, privations, and mind-dependent relations—all of which are, once more in the wake of Aristotle, outside the real being, which is the object of metaphysics.

As for Suárez's place in the history of philosophy, it is fair to say that through his selection of issues and persons before himself he largely shaped the trans-

---

4 Cf. Jesús Iturrioz, S.J., "Fuentes de la metafísica de Suárez," *Pensamiento*, numero extraordinario (Madrid, 1948), pp. 31-89, esp. p. 39.

5 Ibid., p. 40.

6 For an appraisal of this side of Suárez by a great modern historian of philosophy, cf. Etienne Gilson, *Being and Some Philosophers*, 2nd edition (Toronto: Pontifical Institute of Mediaeval Studies, 1952), p. 99.

7 Cf. *Metaphysics* 6.4.1027b33-1028a3.

mission of that history. In this, he had enormous authority among Catholic Scholastics, even for writers who disagreed with him.[8] As might be expected, however, he was most influential among his Jesuit Order-brothers.[9] *Pari passu* with the growth and activity of the Society of Jesus,[10] Suárez's metaphysics spread from the Catholic schools of Spain, Portugal, and Italy to northern European countries.[11] Beyond Catholicism, it crossed to the Lutheran universities of Germany,[12] where the *Disputationes metaphysicae*, of which seventeen editions appeared between 1597 and 1636,[13] was studied, by those especially who embraced what had been Philip Melanchthon's (1497-1560) conciliatory attitude toward philosophy.[14] In similar way, Suárez had major influence in

8 For example, John Poinsot (a.k.a. John of St. Thomas, O.P. [1589-1644]) in his *Cursus philosophicus* has cited Suárez 167 times; cf. Ioannis a Sancto Thoma, O.P., *Cursus philosophicus Thomisticus*, ed. B. Reiser, O.S.B. (Taurini: Marietti, 1930-37), tomus III, pp. 492-5.

9 Among those he influenced in the seventeenth-century, we can mention: Pedro Hurtado de Mendoza (1578-1641), Francisco de Oviedo (1602-1651), Rodrigo de Arriaga (1592-1667), Sylvester Mauro (1619-1687), and Luis de Lossada (1681-1748). Hurtado, for example, refers to Suárez as "the brightest light not only of the Society and of Spain, but even of the whole Church." (... *P. Francisc. Suarez clarissimum non solum Societatis, et Hispaniae lumen, sed etiam Ecclesiae totius,* ...); cf. *Universa philosophia, Metaphysica*, Prooemium, disp. 1, sec. 1, n. 48, nova editio (Lugduni: Sumpt. L. Prost Heredis Rovilli, 1624), p. 700.

10 In the year of its foundation the Society had just ten members. When St. Ignatius died in 1566, that numbr had grown to 1000. In 1580, it was 5000, and by 1600, the Order numbered 13,112 members, in 436 houses, spread through 37 provinces; cf. E.L. Lampe, "Counter Reformation," *New Catholic Encyclopedia* (New York: McGraw-Hill, 1967), vol. IV, p. 387.

11 On the northern expansion of the Jesuits, see Bernhard Duhr, *Geschichte der Jesuiten in den Landern deutscher Zunge*, Vols. I and II, Freiburg im B.: Herder, 1907-1913.

12 For example, in Helmstedt, Jena, Marburg (Lutheran until 1605 and after 1624), Giessen, etc.

13 For this, see Joaquín Iriarte, S.J., "La proyección sobre Europa de una gran metafísica, o Suárez en la filosofía de los dias del Barocco," *Razón y Fe*, numero extraordinario (1948), 229-65, p. 236. Iriarte regards this astounding diffusion of Suarez's 2000 page work as perhaps unique in the history of philosophy and he compares it with the early editions of Descartes's *Meditationes*: ""Descartes, por ejemplo, en todo el siglo XVII alcanzó cuatro ediciones del conjunto total de sus Obras filosóficas. Y de sus 'Meditaciones Metafísicas,' por separado, en ese mismo siglo (1641-1700), nueve ediciones. Meditaciones que no son sino un folleto, después de todo," *ibid.*, note 6.

14 For much of this, see: Karl Eschweiler, "Die Philosophie der spanischen Spätscholastik auf der Universitäten des 17 Jahrhunderts," in *Spanische Forschungen der*

the Calvinist tradition of German[15] and Dutch[16] schools, for both metaphys- ics[17] and law.[18] Through the Calvinist tradition that influence passed from the Netherlands, by way of the University of Cambridge, even to colonial New

---

Gorresgesellschaft, Münster i.W.: Aschendorff, 1928, 251-325; Ernst Lewalter, *Spanische-jesuitische und deutschlutherische Metaphysik des 17 Jahrhunderts*, Darm- stadt: Wissenschaftliche Buchgesellschaft, 1967 (reprint of Hamburg, 1935), Max Wundt, *Die deutsche Schulmetaphysik des 17 Jahrhunderts*, Tubingen: J.C. Mohr, 1939, and J. Iriarte, "La proyección. ..." Among those in the Lutheran university world influenced by Suárez, we may mention especially, Jacob Martini (1570-1649), who authored: "Metphysical Divisions and Questions, in which almost all Distinctions of Metaphysical Terms are accurately Explained so that principally Questions from Francisco Suárez and Clemens Timpler are partly Answered, partly Examined, and partly Refuted" (*Partitiones et quaestiones metaphysicae, in quibus fere terminorum metaphysicorum distinctiones accurate explicantur, ut et praecipue quaestiones ex Fr. Suaretz et Cl. Timplero partim resolvuntur, partim examinantur et refutantur*, Wit- tenberg, 1615). and Christoph Scheibler (1589-1653), who was nicknamed "the Protestant Suárez" and whose chief work was an *Opus metaphysicum*, published at Giessen in 1617 and then later in 1633 at Oxford, a work which was used by Spinoza among others.

15 For example, in Heidelberg, Steinfurt, Herborn, Marburg (Calvinist from 1605 to 1624), Leyden, Franeker, etc. Among those influenced here to some degree by Suárez were Bartholomaeus Keckermann (1572-1609) and Clemens Timpler (1567-1624), who is actually at pains to separate himself from Suárez on the central point of the object of metaphysics, which for Timpler is "every intelligible" (*omne intelligibile*) rather than "being insofar as it is real being."

16 For this, cf. Paul Dibon, *La philosophie néerlandaise au siècle d'or, tome I: L'enseignment philosophique dans les universités à l'époque précartésienne (1575-1650)*, (Paris/Am- sterdam/Londres/New York, 1954), p. 42: "La *Disputatio*, si florissante dans les universités médiévales, a survécu à la Renaissance et Suarez apparait, à la fin du 16ᵉ siècle, comme un maître incontesté en cet art traditionnel. Où trouverait-on en effet examen plus exhaustif des arguments et forme syllogistique plus rigoureuse dans la solution de la question que dans les *Disputationes metaphysicae* du jésuite espagnol?"

17 For Suárez's influence in the Netherlands with special regard to the metaphysical demonstration of God's existence and further knowledge of divine attributes, see Asa Goudriaan, *Philosophische Gotteserkenntnis bei Suárez und Descartes in Zusam- menhang mit der niederländischen reformierten Theologie und Philosophie des 17. Jahrhunderts* (Leiden/Boston/Köln: Brill, 1999), esp. pp. 1-167.

18 For Suárez as a forerunner here of the famous Dutch jurisprudent, Hugo Grotius, see: Paola Negro, "Intorno alle fonti scolastiche in Hugo Grotius," in *Dalla prima alla seconda Scolastica*, a cura di A. Ghisalberti (Bologna: Edizioni Studio Domeni- cano, 2000), pp. 200-251, esp. 207-208, 217-218, 228-236, and 250-251.

England,[19] where Suárez the historian and the thinker was well known and important for philosophical and theological development.

In all probability, it was Suarezian metaphysics that René Descartes (1596-1650) first learned from his Jesuit teachers at La Flèche.[20] While he is short on explicit citations, Descartes has on at least one occasion referred to the

---

19 Thus, the Venice, 1605 edition of the *Disputationes* is listed by Arthur O. Norton, in his "Harvard Text-Books and Reference Books of the Seventeenth Century," *Publications of the Colonial Society of Massachusetts*, vol. 28 (April, 1933), p. 429. Again, Thomas G. Wright (*Literary Culture in Early New England, 1620-1730* [New Haven: Yale University Press, 1920]) lists (p. 276) a copy of the "*Metaphysicarum Disputationes*" in the Harvard College Catalogue of 1723, plus (p. 271) a copy of Scheibler's [dubbed "the Protestant Suárez" by his contemporaries], *Synopsis Philosophiae*, as among the books originally bequeathed by John Harvard to Harvard College. Also, cf.: "Joseph Cooke ([Harvard] A.B. 1660), a few days before his graduation 'suis addidit' the *Metaphysicae Disputationes* of Suarez, ...", Samuel Eliot Morison, *Harvard College in the Seventeenth Century* (Cambridge: MA, Harvard University Press, 1936), p. 253; and: "The Reverend Benjamin Bunker of Malden [Massachusetts] left in 1669 about 80 volumes on religion and theology (including Suarez's *Metaphysica*), ..." idem, *The Intellectual Life of Colonial New England* (Ithaca: Great Seal Press, second printing 1961), p. 139; Morison cites his authority for this as "Ms. Middlesex Probate Court Files, docket 3508. While much of such evidence is sporadic or even anecdotal, it confirms the influence of Suárez on seventeenth-century Harvard and New England and it fits well with the view of Perry Miller: "... though Puritan literature abounds with condemnations of scholasticism, almost no limits can be set to its actual influence." Perry Miller, *The New England Mind: The Seventeenth Century* (Cambridge, MA: Harvard Press, 1954), p. 104. For more confirmation of the place of Suárez, see Norman Fiering, *Moral Philosophy at Seventeenth-Century Harvard* (Chapel Hill: University of North Carolina Press, 1981), p. 120.

20 On this, cf.: "Descartes, who was educated by the Jesuits, certainly studied Suárez's work, and a considerable amount of the framework for the Meditations (particularly the reasoning in the Third Meditations) bears the clear imprint of Suárez's ideas." R. Ariew/J. Cottingham/T. Sorell (eds.), *Descartes' Meditations. Background Source Materials* (Cambridge, 1998), p. 29, as cited by A. Goudriaan, *Philosophische Gotteserkenntnis ...*, p. 1, note 2.

20bis Cf. *Reply to the Fourth Objections*, where Descartes cites Suárez, *DM* IX, 2, 4; in *Oeuvres de Descartes*, ed. Adam-Tannery (1897 sq.), VII, 235; also see Leonard Gilen, S.J., "Über die Beziehungen Descartes' zur zeitgenössischen Scholastik," *Scholastik*, XXXII (1957), esp. p. 54, n. 71. For some influence of Suárez on the *esse objectivum* doctrine of Descartes, cf. J.-F. Courtine, "La doctrine cartésienne de l'idée et ses sources scolastiques," in *Les catégories de l'être: Études de philosophie ancienne et médiévale* (Paris: PUF, 2003), pp. 241-65.

Disputationes, [20bis] of which he is believed to have owned a copy.[21] Gottfried Wilhelm Leibniz (1649-1716) boasted that when he was young he had read Suárez "like a novel."[22] Again, Leibniz's independent disciple, Christian Wolff (1679- 1754), whose *Ontologia* was for Immanuel Kant (1724-1804) a para-digm of pre-critical metaphysics,[23] says that it was "Francisco Suárez, of the Society of Jesus, who among Scholastics pondered metaphysical questions with particular penetration."[24] Beyond all doubt Wolff was in his own metaphysics very much in debt to Suárez.[25] In the nineteenth century, Arthur Schopen-hauer (1788-1860) often cited Suárez's doctrine that a final cause moves not according to its real being but through its "being known" (*esse cognitum*),[26] and in his main work, Die Welt als Wille und Vorstellung, Schopenhauer labels the Disputationes "an authentic compendium of the whole Scholastic tradi-tion."[27] Again, Franz Brentano (1838-1917), in his 1862 work on the various meanings of being according to Aristotle, has recommended the *Disputationes*

21 Étienne Gilson, *Being and Some Philosophers,* 2nd edition (Toronto: Pontifical Institute of Mediaeval Studies, 1952), p. 109.

22 See *Vita Leibnitii a seipso*, in Foucher de Careil, *Nouvelles lettres et opuscles inédits de Leibnitz* (Paris, 1857), p. 382-383; as cited by L. Mahieu, *François Suarez, sa philosophie et les rapports qu'elle a avec sa théologie* (Paris, 1921), p. 517-518. Also cf. P. Menard, S.J., "Comment Leibniz se trouva placé dans le sillage de Suarez," *Archives de Philosophie*, XVIII, cahier 1 (Paris, 1949), pp. 7-32; Menard (esp. pp. 22-30) has much of interest to say about Suárez's *Disputationes* in the Protestant universities of Germany. On the relation between Leibniz and Suárez with particular reference to the doctrine of individuation, see J.-F. Courtine, *Suarez et le système de la métaphysique* (Paris: Presses Universitaires de France, 1990), esp. pp. 496-519.

23 Cf. Gilson, *Being* ..., p. 119.

24 Cf. C. Wolff, *Philosophia prima sive ontologia*, I, 2, 3, n. 169 (Francofurti et Lipsiae, 1736), p. 138.

25 Cf. Gilson, *Being* ..., pp. 112-120. On Suarezian metaphysics as it passes through Wolff to Kant, see the excellent work of Ludger Honnefelder, *Scientia Transcendens: Die formale Bestimmung der Seiendheit und Realität in der Metaphysik des Mittelalters und der Neuzeit (Duns Scotus—Suárez—Wolff—Kant—Peirce)*, (Hamburg: Felix Meiner Verlag, 1990), esp. pp. 200-381.

26 For this, see M. Frischeisen-Köhler and Willy Moog, *Die Philosophie der Neuzeit bis zum Ende des xviii Jahrhunderts*, in *Friedrich Ueberwegs Grundriss der Geschichte der Philosophie*, 14 Auflage, vol. 3 (Basel: Schwabe, 1957), p. 215.

27 Cf. *Arthur Schopenhauers sämtliche Werke*, ed. P. Deussen, I (Munchen, 1911), 134, 148, 181, 500; cited by Nikolaus Junk, *Die Bewegungslehre des Franz Suarez* (Inns-bruck/Leipzig: F. Rauch, 1938), p. 13. Let us also note that in Überweg, volume III, we read that Suárez's doctrine of the end moving by its "being known" (*esse cognitum*) strongly influenced Schopenhauer.

metaphysicae to anyone who wants to understand medieval views on Aristotle.[28] And finally here, for the twentieth-century Martin Heidegger (1889-1976) Suárez was the main source through which Greek ontology passed from the middle ages to usher in the metaphysics and the transcendental philosophy of modern times.[29] In this vein, he has written:

> Direct influence on the development of modern metaphysics was exercised by one theologian and philosopher who, in the 16th century, with quite specific theological intentions, set himself the task of interpreting Aristotelian metaphysics anew: the Spanish Jesuit Franz Suarez. Suarez's significance as a theologian and philosopher is far from being acknowledged to the extent merited by this thinker, who must be placed even above Aquinas in terms of his acumen and independence of questioning. His significance for the development and formation of modern metaphysics is not merely formal in the sense that under his influence the discipline of metaphysics took shape in a specific form. Just as important is his moulding of the problems concerning content, problems which then reawakened in modern philosophy.[30]

B. Some Thoughts on Suárez as a Disciple of Aristotle

As mentioned, Suárez has cited Aristotle over 1700 times in the course of the *Disputationes*. But any consideration of Suárez as a disciple and commentator on Aristotle should begin with a brief adversion to the *Doctor eximius'* background as a Jesuit. Two things especially stand out here: (1) St. Ignatius' own regard for Aristotle and his desire that the members of his Order be trained in and

---

28 For this, see Brentano, *Von der mannigfachen Bedeutung des Seienden nach Aristoteles* (Freiburg im Breisgau: Herder, 1862, reprint: Hildesheim: G. Olms, 1960), p. 3, n. 6; translated by Rolf George: *On the Several Senses of Being in Aristotle* (Berkeley: University of California Press, 1975), p. 150, n. 6.

29 *Sein und Zeit* (Halle: M. Niemeyer, 1941), p. 22, tr. J. McQuarrie and E. Robinson, *Being and Time* (New York: Harper, 1962), p. 43; also cf.: *Die Frage nach dem Ding* (Tübingen: M. Niemeyer, 1962), p. 77. For some of what is involved in this, see my article, "Heidegger and Scholastic Metaphysics," *The Modern Schoolman*, 49 (1972), pp. 201-220. On the question of the relation between Suárez's metaphysics and Heidegger's "onto-theo-logical" conception of metaphysics, cf. A. Goudriaan, *Philosophische Gotteserkenntnis ...*, esp. 8-10.

30 Martin Heidegger, *The Fundamental Concepts of Metaphysics: World, Finitude, Solitude*, translated by William McNeill and Nicholas Walker (Bloomington and Indianapolis: Indiana University Press, 1995), p. 51; for the original German, cf. Heidegger, *Die Grundbegriffe der Metaphysik: Welt—Endlichkeit—Einsamkeit*, in *Gesamtausgabe, II. Abteilung: Vorlesungen 1923-1944*, Band 29/30 (Frankfurt am Main: Vittorio Klostermann, 1976), p. 78.

adhere to Aristotelian philosophy wherever possible, and (2) the emphasis on Aristotle in the *Ratio studiorum* (1599), which was from its adoption the guiding rule of Jesuit studies in philosophy.[31] While the *Disputationes metaphysicae* was published before the final version of the *Ratio* appeared, nevertheless, the discussions leading to its adoption, in which discussions Suarez took some part, reflected both Ignatius' wishes and the actual practice of the Jesuits.

Suárez's *Disputationes metaphysicae* was perhaps the broadest and deepest stream through which medieval Aristotelianism flowed into the theoretical philosophy of modern times. Almost without exception the citations of Aristotle in the *Disputationes* are accurate. But three things more should be said. One is Suárez's criticism of the earlier use of Aristotle and the techniques of Aristotelian commentaries, as well as his expressed intention to present metaphysics in a more systematic (but yet obviously an Aristotelian way). This we find in the prologue to Disputations 1 and 2, where it seems reminiscent of St. Thomas' prologue to the *Summa Theologiae*, in which the Angelic Doctor has criticised the common practice of commenting on texts, the most notable of which was the *Sentences* of Peter the Lombard.[32]

Two is the fact that Suarez, while ever respectful of Aristotle, is not his slavish follower. He is very much aware of the number and variety of Aristotelian commentators who wrote before himself. And while he usually does follow or at least find support in Aristotle's text, he knows that the pagan Aristotle will not always jibe with his own intention of presenting a Christian philosophy. For that reason, he is at times very willing to express his own opinion—regardless of what Aristotle might have thought.[33] In this, the *Doctor eximius* was not at odds with the rule for a Professor of Philosophy stated in the *Ratio* of 1599:

> In matters of any importance let him not depart from Aristotle unless something occurs which is foreign to the doctrine which academies everywhere approve of; much more if it is opposed to the orthodox faith, and if there

31 On this, see Edward A. Fitzpatrick, *St. Ignatius and the Ratio Studiorum* (New York and London: McGraw-Hill, 1933), pp. 22, 107, 168, and 171. For the latest English translation of the *Ratio*, cf. Claude N. Pavur, S.J., *Ratio atque Institutio Studiorum Societatis Jesu: The Official Plan for Jesuit Education*, St. Louis: Institute for Jesuit Sources, 2005.

32 For this, cf. S. Thomae Aquinatis, *Summa Theologiae, Prologus*, in *Opera omnia*, tomus iv (Romae: Ex Typographia Polyglotta, S.C. De Propaganda Fidei, 1888), p. 5.

33 Cf. e.g., *DM* 20, 1, nn. 24-6, vol. 25, pp. 751-53; *DM* 29, 1, n. 8, vol. 26, p. 23; *DM* 30, 16, n. 56, pp. 202-203; and ibid., 17, n. 5, p. 208.

are any arguments of this or any other philosopher against the faith, he will endeavor earnestly to refute them according to the Lateran Council.[34]

Three is the important and often overlooked fact that Suárez attached to his *Disputationes* a moderately sized commentary (*per modum quaestionis*) on the first 12 books of Aristotle's *Metaphysics*. This commentary, labeled a "Most Ample Index to the *Metaphysics* of Aristotle" (*Index locupletissimus in Metaphysicam Aristotelis*), of which I recently published a translation, is very valuable for its cross references to the *Disputationes*, and is also useful to determine Suárez's understanding of and faithfulness to the text of Aristotle.[35] Unfortunately, with regard to relation it adds nothing beyond the forty-seventh Disputation.[36]

More on Suarez's attitude to Aristotle as well as his transmission of Aristotelianism can be gleaned from any of his other works. These include his "Treatise on the Soul" (*Tractatus de Anima*),[37] which while it is not a literal commentary on Aristotle's *de Anima* does for the most part present Aristotle's doctrine, even if it is in a benign way when that doctrine sometimes goes astray (as for example, with respect to the immortality of the soul). Among other writings that are suffused with Aristotle's doctrine are his work "On Laws" (*De legibus*),[38] his treatise "On the Voluntary and the Involuntary" (*De voluntario*

---

34 Cf. Fitzpatrick, *St. Ignatius* ..., p. 168.

35 In the Index and the Disputations, Suárez was using only the first 12 books of the *Metaphysics*. While this was common in the Middle Ages, by Suarez's time books 13 and 14 were widely available. Also from the Index we can see that he uses Fonseca's translation for the early books of the *Metaphysics* and then relies on older translations by William of Moerbeke (ca. 1470-1538), Cardinal Bessarion (ca. 1403-1472), and John Argyropolous (ca. 1415-1487) for the rest. He refers to Fonseca's edition as "elegant" (*Index locupletissimus*, I, c. 7, vol. 25, p. iv) and in those passages from *Metaphysics* V, c. 15, which he has translated in Disputation 47 he has followed Fonseca. But as for Fonseca's commentary, he can take it or leave it in different contexts, as will be apparent from reading Disputation 47.

36 Thus, with regard to *Metaphysics*, V, c. 15, the *Doctor eximius* says: "We treat this Chapter at great length in *Disputation 47*, and therefore there is no need to note anything now." For this, cf. Francisco Suárez, *A Commentary on Aristotle's Metaphysics (Index locupletissimus in Metaphysicam Aristotelis)*, translated from the Latin with an Introduction and Notes by John P. Doyle (Milwaukee: Marquette University Press, 2004), p. 93.

37 For a critical edition, cf. *Commentaria una cum quaestionibus in libros Aristotelis de Anima*, Introducción y edición crítica por Salvador Castellote, Tomo I Madrid: Sociedad de estudios y publicaciones, 1978; tomo II: Madrid: Labor, 1981; tomo III: Madrid, Fundación Xavier Zubiri, 1991.

38 Cf. Vivès edition, volumes 5 and 6.

et involuntario),[39] his treatise "On the Goodness and Malice of Human Acts"
(*De bonitate et malitia humanorum actuum*),[40] as well as his theological writings
on divine grace[41] and the sacraments.[42]

C. Relation in Aristotelian Philosophy— A Broad Overview

1. There are two main places in which Aristotle has dealt with the category
of relation. These are: (a) *Categories*, Chapter 7, and (b) *Metaphysics*, Book V,
Chapter 15. As will become apparent, these places will be central for Suárez's
treatment of relation in Disputation 47.

2. At the lowest level of reality, as Aristotle perceives it, there is potency or
matter.[43] Here we have Aristotle's answer to Parmenides and also the basis on
which he will make motion intelligible—more, that is to say, than the flux of
Heraclitus or Cratylus. To explain: Parmenides left us with a stark choice "is
or is not (ἔστιν ἢ οὐκ ἔστιν),"[44] a choice which Aristotle sidesteps with the
recognition of potency. Things are not only what they are but also what they
are able to be. *Able to be* is nothing in comparison with the actual reality of a
thing, but it is not the absolute nothing of Parmenides' "is not." Again, as we
shall see presently, the recognition of the potential will permit an intellectual
mastery of motion which will overcome the unintelligible flux of Heraclitus.

For us now the most important point is that potency or matter is not an
absolute reality or being. Instead, while it obviously transcends the category of
relation, matter is *relational*. Aristotle tells us that it is among the class of things
which are "toward something" (πρός τι).[45] This is to say that matter exists only
as relative to a counterpart actuality or form. Its reality is encompassed and
confined by form, which form is being for Aristotle. But not only its reality;
also matter's ability to be understood and to be explained are relative to form.
To illustrate: *bronze* is matter for the statue not as it is bronze—for precisely
as such it is form—but rather only insofar as it is able to become a statue, or is

---

39 Cf. e.g. Disputation V, "On Circumstances," vol. 4, pp. 233-41.
40 Cf. Vivès edition, vol. 4, pp. 277-454. In this work and others it is not so much a
   question of Suárez citing Aristotle as it is working within his metaphysics, psychol-
   ogy, ethics, and theory of scientific demonstration.
41 For example, cf. the Vivès edition, volumes 7, 8, and 9.
42 Cf. Vivès volumes 2-23.
43 On this equivalence, cf. "ὕλην δὲ λέγω ἢ μὴ τόδε τι οὖσα ἐνεργείᾳ,
   δυνάμει ἐστὶ τόδε τι" *Metaphysics* 8.1.1042a27; cf. ibid. 14.4.1092a3; ibid.
   8.6.1045a33.
44 *Fr.* 8, l. 16; *DK* I, 236.
45 "ἔτι τῶν πρός τι ἡ ὕλη" *Physics* 2.2.194b9-10.

in potency to be formed as a statue. Accordingly, if one is going to understand or explain bronze as material he must relate it to the statue.

The next level is that of change or more particularly motion itself, which Aristotle, in opposition to the flux of Heraclitus and Cratylus, defines as "the act of a being in potency precisely insofar as it is in potency."[46] Motion (or change more broadly) is a kind of μετάξυ τι, a "middle something" between potency and actuality. It is imperfect actuality. Further, motion is not an absolute—there is no motion apart from things.[47] The other side of this is that motion or change, like potency, while not in the category of relation is nevertheless relational. Most obviously, it is what it is, or it is specified or named, in relation to its terminus.[48] From another angle, since act is equated with form and form is equated with being[49] (in the sense that there is no act beyond form[50]—and that to be is to be something[51] stable, definite, fixed, formal, or even form itself[52])—motion or change, far from an unintelligible flux, can be thought of as "the act of a form in matter, precisely insofar as it is in matter," "the form of a form in matter precisely insofar as it is in matter," "the being of a being in potency precisely as it is in potency," or, stretching beyond anything which Aristotle ever said explicitly, as "the being of a being in relation precisely insofar as it is in relation."

In contrast to potency as well as to motion or change, the next level is comparatively absolute. This is the level of accidental actuality or form—the level[53] of the categories of accident. At this level we have the encompassing,

---

46 "ἡ τοῦ δυνάμει ὄντος ἐντελέχει, ᾗ τοιοῦτον, κίνησίς ἐστιν." *Physics* 3.1.201a10.

47 "οὐκ ἔστι δέ τις κίνησις παρὰ τὰ πράγματα." *Physics* 3.1.200b32.

48 Cf. "μᾶλλον γὰρ εἰς ὃ ἢ ἐξ οὗ κινεῖται ὀνομάζεται ἡ μεταβολή" *Physics* 5.1.224b7-8.

49 Cf. *Metaphysics* 9.8.1050a4-7.

50 This is unlike the well known view of St. Thomas Aquinas that "to be is the actuality of all forms" (*esse est actualitas omnium formarum*); cf. *De potentia* VII, 2, ad 9; *Summa Theol.* I, 3, 4; ibid., I, 4, 1, ad 3; ibid., I, 5, 1; and *Compendium theologiae*, c. 11.

51 In this way, there is no difference between something and being something, e.g. "one man," "man," and "being man" are all the same; cf. "ταὐτὸ γὰρ εἷς ἄνθρωπος καὶ ὢν ἄνθρωπος καὶ ἄνθρωπος" (*Metaphysics* 4.2.1003b26-27).

52 Cf. e.g. *Metaphysics* 7.7.1032b1-2, where form (εἶδος) is called the essence (τὸ τί ἦν εἶναι) and the primary being (πρωτὴ οὐσία) of each thing. For some of what is involved here, cf. Joseph Owens, C.SS.R., *The Doctrine of Being in the Aristotelian Metaphysics*, third edition (Toronto: Pontifical Institute of Mediaeval Studies, 1978), pp. 466-8.

53 Or, better, "levels."

confining, specifying, and explanatory reality required for superficial or accidental change. Once more, however, we have not reached totally absolute reality. Again the reality of accidents is relational, material, or potential. Even the so-called "absolute" accidents of quantity and quality[54] are real only in relation to substance. That is to say that there is no absolute quantity apart from a quantified substance nor any absolute quality except in a qualified substance.

The next level is that of substance, which is in some way absolute when compared with accidents—but, again, not totally absolute. For at this level, the substance in question is still material, subject to change, and to that extent potential, and relative rather than absolute. Therefore, we have not here reached an ultimate absolute reality but rather one which calls out for some completion beyond itself.

At this point we emerge from immanence to transcendence. The completion called for is causal and comes only at the level of immaterial, that is purely formal, purely actual, and purely absolute substance. This is the level of Aristotle's "separate substance." Separate from matter or potency and with all lesser and lower grades of reality or being depending on it, separate substance is independent of all else.

But going back to real being in the categories, let us say that while purely absolute reality is found only when we arrive at the ultimate prime mover or at least at separate substance, there are before that three comparatively absolute levels. These are material substance, quantity and quality, which in comparison with relation, and the last six categories that in various ways presuppose or include relation, have a measure of independence. Thus, relation, action, passion, time, place, position, and possession—are all either immediately or mediately relational. But then going farther back to the distinction of real being from beings of reason and the evident ability which human beings have to relate different items, the core question becomes that of the reality of the category of relation. If it is not real, but rather mind-dependent, what does that say about Aristotle's category doctrine and still more about the constitution of reality itself? If relation is not real, anterior to any human consideration, how can we conceive even the relational character of quantity, quality, and material substance, as well as that of matter and motion—let alone that of the last six categories? If, on the other side, relation is real anterior to our consideration, what is its reality and how can it be conceived? How can it be distinguished from its mind-dependent image which is a being of reason? In Section 2 of the forty-seventh Disputation we have Suárez's choice and answer to this all

---

54 Cf. *DM* 39, 1, n. 4, vol. 26, p. 506; ibid., n. 18, p. 510.

important question of the reality of a categorical relation. In the sixth Section of Disputation 54, he will return to the issue and deal at more length with relations of reason.

3. There are some connected issues here. The first of these is the common Aristotelian division of being into real being and being of reason. Immediately following is Aristotle's doctrine of the categories and the basic question about their nature which Aristotle left for his disciples. This question will embrace the role of the knower and namer, as well as of knowledge, predication, and denomination in the constitution of the categories, and it will center on relation and the last six categories of action, passion, time,[55] place,[56] disposition, and possession (*habitus*).

(a) Background here is furnished by the Aristotelian divisions of being in *Metaphysics* V (Δ), Chapter 7, and in *Metaphysics* VI (Σ), Chapter 2. In the first of these places, Aristotle has divided being into "incidental being" or "being by accident" (τὸ ὄν κατὰ συμβεβηκός) and "being *per se*" (τὸ ὄν καθ᾽ αὐτό).[57] He has gone on to subdivide being *per se* according to the various categories of being ([κατὰ] τὰ σχήματα τῆς κατηγορίας)[58] and centrally to distinguish such from "being as true (τὸ ὄν ὡς ἀληθές)."[59] Then he has distinguished being in potency from being in act.[60] In *Metaphysics* VI, Chapter 2, he has spoken of four members under being "as said in an unqualified way" (τὸ ὄν τὸ ἁπλῶς λεγόμενον). These are: (1) incidental being (τὸ ὄν κατὰ συμβεβηκός); (2) being as true (τὸ ὄν ὡς ἀληθές); (3) being in the categories, and (4) being as potential and actual.[61] Of these members, being

---

55 Or "when" (*quando*).

56 Or "where" (*ubi*).

57 *Metaphysics* 5.7.1017a7-8.

58 Ibid., 1017a23. In the following sentence Aristotle has listed substance and seven categories of accident. His omission of the last two categories of disposition and possession has been noted by Suárez, who has cited Averroes (Cf. *In lib. Metaphys.* V, t. 14 [ed. Venetiis, 1574] fol. 117ra) to the effect "that these two categories are of little importance and [worthy] of almost no consideration, and therefore" [Suárez continues] "we discuss them [only] most briefly in *Disputations 52 and 53* of this work." *DM, Index locupletissimus*, V, c. 7, q. 4, vol. 25, p. xxi; cf. Francisco Suárez, *A Commentary on Aristotle's Metaphysics ...*, p. 88. Also see, *DM* 48, [prol.], n. 1, vol. 26, p. 867.

59 Ibid., 1017a31-35.

60 "ἔτι τὸ εἶναι σημαίνει καὶ τὸ ὄν τὸ μὲν δυνάμει, τὸ δ᾽ ἐντελεχείᾳ ..." ibid., 1017a35-b1.

61 See *Metaphysics* 6.2.1026a33-b2.

in the categories is being in the most important way (κυρίως).[62] Excluded from metaphysical consideration were incidental being and being as true.[63] Since potentiality and actuality are found throughout the categories and since actuality is prior to potentiality, the concern of metaphysics was thus focused on actual categorical being.[64]

(b) This immediately raises a question, which, at least from the time of Simplicius (fl. ca. 529 AD), Aristotle's interpreters asked about the nature of his categories. As raised by Simplicius the issue was whether the categories are meant to be divisions of simple terms (ἁπλαῖ φωναί), of simple concepts (ἁπλᾶ νοήματα), or of things themselves (πράγματα, ὄντα).[65] This question, which was known to the Latins from Boethius (ca. 480—524) on,[66] was

---

62 Ibid. 4.1027b31.

63 See esp. *Metaphysics* 6.4.1027b34-1028a3; ibid. 11.8.1065a22-24.

64 For this, cf. Theo Kobusch, *Sein und Sprache: Historische Grundlegung einer Ontologie der Sprache* (Leiden/New York: E.J. Brill, 1987), p. 25.

65 Cf. *In Aristotelis Categorias*, ed. Karolus Kalbfleisch, in *Commentaria in Aristotelem Graeca*, VIII (Berlin, 1907), p. 9, 8; and Simplicius, *Commentaire sur les Catégories d' Aristote. Traduction de Guillaume de Moerbeke*, prologus, ed. A. Pattin, *Corpus Latinum Commentariorum in Aristotelem Graecorum* V/l, Paris/Louvain: Publ. Universitaires/Nauwelaerts 1971, 12-18; for a wider study, cf. Philippe Hoffmann, "Les Analyses de l'enoncé catégories et parties du discours selon les commentateurs néoplatoniciens," in *Théories de la phrase et de la proposition de Platon à Averroès*, éd. P. Büttgen et al. (Paris: Éditions Rue d'Ulm, 1999), pp. 209-48. While Simplicius is most associated with this problem, its roots go farther back in Greek thought. On this, cf. Alain de Libera, *La querelle des universaux de Platon à la fin du Moyen Age* (Paris: Éditions du Seuil, 1996), p. 48, who traces it at least to Clement of Alexandria (ca. 150-215), *Stromata*, VIII, 8, 23, and who has cited on this J. Pépin, "Clément d'Alexandrie, les *Catégories* d'Aristote et le Fragment 60 d'Heraclite," in P. Aubenque (éd.), *Concepts et Catégories dans la pensée antique* (Paris: Vrin, 1980), pp. 271-84, esp. 271-9. De Libera himself is at pains to link this problem with that of "the universals" in the Middle Ages. Also here, on the role of Simplicius and some of his predecessors, especially Plotinus, cf. Frans A.J. De Haas, "Context and Strategy of Plotinus' Treatise on the Genera of Being (Enn. VI 1-3 [42-44]", in *Aristotele e i suoi esegeti neoplatonici: Logica e ontologia nelle interpretazioni greche e arabe*, Atti del Convegno Internazionale Roma, 19-20 Ottobre 2001, a cura di Vincenza Celluprica e Cristina D'Ancona, con la collaborazione di Riccardo Chiaradonna (Napoli: Istituto per il Lessico Intellettuale Europeo e Storia delle Idee, 2004), pp. 37-53.

66 [67] Cf. A.M.S. Boethius, *In Categorias Aristotelis libri quatuor* I, PL 64, 159C-161A, as cited by Dominik Perler, "Peter Aureol vs. Hervaeus Natalis on Intentionality: A Text Edition with Introductory Remarks," *Archives d'Histoire doctrinale et littéraire du Moyen Age*, 61 (1994), p. 253, note 9.

surely in the mind of Suárez and has importance for his doctrine of relation, especially inasmuch as the central question of Disputation 47 concerns the reality of relation and in Disputation 54, Section 6, the basic premiss is the mind-dependent character of some relations. This goes right along with the *Doctor eximius'* espousal of what looks like a nominalistic position on what a relation adds to its foundation and also a passage in which he has denied the extra mental reality of all the categories, save substance, quantity, and quality.[67]

(c) While Simplicius' question concerns all the categories, it has particular application to the category of relation[68] and then to the last six categories of action, passion, time, place, disposition, and possession. Are these categories real beings, independent of human knowers and namers or are they just the opposite, arising in the wake of human considerations and their linguistic expressions? Again, the question centers on relation, which is listed as a category

---

67 Cf. "Next I will explain that, as is clear from metaphysics, no category offers of itself its own entity, distinct from all the rest, except substance, quantity, and quality. But all the other [categories] are modes of these." (*Deinde ita declaro, quia, ut ex Metaphysica constat, nullum praedicamentum affert per se entitatem suam, distinctam ab omnibus reliquis, nisi substantia, quantitas, aut qualitas; reliqua autem omnia sunt modi istorum;* ...) Suárez, *De Eucharistia*, Disp. 47, s. 1, n. 4, vol. 22, p. 45. With this we may compare and contrast, William of Ockham's view that only the categories of substance and quality have distinct real things corresponding to them; see, for example, his interpretation of Aristotle: "He wished also to say that every thing is either a substance or a quality." (*Voluit etiam ponere quod omnis res vel est substantia vel qualitas.*) Guillelmi de Ockham, *Summa Logicae*, P. I, c. 45, ed. P. Boehner, G. Gál, et S. Brown (St. Bonaventure, N.Y., 1974), p. 144, ll. 156-7; also: "However, there are certain things in the category of quality which do not signify things distinct from substance, in such way that such a thing is not a substance, for examples: 'whiteness' and 'blackness,' 'color,' 'knowledge,' 'light,' and things of this kind." (*Sunt autem quaedam in genere qualitatis quae important res distinctas a substantia, ita quod quod illa res non est substantia, sicut sunt 'albedo' et 'nigredo', 'color', 'scientia' 'lux,' et huiusmodi.*) ibid., c. 55, p. 180, ll. 14-16. On Ockham's doctrine here, see Gyula Klima, "Ockham's Semantics and the Ontology of the Categories," in *The Cambridge Companion to Ockham*, ed. Paul Vincent Spade (Cambridge: Cambridge University Press, 1999), pp. 118-42.

68 In the wake of Plotinus (205-27), who contrasts the Stoic reduction of relation to something merely rational to his own realistic understanding (cf. *Enneads* VI, 1, 6-9), Simplicius tells us that some doubt whether relation is a reality or only a spoken term (*In Aristotelis Categorias*, c. 7, ed. C. Kalbfleisch, p. 169, ll. 1-2). Simplicius himself defends the reality of relation not less than that of the other categories. Indeed, without real relations substance and the other categories would not be categories or have any community with respect to one another (ibid.,ll. 10-12).

but which seems to transcend all categories. Is it a real being or is it merely mind-dependent? Or is it both? And if so, how are these two themselves connected or related? Specifically, is there one, even univocal, notion of relation that covers the span between real and merely rational relations, or is there nothing more than a community of name between them? As for the six ultimate categories, following St. Thomas Aquinas,[69] Suárez denies that the last four can found relations,[70] and in opposition to Duns Scotus[71] and others,[72] refuses to reduce them to relation,[73] except perhaps to a relation as a manner of speaking (that is, a relation *secundum dici*).[74] But nevertheless, relation is deeply embedded in them.[75] Thus "passion" may be identified with change or

69 *In duodecim libros Metaphysicorum Aristotelis expositio*, V, l. 17, ed. M. R. Cathala et R. Spiazzi (Taurini: Marietti, 1950), p. 266, n. 1005. For treatment of St. Thomas' position on the last six categories, cf. A. Krempel, *La doctrine de la relation chez saint Thomas, Exposé historique et systématique*, Chapitre XX (Paris: Librarie Philosophique J. Vrin, 1952), pp. 426-52.

70 Cf. *DM* 47, Section 11, nn. 4 and 11, below.

71 For Scotus' doctrine of extrinsically advenient relations here, see *Quaestiones Quodlibetales*, XI, art. 4, n. 34, in *Obras del Doctor Sutil Juan Duns Escoto*, edicion bilingüe, Cuestiones cuodlibetales, introducción, resúmenes y versión de Felix Alluntis, O.F.M. (Madrid: Biblioteca de Autores Cristianos, 1968), pp. 416-417; and John Duns Scotus, *God and Creatures: The Quodlibetal Questions*, translated with and Introduction, Notes, and Glossary by Felix Alluntis, O.F.M. and Allan B. Wolter, O.F.M. (Washington, D.C.: The Catholic University of America Press—reprint of Princeton University edition of 1975), p. 266. Also, cf. Mark G. Henninger, *Relations, Medieval Theories 1250-1325* (Oxford: Clarendon Press, 1989), p. 105.

72 See, for example, Walter Chatton and Pseudo-Richard of Campsall, as reported by Armand Maurer, *The Philosophy of William of Ockham in the Light of its Principles* (Toronto: Pontifical Institute of Mediaeval Studies, 1999), p. 54, note 123. For exact references to Walter and Ps-Richard on each of these categories, cf. the notes given by the editors of Ockham's *Summa Logicae* (St. Bonaventure, 1974), cc. 57-62, pp. 183-193. For St. Albert the Great, Giles of Rome, and other Scholastics on the relative character of the last six categories, cf. A. Krempel, *La doctrine de la relation* ..., pp. 432-6.

73 Cf. *DM* 50, 12, n. 2, vol. 26, p. 966; *DM* 51, 1, n. 6, p. 974, and *DM* 52, 1, n. 3, p. 1007.

74 Cf. *DM* 39, 1, n. 4, vol. 26, p. 506; ibid., n. 18, p. 510. On relation *secundum dici*, cf. *DM* 47, Section 3, below.

75 See *DM* 47, Prologue, and Section 1, n. 6, below. On this, cf. St. Thomas: "'When' consists in some kind of relation to time. Indeed, 'where' [is related] to place. 'Position' implies an order of parts and 'habit' [implies] a relation of one having to what is had." (*Quando consistit in aliquali relatione ad tempus. Ubi vero, ad locum. Positio*

motion[76] and just as evidently exhibit the relational character we have noted in that. Any counterpart "action" would appear to be nothing more than passion as considered to be related to an agent from which it stems. "Time" evidently involves a compound relation inasmuch as it is nothing more than the numbering of motion according to before and after. "Place" likewise as connoting the first surface of the containing body is again a kind of relational μετάξυ τι—"something between" the container and the contained. "Disposition" also seems relational in its core as nothing else but an order of parts among themselves. And, finally, "Possession" or "Habitus" seems to be something relative between a human haver and what he has or possesses.

At very least, without pinning the matter down at all points, it is safe to say that relation is central to any overall understanding of Aristotle's doctrine of the categories and even more to any understanding of his wider doctrine beyond.

D. Suárez on Relation

1. As I have mentioned, there are two principal places in the *Disputationes metaphysicae* in which Suárez treats relation. These are the present Disputation 47 and then Disputation 54, Section 6. The obvious dividing line between them is that between real being in the categories and "being as true" which by Suárez's time has come to be identified with being of reason.[77] But even as we say this, it is important once again to note that real relation extends beyond the category of relation and also that in the Second Section, Paragraph 22, of Disputation 47 Suárez will come exceedingly close to a reduction of real relation to a simple act of the knower, that is, a connotation.

2. There are other places in the *Disputationes* where in various ways Suárez has touched upon relation. While I have not explored them all in the present work, they do frequently shine added light on this work. For examples, let me mention his treatment of "prior and posterior" in the *Index locupletissimus*

---

autem ordinem partium importat. Habitus autem relationem habentis ad habitum.) *In XII libros Metaph.*, V, l. 17, n. 1005.

76 Cf. Aristotle's dictum that motion is in the *mobile*; *Physics* 3.3.202a13-14; also, ibid., 3.1.201a10-b15.

77 For some of the history of this identification, cf. Theo Kobusch, "Ens inquantum ens und ens rationis: ein aristotelisches Problem in der Philosophie des Duns Scotus und Wilhelm von Ockham," in *Aristotle in Britain during the Middle Ages: Proceedings of the International Conference at Cambridge, 8-11 April 1994 organized by the Société internationale pour l'étude de la philosophie médiévale*, edited by John Marenbon (Turnhout: Brepols, 1996), pp. 157-175, esp. 158-9.

at Book Five, Chapter 11;[78] his discussion—in the context of his treatment of distinction—of relation and its terminus;[79] his discussion of relation in the context of truth;[80] various points he makes about relation in treating transcendental goodness;[81] his contrast of finite created relations and infinite divine relations as regards the essences in which they are found;[82] the divine relations of paternity and filiation as dissimilar;[83] or within a context of his discussion of quantity, a further discussion of the characters of "measure" and "measured,"[84] etc.

3. As may be gathered from some of the examples just mentioned, there are Christian dimensions of relation both in Suárez's sources and in his own teaching. These are linked particularly with the doctrines of the Trinity and the Incarnation. On both these themes, besides what he has said in the *Disputationes*,[85] he has written special works, which contain much on the subject of relation.

Thus, he has left us "Twelve Books on the Mystery of the Most Holy Trinity," filling almost 300 pages in the first volume of his *Opera omnia*.[86] Of special interest here is the character of relation inasmuch as it is constitutive of the persons of the Trinity.[87] Or again, the doctrine that each divine person is a subsisting relation;[88] that there are only four real relations in God;[89] equality, not inequality, but rather diversity among divine relations;[90] as well as various other matters.

---

78 See *Index* ..., V, c. 11, q. 1, vol. 25, p. xxii; Francisco Suárez, *A Commentary* ..., pp. 89-90.

79 *DM* 7, 2, n. 26, vol. 25, p. 270.

80 *DM* 8, 2, nn. 3-9, vol. 25, pp. 278-9.

81 For example, cf. *DM* 10, 1, nn. 3-5, vol. 25, p. 329; ibid., 3, nn. 11-15, pp. 350-51.

82 *DM* 28, 2, nn. 5,6, 8-13, vol. 26, pp. 9-12.

83 *DM* 29, 3, nn. 16-17, vol. 26, p. 53.

84 *DM* 40, 3, nn. 9-10, vol. 26, pp. 540-41.

85 As regards relation and the Trinity, cf. *DM* 7, 2, n. 27, vol. 25, p. 270; *DM* 10, 3, nn. 16-18, pp. 351-2; *DM* 28, 2, nn. 5,6, 8-13, vol. 26, pp. 9-12; *DM* 29, 3, nn. 16-17, vol. 26, p. 53; and *DM* 47, 4, n. 21, below. As regards relation and the Incarnation, see, e.g.: *DM* 47, 4, n. 9, below.

86 Cf. *Tractatus de sanctissimo Trinitatis mysterio, in duodecim libros divisus*, in *Opera omnia*, vol. 1, pp. 531-822.

87 Cf. ibid. VII, c. 7, nn. 9-10, vol. 1, pp. 706-707.

88 Ibid., V, c. 2, n. 3, p. 655.

89 Ibid., V, c. 2, n. 2, p. 654.

90 Ibid., III, c. 10, nn. 10-11, p. 610.

The work on the Incarnation, in the form of Commentaries and Disputations on the Third Part of the *Summa Theologiae* of St. Thomas Aquinas, takes up three full volumes (17, 18, and 19) of the Vivès edition of the *Opera*. Historically, it was the first of Suárez's published works, the first tome of which appeared at Alcalá in 1590.[91] After two years, he completed the work with a second tome, this time titled, "On the Mysteries of Christ's Life."[92] Central items here concern the sonship of Christ in relation to the Virgin Mary and to God the Father as well as the maternity of Mary and the paternity of God with respect to Christ.[93] Of particular interest in this work, and perhaps in the Treatise on the Trinity as well, is Suárez's view that a categorical relation is a mode or a formality, which is added to its foundation.[94] As we shall see, the doctrine given below in Section 2 of Disputation 47 is in direct contradiction to this view.

E. Summaries of the Sections of Disputation 47.

This portion of my Introduction owes much to the summary given by Sergio Rábade Romeo and his associates in their edition with Spanish translation of the *Disputationes metaphysicae*.[95] As they correctly lay it out, the Forty-Seventh Disputation can be articulated as follows:

1. Relation in general—its existence, its essence, and its division (Sections 1-4).

2. Categorical Relation—its essential definition, its subject, foundation, and terminus (Sections 5-9).

---

91 Cf. *Commentariorum ac disputationum in tertiam partem divi Thomae. Tomus primus*, Compluti: P. Madrigal, 1590. In this volume, Suárez commented on the first 26 questions of the Third part of the Summa of St. Thomas.

92 This may be found in volume 19 of the Vivès edition. It concerns Questions 27 to 59 of the Third Part of the *Summa*.

93 Cf. e.g. *Commentarii et disputationes P. Francisci Suarez e Societate Jesu, in Tertiam Partem D. Thomae, a Quaestione vigesima septima ad quinqugesimam nonam*, Q. 35, a. 5, Disputatio XII ("On the Relations which from the Nativity of Christ follow between Him and His Mother"—*De Relationibus quae ex Christi nativitate inter eum et matrem consequuntur*.), vol. 19, pp. 200-208. In the course of this Disputation, Suárez has treated the maternity of Mary and the dual sonship of Christ.

94 Cf. ibid., in Qu. 2, art. 8, p. 328; ibid., Disp. 8, s. 3, n. 21, p. 354; and Disp. 11, s. 2, n. 16, p. 440. Also, see *Tractatus de Trinitate*, VII, c. 4, n. 7, vol. 1, p. 698.

95 Cf. Francisco Suárez, *Disputaciones metafísicas*, edición y traducción de Sergio Rábade Romeo, Salvador Caballero Sánchez y Antonio Puigcerver Zanón, 7 vols. (Madrid: Editorial Gredos, 1960-1966), vol. 6, pp. 631-4.

3. The Aristotelian division of relative beings, based on a threefold foundation (Sections 10-15).

4. The question of whether one relation can be the terminus of another (Section 16).

5. The structure of the category of relation (Section 17).

6. The properties of relation (Section 18).

And then descending to the different Sections in turn:

Section I

Beginning with the issue of the real existence of relation, Suárez enumerates up to five reasons for doubting such existence (paragraphs 1-7). He then presents three different opinions: (1) there are no true real relations (paragraph 8); (2) relations exist, but they do not constitute a special category of being (paragraph 9); and (3) in created things there are real relations, which make up a proper and special category (paragraph 10). This last is the most accepted opinion and it is demonstrated by the teachings of the Catholic Faith and by rational arguments (paragraphs 11-15).

Section II

This is the key Section, in which the reality of a relation is directly addressed. It is first necessary to clarify how a real categorical relation is distinguished from substance and all absolute accidents in order to explain the reality and the nature of created relations (paragraph 1). In this regard, Suárez presents and rejects four different opinions (paragraphs 2-10). He then lingers with another opinion—held by many, especially Nominalists—which defends a distinction of reason with a basis in reality between relation and its absolute foundation (paragraphs 11-17). Next, without approving the distinction between the "being in" and the "being toward" of a relation, he admits the indicated Nominalist opinion (paragraph 22). Finally, he answers the arguments of the other opinions (paragraph 23) and the arguments remaining from Section 1 (paragraphs 24-25).

Section III

The Third Section treats the divisions of relation (paragraph 1). The first division is into real relation and relation of reason. It is only real relation which constitutes the category "toward something" (paragraphs 2-5). The second division is into relation "according to being said" and relation "according to being" (paragraphs 6-9). The third division is into transcendental relation and categorical relation (paragraphs 10-13).

Section IV

Suárez tells us that it is very difficult to explain the difference between categorical and transcendental relations (paragraph 1). It is possible to think of some differences that should be rejected (paragraphs 2-8). Others can be admitted (paragraphs 9-15). From this the inference is that the category "toward something" includes only relations that are categorical in a proper sense (paragraph 16). The remaining paragraphs (17-21) of this Section contain the reply to a difficulty raised in Section 1.

Section V

In this Section the *Doctor eximius* explains the essence and the proper definition of a categorical relation (paragraphs 1-4), and also explains as well as resolves the difficulties which the mentioned division encounters (paragraphs 5-13).

Section VI

This short Section is limited to proving that a categorical relation requires a subject, a foundation, and a terminus (paragraphs 1-6).

Section VII

As was said in the just preceding Section, a categorical relation needs a foundation (paragraph 1), which in some way is distinguished from the subject of a relation (paragraphs 2-3). This foundation can be either an accident or the substance itself (paragraphs 4-9). Although the question is discussed, Suárez prefers not to separate a foundation from a reason for being founded (paragraphs 10-14).

Section VIII

For a categorical relation there is also required a real terminus (paragraph 1). But must this terminus exist in actuality? There are reasons to doubt that (paragraph 2), and one author has thought that a terminus that is real and really existing is not necessary (paragraph 3). Suárez maintains the contrary, and in so doing he follows the common opinion of philosophers and theologians (paragraphs 4-7). He answers the arguments of Gregory of Rimini (paragraph 8), and he rejects the opinion that the terminus belongs to the essence of a relation (paragraphs 9-12). Finally, he affirms that not even by the absolute power of God can a relation remain without a terminus (paragraphs 13-14).

Section IX

For a real relation it is necessary that the foundation and the terminus, formally considered, be distinguished with a real distinction, although this does not have to be equal in all cases (paragraphs 1-6).

Section X

Suárez proposes to examine the division which Aristotle has made of relation looking at a threefold foundation (paragraph 1). Having first explained the Aristotelian doctrine (paragraphs 2-4), he raises the two main questions which arise with respect to that doctrine: (1) whether each one of the members of the stated division is designated in a fitting manner, and (2) whether the division includes the whole range of categorical relations. With regard to the first, there are various arguments which present difficulty (paragraphs 5-10), and the same is true with regard to the second (paragraph 11). Nevertheless, the two questions are answered in the sense of approving the division which Aristotle has made (paragraphs 12-16).

Section XI

It is necessary to answer each one of the difficulties of the preceding Section (paragraph 1). Beginning with the first class of relations, which is founded on unity (paragraphs 2-3), it is affirmed that a relation of unity can be founded on the realities of all the categories (paragraph 4) and there is explained the sense in which one relation can be the foundation of another (paragraphs 5-13). In passing, he explains to which class relations of identity, similarity, and equality belong (paragraphs 14-15). The Section ends by affirming that generic unity can found a real relation (paragraphs 16-19) and by indicating the characteristics of relations of the first class (paragraphs 20-21).

Section XII

In order to treat the second class of relations (paragraph 1), the problem is raised of whether all the relations of this class are real (paragraph 2). Suárez replies by setting up some distinctions (paragraphs 3-4). He concerns himself then with the proximate foundation of paternity (paragraphs 5-6), and of the relation of agent (paragraphs 7-8), whether it is in act (paragraph 9) or in potency (paragraphs 10-14).

Section XIII

Regarding the third class of relations, founded upon the character of measure (paragraph 1), Suárez presents and resolves a difficulty about the authentic thought of Aristotle (paragraphs 2-9).

Section XIV

Is the Aristotelian division sufficient and adequate? (paragraph 1). To answer this question, Suárez indicates how all real relations are reduced to the three kinds, which make up the stated division (paragraphs 2-8).

Section XV

After indicating the double sense in which non-mutual relations can be taken (paragraph 1), Suárez makes a division between reciprocal and non-reciprocal relations (paragraph 2) and raises a difficulty in their regard (paragraphs 3-7). To resolve this difficulty, he affirms that there are some non-mutual relations, which are properly found in the third Aristotelian class of relations (paragraph 8). Then he replies to opposing arguments (paragraphs 9-12) and resolves difficulties proposed at the beginning (paragraphs 13-15). Next, he presents the opinion of the Nominalists about relations in God from time (paragraph 16) and, against them, denies that such relations are real (paragraphs 17-29).

Section XVI

This Section concerns the question of whether the formal terminus of one relation is another relation or has an absolute character (paragraph 1). Having explained the title of the Section (paragraph 2), Suárez presents and explains different opinions (paragraphs 3-5). He crystallizes his thought in the following assertions: (1) in non mutual relatives, the reason why one extreme is the terminus of the relation of the other is not a relation that is opposite to that of the other, but the very entity itself or a property of that terminus (paragraphs 6-13); (2) In mutual relations, the *raison d'être* of a terminus is also some absolute character that constitutes the formal foundation of the opposite relation (paragraphs 14-22). With this an answer is given to the bases of the other opinions, explaining the sense in which relatives are simultaneous in nature, in knowledge, and in definition (paragraphs 23-34), and finally treating of the termini of the divine relations (paragraphs 35-38), and of relative opposition (paragraphs 39-40).

Section XVII

It is proposed to treat the structuring of the category, "toward something" (paragraph 1). The first difficulty is in knowing how all relatives can be reduced to one single genus (paragraph 2). There is accepted the possibility of one single supreme genus which includes all relatives (paragraph 3) and there is adduced the solution which some offer to the motive for doubting (paragraphs 4-5). This solution is probable even though it supposes a false basis (paragraph 6). Suárez affirms that the relative in general is not in an order to another as to its correlative (paragraphs 7-8), that the relative in general has a terminus in general which corresponds to it (paragraph 8), and that the common character of terminus does not constitute a proper category (paragraph 10). Afterwards, he raises the question of the contraction of the supreme genus of relatives into its inferiors (paragraphs 11-14), the question of the origin of the essential and specific difference of relations (paragraph 15), and the question of the simultaneity of various relations—which differ only numerically—in the same subject (paragraphs 16-23). He ends the Section by rejecting an opinion about the relation that a son has with respect to a father and a mother (paragraphs 24-28).

Section XVIII

This is the shortest Section. It designates as properties of all relatives: not having a contrary; being susceptible of more or less; receiving the designation of "convertibles"; being simultaneous in nature; and also being simultaneous in knowledge and definition (paragraphs 1-6).

II. Translator's Notes

The hardest task for me translating the Forty-Seventh Disputation came from the terminology which Suárez employed to designate *relation*. Thus, he used a roughly synonymous variety of names and expressions which I had to bear in mind.[96] These, and the translations I normally gave them, included: "*Ad aliquid*" ("Toward something"); "*Relatio*" ("Relation"); "*Respectus*" ("Respect"); "*Habitudo*" ("Disposition" or "Relation"); "*Habitudo ad*" ("Disposition toward"); "*Ordo*" ("Order"); "*Ordinare*" ("to order"); "*Comparatio*" ("Comparison" or "relation"); "*Referre*" ("to refer" or "to relate"); and "*Se habere ad*" ("to have oneself toward," "to have themselves toward," or "to be related").[97] For the

---

96 Note that Krempel, in the chapter (6) he has devoted to the Thomistic terminology of relation, has remarked that "in order to convey the idea of relation, Saint Thomas has made use of a score of terms" (*Pour traduire l'idée de relation, saint Thomas dispose d'une vingtaine de termes.*); cf. *La doctrine de la relation ...*, p. 127.

97 Prior to Suárez, the only attempt to distinguish among "relatio," "respectus," and "habitudo" which I have found was that given by the Scotist, Anthony Trombetta, O.F.M. (1436-1517), against the background of the Scotistic distinction of intrinsically and extrinsically advenient relations. Trombetta's almost unintelligible text I have transcribed and translated as follows: "... properly and correctly speaking, according to the way of the Subtle Doctor [i.e. Duns Scotus] a respect which is essentially in the category of relation is called a relation. But respects which are outside the category of relation are called dispositions and respects and not properly relations. For this it should be noted that these have themselves in order: relative, relation, respect, and disposition, among which the character [or formality] of

most part, when I thought it would help the reader, I enclosed the Latin word or phrase (usually in nominative case) within parentheses. Yet other problems came from various forms of "real," "really," or "in the nature of things." Thus, Suárez used *"realis, reale," "realiter," "ex natura rei," "in rerum natura," "in re," "in re ipsa," "ex re ipsa,"*, *"in ente reali," "a parte rei,"* etc., interchangeably or in ways that were impossible to distinguish. At the same time, I was very much aware of levels of reality—existential, essential, actual, possible, or intentional—which might need to be distinguished. Wherever I

---

relative is most basic. Hence every relative is a relation. Or it includes a relation. For a relative [thing] beyond the relation which it includes also includes something absolute, which is said to be referred through that relation. But a relation does not include something absolute. Likewise, every relation is a respect, and not every respect is a relation, because a relation is an intrinsically advenient respect which arises from the nature of a foundation when a terminus has been posited. However, a respect is something common to an intrinsically advenient respect and also to one which is extrinsically advenient. Likewise, every respect is a disposition, but not every disposition is a respect. For between a subject and a proper attribute there is a disposition and yet there is not a respect. Likewise, circumscribing all relations, there is some disposition of the Divine Essence to its Attributes (such as [a disposition] of a foundation to what is founded), and yet this is not a respect, since it is repugnant to the [divine] Essence as Essence that it be referred to something. From this it follows that speaking properly about relation only an intrinsically advenient respect is a relation according to the way of the Doctor." (... *proprie relationes. Pro quo est notandum quod ista se habent per ordinem relativum: relatio, respectus et habitudo, inter quas rationes ratio relativi est infima. Unde omne relativum est relatio vel includit relationem. Relativum enim ultra relationem qua(m) includit, etiam includit aliquod absolutum, quod denominatur referri per ipsam relationem; sed relatio non includit aliquod absolutum. Similiter omnis relatio est respectus, et non omnis respectus est relatio, quia relatio est respectus intrinsecus adveniens, qui oritur ex natura fundamenti, posito termino. Respectus autem est quiddam commune ad respectum intrinsecus advenientem et etiam extrinsecus advenientem. Similiter omnis respectus est habitudo, non omnis habitudo est respectus; quia inter subiectum et propriam passionem est habitudo; et tamen non est respectus. Similiter, circunscriptis omnibus relationibus, essentiae divinae ad attributa est aliqua habitudo (qualis est fundamenti ad fundatum), et tamen non est aliquis respectus, quia repugnat essentiae ut essentia est ad aliquid referri. Ex quo sequitur quod loquendo proprie de relatione, solum respectus intrinsecus adveniens est relatio secundum viam Doctoris.*) Magistri Antonii Trombete in tractatum formalitatum Scoti sententia, Art. I, Venetiis, 1505, fol. 3ra. On Scotus' doctrine of intrinsically and extrinsically advenient relations, which Suárez rejects, see DM 47, Section 16, paragraph 17, below. For Krempel tracing distinctions in the Thomistic use of *"respectus," "habitudo," "proportio," "ordo,"* and similar terms, cf. *La doctrine de relation ...*, pp. 101-114.

could, I looked to the context for help. But that still left me at times rather queasy about the results.

Add to these: "*per se*," which in different places I translated: "through itself," "essentially," "necessarily," or "directly."[98] And then, there was every Latin translator's nightmare: "*ratio*"—which depending on contexts and nuances I rendered as: "reason," "reasoning," "argument," "concept," "nature," "character," "feature," "aspect," "facet," etc. etc.

A second hard task was furnished by Suárez's references, especially his cross-references to other places in Disputation 47 or in the *Disputatationes metaphysicae* as a whole. In this last connection, particularly difficult was his practice of referring to places "above" and "below." While usually it was possible to locate these places, at times I was not able with certainty to identify the passage to which Suárez was referring. I did the best I could, but on occasion I simply could not fix on the passage which he had in mind.

The only other thing which I would now remark is that throughout the work I did take the liberty of breaking Suárez's often interminable paragraphs down into more manageable and, I hope, more intelligible ones.

For all of this, as well as for the often hesitant and tenuous character of my translation, I ask the reader's indulgence.

---

98 In this connection, let me call the reader's attention to DM 47, Section 2, n. 9, below, where I have noted Suárez's use of "primo," "per se," and "essentialiter" in one series.

Disputation 47

English Translation

In General about Real Relation

After the two preceding categories (*genera*)[1] of quantity and quality, Aristotle, in *Metaphysics*, Book 5, Chapter 15,[2] treats of "toward something" (*ad aliquid*) not because it is more perfect in entity than all of the six last categories—for Averroes (*Commentator*), in [his commentary] on the *Metaphysics*, Book 12, comment 19,[3] says that among all the categories relation has the least entity,[4] the truth of which will be evident from what will be said. Therefore, Aristotle does not seem to have observed an order of perfection, but rather an order of doctrine, since the doctrine that pertains to this category is more universal and also because it is in a certain way necessary for knowing the other categories inasmuch as they seem in large part to consist of a relation.[5] Add also that very many relations follow closely upon quantity and quality. Therefore, with

1 For Suárez noting the equivalence at times of "genera" and "categories," cf. *DM* 39, 2, n. 29, vol. 26, p. 518.

2 Cf. *Metaphysics* 5.15.1020b26-1021b11.

3 Cf. *Averrois Commentaria et Introductiones in omnes libros Aristotelis cum eorum versione latina* (Venetiis: Apud Junctas, 1562), vol. 8, fol. 306ra. It may be noted that Averroes here says that relation is of such minimal being that some have regarded it as a matter of second intention; cf. "quidam reputaverunt ipsam esse ex secundis intellectis" ibid. This, of course, would be to cross the line which Aristotle has in effect drawn between being in the categories and being as true.

4 Cf. Aristotle, *Metaphysics*, 14.1.1088a 23-4.

5 An "order of doctrine" (*ordo doctrinae*) is something that Suárez often mentions throughout his works but to my knowledge he has not described it at length. The text here is instructive for its understanding. In his "Most Ample Index to the Metaphysics of Aristotle" (*Index locupletissimus in Metaphysicam Aristotelis*), which is joined to the *Disputationes metaphysicae*, he seems to equate the order of doctrine with "proceeding from things more known to those which are less known" and says "that method is everywhere repeated by Aristotle, and to explain it is the proper task of a logician"; cf. *Index*, VII, c. 4, vol. 25, p. xxxi. There he has also distinguished between an order of doctrine for things in themselves, in which metaphysics will be first, and an order of doctrine for us, in which the teaching of metaphysics will come last. For the Aristotelian base of the order of doctrine as it is understood here in Disputation 47, cf. *Posterior Analytics* 1.2.72a1. For much the same understanding as Suárez has here, see John of St. Thomas, *Naturalis philosophiae*, I. pars, qu. 1, art. 3, in *Ioannis a Sancto Thomae, O.P., Cursus philosophicus thomisticus*, nova editio a P. Beato Reiser, O.S.B. (Taurini: Ex Officina Domus Editorialis Marietti, 1933), tom. II, 20-22, who also regards it as an order in which we move from things more universal and confused (which are more known to us) to the more particular and distinct.

regard to relation we shall in general see first whether it exists, what it is,[6] and how many and what properties or causes it has,[7] and then, more in particular, we shall discuss the principal kinds of relations as well as their foundations and termini.
/p. 782/

Section I

Whether Relation Is a True Category (genus) of Real Being,
Distinct from the Rest [of the Categories].
Various Reasons for which Almost Every Problem
Regarding This Category Is Proposed.

1. *First.*—There can be a first reason for doubting inasmuch as relation precisely as such (*relatio ut relatio*) puts nothing real in a thing that is said to be related (*referri*); therefore, it cannot constitute a real category (*genus*) of being. The consequence is evident, because a real category is founded upon a real being, which exists or posits something in the nature of things. But a relation, insofar as it is given in created things (for this is the way in which we are now treating it), cannot be something real in the nature of things, if it does not put such in the thing itself that is related. For neither does it posit anything in the terminus [of the relation], as is self-evident, even though it may perhaps presuppose [something], about which [we will speak] later; nor does it exist (*manet*) in itself, since it is not a substance. Therefore, if it puts nothing in the thing itself that is related, it is *absolutely* nothing real. The antecedent is proven: first, because "toward" (*ad*) [precisely] as "toward" does not express a real characteristic (*ratio*), both because univocally and in an entirely proper way it fits relations of reason,[8] and also because "toward" as "toward" prescinds from "being in" (*esse in*); therefore, as such it puts nothing real in anything. Otherwise, in line with its own proper and ultimate character (*ratio*) it would include "being in" (*inesse*), which is repugnant (*quod repugnat*). Therefore, a relation puts nothing in a thing that it relates. The consequence is clear: for relation precisely as such (*relatio ut relatio*) entails nothing more than "being

---

6 On this, cf. Aristotle, *Posterior Analytics* 1.1.71a11-13, who says there are two ways in which something must be known prior to its scientific consideration. First, we must know *that* it is. And, second, we must know *what* it is.

7 See Section 6, below.

8 This position, which Suárez himself will oppose, is that which will be later embraced as the basis for a unified Semiotics which will bridge between natural and conventional signs; for this, cf. Section 3, n. 2, note 13, below.

toward" (*esse ad*)—as Aristotle says that relatives are those whose whole being ⎫
is to be toward something else.[9]   ⎭

2. *Second.*—Secondly, because a particular relative designation that comes anew to something, does not change that thing nor in reality make it be other than before, for, as Aristotle says in Book 5 of the *Physics*, Text 10, a relation comes without the change of a thing.[10] Therefore, a relation puts nothing in such a thing. The consequence is evident: because it is impossible to understand that something real is newly added to some subject and that this [subject] not be really different than it was before. For, if something is added to it, it has something that it did not have before, but this very thing is to be different than before. Moreover, what some people reply, [namely] that [this thing] does not gain "something" but rather "toward something," seems indeed to be a game of words. For I ask whether that "toward something" is something. For, if it is, then he who gains "toward something" also gains something. Therefore he is in another way and is changed.[11] But if "toward something" is not something, then it is nothing, and this is the point intended.
/col. b/

3. *Third.*—Thirdly, this is further explained. For a relation, as a relation, is nothing apart from what is absolute. Therefore, it is simply nothing. The consequence is evident. For when we ask whether a relation is something real, we are concerned with it insofar as it is distinguished or prescinded from absolute things. Otherwise, how will it be a distinct category (*genus*) of being? But the antecedent is proven: because if we posit, for example, two real white things, they, by virtue of the absolute qualities that they have, are similar between themselves. Therefore, they have that relative designation[12] (*denominatio relativa*) by virtue of absolutes existing or taken together, without any other real addition. Therefore, a relation adds nothing real to absolute things.

Both consequents are manifest: for if a relation is something, it is only on account of that relative denomination (*denominatio relativa*)[13] that seems to intervene between those absolutes. If, therefore, that denomination is taken

9 For this, see *Categories* 7.8a31-32.

10 Cf. *Physics* 5.2.225b11-13.

11 Here Suárez's grammar is inconsistent. Literally, his passage would translate: "he who newly has 'toward something' also newly has something; therefore, he has himself in another way and it has been changed."

12 That is, "similar".

13 For some indication of the ambiguity (between naming and what is named) of Suárez's "denominatio" here, see my article: "Prolegomena to a Study of Extrinsic Denomination in the Work of Francis Suarez, S.J.," *Vivarium*, XXII, 2 (1984), pp. 121-160.

only from absolutes, whatever else is added is imaginary (*fictitium*). Moreover, the antecedent is proven: because, if two white things have been posited in reality, whether you mentally separate every other real thing added to them, or whether we posit that this[14] be separated or impeded by the absolute power of God,[15] those two things will still remain similar between themselves. Nor can the mind conceive anything else, because they necessarily retain a formal unity,[16] and to be similar is nothing else than to have qualities of the same form (*ratio*).

But if someone answers that this is truly said about things that are fundamentally, but not formally similar, he will certainly be begging the question. For this is what we intend, namely, that there is not any other denomination present except that which is called fundamental. For this is enough in order that those things be truly similar, and that other formal denomination either is nothing or, at most, it is a consideration of reason.

4. This last is confirmed: for in this way many comparable denominations are preserved without any intrinsic addition in the thing that is denominated. For in this way God is called creator or lord from time;[17] and in this way a column is said to be right or left; and likewise a wall is said to be seen, etc.[18] By the same reasoning, therefore, every similar denomination can be preserved without the addition of a relation that is something real.

But if someone says that in the stated examples there is no foundation from the side of the things denominated, we shall answer that perhaps this is not altogether true, which we will afterwards explain, and also it is not satisfactory, for if something that does not have a foundation can be denominated relatively from positing something else, even though nothing real is added to it, then much more could a thing that has /p. 783/ some foundation, by virtue of that

---

14 That is, "every other real thing."

15 On Suárez on the absolute versus the ordinary power of God, cf. *DM* 30, s. 17, nn. 32-36 (vol. 26, 216-218). For discussion of the absolute and the ordinary power of God in the Scholastic tradition up to Luther, see Richard P. Desharnais, *The History of the Distinction between God's Absolute and Ordained Power and Its Influence on Martin Luther*, unpublished Ph.D. dissertation, Catholic University of America: Washington, D.C., 1966. Also, cf. Mary Anne Pernoud, "The Theory of the *Potentia Dei* according to Aquinas, Scotus, and Ockham," *Antonianum*, 47 (1972), pp. 69-95.

16 For Suárez on formal unity, see *DM* 6, 1, vol. 25, pp. 201-206.

17 For this cf. *Disp. Metaphys.*, disp. 30, sec. 5, no. 5 (Vol. 26, p. 87); *ibid.*, disp. 47, sec. 15, no. 26 (p. 846).

18 For examples, a voice is said to be *heard*, an odor is said to be *smelled*, or a texture is said to be *felt*. Such designations add nothing real to the things designated.

[foundation] and the co-existence of something else be precisely denominated in this way, without the addition of any relative thing. Therefore, a relation (*respectus*) of this kind is nothing real apart from what is absolute.

5. *Fourth.*—In fourth place, we can argue (and this is a second principal reason for doubting), that, even if we grant that a relation is something real, it still cannot constitute a new category of being, different from other categories. This is proven: for an order to another is intrinsically included in every real concept of created being. For, from its inception, every created being, insofar as it is such, even substance itself, entails a relation (*habitudo*) of essential dependence with respect to uncreated being, and therefore, it is analogically being or substance in comparison with that.[19] Likewise, every accident entails an essential relation (*habitudo*) to a subject, because of which [relation] it is said to be "a being of a being" (*entis ens*) rather than [simply] "a being" (*ens*). Again, in the case of individual categories of accidents, there are found individual relations. For quantity, insofar as it is continuous, entails an essential relation to the termini by which it is continued, and conversely, a point and other similar termini entail an essential relation to the parts whose termini they are. And among qualities, a potency entails an essential relation to its object; and with regard to knowledge, and consequently, with regard to habits and disposition, Aristotle, in the Chapter about Quality, says that they are "toward something."[20]

6. However, he adds, being "toward something" at generic levels (*secundum rationes genericas*) of knowledge, but not at specific levels; *for knowledge*, he says, *is toward the knowable* (*scibile*), *but grammar as such is not toward something else* (*ad aliud*).[21] But this immediately is false. For, even though the names perhaps are not so clearly imposed, nevertheless, in reality just as knowledge in general entails a relation (*habitudo*) to the knowable, in the same way this knowledge [is related] to this object. Moreover, this hardly matters for the present difficulty, since the genus and the species belong to the same category. Therefore, if this specific knowledge is a quality, then knowledge in general is a genus in the category of quality. Therefore, since it is also "toward something," it will be impossible that those things that are "toward something" be located in a special category.

However, what Aristotle immediately adds seems much less satisfactory, namely, that it is not unreasonable for the same thing to be located both under

19 For Suárez's teaching on analogy here, cf. my article: "Suarez on the Analogy of Being," *The Modern Schoolman*, XLVI, pp. 219-249 and 323-341.

20 Cf. *Categories* 8.11a23-24.

21 Ibid., 11a25-30. Also, see Marcello Zanatta, *Aristotele, Le Categorie*, terza edizione (Milano: Biblioteca Universale Rizzoli, 2000), pp. 627-31.

quality and also "toward something," if they both are fitting for it.[22] For the same thing cannot be essentially placed in diverse categories. But knowledge, for example, is not only accidentally but also essentially "toward something". This is first because its whole entity is intrinsically /col. b/ ordered toward the knowable, as Aristotle says in the Chapter, "Toward Something";[23] and second, because otherwise, if knowledge were only accidentally related to the knowable, knowledge itself would not be placed under the category "toward something," but rather that relation that comes to it accidentally [would be so placed], which is contrary to Aristotle, in the same [work], the Chapter, "About Quality."[24]

And the same difficulty is pressing with regard to the last six categories,[25] which, in the opinion of all, include some relation (*relatio*). Thus, with regard to position (*situs*),[26] Aristotle says this in the *Categories*,[27] and about the others we will speak in their own places.[28] Therefore, this character, "toward something," is transcendent, and is included in every entity, especially in every created entity. Therefore, it does not constitute a particular category (*genus*).

7. Two answers are usually given to this last difficulty. The first is that all these [examples] that we have enumerated in the other categories are relative only "according to being said" (*secundum dici*). But those alone that make up a special category are relative "according to being" (*secundum esse*). But this answer will be easily refuted, if we ask what is meant by "relative according to being said." For, either those [examples] of which we are so speaking are named as though they were relative, even though they have in reality no inclination (*habitudo*) among themselves, or certain things are so named, which do have in reality some relation, but of another nature than a real relation. The first cannot be said, one, because knowledge is not only in a manner of speaking but also in reality ordered in its being to what is knowable (*scibile*), and a power is [really ordered] to its object, and likewise with regard to other examples. Also, two, because if these relative denominations or locutions are

---

22 Cf. *Categories* c. 8.11a37-8.
23 Cf. *Categories*, c. 7.7b23-34.
24 Ibid., 8.8b29.
25 That is: action, passion, place, time, position, and possession—the so-called "*sex principia*" (six principles) of medieval philosophy.
26 For Suárez on position, cf. *DM* 52, ed. Vivès vol. 26, pp. 1006-1011.
27 Cf. *Categories*, c. 7, 6b2-3.
28 Thus, action will be treated explicitly in *DM* 48, vol. 26, pp. 867-97; passion in *DM* 49, pp. 897-912; duration and time, or "when" (*quando*), in *DM* 50, pp. 912-72; place or "where" (*ubi*) in *DM* 51, 972-1006; and possession or having (*habitus*), in *DM* 53, 1011-14.

said to be in our manner of speaking and not in reality, the same may be said of every similar denomination, and no probable way will be left for stating that relations of this kind are real, because they are for the most part gathered from denominations of this kind. But if the other choice is taken, one must explain what inclinations (*habitudo*) of this kind are or how they are distinguished from relations or why relations (*relatio*) of a different character from these inclinations (*habitudo*) are necessary.[29]

And in this there is indicated another answer, and its difficulty.[30] For it is usually said that in the mentioned things belonging to other categories there are included transcendental relations (*respectus*), but not genuine categorical relations, which constitute a special category (*genus*). However, in regard to a division of this sort we must immediately ask: why is it necessary to multiply these diverse kinds of relation (*respectus*)? For if a transcendental (*transcendens*)[31] relation (*respectus*) is true and real, it suffices for all relative denominations that are not /p. 784/ purely extrinsic denominations. Therefore, it is superfluous to fashion other relations (*relatio*). At this point, it will be necessary to explain what kind of distinction there is between relations (*respectus*) of this kind, or why one constitutes a special category and another does not.

Various Opinions Are Proposed.

8. *First.*—These seem to be the principal difficulties that generally occur with regard to real relation. But others that could have been offered with regard to the particular kinds of relation are proposed below. Therefore, because of these difficulties there can be two ways of speaking. The first is, that there are no genuine real relations, but all denominations that are explained in the manner of relations are taken from absolutes themselves or from their co-existence. Averroes in *Metaphysics*, Book 12, Comment 19,[32] and Avicenna in Book 3, Chapter 10 of his *Metaphysics*[33] present this opinion, and Aureoli—according

---

29 This is a passage to note for a subtle distinction between "habitudo" and "relatio."

30 This would then be a fifth difficulty.

31 We may note that Suárez, in time before Kant, often uses "transcendental" (*transcendentalis*) and "transcendent" (*transcendens*) interchangeably. On this, cf. Rolf Darge, *Suárez' transzendentale Seinsauslegung und die Metaphysiktradition* (Leiden/Boston: Brill, 2004), esp. 66-70.

32 Cf. *Commentaria* ...(Venetiis: Apud Junctas, 1562), vol. 8, fol. 306rab. Note that Averroes here "presents" this opinion, which is not his own.

33 For this, see *Avicenna Latinus: Liber de philosophia prima sive scientia divina, I-IV*, Tr. 3, c. 10, édition critique de la traduction latine médiévale, par S. Van Riet (Louvain: E. Peeters/Leiden: E.J. Brill, 1977), p. 178.

to Capreolus in [his *Defensiones*] Book 1, Distinction 30, Question 1—has followed it.³⁴

9. *Second*.—Another opinion can be that there are indeed real relations in things, but that they do not constitute a special category of being, but rather that they are a kind of transcendental condition, which can be included in all beings. Soto, in the beginning of [his treatment of] the category, "toward something," relying on Albert and Alexander [of Aphrodisias] in the same context, has attributed this opinion to Zeno and earlier philosophers before Plato.³⁵

10. *Third*.—But now the received opinion, [which is] a kind of common philosophical axiom, is that in created things there are real relations, which constitute a genuine and special category. This was the opinion of Plato,³⁶ and Aristotle followed him, and all his interpreters, Averroes, Simplicius, and the rest of the Greeks and the Latins, followed Aristotle. And the theologians fol-

lowed these, [e.g.] St. Thomas, in [*Summa Theologiae*], Part 1, Question 13, Article 7;³⁷ Question 28, Articles 1 and 2,³⁸ and frequently elsewhere, as well as Capreolus³⁹ and others, in [*Sentences* commentaries], Book 1, Distinction 33; Gregory [of Rimini], extensively in [Book 1], Distinction 28, Question

34 For the arguments of Aureoli, cf. Johannis Capreoli, Tholosani, Ordinis Praedi-
catorum, Thomistarum Principis, *Defensiones theologiae divi Thomae Aquinatis,
In I Sent.*, d. 30, q. 1, a. 1, de novo editae cura et studio RR. PP. Ceslai Paban et
Thomae Pègues, ejusdem ordinis in Conventu Tholosano Professorum, (Turonibus:
Sumptibus Alfred Cattier, Bibliopolae Editoris, 1900), tomus II, pp. 284-88. It is
worth noting that Suárez, like many other late Scholastic authors, usually knows
Aureoli through Capreolus.

35 For this, cf. Dominici Soto Segobiensis, Praedicatoriae Familiae Theologi, ac
Philosophi praestantissimi, *In Porphyrii Isagogen, Aristotelis Categorias, librosque de
Demonstratione, Absolutissima Commentaria ... , in librum Praedicamentorum Aristotelis*, cap. vii (Venetiis: Ex Officina Dominici Guerraei et Io. Baptistae, fratrum,
1587—reprinted Frankfurt: Minerva G.M.B.H., 1967), p. 195.

36 Cf. *Sophist* 255C.

37 Cf. Sancti Thomae Aquinatis, *Opera omnia*, iussu impensaque Leonis XIII P.M.
edita, tomus IV (Romae: Ex Typographia Polyglotta, S.C. de Propaganda Fide,
1888), pp. 152-5.

38 Ibid., pp. 318-319, and 321-322.

39 Cf. *Defensiones, In I Sent.*, d. 30, q. 1, a. 1, ed. Paban-Pègues, tom. II, pp. 282-
310.

1;[40] Henry [of Ghent], in *Quodlibet* 3, Question 4[41] and *Quodlibet* 9, Question 3[42]—not only because of philosophical reasons, but also because this opinion is better fitted for explaining the mystery of the Trinity and may seem to be very much confirmed from that.

11. For Christian Faith teaches that in God there are three real relations, constituting and distinguishing divine persons[43]—from which an evident argument is made that the concept of relation as such, without adding that it is created or uncreated, is not imaginary (*fictitium*) and that for some thing to be related is not an extrinsic denomination resulting from a mental comparison only,[44] but /col. b/ it is something real, since it is something real in God.

And from this it is further, with great probability, inferred that it can also be something real in created things. For it would be repugnant to created things either because of their perfection or because of their imperfection. The first cannot be said, for if relation is not incompatible with the supreme perfection of God, why will it be incompatible with the perfection of a creature?

You say: because that relation of God is substantial, but in a creature it must be accidental. But against this, in fact, it is not more repugnant to a relation as such that it be accidental than that it be substantial. For just as an accident entails being in another, so a substance entails being in itself. If, therefore, with this latter feature (*ratio*) there can be joined "being toward another" (*esse ad aliud*), much more [can it be joined] with the former. And, otherwise, a real accident is not repugnant to a creature as such; therefore, neither will such a relation be repugnant to it, which [relation], even though it is accidental, is something real. But neither can it be repugnant on account of imperfection,

---

40 For this, cf. Gregorii Ariminensis OESA, *Lectura super primum et secundum Sententiarum* (Tomus III, ed. A.D. Trapp et V. Marcolino, Berlin/New York: Walter de Gruyter, 1984), In I Sent. dist. 28-32, qu. 1 additionalis, et q. 1, pp. 79-115.

41 Cf. Henrici Goethals a Gandavo, *Quodlibeta* (Parisiis: Vaenundantur ab Iodoco Badio Ascensio, 1518; reprint, Louvain: Bibliothèque S.J., 1961), *Quodl.* III, q. 4, fol. 51rO.

42 Cf. Henrici de Gandavo, *Quodlibet* IX, qu. 3, ed. R. Macken (Leuven: University Press, 1983), pp. 46-51.

43 See esp. the Decree for the Jacobites at the Council of Florence, February 4, 1442, in Henricus Denzinger et Adolfus Schönmetzer, S.J., *Enchiridion symbolorum definitionum et declarationum de rebus fidei et morum*, editio xxxii (Barcinone/Friburgi/ Romae/ Neo-Eboraci: Herder, 1963), n. 1330, p. 337. In a note here, the editors of the *Enchiridion* tell us that this fundamental Trinitarian doctrine seems to have been first enunciated by St. Anselm of Canterbury, *De processione Spiritus Sancti*, c. 1, ed. F.S. Schmitt, in *S. Ans. Cant. Opera omnia*, vol. 2 (Edinburgh, 1946), pp. 180-181.

44 Note here what is a mind-dependent understanding of extrinsic denomination.

for a relation as a relation does not entail imperfection. But if something of imperfection be added to it, from the very fact that it is accidental, such imperfection is not outside the range of being. Therefore, by this theological argument it seems to be effectively proven that real relations (*respectus*) can be and are *de facto* given in created things.

12. But this is usually proven by arguments derived only from natural reasoning, especially from relative ways of speaking and from denominations that exist in things themselves apart from any fashioning by the intellect,[45] and that therefore are necessarily founded in some real being. However, they are not founded in something absolute; therefore, in something relative; therefore, there is some real relative being in things. The antecedent is clear in these denominations: *greater, lesser, equal, similar, near, far, father, son,* and the like. For all of these plainly entail a reference (*habitudo*) to something else, without which they can neither be nor be understood, and they exist in things themselves, as seems self-evident.

13. But how great is the force of these proofs we will see in what follows. For the second, [that is], the natural argument for the most part depends upon solutions of arguments that we cannot give before we explain many things about the distinction and division of relations (*relatio*). However, the theological argument does not seem sufficiently efficacious for showing categorical relations, since divine relations are outside every category. But if God were in the category of substance, those relations, by the fact that they are personalities of divine nature, would belong or be reduced to that same [category of substance]—just as created personalities or substances /p. 785/ belong to that very category.[46] Hence, the argument from parity (*argumentum a simili*), for example, from divine to created paternity, is not very effective; for divine paternity does not result from or follow on generation, but rather constitutes the person who is the principle of generation. Therefore, that uncreated personality, inasmuch as it is substantial, can be thought to be quasi-transcendental, that is, intimately included in the adequate concept of such a being or [such] a personal substance. Accordingly, from those relations it does not seem possible to infer categorical relations, but at most real transcendental relations intimately included in some beings.

14. But another way to show the relations in question is usually taken especially from the order of the universe, which [order] is something accidental

---

45 For this more mind-independent notion of denomination, cf. my earlier cited article, '*Prolegomena* to a Study of Extrinsic Denomination in the Work of Francis Suarez, S.J."

46 For this, cf. Suárez, *DM* 34, s. 1, ed. Vivès, vol. 26, pp. 348-53.

to those absolute things, of which the universe is comprised. For, even if the elements and the heavens were to be constituted in another order, the absolute things themselves would be the same. The order, therefore, that they now have is something accidental to them. And [this order] is not something fashioned by the mind (*ratio*), for it is self-evidently in things themselves, and it tends to the great perfection of the universe, as Aristotle witnesses in *Metaphysics*, Book 12, Text. 52.[47] And it is only a relation, which necessarily belongs to its own category, because it is not part of the intrinsic nature of any absolute thing, nor can it be indicated to which of the other categories it may belong or be reduced.

Nevertheless, this proof is subject to those difficulties that have been mentioned as part of what is to be discussed. For the order belonging to the perfection of the universe is so great that individual bodies have been constituted in their natural places, which is indeed something absolute in those individuals, and in everything together it entails their co-existence. But that there follows on this a particular accident, which is a real relatio (*relatio*), seems to make no difference as regards the perfection of the universe.

The Resolution of the Question.

15. Nevertheless, we are supposing that the third and common opinion[48] is true and certain in philosophy, which we are now confirming especially by authority. But its reason and demonstration should most of all be taken from those [already mentioned] relative denominations, adding two things.

The first is that those [denominations] are such that they are accidental to absolute created things, and they can be varied in some subject without the loss of its absolute form, which is clear enough in almost all the examples cited above.[49] The second is that these are not merely extrinsic denominations /col. b/, and in this there is difficulty, but it depends upon what will be said below. For it is necessary first to explain the mode of entity of such relations (*relatio*) and denominations.

---

47 Cf. *Metaphysics* 12.10.1075a11-24. Also, see Avicenna, *Liber de prima philosophia*, Tr. 3, c. 10, ed. Van Riet, pp. 178-9.
48 That there are real created relations.
49 Cf. This Section, nn. 4, 6, and 12.

Secton II.
Whether a Real Categorical Relation Is Distinguished Really, or Modally and "From the Nature of the Thing" (*ex natura rei*),[1] From Substance and All Absolute Accidents.[2]

1. This question is extremely necessary in order to explain in what sense created relations are something real and what they are as well as what entity they have. And in its regard there are different opinions.

The First Opinion, Which Posits a Real Distinction, Is Rejected.

2. The first [opinion] teaches that a real relation is always something really distinct from its subject and its foundation. This is the opinion of the older Thomists: Capreolus, in [*Defensiones*], Book 1, Distinction 30, Question 1;[3] Cajetan, [*In Summam Theologiae*], Part 1, Question 28, Article 2;[4] Ferrara [commenting on] *Contra Gentiles*, Book 4, Chapter 14,[5] who base themselves on the words of St. Thomas in the same places and in Question 8, Article 1 of the *De Potentia*,[6] and Book 1, Distinction 33, Question 1, Article 1 [of his *Sentences* commentary],[7] in which passage he has placed the difference between a created and an uncreated relation in the fact that the first is not identified with the substance, *but it is another thing and it produces a composition with that [substance]*, which is not so in the case of an uncreated relation.

---

1 For the various distinctions involved here, cf. DM 7, s. 1, vol. 25, pp. 250-61.

2 "Absolute accidents" here are quality and quantity. All the others are relational.

3 For this, cf. *Defensiones, In I Sent.*, d. 30, q. 1, a. 1, ed. Paban-Pègues, tom. II, pp. 282-310.

4 Cf. Thomas de Vio, O.P., *Commentaria in Summam Theologiae* I, q. 28, a. 2, nn. 8-10, in *S. Thomae Opera*, tomus IV (1888), pp. 323a.

5 Cf. Franciscus de Sylvestris Ferrariensis, *Commentaria in Summam contra gentiles*, IV, c. 14, nn. 12-13, in Sancti Thomae Aquinatis, *Opera omnia*, tomus XV (Romae: Apud Sedem Commissionis Leoninae; Typis Riccardi Garroni, 1930), pp. 62a-63a.

6 Cf. S. Thomae Aquinatis, *Quaestiones disputatae de potentia Dei*, q. 8, a. 1, ad 5, editio ix, cura P. Bazzi *et al.* (Taurini: Marietti, 1953), p. 215b.

7 Cf. S. Thomae Aquinatis, *Scriptum super libros Sententiarum Magistri Petri Lombardi*, I, d. 33, q. 1, a. 1, editio nova cura R.P. Mandonnet, O.P., Tomus I (Parisiis: P. Lethielleux, 1929), p. 765.

However, this opinion, understood of a proper and rigorously real distinction, such as exists among entities that are completely distinct from one another,[8] has no very probable basis. For what is put forward by these authors about the separability of a relation from its foundation,[9] or about the different changes that can take place in these, at most prove a distinction "from the nature of the thing" (*ex natura rei*)—if indeed they prove anything, since perhaps it is more probable that they do not even show that, as we will see in treating the following opinions.

From the arguments of these opinions and from the proofs of our own opinion this [first] opinion will also be sufficiently refuted, although in order to reject it those [arguments] that were proposed in the beginning of the preceding Section can be enough. For those, I think, sufficiently demonstrate that a relation is not a thing that has in itself an entity that is distinct from all absolute entities.

Insofar As It Agrees with the Above [Opinion], the Opinion of Scotus Is Rejected.

3. And the same judgment must be passed on the opinion of Scotus in [the *Ordinatio*] Book 2, Distinction 1, Question 3 [sic],[10] and in Book 3, Distinction 8, Question 1,[11] as regards that part in which it agrees with the preceding [opinion].[12] For he distinguishes certain relations (*relatio*) that can in no way be separated from their foundations, for example, the relation of [being] a creature, from other [relations] that can be separated, for example, the relation of likeness. And these latter, he says, are really distinguished from their foundations, because of that separation. But the former, he says, are not to be distinguished, for, while they are inseparable, there is no other sign of a real distinction, nor does its necessity appear from anything else. However, as regards the first part, it has already been shown that that sign does not indicate

---

8 For this, cf. *DM* 7, s. 1, n. 1, vol. 25, p. 250.

9 For example: two white men have a relation of similarity which is founded in their whitenesses. Take one man away and *ipso facto* the relation of similarity in the first man perishes even though its foundation of whiteness remains in him. Thus, the relation is separable from its foundation.

10 Cf. Ioannis Duns Scoti, O.M., *Quaestiones in lib. II. Sententiarum*, II, d. 1, q. 4, in *Opera omnia* (Lugduni: Sumptibus Laurentii Durand, 1639), tomus vi, pars i, p. 60; idem, *Ordinatio* II, d. 1, q. 5, in *Joannis Duns Scoti Opera omnia*, VII (Civitas Vaticana: Typis Polyglottis Vaticanis, 1973), pp. 101-104, nn. 200-205.

11 Idem, *Quaestiones in III Sent.*, d. 8, q. un. (editio 1639), tomus vii, pars i, p. 213.

12 That is, to the degree in which it affirms a real distinction between a relation and its foundation.

a real distinction, but at most a modal one,[13] especially when the separation is not, so to say, convertible, as is the case in the present instance. For, even though the foundation can remain without the relation, still the relation cannot in any way remain without the foundation.

From this a weighty argument can be taken against this [first] part, and against the whole of the above opinion. I add, moreover, that this sign in the present case is not enough to indicate a modal distinction that is actual and real (*ex natura rei*). For, even though a relative denomination may be taken away with the foundation remaining and with the terminus removed, nevertheless, with both remaining, it cannot be taken away. Therefore, from that sign one cannot effectively conclude that a relation is something distinct from the foundation that is taken away from it when that denomination ceases, because that denomination can include or connote the concomitance or the coexistence of the other extreme and therefore can cease, not because something is taken away from the foundation, but because something is taken away from the terminus.

Accordingly, if some relations are inseparable from their foundations, it is, therefore, because their termini must[14] exist, and therefore when the foundations are posited, it is necessary that relative denominations arise. For example, if by some impossible stroke (*si per impossibile*), a created essence could remain, with God not existing, the relation of the creature to him would cease. Therefore, the fact that it cannot now be separated is not only because of its identity with the foundation, but also because of the intrinsic necessity of the terminus. Therefore, conversely, from the fact that other relations cease, when their termini are taken away, a real (*ex natura rei*) distinction is not correctly inferred, unless it is shown from elsewhere that the destruction alone of that terminus does not suffice for that.

Durandus' Opinion in This Is Not Proven.

4. Accordingly, Durandus, in [his *Sentences* commentary], Book 1, Distinction 30, /col. b/ Question 2, uses another distinction, namely, that there are certain relations (*relatio*) that are true dispositions (*habitudo*) and real respects (*respectus*), following upon their foundations essentially (*per se*), or accidentally, as [for example] inherence follows essentially (*per se*) the nature of an accident, and to touch or to be touched follows accidentally (*per accidens*) on quanti-

---

13 On a modal distinction, cf. *DM 7*, 1, nn. 16-20, vol. 25, pp. 255-7.
14 Literally: "cannot not" (*non possunt non*).

fied bodies; but there are others that are only relative denominations, as [for example] to be equal and to be similar.[15]

He says, therefore, that these latter [relations] are not distinguished in reality from their foundations, nor do they add anything beyond the existence and the concomitance of both absolute extremes—from which mutual coexistence he says there are taken those denominations that he says, nevertheless, pertain to the category of relation (*relatio*) and suffice in order to constitute it.[16] And we will see about this part later.[17]

But about the prior respects (*respectus*) he says that they are distinguished really from their foundations,[18] in which [saying] he agrees with the preceding opinions and he uses the same foundation, namely, the sign of the separability of the foundation from such a respect (*respectus*).[19] About this sign, it has already been said that at most it can show a modal distinction, nor does Durandus intend anything more, as will easily be clear to anyone reading him. He differs only in the use of words—calling that [distinction] real because it is found in things themselves.

5. But with regard to this part of Durandus's opinion, one should note a certain subdivision of the first member, or of a real relation (*habitudo*), which he briefly touches upon in that part, and one should consider also the examples by which he explains both members. For a certain respect (*respectus*), he says, follows by accident on its foundation, for example, touch upon quantity. Another follows directly (*per se*), as, for example, inherence (*inesse*) follows on quantity. And either respect, he says, is to be distinguished from its foundation.[20]

But in the first member and the example,[21] it does not seem that Durandus is speaking consistently. For by what reason does he say that things are called similar or equal? Not by the addition of some respect that is really (*ex natura rei*) distinct, but only by the co-existence of each extreme and a denomination arising from that. Consequently, it should be said that two bodies touch one another by a denomination that has arisen from the co-existence of each

---

15 For this, see D. Durandi, a Sancto Porciano, O.P., *In Petri Lombardi Sententias Theologicas Commentariorum libri IIII*, I, d. 30, q. 2, n. 14 (ed. Venetiis: Ex Typographia Guerraea, 1571; reprint: Ridgewood, NJ: Gregg Press, 1964), vol. 1, f. 84v ab.

16 Ibid., n. 17, f. 85ra.

17 Cf. this Section, n. 6.

18 Durandus, In I Sent., d. 30, q. 2,

19 Ibid., n. 14, f. 84vb.

20 Ibid.

21 That is, "to touch and being touched."

extreme in a certain place, apart from any other respect that is really (*ex natura rei*) distinct. For I am supposing that we are talking about a purely quantitative touch. For a physical touch adds something else, although not only a relation but the physical action of one thing upon another. Therefore, a quantitative touch is nothing else than a certain nearness between two quantities and their termini, in such way /p. 787/ that no other quantity is interposed. But this belongs to two bodies by the very fact that they exist in such places or spaces, without the addition of any mode or respect that is really (*ex natura rei*) distinct, at least according to the doctrine of Durandus himself.

For the same arguments that can prove this with regard to likeness, prove it about touch and about any nearness or distance, namely, that positing two bodies in such places, and prescinding either by the intellect, or by divine power, from every other thing or real mode, it is impossible that those bodies not touch each other. Therefore, the argument is the same with regard to this denomination. And universally it is the same about every respect, which is said by accident to follow on a foundation. For that will be by accident because it is the kind of denomination that requires the co-existence of another extreme, which [co-existence], however, that foundation does not require of itself, as is plainly clear in the mentioned example about touch. Therefore, that denomination can be taken from a co-existence of extremes without any other respect in reality (*in re ipsa*) distinct from the extremes. Or if that is not only a denomination, but also an intrinsic reference (*habitudo*), the same will be so in all those [cases] that Durandus posited in the second member of his principal distinction.

6. In regard to the other member[22] concerning a respect (*respectus*) that directly (*per se*) follows upon a foundation, and about the example of inherence — by the word "respect" (*respectus*) there can be signified that very mode of inherence, or of union, or some categorical relation (*relatio*) that has arisen from this.[23] In the first sense, it is true that that respect is distinguished really (*ex natura rei*) from the form or the thing whose mode it is, which is called the foundation of such a respect—something that has often been said above[24] by us and has been confirmed by the same argument.

However, what Durandus says, namely, that this respect (*respectus*) does not make for a composition in any way with its foundation, is false, as was often

---

22 See paragraph 4, just above.
23 Here we note Suárez himself struggling with the terminology of relation and we can sympathize with him.
24 Cf., e.g., *DM* 7, 1, nn. 17-19, vol. 25, pp. 255-7; and *DM* 34, 4, n. 33, vol. 26, p. 377.

said above, treating about the distinctions of things[25] and about the composition of nature and supposite,[26] as well as in other places. But this respect (*respectus*) is not categorical, but rather transcendental, because that mode of union or of inherence is not something that results from a foundation and a terminus, but is an absolute mode that can be directly (*per se*) caused by some action, even though intimately and essentially it includes a transcendental respect to what can be united (*ad unibilia*), which is also touched upon above and which will be explicitly clarified below, partly in this Disputation[27] and partly when we dispute about action.[28] Consideration, /col. b/ therefore, of that respect in the stated sense is of no importance for the present question.

But if we are talking about a categorical respect that is thought to result between an inherent form and its subject, and in general between those things that are united, the reasoning about such a respect will be the same as that about touching (*contactus*), likeness, and other similar instances, namely, that this is not a thing nor a real mode that is really (*ex natura rei*) distinct from the extremes, but it is only a mutual denomination that has arisen in the extremes from their co-existence under such a manner of existing. This can be easily shown by applying the reasoning developed above.[29] Therefore, speaking properly about a categorical respect (*respectus*), this distinction of Durandus is also not necessary, but it must be said that every categorical relation (*relatio*) either is or is not something distinct.

A Fourth Opinion Is Explained:
About a Modal or a Formal Distinction of a Relation From Its Foundation.

7. There is, therefore, a fourth opinion, which affirms that a real relation (*relatio*) is always actually distinguished from its subject and its foundation, but not altogether really as thing from thing, but modally as a real mode from

---

25 For Suárez's treatment of distinctions, see *DM* 7, ed. Vivès, vol. 25, pp. 250-274. For an English translation, cf. Francis Suarez, *On the Various Kinds of Distinctions (Disputatio VII)*, tr. Cyril Vollert, Milwaukee: Marquette University Press, 1947.

26 For this, cf. *DM* 34 ("About First Substance or Supposite and its Distinction from Nature"), vol. 26, 347-423.

27 See Section 12, below.

28[28] For this, see *DM* 48 ("About Action"), vol. 26, pp. 867-97; esp. Sections 1-4 (pp. 868-93).

29 Cf. this Section, n. 3.

a thing in itself. Javellus, in *Metaphysics*, Book 5, Question 22,[30] and Soto,[31] about the category "toward something" (*ad aliquid*), Question 2,[32] seem to hold this opinion. However, they call this distinction not modal but formal, but still they think it is actually in things before any consideration of the intellect. Fonseca, however, in [his commentary on] *Metaphysics*, Book 5, Chapter 15, Question 2, Section 5, says indeed that a categorical relation (*relatio*) is distinguished from its foundation by a formal distinction in such way that it has its own essential and existential being (*esse essentiae et existentiae*), which is distinct from the being of the foundation. Yet he denies that that distinction is real, or modal, or one of reason only, but [says] that it is another kind of "middle" (*media*), which he indicates is less than a real distinction but more than a modal [distinction].[33] Moreover, he seems to constitute its diversity in the fact that in a modal distinction the mode does not have its own being that is distinct from the being of the thing whose mode it is,[34] but in this formal

---

30 Cf. Chrysostomi Iavelli Canapicii, *In omnibus Metaphysicae libris quaesita testualia metaphysicali modo determinata: in quibus clarissime resolvuntur dubia Aristotelis et Commentatoris, eaque ut plurimum decisa habentur iuxta Thomisticum dogma* ..., V, q. 22 (Venetiis: Apud Haeredes Ioannis Mariae Bonelli, 1576), fols. 118v-122r.

31 Here I am following the reading, "Sotus," from the Salamanca, 1597 and the Mainz, 1605 editions of the *Disputationes* rather than that of the Vivès edition which erroneously gives "Scotus." Cf. R.P Francisci Suarez Societatis Iesu, *Metaphysicarum Disputationum*, tomus posterior (Salmanticae: Apud Ioannem et Andream Renaut, 1597), d. 47, s. 2, n. 7, vol. 2, p. 542a, and Francisci Suarez, e Societate Jesu, *Metaphysicarum Disputationum*, tomus posterior (Moguntiae: Excudebat Balthasarus Lippius, Sumptib. Arnold Mylii, 1605), d. 47, s. 2, n. 7; vol. 2, p. 501b. For the same reading of "Sotus," see also R. Patris Francisci Suarez, e Societate Jesu, *Metaphysicarum Disputationum* (Venetiis: Apud Haeredes Melchioris Sessae, 1610), d. 47, 2, n. 7; vol. 2, p. 501b. Although in this place the pagination of the Mainz and Venice editions is running very close together, this is not entirely true over the whole of the *Disputationes*. Thus the Venice edition has five indices at the beginning of the first volume while Mainz has them all at the end of volume two. Again, even though the page references here are the same, the last line of 501a in the Mainz edition has become the first line of 501 in the Venice edition.

32 Cf. D. Soto, *In librum Praedicamentorum*, c. vii, q. 2, ed. Venetiis, 1587, pp. 215-16.

33 For this, see Pedro Fonseca, S.J., *Commentarii in libros Metaphysicorum Aristotelis Stagiritae*, V, c. 15, q. 2, s. 5 (4 vols., Cologne, 1615-29. [reprint, Hildesheim: G. Olms, 1964]), vol. 2, col. 818. In this place, Fonseca has also cited the passages from Javellus and Soto which Suárez has mentioned here.

34 On modes in Fonseca, cf. *Commentaria in Metaph.*, V, c. 6, q. 6, s. 2, vol. 2, col. 400.

distinction, both extremes have their own being. Again, in this [formal distinction], each extreme is a genuine entity, but in a modal distinction the mode is not an entity. Hence, most of all, he bases his opinion on the fact that a relation (*relatio*) has its own being that is distinct from the being of its foundation. For the being of the foundation is absolute, whereas the being of a relation (*relatio*) is a being that consists /p. 788/ in a disposition (*habitudo*) toward something else (*ad aliud*), as is clear from Aristotle's definition.[35]

8. But, first of all, I do not understand (*percipio*) this middle distinction between real and modal, which is a genuine actual distinction in reality and much greater than a distinction of reason inasmuch as it is said to be even greater than modal. [This is], first, because in a modal distinction, just as a mode is in reality distinguished from that thing whose mode it is, so it has some being of its own, equally and proportionately distinct from the being of that thing, as was explained when we were treating of existence.[36] Again, just as a mode is something existing in things, so it can be said to possess some entity, insofar as by this word there is signified whatever is not nothing.[37] But because its entity is of such a nature and condition that by itself (*per se*) it is not able immediately and directly (*per se*) to constitute a real being, but it necessarily must be joined and identified with some being, which it may affect and modify, it is thus called not a thing, but the mode of a thing.

9. From this then it is clear that among distinctions in reality (*ex natura rei*) there can be no medium between one that is [simply] real and one that is modal, as has been said in general above in the seventh Disputation.[38] And in particular it is explained (*declaratur*) now in the matter of which we are treating. For a real relation, precisely from the fact that it has its own proper being and is something distinct from its foundation, does not have it that it is an entity or a real mode. For that is common to both. Therefore, precisely from that source there is not enough basis to conclude to a greater than modal distinction nor to another degree of entity besides that which is found in real modes. Accordingly, either a real relation has that kind of entity that can be understood to be immediately (*primo*), directly (*per se*) and essentially

---

35 Cf. *Categories* 8.11a23-24.

36 For this, cf. *DM* 31, 11, nn. 30-33, vol. 26, pp. 281-2; for an English translation, cf. Francis Suarez, *On the Essence of Finite Being as such, On the Existence of that Essence and their Distinction*, translated from the Latin with an Introduction, by Norman J. Wells (Milwaukee: Marquette University Press, 1983), esp. pp. 170-173.

37 Cf. *DM* 7, 1, n. 19, vol. 25, p. 257. Also for this extended notion of being as applicable to a mode, see Fonseca, *Commentaria in Metaph.*, V, c. 6, q. 6, s. 2, vol. 2, col. 400.

38   Cf. *DM* 7, 1, n. 21, vol. 25, p. 257.

(*essentialiter*)[39] constituted by a referential character alone, in such a way that on this score (*ex hoc capite*) it is not unreasonable that such an entity be alone without the entity of a foundation—or indeed it has such a mode of entity that it intrinsically demands to be joined to its foundation, and as in its own way affecting that, so that it cannot be otherwise by any potency.

If the first is said, it is evidently concluded to be a true and proper thing, in an altogether real way distinct from its foundation—which this opinion does not admit. But if the second is said, the distinction will not be other than modal, supposing that it is actually in reality. Therefore, just as between those two [things] a medium cannot be thought, so neither between those two distinctions in reality (*ex natura rei*) can a medium be imagined (*excogitari*). For either the extremes of the distinction can be mutually separated in reality (*in re*), and one in turn can be conserved without the other, and thus there is an entirely proper and rigorous real distinction /col. b/—or only one extreme can be separated and remain without the other, but not conversely, and we call this distinction modal. However, apart from these two ways there is no other, for if each extreme is really inseparable from the other there will be a distinction of reason but not [a distinction] in reality (*ex natura rei*).

Therefore, since in the present instance the foundation and the relation are not mutually separable, as is self-evident to all inasmuch as a categorical relation can in no way be understood without its foundation, there cannot be a greater or another distinction, which is actually real, between a relation and its foundation, besides one that is modal. Therefore, even though the mentioned authors use other words, calling this distinction "formal," nevertheless, it is necessary that they are speaking of a modal [distinction], if they are still understanding their opinion to be about an actual distinction that exists in things themselves. For some of them do not sufficiently explain this very thing, as we will say below.[40]

The Opinion in Question Is Argued Persuasively.

10. But the principal basis of this opinion, so explained about a modal distinction, is that which is taken from the mark of separation. For its foundation is so separable from the relation that it can remain in reality without that [relation]; therefore, it is necessary that they be distinguished in reality, at least modally, according to the principles stated above in Disputation 7.[41]

---

39 Here we may note the difference among "primo," "per se," and "essentialiter."
40 Cf. n. 15, this Section.
41 For this, see *DM* 7, 2, nn. 6-10, vol. 25, pp. 263-5.

Secondly, this is sufficiently confirmed by the argument[42] that a relation has its own being (*esse*), which intrinsically consists in a disposition (*habitudo*) toward another. Therefore, it is necessary that in reality itself (*in re ipsa*) it be distinguished from absolute being (*esse*). Thirdly, I explain it in this way: for when with only one white thing existing, for example, which heretofore was similar to nothing, there comes to be another white thing, either that first has some real relative being that it did not have before, or it has nothing new. This second cannot be said, for otherwise a relation is nothing real; for if it was nothing before and if afterwards it receives no real being, it never is anything. Therefore, that relative being that is added must necessarily be distinct from that to which it is added, at least by a modal distinction. For if one thing existed and the other did not yet exist, and afterwards it is added or arises, they cannot be one and the same in reality.

11. Fourthly: for when one thing is said to be similar to another, or one man is said to be the father of another, either these are merely extrinsic denominations, or they are intrinsic. The first cannot /p. 789/ be said. Therefore, necessarily the second must be said. Therefore, some intrinsically denominating form is necessary. Therefore, that must necessarily be distinct in reality, at least modally, from the thing denominated.

The minor[43] is proven first: for if it were an extrinsic denomination, it would not be relative, because it would be an application of an extrinsic form to a denominated subject rather than a disposition of that subject to an extrinsic terminus. Secondly, [the minor is proven] because for this reason a denomination of "clothed," or of "circumscribed by place,"[44] or even of "agent," is not relative with a proper categorical relation (*respectus*). Thirdly, it is [proven] with more difficulty: for otherwise there would not be a less real relation of the creator to a creature than of any created agent to its effect; for an extrinsic denomination can be equally present.

Likewise, the second consequence[45] is clear, because that is called an intrinsic denomination which is taken from an intrinsic form. The final consequence[46] is based upon something, which has been often repeated, [namely], that this denomination can be lost and acquired anew, preserving every absolute form.

---

42 Here for the sake of meaningful English, I have changed Suárez's active voice to a passive voice construction.

43 That is for one thing to be similar or for one man to be father are merely extrinsic denominations.

44 That is, "located."

45 That is, that some intrinsically denominating form is needed.

46 That is, that form must be distinct in reality from the thing denominated.

Therefore the intrinsic and relative form from which it is taken is in some way really distinct from all absolute forms, at least with a modal distinction.

And this opinion, explained in this way and confirmed, is more probable than the others, which posit in reality some actual distinction between a relation and its foundation. And if this is once asserted in the case of some relations, by a logical argument it must be posited in all created and categorical [relations], because there is no sufficient reason to use any distinction, as can be understood from what was said against Scotus and Durandus.[47]

A Fifth Opinion Denying an Actual Distinction In Reality of a Relation from its Foundation.

12. Still, there is another opinion, extremely opposite to these,[48] which denies that a relation is in reality (*in re*) distinguished with some actual distinction from its absolute foundation, but [says that it is distinguished] with only some distinction of reason having some basis in things.

Many theologians teach this opinion, especially the Nominalists, in [their *Sentences* commentaries] I, dist. 30; [cf.] Ockham, [in this place] at question 1,[49] and at dist. 31, question 1;[50] Gregory [of Rimini], at dist. 29, question 2, article 2;[51] and Giles [of Rome][51bis] is clearly of the same opinion in [Sent.] I, dist. 26, question 4, when he says a relation has no proper being beyond the being of [its] foundation, nor does it have any composition joined to that [*ei*]—which cannot be true, except by reason of a complete identity in the thing itself (*in re ipsa*). Silvester [Mazzolini a.k.a. Prierias, O.P.] plainly /col. b/ holds the same view, in his *Conflati [ex angelico doctore S. Thoma]*, Question 1, Dubium 1,[52] where he says that a relation is the same thing as its proximate foundation. And although he adds that they are distinguished formally, he ,

47 Cf. this Section, nn. 3-6, above.
48 That is, the first four opinions presented.
49 Cf. Guillelmi de Ockham, *Scriptum in librum primum Sententiarum ordinatio*, d. 30, q. 1, in *Opera theologica*, vol. 4, ed. Girardus I. Etzkorn et Franciscus E. Kelley (St. Bonaventure, N.Y., 1979), pp. 309-310.
50 Cf. ibid, d. 31, q. un, p. 400.
51 Cf. Gregorii Ariminensis, *Lectura super primum et secundum Sententiarum* (Tomus III, ed. Trapp et Marcolino, Berlin/New York, 1984), *In I Sent*. dist. 28-32, qu. 2, Additio 142, pp. 154-5.
51bis Cf. Egidii Romani, *Primus Sententiarum*, correctus a reverendo magistro Augustino Montifalconio (Venetiis: Impressis sumptibus et expensis heredum quondam Octaviani Scot., 1521), *In Sent*. I, d. 26, quaestio principalis secunda, fol. 141va.
52 The work here is Silvestro Mazzolini, *Conflati ex angelico doctore S. Thoma*, Perusie: Per Hieronymum quondam Francisci Chartularii, 1519, of which I have found one

however, immediately makes it clear enough that this is only a distinction of reason, from a diversity of concepts, insofar as the same thing taken alone is conceived absolutely, but with something else posited, it is conceived relatively, with simply nothing added or varied with respect to the thing itself (*rem ipsam*). But Hervaeus [Natalis, O.P.] teaches and treats this opinion more expressly and better, [*Sent.*] I, dist. 30, art. 1 [sic],[53] and *Quodlibet* 7, question 15,[54] and *Quodlibet* 10, question 1;[55] who also has declared that these relative denominations are taken from the association (*consortio*) of several absolute things, and not from special (*peculiaribus*) entities, or really distinct modes,[56] which they add to those absolute things themselves.

13. And this opinion has a basis in St. Thomas, *Opusculum* 48, Chapter 2, which concerns "toward something" (*ad aliquid*), where he says as follows: "*But when I say that the likeness of Socrates has his whiteness as a foundation, it should not be understood that the likeness of Socrates is some thing in Socrates other than that whiteness itself, but it is only that whiteness itself as it is related to the whiteness of Plato as to a terminus.*"[57] And this he immediately confirms by

---

copy listed as owned by Bowdoin College, Maine, which I have not been able to see.

53 Cf. Hervei Natalis Britonis, *In quatuor libros sententiarum, Commentaria, In I Sent.*, d. 29, q. 1, ad 2 (Parisiis: Apud Viduam Moreau, 1647), p. 126a.

54 For this, see: Hervaeus Natalis, *Quodlibetum VII, q. 15*, in *Quolibeta Hervei: subtilissima Hervei Natalis Britonis theologi acutissimi quolibeta undecim cum octo ipsius profundissimis tractatibus infra per ordinem descriptis. Quorum omnia: demptis tantum quatuor quolibetis: nunc primum impressa: atque in lucem prodita fuerunt: summaque diligentia castigata. Additis quampluribus in margine notabilibus: necnon eleganti tabula: que secundum alphabeti ordinem omnes principales quaestiones mirifice demonstrat. Tractatus VIII, videlicet. De beatitudine. De verbo. De eternitate mundi. De materia celi. De relationibus. De pluralitate formarum. De virtutibus. De motu angeli* (Venetiis: Georgium Arrivabenum, 1513; rep., Ridgewood, NJ: Gregg Press, 1966), fol. 143va.

55 Cf. ibid, *Quodlibetum X*, q. 1, fols. 169vb-170rb.

56 In passing, let us note this refusal to regard a relation as a mode of its foundation.

57 For this, see the spurious work, *Summa totius logicae Aristotelis*, Tract. V, c. 2, in *S. Thomae Aquinatis, O.P., Opuscula omnia, genuina quidem necnon spuria melioris notae debito ordine collecta cura et studio R.P. Petri Mandonnet, O.P., Tomus quintus, opuscula spuria* (Parisiis: Sumptibus P. Lethielleux, 1927), p. 50. It is noteworthy that this work, which was falsely attributed to St. Thomas in the 1570 *Editio Princeps* of his works, has been afterwards attributed by Quétif-Échard as likely belonging to Hervaeus Natalis; cf. Jacobus Quétif et Jacobus Échard, *Scriptores Ordinis Praedicatorum recensiti, notisque historicis et criticis illustrati*, tomus primus (Lutetiae

the reasoning made above, namely, that otherwise a likeness could not come to anything without its mutation, which argument is probative both of a real mode, which is really distinct and also of a genuine reality. Hence also this opinion is founded upon the dictum of the Philosopher, in *Physics*, Book 5, Text 10,[58] that a relation comes to a thing, with that thing itself remaining unchanged. And in a similar way the same opinion is taken from Anselm, in the *Monologium*, Chapter 24,[59] to which place we will refer below[60] when we treat more at length of non-mutual relations (*relationibus*); and a very similar [opinion is found] in Augustine, *On the City of God* [sic], Book 5, Chapter 16.[61] Finally, the words of Damascene, in his *Dialectics*, Chapter 52 [sic], lend support to this opinion: *"It is necessary that those things which are said "toward something"* (ad aliquid), *be first reduced to another category as they are separately considered, and then afterwards as having a disposition* (habitudinem) *and affection to something else, [be reduced] to those things that are to be referred to something. Indeed, it is necessary that something first be without a disposition and relation and then to consider a disposition in it."*[62] This opinion of Damascene, I think,

---

Parisiorum: Apud J.P. Christophorum Ballard et Nicolaum Simart, 1719), p. 536a. The obvious lesson to draw from this it that Hervaeus had great influence here on Suárez.

58 Cf. *Physics* 5.2.225b11-13; also, see *Metaphysics* 11.12.1068a11-13. For Suárez's recognition of the dependence of *Metaphysics*, Book 11, on the *Physics*, cf. *DM, Index locupletissimus*, Lib. XI, vol. 25, pp. lx-lxi, an English translation in: Francisco Suárez, *A Commentary on Aristotle's Metaphysics (Index locupletissimus in Metaphysicam Aristotelis)*, translated from the Latin with an Introduction and Notes by John P. Doyle (Milwaukee: Marquette University Press, 2004), pp. 203-206.

59 Cf. *Monologium*, Cap. 25, in *Obras Completas de San Anselmo*, traducidas por primera vez al castellano. Texto latino de la edición critica del P. Schmitt, O.S.B. (Madrid: Biblioteca de Autores Cristianos, 1952), vol. 1, p. 258. In this place, Anselm says that God is unchanged even though creatures, which are related to Him, may come and go.

60 Cf. Section 15, n. 16.

61 Actually, this should be *De Trinitate*, V, c. 16, n. 17, in *Obras de San Augustin en edición bilingüe*, tomo V, *Tratado sobre la Santísima Trinidad*, primera versión española, introducción y notas del Padre Fr. Luis Arias, O.S.A., segunda edición (Madrid: Biblioteca de Autores Cristianos, 1956), pp. 426-29.

62 Cf. St. John Damascene, *Dialectica*, Chapter 50, in ΙΩΑΝΝΟΥ ΤΟΥ ΔΑΜΑΣΚΗ-ΝΟΥ, ΤΑ ΕΥΡΙΣΚΟΜΕΝΑ ΠΑΝΤΑ, Sancti Patris Nostri, Joannis Damasceni, Monachi, et Presbyteri Hierosolymitani, *Opera omnia*, opera et studio P. Michaelis Lequien, in *Patrologia Graeca*, vol. 94 (Paris: Apud J.P. Migne, 1860), col. 631 C.

must be understood about non-subsisting relations, because the reasoning is different about those which are subsisting.[63]

14. The principal arguments for this [last] opinion are those by which the other opinions, which posit a distinction in reality (*in re*), are disproven. For with these set aside, this opinion is concluded to from a sufficient enumeration of parts.

Second, [it is concluded to] from the matter itself (*ex re ipsa*), /p. 790/ because this distinction of reason and this way of denomination suffices for all things that are said relatively of absolute things, as the arguments posited in the first place at the beginning of the preceding Section seem also to prove. But if this is enough, it is superfluous to add anything more; for a distinction or a multiplication of things or of real modes should not be fashioned or asserted without necessity or sufficient reason.[64]

15. In the third place, we can turn around that argument about separability.[65] For positing two white things, for example, it is impossible even with absolute power[66] to bring it about that they are not similar. Therefore, this denomination [of "similar"] is not taken from some thing or real mode[67] that is really distinct from both white things taken together. Otherwise, why would it be contradictory (*repugaret*) for God to take away that mode, if it is in reality distinct, or why could he not impede the resultance (*resultantiam*) of such a mode? For if this is with respect to a distinct thing, it is some sort of efficiency, which cannot be without the influence of God. Therefore, God could suspend his influence and block that resultance.

Some, such as [Francis of] Mayronnes, in [his *Sentences* commentary], Book 1, Distinction 29, Question 2,[68] convinced by the argument[69] concede this. But then I ask whether those two white things remain similar or not? This latter cannot be mentally conceived, since they retain the same unity in whiteness.

---

63 That is about the relations which are constitutive of divine persons. On such relations, cf. Suárez, *De sanctissimo Trinitatis mysterio* III, c. 9, n. 16, vol. 1, p. 606. Also, cf. below, n. 21, this Section.

64 This, of course, is a version of "Ockham's razor." On the role of the razor in Ockham cf. Armand Maurer, "Ockham's Razor and Dialectical Reasoning," *Mediaeval Studies*, vol. 58 (1996), pp. 49-65. Again, note the refusal here to reduce a relation to a mode of its foundation.

65 Cf. n. 4, this Section.

66 That is, even by the Absolute Power of God.

67 Again, a relation is not simply an added mode.

68 Cf. Francisci de Mayronis, O.M., *In quatuor libros Sententiarum*, I, 29 (Venetiis: Impensa heredum domini Octaviani Scoti, 1520), f. 89v.

69 That is, about separability.

But if the first is said, it is proven that that distinct mode and the advent that is now imagined are found without a foundation, since a true likeness remains without these. It is a sign therefore that this denomination[70] is taken only from these absolutes, which co-exist and hold themselves in the same way.

Hence, as I was saying above,[71] the fact that through the removal of the terminus that denomination ceases is no argument that the likeness is some real mode that is really distinct from the whiteness, but it is an argument only that the terminus itself is in reality distinct from the foundation and that it in some way concurs or is necessary in order to complete such a denomination. For it is enough that when that is removed the denomination ceases, even if no reality is taken away from the thing denominated. Therefore, from the inseparability of a relation, when the foundation and the terminus are posited, there is rather inferred a real identity in every way, or (what is the same) there is inferred that a relative denomination adds nothing beyond all the absolute things.

16. *How Some May Deny That the Foundation Is Changed by the Acquisition of a Relation.*—In the fourth place, the argument that one thing becomes similar or equal to another without any change in itself [simply] by the positing of the other, carries great weight (*urget*). For whether similarity is a thing /col. b/ entirely distinct or a real mode that is really distinct, it cannot come anew to something without a change of that thing.

Some answer that a relative (*respectivum*) mode does not suffice, for the reason that it is not something but "toward something" (*ad aliquid*), and because the whole foundation from which that relation possesses its entity already pre-exists in the thing. But this is not satisfactory, because those words, namely, that a relation is not something but "toward something" either involve contradiction (*repugnantiam*), or they are extremely equivocal and not at all relevant.

For if "not to be something" is taken absolutely and transcendentally (*transcendenter*), it clearly follows that relation is nothing, and to be toward something is nothing real, as I argued above.[72] But if "to be something" is taken in a more restricted way, so that it is the same as to be a thing or an absolute mode, the question is begged, and the argument is not solved but rather avoided. For, even though a relation is not something absolute, if it is, however, something real, [something] new, and really distinct from everything that existed before, then by reason of that a thing is truly, properly, and intrinsically other than it was in fact before. Therefore, it is truly changed.[73]

---

70 That is, "similar."
71 Cf. n. 3, this Section.
72 Cf. Section 1, nn. 1-3, above.
73 This, of course, will contradict Aristotle, in *Physics* 5.2.

Neither again does it suffice in order to avoid a change that the whole foundation of a relation pre-exist, because we did not say that the thing is changed on account of the foundation, but on account of that which is added to the foundation, which is said to be something real and really distinct from that [foundation]. Hence, according to this opinion, it cannot logically be said that a relation has its own proper or modal entity formally from that foundation, but at most [only] radically, insofar as the relation flows from that foundation when the terminus is posited.[74] But this does not exclude a true change, since something new and distinct happens in the thing, even if it remains intrinsic.[75]

17. *How They Explain Aristotle Who Say That the Foundation Is Changed through the Resultance (resultantiam) of a Relation.*—Hence, some finally say that through the advent (*adventum*) of a new relation (*relationis*) or of a relative denomination there is produced in the thing itself that is related a genuinely

---

74 This seems to be the position which St. Thomas has taken in his commentary on *Physics* 5.2; cf.: "Hence it must be said that if someone through his own changing becomes equal to me, while I do not change, that equality was first in me in some way, as in its root from which it has real being. For from the fact that I have such a quantity, it belongs to me that I am equal to all those who have the same quantity. When, therefore, someone newly receives that quantity, that common root of equality is determined in regard to that person and then nothing comes to me anew from this that I begin to be equal to another through his changing." ("*Unde dicendum est quod si aliquis per suam mutationem efficiatur mihi aequalis, me non mutato, ista aequalitas primo erat in me quodammodo, sicut in sua radice, ex qua habet esse reale: ex hoc enim quod habeo talem quantitatem, competit mihi quod sim aequalis omnibus illis, qui eamdem quantitatem habent. Cum ergo aliquis de novo accipit illam quantitatem, ista communis radix aequalitatis determinatur ad istum: et ideo nihil advenit mihi de novo per hoc quod incipio esse alteri aequalis per eius mutationem.*") S. Thomae Aquinatis, *In octo libros Physicorum Aristotelis expositio*, cura et studio P.M. Maggiolo, O.P. (Taurini: Marietti, 1954), V, l. 3, p. 330, n. 667. For a parallel passage, cf. S. Thomae Aquinatis, *In duodecim libros Metaphysicorum Aristotelis expositio*, ed. Cathala-Spiazzi (Taurini: Marietti, 1950), XI, l. 12, p. 561, n. 2385. For places in which St. Thomas speaks of powers as rooted in the essence of the soul, see: *Quaestiones disputatae de veritate*, q. 14, a. 5; ibid., q. 22, a. 10, ad 2, and *Summa Theologiae*, I, q. 77, a. 8. Note also that St. Thomas understands such powers to flow from the soul or to "result" from it; cf. *Summa Theologiae*, I, q. 77, a. 6 and 7, esp. ad 1.

75 This would seem at variance with the text from St. Thomas' commentary on the *Physics*, just recorded in the immediately preceding note. However, for a resolution of this, see the text cited from St. Thomas' commentary on the *Metaphysics*, i.e., XI, l. 12, n. 2385.

real change, not indeed through a genuine action but through an intrinsic emanation (*dimanationem*).[76] But [they say] that Aristotle did not speak generally

---

76 "Dimanatio" is literally "an emanation or a flowing out of." For example, in *DM*
18, Sections 3 and 7, Suárez regards water growing cold as a "natural resultance or
emanation" (*resultantia naturalis, dimanatio naturalis*). Generally, such is the flowing of a property from a substantial form. In this emanation, there is according
to Suárez (*DM* 18, 3, n. 7 [vol. 25, 617]) a certain efficiency which is a separate
and distinct action from the original action whereby the substance, here water, is
generated (ibid., n. 8). Consequently, it requires a proximate principle, namely, the
substance itself which is the term of the prior act of generation (ibid.). Nevertheless,
the action of resultance does not take place without the concurrence of the First
Cause (ibid., n. 13 [p. 619]). Indeed, more than this, since such natural resultance
is entirely intrinsic to the complete thing involved, e.g. water, and since in a certain
sense it belongs to the complete production of that thing, it is customary to attribute it to the generating cause and not in any way to the thing itself except insofar
as this latter takes the place of the generator and is, as it were, his instrument; cf.
"... natural resultance is completely intrinsic and in a certain way belongs to the
complete production of the thing. For it tends only to constituting the thing in
the connatural condition which is due to it by virtue of generation; ... Hence, it is
common also as a rule to say that natural resultance is attributed to the generator,
and is not from an intrinsic form or property, except inasmuch as such takes the
place of the generator and as, as it were, his instrument." (*...resultantia naturalis est
omnino intrinseca, et quodammodo pertinet ad consummatam rei productionem, quia
solum tendit ad constituendam rem in connaturali statu per se sibi debito ex vi generationis; ... Unde etiam communiter dici solet naturalem resultantiam tribui generanti,
et non esse a forma vel proprietate intrinseca, nisi quatenus vicem obtinet generantis,
et est quasi intrumentum ejus.*") *DM* 18, 3, n. 26 (25, p. 619); also ibid., 7, n. 18
(633); 7, n. 26 (638). Other examples of such dimanation would be in motion of
the heavens or the natural downward motion of a stone; cf. "... the same thing,
therefore, can happen in the case of local motion; and in this way heaven [i.e. the
heavenly spheres] can be moved not by anything else than by itself through its own
form as some innate power, just as downward motion results in a stone from its
intrinsic gravity." ("*... idem ergo accidere potest in motu locali; atque ita dici potest
coelum non ab alio quam a seipso moveri per formam suam aut aliquam virtutem in-
natam, ex qua talis motus resultat, sicut motus deorsum resultat in lapide ex intrinseca
gravitate.*") *DM* 29, 1, n. 7 (vol. 26, p. 23). In this last passage, Suárez presupposes
the Aristotelian distinction between natural and violent motion. Obviously, in a
case of violent motion there is an external mover required; cf. *DM* 18, 7, n. 20
(25, 636). But in the case of natural movement it would seem that the principle of
movement is intrinsic. For this reason, such thinkers as Duns Scotus, Gregory of
Rimini, John Buridan, and Albert of Saxony, have conceived the motions of heavy
and light bodies to their respective natural places to be instances of self-movement

about just any change as that is most commonly understood, but about that

(ibid., n. 21). On the other hand, St. Thomas and his disciples have held that even here the motion is to be principally attributed to an external cause, namely, the original generator of the heavy or light body in question (ibid). This Suárez calls "the common opinion" (*communis sententia*) and his own final option is to accept it in a qualified sense: "And this opinion when it is correctly explained is true; ..." (*"Et haec sententia recte explicata vera est*; ...) proximate intrinsic cause of such movement: "It must be said, therefore, that as often as an inanimate thing tends to its natural place, intrinsic gravity or levity is the proximate, but not the main, principle of that motion." (*"Dicendum est ergo, quotiescumque res inanimata tendit in suum locum naturalem, intrinsecum gravitatem vel levitatem esse principium proximum, non vero principale, illius motus*") ibid., n. 23 (637); "But, nevertheless, it should finally be added that this natural motion is principally to be attributed to the generator, who has given the form, and by means of that, the gravity by which the motion results; just as to one projecting and impressing an impetus there is attributed the motion which flows from that. For just as an impressed impetus, even though it is a true motive power, and has in itself sufficient force for that motion, but is not moved except as an instrument of, and in place of, the one projecting, so gravity does not move except as the instrument of, and in place of, the one generating." (*"Nihilominus tamen, addendum est ultimo, hunc motum naturalem principaliter esse tribuendum generanti, qui formam, et mediante illa, gravitatem indidit a qua motus resultat; sicut projicienti et imprimenti impetum tribuitur motus qui ab illo manat. Quia ut impetus impressus, licet sic vera virtus motiva, et in se habeat sufficientem vim ad illum motum, nihilominus non movetur nisi ut instrumentum projicientis, et vice ejus, ita gravitas non movet nisi ut instrumentum generantis, et vice ejus.*") ibid., n. 26 (p. 638). So understood, natural motion then does not violate the Aristotelian principle, "Whatever is moved is moved by another." However, as in the case of water growing cold, to verify the principle here will involve its extension from the physical plane of motion to the metaphysical plane of substantial generation; cf. "Hence that dictum of Aristotle: 'Everything which is moved, is moved by another,' although it is understood about what is proximately and essentially moving is not always verified about another subject, nevertheless, when it is indifferently understood about some mover, either proximate, or remote, particular or universal, it will always be found that every moveable thing is moved by some distinct subject, or (to use metaphysical terms) every thing which is acted upon is acted upon by some efficient [cause] which is 'suppositally' distinct. However, this cannot be demonstrated by a purely physical medium, but by one which is metaphysical, namely, because no particular agent cause has the power to act from itself, but [has it] from another subject and it cannot act without the concurrence of a superior cause, as will be shown below from from we will say about God or the First Cause." (*"Unde illud Aristotelis: Omne quod movetur, ab alio movetur, quamvis intellectum de proximo movente et per se, non semper verificatur de alio supposito, tamen indifferenter intellectum de aliquo movente, sive proximo, sive remoto, particulari, aut universali, semper invenietur quodlibet mobile* [change] that comes about through a proper action and passion.

However, even though this answer proceeds in a logical way, given the opinion in question, and [even though] it can be easily defended in order to escape from Aristotle's assertion in the cited place from *Physics*, Book 5,[77] nevertheless considered by itself, it indeed says something that is most difficult to believe /p, 79l/ and [something that is] founded upon no evident sign or experience, namely, that as often as someone newly becomes white or hot, there blossoms in all the other hot or white things that exist in the world something new and real, which truly and properly inheres in each one. For as seems sufficiently proven above,[78] for those bare denominations, "similar," "equal," and the like, that advent (*resultantia*) of a new real mode and entity is not necessary.[79] But apart from this indication (*signo*) there is no other from which it can be inferred. Therefore, it is imagined gratuitously and without probability.

Add that whatever that change or acquisition of that new real mode or entity is, it cannot be without efficiency, at least by way of resultance (*resultantiae*), because every change, in the manner in which it is such, includes a proportionate action. I ask, therefore, whether that efficiency is from the terminus itself upon the foundation or from that very foundation upon itself by a natural resultance (*resultantiam*)?

The first [alternative] is asserted by no one; nor is it probable. For how would a terminus act simultaneously on almost infinite things that are so very distant? Again, [it is not probable], because if a relation were to come about in this way, nothing would be lacking to it that would not come about through a genuine action and directly (*per se*) from an extrinsic agent. Finally, because a relation belongs intrinsically to a thing, when a foundation and a terminus are posited, it does not, therefore, depend upon the efficacy of an extrinsic agent.

The second [alternative] also can be disproven: for such efficacy, even if it is from an intrinsic principle, will be through a proper action and consequently

---

moveri ab aliquo supposito distincto, vel (ut terminis metaphysicis utamur) quodlibet patiens pati ab aliquo efficiente suppositaliter distincto. Hoc tamen demonstrari non potest per medium pure physicum, sed per metaphysicum, scilicet, quia nulla causa agens particularis habet a se virtutem agendi, sed ab alio supposito, neque etiam potest per se agere sine concursu superioris causa, ut infra constabit ex his quae de Deo et prima causa dicemus.") ibid., n. 52 (p. 8). Note here that rather than using the principle *Whatever is moved is moved by another* to prove the existence of God, Suarez uses God and the Divine Concursus to show the universal applicability of this principle.

77 That is: *Physics* 5.2.225b11-13.

78 Cf. this Section, nn. 5, 12, 14, and 15, above.

79 Once more, note that a real relation is not simply an added mode.

through a proper change. For although such resultance (*resultantia*) exists only when the terminus is posited, that will be only because the terminus is either a necessary condition in order that the relation result or a kind of specifying object (*objectum specificans*), without which [the relation] cannot exist.

But this does not prevent that the resultance, which comes about from the foundation, be through a proper action, which comes about in such a subject apart from any other action which may then intervene in that [subject]. For example, a descent downwards naturally results from the gravity of a stone, when every impediment is removed, and nevertheless it comes about through a proper action and change.

Lastly, an argument often touched on above has a place here: that such resultance and any efficiency whatever cannot exist without the concurrence of God,[80] which [concurrence] he can suspend. Yet even though we stipulate that he is suspending that [concurrence], and that consequently no real resultance occurs, still we understand things to be similar or equal, when such extremes are posited. Therefore, there is no indication that such a resultance or change takes place.[81]

/col. b/

An Opinion Is Treated That Distinguishes between the "Being in" And the "Being toward" of a Relation.

18. Accordingly, others,[82] for the purpose of answering this difficulty,[83] use a certain distinction. And this can be adduced as the sixth opinion in the present question we are treating about the distinction of a relation and its foundation.

In a relation, then, they distinguish "being in" and "being toward," and they say that a relation [considered] according to "being in" does not result properly nor blossom (*pullulare*) from the foundation, but it results only according to "being toward" as "toward," and therefore, the foundation is not changed by such a resultance,[84] because a thing is changed only by that which is new *in* it, and thus according to "being in." From this distinction it clearly comes about that a relation, according to "being in," is not really distinguished from its

---

80 Cf. *DM* 18, 3, n. 13 (vol. 25, 61).

81 Suárez's position thus is that no resultance or any other change is required in the thing which comes to be related.

82 For a possible identification of these unidentified "others," see Suárez, *De Sanctissimo Trinitatis mysterio* V, c. 1, n. 7, vol. 1, 654, in which place a similar opinion to attributed to certain "Thomists."

83 See nn. 17 and 20, this Section.

84 Which, then, agrees with Aristotle, *Physics*, 5.2.

foundation, because it necessarily belongs to it, even before its terminus exists or independently from the terminus. But indeed "being toward" is distinguished really, and therefore it can result from the foundation, once the terminus is posited.

19. *How Many Inconsistencies Arise from the Presented Opinion.—First.—* Wherefore, this opinion involves many impossible things that cannot be sufficiently understood. First, it follows from it that in one and the same relation there must be actually and really distinguished "being in" and "being toward."[85] For "being in" is said to be in reality (*in re*) the same and not distinct from the foundation, but "being toward" is said to be actually distinct in reality (*in re*) from the foundation. Therefore, "being in" and "being toward" will be actually distinct from one another, because things that are so compared to one third thing that one is the same with that, while the other is not, cannot between themselves be the same.[86] But [this] consequent is impossible, because "being in" and "being toward" are related (*comparantur*) as superior and inferior, or as common or transcendent and a mode that determines or modifies that[87] which cannot be distinct in reality, as was taught above.[88]

20. *Second.*—There is a second inconsistency: because it follows [from this position] that the "being toward" of a real created relation as such is not an accident of anything and consequently it does not constitute a genuine real accident—which is against the nature (*ratio*) of this category. The consequence is clear, because that "being toward" does not essentially include "being in,"

---

85 For a position which is *prima facie* close to this, but which does not make the application under discussion here, cf.: "... to be in something is one thing; to be toward something is another" ("... aliud enim est esse in aliquo, aliud esse ad aliquid,") Franciscus Toletus, S.J., *Commentaria in lib. Categoriarum Aristotelis*, Cap. VII, q. 2 (Coloniae Agrippinae, In Officium Birckmannica, Sumptibus H. Myli, 1615), p. 249. On Toletus, cf. my entry, "Toletus, Franciscus (1533-96)," in *Routledge Encylopedia of Philosophy* (London/New York: Routledge, 1998), IX, pp. 433-435.

86 For Suárez, in another place, having difficulty with the range of the principle of comparative identity which is operative here, see his *Tractatus de Sanctissimo Trinitate* IV, c. 3, vol. 1, pp. 622-4. Also see: *DM* 7, 3, n. 8, vol. 25, p. 274. On this difficulty, cf. Pedro Descoqs, S.J., *Institutiones Metaphysicae Generalis: Éléments d'ontologie*, tomus primus(Paris: Beauchesne, 1925), pp. 470-72; A. Michel, "Relations divines," *Dictionnaire de Théologie Catholique*, tome XIII, deuxième partie (Paris: Letouzey et Ané, 1937), esp. cols. 2155-56; and José Hellin, "Principio de identidad comparada," *Espiritu*, 24 (1975), pp. 135-142.

87 Suárez's point here is that "being in" is the common or transcendent mark of all accidents, while "being toward" introduces a particular restriction for one kind of accident.

88 Cf. n. 15, this Section.

since it is really distinguished and prescinded from that. Again, if that "being toward" were an accident of something, it would affect that something and would come to it anew, and then the difficulty we are treating returns, namely, that from the advent (*resultantia*) of that "being toward" /p. 792/ the thing or the foundation from which it results would be changed.

But they say that "being toward" as "toward" is not anything real, and so it is not strange that it is not an accident; neither does it inhere, nor does it change the relative thing that it denominates. But this is not said either truly or logically, if we are using univocal terms,[89] and especially according to the mentioned opinion, which supposes a real relation to be something in reality itself (*in re ipsa*) that is in things and to some extent (*secundum aliquid sui*) is distinguished in reality (*in re ipsa*) from the foundation. For, although if one is speaking of "being toward" as it is attributed to relations of reason, it is not something real, nevertheless, as I will show below, that is only equivocally, or at most according to a certain analogy of proportionality,[90] called "being toward," about which we are not talking now, but [rather we are talking] about a true "being toward," which constitutes a real category of accident. But this [latter] must be something real; otherwise, how could it constitute a true real accident? Or how could a relation be an intrinsic form referring its subject to a terminus, if it would not affect that [subject] according to its own proper character and consequently also according to that very "being toward"?

21. This is confirmed, because with regard to this the argument (*ratio*) is almost the same as it is about "being in." For, as it is attributed to beings of reason,[91] it can be taken either equivocally or analogically. For in this way blindness is said to be in an eye; therefore, as such, "being in" does not mean

---

89 That is, using the terms consistently in the same sense.

90 For Suárez, an analogy of proportionality is one which involves a comparison between two relations. For example, when one speaks of a "smiling meadow" by comparing the verdure of a meadow with the smile of a man, the verdure is said to be related to the meadow as a smile is to a man; cf. *DM* 28, 3, n. 11, vol. 26, p. 16. And "... every genuine analogy of proportionality includes something metaphorical and improper." ibid. For other places where Suárez has explicitly mentioned the extrinsic and improper character of metaphor, cf. *DM* 8, 7, nn. 21 and 22, vol. 25, pp. 302-03; *DM* 32, 2, n. 13, vol. 26, p. 323; and *DM* 39, 3, n. 1, p. 523. For proportionality as "a relation of a relation," for example, the likeness in being double which is involved between four and eight in respect to three and six; cf. Section 11, n. 6, below.

91 For Suárez on beings of reason, see Disputation 54, vol. 26, pp. 1014-1041; for an English translation, cf. Francisco Suárez, S.J., *On Beings of Reason (De Entibus Rationis) Metaphysical Disputation LIV*, translated from the Latin, with an Introduction and Notes, by John P. Doyle, Milwaukee: Marquette University Press, 1995.

something real. But nevertheless, true "being in," which constitutes a real accident, is real. Therefore, in like manner, we should philosophize about true "being toward," which doubtless is a certain real thing. Hence it happens that it must be necessarily or intrinsically subsisting—which cannot be said about the relation, on which we are focused, which is accidental or intrinsically inhering. Therefore, if the "being toward" of a real relation is something distinct in reality (*ex natura rei*) from the foundation of such a relation, also "being in" which is proper and intrinsic to such a relation will be distinct, or conversely, if no "being in" of a relation is distinguished really from its foundation, then neither is any "being toward" distinguished.

Hence, I finally argue that it is impossible that a relation as regards "being toward" result from its foundation, as something real that is from the nature of things distinct from that, unless that real thing, whatever it may be, is somewhere inherent (*alicubi insit*). For either it exists in itself, and then it will be subsistent, or it is sustained by something, and then it will inhere in that. Therefore, either it inheres in the terminus, which self-evidently cannot be said, or it inheres in its proper subject or foundation, and then such "being toward" will be distinguished /col. b/ from that, also according to its own "being in," which it intrinsically includes. Therefore, that distinction is useless for explaining the present matter. Moreover, through it the difficulty mentioned[92] is not avoided, [namely], that through a resulting relation the thing related will be changed in some way, if a relation according to a proper real being is something in the nature of things actually distinct from its foundation.

When It Is Appropriately Explained, the Fifth Opinion Is Approved.
22. Therefore, among these opinions, the one that is most proven is the fifth, which Hervaeus and some other Thomists have taught, from the sense of which the Nominalists scarcely separate themselves—and Aristotle and St. Thomas are much in favor of it, as we have seen.[93] However, this opinion is to be interpreted so that it not be understood that the formal character of a relation is nothing or that a relative denomination is merely extrinsic, taken from some absolute form. For according to this [understanding] the real category of relation (*ad aliquid*) would be demolished and destroyed. But it must be understood that relation indeed entails some form that is real and intrinsically denominating a proper relative thing (*relativum*), which [relative thing] it constitutes [as relative].

---

92 Cf. n. 17, this Section.
93 Cf. n. 13, this Section, where, it may be recalled, Suárez has cited the pseudo-Thomistic work, the *Summa totius Aristotelis logicae*.

However, it is not some thing or mode,[94] physically distinct from every absolute form, but it is in reality some absolute form, not however taken absolutely, but as respecting another [form], which the relative denomination includes or connotes.[95] Thus, for example, similarity is some real form existing in the thing that is denominated "similar," but it is not, however, in reality distinct from whiteness, with regard to that which it posits in the thing that is called similar, but only with regard to the terminus that it connotes. And thus, similarity is in reality not other than that whiteness itself as respecting another whiteness as it is of the same or similar character.

And this distinction of reason is enough, both for diverse forms of speaking and also for a distinction of categories. For, as we have said above,[96] a categorical distinction is sometimes only a distinction of reason with some foundation in reality, as, for example, with regard to action and passion,[97] and as we will say below with regard to other categories.[98] And this opinion will be made more clear both from the solution of the arguments [against it] and also in the following Sections.

---

94 Again, let us note Suárez's refusal to reduce a relation to a mode which is added to its foundation.

95 For some wider historical background here, cf. Paul Vincent Spade, "Ockham's Distinction between Absolute and Connotative Terms," *Vivarium*, 13 (1975), pp. 55-76. Also, cf. Mark G. Henninger, S.J., *Relations, Medieval Theories 1250-1325* (Oxford: Clarendon Press, 1989), esp. Chapter 7, "Relative Terms as Connotative: William of Ockham," pp. 119-49.

96 Cf. *DM* 39, s. 2, nn. 22-23, vol. 26, pp. 516-517, in which place there is, among other references, one to *De veritate*, I, a. 1, where St. Thomas has laid out his doctrine regarding the distinction of categories and most especially regarding the transcendental attributes of being. From this, and many places in Suárez, we can conclude that the same kind of distinction, which is operative here between a relation and its foundation, will suffice for a distinction of categories and also for a distinction between being and its transcendental properties, as well as among those properties themselves. Again, on the Suarezian doctrine of transcendentals, cf. Rolf Darge, *Suárez' transzendentale Seinsauslegung* ... (2004), whose special merit is to show that the core distinction which Suárez finds between being and its transcendental properties does not require a Scotistic "absolutely simple" (*simpliciter simplex*) concept of being that would be differentiated by modes which would be outside it.

97 Cf. Aristotle, *Physics* 3.3.202b19-22; also see *Metaphysics* 11.9.1066a30-34.

98 He is talking here about time, place, disposition, and possession. For the distinction of reason with a foundation in reality that is involved in the distinction of the last six categories, cf. *DM* 39, 2, nn. 21-23, vol. 26, pp. 516-517.

Reply to the Bases of the Other Opinions.

23. Therefore, the bases of the first, second, third, and sixth opinions have been touched upon among those things that had to be presented and opposed, and they have been answered. Neither /p. 793/ does any other argument occur, which in their favor could produce any difficulty, to which there is need to respond. Therefore, only the arguments of the fourth opinion[99] remain to be answered.

And indeed, the first [argument], about the separability of a relation from its foundation has already been answered. For we deny that a relation is ever separated from its foundation as regards something real that is intrinsic to it. But it happens only that the terminus may be separated or destroyed, and when this is removed the relative denomination also ceases—not because some part of a thing or some real mode is taken away from that relative [thing], but because the relative denomination includes in some way the terminus, without which it does not remain actually, but only fundamentally, or in proximate aptitude.

To the second [argument] the answer is that the being of a relation is not in reality different from the being of its foundation; however, they are conceptually distinguished insofar as that being is conceived as in some way including or connoting the terminus to which it refers.

To the third [argument] I answer: when one white thing newly comes into existence, nothing real is newly added to another white thing, as has been stated and proven. Nor does it follow from this that a relation of likeness is nothing; rather it follows only that it is not something distinct from the whiteness, which was hitherto in such a white thing. But when it is further objected that before there was in that thing no likeness and that afterwards there is a likeness, and that therefore either the likeness is nothing real or that something real is newly in that white thing: the answer lies in denying the consequence with respect to both parts. For besides those two choices, there is also a third, namely, that something real exists anew, not in the thing that was white before, but in a terminus that has newly become white, a terminus that in some way that reality that is likeness includes or connotes under the aspect and concept of likeness and not under the aspect of whiteness.[100]

To the fourth [argument][101] the answer is that those denominations are, as is correctly proven there, not merely extrinsic. Accordingly, we concede that a denomination of this kind is from some intrinsic form, but as including or

---

99 See n. 10, this Section.
100 For this position, cf. Hervaeus Natalis, *Quolibet* 1, q. 9, ed. Zimara, fol. 21rb-va; *Quolibet* 2, q. 7, fol. 47vb.
101 Cf. n. 11, this Section.

connoting some other extrinsic [form] in an extrinsic terminus. For this reason, the ultimate consequence is denied, namely, that this form denominating in this way with respect (*habitudo*) to something extrinsic, must be really (*ex natura rei*) distinct, at least modally, from every absolute form. For with an extrinsic terminus presupposed, that absolute form itself in reality (*secundum rem*) is enough to give such a denomination, which can be taken away or can cease by the simple removal of the extrinsic terminus, as has been said. /col. b/

The Arguments Remaining from the First Section Are Answered.

24. *First.—Second.—Third.*—Also from what has been said in this Section many of the arguments are resolved that were proposed at the beginning of the preceding Section.[102] For with regard to the first,[103] it has now been explained how the "being toward" of a real and accidental relation is something in the thing itself that is said to be referred. And it is false that "being toward" is said univocally about relations of reason and real [relations]. Likewise, it is false that true "being toward" can be prescinded from "being in" so that it does not intrinsically include that, in the way in which we have said above[104] that modes of being cannot be so prescinded from being that they do not include that [being] in themselves.

Again, with respect to the second argument,[105] namely, that a relation may come without a change of the foundation, sufficiently many things have been said. For we concede that from this it is correctly concluded that a relation is not something really distinct from its foundation, but not that it is not something real.

Hence, [in reply] to the third [argument][106] the first consequence is denied (that is, a relation is nothing apart from absolutes, therefore, it is simply nothing) if in the antecedent the words "apart from" indicate an actual real distinction. For although a relation is not something distinct in reality from absolutes, it can be something that is distinct rationally. Neither does it matter that a relation as a relation is prescinded from absolute things, because it is not prescinded as something fashioned by the mind nor even as something precise and distinct in reality, but as something that is true and real but prescinded only by reason. For often there is a distinction of reason between extremes

---

102 Cf. Section 1, nn. 1-3.
103 Ibid., n. 1.
104 Cf. e.g. *DM* 2, 5, n. 8, vol. 25, p. 95; and *DM* 32, 1, nn. 13-19, vol. 26, pp. 315-18.
105 Ibid., n. 2.
106 Ibid., n. 3.

that are true and real, which is enough to constitute [different] categories.[107] Hence, all the proofs that are brought forward in the third argument are useful for explaining how a real relation does not add [another] thing to absolute things or a real mode that is really (*ex natura rei*) distinct from those [absolute things],[108] but they are not at all valid for concluding that a relation of this kind is completely nothing.

25. *Something To Note.*—But two things should be avoided in those arguments. The first is that when it is said that a relative denomination arises from the co-existence of a number of absolutes without any real addition, it should not be understood that this denomination is equally and simultaneously taken from a number of absolute forms, one of which is intrinsic and another extrinsic. But it must be understood that that denomination requires indeed an association (*consortium*) or a co-existence of such things or /p. 794/ forms, but in each extreme it is taken from a form that is proper insofar as this respects another [form]—which as such has the character of a relation, even though in reality it is not other than that absolute form itself.

Second, (on account of the example that is there brought forth about God insofar as he is denominated lord, creator, etc.) care should be taken lest one think that denominations of this kind are of the same manner and character in all things. For that cannot be true, according to the common opinion, which distinguishes relations as mutual and non-mutual, which distinction would be null if all the denominations in question were in the same manner in all extremes. However, it is not easy to explain what this diversity is, according to the doctrine and the opinion that we are defending. Therefore, about this matter

---

107 For example, cf. the distinct categories of action and passion.

108 This doctrine, which is consistent throughout this Section and throughout Disputation 47, contrasts sharply with what Suárez has said in his earliest work, on the relation of union in the Incarnation; cf.: "... thus this question coincides with the general metaphysical question about the distinction of a relation from its foundation, ... But, indeed, I think that there is some real distinction, not, to be sure, as of things which are entirely distinct, but as of diverse formal features, or of a mode and a thing of which it is a mode." (... *sic coincidit quaestio haec cum generali quaestione metaphysica de distinctione relationis a suo fundamento* ... *Ego vero sentio esse quidem distinctionem aliquam ex natura rei, non quidem tanquam rerum ominino distinctarum, sed tanquam formalium rationum diversarum, seu tanquam modi, et rei cujus est modus.*), *Commentaria ac disputationes in Tertiam Partem D. Thomae, scilicet, Opus de Incarnatione*, Qu. 2, art. 8, in *Opera omnia*, vol. 18, p. 328; ibid., Disp. 8, s. 3, n. 21, p. 354; and Disp. 11, s. 2, n. 16, p. 440. Also, see *Tractatus de Trinitate*, VII, c. 4, n. 7, vol. 1, p. 698. Evidently, the *Doctor eximius* has undergone some development here on his central understanding of the reality of relation.

we will compose a special Section below.[109] Now we are only saying that when in a thing denominated there is some proper and proportionate foundation of such a denomination, then it results from a proper real relation, but when it is attributed to a thing without such a foundation, then the denomination is extrinsic or conceptual.

---

109 That is, Section 15.

Section III.
How Many Kinds of Relation There Are, and Which Is Truly Categorical.

1. This question is proposed because of the difficulty that was touched upon in the fourth argument advanced in the First Section.[1] In order to answer this, some distinctions of relatives must be put forward and explained, so that putting aside those things that do not pertain to this category, we may conclude how there could be a genus of real accident that would be diverse from other [genera of accidents] and constituting a genuine category, "toward something."

The First Division of Relation into Real and Rational.

2. Relation is usually divided into that which is real or that which is only rational, which some interpret such that they teach that the categorical genus, "toward something" (*Ad aliquid*) includes both relations and that this division is therefore univocal, indeed that it is a division of a genus into its species. This opinion St. Thomas seems to favor in *Summa Theologiae*, I, q. 28, a. 1, where he says this: *"It must be taken into account that only in those things that are said 'toward something' are some found to be according to reason only and not according to reality."*[2]

Therefore, he feels that those things that are related only according to reason are truly and univocally "toward something." /col. b/ For if it were a case simply of an equivocal or an analogous denomination, some things [which would be] only according to reason would be found in other categories, for example, blindness in [the category of] quality, and similar things in other categories. The same position can be taken from [St. Thomas] article 2 of the same question [i.e. *Summa* I, q. 28],[3] from Question 13, article, 7;[4] from *Quodlibet* I, art. 2 [sic];[5] *Quodlibet* IX, art. 5 [sic];[6] *De Potentia*, question 2, article 5,[7] and often elsewhere.

---

1 Cf. Section 1, n. 5, above.
2 Cf. S. Thomae Aquinatis, *Opera omnia*, tomus IV, p. 318b.
3 Cf. ibid., p. 321a.
4 Cf. ibid., pp. 152b-153a.
5 Cf. Sancti Thomae Aquinatis, *Quaestiones de Quolibet*, I, q. 2, a. 1, in *Opera omnia*, tomus xxv, vol. 2 (Roma: Commissio Leonina, 1996), p. 178b.
6 Cf. ibid., IX, q. 2, a. 4, in *Opera omnia*, tomus xxv, vol.1, p. 96b.
7 Cf. *Quaestiones disputatae de potentia Dei*, q. 2, a. 5, ed. ix, cura Bazzi et al., p. 35b.

In line with this, Cajetan [a.k.a. Tommaso de Vio, O.P.], at the mentioned places in the First Part [of *Summa Theologiae*] evidently thinks that "being toward" is said univocally of both a real and a rational relation.[8] Earlier Capreolus [John Capreolus, O.P.] seems to have taught the same thing in [his *Defensiones* ...], I, dist. 33 [sic], question 1,[9] and Deça [Diego de Deza, O.P. (d. 1523)] appears to follow [him] there, at question 1, note 4.[10] Also [the same is found in] Ferrara [Franciscus de Sylvestris Ferrariensis], [commenting on] *Summa contra Gentiles*, IV, chapter 14,[11] and more explicitly, in Soncinas [Paulus Barbus Soncinas, O.P.], *Metaphysics* V, question 26, conclusion 2[12]—who bring forward other texts of St. Thomas. Their basis is that the definition of relatives that Aristotle has given and the properties that follow upon that, fit both relations of reason and also real relations.[13]

This is clear, because those things are said to be relative whose whole being is such as "to have itself toward another." But this is entirely and most properly fitting for relations of reason. For although the being of these is more imperfect and diminished than the being of real relatives, nevertheless, their being, such as it is, consists entirely in a disposition (*habitudo*) toward something else, just as properly as does the being of a real relation. Thus it turns out that, just like

---

8 Cf. *Commentaria in Summam Theologiae* I, q. 28, a. 1, nn. 6-7, in *S. Thomae Opera*, tomus IV (1888), pp. 319b-20a; ibid., In I, q. 13, a. 7, n. 10, p. 155b.

9 Cf. *Defensiones, In I. Sent.*, d. 30, q. 1, a. 2, ed. Paban-Pègues, tom. II, pp. 310-312.

10 Cf. Didaci Deza, O.P., *Nouarum deffensionum doctrine ... Beati Thome de Aquino super primo libro sententiarum questiones profundissime ac vtilissime*, I, d. 33, q. 1, a. 3, not. 4 (Hispali: Arte et Ingenio Iacobi Kronberger, 1517), tom. I, fol. 237v-238r.

11 Cf. *Commentaria in Summam contra gentiles*, IV, c. 14, n. 18, in *S. Thomae Aquinatis, Opera omnia*, tomus XV (1930), pp. 64b-65b.

12 Pauli Soncinatis, O.P., *Quaestiones metaphysicales acutissimae*, V, q. 26 (Venetiis, 1588; reprinted: Frankfurt: Minerva, 1967), p. 86b.

13 In the seventeenth century, this position will be again taken up by John of St. Thomas and it will become for him the basis of a unified semiotic bridging between natural and conventional signs. For this, see John Deely, in *Tractatus de Signis: The Semiotic of John Poinsot*. Interpretive Arrangement by John N. Deely in consultation with Ralph Austin Powell (Berkeley, 1985), pp. 44-5, n. 2; also see Deely, *Introducing Semiotic: its History and Doctrine* (Bloomington: Indiana University Press, 1982), esp. pp. 168-73; idem, *Four Ages of Understanding: The First Postmodern Survey of Philosophy from Ancient Times to the Turn of the Twenty-first Century* (Toronto/Buffalo/London: University of Toronto Press, 2001), esp. pp. 371, 440-2, 464, 476, 694, and 724.

a real relation, a relation of reason can be neither known nor defined without a disposition to something else.

Only Real Relations Make Up the Category, "Toward Something."

3. Nevertheless, we have to say, that only real relations make up the category, "toward something." This is evident enough from what has been taught above[14] with regard to the concept of being and its division into nine supreme categories [of accident]. For we have shown that being not only is not univocal between real being and being of reason, but it also does not have one concept even analogously common to these, but that it is equivocal or at best analogous with an analogy of proportionality.[15] And for this reason also we say the object of metaphysics is not being as common to real being and being of reason, but to real being only;[16] and this also we have shown to be divided into ten supreme kinds.[17] Since, therefore, relations of reason are not real beings, and consequently not true beings, they cannot belong to the category, "toward something."

I add, further: they cannot have a univocal /p. 795/ agreement with real relations, if we suppose these to be true real beings, as was supposed above[18] from the common opinion and will be gradually explained and proven in the discussion of this subject. But the reason is that since a being of reason is nothing, it cannot have a true likeness or agreement with real being, on which agreement the univocity and the unity of a concept is ordinarily based. There- fore, there cannot be any true and essential concept common to real being and being of reason. Hence, Soncinas, in *Metaphysics* IV, questions 5 and 6,[19] rightly approves the dictum of Hervaeus (although by a typographer's error it is attributed to Henry [of Ghent][20]) in *Quodlibet* 3, q. 1, article one—at the end: *"Being" cannot be univocal between real being and being of reason, any more than "man" can be univocal between a living and a dead man.*[21] But this dictum has the same measure of truth with respect to being in common and with respect to the particular kind of being that is *relation*. For just as a being of reason is not a true, but rather a fictitious being, so a relation of reason is

---

14 Cf. esp. *DM* 39, 3, nn. 12-15, vol. 26, pp. 526-8.
15 Cf. Section 2, note 62, above.
16 Cf. *DM* 1, 1, n. 26, vol. 25, p. 11; ibid., n. 6, pp. 3-4.
17 Cf. *DM* 32, 1, nn. 4-5, vol. 26, p. 313.
18 Cf. Section 1, n. 15.
19 Pauli Soncinatis, O.P., *Quaestiones metaphysicales* ..., V, q. 5 (Venetiis, 1588), p. 10b and q. 6, p. 11.
20 Ibid. p. 10b.
21²¹ Cf. Hervaeus Natalis, *Quodlibetum* III, q. 1, a. 1 (Venetiis, 1513), fol. 68vb.

not a true relation but one that is fictitious or, as it were, fashioned by the intellect.

4. *An Objection Is Met.*—Someone perhaps will say: this is true as regards the integral and complete concept of relation, about which the argument advanced proceeds, because in this kind of concept of a real relation there is included the fact that it is a true being and a real accident; however, [the argument] does not proceed in the same way with regard to the precise concept of that mode, or constituent of relation, which is signified through this expression, "*to be toward*"; for such a concept of its nature prescinds from the character[s] (*ratione*) of being and of accident.

The cited authors seem to have spoken in this sense, and Henry seems to agree with them in *Quodlibet 9*, question 3, where he has argued most obscurely about this subject. But among other things he says: "*To be toward another*" of itself admits no distinction or diversity, whether it might be in God or in creatures, in relations according to reality or in relations according to reason.[22]

However, against this evasion the argument made has the same force. For that "being toward," insofar as it is a mode that is constitutive of a real relation, is either itself also a real mode, or it is only a being of reason. This second cannot be said, for otherwise a real relation will not have a real proper and formal constitutive [principle], which implies a contradiction. For how can a real being as such be constituted through what is not real?

About this matter, we have said much above at Disputation 2, treating of the modes that contract being.[23] However, if that "being toward" in a real relation is a real mode, again I ask whether in a relation of reason it is also a true and real mode or only one fashioned by the intellect? /col. b/ The first cannot be said, because it contradicts a relation of reason, of whose essence it is not to entail a disposition existing in reality but [only] in the mind's comparison or denomination. Again, [it cannot be said] because it implies a contradiction that a fictitious being, existing only objectively in the intellect, be constituted by a mode that is real and existing in reality itself. Thus, that "being toward" in a relation of reason is a pure being of reason. Therefore, just as a common or univocal concept cannot be granted between real being and being of reason, or between a real relation and a relation of reason, according to the complete concept of relation, so neither can "being toward," conceived precisely as such, signify one common and univocal concept for the "being toward" of a real relation and of a relation of reason. For there cannot be a truer likeness and agreement between these than between any other real beings and beings

---

22 Cf. Henrici de Gandavo, *Quodlibet* IX, qu. 3, ed. R. Macken (1983), p. 55.
23 Cf. *DM* 2, 2, n. 21, vol. 25, p. 77; ibid., 6, nn. 7-12, pp. 100-102.

of reason. Neither can it be understood in them more than in others of what kind would be that concept abstracting from real being and being of reason, or of what kind could be the contraction or the determination of such a concept to real being through a real mode and to being of reason through a rational mode.

5. *Only Real Relation Is Properly "Toward Something."—The Text of St. Thomas Explained.*—Therefore, it should be said that only a real relation is truly and properly "toward something," while a relation of reason is not, but is conceived "as if" (*ac si*) it were "toward something." And therefore, only real relations belong to the category proper. Relations of reason, however, are not to be placed in a real category, but they are to be explained by analogy and proportion to real relations, as we will say more in detail in the final Disputation of this work.[24] Nor does St. Thomas intend to oppose this in the cited texts. For he has never said either that a relation of reason is univocally a relation in the same way as a real relation or that "being toward another" is not something real in a real relation. But he has said only that the nature of a real relation is such that by a likeness and proportion to it beings of reason can be fashioned in the manner of relations by the intellect with some foundation in reality, rather than in the manner of quantity or quality, etc.

This, he says, results from the fact that relation as relation signifies only a respect toward another. In this context, the word "only" does not exclude concomitants; hence it cannot exclude the transcendental character (*rationem*) of being, or of accident if the relation is accidental. But because a relation, insofar as it is precisely conceived or signified as it is "toward something," is neither conceived nor signified /p. 796/ explicitly as inhering, St. Thomas, therefore, says that as such it expresses only a respect toward another—not because in reality it is not something in itself or something existing in a subject but because in conceiving or signifying it in this way nothing else is expressed. Therefore, it also happens that beings of reason can be conceived according to the mode of relation, not because in such a [conceived] relation there is a real relation, or a real "being toward," such as there is in a real relation, but because it is conceived after the manner of or in proportion to that. Hence, St. Thomas himself, after he said that relation according to its proper rationale (*rationem*) signifies only a respect to something else, adds that this respect sometimes is in reality itself, but sometime it is *only in the apprehension of the reason comparing one thing with another.*[25]

---

24 Cf. *DM* 54, s. 6, in *Opera omnia*, vol. 26, pp. 1039-41.
25 For this, see *Summa Theologiae* I, q. 28, a. 1, in *Opera*, tomus IV, p. 318b. While St. Thomas does not use the word "univocal" here, in another place he equates the

But to the argument of that opinion [i.e. of the Thomists] it is easy to reply: by denying that the proper rationale of relation is truly found in a relation of reason, because in such a relation there is neither a true disposition (*habitudo*) nor a true "being toward something," but it is only apprehended "as if" it were "toward something."

A Second Division of Relation: "According to Being Said" And "According to Being"

6. There is a second division of relation into relation "according to being" (*secundum esse*) and [relation] "according to being said" (*secundum dici*). This division has its basis in Aristotle, the Chapter on "Toward Something," where he first gives the definition common to relatives "according to being said"[26] and then gives the proper definition of relatives "according to being."[27] A relation, then, "according to being said" is usually defined as something that is conceived, explained, or said in the manner of a respect (*per modum respectus*), although in reality it does not have a true respect. But a relation "according to being" is said to be one that in fact has true being with a disposition to another [thing].

7. *Relation "According to Being Said" As It Is Explained by Some.*—From this, some, not without probability, have thought that a relation "according to being said" is the same as a relation of reason. Henry [of Ghent] in his *Quodlibet 3*, Question 4, indicates this from Avicenna saying, in Book 3 of his *Metaphysics*, that a relation "according to being said" is one which has being only in the intellect and belongs to things that are not simply and absolutely "toward something" but only insofar as they are conceived by the intellect.[28] And this seems reasonable. For as we conceive, so do we speak. But relations "according to being said" are called such only because they are so said or explained by us as if they were relations, even though they are not. Therefore, that /col. b/ way of speaking about these relations presupposes our way of conceiving, from which it arises that these are doubtless conceived by us with a relation and a disposition [toward] or in the way of a relation and a disposition [toward], even though truly and in reality they do not have a disposition [toward]. But it is in this that the rationale (*ratio*) and the essence of a relation of reason

---

phrase "according to its proper rationale" (*secundum propriam rationem*) with being predicated "univocally" (*univoce*); cf. ibid., q. 16, a. 6, p. 213a.

26 *Categories* c. 7.6a36-7.

27 Ibid., 8a31-32.

28 Cf. Henricus a Gandavo, *Quodlibet.* III, q. 4 (ed. 1518), fol. 51rN. For Avicenna, see *Avicenna Latinus: Liber de philosophia prima sive scientia divina, I-IV*, Tr. 3, c. 10, édition critique par S. Van Riet (1977), p. 182, ll. 72-3.

consists; therefore, a relation "according to being said" is the same as a relation of reason.

8. *The True Essence of a Relation "According to Being Said."*—But, nevertheless, this division is not commonly understood in this way. For a relation of reason, in that way in which it is, is thought to be a relation "according to the being," which is proportionate to itself, as is clear with regard to the relation of genus and species, as well as similar [relations]. For in that way in which these are thought, they not only are said, but they also are "toward something." And, conversely, a relation "according to being said" is not limited to a relation of reason, but is said of any real thing whatever whose being is absolute and [which at the same time] is explained by us only by way of a disposition [toward] (*habitudinis*) or a relative relation [sic]. For in this way we say that divine omnipotence is relative "according to being said," not on account of a relation of reason that we imagine in it, but because we conceive it and explain it, only with the concomitance of something else to which it is in potency and by way of its having a disposition toward that thing.

Hence, even though it may be true that this way of saying or speaking presupposes a way of conceiving, nevertheless, that way of conceiving is not such that from it there necessarily results or is apprehended a relation of reason. For it is not a reflex or a comparative concept, but rather it is a direct concept of an absolute thing, which is, however, imperfectly conceived in the manner of those things that have a disposition toward other things. In this way of conceiving, there is not attributed to that object that is known any disposition [toward], either real or rational, but only from the side of the one conceiving there is a concept produced by a certain imitation and analogy with concepts of relative things. For example, when we conceive a spiritual thing in the manner of something corporeal, we do not attribute real corporeity to an object; otherwise, the conception would be false. Again, we do not imagine or think some being of reason in that object; for, of what sort would that be? Therefore, we only conceive one thing by analogy with another. So then sometimes we conceive an absolute thing in the manner of something relative, and we speak of it as though it were relative, and therefore it is said to be relative only "according to being said."

Hence, it is clear that relations only "according to being said" are outside the genus of relation, and they cannot essentially /p. 797/ belong to the category, "toward something." Indeed, under that character they belong to no category; for from the fact that a thing is imperfectly conceived or said by us it does not receive a special nature by virtue of which it must be located in a special category. And therefore, Aristotle, in the category "toward something," as Boethius and others note in that place, after the exclusion of the first definition of relatives, which was common even to relatives "according to being said," added a second [definition][29] that is proper to relatives "according to being".

9. *Relations "According to Being Said" Are Diverse from Categorical and Transcendental [Relations].*—To be sure, there are some who think that this division of relation "according to being said" and "according to being" coincides with another division of relation into transcendental and categorical, in such way that only a transcendental relation is a relation "according to being said," whereas every relation "according to being" is categorical (we are speaking of created [relations]).

But even though this opinion seems to be carried about in the mouths of almost all, it is not proven to me. For I think that transcendental relations include in reality and, in their being true and real, dispositions [toward] (*habitudines*), which I will show a little below. However, relations that are only "according to being said," when they are taken properly and with rigor, are distinguished from all relations "according to being," whether these are transcendental or categorical. For they do not require in a thing that is so conceived or relatively denominated any true disposition toward, which by reason of its own being belongs to that thing, but [they require] only a denomination from our way of conceiving and speaking, as we have explained.

Thus, in the posited example about the power of God, it is more probable that it does not include even a transcendental respect, albeit [that power] may be called relative "according to being said." Therefore, a relation "according only to being said" is not the same as a transcendental relation. Indeed, it is even [sharply] distinguished (*condistinguitur*) from that, if it is taken with precision, as it should be taken. I am adding this, because a transcendental relation can also be called a relation "according to being said," since we also speak of it in the manner of relatives. Indeed, a categorical relation will also be a relation "according to being said," since it too is said with a disposition toward something else. In order, therefore, that the division be properly made, a relation "according to being said" must be taken with exclusion and precision in such way that only in that "being said" (*dici*) it seems to have a disposition [toward], but in "being" (*esse*) it has no [disposition toward], either transcendental or categorical.

You say: if a thing is so absolute that in its being /col. b/ it has no disposition [toward], even one that is transcendental, why will it be necessary that it be conceived or said with a disposition, since each thing can be conceived in that way in which it is apart from everything that is outside its essence? The answer is: this often results from our imperfect way of conceiving inasmuch as

---

29 Cf. *Categories* c. 7.8a31-32.

we cannot conceive things as they themselves are. I further add that sometimes it happens that a thing even perfectly conceived cannot be known without the concomitance of other things, even if they are outside its essence, not because of a disposition [toward] or a dependence, but because of another higher connection in the nature of a cause that is eminently containing its effects. In this way, theologians say that God cannot be perfectly seen or comprehended unless creatures are known in Him—about which [we speak] elsewhere.

A Third Division: Between Transcendental and Categorical Relation.

10. Thirdly and principally, relations which are real and "according to being" are divided into transcendental and categorical, which division is most of all necessary in order to conclude and to explain what we intend in the present Section. For up to now it is clear only that a relation that belongs to this category, "toward something," must be real and "according to being." But now it remains to be seen whether every relation of this kind belongs to this category. Indeed, from the fourth argument that was proposed in the First Section it is clear that not every disposition [toward] that is real and "according to being" can belong to one definite category. And therefore this division is being proposed by which it is signified that there is a certain mode of real disposition [toward], which has a particular and definite mode of being, which constitutes a particular category of being, and categorical relations are of this kind. But besides these there are other also true and real dispositions [toward], which essentially belong to various and indeed almost all categories (*genera*) of beings, which are then called "transcendental" and are distinguished from categorical [relations] because they do not belong to a certain category but rather wander through all [categories].

11. First of all, then, this division as so explained needs to be shown with regard to its individual members. To be sure, as was said in the First Section, from the traditional division of the categories and from the common opinion of all, we are presupposing that there are some categorical relations. But that, besides these, there are transcendental relations, /p. 798/ which are not only "according to being said," but also true and real dispositions [toward] "according to being," is sufficiently proven by induction and by the discussion formulated in that fourth argument proposed in the First Section.[30]

And this can be confirmed; for in the category of substance matter and form have between themselves a true and real disposition [toward], which is essentially included in their proper being, and therefore one is defined by reference (*habitudo*) to the other, and from this they receive their specification. The same reasoning is valid with respect to accidental potencies that are

---

30 Cf. Section 1, n. 5, above.

essentially and immediately (*per se primo*) instituted for and ordered toward their acts. It is also the case with regard to operative habits, about which it was shown above that by their nature they are specified through a disposition toward their acts or objects, because without doubt they include in their being a true disposition toward their acts, and through the medium of these, toward their objects.[31] Therefore, these transcendental respects (*respectus*) are true and following upon the real being of those things to which they belong. Therefore, just as the induction that was made is based upon more common and more received opinions, so also this doctrine should be regarded as one which is commonly approved by the [Scholastic] Doctors.

Especially in its favor one should note the words of St. Thomas in [*Summa theologiae*], Part 1, Question 28, Article 1, where he writes as follows: "Those things that are said 'toward something' signify according to their proper nature only a respect to something else, which respect indeed is sometimes in the very nature of things (*in ipsa natura rei*), as for example when any two things are according to their nature ordered to each other and have an inclination to one another. And relations of this kind have to be real. For instance, in a heavy body there is an inclination and an order to the middle place [in the universe]; hence there is a certain respect in that heavy body with regard to the middle place. And the situation is similar in the case of other things of this kind."[32] This reasoning of St. Thomas is equally and especially valid as regards a transcendental respect. For in that case especially there are found things that are ordered to one another. Indeed, the example of St. Thomas is best understood and verified about a transcendental respect. For an inclination of gravity and a propensity to the middle place does not belong to the category of relation, but [rather to the category] of quality. For it is the proper essence of such a quality.

12. *Objection.—First Response.—A Truer Response.*—You will say: no real respect is included in the concept of an absolute thing; but this transcendental respect is included in the concept of an absolute thing; therefore, it is not a true respect "according to being," but only according to our mode of speaking and conceiving. For on this argument they are most of all dependent who feel about these transcendental respects /col. b/ in such way that they think they consist only in words. Indeed, some reply—and this can be taken from

---

31 On habits as specified by acts, and acts in turn by objects, cf. *DM* 44, 8, n. 15, vol. 26, p. 685; on habits taking their species and unity from acts, cf. ibid., s. 7, pp. 679-681. For some wider implications of this doctrine, cf. John P. Doyle, "Suárez on the Unity of a Scientific Habit," *The American Catholic Philosophical Quarterly*, 65 (1991), pp. 309-331.
32 Cf. *Summa Theologiae* I, 28, a. 1, in *Opera*, tomus IV, p. 318b.

[Duns] Scotus, in [his *Sentences* commentary] Book 4, Distinction 12, the only Question [sic][33]—that respects of this kind follow upon absolute things, but they do not belong to the intrinsic nature of those things.[34] For this reason, Scotus denies that aptitudinal inherence is of the essence of an accident, since [that inherence] is a true respect.[35] According to this reply, these respects would not be outside the range of the category, "toward something." Hence, they could not properly be called "transcendental," nor could they be distinguished from categorical [relations], because it is not against the nature of a definite category that things contained in it follow from things of other categories, if [those categories] are not of the essence of those things but are rather properties following them.

However, we may better reply with Cajetan, [in his Commentary on] *De Ente et essentia*, Chapter 7, Question 15 [sic], that it is not against the concept of an absolute thing that in its essential rationale it include a transcendental respect that is proportioned to its nature.[36] For, in fact, aptitudinal inherence is not a property following upon the nature of an accident, but it is its intrinsic essence, as was shown above.[37] Rather it is, indeed, probable that in created beings there is none so absolute that it does not intimately include in its essence some transcendental respect, at least insofar as it is a being by participation, which depends upon a Being by essence. For, even though the actual dependence is something that is really distinct from created being itself, nevertheless, that aptitude and necessity of depending is intrinsic and essential to that [created being]. Moreover, it does not seem that it can be conceived or exist without a transcendental respect and a disposition toward that on which it depends, in which [transcendental] respect the potentiality and imperfection of created being as such seem most of all to consist.

13. But whatever may be the case about complete beings, such as whole substances, especially those that are simple and immaterial, which among created beings seem to be most of all absolute—out of all the others, which are called incomplete—there is none so absolute that it does not essentially include some transcendental respect. And the reason is that all those things of their nature have been made to be toward another or on account of another. For matter is

---

33 In the 1639 edition of Duns Scotus' *Opera omnia*, there are six questions comprising this Distinction; cf. tomus viii, pp. 698-785.

34 Cf. *Quaestiones in IV Sent.*, d. 12, q. 1 (editio 1639), tomus viii, p. 711.

35 Cf. ibid., pp. 719-24.

36 Cf. Thomae de Vio, Caietani, Ordinis Praedicatorum, *In De Ente et Essentia D. Thomae Aquinatis commentaria*, c. 7, q. 16, cura et studio P.M.-H. Laurent (Taurini: Marietti, 1934), n. 136, p. 222.

37 *DM* 37, 2, n. 9, vol. 26, p. 495.

on account of form, while form is in order to actuate matter and to complete the composite, and an accident is for a substance, potency is for act, an act is on account of an object, and likewise as regards the rest. Moreover, each thing receives a mode of entity which is accommodated /p. 799/ to its primary purpose and constitution. Therefore, since all these things are essentially and immediately (*per se primo*) ordered to other things, they thus receive a mode of entity such that they intimately include a disposition toward another, and this is a proper transcendental disposition or respect. So, among real, true, and "according to being" (*secundum esse*) dispositions [toward] there are some which are transcendental, which cannot be reduced to a definite category and which thus are distinguished from categorical [relations].

Section IV.
How a Categorical Respect Differs From a Transcendental Respect.

1. But there occurs a great difficulty: to explain the difference between these two orders of respects, and consequently [great difficulty] to explain the reason why it is necessary besides transcendental respects to admit [ones which are] categorical.

Some Differences are Proposed between the Respects in Question.

2. Therefore, various differences can be imagined among respects of this kind. The first, which includes several [others], is that a transcendental relation (*relatio*) does not require those conditions that a categorical relation demands, which [conditions], as we will see below, are principally three. First: that a categorical relation requires some real absolute foundation, for example, likeness [requires] whiteness, or paternity [requires] the power of generating or [actual] generation. Second: that it requires a terminus that is real and really existing. Third: that it requires a real distinction, or at least one that is "from the nature of the thing" (*ex natura rei*)[1] between the foundation and the terminus. However, a transcendental respect essentially (*per se*) requires none of these conditions. For the divine knowledge, to give an example, entails a transcendental disposition toward the divine essence, as toward its proper object, and divine love [entails the same] toward divine goodness, and nevertheless, there is among them no distinction "from the nature of the thing," but one of reason only. Again, a transcendental respect does not always require a real terminus, but sometimes it can be toward a fictitious being or a being of reason, or toward some extrinsic denomination. For example, the concept or the thought of a being of reason or of a privation, as such entails a transcendental disposition toward that object, which, however, is not a real being.

Often also this transcendental respect, even if it is toward a real terminus, still does not require the real existence of that [terminus]. For example, the

---

1 On its face, the difference here seems to be between a distinction among really existing things and a distinction between facets or formalities of the same thing. That is to say that a distinction "from the nature of the thing" (*ex natura rei*) is a Scotistic-like formal distinction. That would be a distinction which Suárez himself would not accept, but one which he would include here for the sake of the argument.

scientific knowledge of a future eclipse /col. b/ entails a real transcendental disposition toward that [eclipse], even though this does not exist. And the same is true in any knowledge at all of a possible object, and in the case of a potency with respect to a non-existing act. Finally, this transcendental respect requires no foundation; for the transcendental respect of matter to form has no foundation, but rather is intimately included in matter itself. And the same is true of the respect of form to matter, of knowledge to an object, and of similar things. The reason is evident: for this transcendental respect does not come to some thing that is already constituted in its essential being, but it is a kind of difference (*quasi differentia*) constituting and completing the essence of that thing whose respect it is said to be. And, therefore, just as that thing, inasmuch as it is absolute, does not require another foundation in order to exist—besides its proper subject, if perhaps it is an accidental entity—so also this transcendental respect does not pre-require another foundation, but rather it constitutes the thing itself, which can be the foundation of other categorical relations.

3. And from this another difference can be gathered. For a categorical relation is a certain accidental form, coming to a foundation that is fully constituted in its essential and absolute being, to which [being] it is compared as a complete form in its own accidental category (*genere*), affecting [that being] and referring it to something else. But a transcendental respect is not compared as an accident nor as a complete form to that thing that it is proximately actuating and of which it is a respect. But it is compared as an essential difference, and consequently something that is an incomplete being in that category (*genere*) to which that thing that it actuates and completes belongs. And it does not properly refer that thing to another as ordered or related to that other by way of a metaphysical difference.

Objections against the Stated Differences.

4. But these differences are in part not true, and in part they do not seem satisfactory. For what is said in the first difference, [namely] that a transcendental respect of the same thing to itself is found only by reason of a distinction of reason, is not true. Otherwise, it could also be said that the identity of a thing with itself is a transcendental respect and that for it a distinction of reason is enough. But if you say that there is required a "distinction of reasoned reason" (*distinctio rationis ratiocinatae*),[2] which is founded in reality, at least it follows that between a generic and a specific character there is a real /p. 800/ transcendental respect of act and potency, because a genus and a difference are distinguished conceptually with a foundation in reality.

---

2 For this, cf. *DM* 7, 1, nn. 4-5, vol. 25, p. 251.

Again, the examples introduced are false. For God's knowledge or love do not entail a real respect, even a transcendental one to God himself as to their primary object, but rather that knowledge and love are most absolute apart from every real respect, since essentially and immediately (*per se primo*) they have no respect to any object outside themselves. Hence, just as in that case the act and its object are distinguished only conceptually, so the only respect of the act to its object is a conceptual one. And the general reason is that since a respect and a disposition [toward] are like a certain tendency toward another thing, there cannot be a true and real respect of the same thing toward itself, without an intervening distinction [within that thing], at least one which is "from the nature of the thing" (*ex natura rei*).

5. *In What Way a Transcendental Respect Can Be Terminated at a Being of Reason. Some Transcendental Respects Require the Existence of their Termini.*—But, what is further said, namely, that there can sometimes be a transcendental respect toward a being of reason, is indeed true when that respect is toward something that is in the mode of an object, for which *objective being* (*esse objectivum*) is enough in order that it can have the character of a terminus of a transcendental disposition [toward]. And by the same reasoning the other part also is true, namely, that a transcendental respect can sometimes tend to a real thing or essence not actually existing, because for the character of an object *essential being* (*esse essentiae*) is often enough, apart from *existential being* (*esse existentiae*).

However, it is not always true that no transcendental respect requires a real, i.e. a really existing, terminus. For, first of all, an act of vision or of created intellection that is intuitive and natural entails a transcendental disposition toward an actually existing thing, and it cannot be or be conserved without that. Second, an actual mode of union entails a transcendental respect to a terminus or rather the extreme of the union, in which it requires both reality and actual existence, in such way that a real actual union can neither be nor be understood unless the thing with which there is the union actually exists, as was often indicated above.[3] Again, action as action, and passion as passion, entail transcendental respects to a real actually existing agent or patient, without which they could neither be nor be understood. And finally, a creature, apart from any categorical relation, from the fact alone that it is a participated and dependent being entails an essential transcendental disposition toward /col. b/ an actually existing first cause and being by essence. It is not therefore of the essence of a transcendental respect that it not require real and actual existence

---

3 Cf. e.g. *DM* 16, 1, n. 24, vol. 25, p. 574. On various meanings of "union," cf. ibid., 15, 6, n. 10, p. 521.

in its terminus. Therefore, from that difference alone the conclusion is that among transcendental respects there are some that do not require a real or actually existing terminus, even as there are others that may have and demand a terminus of this kind, in the case of which that second difference has no place.

6. But if you say that the difference consists in the fact that a transcendental respect of itself does not require such a terminus, although for some particular reason it can have that, but a categorical respect, from its full nature demands a terminus of this kind, one can object against this that this doctrine supposes that among respects to termini that really exist certain ones are transcendental and others are categorical, and they differ in the reason why they require such a terminus. But it is indeed this very thing that we are asking and that does not seem to be sufficiently explained, namely, of what sort is this diverse character in these respects that are demanding a similar terminus and what need is there to multiply these [respects]? For that distinction of transcendental respects having real or not real, existing or not existing, termini seems sufficient to explain all dispositions [toward] of things.

7. Moreover, what was asserted about a real foundation is not less obscure and uncertain. First of all, because not every categorical relation requires a real foundation that is really (*ex natura rei*) distinct from its subject, but only that [relation] that belongs to a substance by some mediating accident, as is clear, for example, with regard to a relation of specific identity between two men or souls, which relation is thought to be categorical and is immediately founded upon a substantial nature itself, about which [we will speak] more at length below.[4]

Second, a categorical relation that belongs to a substance by means of an accident, even though as compared to the substance, may be said to have another proximate foundation, namely, that accident by the medium of which it belongs to the substance, nevertheless, with regard to that accident itself, it belongs to that immediately and without any other foundation, as, for example, likeness [belongs] to whiteness; otherwise, it would be necessary to proceed to infinity. But the same thing is found proportionally in transcendental relations; therefore, there is no distinction.

The minor [premiss] is explained: for if there are transcendental relations included in substances themselves, these [relations] /p. 801/ do not require another foundation. However, there are many others that do not belong to substances, except by the medium of accidents, and those [relations] also have a foundation with respect to a substance, although with respect to a [mediating]

---

4   Cf. below: Section 7, n. 5; Section 9, n. 4; Section 16, n. 12.

accident they do not have that [foundation], but they immediately belong to such accidents. For example, the relation of knowledge to a knowable object belongs to the knower by the medium of the knowledge, but it is in the knowledge immediately. Therefore, in the need of a foundation there seems to be no distinction between transcendental and categorical respects.

8. *An Objection against the Last Mentioned Difference.*—Finally, the last difference also is hard to explain. For either a respect is compared to a form or to an essence proximately constituted by that [form], or to the subject of such a form. If the comparison is made in the first way, a respect, whether categorical or transcendental, is essential to the form or the essence constituted by it,[5] and it is compared to that [form or essence] in the manner of a difference that constitutes it. Hence, also speaking of the supreme genus itself of categorical relation, it is said to be constituted by that very "being toward" as by an essential mode that determines a common accidental character and is formally and essentially constituting such an essence. Therefore, in this there is no difference between a transcendental and a categorical respect.

But if the comparison is made in the second way, just as a categorical respect is accidental to some subject, also a transcendental respect can be so. For example, the respect of knowledge to an object, even though it is essential to the knowledge, is however accidental to the knower. Hence, even though that respect, considered metaphysically, is not a physical form referring [its] subject to something else, but is rather a difference constituting some form, nevertheless, that form that is constituted by such a respect is a respective physical form that refers the subject to its terminus. For a respective form cannot inform some subject as its ultimate form (*secundum ultimam rationem suam*) unless it refers that subject to the terminus that that form in its own way respects. For example, in the case of gravity, which we brought up above from St. Thomas,[6] just as gravity is an inclination to the lowest place, in which it includes a transcendental respect to that place, so by affecting and informing the heavy thing itself it inclines that thing, and this is to relate (*referre*) it toward the center [of the universe]. And the same is true about any potency and any knowledge, and the like.

It is very obscure and difficult, therefore, from these differences to gather the proper concepts of a transcendental and a categorical relation, as well as

---

5 Here Suárez changes his expression from "ipsam" (whose antecedent is "formam") to "ipsum" (whose antecedent should be "respectus"). However, the sense demands that the antecedent in both instances be "formam" or "formae" depending on the context.

6 See Section 3, n. 11. For St. Thomas, cf. *Summa Theologiae* I, 28, 1, in *Opera*, tomus IV, p. 318b.

their /col. b/ distinction, and the true necessity to admit categorical apart from transcendental relations.

Another Difference Given by Cajetan Between the Respects in Question Is Explained.

9. In another way, therefore, Cajetan, in his little work on *De Ente et essentia*, Chapter 7, Question 15 [sic], touching on this division of real respects into transcendental and categorical, explains the difference between them from the side of their termini. For a categorical respect, he says, is one that respects its terminus purely under the character of a terminus. But a transcendental [respect] respects something else, not purely as a terminus, but under a certain other definite character of subject, or object, or of efficient [cause], or of end.[7] This difference seems better suited for explaining this matter, inasmuch as every respect takes its species from its terminus, or from that thing toward which it tends. Therefore, if there is any distinction between these two orders of respect, it seems that it should be taken from the termini.

It is not, however, easy to explain how the designated difference is a general one and in what it properly consists or what is implied by it. The reason for the difficulty as regards the first part is that motion, action, and passion entail a transcendental respect to a terminus, and yet they respect it only under the pure character of a terminus. Likewise, the hypostatic union,[8] for example, entails a transcendental disposition toward the divine Word, and still it respects that Word only under the pure character of a terminus. But the reason for the difficulty with regard to the second part is that every respect, if it is taken abstractly and in general, only entails a disposition to something else under the character of a terminus by abstracting from other characters. If, however, it is taken in a restricted way, for instance as it is such or such a respect, whether that transcendental or categorical, it entails a disposition to a certain kind of terminus, which may be either a cause, or an effect, or an object, or may have some other particular character of terminus. For example, the respect of

---

7 Cf. Cajetan, *In De Ente et Essentia*, ed. Laurent, n. 136, p. 222.

8 This is the substantial union of Divine and human nature in the one hypostasis or person, which is Jesus Christ, the Son of God. On this, see Henricus Denzinger et Adolfus Schönmetzer, S.J., *Enchiridion symbolorum definitionum et declarationum de rebus fidei et morum*, editio xxxii (Barcinone/Friburgi/Romae/ Neo-Eboraci: Herder, 1963), n. 302, p. 108. Also, cf. A. Michel, "Hypostatique (Union)," in *Dictionnaire de théologie catholique*, tome septième (Paris: Letouzey et Ané, 1927), cols. 437-568. For Suárez on the hypostatic union, cf. esp. *Tertia pars Summae Theologiae Doctoris Sancti Thomae Aquinatis, cum commentariis et disputationibus P. Francisci Suarez e Societate Jesu*, disp. 8, in *Opera omnia*, vol. 17, pp. 328-370.

paternity, even though it is called categorical, respects a certain kind of terminus that is caused or produced by a father, and the same is so with regard to other [respects].

The Stated Distinction Is Defended and Proven.

10. To the first argument the answer is that it suffers from equivocity. For a categorical relation is said to respect something else as purely a terminus inasmuch as in regard to that thing it exercises no other task except that of respecting only. But in this way it cannot be said that motion, or action, or passion, is a pure respect to a terminus. /p. 802/ For the disposition of a motion to a terminus is a disposition to the way through which that terminus is constituted in being. Hence it does not involve a disposition to a terminus as [to something that is] only to be respected, but as [to something] to be constituted through that (*per ipsum*) [motion]. And thus it does not respect [something] as purely a terminus in the sense spoken of. And the same is true proportionately of action and passion. However, the hypostatic union is said by theologians to pertain to the Word as a pure terminus, so that by that term "pure" they exclude all proper causality that the Word as such has with regard to such a union. Nevertheless, the Word is not purely the terminus of that union in the sense in which we are speaking here about the terminus of a categorical relation. For that union, as it is a real mode of human nature does not respect the Word in any way whatever, but it really conjoins human nature to that Word and really attains the Word itself as the other extreme of that union on which it intimately and really, although without proper causality, depends. In this way, therefore, it universally belongs to a form or to an absolute mode that includes a transcendental respect that it exercises some real function in regard to that to which it entails a respect, either by causing, or uniting, or representing that thing, or by causing some other similar thing, and for this reason it is said to not respect that thing as purely a terminus. However, a categorical relation respects a terminus in such a way that in its regard it exercises no other task except purely to respect, as is clear in the similitude of one white thing to another, and in this way it is said to be proper to such a relation to respect something else as purely a terminus.

11. From this the reply is also clear to the second argument, in which again there is an equivocity. For to respect something else as purely a terminus is not to respect a terminus abstractly and in general as seems to be supposed in the argument. For it is clear that categorical relations that are specific and of diverse natures tend also to termini that are specific and of diverse natures. However, it is common to all of those that, with regard to those termini even as they are such, they exercise no other task beyond respecting them [i.e. the

termini]. And, therefore, they always respect them purely as termini, even if they respect them under their own natures. This is different in the case of a transcendental respect, as has been explained. Therefore, this difference explained in this way seems to be true and universal and seems to correctly explain the proper task of a categorical relation, which is to formally relate (*referre*) or to respect (*respicere*) something else, [which differs] from the task and function of a transcendental respect, which is to constitute a form or a nature /col. b/ causing something or operating in some way in regard to the thing to which it entails a disposition, or conversely.

Another Difference Is Inferred from the Preceding [One].

12. And from this there arises another difference that is commonly accepted, which although it may seem to be *a posteriori*, does, nevertheless, contribute to explaining the nature of these respects. Thus, a categorical respect is such that of its nature it is not directly (*per se*) intended, and therefore it never directly (*per se*) occurs by virtue of the action of some agent. But, if the foundation and the terminus are posited, it follows, as Aristotle (with whom in this the rest agree) attests in Book 5 of the *Physics*.[9] However, a transcendental respect often is directly in a most special way intended by nature, and therefore the form that essentially includes such a respect often comes to be formally as well as directly and immediately (*per se primo*) by a proper action. Through heating, for instance, heat comes to be as inhering, in which there is intimately included a transcendental respect.[10] And by the action of seeing there is produced an act that includes a transcendental disposition toward an object. And by a unitive action there is produced a mode of union that includes a transcendental disposition toward [the parts] that are unitable. And the same can be seen in many other instances.

And this same thing is perhaps what Scotus distinguished with regard to extrinsically and intrinsically occurring relations, when he said that an action can be directly terminated at the former, but not at the latter, which alone are categorical.[11] About this division, phrased in these words, we will speak in the

---

9 Cf. *Physics* 5.2.225b11-13.

10 That is, the relation of inherence.

11 Cf. Duns Scotus, *In IV Sent.*, d. 13, q. 1, nn. 9-11 (ed. Lugduni, 1639), tomus viii, p. 793; ibid., d. 6, q. 10, p. 352; *In III Sent.* d. 1, q. 1, nn. 14-15, tomus vii, pars prima, p. 23; and *Questiones Quodlibetales*, q. 11, a. 4, n. 34, in *Obras del Doctor Sutil Juan Duns Escoto*, edicion bilingüe, *Cuestiones Cuodlibetales*, ed. Felix Alluntis, O.F.M. (Madrid: Biblioteca de Autores Cristianos, 1968), a. 4, n. 34, pp. 416-17.

following Disputation,[12] which will be the first about the six last categories, on account of which Scotus seems most of all to have invented that distinction. But that it be phrased in these words is not necessary for us, and the matter itself is not limited to the six last categories, but it is found also in other [categories], as we will see there.

13. Therefore, the reason for this distinction between categorical and transcendental relations is that a categorical relation is not set up in the nature of things in order to perform some particular task, but it is said only to accompany other things for this, so that some things respect one another by virtue of some character or real foundation that is presupposed in them. And therefore such a relation is nothing else but a respect that arises when a foundation and a terminus are posited, but it is never directly (*per se*) produced. However, a transcendental respect belongs to some form or entity, or mode of being, insofar as it has been by nature directly instituted and ordered to some particular task that can be directly intended by some action. Therefore, that respect also /p. 803/ can be directly produced by an action as included in a form that entails such a respect. For since such a form in its own specific concept includes that respect, that respect cannot be less directly intended or less directly produced than the form itself, because the action and intention of the agent directly tends toward the whole form up to its specific character.

Another Difference between the Respects in Question.

14. And from this also it comes about that a pure categorical relation is never a principle of acting, both because, just as it never directly (*per se*) comes to be, so also it never directly acts; and also because, as we have said, it is not by nature instituted on account of some special task that is necessary for the being or the becoming of a thing, but it is only a certain respect that results consequently, whereas principles of acting are directly instituted and ordered toward a special task. However, a form that entails a transcendental respect, even according to its proper respective character, is often directly a principle of acting, as is clear with regard to knowledge, a power, and the like.

A Fourth Difference, and an Explanation of the Others.

15. Finally, from what has been said it is understood that a categorical respect must be conceived as a certain minimal and accidental form that does not give a subject any being except to respect something else, and it does not serve for anything more in nature. However, a transcendental respect must not be conceived as some whole form whose function is only to refer, but it is

---

12 For this, cf. *DM* 48, 1, nn. 2-8, vol. 26, pp. 868-70.

an essential mode or a difference of some form or entity, insofar as it has been instituted directly and immediately (*per se primo*) for causing or operating in some manner with regard to other things, or conversely, insofar as it depends essentially upon another thing.

And according to this way of explaining these respects, the difference treated above can be reduced to the same sense, because a transcendental respect is always intrinsic and essential to some entity, comprehending also under "entity" real modes.[13] However, a categorical relation has the proper and particular character of an accident. And so also the two other differences taken from the side of the foundation and the reality or existence of the terminus can be reduced to an acceptable sense.

Which Relations Belong to the Category, "Toward Something."

16. Finally, from these differences it is concluded that transcendental respects, even if they are truly /col. b/ in things according to their proper being, do not belong to some one special category, because those things or natures or essences to which they belong are ordered to various tasks that are sometimes utterly diverse, and therefore they are reduced to various categories, according to their diverse conditions and natures. And therefore the category, "toward something," embraces only those relations that properly and in a special way are called categorical; for all of these agree among themselves and are distinguished from the others in their special way of purely referring the thing that they affect. And therefore generally they also agree in the way in which they begin to be by the co-existence of the extremes or of the foundation and the terminus, and in other conditions that they require, as will be clearer from the discussion in the following Section.

Response to the Fourth Difficulty Left from the First Section.14

17. *Science:*[15] *Whether according to Aristotle It Belongs to the Category of Relation.—It Is Necessary That Single Sciences Be Referred to Single Objects.*—Also from what has been said, the difficulty touched upon in the fourth argument of the First Section has been resolved. For those respects on the basis of which the induction was there made are all transcendental, and as such we say they do not belong to a special category. Hence in that special example that was mentioned in that place about knowledge insofar as it entails a respect to the

---

13 For the Suarezian doctrine of modes, see J.I. Alcorta, *La Teoría de los modos en Suárez*, Madrid: CSIC—Instituto Luis Vives, 1949.
14 That is, Section 1, n. 5.
15 Or "knowledge."

knowable (*scibile*), I confess that the answers there, which were taken from Aristotle, in the Chapter on Quality,[16] do have great difficulty. For the first [answer] seems sufficiently disproved by the objections made there, which [objections] can be confirmed by the testimony of the same Aristotle, in Book 4, Chapter 1, Place 4, of the *Topics,* where he generally says that genus and species must be in the same division, namely, categorical, and in particular he uses the example of "toward something" (*Ad aliquid*): *For (*he says*) the genera of those things that are 'toward something' must have species that are also 'toward something,' and conversely.*[17] He says the same about quality, and he repeats the same in the *Topics,* Book 6,[18] Chapter 4, Place 39,[19] where he says as follows: *"Furthermore, in those things that are "toward something" we must consider that if a genus is assigned in relation to something, a species also is assigned to that same thing, for example, opinion and the object of opinion (opinatum) and a certain opinion with regard to a certain object of opinion ...*[20] *Moreover, if it is not so assigned, it is clear that an error has been made."*[21] And the same is evident from the rules stated by Aristotle in the *Antepredicaments,*[22] Chapter 3,[23] especially

---

16 Cf. *Categories* c. 8.8b25-11a38.

17 This is not an exact quotation, but it does seem to summarize the doctrine of *Topica* 4.1.120b36-121a9. However, in opposition to Suárez's "conversely" (*e converso*), cf. *Topica* 4.4.124b15-23.

18 Here the Vivès edition, which Rabade *et al.* follow, reads "5." But I am following the Salamanca, 1597, Mainz 1605, and Venice 1609 editions to read "6." The Venice 1751 edition has "5."

19 Cf. Aristotle, *Topica* 6.9.147a24-28.

20 There is an omission or an ellipsis here which Suárez has made in the text of Aristotle which has not been marked in any edition of the *Disputationes metaphysicae* which I have seen.

21 Suárez, with the omission noted just above, has here followed the translation of the *Topics* by Abraham de Balmes, as given in *Aristotelis Opera cum Averrois Commentariis* (Venetiis: Apud Junctas, 1562-74), vol. 1, p. 3, fol. 104vb.

22 The *Antepredicaments* are Chapters 1-4 of Aristotle's *Categories.*

23 Chapter 3 of the *Antepredicaments* was, in medieval translations, entitled: *De Regulis,* i.e. "About Rules."

this: *Genera which are not posited subalternately*[24] *do not have the same differences.*[25]

And in the present case, it is sufficiently evident from the matter itself. For every /p. 804/ science, in line with its proper and specific character, entails a proper disposition toward its own proper object. For what Soto, explaining that passage of Aristotle, says in the case of the category of quality, that although knowledge as such entails a disposition to a knowable object (*scibile*) as what is measurable to a measure, nevertheless, particular knowledges do not entail proper relations of something measurable to their objects,[26] this, I say, is false and contrary to the explicit words of Aristotle in the mentioned place from Book 6 of the *Topics*, as well as against evident reason. For just as the truth of knowledge in general is measured from a knowable object in general, so the truth of this knowledge [is measured] from this knowable object. Likewise, because a determinate knowledge takes its species from a disposition to its own object, therefore, not only as knowledge but also as such a knowledge, it entails a respect to such a knowable object.

18. Accordingly, it must be said that Aristotle did not approve that first answer, and therefore he added a second, namely, that the same thing that is knowledge is located in different categories, namely, [the category] of quality and of "toward something," at least under different aspects; for under one and the same aspect one thing cannot be put in different categories.[27] But even against this answer the objections added above press very much, and therefore some feel that Aristotle there did not voice his own opinion but spoke according to the opinion of those who embraced the first definition of relatives, which he gave in the Chapter, "Toward Something," namely, that all things that are in any way said "toward something" belong to the category, "toward

---

24 That is, one "under" (*sub*) "another" (*altero*). Aristotle give the examples of "animal" and "knowledge" as two genera which are not subordinate to one another. Accordingly, the differences of "animal," which are "footed," "two-footed," "winged", "aquatic," etc. will not be differences for "knowledge". Thus, while we may find "two-footed animals" we will never find "two-footed knowledges."

25 Cf. "τῶν ἑτέρων γενῶν καὶ μὴ ὑπ᾽ἄλληλα τεταγμένων ἕτεραι τῷ εἴδει καὶ αἱ διαφοραί, ... " *Categories* 3.1b16-17. Suárez's translation here is not exact. Its source seems to be Domingo Soto, *In Porphyrii Isagogen, Aristotelis Categorias, librosque de Demonstratione, Absolutissima Commentaria ... , in librum Praedicamentorum Aristotelis*, cap. ii (Venetiis 1587), p. 195.

26 For this, cf. D. Soto, *In librum Praedicamentorum*, c. viii, ed. Venetiis, 1587, p. 227a.

27 Cf. *Categories* c. 8.11a20-38.

something."[28] For in accord with that [definition] he added in the same place that habit, disposition (*dispositio*), and knowledge are "toward something."[29] But afterwards he does not approve of that definition, and therefore he should not be thought to approve all things that follow from it, even though he may suggest how one should speak in accord with it.

But neither is the other answer satisfactory, that is, that these are relatives only "according to being said" (*secundum dici*), for it is sufficiently manifest that in the proper being of these things there is included a respect. Therefore, the true response is that which has been proposed in the last place in the same fourth argument, namely, that knowledge, and other things of this kind, in line with their essential nature do not entail a categorical respect, but one which is transcendental only, and therefore as such they do not belong to the category, "toward something." But insofar as there can be added to knowledge some pure accidental respect, which is outside its essence, as such it does not belong to /col. b/ the category of quality, but [to that of] "toward something." In this sense the second answer of Aristotle could also be explained.

19. *What Is the Reason to Posit Categorical Relations.*—But there was a last answer, which was produced through a questioning in that fourth argument, namely, why it is necessary to add and to admit accidental and categorical respects of this kind, besides transcendental ones. For if the arguments by which it is usually proven by the [Scholastic] doctors that there are real relations are carefully considered, they certainly very much prove that there are in things respects of this kind, i.e. according to being (*secundum esse*), as may most of all be seen from St. Thomas, in [*Summa Theologiae*] Part 1, Question 13, Article 7,[30] and Question 28, Articles 1[31] and 2;[32] and [Duns] Scotus, in [his *Sentences* commentary], Book 2, Distinction 1,[33] and from others cited above. But that besides transcendental relations there are categorical ones that are distinct from these does not seem possible to demonstrate.

Nevertheless, the common consensus of philosophers is enough that we should not in any way back away from that opinion. Moreover, the reason for introducing and admitting respects of this kind was that we find many accidental respective predications that are not taken from transcendental respects

---

28 Ibid., c. 7.6a36-37.

29 Ibid., 6b2-3.

30 Cf. S. Thomae Aquinatis, *Opera omnia*, tomus IV, p. 153a.

31 Ibid., p. 318b.

32 Ibid., p. 321b.

33 Cf. *Quaestiones in lib. II. Sententiarum*, II, d. 1, q. 4, in *Opera omnia* (1639), tomus vi, pars i, p. 60; idem, *Ordinatio* II, d. 1, q. 5, in *Opera omnia*, VII (1973), pp. 101-104, nn. 200-205.

alone, for example, *to be a father,* [or to be] *similar, equal,* etc. Neither have they arisen from some apprehension or fiction of the intellect, but rather from things themselves in which there are forms from which such denominations and predications arise. Neither again are such denominations extrinsic, that is, derived from extrinsic things or forms; for a thing is not said to be similar to another thing through that which is in the other, but through that which it has in itself—and so it is with the rest [of those denominations]. From this, then it is understood that denominations of this kind are derived from certain respects that result from the co-existence of a number of things that have a sufficient foundation for that, [respects] whose sole function is to refer and to order one thing to another, in such way that one respects another by reason of some foundation that is presupposed in it. And these respects, because they have a special mode of causing, have been located in a special category.

20. But I add that this common opinion and its reasoning become easier and more probable if we say that these categorical relations are not new things or real modes that are really (*ex natura rei*) distinct from those things in which they are said to be founded, but that those things have a twofold way of de-nominating. One is direct (*per se*) and, as I may say, from their primary /p. 805/ constitution, and the other is as it were resulting from the co-existence of one thing with another. The first way of denomination is either completely absolute, or if it includes a respect, it will be a transcendental one, which most often does not demand the co-existence of the other extreme to which it tends. And when it does require that, it is not therefore because such a respect arises as it were by accident from the co-existence of those extremes, but because the thing itself has been essentially (*per se*) constituted in order to exercise some function with regard to another thing, which function it can exercise only with regard to an existing thing. And explained in this way, the particular difference of transcendental relations[34] that was mentioned above is best (*optima*).

The second [kind of] denomination is in a particular way respective and of an accidental kind, because the fact that one thing co-exists with another, precisely looking at the concept and the character of the co-existence, is outside the concept of each thing and therefore also the denomination that requires this co-existence for no other cause except that this denomination itself results from it, is accidental. Therefore, even though in the thing it is taken from the same entity, nevertheless, because it is accidental, it has enough foundation for a distinction that the intellect conceives that entity in the manner of two forms. And finally, because that denomination is taken from things themselves, it also is enough that by reason of it a special category of real and respective

---

34 That, unlike categorical relations, their being is not purely "being toward."

accident is constituted. Therefore, in this way a sufficient reason seems to be given both for the aforesaid division and for the constitution of the category, "toward something."

21. *Divine Relations—Of What Kind They Are.*—But in this place there occurs a theological difficulty with regard to divine relations. How can the given doctrine be applied to them, and to which member of the mentioned division should they be relegated? But this debate does not pertain to us, nor is it necessary that everything which was said previously have an application in the case of these [divine] relations, since these relations are not accidental but rather substantial.

However, it is certain that they are not relations only "according to being said" but rather "according to being." Nor are they properly and rigorously categorical relations, since they are infinite substances and [are] of a higher order. And therefore they cannot be located in any category. In line with this, neither also do they have that imperfection or mode of being by resultance from a foundation and a terminus. But they are, either of themselves, like the relation of a producer, for example, paternity, or they are directly (*per se*) produced by a proper production, or (to speak according to our way of conceiving) they are co-produced, and formally speaking, they are directly attained through /col. b/ the origins themselves, as filiation and passive procession. Those relations, therefore, are of a higher order, eminently embracing whatever perfection and necessary property there is found in both a transcendental and a categorical respect, excluding imperfections.

Section V.
What is the Essence and the Proper Definition Of "Toward Something" Itself or Of a Categorical Relation.

1. The things we have up to now discussed almost entirely pertain to explaining and defining the question whether there is any real categorical relation, about which we are now treating. However, along the way we have touched upon many things from which it will be more easy for us to explain the essence of this relation and the definition that Aristotle accepts in this matter.

The Definition of a Categorical Relation.

2. It must therefore be said that a relation (speaking only of one that is categorical) is an accident whose whole being is to be toward something else, or to have itself toward something else, or to respect something else. This definition is taken from Aristotle, in the *Categories*, the Chapter, "Toward Something," where he assigns for those things that are toward something two definitions, which differ in only one word. The first definition is: *Those things are "toward something" which are said to be that which they are of other things or toward something in some way.*[1] The second is: *Those things are "toward something" whose being is to have themselves toward something.*[2] Therefore, the whole difference is in those words, "are said" (*dicuntur*)[3]. This indeed is frequently, especially in the customary usage of philosophers, taken for the word "being," as Aristotle himself has said: *A quality is that by which certain things are said to be such* (*quales*). And, therefore, many do not want to care very much about a distinction or a diversity between those descriptions. Yet, nevertheless, according to the mind of Aristotle it is clear that they are diverse and in the first one the words "are said" (*dicuntur*) are taken with rigor and propriety, and beyond that under the disjunction in that definition it is posited that those things are "toward something" *which are that which they are of others or in*

---

1 Cf. "Πρός τι δὲ τὰ τοιαῦτα λέγεται, ὅσα αὐτὰ ἅπερ ἐστὶν ἑτέρων εἶναι λέγεται ἢ ὁπωσοῦν ἄλλως πρὸς ἕτερον." *Categories*, 7.6a36-7. I have not found a Latin translation that Suárez is exactly reproducing here.

2 Cf. "ἀλλ' ἔστι τὰ πρός τι οἷς τὸ εἶναι ταὐτόν ἐστι τῷ πρός τί πως ἔχειν," *Categories* 7.31-2. Again, I have not found a source Latin translation for Suárez here.

3 Here there is one word, "dicuntur" in Latin, "λέγεται" in Greek, which requires at least two words, "are said," to be translated into English.

some way are said to be of others, in such way that it is indicated that it is not of the nature of a relation that it be toward another, but that it be or be said [toward another]. And Aristotle wanted to correct this in the second definition, so that in the proper definition of the category "toward something" only relations "according to being" (*secundum esse*) and not relatives "according to being said" (*secundum dici*) are comprehended. Therefore, from that second definition our own [definition] is derived, or rather it is the same as that; for it is only for the sake of greater clarity /p. 806/ through a certain proportion of genus and difference that it has been established and composed.

3. *What is the Genus in the Definition of Relation*—Therefore, *accident* is put in the place of a genus in that definition. Through this there is first of all excluded divine relations which are not accidents but substances. Then there are excluded all created substances, which cannot be categorical relations, as is clear from what has been said in the preceding Section. Again, relations of reason are excluded, which properly and without qualification cannot be called accidents, since an accident, said simply, is contained under real being.[4] Neither do I accept what Cajetan [in commenting on *Summa Theologiae*] Part 1, Question 13, Article 7, indicates, namely, that the definition given of relatives in the categories is common to relatives of reason and real relatives, because it has been given (he says)[5] about them insofar as they imply "toward" and in such way that they abstract from real being.[6] For this contradicts Aristotle who first divided real being and posited "toward something" as one of its members[7] and then afterwards defined it.[8] Moreover, from that opinion it follows that either relations of reason are placed in the category, "toward something," or that that definition extends more broadly than what its defines. Therefore, although Aristotle did not explicitly posit the word "accident" in that definition, nevertheless, he tacitly understood it from the earlier division of being into nine categories. From that, or especially because also the later phrase, namely, "being toward," taken properly and with rigor, does not pertain to relations of reason, but only [pertains to them] through a kind of analogous imitation or proportion, as was explained above,[9] and therefore also through

---

4 In passing, we may note Suárez's realistic assessment of accidents and thus of the categories as such.

5 While I have no doubt about Suárez's understanding here of Cajetan, I have not found it in so many words.

6 Cf. *Commentaria*, in I, q. 13, a. 7, n. 10, in *S. Thomae Opera*, tomus IV (1888), p. 155b.

7 Cf. *Categories* 4.1b25-27; *Metaphysics* 5.7.1017a7-27.

8 Cf. Categories 7.6a36-7; and *Metaphysics* 5.15.1020b26-1021b11.

9 Cf. Section 3, n. 5, above.

that phrase, taken properly, there could be excluded relations of reason, which not so much are as are apprehended to be "toward something."

4. *What the Difference Is in the Definition of Relation.*—The second part of that definition,[10] which takes the place of a difference, separates this category from other categories of accident, for since they are absolute, they have their being in another, but not toward another, which is proper to relation. But immediately two difficulties surface.

The First Difficulty with regard to the Definition.

5. The first is that the whole definition belongs [also] to transcendental relatives, for knowledge has its whole being toward another. To this difficulty the usual common response is that beings of this kind have been excluded by Aristotle in the second definition by taking away the words "are said," which were in the first [definition]. But /col. b/ this response is not consonant with the doctrine given by us in the above Section;[11] for beings of this kind, also conceived as they are in themselves, include in their essential concepts a disposition toward another. Therefore, they are not only *said*, but they also truly *are* toward another. Therefore, even after those words, "are said," are taken away from the definition, the definition truly belongs to those [beings of this kind]. Finally, those words have been taken away solely in order to exclude relatives "according to being said." However, we have shown that these are not simply relatives "according to being said," but also "according to being." Therefore, they have not been sufficiently excluded. Therefore, I think that transcendental respects of this kind must be excluded through that phrase: "whose total being is being toward another," if it is understood in the proper way, which we have explained at the end of the preceding Section. For those beings that include a transcendental respect are not so "toward another" that their whole being is placed in a pure respect toward another, and, thus, they do not respect another under the pure character of a terminus, but under some other character and by exercising in its regard some function for which things of this kind have been essentially (*per se*) constituted. But the relation that is here defined has its whole essence in a pure respect to another, and therefore it particularly belongs to it that its whole being be toward another as to a pure terminus of such a respect or disposition.

---

10 Cf. n. 2, this Section.
11 Cf. Section 3, n. 9, above.

If a Relation Has a "Being in"—How It Is Totally "toward Another."

6. But then there arises a second difficulty, which adds to the first, for this latter part of the definition seems to contradict the prior part. For if a relation is an accident, its whole being cannot then consist in a disposition toward another. For it is necessary that something of its being be in a subject, so that in that way it can be an accident, since the being (*esse*) of an accident is "being in" (*inesse*).

To this difficulty some reply that when a relation is said to have its whole being toward another this must be understood about the proper being of a relation as such, which is *being toward*, and not about the being that it has in common with other accidents, which is *being in*. And from this has arisen the opinion treated above[12] about the distinction between the "being toward" and the "being in" of a relation and [the view] that "being toward" abstracts from every real being and of itself is univocally common to relations of reason and real relations.[13]

However, this reply has been sufficiently refuted from what was said above[14] against the said opinion. *First*, because not only is it of the nature of an accident, as it exists in a certain thing /p. 807/ that it be in it according to some generic or common character, but [that it be in it] also according to its proper [character] and insofar as it is a certain kind of form in the nature of things. Indeed, it is impossible that a form inform or affect [anything] according to a common character and not some proper character, since these characters are not distinguished in actual reality (*a parte rei*). *Second*, because otherwise a relation would not give a proper formal relative effect to its subject, since an accident does not give a formal effect except by inhering and affecting. If, therefore, a relation does not inhere (*non inest*) according to its proper character, it does not confer a proper and specific formal effect. *Third*, because if that real proper being of a relation, which is said "to be toward," would not "be in," it would be nothing real in the nature of things and, consequently, a categorical relation according to what properly constitutes it would not be anything real. Hence, St. Thomas, correctly, in [his Commentary on the *Sentences*], Book 1, Distinction 25, Question 1, Article 4, in Reply to the Third Objection, says that a real relation, in line with its proper quidditative character, posits something in that thing whose relation it is, even though that which it posits is not absolute.[15] This he has taught more at length in another work, *On the Sentences*

---

12 Cf. Section 2, nn. 18-21.

13 Cf. Section 3, n. 2.

14 Cf. Section 2, nn. 18-21.

15 Cf. S. Thomae Aquinatis, *Scriptum in lib. Sent.*, I, d. 25, q. 1, a. 1, ed. Mandonnet, tomus I, p. 613.

to Annibaldus, Book 1, Distinction 25, Article 4, to the Third Objection, saying: *"Even though a relation does not posit from that respect*[16] *anything absolute, still it does posit something relative, and therefore a relation is a certain thing. For if according to the character of relation or respect it did not posit something, since according to its being by reason of which it posits something inherent, it would not fall within the category of relation, it would not be any kind of being."*[17]

7. Therefore to the stated difficulty we must concede that a relation in its whole being is an accident. For this character, as we have said above,[18] is, as it were, transcendental with regard to nine categories. Hence, when it is said that the whole being of a relation is to be toward another, the exclusive word that is there virtually contained does not exclude concomitant things or extrinsic and transcendental characters. Accordingly, just as it does not exclude the character of real being so neither [does it exclude] the character of accident and of being inherent. Therefore, it excludes only absolute being and indicates that the being of a relation as such does not stay in the subject that in its own way it affects and denominates but rather it orders that [subject] to a terminus, and in this is placed the whole formal character of a relation. Thus, even though, similarity, for example, according to its whole, and even relative, character, must be conceived /col. b/ as a form that affects the thing that it denominates as similar, nevertheless, its whole affecting of that [thing] is posited in this that it orders that thing and refers it to another, and in this sense the whole being of a relation is said to be and to have itself toward another.

8. *An Objection.—It Is Resolved.*—You will say: this is common to those forms or modes that are real and absolute and that include a transcendental respect. For knowledge so exists in and affects the knower that in its own way

---

16 That is, the respect by which in the Trinity a relation distinguishes the Father from the Son.

17 For this, cf. Sancti Thomae Aquinatis, *Opuscula alia dubia, vol. primum, Scriptum super libris Magistri Sententiarum ad Hannibaldum Hannibaldensem Romanum, Episcopum Cardinalem*, I, d. 25, a. 4, ad 3, in Sancti Thomae Aquinatis, *Opera omnia*, tomus xxii (Parmae: Typis Petri Fiaccadori, 1868; reprint: New York: Musurgia Publishers, 1950), p. 75a. For greater understanding of what is involved here, let me translate the objection which is being answered here as follows: "The Father and the Son are distinguished only by relations. But a relation as regards the respect by which it distinguishes does not posit 'something' (*aliquid*) but 'toward something' (*ad aliquid*). Therefore, from the fact that they [Father and Son] are distinguished by relations, they are not said to be three beings (*entes*) or three things." ibid., p. 74b. On Annibaldus and this work which bears his name, cf. P. Mandonnet, "Annibal des Annibaldi," *Dictionnaire de Théologie Catholique*, tome premier, deuxième partie (Paris: Librairie Letouzey et Ané, 1931), cols. 1321-23.

18 Cf. *DM* 37, 1, nn. 1-5, vol. 26, pp. 491-3; and *DM* 39, 3, nn. 17-18, pp. 528-9.

it orders him to a knowable object, and it cannot otherwise exercise its formal effect. And the same is true about a potency, a union, and similar things.

This is answered by conceding that in this there is some similarity and proportion, on account of which these forms are said to include some respect "according to being" (*secundum esse*), even though it is transcendental. But the difference is the same one that was mentioned above:[19] that categorical relations consist in a pure respect, but other forms or qualities give some proper absolute being exercising some function to which their natures are ordered, in which also they include some disposition [toward], and therefore they do not have their total being toward another as do categorical relations.

Whether the Essence of a Relation Is to Refer Actually or in Aptitude.

9. But finally it can be objected that if a relation is considered abstractly, as it is a certain form that refers a subject or a foundation to a terminus, in this way it is not of its nature that it refer actually but that it be apt to refer; and, therefore, its whole being does not consist in "being toward" a terminus. The consequence is clear: because being toward a terminus implies an actual exercise (so to speak) of a certain disposition toward a terminus. But the antecedent is evident, both because the common nature of an accident is not to actually effect [something] but rather [to do so] in aptitude, and also because the mind can conceive a complete relation as affecting and not yet referring a subject. In this way, the theologians also say that in God paternity is conceived as constituting the first person and as it were adhering to him before referring him. Therefore, the nature of a relation does not consist in an actual respect.

10. The answer is that the antecedent is false. For a thing is not constituted as apt to refer by a relation as such, but rather by the proximate foundation of a relation. Moreover, the proper formal effect of a relation is to actually refer. Otherwise, it would not be distinguished, even according to its formal nature, from the foundation, and it would not require the coexistence /p. 808/ of a terminus. Neither would its whole being truly be said to be located in a respect to something else.

11. In answer then to the first proof of the antecedent: first, it is one thing to consider whether the formal effect of an accident is actually to constitute something and another thing [to ask] whether it is of the essence of an accident actually to exercise its own formal effect. For these two things are distinct. For we truly say that the formal effect of whiteness is to constitute a white thing actually and not only in aptitude, even though absolutely it is not of the essential nature of whiteness that it actually impart such a formal

---

19 Cf. Section 4, n. 10.

effect. Hence, it also can be said that, although, simply speaking, it is not of the nature of whiteness to actually constitute a white thing, nevertheless, it is of the nature of whiteness, as affecting and informing a subject, to actually constitute a white thing. In this way, then, in the present case, we are saying that the formal effect of a relation is to actually refer, because this is what that relation directly, immediately, and formally confers upon the subject that in its own way it affects.

12. *The Essence of Relation Is Located in the Actual Affecting (in actuali affectione) of a Subject.*—But I add then that it is not common to every accident to affect only in aptitude, but there are certain ones of whose essential concept it is that they cannot exist in the nature of things without affecting, as we said above with regard to accidental modes.[20] Relations then are contained in this second class, because they cannot exist in the nature of things without actually referring, by the fact that they cannot be conserved separate from every subject, because, as has been shown,[21] in reality they are not distinguished from their proximate subjects.

Yet there is no lack of those who teach the opposite, for example, [John] Major, in [his *Sentences* commentary], Book 4, Distinction 12, Question 3 [sic];[22] and Ledesma, in the First Part of Book 4, Question 28, Article 2, Doubt

---

20 Cf. *DM* 16, 1, nn. 21-22, vol. 25, p. 573.

21 Cf. Section 2, above.

22 For this, see Joannes Maior, *Quartus sententiarum*, d. 12, q. 1 (Parisiis: Apud Ponset le Preux, 1509) fol. 57vb-58ra, where Major's basic argument is: "every accident can be without a subject. This is evident inasmuch as a subject is extrinsic to an accident, that is, it is not a part of it nor is [the accident] essentially depending on a subject as it depends upon God. This is certain about some accidents, for example, quantity, and the reasoning is the same for all accidents. Therefore, [God] can produce every accident without a subject and can conserve it apart from a subject." (*dico conclusive ... quodlibet accidens potest esse sine subiecto. Patet cum subiectum sit extrinsecum accidenti, puta non est pars eius nec essentialiter dependet a subiecto sicut a Deo. De aliquibus accidentibus hoc certum est ut de quantitate et aequa est ratio in omnibus; ergo omne accidens potest facere sine subiecto et eum conservare extra subiectum.*) Also, cf. idem, *In Primum sententiarum*, dd. 30-31, q. unica (Parisius: Apud. Io. Badium, 1519), fol. 89rb-va. Also see *In Secundum sententiarium*, d. 12, q. 2, ed. secunda (Parisius: Apud Iohannem Granion, 1519), fol. 64rb, where Major says that by his absolute power God can create prime matter apart from form, just as "whenever there are two created things which are really distinct, and of which one is not a part of the other, God can create either of them without the other and He can conserve either of them without the other" (*quandocumque duae sunt res creatae realiter distinctae, quarum neutra est pars alterius, Deus potest quamcumque illarum producere sine alia, et quamcumque illarum conservare sine reliqua*). Here, I

4,[23] who say that God can conserve a created paternity, for instance, without its proper subject, either as essentially separate or in another subject. For they think that paternity is a thing that is totally distinct from other things, and therefore they are speaking logically, especially with regard to the first part. For with regard to the second [part] it appears to be impossible that this paternity

---

am reminded of the sarcasm directed at Maior by Philip Melanchthon, which reads in part: "I have seen the Commentaries of John Maior (about the morals of the man I am not judging) on the *Sentences* of the Lombard, a man [i.e. Maior] whom they say now reigns among the theologians of Paris. Good God, what wagonloads of nonsense! For how many pages does he dispute whether for horseback-riding a horse is required? ..." (*Vidi Joannis Maioris commentarios (de moribus hominis non judico) in Sententias Longobardicas* [sic], *quem nunc inter Lutetiae theologos regnare aiunt: Bone Deus, quae plaustra nugarum! Quot paginis disputat, utrum ad equitandum requiritur equus?* ...) *Adversus furiosorum Parisiensium Theologastrorum decretum Philippi Melanthonis pro Luthero Apologia: Opera* t. II, Wittenberg, 1562, p. 83; cited by Ricardo G. Villoslada, S.I., *La universidad de Paris durante los estudios de Francisco de Vitoria, O.P. (1507-1522)*, (Romae: Apud Aedes Universitatis Gregorianae, 1938), p. 138.

23 I have not found this reference. There were two Ledesmas, both Dominicans, that Suárez might have seen. The first was Martin (1509-1574), who authored *Commentaria in IV Sententiarum*, 2 vols., Coimbra, 1555-1560), the first volume of which was also named: "Prima quartae" (That is, "The first of the fourth [part?]." I have not seen this extremely rare volume and the problem I have beforehand is that if it is a Commentary on the *Sentences*, it should be divided by Distinctions rather than by Questions, as Suárez cites it. The second Ledesma was Pedro (1544-1616), who authored in Spanish: *Primera parte de la Summa, en la qual va cifrado todo lo que pertenece a los siete sacramentos, con todos los casos y dudas morales que se pueden ofrecer resueltas y determinadas*, Salamanca: Juan y Andrés Renaut, 1598. While this work appeared in the year following the first appearance of Suárez's *Disputationes metaphysicae*, both works had the same publisher and it is perhaps conceivable that Suárez saw the work of Pedro de Ledesma in preparation while his own work was being printed. However, in this case also, the divisions of the work, into separate treatises in turn divided into chapters, do not correspond to Suárez's reference here. The closest I have so far come to what is needed is Pedro de Ledesma, in his *Tratado del Sacramento del Altar, que se llama Eucharistia, Cap. VIII, De los acidentes que quedan en este sacramento* (page 68 of Salamanca: En Emprenta de Antonio Ramirez, viuda, 1621, edition of the *Primera parte*), where Pedro speaks of the accidents in the Eucharist, which by divine power can exist apart from the substances of bread and wine. However, in this place he does not mention relation in general or paternity in particular. For information on the two Ledesmas, cf. Gonzalo Diaz Diaz, *Hombres y documentos de la filosofía española*, vol. iv (Madrid: Consejo Superior de Investigaciones Científicas, 1991), pp. 624-5.

be located in him who has not begotten this son. Otherwise, either it would constitute him a father who did not beget, or it would inhere in someone to whom it would not give its own formal effect. But both of these are impossible.

Moreover, just as it is truer that a relation is not a thing that is distinct from its foundation, so also it is truer that it cannot be separated or essentially conserved apart from that [foundation]. But if sometimes a relation is really distinguished from a remote subject, this is insofar as the proximate foundation /col. b/ of the relation is some thing that is distinct from a remote subject. Hence, such a relation can also be conserved separate from such a subject to that degree that the thing that is its foundation can be conserved without that subject. But then a relation that is conserved in this way affects its own foundation in the manner of a subject and actually refers that [foundation]. In this manner, a consecrated quantity[24] is equal to another [quantity], and a separated whiteness would be similar to another [whiteness]. And so there can never be an actual relation without it actually referring to something else.

13. The answer to the second proof[25] is that it is impossible to conceive a relation with its own formal effect fully and properly conceived, without it being conceived as actually referring—just as it is impossible to conceive whiteness, with its formal effect fully conceived, without it being conceived as constituting an actual white thing, because a thing cannot be fully conceived without that which is part of its essential nature. However, it is possible sometimes that our intellect, conceiving some form as affecting does not distinctly, properly, and fully, conceive its formal effect, but only [conceives it] confusedly, staying within this common concept of affecting or inhering. For because this concept is quasi-transcendent and included in every mode or difference of form, the whole form, therefore, as affecting, can be conceived only confusedly with regard to its effect. For example, if someone conceives that whiteness, in line with its total being, is a form adhering in a subject and informing that [subject], he does not indeed conceive it as actually constituting a white thing, not because that is not the formal effect of whiteness, but because he is conceiving its effect in a diminished and confused way.

---

24 According to Catholic doctrine, in the Eucharistic consecration, the accidents, including quantity and the quality of whiteness of bread, remain even though their substrates do not. This will permit the quantity of one consecrated host to be equal to another or the whiteness of one to be similar to that of another. On this, cf. F. Jansen, "Eucharistiques (Accidents)," in *Dictionnaire de théologie catholique*, 5, 2ᵉ partie (Paris: Letouzey et Ané, 1939, cols. 1368-1452, esp. 1418-22. For Suárez, cf. *De Eucharistia*, Qu. 77, aa. 1-2, Disp. 56, ss. 1-3, vol. 21, pp. 275-87.

25 See n. 9, this Section.

In this way, therefore, a relation can be conceived inasmuch as in its totality it affects or adheres in or constitutes something, even if it is not understood as actually referring, not because the formal effect of a relation is not actually to refer, but because then the formal effect of a relation is not conceived with a proper and adequate concept, but with one that is confused and common. And in this way it happens for us when we conceive paternity in God as prior to the act of referring to the Son, about which matter the Theologians debate at length.

Section VI.
About the Subject, the Foundation, and the Terminus Required for a Categorical Relation.

1. *Whether There Is a Final Cause of Relation.—Whether it has an Efficient Cause.—What Is the Material Cause of a Relation.* We have explained /p. 809/ whether there is and what is a categorical relation. Now it is necessary to explain its causes or principles, of what kind they are and how they can belong to it.[1] For since this relation is not as such (*per se*) intended in things, it properly does not have a final cause, although in that way in which it is it can be said to be on account of its formal effect or on account of its terminus.

And for a similar reason, since it is not directly made but rather results or formally follows when the foundation and the terminus are posited, it neither has nor requires an efficient cause, besides those that effect the foundation and the terminus—unless someone wishes to attribute to that foundation or terminus some efficiency with regard to relation, at least through a natural resultance, which would be probable with respect to the foundation, if the relation would be a mode that would be really (*ex natura rei*) distinct from that. However, because we suppose the opposite to be true, therefore we do not think that there is here an effective resultance, but a quasi-formal one.

Again, since relation itself is a certain form, it does not have another proper and physical formal cause, but it has its own quiddity and metaphysical formal nature, which we have already explained. It also has a terminus, which, insofar as it is specifying, shares in a certain way the character of a form.

But the foundation and the subject seem to constitute a material cause, and therefore in these three—the subject, the foundation, and the terminus—all principles and causes of relations have been posited. Therefore, we must speak of these individually, and then afterwards it will be evident how from the variety of these, diverse genera and species of relations can be distinguished.

About the Subject of Accidental Relations.[2]

2. First, therefore, it must be said that every categorical relation requires some real subject. Taken in general, this assertion is clear, for a relation is an accident, as has been said. But every accident requires some subject. Therefore.

Again, a relation is a certain form. But every form informs something. But that which it informs is called its subject, especially if it inheres in that and

---

1 For this order of proceeding, cf. the prologue to Section 1, above.

2 Said another way, this is a question of the material cause of a relation.

depends upon it—which we have shown about a relation, even as it is a relation.

It is necessary, however, to note that we can speak about relation in the abstract or in the concrete, just as [we can] about other accidents. So in general the word "relation" itself is abstract and in particular so are the words "paternity," "similarity," etc. And likewise "relative" in general is /col. b/ something concrete, and in particular "father," "similar," and the like. When therefore we say that relation requires a subject, it is necessary to understand this about relation in the abstract; for a relative in the concrete does not properly have a subject, but rather it is something that consists of a subject and a relation, if it is formally taken as it is relative, or as a certain composite of relation and its subject. For sometimes the subject of a relation is customarily called a relative denominatively rather than formally, that is, as affected, not as constituted by a relation. Therefore, more properly and more formally it is said about what is itself constituted. For that which is affected by a relation is not properly said itself to be relative, and also it is often called the extreme of a relation, because a relative disposition is as it were enclosed between two subjects of relations, as between two extremes.

It Is Shown, against Henry, That One Relation, Even as Regards "Being Toward," Can Be in Only One Subject.

3. But here it can be asked whether one relation has one subject and of what sort that is. I am asking this principally because of Henry [of Ghent], who in his *Quodlibet* 9, Question 3, thinks that a relation as regards its proper "being toward" is one and the same between the two extremes which are related (*referuntur*). For a relation, according to its proper nature, is a kind of medium between related extremes, and, therefore, just as Aristotle has said that the road is the same from Athens to Thebes as from Thebes to Athens,[3] so Henry says that the disposition of any two extremes that relate to one another (*ad invicem se habentium*) is one and the same, that is, [the relation] of father to son and of son to father, or of two brothers or of similar things to one another.[4]

But if you object that the relation of a father, for example, is paternity and [the relation] of a son is filiation, and that it is always (*in universum*) necessary that they be distinguished from their foundations, because one and the same accident cannot be in diverse subjects, he answers as follows. Relations, considered as existing in foundations and as insepaable from those founda-

---

3 Cf. Aristotle, *Physics* 3.3.202b13-14.

4 Cf. Henrici de Gandavo, *Quodlibet* IX, qu. 3, ed. Macken (1983), p. 52 ll. 71-76.

tions, are multiplied according to the distinction and the plurality of those foundations, but nevertheless, insofar as a relation is a certain medium and a kind of interval between two things having a disposition between themselves,[5] in this way it is one and the same for both.

4. However, either this distinction and the whole opinion is only a matter of words or it is unintelligible. For how can it happen that an accident that is numerically one and the same be in subjects /p. 810/ that are really distinct and not united among themselves, but are entirely disjointed and even separate in place? For either this relation is said to be one, with a true and proper unity, like a simple form, and the argument that was made to prove that one and the same relation cannot exist simultaneously in both extremes proceeds in this sense. Or that relation is said to be one only by a certain collection, because, that is, from both relations existing in both extremes there coalesces a complete disposition and a kind of connection in both extremes, and in this way that relation is called one only in name, which is a way of speaking that is unusual and therefore it should be avoided. Moreover, according to that [way of speaking] it should logically be said that such a disposition, in the way in which it is one, has one subject, not simply, but by the bundling of both extremes that are ordered to one another.

But if someone says that that mutual disposition of both extremes is simply one, but it is not in them as in subjects but is only between them, which Henry indicates more, this certainly is more evidently false and less intelligible. For either that interval, or mutual disposition, is something of reason only, and thus it is irrelevant for a real relation, as Gregory [of Rimini], in [his *Sentences* commentary], Book 1, Distinction 28, Question 1, correctly shows against [Petrus] Aureoli.[6] Or it is something real, and thus it is either something that subsists in itself, which cannot be said, or it necessarily is in some subject. But it can only be in the extremes that are related between themselves or in some one of those extremes. Or, finally, it is something abstracting from real being and being of reason, as Henry indicates,[7] and this is simply false, as was shown above.[8] And even if we were to grant that as it is in our concept it can be abstracted, nevertheless in individual relations it would not be possible to abstract. Therefore, it is necessary that in real and accidental relations there

---

5 Ibid., ll. 69-70; p. 53, ll. 94-97; p. 54, ll. 8-10.
6 Cf. Gregorii Ariminensis, *Lectura ... In I Sent.* dist. 28-32, qu. 1, Additio 129, tomus III, pp. 86-7; ibid., ad 3, p. 90. Here we may note another indirect approach by Suárez to Aureoli, this time through Gregory of Rimini.
7 Cf. *Quodlibet* 9, q. 3, ed. Macken, p. 55, ll. 58-59.
8 Cf. Section 3, n. 3, above.

be something real and accidental, and then the stated argument recurs—that it must be in some one subject.

How There Can Be Several Subordinated Subjects of One Relation.

5. *What Order Relations Observe in the Denomination of a Subject.*—Therefore, we must speak in another way and must distinguish with regard to subjects. For there can be several subjects of diverse character subordinated among themselves or of the same character and equally affected immediately by a relation. Therefore, in this second way it cannot happen that one relation be in several subjects, as the argument made against Henry[9] proves, which [argument] is universal with regard to any accident at all that has in reality /col. b/ a true and proper unity.

However, in the first way there can be distinguished several subjects of one relation, one [subject] proximate and another remote. For example, the relation of equality is proximately in quantity, but remotely in substance; and the relation of similarity is proximately in quality and remotely in quantity, and even more remotely in substance. However, a relation of this kind directly and properly affects only the proximate subject in which in its own mode it exists. But it is related (*comparatur*) to a remote subject by means of the proximate one insofar as this inheres and is sustained in that. For already above, in Disputation 14, we have shown that one accident can proximately inhere in another, and not affect the substance in itself, but only insofar as that accident in which the other inheres is sustained in the substance.[10] In this way then one relation can immediately be in some accidental subject and remotely in another or in a substance. But whether this is common in all relations, we shall see very soon.

6. However, as regards the denomination of a relation[11] a certain variety must be considered among relations. For sometimes a relation equally and in the same way denominates a proximate and a remote subject, as quantity is called equal, as is also a material substance, and whiteness is called similar, and a white thing itself or also a subject, such as a man or a wall [is called similar]. But sometimes a relation denominates a proximate and not a remote subject, as the intellect is said to be referred by a relation of potency to its own act, but the soul[12] is not like this. And so it is with regard to other things.

---

9 See n. 4, just preceding.

10 Cf. *DM* 14, 4, nn. 6-7, vol. 25, p. 495.

11 That is, what a relation denominates rather than what is denominated as a relation.

12 Which is the substrate or the subject of the intellect.

But conversely, sometimes a relation denominates a remote subject or the supposit itself, and not a proximate [subject], as filiation denominates a supposit, namely, a son, but not humanity, even though it is probable that it proximately inheres in humanity. And paternity is proximately said to be in potency, and yet it does not denominate a father unless the same is supposed. But the reason for this variety comes from a diversity of foundations, which sometimes are compared according to the same proportion to the termini of relations, but sometimes according to a diverse [proportion], as will become more clear below in explaining the different kinds of relations. Sometimes also it results from this that a relation follows its own proximate foundation and denominates that, not insofar as it affects or denominates another subject, but according to its own precise and abstract nature, in which way the relation of inhering belongs to an accident. But sometimes a relation follows the foundation only inasmuch as it affects or denominates /p. 811/ a certain subject or supposit, but sometimes [it follows it] indifferently under both features. And this is [enough] about the subject of a relation.

Section VII.

About the Foundation of a Categorical Relation.[1]

1. *A Real Relation Requires a Real Foundation.*—As regards the foundation of a relation it must first be stated as a general rule (*in communi*) that every real relation needs some real foundation. So it is supposed almost without proof or discussion by all who write on this subject. And the reason seems to be that a relation of itself does not have its own entity, since it has been shown that it is not a thing that is distinct from absolutes. Therefore, it is necessary that it have that [entity], at least identically and really, from something else. But it does not have it from a terminus; for a terminus is something extrinsic and distinct, whereas the entity of a thing is intrinsic. Therefore, a real relation has its entity from a real foundation. Thus, it always requires that [foundation].

This is confirmed and more fully explained, because a relation is of such a nature that it neither comes to be through itself, nor is it directly intended in nature. Therefore, it follows and as it were results in a subject when a terminus is posited. Therefore, it requires in the subject some real reason or cause on account of which such a relation results when such a terminus is posited. That cause then is called the real foundation of the relation.

About the Distinction of the Foundation from the Subject of a Relation.

2. But in order that this assertion be more fully explained, first of all it can be asked whether it is necessary that this foundation be in reality distinct from the subject of the relation. However, this can be understood either about the proximate subject of inhesion or about the remote and as it were the fundamental subject, which is the substance itself. And indeed about the prior subject it is certain that it is not necessary that apart from it there is another foundation of the relation that is really distinct from it; otherwise, it would be necessary to regress to infinity. Hence, it is certain that the relation of equality, which exists in a quantity, even one which is separate from substance,[2] does not have another foundation apart from that quantity. For it cannot be imagined of what kind that is. Nor would we stop in that further foundation, for it also would be a proximate subject and thus with respect to it we would have to seek another foundation. Or if we were to stop in that, for a greater reason we should stop in the quantity itself.

---

1 Note that Suárez is still dealing here with the material causality of a relation.

2 We may relate this immediately to what was said in Section 5, n. 12, above, about a consecrated quantity.

The difficulty therefore concerns /col. b/ the principal and fundamental subject, which is to ask whether with respect to substance every real relation requires some accidental foundation which is distinct in the thing itself (*in re ipsa*), at least "from the nature of the thing" (*ex natura rei*),[3] from that substance. For many seem to think so. And the reason can be that relation is an accident, and therefore it must belong to a substance by the medium of an accident in which it is founded. The consequence is evident, because a relation, as was said above,[4] is not distinguished in reality (*a parte rei*) from its proximate foundation. Therefore, inasmuch as it is an accident, it must be proximately founded in an accident; for if it were immediately to belong to a substance, it would be the same in reality (*in re*) with that [substance], and thus it would not be an accident but rather a substance.

3. Therefore, St. Thomas, in *De Potentia*, Question 8, Article 2, in answer to the First Objection, says that no relation can be the same as a substance that is in a genus, that is, [the same] as a created substance.[5] And in *Contra Gentiles*, Book 4, Chapter 14, toward the end, he says that in creatures relations have a dependent being, because their being is other than the being of a substance,[6] and afterwards he says: "*A relation which really comes to a substance has both an ultimate and a most imperfect being; an ultimate being because not only does it prerequire the being of the substance but also the being of other accidents, from which the relation is caused.*"[7] Therefore, from the opinion of St. Thomas, a relation always supposes in a substance another accident on which it may be founded.

Hence [in *Summa Theologiae*], Part 1, Question 28, Article 2, in answer to Objection 2,[8] he says that for a relation in creatures there is always supposed something absolute, which is some thing other than the relation itself. This, according to what was said above,[9] cannot be verified by reason of the proximate foundation alone. Therefore, [it is verified] at least by reason of

---

3 Here I acknowledge some insecurity in translating. Both the phrase "*in re ipsa*" and the phrase "*in natura rei*" can be translated as "in reality." Or they can be rendered literally, as I have done here, as "in the thing itself" or "in the nature of the thing."

4 See Section 2, nn. 2-11, and 22-24, above.

5 Cf. *Quaestiones disputatae de potentia Dei*, q. 8, a. 2, ad 1, ed. Bazzi et al., pp. 217-218. Of course, the Divine Substance is not in any genus; ibid.

6 Cf. S. Thomae Aquinatis, *Summa contra Gentiles*, IV, c. 14, in *Opera omnia*, tomus xv (Romae: Typis R. Garrone, 1930), p. 57b.

7 Ibid.

8 Cf. S. Thomae Aquinatis, *Opera omnia*, tomus IV, p. 321b.

9 Cf. Section 2, nn. 2-11, and 22-24, plus Section 4, n. 7, above.

the substance, which is what St. Thomas principally intended in that place. Therefore, between a substance and a relation there is always interposed some other foundation, by reason of which a relation can be a thing different from the substance itself.

And this is confirmed from Aristotle, in his *Metaphysics*, Book 5, where when enumerating the foundations of relations he always posits something distinct from substance, namely, quality, action, or something of this kind.[10] It is again confirmed because otherwise relations could be founded and based in matter alone, which is manifestly false, expecially according to the common opinion that denies that any accident can be in prime matter alone.

Some Relations Can Be in Reality (in re ipsa) Immediately Founded on Substance.

4. Nevertheless, it must be said that it is not necessary that the proximate foundation of a relation be some accident, or some thing, /p. 812/ or real mode that is really (*ex natura rei*) distinct from the primary subject of the relation. This is the common opinion, as I will say in what follows soon. But I am proving it first, because there is no cause or reason of this necessity. For the reasons by which it was proven above[11] that a real relation requires a foundation do not prove that it is necessary that the foundation be in reality distinct from the subject. For, although in the subject there is required a real cause or reason on account of which when the terminus is posited the relation follows, nevertheless, that reason or cause can be the intrinsic nature itself of such a subject, and not some thing or mode that is superadded to that. For, why, just as quantity from its natural condition and nature has a sufficient reason because of which certain relations follow on it, and likewise quality, could not a substance also have something similar through itself?

5. Hence, I argue secondly by induction. For just as two quantities or two whitenesses are really related (*referuntur*) by a relation of similarity or equality, so two substances [may be related] by a relation of specific identity. Therefore, this relation is in a substance without an accidental foundation that is really (*ex natura rei*) distinct from that [substance]. The consequence is evident: both because one substance is of the same species with another not by reason of some accident but by reason of its own entity and proper nature, and also because just as between whiteness and similarity there is no medium, so there is none between a substantial nature and a relation of specific identity. But the antecedent is taken from St. Thomas [in *Summa Theologiae*], Part 1, Question

---

10 Cf. Aristotle, *Metaphysics* 5.15.1020b26-32.
11 Cf. Section 6, above.

28, Article 1, in answer to Objection 2,[12] and it is explicitly the position of Aristotle in *Metaphysics*, Book 5, Text [sic] 15, where he is thinking in the same way about identity in substance as about similarity in quality and equality in quantity.[13] From this also there is taken an argument by parity of reason. For there is as much agreement between two substances as between two whitenesses or [two] quantities. Again, there is as much proportion, because they are equally of the same order. Therefore, specific identity in a substance is as much a real relation as are similarity and equality in quantity and quality. And in this way the Thomists frequently teach, [for example] Soncinas, in *Metaphysics*, Book 5, Question 35,[14] and Javelli, in *Metaphysics*, Book 5, Question 21.[15]

6. *In What the Relation of Creature Is Founded.*—Another example concerns the relation of creation. For, from the opinion of all, it is real and categorical, and still it is immediately founded in a substance. St. Thomas expressly teaches this in *De Potentia*, Question 7, Article 9, in answer to Objection 4, where he says as follows: "A creature is related (*refertur*) according to its substance as according to a cause of the /col. b/ relation, but formally according to the relation itself, just as something is said to be similar according to quality causally, and according to similarity formally."[16] And the same thing is taken from *De Potentia*, Question 3, Article 3;[17] and from Cajetan [commenting on *Summa Theologiae*], Part 1, Question 45, Article 3;[18] Ferrara [commenting on] *Contra Gentiles*, Book 4, Chapter 14;[19] Soncinas, in *Metaphysics*, Book 5, Question 31;[20] and Javelli, [in *Metaphysics*, Book 5], Question 21.[21]

---

12 Cf. S. Thomae Aquinatis, *Opera omnia*, tomus IV, p. 319a.

13 Cf. *Metaphysics* 5.15.1021a9-12.

14 Cf. Pauli Soncinatis, O.P., *Quaestiones metaphysicales*, V, q. 35 (Venetiis, 1588), p. 99a.

15 For this, cf. Chrysostomi Iavelli Canapicii, *In omnibus Metaphysicae libris quaesita* ..., V, q. 21 (Venetiis, 1576), fol. 115r.

16 Cf. S. Thomae Aquinatis, *Quaestiones disputatae de potentia Dei*, q. 7, a. 9, ad 4, ed. Bazzi *et al.*, p. 208.

17 Ibid., pp. 42-44.

18 Cf. Cajetan, *Commentaria*, in I, q. 45, a. 3, nn. 3-5, in *S. Thomae Opera*, tomus IV (1888), p. 467.

19 Cf. Ferrara, *Commentaria in Summam contra gentiles*, IV, c. 14, n. 12, in S. Thomae Aquinatis, *Opera omnia*, tomus XV (1930), p. 62ab.

20 Cf. *Quaestiones metaphysicales* ..., V, q. 31 (Venetiis, 1588), pp. 93b-94b; in this place, Soncinas asks, "Whether a relation can be founded immediately upon a substance?" and he answers that some relations can be so immediately founded.

21 Cf. Chrysostomi Iavelli Canapicii, *In omnibus Metaphysicae libris* ..., V, q. 21 (Venetiis, 1576), fol. 116v.

And it is evident by reason, for substance, according to itself, immediately terminates God's creation. Therefore through itself it is immediately referred to God by a relation of creature.

You will say that passive creation is a certain mode that is really distinct from a terminus, in which that relation can be proximately founded and not immediately in substance. I answer first: although the whole may be conceded, nevertheless, there is no accident that is the foundation of that relation, because that creative dependence is not an accident, as I have said above.[22] Moreover, although it is true that in that dependence there can be founded a certain proper relation, nevertheless it is not therefore excluded that the substance itself through itself be referred causally or fundamentally to God, insofar as it itself by reason of its own being essentially demands that dependence and terminates it through itself.

7. And this is confirmed in the relation of sonship, which cannot be so founded in active or passive generation so that it is proximately in that [generation]. For when the actual generation has been transacted, there remains the relation of sonship. Nor can it be founded in another accident, since there is none that is its cause. It is founded, therefore, in the substance itself. But the reason is that the substance itself of a creature, insofar as it is creatable or generable by another cause, is sufficient that in it a relation can be founded, if it is created or generated by such a cause.

8. *What Accident Can Be the Same as Substance.*—To the arguments to the contrary, from what was said above about the division of being into substance and accident,[23] the answer is that a proper physical accident cannot in reality (*in re*) be altogether the same as a substance. But a categorical accident can sometimes be distinguished only by "reasoned reason" (*ratione ratiocinata*), as is clear with regard to duration. So therefore it must be said that relations that are proximately founded in substance are not accidents that are physical and according to their own entity, but are only categorical accidents with respect to a figure and mode of predication, inasmuch as according to their formal nature they are outside the nature of substance, and therefore it is reasonable that such relations not be distinguished in reality from substance.

9. But the texts cited there [above][24] from St. Thomas /p. 813/ persuade with probability that he thought a real relation was in some way really (*ex natura rei*) distinguished from its foundation, which is a probable opinion. For, indeed, in *Contra Gentiles*, Book 4, he says the such a relation belongs to

---

22 Cf. *DM* 20, 4, n. 28, vol. 25, p. 777.
23 Cf. *DM* 32: "About the Division of Created Being into Substance and Accident" (*De divisione entis creati in substantiam et accidens*), vol. 26, pp. 312-29.
24 See n. 3, this Section.

a substance by the medium of another accident—which cannot be universally true, even if that opinion is supposed; therefore it is probable to me that he is speaking about relations that are physically and really accidents, and therefore perhaps he is calling that a relation which really comes to a substance. For he is speaking there in this way, and therefore he also gives examples in cases of similarity and equality, but not in other cases.

Ferrara explains it in another way: when St. Thomas says that a relation pre-requires in a substance the being of other accidents, it is understood either according to a thing or according to a mode.[25] But this [explanation] is forced. And it cannot be fitted to all of these relations, as is clear with regard to the relation of act and potency that is between matter and form, or the relation of substantial union, and similar [relations].

To the text of Aristotle,[26] the answer is that it rather proves the contrary; but in the following Section we will explain how the division of foundations of relation given by him should be understood. To the ultimate confirmation we concede that many relations can be proximately in matter, for example, the relation of potency, the relation of material cause, the relation of union, of creature, and similar ones. And whatever about physical accidents, about these categorical ones, and those that are distinct only by reason, there is nothing unreasonable in their being proximately in matter, as seems self-evident.

About the Reason of Founding and a Comparison of That to the Foundation.

10. *Arguments Proving That the Foundation and the Reason of Founding are the Same.*—But further inquiry can be made about the foundation of a relation: whether it is the same as the "reason of founding," or whether these are diverse; or if they are diverse, what is the character and the necessity of each. But there is cause to question inasmuch as the foundation of a relation seems to be nothing other than that by the medium of which the relation belongs to a subject. But this very foundation is the reason of founding or of receiving the relation. Therefore, these are not distinguished. Again [there is cause to question] because, if besides the foundation there would be need for another reason of founding to intervene, there would be no end to these foundations or reasons which would have to be assigned. For there is no reason why they would rather be two, than three, or four. Therefore, we should stay with a single foundation, which itself is the reason of founding.

---

25 Cf. Ferrara, *Commentaria in Summam contra gentiles*, IV, c. 14, n. 11, in S. Thomae Aquinatis, *Opera omnia*, tomus XV, p. 62a.
26 *Metaphysics* 5.15.1020b26-32, as cited in n. 3, this Section.

Indeed, as we have said, this foundation need not always be distinct in reality (*re*) /col. b/ from the subject of the relation, but [distinct] by reason is enough sometimes. For it is called the subject insofar as it is that in which the relation exists. But [it is called] the foundation inasmuch as it has a certain character on which the relation follows when the terminus is posited or insofar as the relation has its entity from that.

11. *Reasons Supporting the Opposite.*—But on the opposite side is the fact that most often authors speak about these as about distinct things and they suggest that the reason of founding is something required in the foundation itself or beyond the foundation and the terminus in order that the relation result. For example, for the relation of paternity there is required the action of generating, which is not the foundation, because paternity does not have its entity from that, since the action of generating is in the generated son, while paternity is in the father. It is therefore the reason of founding.

12. *The Mind of the Author.*—On this subject there can be some verbal diversity. For among authors sometimes these words appear to be confused and to be taken for the same thing, while sometimes they are attributed to different things. Therefore, we will first explain how the reality stands, and then we will fit the use of words [to that].

Thus in every real relation there is required from the side of the subject some thing that is by its nature apt and fitted in such way that it can found a respect to something else, so that from that the relation proximately has its own reality in the way in which we have explained. A thing of this kind, therefore, is properly called the foundation of the relation in any genus of relations. But it does happen in the case of some relations that in addition to the whole entity of the subject and the foundation there is required some other condition mediating between the foundation and the terminus and in reality (*in re ipsa*) distinct from them in such way that among those things the relation can arise. And in this way there is necessary an action or a generation for the relation of an agent or of a father, and perhaps in the same way matter supposes a mode of union for a relation of union [with form]. For that a condition of this kind is absolutely necessary can be easily explained in the case of action. For if Peter and Paul (who are now father and son) were immediately created by God with all the absolute properties /p. 814/ that they now have, and if between them there were not to intervene an action of generation and of procession of the one from the other, a relation would not have arisen between them, nor could it come about from the absolute power [of God] that it would arise. But now, with that condition alone added, immediately the relation results. Therefore, that condition is absolutely necessary. And nevertheless, it is not a foundation, understanding by that word,[27] that in which and from which the relation proximately has its own entity. Hence, it has come about that such a condition has been called *the reason of founding*, either because there is not any other special name by which it may be named, besides that common one by which it is called a necessary condition, or because that condition is as it were ultimately or proximately required in order that the relation bud forth (*pullelet*). In actual reality, however, it is not so much called the reason of founding as a necessary condition. For the nature (*ratio*) of some thing is properly said to be that which has some direct (*per se*) influence on that thing, especially formal or effective [influence] according to reality or reason. To be sure, this condition in the present [instance] does not have such influence for the relation of paternity, since it is outside the father himself and has no proper causality on him. Therefore it is more properly a necessary condition.

13. However, this is not general in all relations that, in order to arise, they require similar conditions that are really (*ex natura rei*) distinct from foundations and termini actually existing. For between two white things, by whatever they have been made, wherever they exist, and whatever other conditions they may have, there immediately arises a relation of similarity; and the same is true about the relation of knowledge (*scientia*) to the knowable (*scibile*),[28] and about similar things. And so, a reason of founding of this kind, even though we call it by this word, "condition," is not necessary in all relations.

However, it is common to all foundations of relation that they have some natural property, or condition, by reason of which they are apt for founding the relation, which property with respect to such a foundation can be called the reason of founding. So, for example, it is natural to created knowledge that it be measurable by a knowable, by reason of which it can found a relation to that [knowable]. Similarly, to a certain kind of form, for example, whiteness, it is natural that it have a certain kind of formal unity such as another form of the same species can also have. This, then, is the reason why such a form can found a relation of similarity.

And in this way in the relation of paternity, or of any created agent, it should also necessarily be thought that there is some /col. b/ reason of founding that essentially (*per se*) belongs to the foundation itself. For let us posit that such a foundation is the principle itself, whether proximate or principal, of an efficient causation. In this very principle some reason must be considered on account of which it can be the foundation of a relation. For in the divine action *ad extra*,[29] even though in God there is a true principle of efficiently causing, a real relation in God himself does not however result, because that principle is not an apt foundation of that relation, as we will say below.[30] Therefore, if a created efficient principle is an apt foundation, it is necessary that there be designated in it some intrinsic connatural reason on account of which it is by nature an apt foundation of a real relation, as, for example, that it is a principle essentially ordered to action or something of this kind, about which we will see below.[31]

14. Accordingly, with respect to the issue itself, it is clear that in every foundation there is present an essential and intrinsic reason of founding. Again, it is clear that these two items are not physically distinct in the thing itself; but they are metaphysically or conceptually (*ratione*)[32] distinguished in order to explain features of things, and in this way they can also be denominated by different words. But we, however, are including these reasons of founding in the foundations lest we seem to multiply things. Hence, certain people speak in this way that they say that a foundation, formally speaking, is not, for example, absolutely a quality but a quality "as one" (*ut unam*); see Hispalensis [i.e. Diego Deza], in [his Commentary on the *Sentences*], Book 1, Distinction 13, Question 1, Article 3, Notabile 4.[33] But when it is present, we call this necessary condition by this common name. But now there occurred here the question about the distinction of foundations or reasons of founding, given by Aristotle, in *Metaphysics*, Book 5, Chapter 15.[34] However, because this demands more extended discussion, we will treat of it in its own Section,[35] after that which follows.

---

29 That is to say, God's action with regard to things outside Himself.

30 Cf. Section 15, nn. 17-20, below.

31 Cf. Section 15, n. 16, below.

32 Here and elsewhere, one may note the affinity for Suárez of "metaphysical" and "conceptual."

33 Cf. D. Deza, O.P., *Nouarum deffensionum doctrine ... Beati Thome de Aquino ...*, I, d. 13, q. 1, a. 3, not. 4 (Hispali, 1517), tom. I, fol. 132r.

34 Cf. 1020b26-32.

35 That is, Section 10, below.

Section VIII.
About the Terminus of a Categorical Relation.

1. *A Real Relation Requires a Real Terminus.*—First of all, it must be said that for a categorical relation some real terminus is necessary. This assertion, taken in general, is common to almost all, and it can be easily inferred from the intrinsic character of a relation. For since its essence is to be (*se habere*) toward another according to its essential being, in this there is included a terminus. And since this relation is categorical and real, its terminus must be real. But in the conditions to be explained /p. 815/, which are required on the side of the terminus for the being of a relation, and in what way a terminus of this kind concurs with the essence of relation, there are usually treated many things which we should briefly indicate and explain.[1]

Whether an Actually Existing Terminus Is Required.

2. *The Reason for Doubting.*—The first [question] is whether the terminus of a real categorical relation need be a real actually existing terminus. And the reason for the difficulty is that, as was said above,[2] there can be a real transcendental order to a thing that does not exist, indeed, to that which is not a true being, but rather a being of reason. What therefore does a categorical relation have that it cannot respect a similar terminus?

And this is confirmed and explained, since knowledge respects a knowable equally when it does not exist and when it exists, because knowledge abstracts from singular things and from existence.[3] Likewise, the productive is related (*refertur*) to the producible, as Aristotle says in the *Metaphysics*, Book 5,[4] but the producible as such does not require existence. Again, an image, and a phantasm, and like things, equally represent an existing and a non-existing thing, and an existing whiteness is as similar in essence to another possible whiteness as to an existing one, for it has the same agreement in nature and essence with that. Similarly, the effect of a final cause equally depends on an existing and a non-existing end.

Finally, an *a priori* reason can be that neither on the part of a relation, nor on the part of a terminus, nor from the task of terminating, does this actual existence of the terminus seem necessary. The first is evident, because a relation

---

1 Here, for the sake of readable English, I have changed Suárez's passive voice construction to one that is active.
2 Cf., e.g., Section 4, n. 2, above.
3 This is especially true of that kind of knowledge which is science.
4 Cf. *Metaphysics* 5.15.1020b30.

has its entity from the foundation; therefore, from that viewpoint this suffices for the existence of the relation. The second is clear, because to actually terminate only expresses an extrinsic denomination from the disposition of another thing to the thing that is said to terminate [that other thing]. Therefore, from that point of view, such a denomination can fall upon a non-existing thing.

3. *The Opinion of Some.*—And in [his Commentary on the *Sentences*] Book 1, Distinction 28, Question 23 [sic], Gregory [of Rimini] follows this opinion, who also adds that, conversely, non-being can also be really related (*referri*) to being.[5] For he thinks that real relatives are always mutual—which foundation [of his opinion] is false, as we shall see below. And that consequent, which he infers, is extremely improbable. For who can understand that what is actually nothing is referred by a real relation, or how can an accident exist without a real subject?

Finally, nothing is actually real, unless it actually exists. Therefore, neither can a relation be actually real unless it belongs to an actual existent /col. b/, because it cannot otherwise exist, unless it also subsists. Therefore, regarding a real correlative, the opinion that it can be a non-being is improbable, as is clear also from the two preceding Sections. But as regards a terminus it is less improbable.

It Is Shown That an Actually Existing Terminus Is Required.

4. Nevertheless, it must be said that for a categorical relation a terminus that is real and really existing is necessary. This is the common opinion, both of the philosophers and interpreters of Aristotle in the *Categories*, the Chapter, "Toward Something" and in the *Metaphysics*, Book 5, Chapter 15, and also of the theologians, as it clear from St. Thomas, [in *Summa Theologiae*], Part 1, Question 13, Article 7, where he says that all relations that are between being and non-being are [relations] of reason, because reason forms them when it apprehends non-being as a certain extreme.[6] [He has said] the same in Question 28, Article 1, in reply to Objection 2 [sic],[7] and in *Contra Gentiles*, Book 2, Chapter 12, Argument 3,[8] and *De Potentia*, Question 3, Article 3, in reply to Objection 5, where he adduces Avicenna, in Tractate 3, the last Chapter, of

---

5 For this, cf. Gregorii Ariminensis, *Lectura ... In I Sent.* dist. 28-32, qu. 3; tomus III, pp. 166-170.

6 Cf. *Summa Theologiae* I, 13, 7, in *Opera omnia*, tomus IV, p. 153a.

7 Cf. ibid., p. 319a.

8 Cf. S. Thomae Aquinatis, *Summa Contra Gentiles* II, c. 12, in *Opera omnia*, tomus xiii (Romae: Typis Riccardi Garroni, 1918), p. 290b.

his *Metaphysics*.[9] And all the Thomists think the same, [for example]: Cajetan and Ferrara at the cited places;[10] Soncinas, in *Metaphysics*, Book 5, Question 27;[11] and Capreolus, in [*Defensiones*], Book 1, Distinction 7, Question 2[12] and more extensively in Distinctions 13[13] and 20.[14] [For the same, see]] Scotus and others, in [commenting on the *Sentences*], Book 1, Distinction 13;[15] and [Francis of] Mayronnes, Distinction 29, Questions 6 and 8,[16] who, however, makes use of a certain distinction. For he says that to non-being there can be a fundamental relation, but not a formal relation. But through this latter he understands a categorical relation, and thus he himself explains himself, where he openly consents to the stated assertion. But what he understands by a fundamental relation, he does not explain. However, if (as it appears) he understands some transcendental respect, his opinion is not displeasing to me. For already above[17] we have shown that real transcendental relations can be not only to non-existing termini, but also [to termini] that are not real beings according to essence.[18] And the arguments of Gregory also sufficiently prove this. For a potency that is directly and immediately (*per se primo*) ordered to an act has without doubt a transcendental order to that [act], even if it is possible and not yet existing. Knowledge also has a relation to the knowable (*scibile*),[19] which, essentially speaking, not only does not necessarily exist, but is also something universal that abstracts from singulars, [something] which cannot exist in that way.

---

9 Cf. S. Thomae Aquinatis, *Quaest. disp. de potentia Dei*, q. 3, a. 3, ad 5, ed. Bazzi et al. (1949), p. 44a. For Avicenna, see *Avicenna Latinus: Liber de philosophia prima sive scientia divina, I-IV*, Tr. 3, c. 10, éd. S. Van Riet (1977), p. 183, ll. 96-98.

10 Cf. Cajetan, *Commentaria*, in I, q. 13, a. 7, n. 5, in *S. Thomae Opera*, tomus IV (1888), p. 154b; Ferrara, *Commentaria, In Contra gentiles*, II, c. 12, n. 3, in *S. Thomae Opera*, tomus XIII (1918), p. 291ab.

11 Cf. *Quaestiones metaphysicales ...*, V, q. 27, p. 87b.

12 Cf. *Defensiones, In I Sent.*, d. 7, q. 1, a. 2, ed. Paban-Pègues, tom. i, pp. 296 and 297.

13 Cf. ibid., I, d. 13, q. 1, a. 2, tomus ii, pp. 56b-57a.

14 Cf. ibid., d. 20, q. 1, a. un., p. 168.

15 Cf. Duns Scotus, *Ordinatio* I, d. 13, q. un., in *Opera omnia*, tomus v (ed. Vat., 1959), pp. 120-21, n. 99.

16 Cf. *In quatuor libros Sententiarum*, I, 29, qq. 6 and 8 (Venetiis, 1520), ff. 91va-92ra and 92vb-93rb.

17 See Section 4, n. 2, above.

18 Here, Suárez has in mind the difference between a possible thing and a pure fiction, such as a goatstag, a chimera, or something like a square circle.

19 Or "the scientifically knowable".

5. Some Arguments Are Laid Out, by Which the Assertion Is Usually Proven.—
Therefore, it is not easy to bring forth convincing arguments that /p. 816/
might prove the stated assertion in the case of categorical relations. For those
that are commonly and usually brought forth seem to proceed equally about
transcendental [relations], as, for example, that no real being can be ordered
to non-being. Again, because otherwise it could be ordered to a being of
reason, which is repugnant, since a being of reason depends upon a fiction of
the intellect. Again, because a relation is a kind of nexus between extremes, it
therefore cannot be real unless it is between real extremes.

These arguments, and similar ones, if they are efficacious have a place in
the case of transcendental respects. However, it is clear that they do not have
cogency in their instance, because it is not repugnant that a real being have a
transcendental order to a non-actual being. First, because a power can have
an order to a possible being, although it does not respect that according to its
possibility alone, but in an order to [its] act, in such way, however, that the very
disposition of the power is prior to and independent of the actual existence
of the act or of the object. Likewise, non-being, insofar as it can be thought,
can also terminate a transcendental disposition of thought or of knowledge
toward itself. And in this way, although non-being of itself does not seem apt
to be a terminus of a real disposition, nevertheless, insofar as some action can

be exercised with respect to it, that action itself, or a habit or a power, which
are principles ordered to that action, can entail a transcendental disposition to
a thing that does not exist. And for a similar reason some act of the intellect
can entail a transcendental respect to some being of reason,[20] because, that is,
this can be a sufficient object of such an act. And therefore for a disposition
of this kind not only is there no problem that a being of reason is something
fashioned by the intellect, but also in this very fact that transcendental disposition is founded.

6. But it is correctly proven by that argument that no other things can have
transcendental dispositions toward beings of reason besides those acts of the
mind by which those very beings of reason are thought or imagined, under
which I include some acts of the imagination insofar as through them imaginary and impossible beings can be fashioned and represented.[21] And the same

---

20 This can be even to a pure fiction.

21 Note this extension of the power of imagination to produce even impossible ob-
jects. On this cf.: *DM* 54, 2, n. 18, in *Opera*, vol. 26, pp. 1023-4; and Suárez, *De
Trinitate*, IX, c. 2, n. 11, in vol. 1, p. 725. For a wider context here, see my essay,
"Gedankendinge bei den Jesuiten des 17. Jh.," in *Imagination—Fiktion—Kreation:
Das kulturschaffende Vermögen der Phantasie*, hrsg. von Thomas Dewender und
Thomas Welt (München/Leipzig: K.G. Saur, 2003), pp. 213-228. For a general

will be true of acts of the will, insofar as they can be employed with regard to beings of reason, or, if the opinion of Scotus[22] is true, because beings of reason can be made through them. Finally, that also in its own way can be extended to habits that are proportioned to those acts inasmuch as they essentially (*per se*) entail an order to the same objects. Therefore, in all of these there is found this /col. b/ disposition, because of a transcendental order to an object.

But other things, which cannot have beings of reason for objects, cannot have a real transcendental disposition toward them. For, as we have shown above,[23] a transcendental disposition is always in accordance with some real function, which actively or passively may be reduced to some kind of cause. But with regard to a being of reason no real function can be exercised, except insofar as it is taken in the role of an object.[24]

Finally, a categorical relation is not properly a nexus or a union, but only something like a tendency that can only be extrinsically terminated at something else, and, therefore, on this score, it is not repugnant that it be of a being to a non-being. Therefore, just as these arguments are dissolved in the case of transcendental relations, so they seem to be solvable in the case of categorical ones.

7. *An Argument Proving the Assertion.*—Therefore, some proper argument must be sought, which proceeds in a special way with regard to categorical relations. And first indeed we can argue from accepted principles as regards these relations: to wit, that a relation and its terminus are simultaneous in time, and that when the correlative or the terminus is removed the relation is removed, and that when the terminus is posited, if the foundation is presupposed, the relation arises. For these are all taken from Aristotle and from common opinion. But all of these suppose the real existence of the terminus, for they include the co-existence of the extremes, which supposes the existence of both.

However, a proper argument should be taken from what was said above[25] about the being (*esse*) and essence of this [kind of] relation, namely, that it consists in a pure respect and does not naturally have any other function, and, therefore, it is not directly (*per se*) intended, but it is merely resulting, as a kind

treatment of Suárez on imagination, cf. J. B. South, "Francisco Suárez on Imagination," *Vivarium*, 39 (2001), 119-158.

22 For this, cf. Duns Scotus, *Ordinatio* II, d. 1, q. 1, tomus vii (ed. Vat., 1973), p. 8, n. 15; pp. 18-19, n. 32; p. 21, n. 36. For Suárez's rejection of the will as productive of such items, cf. *DM* 54, 2, n. 17, vol. 26, p. 1023.

23 Cf. Section 3, n. 11, and Section 4, n. 11, above.

24 On causes of beings of reason, see *DM* 54, s. 2, vol. 26, pp. 1018-26; esp. ibid., n. 1, p. 1018.

25 Cf. Section 4, n. 10, above.

of accident to things besides all that which from themselves and from an intention of nature belongs to them. For from the nature of this relation so explained it is plainly inferred that it as such does not exist unless the co-existence of its foundation and terminus are supposed, from which [co-existence] it results. This is both because it does not have the mode of production of natural things and also because only for this reason can it have the character of an accident. For other respects that can be toward non-beings are essential and belong to the categories of those things of which they are essential differences.

This argument has some efficacy, even in the opinion of those who think that this relation is some mode that is really distinct from its foundation and terminus. For these easily fit to themselves this discussion that has been made. Only for them it is difficult to give the nature /p. 817/ of such an entity or distinct mode. But in [the context of] our opinion [the argument] can be more cogent, for if a categorical relation in reality (*in re*) is nothing else than the foundation itself, as it accidentally gives a relative denomination, then it cannot give that in reality unless the terminus co-exists. For every other denomination either will be completely absolute and essential, and consequently, at most it will be transcendentally relative (*respectiva*), or it will not be a denomination taken from those things themselves alone, but from a comparison of our reason. Because of this then, for a categorical relation a terminus that is real and really existing is always necessary.

The Arguments of the Opposite Opinion Are Refuted.

8. But the arguments of the opposite opinion, if they are carefully considered, proceed only with regard to a transcendental respect, and now the difference between that and a categorical relation has been sufficiently explained. Hence, the answer to the last argument is that a real terminus is required for a categorical relation from the nature and the mode of such a relation, which consists only in a pure respect that has arisen from the co-existence of the extremes. Hence, even though it is true that the actual termination itself posits nothing in the terminus, it, nevertheless, necessarily supposes in that terminus an entity that is so proportioned that from its being posited together with the terminus the relation can arise, and [it supposes] that the relation itself have a kind of object to which it can relate (*respicere*).

Accordingly, just as we said about the foundation that in it there could be conceptually (*secundum rationem*) distinguished the thing that founds the relation and the reason or the aptitude of founding, so on the part of the terminus there can be distinguished a thing or a form of the terminus and a reason for terminating that is in such a form.

But now in this place the question suggests itself: of what sort should this form and reason for terminating be, and especially whether it is absolute or relative (*respectiva*). But because this question is more extensive and supposes many things that are to be treated in the following Section, it will therefore, be discussed after that.

How the Terminus Is of the Essence of a Relation Is Deduced From What Has Been Said.

9. *The Opinion of Some.*—*The Opinion of Others.*—But from the aforesaid refutation and its argument it can be first understood that a real terminus of this kind in some way belongs to the essence of a relation, although in this there is some diversity among authors, [a diversity] which is more in the way of speaking than in reality (*in re*). For certain ones absolutely deny that a terminus is of the essence of a /col. b/ relation, as [for example] Francis of Mayronnes, in [his *Sentences* commentary], Book 1, Distinction 29, Question 5;[26] which in part also Soncinas thinks, in his *Metaphysics*, Book 5, Question 33;[27] and Cajetan, in his *De Praedicabilibus*, the Chapter on Species.[28] And the reason can be because a terminus is completely outside that relation itself and is a thing that is distinct from that. Therefore, it cannot be of the essence of that [relation], because what is of the essence is completely intrinsic and the same as the thing of whose essence it is. But others say that a terminus is of the essence of a relation, which is the common opinion of the Peripatetics, as [in the place cited just] above, Cajetan says,[29] and [also] Nifo, in his *Metaphysics*, Book 5, Disputation 16.[30] And the reason is because the whole being of a relation is to be toward a terminus; therefore, a terminus is of the essence of a relation.

10. *The Author's Opinion.*—Nevertheless, as I have said, there can hardly be disagreement on the fact. For a terminus is not an intrinsic part, neither a genus nor an intrinsic difference of a relation. Hence, it cannot be of its essence in the mentioned sense; and in this all agree. Moreover, it is certain

---

26 Cf. *In quatuor libros Sententiarum* I, d. 29, q. 5 (Venetiis, 1520), f. 91ra-va.

27 Cf. *Quaestiones metaphysicales ...*, V, q. 33, pp. 96-97a.

28 For this, possibly cf. Thomas de Vio Cardinalis Caietanus (1469-1534), *Scripta philosophica: Commentaria in Porphyrii Isagogen ad Praedicamenta Aristotelis*, c. 1, ed. Isnardus M. Marega, O.P. (Romae: Apud Institutum "Angelicum", 1934), p. 30.

29 Cf. ibid., p. 31.

30 Cf. A. Nifo, in *Dilucidarium Augustini Niphi, Suessani Philosophi solertissimi, Metaphysicarum disputationum, in Aristotelis Decem et quatuor Libros Metaphysicorum*, L. V, disp. 16 (Venetiis: Apud Hieronymum Scotum, 1559; reprint: Frankfurt am Main: Minerva, 1967) pp. 155-6.

that a categorical relation, as such, exists only while it is respecting or tending toward a terminus, and its essence consists in this. Hence, under that aspect, it can be said in some way to include in its essence the terminus, because it cannot be separated from that, nor can it be conceived according to its proper concept unless the terminus is included in such a concept. And in this sense all the ancients have spoken, who, for this reason, do not so much say that the terminus is of the essence as that it is of the quidditative concept of a relation, which Cajetan[31] and Soncinas[32] also admit.

11. *A Categorical Relative Can Be Defined Only by an Order to a Terminus.*—These[33] correctly infer that a relation cannot be defined according to its proper character unless the terminus of the relation is stated in the definition; for a thing should be so defined as it essentially is. But the essence of a relation is such that it cannot be separated from a terminus; therefore, neither can its definition be separated from a terminus; therefore, it must necessarily include in itself a terminus. And in this, Mayronnes [as cited] above[34] is not thinking correctly; for he seems to say that a relation can be defined without the addition of a terminus, in which he is also dissenting from Scotus, as is clear from the same [Scotus] in [commenting on the *Sentences*], Book 1, Distinction 30.[35] But it should be carefully observed, that we have always been speaking about the terminus of a relation and not about a correlative, in such way that we are abstracting from the question whether the correlative itself is the terminus, which [question] we will treat below.[36] And there we will also see whether this can also be extended to a correlative as such, even if it is not a formal /p. 818/ terminus. And again there we will also solve the problem that is occurring here, whether a terminus is prior in cognition to a relation and in what way correlatives can be simultaneous in cognition and definition without committing a [vicious] circle.

12. *Transcendental Respects, How They Respect a Terminus.*—Lastly, it should be observed, that this doctrine is in some way general, also for transcendental respects. For those also, and the forms or entities of whose essence they are, cannot be adequately and essentially defined without the addition of that thing that they respect, which under that aspect can be called a terminus. But the

---

31 Cf. Cajetan, *Commentaria in Porphyrii Isagogen* ..., c. 1, ed. Marega, p. 30.

32 Cf. *Quaestiones metaphysicales* ..., V, q. 33, p. 96b.

33 That is, Cajetan and Soncinas.

34 Cf. n. 9, this Section.

35 Cf. *Ordinatio* I, d. 30, q. 1-2, in *Opera omnia*, tomus vi (ed. Vat., 1963), p. 183, n. 35.

36 See Section 9, n. 3; Section 15, n. 13; and Section 16, nn. 3, 8, 9, 23, 32, 33, 34, 35, and 39, below.

difference is that a categorical relation, from its peculiar and proper nature requires an actually existing terminus, both in order that it result from that [terminus] in its own genus and also that it respect that [terminus] under the precise aspect of terminus. But a transcendental relation neither results from a terminus, properly speaking, nor does it respect it under the precise aspect of terminus, but always with some other added character of object, of cause, or some other similar thing. And thus there is in some way a more intrinsic and formal disposition to a terminus, especially one that exists, in a categorical relation than in a transcendental respect.

Even by the Absolute Power [of God], A Relation Cannot Remain without a Terminus.

13. Secondly, the question is resolved: whether the dependence of a relation upon the existence of its terminus is so great that not only from its nature does it require that [dependence], but that even by the absolute power [of God] it cannot be conserved without it. For this seems difficult to believe, inasmuch as since they are distinct things, as we are supposing, and the foundation does not intrinsically compose the relation, and it does not have a real influence on that [relation], no sufficient reason can be given on account of which God could not conserve a relation without a terminus.

Nevertheless, it still must be said that a categorical relation cannot by any power be conserved as such without its actual terminus. Almost all writers teach this. But the reason is that in the formal effect itself of a relation there is involved in some way a real and actual terminus.

However, it has been shown above[37] that a relation cannot be conserved in reality (*in rerum natura*) if it is not exercising its formal effect. Therefore, a relation cannot actually be conserved without its actual terminus. The consequence is clear, because a formal effect cannot be conserved without all things that are directly (*per se*) and essentially required for it. /col. b/ But the major is evident, because the formal effect of a relation is actually to refer to a terminus; but in this effect there is included the terminus itself; just as motion or action cannot exist without a proper terminus, by the fact that [each of these] is an actual way toward that [terminus].

14. And this is far more easy to understand in [line with] our opinion, namely, that a relation is not a thing or a real mode that is distinct from the foundation and added to it, but it is the very entity of the foundation as so denominating a subject. For since that denomination is purely respective, it consists only in a certain disposition that has arisen from the co-existence of a terminus.

---

37 Cf. Section 5, n. 6.

Therefore, it is not strange that such entity of the foundation could in no way confer that denomination unless the co-existence of the terminus be posited. And thus there is easily solved the reason for doubt to the contrary. For there is no entity here present that God could not conserve without another that is really distinct. For he can conserve the whole entity of the foundation without the terminus. He cannot, however, conserve that entity under such a character and denomination, because according to that it involves the terminus itself. Indeed, in the thing itself it adds nothing distinct besides the co-existence of the terminus.

Section IX.
What Distinction Is Necessary
Between a Foundation and a Terminus?

1. This question is also easily resolved from what has been said up to now. For certain people think that a real distinction is necessary between them. For example, Soncinas, in his *Metaphysics*,[1] who indicates that there must be a distinction in every way, so that it is not enough that they be distinguished as a whole and a part. This is principally based upon the fact that otherwise a whole continuum would be related by infinite real relations of diverse proportions of greater inequality to infinite proportional parts, which is unreasonable. Hence, with a similar argument, St. Thomas, in *Contra Gentiles*, Book 2, Chapter 12, Argument 3, proves that one quantity cannot be referred by a real relation to a possible greater quantity, because otherwise it would have at once infinite relations since numbers or greater quantities can be multiplied to infinity.[2]

2. But others think that no distinction in reality is necessary, which can especially be seen in a relation of identity of the same thing with itself. For just as much as properly and really (*a parte rei*), without any fiction of the intellect, some being is the same as itself, so it is diverse from something else, or similar to another thing. Therefore, just as much is the one a real relation as is the other. And /p. 819/ some think this most of all [is true] if the same thing happens to be the foundation in diverse subjects. So, for example, if the same whiteness were to be in two men, they say that they would be related between themselves by a real likeness, because the foundation is distinguished from the terminus that terminates, even if it is not distinguished from the reason itself of terminating. And Scotus thinks this, in [commenting on the *Sentences*], Book 1, Distinction 31,[3] and in *Quodlibetal Question 6*.[4]

---

1 Cf. *Quaestiones metaphysicales*, V, q. 26, p. 87a.

2 Cf. S. Thomae Aquinatis, *Summa contra Gentiles*, II, c. 12, in *Opera omnia*, tomus xiii (Romae: Typis R. Garrone, 1918), p. 290b.

3 I do not find Scotus making this precise point in this cited place; cf. *Ordinatio* I, d. 31, q. un., tomus vi (1963), pp. 208-208, nn. 12-15.

4 Cf. Duns Scotus, *Quaestiones quodlibetales*, q. 6, a. 2, ad 2, in *Obras del Doctor Sutil, edicion bilingüe, Cuestiones cuodlibetales*, introducción, resúmenes y versión de Felix Alluntis, O.F.M. (Madrid: Biblioteca de Autores Cristianos, 1968), n. [27] 65, p. 237.

The Resolution.

3. But it must be said that for a real relation it is necessary that the foundation and the terminus as such (*formaliter sumptus*) be distinguished in reality (*in re ipsa*). This is the opinion of St. Thomas, [in *Summa Theologiae*], Part 1, Question 42, Article 1, in reply to Objection 3,[5] where, for this reason, he denies that the equality among the divine persons is a real relation. He also denies that the same thing is related to itself by a real relation, and all Thomists follow this. And that some distinction in reality (*in re*) is required between real correlatives is almost a self-evident principle in metaphysics. For correlatives are considered to be really opposite [to one another], but the same thing is not opposed to itself; therefore, it is necessary that correlatives be really (*in re*) distinguished in some way. Hence, it is necessary also that real opposite relations be really distinct in some way, both because of their opposition, and also because each relation is in reality the same as its own extreme, as was shown above.[6] Therefore, if the extremes are distinct, so also are the relations.

Accordingly, if the terminus of a relation is an opposite relation, it is sufficiently inferred from this that the relation and the terminus must be really distinct. But if the formal terminus of a relation is some absolute form, it must also be concluded that they are distinguished in reality (*in re*). For a formal terminus of this kind can only be the foundation of the opposite relation, as I will say below.[7] But it is not less necessary that the foundation of one relation be distinguished from the opposite relation than that those opposite relations themselves [be distinguished]. Therefore.

The minor [premiss] is proven: because the relation and the foundation are really (*in re*) the same. Therefore, inasmuch as a relation is distinguished from an opposite relation, so much is the foundation of one relation distinguished in reality from the opposite of that [relation]. Therefore, it is also equally distinguished from the foundation of the opposite relation. Again, because not only relations, but also the extremes or the subjects of relations must be distinct in reality, because a real and true disposition cannot be understood to exist between things that are not distinguished in reality, since every disposition [toward], as is clear from the term itself,[8] postulates extremes. But extremes involve a plurality, and, consequently, some /col. b/ real distinction.

Finally, this is contained in the very definition of relatives that they must be toward another. But if the subjects of opposite relations must be mutually

---

5 Cf. S. Thomae Aquinatis, *Opera omnia*, tomus IV, p. 436ab.

6 Cf. Section 2, nn. 12, 13, and 22.

7 Cf. Section 10, n. 14; and Section 11, nn. 3, 9-10.

8 Note this for comment on the meaning of "habitudo." In this context, at least, it is a "disposition" with the added implication of one extreme "toward" another.

distinct, this is most of all true about the subjects or the proximate foundations in which the relations proximately exist. For to them do they proximately give their own proper and formal dispositions. Therefore, this distinction is most of all required between those foundations of opposite relations, and consequently also between the relations themselves, and finally between a relation and a terminus.

How Great the Aforesaid Distinction Must Be.

4. But it can be asked how great this distinction must be. Briefly, however, I think that it is not necessary that it be equal in all cases, but it must be thought to be according to the nature of the foundations and the manner of the relations. For often this distinction must be real and supposital,[9] as in the relation of father and son. For, because such relations are founded upon a real procession of one supposit, and one supposit can proceed only from another supposit, therefore, such a relation requires a real distinction of supposits. And likewise, a relation of specific identity requires a real distinction of substantial natures, and consequently also of supposits, apart from miracles. And the same is true, with proportion observed, about a relation of equality or of likeness. For they require a real distinction of such forms, and consequently, a real (*ex natura rei*) [distinction] of subjects. But for some relations I think that a modal distinction is enough. For, just as there is a true efficiency or an emanation between a thing and a mode, so there can also be a true relation. Again, because a modal distinction is a true distinction, and it suffices for opposition or a disposition (*habitudinem*), on account of which there is a necessary distinction between a relation and its terminus.

5. But it can be asked, on account of the argument of Soncinas[10] about an infinity of relations, whether a distinction between whole and parts is enough. Hence, it could be said that although a distinction between a whole and a part, insofar as it is in some way real, is greater than a modal distinction, nevertheless, insofar as the extremes are not so distinct, but one is included in the other, it is less sufficient for founding a real relation. But this is difficult to believe, first, because absolutely that distinction is truly in reality and it is /p. 820/ greater than a modal one. Again, [it is difficult to believe] because a material or a formal cause seem really to be related (*referri*) to their effect, which is the composite itself, from which, however, they are distinguished only as a part from a whole. Again, [it is difficult] because two halves of the same continuum seem to be related between themselves by a real relation of equality. For in

---

9 "Supposital" seems equivalent to "individual."
10 See n. 1, this Section.

reality (*in re*) they are truly distinguished, and not as including and included, but as distinct, and if they were only contiguous, they would be related by a real relation. However, a union by continuation cannot impede this relation. For the union is greater between a thing and a mode or between matter and form, because a union does not take away all distinction. But if those halves are related between themselves with a real relation, the same will be true about their halves related between themselves, and thus also there follows an infinity of relations. Nor does there seem to be anything unreasonable that in a continuum there may thus be infinite relations just as there are infinite points or parts, because relations add nothing real to foundations themselves.

The Solution of the Arguments.

6. *The Same Thing Is Related to Itself only by a Relation of Reason.—Whether Two Things Which Are White with the Same Whiteness Are Relatives through a Real Relation of Likeness.*—Through these [remarks], therefore, an answer is given to the prior opinion. But to the posterior [opinion][11] we deny that the identity of the same thing with itself is a real relation; but rather it is one of reason only. Moreover, that a thing be said to be the same as itself without a relation of reason is either false, because a comparison of the intellect is necessary by which the same thing is compared to itself in such a way as if it were two extremes, or indeed if this comparison be excluded, there is in reality (*in re*) only the thing itself and the denial of a distinction that only this very identity of the thing can add, as was seen above in Disputation 8 [sic].[12]

And I think the same about the genuine likeness between two white subjects, if they were to have a numerically same whiteness, because that agreement that they would have in whiteness would rather be an identity in a numerically same form. In order that this may be better understood, we can in that case distinguish agreement in the form of whiteness or in a union with the same form. The first agreement is a certain identity and, therefore, it is not a real relation. But the latter [agreement] can be a likeness and a relation, because even though the form is the same, the union with diverse subjects is necessarily diverse, and, therefore, in its regard there is a sufficient distinction in order that a likeness or a real relation can be founded. For example, if there were two humanities united to the Divine Word, there seems to be no /col. b/ doubt that they would be truly similar in the hypostatic union,[13] which would not be numerically the same in them, but rather distinct, and therefore

---

11 See n. 2, this Section.
12 For this, see *DM* 7, 3, n. 2, vol. 25, pp. 271-2.
13 Cf. Section 4, note 4, above.

under that aspect they could be related with a real relation. But an argument cannot be taken from this with respect to the divine relations insofar as they are terminating (as in our way we may say) the same essence of God, because they do not terminate [that essence] through a union but rather by a most simple identity.

Section X.
Whether Three Kinds of Relations on Three Foundations Were Correctly Distinguished by Aristotle.

1. In this Section we must examine the doctrine of Aristotle in *Metaphysics*, Book 5, Chapter 15, where treating of "toward something," he reduces all classes of relatives to three, which he distinguishes from three foundations or reasons of founding a relation.[1]

Aristotle's Division and Doctrine Are Proposed.

2. Which Relations Aristotle Locates in the First Class.—In the first class he puts those relations that he says are founded in unity or multitude, which afterwards he subdivides into various species.[2] For in unity he says are founded equality, similarity, and generally the identity of those things whose substance is one. For those things are called similar that have one quality; [those are called] equal that have one quantity; while [those are called] the same that have one substance, which can be understood either properly and with rigor about substance or generally about essence, which we will see below.[3] But in number he says are founded all relations that in some way are said according to quantity and that recede from unity; for example, all proportions among unequal numbers, whether those [proportions] are indicated in an indefinite or general way, such as: *exceeding, multiple*, etc., or definitely, such as: *double, triple*, etc. Therefore, even though these relations can also be found among continuous quantities, they are, nevertheless, said to be founded in number inasmuch as they require diversity in quantity. And by the same reason, all relations of dissimilarity, distinction, and the like, pertain to the same foundation, because they are in some way founded in number; for here unity and number are not taken with rigor for quantity, but more generally. To be sure, it must be taken into account that Aristotle always speaks of these relatives in the plural, for speaking most properly, both opposite relations of this class are those that require in their foundation either a number or /p. 821/ some unity of several things (for this unity must be so understood). Therefore, if we speak of singular relations, each one requires a foundation, not that it simply be a number, but that with another it compose a number or has unity.

---

1 Cf. *Metaphysics* 5.15.1020b26-32.
2 Ibid., 1020b33-1021a14.
3 Cf. n. 6, this Section.

3. *Which Relations Are in the Second Class.*—In the second class Aristotle puts those relatives that are founded on the potency of acting and suffering,[4] or on the actualizations (*actiones*) of those, which he then distinguishes into various species, which he takes in part either from the fact that the relations are founded only in the power, abstracting from the action, or as they are subject to action. And he uses as examples: able to heat and heatable, heating and heated.[5]

In these, it is necessary to note two things: one is that when Aristotle puts a real relation between a potency and a possible, he never speaks of a possible effect taken objectively, as Gregory [of Rimini] cited above seems to have thought, who from this example of Aristotle concluded that there are real relations to termini that do not exist but which are possible.[6] But Aristotle openly speaks about a passive potency or a heatable subject, as he explains in these words: *"And in a word, the active [in relation] to the passive;*[7] and below: *"But the active and the passive are said from active and passive potency and the actions of potencies, such as, what can heat [in relation] to what can be heated."*[8]

From this, secondly, one must consider that to be a real terminus of a relation of an active potency as such, abstracting from action, is something other than the terminus of an active potency as it is existing under action or as it is acting. For the first terminus is a passive potency, and otherwise it cannot be a real terminus. But the second is the effect itself, as now flowing from an acting potency. But again, Aristotle adds that this relation that is founded on a potency under action is varied according to various differences of time.[9] For one is founded in present action, for example, the relation of building, heating, etc. Another [is founded] in past action, for example, the relation of a father.

---

4 Or, "being acted upon."

5 Cf. ibid., 1021a14-26. Note that Suárez's Latin words here: "calefactivum," "calefactibile," "calefaciens," and "calefactum" can be rendered adjectivally, as I have done here, or substantively, as "what can heat," "what can be heated," "what is heating", and "what is heated."

6 Cf. Gregorii Ariminensis, *Lectura ... In I Sent.* dist. 28-32, qu. 3, tomus III (1984), p. 167.

7 Cf. 'καὶ ὅλως τὸ ποιητικὸν πρὸς τὸ παθητικόν." *Metaphysics* 5.15.1020b30. For his translation here, Suárez is following Fonseca: *In Metaphys.* V, c. 15, tomus II, col. 784.

8 "τὰ δὲ ποιητικὰ καὶ παθητικὰ κατὰ δύναμιν ποιητικὴν καὶ ἐνεργείας τὰς τῶν δυνάμεων, οἷον τὸ θερμαντικὸν πρὸς τὸ θερμαντὸν ὅτι δύναται, ..." ibid., 1021a14-17. Again, Suárez is following Fonseca's translation: *In Metaphy.* V, c. 15, tomus II, col. 788.

9 Cf. *Metaphysics* 5.15.1021a21-25.

And a third [is founded] in future action, as (he says) *"what is going to do"* [in relation] *"to what will be done,"*[10] which contains a difficulty that will need to be treated below.[11]

4. *What Relations Are in the Third Class.*—In the third class Aristotle puts relations that he calls of the measurable to the measure, as (he says) are the relations of knowledge to the knowable (*scibile*), of intellect to the intelligible, and of sight to the seeable.[12] However, he indicates a difference to be noted (which gives occasion for serious questions) between this class and the two previous ones. For in the previous ones (he says) each relative is said "toward something" /col. b/ because that toward which each one is is said to be other, and not because another [is said to be] toward it. But, in the third class, even though one of the relatives is said to be "toward something" because it truly is toward something else, the other [relative], however, which corresponds to it, is not said to be toward something because it truly is toward another, but rather because another is toward it. For example, knowledge and the knowable (*scibile*), although they are said toward another, [this is] nevertheless in a different way. For knowledge is so said, because it truly is toward another; but the knowable is certainly not [so said], but only because knowledge is toward it. And the same is true about the intellect and the intelligible, and in similar cases. This difference Aristotle did not prove by any argument, but hands it on as obvious.

Is the Division Properly Given?

5. *What Reasons Engender Difficulty.—First.*—This is Aristotle's division and his doctrine, about which two things principally occur to be explained, in which [things] various difficulties are broached. First, whether the individual members of the division are properly designated. Second, whether the division is adequate for categorical relation in such way that it sufficiently embraces the whole range of that relation.

As regards the prior question, a first reason for doubting is that relations of the first class do not seem to be real; therefore. The antecedent is proven first with regard to relations of unity, because that unity in which they are founded is not real, but a matter of reason only; therefore, a relation founded on that cannot be real. The [new] antecedent is clear, because that is not numerical unity, for this founds an identity of the same thing with itself, which, as we have said above, is a relation of reason.[13] Therefore, it is specific unity or another

10"τὸ ποιῆσον πρὸς τὸ ποιησόμενον" ibid., 23.
11 Cf. Section 12, n. 2, below.
12 Cf. *Metaphysics* 5.15.1021a26-b2.
13 Cf. *DM* 7, 3, n. 2, vol. 25, p. 272.

higher[14] unity, but every other, besides numerical, unity is a unity of reason. Nor does it matter if someone says that formal unity is real; for this also is not real except insofar as it is in reality (*in re*) the same as numerical [unity], even though they are distinguished by reason. Hence, [formal unity] is multiplied in things as much as is numerical unity itself, as was seen above.[15] Therefore, it cannot be the foundation of a real relation any more than numerical unity.

And this is confirmed and explained: for the unity that is the foundation of a relation must be a unity of several things, since the unity of each one as such does not found a relation to another; therefore, it must be a unity of several things. But every unity of several things that are distinct in reality (*in re*) is a unity of reason. Therefore.

You will say that this is true of, as it were, positive and universal unity, however, a negative unity, by which one thing is not other than another in some form or property, does exist in things themselves. For in this way /p. 822/ some Thomists answer, [for example], Capreolus, in [*Defensiones*], Book 1, Distinction 30, Question 1;[16] Soncinas, in *Metaphysics*, Book 5, Question 34;[17] and Cajetan, [commenting on] *De Ente et essentia*, Question 7 [sic].[18] But against this, since a negation or a privation cannot found a real relation any more than a being of reason [can]—since a privation taken according to itself is also a being of reason and posits nothing real in things—therefore it cannot found a real relation.

And this argument seems also to prove that a relation founded on number cannot be real, because its proximate reason of founding is a kind of negation, for a number or a multitude is established by a distinction, but a distinction or a division formally consists in a negation, as was seen above.[19] And this is made plain by examples. For inequality, for instance, is proximately founded in the fact that this quantity does not have something that another has. But this is a negation. Likewise, dissimilarity is proximately founded in the fact that this quality does not have the essence that another has, and conversely.

6. *Second.*—I argue in a second principal way: for if specific unity is a sufficient foundation for a relation, many absurd things follow. The *first* is that between things of the individual categories, insofar as they are of the same species, there arises a relation of identity or of similarity. Aristotle himself seems

---

14 For example, *generic*, or *analogical*; cf. *Metaphysics* 5.6.1016b31-32.

15 Cf. *DM* 6, 1, nn. 8-12, vol. 25, pp. 203-204.

16 Cf. *Defensiones, In I Sent.*, d. 30, q. 1, a. 1, ed. Paban-Pègues, tom. II, pp. 299b-300a.

17 Cf. *Quaestiones metaphysicales ...*, V, qq. 34-35, pp. 97-99a.

18 Cf. *In De Ente et Essentia*, c. 4, q. 6, ed. Laurent, n. 60, p. 93.

19 Cf. *DM* 4, 6, nn. 2-3, vol. 25, p. 135.

to have conceded this, when he said: "those things are the same, of which there is one substance,"[20] that is, an essence, and he locates all these in this class. Nor does it matter if someone understands by the term "substance" not the essence but a proper substance, since at least for equal reason a sufficient argument is taken. For two actions or two places (*ubi*), are as similar as two whitenesses. But the falsity of the consequent is proven inasmuch as from it the fact would come about that two relations of the same species, for example, two paternities, are related by a real relation of similitude; for the argument is completely the same. But the consequent is false, because a relation cannot be founded upon a relation. Otherwise, in every relation there would be infinite relations; for just as the first founds the second, so also the second could found a third. For it will be similar, or dissimilar, or distinct, from the others, and the same will be true of the third with respect to a fourth, and so to infinity. *Secondly*, it follows that between two quantities of two feet there are two real relations, the one of identity, insofar as they are of the same essence, and the other of equality, insofar as they are of the same size. And the first could be lost while the second would remain; for between a two-foot and a three-foot quantity there is a similarity /col. b/ of essence, although there is not equality. Likewise, it should be said that an intensified and an abated heat are related by one real relation of identity in essence and another of dissimilarity by intension, and similar things, which seem absurd.

7. *Thirdly* it follows that not only a specific similarity but also a generic or analogous one can found a genuine real relation. For the argument is proportional. For even though a generic similarity is not as great as a specific one, still it is a true similarity and unity. Therefore, it will found a real relation, although not of the same character nor perhaps as perfect. Again, [this is so] because if a generic unity, because of various specific differences, is not enough for this relation, neither would a specific unity suffice, because of various individual differences; for they keep the same proportion in real identity and a distinction of reason. The argument, therefore, is the same. Thus, just as a specific unity founds a relation of reason, so does a generic [unity].

The consequent is false, both because things that are distinct in species, even though they agree in genus, are simply dissimilar rather than similar, as for example, whiteness and blackness, and also because otherwise, since the agreements and differences of things can be multiplied to infinity through abstractions of the intellect, also the relations of similarity or dissimilarity would be infinite in one thing, either with respect to another with which it agrees in a specific difference and in all superior predicates, or with respect to

---

20 *Metaphysics* 5.15.1021a11.

diverse things, insofar as it is similar in species to one and [similar] to another in a proximate or remote genus.

And the same difficulty, with proportion observed, is found in relations that are said to be founded in number or in disagreement. For one relation will be to a thing that is distinct in the ultimate species, and others will be to various things that are diverse in one or another genus, which things can be multiplied almost to infinity.

I add also that it seems incredible that all the proportions that arithmeticians see among numbers are real. This is both because no one adequate subject of such a relation can be assigned, since a whole number does not have in reality a true and real unity, and also because they seem to be comparisons and considerations of the intellect rather than real dispositions [toward]. However, Aristotle counts all these equally as species contained under this class.[21]

8. *A Third Difficulty against the First Class of Relations.*—There is a third principal difficulty with regard to the same class. For either relations of this kind /p. 823/ are some things or real modes that are added to those absolute forms themselves or they are not. The first cannot be said, as was generally said above[22] about this whole category. And in a special way about this class the two first difficulties here proposed seem sufficiently to prove that, because infinite modes are multiplied in the same thing, which modes are not only unnecessary, but they can neither be understood nor reduced to some definite concept (*certam rationem*). Again [it cannot be said], because unity among things of this kind is not something other than the things themselves. Why therefore will a feature (*ratio*) result from this as something different? But if there are no modes that are distinct in reality (*in re*) there cannot be real dispositions [toward], but a mere co-existence of several absolute things of certain conditions.

This is proven, because a real disposition [toward] cannot belong to a thing unless either it is intrinsic to it and from itself, or it is added to it. In the present case, however, when one whiteness becomes similar to another there is not added to it an intrinsic real disposition [toward], since if it were added, it would be really (*ex natura rei*) distinct, for an addition in reality cannot be understood without a distinction between that which is added and that to which it is added. Again, neither is that disposition [toward] intrinsic and essential to whiteness, both because it can absolutely be without that and also because every intrinsic and essential disposition [toward] of an absolute thing is transcendental. But one whiteness has no transcendental disposition toward

---

21 Cf. *Metaphysics* 5.15.1020b33-1021a14.
22 Cf. Section 2, nn. 7-9, above.

another. And, therefore, there is a greater reason for doubting in the case of these absolute forms than in these that include a transcendental respect. For in these latter it can be understood in some way that without a real addition the same respect, under different aspects, is both transcendental and categorical. However, in the former absolute things it seems that in no way there can be understood a real disposition [toward], if nothing intrinsic is added to them, as in fact it is not added. Therefore, this first class of relations seems at least more to contain relations of reason, or extrinsic denominations, and modes of speaking that have arisen from various comparisons by our intellect among diverse things, rather than true and real dispositions [toward].

9. *Fourth.*—There is a *fourth* difficulty as regards the second class, in which, in order that we may begin from the more difficult things, what Aristotle says seems plainly false, [that is], that the relation of a cause that is about to cause to its future effect is under this class.[23] For that cannot be a real relation. This is *first*, because the terminus is not actually existing; for what is future does not yet exist. Indeed, it is not yet becoming; otherwise, it would not be a relation of a cause about to operate, but rather of [a cause] that is operating. It is *second*, because the reason of founding /col. b/ or the necessary condition, namely, the action, does not yet exist. But that this condition is necessary is clear, because otherwise there would in no way be a relation of one acting, or of one about to act, but only of one able to act.

Then it is also difficult [to understand] in what way a relation founded upon a past action is real. This is first, because that action does not exist now; therefore, it cannot be the foundation or the reason of some relation. It is second, because the fact that Peter, for instance, generated Paul is only an extrinsic denomination from a past action; how, therefore, can a real intrinsic respect be founded on that? This is most of all because that denomination is said equally whether the generated son is alive or not; for it is always true to say that Peter generated Paul. Indeed, if we attend to the mode of speaking, he is called his father in the same way. And from this again it is also difficult [to understand] that a relation of agent, even a present relation, is real in the agent himself, since an action is not in an agent[24] and consequently it denominates the agent extrinsically.

And this is confirmed, because Aristotle says that in the third class the relation of a knowable object (*scibilis*) is not real, from the fact that a thing is called knowable through a disposition of knowledge toward it.[25] But also an agent is in this way denominated through the disposition of an action, which is in

23 Cf. *Metaphysics* 5.15.1021a14-19.
24 Cf. Aristotle, *De Anima* 3.3.426a9-10.
25 *Metaphysics* 5.15.1021a29-32.

a patient, toward the principle itself of acting. Therefore, for an equal reason, there will not result in that principle of acting any relation that will be intrinsic to the agent itself.

Finally, about the relation of an agent in potency, as such, it can also be doubted, at least when the principle of acting is essentially (*per se*) instituted for that task. For then it does not have a transcendental disposition to a thing in potency or to a possible effect. Therefore, neither will it have a categorical [disposition toward these]. The consequence is based upon the third difficulty proposed above.[26]

10. *Fifth.*—There is a fifth difficulty with regard to the third class, in which it can be first doubted about the distinction assigned by Aristotle between this class and the others. But this requires a special Section, which we will treat below.[27]

Now there is a particular difficulty: in what way the character of a measure can be the foundation of a real relation, since that character of a measure is not real, but one of reason only, as was shown above, when we were treating of quantity.[28] But if you say that in that place we were talking about a measure of quantity, but here we are talking about a measure of truth, this rather increases the difficulty. For much less can this character of measure be real, as is clear because knowledge or a judgment of the intellect is equally measured by an existing or a non-existing object.[29] Again, the measuring is not /p. 824/ some action, nor is it something real (*aliquid rei*), as will be clear when we are discussing individual categories.

Is the Division in Question Sufficient?

11. *Sixth.*—There is a sixth and last difficulty inasmuch as all relations do not seem to be sufficiently included under these three classes. For there are others that do not seem to be less real than those that are contained in the aforementioned classes. This assumption is clear first about the relation of appetite to the appetible, and of all things that are contained under this kind, as for example, [the relation] of love to the lovable, of desire to the desirable, etc. For, as is clear, these relations are not founded in unity or in action. Neither [are they founded] on the character of measure, for in love there is not a truth that is measured by a lovable object. But if you say not the truth, but the

---

26 Cf. n. 8, this Section.
27 Cf. Section 15, below.
28 Cf. *DM* 40, 3, n. 6, vol. 26, pp. 539-40.
29 For some background here, cf. my article: "Suarez on Beings of Reason and Truth (1)," *Vivarium*, XXV (1987), pp. 47-75; and (2) *Vivarium*, XXVI (1988) pp. 51-72.

perfection, or moral goodness (*honestas*), of love is measured from a lovable object, certainly in this way a relation of measure will be present between every effect and cause, either a formal [cause], which is the intrinsic measure of the perfection of a thing, or efficient, exemplar, or final [causes], which can be extrinsic measures. And, of one genus, the more imperfect species are related to a supreme species by a relation of what is measured to their measure.

Moreover, a relation of union seems to belong to none of the aforementioned classes. For, most of all, [it would seem to belong] to the first class (because about the other [classes] it appears there can be no doubt). But neither can it belong to that. For the agreement or the unity of which we were speaking in that place is one thing, but a union or conjunction, which can be of things altogether distinct, as the relation of union, for example, of humanity and the [divine] Word, and other similar ones, is something else. There is almost a similar difficulty about relations of contact, nearness, and distance, and finally about relations of final, formal, and material cause. For all of these do not have those foundations.[30]

The Division Given by Aristotle Is Defended.

12. These are the principal difficulties which occur in regard to the division in question, notwithstanding which, Aristotle's doctrine or division should be embraced and fittingly explained, which [doctrine or division] all of his inter-preters and writers of metaphysical questions follow, and theologians also, as is clear from St. Thomas, [in *Summa Theologiae*], Part 1, Question 13, Article 7,[31] and Question 28, Article 1,[32] and *Contra Gentiles*, Book 2, Chapters 11 and 12;[33] in which places Cajetan[34] and Ferrara[35] discuss many things about these relations, [and] Capreolus and Hispalensis, in Book 1, partly in Distinction

---

30 That is, unity, action-passion, and measure.

31 Cf. S. Thomae Aquinatis, *Opera omnia*, tomus IV, pp. 152-154.

32 Ibid., pp. 318-319.

33 Cf. *Opera omnia*, tomus XIII (1918), pp. 287 and 290-91.

34 Cf. *In Summam Theol.* I, 13, 7, in S. Thomae, *Opera omnia*, tomus IV (1888), pp. 154-57; ibid., I, 28, 1, pp. 319-320.

35 Cf. *Commentaria in Contra Gentiles*, II, cc. 11 and 12, in *S. Thomae Opera*, tomus XIII, pp. 287-90 and 291-92.

19[36] and partly in Distinctions 30[37] /col. b/ and 31,[38] where also does Scotus[39] and other theologians, and in other places cited above.

Apart from the authority of Aristotle, the basis is that relations belonging to singular things of these classes are real, as is clear from the common consent of all philosophers and what has been said above about the entity of these relations.[40] For if these are real relations, [this is true of] especially similarity or paternity or of the relation of knowledge to a knowable, which are relations belonging to the three classes in question, for if these relations are not real and categorical, what kind could there be that could rationally be thought to be such?

This, therefore, is enough in order that these three classes be placed in the category, "toward another," whether there are some relations of reason that are analogous (*habeant proportionem*) with these classes, or not. For if they do not exist, it will be evident enough that these classes are entirely real, whereas if they do exist, they will not pertain directly to these classes as these divide the category, "toward something," but they will have a certain analogy or proportionality[41] with these.

13. However, that these classes in relative character are distinct among themselves, seems first known sufficiently from the denominations themselves that they impart; for they are very much diverse. Then the matter itself is best explained by Aristotle from the foundations themselves or from reasons of founding. For since one of the principal causes of a relation is its foundation (since, indeed, it has its entity from that), there can be no greater indication of the distinction of relations than a distinction of formal and especially proximate foundations, about which we must speak. For a remote foundation, or rather a subject, does not essentially (*per se*) so concur for a relation, and therefore its distinction is not in this way a sufficient foundation for distinguishing relations. But that the foundations of those three classes are completely distinct is

36 For Capreolus, possibly cf. *Defensiones, In I Sent.*, d. 19, q. un., ed. Paban-Pègues, tom. II, p. 151b. I have not been able to find the reference in Hispalensis.

37 Cf. Capreolus, *Defensiones, In I. Sent.*, d. 30, q. 1, a. 1, ed. Paban-Pègues, tom. II, p. 282b. For Hispalensis, see *Nouarum deffensionum doctrine ... Beati Thome de Aquino ...*, I, d. 30, q. 1, fols. 214rb-215rb.

38 Cf. Capreolus, *Defensiones, In I Sent.*, d. 31, q. 1, a. 1, ed. Paban-Pègues, tom. II, pp. 318-319. For Hispalensis, see *Nouarum deffensionum doctrine ... Beati Thome de Aquino ...*, I, d. 31, q. 1, fol. 230va.

39 Cf. *Ordinatio* I, d. 1, in *Opera omnia* tom. v (ed. Vat., 1959), pp. 265-303; ibid. dd. 30-31, tom. vi (1963), pp. 169-222.

40 Cf. Section 2, n. 22, above.

41 Cf. Section 2, note 62, above.

even self-evident. Rightly, therefore, that distinction of relations is taken from their distinction.

14. You will say: rather the distinction of relations should have been taken from their termini. For things that have an essential disposition toward another take their specification from that, for example, motions from their termini, powers and habits from their objects.

The answer is first that this is true about a specific and ultimate distinction; however, a generic, or a subalternate, distinction can sometimes be taken from elsewhere. The answer is second that in that distinction formal termini are not left aside, but they are either expressly, or at least implicitly, signified to be in those three classes. For when a relation /p. 825/ of the first class is said to be founded in unity, it is included in this that it is also terminated at another, insofar as it is in some way one. For, as I will show below, that which is the foundation of a relation in one relative to another is also the reason of terminating the relation of the other.[42] And, by a similar reasoning, when in the second class it is said that a relation is founded in a potency, by this very fact, it is indicated also to be terminated at a potency, or at an effect if the relation is founded not in a bare potency but as such is under action. For in this way a relation of an active potency is terminated at one that is passive, and *vice versa*. But the relation of an acting potency is terminated at its effect.

However, in the third class, it is more clearly evident that a relation of a measurable is terminated at a measure. Therefore, that distinction is not so taken from foundations, without termini also being included. For, since these are two principles that are in their own way intrinsic to relations, neither can be excluded from the constitution and distinction of those relations. But the foundation is quasi-material, whereas the terminus is quasi-formal, because it is the ultimate thing toward which the relation tends.

About the Sufficiency of the Stated Division.

15. *The First Reason of Sufficiency.—To How Many Difficulties the Asserted Reason of Sufficiency Is Subject.*—Finally, all the cited authors teach that this division is sufficient and embracing all species of relations that can belong to the category, "toward something." But the reason of its sufficiency St. Thomas gives in [his commentary on] *Metaphysics*, Book 5, Lecture 17—for in three ways only is it possible that one thing be ordered to another. These are, either according to being (*esse*) insofar as one thing depends in being on another, and in this way there is the third class, or according to active and passive unity, insofar as one thing receives from another, or confers something on another,

---

42 Cf. Section 16, n. 20-21, 31, 35, and 36.

and in this way there is the second class; or insofar as the quantity of one thing can be measured by another, and in this way there is the first class.[43]

But this reasoning is difficult. For a disposition to something else according to dependence in being, if it is taken generally, seems to pertain more to the second class, since an effect depends in being upon its cause. But if it is taken according to a special mode of dependence on an object, which is that of knowledge or of a potency, in this way there must be distinguished as many modes of relatives as there are modes of dependences. For why rather does that mode of dependence constitute a special class of relatives and not others?

Again, it seems false that quantity, as it has the character of a measure, founds the first /col. b/ class. This is first because Aristotle is not assigning there the character of measure, but of unity or number, which is a very different character. For when two quantities are called equal, one is not the measure of the other, nor *vice versa*, nor is this looked at between them, but rather the character of unity. And the same *a fortiori* is true about similarity or identity, and therefore, as we have said, unity there is not taken quantitatively, but more generally. It is true also, second, because the character of a measure is not essentially (*per se*) apt for founding a real relation, since it is only an extrinsic denomination of reason, as was mentioned above.[44]

16. *The Second Reason of Sufficiency.—How Many Difficulties There Are in It.*—Alexander of Hales, in the same place, indicates a reason for this distinction, when he says that the division has been taken from three universal modes of being, which are: the same and the other, with regard to the first [class]; potency or act, with regard to the second [class]; and (he says) the perfect or the imperfect, with regard to the third [class], in the way in which the imperfect is measured by the perfect and the diminished by the complete. And because these three modes sufficiently vary the nature of the foundations, there are, therefore, three species of relation.[45]

But what he says is difficult, namely, that the third member is taken from a mode of being insofar as it is perfect or imperfect. For, although a sense is referred to a sensible according to that class, it is not measured by that [sensible] as the imperfect by the perfect, but it is said to be measured only as by a specifying terminus, which can sometimes be more perfect, sometimes equal,

43 Cf. S. Thomae Aquinatis, *In duodecim libros Metaphysicorum Aristotelis expositio*, ed. Cathala-Spiazzi, V, l. 17, p. 266, n. 1004.

44 Cf. *DM* 40, 3, n. 8, vol. 26, p. 540.

45 Cf. [Pseudo] Alexandri de Ales, O.M. [actually, Alessandro Bonini, aka Alexander of Alexandria (ca. 1270-1314)], *In duodecim Aristotelis Metaphysicae libros dilucidissima expositio*, V, t. 20 (Venetiis: Apud Simonem Galignanum de Karera, 1572), ff. 138b-139a. Note that in this edition folio 139 is erroneously labeled as "143."

and sometimes less perfect, as is seen also in the case of the intellect and the intelligible. Then, even though he asserts that these three classes sufficiently divide the foundations of relations, he does not however give a reason for the sufficiency, nor does he by virtue of that explanation explain their distinction among themselves. For potency and act also are compared as perfect and imperfect, and potency can be said to be measured by act, insofar as it is proportioned and commensurate to that act—because of which potencies are also said to be specified by acts.

Therefore, I think that Aristotle did not have any other reason for the sufficiency besides a certain induction by which he understood that no relation was found that could not be reduced to some one of the stated heads, which cannot better become evident than by responding to the difficulties mentioned. For if we find no relation which does not have one of those foundations, it will be sign enough for us that the division is sufficient.

/p. 826/

Section XI.
About the First Class of Relations, Founded in Number or Unity.

1. For the sake of greater clarity, we will respond almost with individual Sections to the individual difficulties proposed in the Section above.[1]

2. To the first [difficulty][2] then the answer is that it is one thing to speak about two relations of two extremes that are said to be founded in unity, but another thing [to speak] of each of them. For each of two relations of similitude, for instance, is founded in one quality insofar as it is in itself one by a formal unity, not indeed with regard to that which unity adds beyond being, for that is a negation, and therefore it cannot found a real relation, as the argument correctly proves, but with regard to that positive character of being that underlies that negation.

But speaking of both relations of two extremes, they are said to be founded in their unity, because the reason why those two relations simultaneously arise, when those two extremes are posited, is not only because the individual extremes have such a unity between themselves, but also because that unity is of the same nature in both, which is the same as saying that therefore they are related between themselves because they have a real agreement. And although this agreement is not some real unity of the two extremes between themselves, as is also correctly assumed in the argument, speaking of proper and formal unity, however, there is given in reality a foundation of that unity, whether with regard to a negation, or with regard to a unity of reason, and that foundation is enough in order that such relations arise in those extremes.

3. And in a similar way we must respond to the second part about relations that are founded in multitude, distinction, or diversity. For, although because of that argument it has seemed to many that those relations are not real, but are rather [relations] of reason inasmuch as they do not have a real proximate foundation or a formal terminus, nevertheless, when one is speaking in accord with the common opinion and in a reasonable way (*consequenter*), it is more truly said that the argument is the same about these relations and about those that are founded in unity. For just as distinction includes negation, so also does unity.[3] And, conversely, just as the negation that unity entails supposes an entity, which can be the foundation of a relation, so also a real distinction

---

1 That is, Section 10, just preceding.

2 Ibid., n. 5.

3 For this, cf. *DM* 4, 1, n. 12, vol. 25, p. 118. Also, see Darge, *Suárez' transzendentale Seinsauslegung* ..., pp. 199-216.

is between real extremes, in which the negation there included is founded. In those [extremes] /col. b/, therefore, as they are such, a real relation also could be founded.

Hence, in the examples brought forth there, although it is true that in a relation of inequality one extreme lacks some part of the magnitude of the other extreme, still, the relation is not founded formally in that lack, but rather in the fact that this quantity is so great and that is so great. And the same is true of dissimilarity. For it presupposes two essences, one of which is not the other. However, it is not proximately founded in that negation, but in those essences themselves insofar as according to their formal unities they are essentially more than one.

This is clarified by an example: for light and dark also have dissimilarity as regards that negation, since the form of light is not in one which is in the other. But, nevertheless, there is no real relation of dissimilarity between them, because from the side of the second extreme[4] there is neither the foundation nor the positive formal terminus of such a relation.

A Relation of Unity Can Be Founded in Things of all Categories.

4. In the second difficulty,[5] many things are touched which could raise particular questions. Nevertheless, let us quickly pass through them, lest we delay too much in explaining the most minute things. First, therefore, there is a question about whether a relation of similarity and other [relations] of this kind can be founded in only quantity and quality, or also in things of other categories. And indeed about substance we have already seen in the preceding Section that the argument is the same on this score as about quantity and quality. And the argument made there seems to me to conclude about any thing or mode or entity whatever, especially if such are absolute, that we might for the moment omit relations. For why are two heats[6] really similar—and as such they are really related—and not two heatings,[7] or two places (*ubi*),[8] and any other similar things. Again, between two actions there is a true and positive contrariety. But this is a relation, which belongs to this class. For it is founded in a sort of special mode of distinction. Therefore, as regards the other categories beyond "toward something," we easily concede the inference made there. Neither against this consequent, as regards this part, is anything there objected. It is true that St. Thomas, [commenting on] *Metaphysics*, Book

---

4 That is, the dark.
5 Cf. Section 10, n. 6, above.
6 Which would be in the category of quality.
7 Which would be in the category of action.
8 Which would be in the category of place.

5, Lecture 17, completely excludes the last four categories, in such way that they cannot be foundations of relations, "*because,*" he says, "*they rather follow relation than they are able to cause relation.*"[9] But it can be explained that this is understood about those categories according to their own proper /p. 827/ natures, but not insofar as they have a proportion or an agreement with others in the character of unity or of distinction.

How One Relation Can Found Another.

5. *The First Opinion.*—But there is a greater difficulty about relations themselves, in which a second general difficulty is suggested: whether a relation can be founded on a relation? For it is the opinion of many that a relation can never be founded on a relation. St. Thomas thinks this way, in [*Summa Theologiae*], Part 1, Question 42, Article 4 [sic];[10] and *Contra Gentiles*, Book 2, Chapter 13;[11] and *De Potentia*, Question 7, Article 11;[12] and in [commenting on the *Sentences*], Book 1, Distinction 3 [sic],[13] Question 1, Article 1.[14] And more frequently the Thomists follow that, [for example], Soncinas, in *Metaphysics*, Book 5, Question 29, in Reply to Objection 1;[15] and Ferrara, [commenting on] *Contra Gentiles*, Book 4, Chapter 11.[16] The principal basis is the point about a process to infinity that would follow from this.[17] Just as for a similar reason, there cannot be an action toward an action, nor a motion toward a motion, and universally proceeding from the formal effect to the form, if the form itself in some way participates the effect or its denomination, we must make a stand in that, so that it is such through itself. This is usually said in another way, in proceeding from a "which" (*quod*) to a "by which" (*quo*), we must stand in the "by which" (*quo*). Therefore, since it is a relation by which something relative is related, we must stop with that in such way that it is not related by another relation.

---

9 Cf. S. Thomae Aquinatis, *In duodecim libros Metaphysicorum Aristotelis expositio,* ed. Cathala-Spiazzi, V, l. 17, p. 266, n. 1005.
10 Cf. *Summa Theologiae* I, q. 42, a. 1, ad 4, in *Opera,* tomus IV, p. 436b.
11 Cf. S. Thomae Aquinatis, *Opera omnia,* tomus XIII, p. 293a.
12 Cf. *Quaestiones disputatae de potentia Dei,* q. 7, a. 11, ed. P. Bazzi *et al.,* p. 212; also see ibid., a. 9, ad 2, p. 208b.
13 Here, the Vivès, the Salamanca, 1597, the Mainz, 1605, and the Venice, 1610, editions all read "3" instead of the correct "31."
14 Cf. S. Thomae Aquinatis, *Scriptum in lib. Sent.,* I, d. 31, q. 1, a. 1, ed. Mandonnet, tomus i, p. 719.
15 Cf. *Quaestiones metaphysicales ...,* V, q. 29, p. 92a.
16 Cf. *Commentaria in Contra Gentiles* IV, c. 11, n. 25, tomus XV, p. 45b.
17 Cf. Section 10, n. 6, above.

And this can be confirmed by a theological argument. For otherwise among the divine relations there would be a variety of real relations, namely, of real distinction and quasi specific dissimilarity in the relative character, and of generic similarity in the same [character], and other [relations] of this kind, which is against the common teaching of theologians, who acknowledge only four real relations in God.[18]

6. *The Second Opinion.*—Scotus, in [his *Sentences* commentary], Book 2, Distinction 1, Questions 4 and 5,[19] and in Book 4, Distinction 6, Question 10,[20] holds a contrary opinion. Lychetus and Mayronnes follow him in these places,[21] as does Mayronnes also in Book 1, Distinction 29, Question 4;[22] Antonio Andreas, in *Metaphysics*, Book 5, Question 13 [sic],[23] and the book

---

18 These would be the relations of paternity, filiation, spiration, and spiratus. The relation of paternity would be constitutive of the Father; filiation would constitute the Son; spiration would be the mutual love of the Father and Son, which would give rise to the Holy Spirit (the one breathed forth [spiratus].

19 Cf. *Ordinatio* II, d. 1, q. 4-5, in *Opera omnia*, tomus vii (ed. Vat., 1973), p. 119, n. 239; pp. 133-4, nn. 268-71.

20 Cf. *Quaestiones in IV Sent.*, d. 6, q. 10, in *Opera omnia* (1639), tomus viii, pp. 353-4.

21 Actually, Lychetus did not comment of Book IV of Scotus' *Commentary on the Sentences*. For this, see the brief letter, dated May 14, 1636, of Fr. Ioannes Baptista a Campanea, Minister General of the *Ordo Minorum* to the Irish Franciscan, Anthony Hickey, which is given in the front matter of Tome 8 of Ioannis Duns Scoti, Doctoris subtilis, Ordinis Minorum, *Quaestiones in Lib. IV. Sententiarum*, Lugduni: Sumptibus Laurentii Durand, 1639. As for Mayronnes: I cannot find him directly commenting on Scotus' text here, i.e. *In IV Sent.*, d. 6, q. 10. Instead, he comments up to only Scotus' Question 9; cf. Francis of Mayronnes, *In quatuor libros Sententiarum* IV, d. 6, q. 4 [sic] (Venetiis, 1520), f. 182ra.

22 Cf. *In quatuor libros Sententiarum* I, d. 29, q. 4 (Venetiis, 1520), f. 90ra. Here the Vivès, the Salamanca, 1597, and the Mainz, 1605, editions of Suárez read: "q. 6."

23 For this, cf. [Pseudo] Scotus [aka Antonio Andreas, O.M.], *In XII libros Metaphysicorum Aristotelis expositio*, V, q. 11, in Ioannis Duns Scoti, *Opera omnia* (Lugduni, 1639), tomus iv, p. 635a. On Antonio Andreas as author of the *Expositio* here, cf. E. Gilson, *Jean Duns Scot: Introduction à ses positions fondamentales* (Paris: Librairie Philosophique J. Vrin, 1952), p. 674. It is noteworthy that while Suárez does not have this reference exactly correct, he was aware that Antonius Andreas had some role in the preparation of the *Expositio* attributed to Scotus; cf. *DM, Index locupletissimus*, X, c. 4, vol. 25, p. lv b. In this he anticipates Luke Wadding and his colleague, Cavellus (i.e. Hugh McCaughwell), who, in a "Judgment" (*Judicium*) prefixed to tome IV of the 1639 edition of Scotus's *Opera omnia*, has asserted that Scotus authored the *Expositio* while Antonio Andreas corrected it, ordered it, and

On the Six Principles, Question 10.[24] The basis was touched upon by us in the aforesaid difficulty. For no sufficient reason appears on account of which a likeness between two paternities is not as much a true relation as between two whitenesses, since in reality (*in re ipsa*) they have the same manner of agreement and of formal unity, and they are also denominated in the same way as alike. For if someone wants to say that two paternities are denominated similar only fundamentally or negatively, that is, because they do not have a diverse character, he who so responds /col. b/ presents an occasion that about any similar things the same can be said, or he needs to give a sufficient reason for the difference [in this case], which certainly does not appear.

The same argument is valid about the relation of dissimilarity, which can exist between paternity and the relation of science, for example. Again, arithmeticians posit a proportionality founded on two proportions, for just as four is to eight, so three is to six. But a proportion is only a relation. Proportionality, therefore, seems to be nothing else than a likeness of proportions, which is a relation of a relation.[25] And this argument seems certainly to prove, speaking logically (*consequenter*), that one relation can be really related to another through relations that belong to this first class. Therefore, just as the one and the many transcend all categories, so also relations of this first kind can be found in things of all categories, not so that they are of the essence of those things, but as founded on those things themselves.

7. A Third Opinion, Which Reconciles the Two Preceding Ones.—But some try to bring these opinions to an agreement, both because of the authority of St. Thomas and on account of the force of the reasons. For they say that one relation can be really related to another, not, however, by another relation, but by itself in order that a process to infinity be avoided and that the same thing be simultaneously "that by which" (*quo*) and "which" (*quod*). And in this way

---

in places added to it. Antonio Andreas did author a *Questiones super xii libros Metaphysicae Aristotelis*, ed. Venice: Johannes et Gregorius de Gregoriis, 1495, which I have seen, but in which the point in question is not made.

24 For this, cf. Antonio Andreas, O.F.M., *Scriptum super librum Sex principiorum*, ed. Joannes Maria Mapellus Vincentinus (Venetiis, 1508), fol. 52vab; I can find no obvious division of this work into *Questions*. For a critical edition of the original book, *On the Six Principles*, cf. A. Heysse, *Liber de sex principiis. Gilberto Porretano ascriptus*, in *Opuscula et textus*, Münster i. W. 1929 (revised 1953); cf. c. 4, pp. 18-19, for the passage on which Antonio is commenting here. On the incorrect character of the ascription of the book to Gilbert de la Porrée, cf. L. Minio-Paluello, *Magister Sex Principiorum*, in: *Studi Medievali*, terza serie, VI (1965), 123-155.

25 That is, a likeness in relation.

a relation is not properly founding a relation, since the relation that is related and that by which it is related are not different.

However, conceptually, it can be said to found, insofar as it is distinguished according to reason into that which is related and that by which it is related. Cajetan favors this opinion, [commenting on *Summa Theologiae*], Part 1, Question 42, Article 1, based on the words of St. Thomas, in answer to Objection 4, which are as follows: "*One relation is not related to another through some other relation.*"[26] About this, Cajetan adds, that from this condition of a relation, namely, that it is not founded upon another relation, it does not follow that relations of relations are not real, but that they are not other than their foundations.[27] From this, he adds that if the divine relations were not otherwise to have identity in [the divine] nature, they could be related by a real relation of equality. But then the equality of the Son to the Father would be filiation itself, and of the Father to the Son, paternity itself.[28]

8. *The Opinion of the Author.*—However, this opinion does not seem to be totally sustainable. For, in order that a form be by itself sufficient to receive some denomination, or (as they say) in order that it have itself as "by which" (*quo*) and "which" (*quod*), it is necessary that that denomination /p. 828/ be both of the same character as the form in question and also intrinsic and inseparable from it, as is clear in the case of action, which comes to be by itself inasmuch as the nature of action is that it come to be, when through it something comes to be, and in the case of quantity which is intrinsically by itself quantified.

But if one relation is really related to another, often that respect [to the other] is of a very different character from the proper character and formal effect of such a relation, and it is extrinsic and accidental to that. Therefore, that relation cannot through itself be so related, but [it is so] rather through another relation. The minor is proven: because the formal character and effect of paternity is to relate to a son. When, however, this [paternity] is said to be similar to another paternity, if it is really related to that, this is a formal effect of a very diverse character, since it tends toward a terminus of a diverse character, and it has a reason of founding that is also of a diverse character. Again, this denomination, "similar," is accidental to paternity. For if there were no other paternity in the world, it would not be denominated as similar, nor would it be related in that way. Therefore, when it is so related, it is related not by itself but by another relation.

---

26 *Summa Theologiae* I, q. 42, a. 1, ad 4; in *Opera omnia*, tomus IV (1888), p. 436b.
27 Cf. *Commentaria*, in I, 42, 1, n. 9; tomus IV, 437b.
28 Ibid.

9. And this is confirmed, for when one relation is said to be really related to another, but not through another relation, either this is understood to be not through another that is distinct either in reality or by reason, and this is evidently proven to be false by the argument that has been made. For what can be a greater distinction of reason than that which is from termini of diverse characters and which is enough that one relation be accidental to the other? Or the meaning is that it is not related by another relation that is really distinct but [by one which is distinct] by reason only, and this is not something special to a relation. For above[29] we said that relations by which absolute things are related are distinguished only by reason from their absolute foundations.

Or if someone contends that an absolute foundation is related by a relation that is real and really distinct, but one relation can be related by a real relation that is, however, not really distinct, first he is supposing something false, and then it is necessary that he give some reason for this difference, which up to now no one has given. For what certain people say: that a relation is the most minute entity and, therefore, that it cannot found another [relation] that is really distinct, is not satisfactory. This is because, first, the relation that is founded is also of the most minute entity, and then, second, because the first relation is now supposed to be founded in the absolute thing. And, therefore, it is not strange that it could found another proportionate [relation], just as also motion or time is of a sufficiently diminished entity and, nevertheless, can found a relation.

10. Therefore, it seems that we must distinguish. For there are certain respects intimately included in relations themselves and inseparable from those relations themselves according to their proper natures. But others are accidental. The first are [ordered] only toward proper termini or toward opposite relations; but the second are toward other termini, which are simply accidental to the being of such a relation.

An example may be in paternity, which, by the very fact that it relates a father to a son, intrinsically and inseparably includes an opposition with sonship, and consequently also a distinction. For a distinction is like something superior that is included in opposition. Opposition, however, is something that is included in correlation. But a relation (*respectus*) of one paternity to another in the feature of being similar is not so included in the proper nature of paternity. And one paternity is an accidental and extrinsic terminus with respect to the other paternity.

---

29 Cf. Section 2, n. 22.

11. Therefore, about the first relations (*respectibus*),[30] what Cajetan says[31] is fitting enough, namely, that although in all of those a same relation is related, it is related not by another relation but by itself, since in its full nature it includes all those. However, about relations of the second kind, I do not see how it can reasonably (*consequenter*) be denied that one relation can be related through another and therefore can in itself found the other. For it does not seem that it can be denied that a relation is also really related in that way, as the arguments that were made prove. Moreover, it cannot be said that in that way it is related through itself, as what we have said against the last opinion argues persuasively.

But from this I further add that just as above I explained St. Thomas' denying that relations are founded on the four last categories, so also can it be explained as regards relations [themselves]. For relations, in line with their proper and intrinsic nature, are not related by a relation which is distinct from themselves, nor do they found such a relation. However, insofar as in some way they participate, or agree with quantity, in unity or multitude, in this way it is not unreasonable that they be related by a relation of similarity, and by others like that, and the bases of the second opinion seem to prove only this.

12. *If One Relation Founds Another, Whether It Is Necessary To Regress to Infinity.*—However, to the argument about a process to infinity,[32] first, it can be answered that there is no great problem admitting it in relations, as we said above in regard to the relations of parts or points. But here it may seem to have some greater difficulty, because between the foundation and the relation there is an /p. 829/ essential (*per se*) order. However, in things that are essentially ordered it does not seem possible to proceed to infinity, as Aristotle teaches in Book 2 [of the *Metaphysics*].[33] One can answer, indeed, that this is true in the case of things that are distinct in reality, but not in the case of those that are distinguished by reason.

Secondly, [the argument] can be answered by denying the process to infinity, because we must stand with that relation that receives the same denomination that the foundation gives and necessarily and intrinsically brings that with itself. So, for example, although paternity is related by similarity, and that similarity is similar to another of the same species, it is not necessary that it be similar by another relation, but by itself, because that denomination is of the same nature, and it brings that nature intrinsically with itself. For it is not possible to relate one paternity to another that is similar without another rela-

---

30 See n. 10, just preceding.
31 Cf. n. 7, this Section.
32 Cf. Section 10, n. 6, above.
33 Cf. *Metaphysics* 2.2.994a1-b31.

tion corresponding to it to which it itself is similar. And this is at most what the examples[34] of action, motion, and the like, prove.

13. But if the objection is pursued to the effect that any relation is capable of another relative denomination of a diverse nature, for a relation of similitude can be dissimilar to another [relation] and *vice versa*, I answer that relations that are founded in the same absolute foundation, since they are only rationally distinguished, can mutually so relate to and denominate themselves. Hence, inasmuch as those denominations of diverse characters are finite, it is not necessary because of them to admit infinite relations or a process to infinity.

But about divine relations[35] the reasoning is different, because excluding the identity of the [divine] essence, in which there is not founded a real relation but rather one of reason, they do not have among themselves a true and real likeness, but rather distinction and dissimilarity, which they [each] include in their proper relations. Therefore, they are not related among themselves by another relation, but by themselves. But this discussion belongs in another place.

About Relations of Identity, Similarity, and Equality.

14. Third, in that difficulty[36] it is asked what is a proper relation of identity, of similarity, and of equality, and whether they can belong to the same thing in diverse respects. To this we must briefly say that a relation of identity is properly essential identity, less than numerical, in order that we may now abstract from specific and all superior [identities], about which [we will speak] soon. This is clear from Aristotle who says that those things are the same whose substance, that is, essence, is one.[37] Therefore, to the argument made there it should be conceded that two qualities, as they are of the same essential species /col. b/, are properly related with a relation of identity. For there is the same nature in them that is in other beings of the same species. Consequently, therefore, it should also be said that a proper relation of similarity (looking at the thing itself, whatever about the use of words) is that which belongs to qualities by reason of intension, but a relation of equality is that which belongs to quantities by reason of actual extension.

Finally (what further explains this matter) it should be admitted that in the same quality the relation of identity that is founded in its essence as such is one thing, but the relation of similarity, founded in a unity of intension, is another, so that this is separable from that because a unity of essence can remain without an intension. Indeed, also conversely, although in respect to

---

34 Cf. n. 9, this Section.
35 Cf. n. 5, this Section.
36 Cf. Section 10, n. 6, above.
37 Cf. *Metaphysics* 5.15.1021a11.

another whiteness one whiteness cannot be similar in intension without also being one in essence, nevertheless, with respect to blackness a whiteness and a blackness [each] as eight degrees can be called similar in their mode or grade of intension, even if they are dissimilar or, rather, diverse in essence. Neither is it a problem for relations of this kind to be multiplied, especially if it is true that things or real modes that are really distinct are not multiplied because of this.

15. And we should think in the same way about relations of equality and specific identity in continuous quantity. For there is the same proportional reasoning as is explained in the stated argument. However, I say in continuous quantity, because in numbers a relation of equality and of specific identity do not seem diverse, because two couples (*binarii*), for example, from their proper essential characters have equality, and it is not possible, not only in reality but also by reason, that the relation of specific identity between them be separated from the relation of equality. And the reason seems to be that discrete quantity does not have another proper essence or species apart from such actual extension, or numerability, and in its case a species of such a kind is not separable from a multitude of such a kind. This is otherwise in continuous quantity, for keeping its proper essential extension it can exist in a greater or lesser size.

Whether a Generic Unity Founds a Real Relation.

16. *It Is Affirmatively Answered.*—Fourthly, it is asked in that argument,[38] whether relations of this first class, which pertain to unity, are founded on specific unity alone, or also /p. 830/ in generic [unity]. And although either side can be easily discussed, as was suggested there, and conjectures could be multiplied against both sides, nevertheless, briefly I think it should be said that not only specific unity, but also generic, suffices for a relation of similarity.

This is the explicit opinion of St. Thomas, [in *Summa Theologiae*], Part 1, Question 28, Article 1, in Reply to Objection 2, where he says: "*The relation which is implied by this word, 'same', is a relation of reason only, if it is taken as simply the same; however, it is otherwise when some things are said to be the same not in number, but in the nature of a genus or a species.*"[39] Antonio Andreas, in [his commentary on] the *Metaphysics*, Book 5, Question 13 [sic], in Reply to Objection 3,[40] also follows this. And the reasons presented within the statement

---

38 Cf. Section 10, n. 7, above.

39 Cf. *Summa Theologiae* I, q. 28, a. 1, ad 2, in *Opera*, tomus IV, p. 319a.

40 For this, cf. [Pseudo] Scotus [aka Antonio Andreas, O.M.], *In XII libros Metaphysicorum Aristotelis expositio*, V, q. 12, in Ioannis Duns Scoti, *Opera omnia* (Lugduni, 1639), tomus iv, pp. 643b, 644b, and 646a. Also, see: *Questiones super xii libros Metaphysicae Aristotelis*, V, q. 14, ad 3 (Venice, 1495), fol. 26rab.

of the question (*argumentandum*)[41] show this in a fairly probable way. Nor does it matter that things that are different in species are without qualification rather called dissimilar than similar. For from this it follows only that a relation of generic similarity, precisely taken, is not, so to speak, as potent for denominating as a specific relation of similarity or dissimilarity. Nevertheless, it does impart its own denomination, that is, of a certain kind of similarity, namely, generic.

17. However, it seems probable enough that these relations of similarity in species or genus are properly diverse only with regard to diverse things, or when each is adequate to its terminus as well as to its proper and formal foundation. So, for example, although two men may be similar in species and genus, it is not necessary that they be related by a double real relation, because in one adequate relation, namely, of specific similarity, both respects are included, because that relation as it exists in reality (*in re*), is not founded solely on an ultimate difference, but it is founded in a particular form that gives a particular specific being. However, the relation by which a man is similar to a horse in the nature of animal is diverse in kind (*specie*) from that by which one man is similar to another. However, that also includes every other relation of similarity that can be imagined between a man and a horse as in the superior degrees included in the nature of an animal. And proportionally in the same way we should philosophize in other instances. And thus there is easily avoided not only an infinity, but also a too great multitude of relations, for they are multiplied only according to the multitude and the formal distinction of termini or of unities.

18. *Whether an Analogical Unity Founds a Categorical Relation.*—But it can be rightly asked: whether a relation of this kind can sometimes be founded on an analogical unity, especially on that /col. b/ which involves one objective concept intrinsically belonging to each of the analogates. For as regards other modes of analogy, it is certain that this does not suffice for a real relation, because [that imagined relation] is not founded upon some proper similarity, but on [one that is] metaphorical, which principally comes about through a comparison by our intellect. But in the first kind of analogy it is not improbable that there can be among the analogates a real relation that is founded upon such a unity, because among the extremes [that is, the analogates] there is some real agreement.[42] Hence, St. Thomas sometimes indicates that the effects of

---

41 See Section 10, n. 7, above.

42 Here we may note the realistic character of the objective concept which intrinsically belongs to a number of real things. While at times, in different contexts, Suárez seems undecided or even vacillating about the mental or extramental status of the objective concept, it should be noted here how he contrasts it with a merely meta-

God are related to God by some real relation of likeness or of image, as can be gathered from [*Summa Theologiae*], Part 1, Question 4, Article 3, in Reply to Objection 4,[43] together with what Cajetan in an acute way notes there.[44] Again [this is indicated] from the same St. Thomas, in Part 1, Question 93, Article 1, in Reply to the Last Objection,[45] and in *De Potentia*, Question 7, Article 6, where he says that there are in creatures various relations to God, insofar as he produces them diverse from himself, although in some ways like to himself.[46] Antonio Andreas, as cited above,[47] also thinks the same.

19. Lastly, in this difficulty[48] there is a question as to whether these relations, as they are properly founded in multitude and have their place among various numbers, are real relations or only denominations from comparisons that our intellect makes. And, indeed, if we note the common way of speaking of Aristotle and other philosophers, there is no doubt that they think in the same manner about these relations as about other real ones that belong to this first class. For denominations of equality or of inequality are taken in the same way from things themselves.

However, if a relation is a thing or a mode that is really (*ex natura rei*) distinct from its foundation, it is difficult to explain such a real relation as founded in two things or in three things. For it cannot be truly one and simple in a totality of two things. For what subject would it be? Neither indeed can it be in one unity rather than in another, since there is no reason for disparity, nor [can it be] in all together, since one accident cannot as a whole be in many subjects at the same time, and in each of them, as is self-evident. This is especially because no unity is double or triple in such way that there can be in it alone the whole relation of double or triple. But neither can it be partly in one subject and partly in another; otherwise, it would not be truly one and simple, but rather composite in the same way as a number.[49] However, it cannot be composed in that way, if a relation is a thing or a distinct mode;

---

phorical term. This has enormous ramifications for analogy and for being itself, both real (actual or possible), or merely intentional (e.g. impossible objects).

43 *Summa Theologiae* I, q. 4, a. 3, ad 4, in *Opera omnia*, tomus IV, p. 54b.

44 Cf. Cajetan, *Commentaria*, in I, 4, 3, n. 5, in S. Thomae, *Opera*, tomus IV, p. 55a.

45 Cf. *Summa Theologiae* I, q. 93, a. 1, ad 3, in *Opera omnia*, tomus V (Romae, 1889), p. 402ab.

46 Cf. *Quaestiones disputatae de potentia Dei*, q. 7, a. 6, ed. viii revisa, P. Bazzi et al. (Taurini: Marietti, 1949), p. 202; ibid., ad 5.

47 Cf. n. 16, this Section.

48 Cf. Section 10, n. 7, above.

49 That is: a number is composed of units.

otherwise, in any unity whatever there would arise a special entity or a mode that, taken essentially (*per se*), would be one relation and would with others compose one [relation] only /p. 831/ "to a certain degree" (*secundum quid*), in that way in which a number is one. But this cannot be, because in no unity, taken essentially, is there a reason or a basis from which such a mode results.

But if a relation is not some mode that is really added to its foundation, it is easily understood that a number, in the way in which it is in things, and according to the imperfect unity that it has, can be compared and related in the way of one extreme to another number as equal or double, or in some other similar way. For the foundation of that relation in particular numbers is nothing other than a discrete quantity itself, as it has a certain unity, or a diversity from another [discrete quantity], and that [first] quantity in reality (*in re*) is the relation itself insofar as it can give a denomination to a subject in an order to a similar or dissimilar terminus.

Of What Kind Are the Relations That Belong to the First Class.

20. In reply to the third difficulty,[50] it must be said that it is not necessary that a relation of this first kind be either really (*realiter*) added to the foundation itself, as something really (*ex natura rei*) distinct from that, or a mere extrinsic denomination from the co-existence of the other extreme. For between these two a medium can be found, namely, that there be an intrinsic denomination that includes the co-existence of another extreme to which it entails a disposition.

However, when it is asked about this disposition, whether it is presupposed intrinsically in the foundation, even when the terminus does not exist (although in that case it does not have the nature of a categorical relation, but of a transcendental one), or whether it is added anew when the terminus is posited, it must be said that it is not presupposed properly under the character of a disposition [toward] or a relation, either categorical or transcendental. For, as was correctly proven in that third difficulty,[51] the foundation of this first class does not essentially (*per se*) include a transcendental disposition [toward]. Therefore, no formal disposition is presupposed intrinsically in such a foundation, and also it is not really and intrinsically added, when a terminus is posited.

21. It must be said, therefore, that this disposition is presupposed fundamentally and quasi-inchoatively by virtue of the foundation, but it is completed by the positing of the terminus. "Is completed," I say, not by an extrinsic addition,

---

50 Cf. Section 10, n. 8, above.
51 Ibid.

but only by the extrinsic positing of the terminus. For the foundation itself is apt of itself to give a relative denomination of this kind, and for this reason it is said to contain a quasi-inchoate relative /col. b/ disposition. In order, however, that it actually give that denomination, it requires an actually existing terminus, and therefore, when the terminus is posited, that denomination is immediately completed, without another intrinsic and real addition. But the relative disposition in the present case is not anything other than this same relative denomination, or the form itself, insofar as it is actually giving that [denomination]. However, what condition is necessary in the foundation, in order that on its part it be apt to give this denomination, we will say in the following Section. And [this suffices] up to now for the first member of that division.[52]

---

52 That is, the first of the three classes of categorical relations.

Section XII.
About the Second Class of Relations
Founded in Potency and Action.

1. Concerning the second class of relations many things are touched on in the fourth difficulty that was stated above.[1] Speaking in general about these relations, it is certain that they are real and categorical. For this is the way that all the Doctors think, and this is the way they explain Aristotle. For if between some extremes all things necessary for a relation of this kind[2] concur, [it will be] especially between these, as can be evident from what has been said and as will be more evident from what will be said. But in particular there are two [questions] that have difficulty here. The first is whether all the relations that Aristotle, for example, numbers in that class are truly real and categorical. The second is what is the proper foundation of such relations.

Whether All Relations of the Second Class Are Real.

2. Concerning the first part, the first objection is surely difficult, which in the fourth difficulty[3] is made against that member that pertains to relations founded in future action, which are said to be: "*between that which is going to do and that which will be done.*" For these are Aristotle's words.[4] But the objection that is made, as I see it, concludes that such a relation cannot be real, for lack of a terminus and of a proximate required condition. Hence, I think it must be said that not all the examples that Aristotle has posited there are in rigor about real and categorical relations. For he himself does not in that place intend to give a proper and rigorous coordination of the category, "toward something," but rather to explain all modes of relatives and to reduce them to certain heads, whether they are proper real relatives or only imitate those, according to our /p. 832/ way of speaking.

And this can be confirmed. For in the same place he says that to this second class certain relatives belong, which are said according to a privation of potency, for instance, the impossible,[5] and similar things. However, it is clear

---

1 Cf. Section 10, n. 9, above.

2 That is, one which is real and categorical.

3 Ibid.

4 Cf. *Metaphysics* 5.15.1021a23.

5 This is worth noting, especially in view of later debate among 17th century Jesuits; on this, cf. my article: "Another God, Chimerae, Goat-Stags, and Man-Lions: A Seventeenth-Century Debate about Impossible Objects," *The Review of Metaphysics*, XLVIII (1995), pp. 771-808.

that these are not true real relatives, since the privation of a potency is not a real foundation. Therefore, they are put in this class only through a certain reduction. Accordingly, I think the same should be said about relations that are said to be founded in future action.

3. But about a relation that has arisen from a past action, which lacks an actually existing terminus, we must think otherwise. For that relation is real and categorical, and it endures as long as the effect and the cause actually exist, as the common opinion holds. For in that case there are present real extremes that are apt to be able to have between them a real order[6] (for we are treating now of created causes) and already there has been placed in reality all things that are necessary for that order or relation, as will become evident in solving the proposed difficulty.

4. In this, first of all, the question is how a relation that remains can be founded in a past action, which now does not exist. It must be said that it is not founded in that as in a proper foundation in which it exists or from which it has its entity, but which is the reason of founding such a relation, or, as we said above,[7] the condition required in order that such a relation result. However, it is not such that the relation depends on it as if in becoming and in being, and, therefore, it is not strange that when the action has been completed the relation may remain. But that condition is required, not only because through it the necessary terminus for such a relation is posited as regards its absolute entity only. For it could be posited in reality (*in rerum natura*) through another action which would not have been enough in order that the said relation would arise. It is, therefore, necessary because through it a cause has exercised influence unto such an effect. From this influence [the cause] remains ordered to that effect and respectively denominated from the relation that arises, or from its own power of acting insofar as in a special way it exercised influence into that effect.

About the Proximate Foundation of Paternity.

5. Hence it is usually debated in what principle such a relation inheres proximately and with what it is identified: whether, that is, it exists in proximate and accidental or in principal and substantial potency. For many think it is in a proximate principle, or in the potency of generating, which can become probable by evident arguments. Others, /col. b/ however, think a principal and substantial principle identifies this relation with itself. But perhaps it is true

---

6 Note here that for Suárez reality is first found at the level of an aptitude for existing; cf. DM 3, 2, n. 4, vol. 25, p. 108b. On this see my article: "Suárez and the Reality of the Possibles, *The Modern Schoolman*, 46 (1967), pp. 29–40.

7 Cf. Section 7, n. 12, above.

that on each principle there follows a relation that is fitted to that [principle], because the argument is equal with regard to both. For a relation of potency, taken absolutely and abstracting from act, exists in both. Therefore, also in each of them, as it is under its own act, some relation follows.

However, I think that a proper relation of paternity is that which proximately is in the substance itself by means of a principal principle. For in a begotten supposit, the relation of sonship without doubt immediately affects the substance itself, or even the supposit itself, as many wish, about which I have treated at length in the Second Tome of [my commentary on] the Third Part.[8] Therefore, since these relations correspond proportionately to themselves, the relation of paternity also proximately affects a substantial principle, and it is identified with that.

Again, because with every really distinct accident excluded, even if by the [absolute] power of God there remains [both] a substantial supposit that has generated[9] and [also] that which has been generated,[10] the relation of paternity endures (otherwise, there would then be no reason for positing that [relation]) since that man [who has generated] truly and properly will be called a father.[11] That, therefore, is a sign that this relation is intimately within the substance itself. Finally, this is most of all in agreement with its mode of denominating; for it denominates only that supposit which is principally acting.

6. *One Who Has Generated, If He Be Deprived of his Son, Does Not Remain a Father.* However, this relation of paternity will not remain after the son has died, as is falsely assumed in that fourth difficulty.[12] Neither truly and properly will he who has lost his sons [sic] be said to be, but rather to have been a father, which is true not only in philosophical rigor, but also seems to be observed in common language. Wherefore, it is not the same to be a father as to have generated. For the latter is an extrinsic denomination from a past action, and therefore it endures, even if the one generated is dead, but the former is a relative denomination, which includes the co-existence of the extremes.

---

8 For this, see Suárez, *Commentaria ac disputationes in tertiam partem D. Thomae, scilicet, opus de Incarnatione*, d. 49, s. 2, nn. 3-4, in *Opera omnia*, vol. 18, pp. 484b-485a; ibid., nn. 7-8, p. 486a; ibid., s. 3, n. 5, p. 502b; ibid., n. 32, p. 512a.

9 That is to say, a father.

10 That is to say, a son.

11 That is to say he will, without any addition, have the relation of paternity.

12 Cf. Section 10, n. 9, above.

Whether the Relation of an Agent Inheres in That [Agent].

7. From this it is *a fortiori* evident (which is further touched on in that fourth difficulty[13]) that the relation of one actually acting and generating is also real. For if this is true after a past action, why not more so while the action is present and enduring?

But two questions can be asked here. One is whether this relation is intrinsically inhering in the agent himself,[14] or only extrinsically denominating [him], just as the action itself.[15] For it seems /p. 833/ this latter is enough for a real relation, and is more in line with the denomination of such a relation. For action itself is real and really denominates an agent, and in this very denomination there is included a certain transcendental disposition toward an effect, for action as action relates to (*respicit*) a terminus, as we shall say below.[16] Therefore, similarly, a relation could be real, even though it denominates the agent himself, only extrinsically and by the medium of an action, as related to a terminus or to his effect.

8. Nevertheless, it must be said that a proper relation, which through itself relates an agent or a generating cause, from the instant in which he actually generates, is intrinsic and immediately inhering in him. First, indeed, because if, after a past action, there remains in an agent cause, a relation that is intrinsically adhering to him, much more will such a relation result and inhere also while the action itself is enduring. Then, because, as St. Thomas teaches, in *Contra Gentiles*, Book 2, Chapter 13, although in other forms extrinsic denominations are found, "*by relation,*" says St. Thomas, "*it is not found that something is denominated as though externally existing, but rather as inhering.*" Hence, he adds: "*Someone is denominated a father, only from a paternity that exists in him.*"[17] The reason for this seems to be that what extrinsically denominates is related to that which it denominates rather than relates that. And in this way action is related to an agent rather than it relates that [agent], even though it is the occasion or the condition in order that a relation result in the agent. Therefore, although it is true that action itself is related to a terminus, it does

---

13 Ibid.

14 While the Latin would admit the translation of "itself" or "himself" I prefer "himself," here and in what follows, in order to keep a better focus on the antecedents of both intensive and reflexive pronouns.

15 On the extrinsic denomination involved in action, cf. my article, "*Prolegomena*' to a Study of Extrinsic Denomination in the Work of Francis Suarez, S.J.," *Vivarium*, xxii (1984), pp. 121-60, esp. pp. 138-9.

16 Cf. *DM* 48, 2, nn. 16-19, vol. 26, pp. 878-9.

17 Cf. S. Thomae Aquinatis, *Summa contra Gentiles*, II, c. 13, in *Opera omnia*, tomus xiii (Romae: R. Garrone, 1918), p. 293a.

not, nevertheless, properly relate the supposit itself that is acting, because it does not denominate that as that in which it is, but as that from which it is. And so it can only be said that it flows from the agent with respect to the terminus. But that is only remotely a respect of the agent himself, as will be more clear from the following question.

Is a Relation the Same in an Agent While an Action Endures and When That [Action] Has Been Completed?

9. *An Affirmative Reply.*—But again it can be asked[18] whether this relation of an actual or a present agent is the same both in species and in number with the relation of a past agent, for example, with paternity. For certain people think they are diverse, and Aristotle seems to favor that, when he says that these relations are varied according to times.[19] And this can be founded in a diverse way of denominating. For one denominates the agent as actual while the other denominates him as one who has acted. Therefore, it seems that one relation endures only /col. b/ as long as the action [endures] and at its ceasing another arises.

However, I think, in a father, for example, (and the same is true in similar cases) it is more truly the numerically same relation that arises in the very moment in which he generates and remains for as long as such a father endures with a son. For if we argue theologically, who will say that the Most Blessed Virgin, in the first instant in which she conceived Christ, had one relation of mother, and then immediately lost that and acquired another?

Moreover, the action of generating is the reason or the condition that, when posited, a relation of paternity results; therefore, I ask whether it is such a reason or condition that the relation of paternity depends on it in becoming and in being conserved, or not? For if it does not depend in being conserved, then when the action of generating is over the same paternity will remain, because there is no reason that it be varied. For the cessation of the action, since it is a certain privation, is not a sufficient reason for a new real relation to result. Neither can a past action be the reason for such a new relation, because that action, when it existed, already had its proportionate relation, while as past it adds only the mentioned privation. Therefore, it is better and more easily said that that relation is one and the same, and in fact it remains afterwards, because it does not depend in being conserved upon the action as such, but on a foundation and a terminus, which were explained in the preceding paragraph. Therefore, paternity as such includes neither a denomination of past

---

18 This is the second question which was indicated in n. 7, this Section.
19 Cf. *Metaphysics* 5.15.1021a21.

nor of present, but it simply refers to him who has being from that man who is denominated a father, abstracting from the fact that the action, through which he has that being, exists or does not exist. For these denominations, as including these temporal respects, are rather from that action itself as present or as past.

About the Relation of an Agent in Potency.

10. Lastly, in this same fourth difficulty,[20] it is asked that we explain of what kind is the relation of an agent in potency, about which we have already said that it cannot be real and categorical in an order to a merely possible effect as such, but in an order to some real passive, and actually existing, potency, because it cannot have any other real terminus. However, in this way all things necessary for a real relation are present.

But some say that this relation does not belong to this second class of relations, but rather to the first, since it is not founded /p. 834/ in action, but precisely in the proportion that exists between two faculties, so that one can act upon the other and the other can be acted upon (*pati*) by the one, which proportion is a kind of unity and, therefore, seems to belong to the first reason of founding.

11. But this opinion is not in agreement with Aristotle, who in the case of this second member never said that relations founded in action belong to it, but rather at the beginning of the chapter said: *"Other things"* (i.e, are called "toward something") *"like able to heat to the heatable, able to cut to the cuttable, and in one word the active to the passive,"*[21] in which he has made no mention of action and passion but of potencies only. But afterwards he has joined them both together, saying: *"Active and passive are said from active and passive potency and the actions of potencies."*[22]

Moreover, a relation that is of an agent potency to a patient is not founded in unity, but in a power to act. For that unity that is the reason of founding in the first class consists in some real and formal agreement between those things that are said to be similar or the same. But between an agent potency and a patient such unity and agreement is not present, except perhaps inasmuch as

---

20 Cf. Section 10, n. 9.

21 Cf. τὰ δ' ὡς τὸ θερμαντικὸν πρὸς τὸ θερμαντὸν καὶ τὸ τμητικὸν πρὸς τὸ τμητόν, καὶ ὅλως τὸ ποιητικὸν πρὸς τὸ παθητικόν. ...," *Metaphysics* 5.15.1020b28-30. Here Suárez follows the Latin translation of Fonseca: *In Metaphys.* V, c. 15, tomus II, col. 784.

22 Cf. "τὰ δὲ ποιητικὰ καὶ παθητικὰ κατὰ δύναμιν ποιητικὴν καὶ παθητικὴν καὶ ἐνεργείας τὰς τῶν δυνάμεων, ...," ibid., 1021a14-16. Again, Suárez here reproduces the Latin of Fonseca: *In Metaphys.* V, c. 15, tomus II, col. 788.

they agree in the generic character of potency, under which character they are not related with a proper relation of an agent potency to a patient, but by a relation of similarity with respect to the generic character. Therefore, that proportion is not a true unity. But if by analogy it is so called, it is of a far different character than the unity which founds the first class of relatives. Therefore, this relation belongs not to the first but to the second class, and it differs from the other which was explained above,[23] because this one follows the character of a potency taken precisely, while that one [follows that character] insofar as it is under act. Hence, this is terminated at a passive potency as such, but that [is terminated] at an effect.

12. *Which Potencies Are Related by a Real Relation That Is Founded upon Action or Passion.*—But a further question is whether this relation is found in every active and passive power, whether this is of a proper potency of the category of quality[24] or is of every other category or of a transcendental character. And, certainly, with regard to essentially and immediately (*per se primo*) ordered categorical potencies, in order that one act upon another or that the other be acted upon by the one, it is not hard to understand that they are most apt for founding a relation between themselves, as long as they are in reality (*in re ipsa*) distinct, because by the very fact that they exist they mutually have respect to one another, by reason of a transcendental order that they have between /col. b/ themselves, by reason (I say) of that as a proximate foundation.

However, I have said, "as long as they are in reality distinct," since a potency that is simultaneously active on itself and passive from itself, even if it is a proper and categorical potency, and has both features essentially and immediately from its constitution, cannot have following them a real relation, in default of the distinction that is necessary for this relation. Hence, neither does such a potency have those features through transcendental dispositions of the same thing to itself, but through a certain eminent disposition to its own act, which it respects under both features. But if such a potency, as active, requires another co-principle in order to act on itself, as the intellect needs a species,[25] then according to that [co-principle] it could be really related to itself alone, in the character of active to passive, not, however, by reason of its own proper and intrinsic activity, on account of the reason mentioned regarding identity.

---

23 Cf. Section 10, n. 2.

24 For potency as the second species of the category of quality, cf. *Categories* 8.9 1 14-27.

25 That is a *species intelligibilis*, which originates from the object of intellection. On six tasks of the intelligible species as a co-principle of intellection; cf. Suárez, *De Divina Substantia*, II, c. 12 ("Whether God is seen through a created species" [*An videatur Deus per speciem creatam*]), nn. 5-13, in *Opera*, vol. 1, pp. 87-9.

However, where a sufficient distinction is present, and the coordination of the potencies is intrinsic and natural, there is no doubt that all things necessary for a real categorical relation (*respectum*) are in concurrence, if the extremes co-exist.

13. *What kind of Active or Passive Power can be related by a Relation of the Second Class.*—But it must be further added that this relation should not be restricted to this kind of potency, but it is present among all created things (for about God I will speak below[26]) that, for whatever reason, have a real power to act and to suffer[27] among themselves. This is evident, both from the general way in which Aristotle speaks, and also from his examples, which also include other kinds of potencies, and also again from the common opinion of interpreters[28] and philosophers.

Finally, also [it is evident] because in order that a categorical relation be present, it is not always necessary that a transcendental relation be supposed in its foundation, as was said in the solution of the third difficulty. Therefore, it is enough in the case proposed that one power (*virtus*) be of the same order with another power (*potentia*), and that by its nature it have a force of acting, which is to have as it were a certain physical dominion over that, in order that from this there can arise a categorical respect or a relative denomination.

14. And from this finally it is understood that the term, "potency," must not in this second foundation be taken strictly, as it is distinguished from "habit." For a habit also, inasmuch as it is a power to perform its acts, is by Aristotle usually included under the name of an active potency,[29] as has been noted often above,[30] and, as such, it can /p. 835/ be the foundation of a real relation, not indeed, to an object,[31] for this pertains to the third class, but either to an act which it effects or to the potency into which it can effect—which feature (*ratio*) pertains to this second class, as is clear by a parity of reasoning (*ratio*) from what has been said.

---

26 Cf. Section 15, nn. 15-22, below.

27 Or, "be acted upon."

28 That is, principally, commentators on Aristotle.

29 Actually, it is customary for Aristotle to distinguish between habit and potency; cf. e.g. *Topics* 4.5.125b20; *Categories* 8.8b26-9a27. For the closest text which I have found for an identification of habit and potency, with which identification Suárez himself disagrees, cf. *Metaphysics* 5.12.1019a26-28.

30 Cf. *DM* 42, 1, n. 3, vol. 25, p. 608. For Suárez's detailed refutation of this, cf. ibid., 4, nn. 7-14, pp. 617-619.

31 For the meaning of "object" here, cf. Section 13, n. 9, and Section 14, nn. 3, 4, and 6, below.

Section XIII.
About the Third Class of Relation
Founded in the Character of Measure.

1. It remains that we explain what is asked in the fifth difficulty,[1] namely, how relations of the third class are said to be founded in the character of measure. For almost all authors speak in this way and they take it from Aristotle in this place.[2]

A Difficulty Is Proposed about the Mind of the Philosopher.

2. If, however, Aristotle is read carefully, he does not seem to be saying that these relations are founded on the character of measure, but among other examples by which he explains this class (*modum*) one is of measurable to measure. For his words are: "*Others like measurable to measure, and knowable (scibile) to knowledge, and sensible to sense,*"[3] where he does not state any foundation for these relations, but only, after he has used those three examples, does he propose this third class of relation. Neither can it be said that in those first words, "*like measurable to measure,*" he is explaining the common character of these relations while he is using the other items as examples and species of this class. For this cannot be fitted to the context.

This is first because Aristotle did not say, "*like knowable to knowledge,*" but [said] only copulatively, "*and knowable to knowledge.*" Also, second, because if he had used these latter words for an example of the prior [relations],[4] he should not have said, "*like knowable to knowledge,*" but rather, "*like knowledge to knowable.*" But he did not say that, but (something that should be carefully considered) he does say that the measurable to the measure, the knowable to knowledge, and the sensible to sense, are [all] related in the same way. However, the knowable is not related to knowledge as is the measurable to the measure.

---

1 Cf. Section 10, n. 10, above.

2 That is, *Metaphysics* 5.15. On this third class of relation, with particular reference to knowledge, in Aristotle and St. Thomas, cf. Horst Seidl, "Bemerkungen zu Erkenntnis al Massverhältnis bei Aristoteles und Thomas von Aquin," in *Mensura, Mass, Zahl, Zahlensymbolik im Mittelalter; Miscellanea Mediaevalia*, Band 16/1, herausgegeben von Albert Zimmermann (Berlin/New York: Walter de Gruyter, 1983), pp. 32-42.

3 Cf. "τὰ δ᾽ ὡς τὸ μετρητὸν πρὸς τὸ μέτρον καὶ ἐπιστητὸν πρὸς ἐπιστήμην καὶ αἰσθητὸν πρὸς αἴσθησιν." *Metaphysics* 5.15.1020b30-32. Here, Suárez again follows the Latin of Fonseca: *In Metaphys.* V, c. 15, tomus II, col. 784.

4 That is of measurable to measure.

For in the way in which the character of measure can be found between these, knowledge is rather measured by the knowable, than *vice versa*.

Add to this, that in this third class Aristotle seems to make no mention of the relations of knowledge to the knowable, or of sense to the sensible, but only of the opposite relations (so to speak), namely, of the knowable to knowledge, and of the sensible to sense, to which he adds the relation of measurable to /col. b/ the measure as similar to those. Therefore, he has not placed the common character of this third class in its being founded on the character of a measure, but in some other character that is common to the measurable, the knowable, and other things of this kind.

3. All of this can be confirmed from the way in which Aristotle afterwards explains this third class of relations. For he posits no other common character except that other relatives are called relative through the relations that they have in themselves, but these alone receive the denomination of relative because other things are said to be toward them, and he repeats the same examples, namely, measurable, knowable, intelligible, although he explains only this last, saying: *"For also the intelligible signifies that the intellect is occupied with it."*[5] Hence, interpreting this text of Aristotle in a simple way, he does not seem to posit in this third class any new real relation that is intrinsically within and relates its subject, but only certain relative denominations, taken from relations that exist in opposite extremes. Therefore, although knowledge to the knowable, and the knowable to knowledge, are said relatively, there belongs to this third class of relatives, according to the mind of Aristotle so explained, only the relation or denomination of the knowable itself, howsoever that may be. However, the relation of knowledge to a knowable [object] seems not to be located by Aristotle in this third class for the reason that knowledge is not said [to be] in a relative way from the fact that something else is related to it, but rather because in itself it truly has a respect toward something else. However, Aristotle puts in the third class only those things that are called relative because other things are related to them.

4. But if you ask: according to this exposition, to which class of relation does the relation of knowledge to the knowable, and of sense to the sensible, etc., belong, the answer could be that that is the relation of a certain effect to its cause in some genus, and thus it is reduced to the second class, as we will directly say[6] in a similar case, when we are solving the sixth difficulty.[7] Or, if

5 Cf. "τὸ τε γὰρ διανοητὸν σημαίνει ὅτι ἔστιν αὐτοῦ διάνοια, ..." *Metaphysics* 5.15.1021a31. Again, the Latin here is that of Fonseca: *In Metaphys.* V, c. 15, tomus II, col. 792.

6 Cf. Section 14, n. 6, below.

7 Cf. Section 10, n. 11, above.

someone were of a mind to reduce every relation that is founded in a proportion to the first class, he could say that the relation of knowledge belongs to that [class]. For it consists in a certain adaptation and proportion to its object.

5. But still objection can be made. For, according to this interpretation, a relation between the measure and the measurable will be intrinsic and real in the measure; but in the measurable it will only be one of reason, or by denomination, toward the measure itself, which is against the common opinion /p. 836/ and against reason. For that which is measured is inferior and thus it is itself ordered to the measure, rather than *vice versa*. This is also clear by induction. For science (*scientia*[8]) is measured by a scientific object (*scibili*) and, therefore, the relation is in the science itself, and cognition is measured in truth by an object, and a creature [is measured] in its being or truth of being from a divine idea, and all these relations are in those things themselves that are measured.

I answer that Aristotle makes the same judgment about the measurable as about the scientifically knowable (*scibili*) and the intelligible; and about all he says that they are said "toward something," *because something other is said toward them.*[9] However, Aristotle seems to be speaking about the measurable by an extrinsic and superadded measure, not by an intrinsic adaptation or proportion, such as is found in the examples that are adduced to the contrary. For that intrinsic commensuration consists only in a certain similarity or adaptation (so to speak), or in a dependence or specification, and in this way it is reduced to the first or the second class of relations. In this way also an image is commensurate with an exemplar by reason of similarity and an effect [is commensurate] to a cause, by reason of dependence or also similarity. But extrinsically a thing is said to be measurable, just as also knowable, or visible, because its quantity can be manifested through the application of an extrinsic measure. And in this way, Aristotle says that a thing is said to be measurable by the relation of something else to itself, because, that is, its quantity can become known through a measure.

6. Neither does it matter whether the measure is quasi-natural or from human institution. For in both ways a thing is formally measurable only through an extrinsic potency and denomination, even though the foundation, or the proportion, which is presupposed for such measurability, is often something intrinsic, and it can be the foundation of some real relation of another kind. So also the visible presupposes some real and intrinsic foundation in a visible

---

8 Here I am translating "scientia" as "science" in order to allow a distinction from "cognition" which immediately follows.

9 Cf. "τὸ δὲ μετρητὸν καὶ τὸ ἐπιστητὸν καὶ τὸ διανοητὸν τῷ ἄλλο πρὸς αὐτὸ λέγεσθαι πρὸς τι λέγονται." *Metaphysics* 5.15.1021a30. For the Latin, cf. Fonseca: *In Metaphys.* V, c. 15, tomus II, col. 792.

object, and indeed the active force of the species, by reason of which [force] it is really related to sight by a relation belonging to the second class. And also in quantitative measures, which are designated through human institution, there is presupposed some foundation of extension and of some real proportion, which has some true relation joined to it, belonging however to the first class, because it is not other than the relation of equality or inequality. So, therefore, that a thing is formally measurable, entails only the relation of something else to it, insofar as by the application of a measure its quantity can /col. b/ become known, even though fundamentally something intrinsic is supposed in the measurable thing.

7. Finally, one can object that from the stated exposition it follows that a certain member from those three that were enumerated by Aristotle does not contain real relations but only ones of reason, and, therefore, they are without cause included among those things which are truly "toward something." The consequence is clear, because according to the stated exposition, in the third class there are only those relations that belong to the relatives not by the fact that they themselves are related, but by the fact that other things are related to them. However, those relations are of reason only.

The answer is that (whatever may be the case about these relations of reason, whether such are necessary in extremes of this kind, which we will see below[10]) Aristotle is not here treating of these relations, but about the various modes in which things are denominated *relative* from things themselves. Accordingly, he distinguishes two general modes, namely, that certain things are denominated because they themselves are related, but others [are so denominated] because other things are related to them. And again, he divides the first member[11] from the double foundation of quantity or unity and of potency, and in this way the three modes of relatives are constituted. And thus it happens that, according to this interpretation, those three modes of relatives are not three classes of real relatives.[12] For the third mode does not add a new class of relation, but it only states a special mode of denomination that redounds from some relations of other classes toward their termini.

Resolution.

8. This whole opinion and the interpretation of this text has been proposed only for the sake of debate (*disputatio*),[13] since in Aristotle's text, looked at

---

10 Cf. *DM* 54, 6, n. 4, vol. 26, p. 1040.

11 That is, things denominated relative because they themselves are related.

12 Here, Rábade *et al.* read "relations"

13 Note that there is nothing acrimonious about the word "disputatio" as Suárez is using it here. It simply signifies something in the nature of classroom discussion or

simply, it seems to have much basis, and relying on reason, it could probably be defended. Nevertheless, we still do not wish to abandon the common opinion, which holds that this third mode of relatives constitutes a third class of real relations that are really existing in one extreme, and they essentially and immediately (*per se primo*) relate that [extreme] to the other, which is not in turn related by a proper real relation that it has in itself, but only terminates the relation of the first (*alterius*), and is denominated from this. For that there are some relations of this kind is both evident by induction in the case of knowledge and the knowable, and the like, and also will be treated more extensively in a following Section.[14]

But that these constitute a class that is diverse from the rest, and that they require a foundation of a different kind, seems directly (*per se*) probable from the fact /p. 837/ that they have a very diverse way of relation (*habitudo*). For just as from effects we know causes, so we can understand that a foundation from which an intrinsic relation arises in both extremes is of a diverse nature from that which can found a relation in only one extreme.

Finally, this foundation is called measure and the measurable, because these relations are most of all founded in certain things that have their perfection commensurate with other things and as such are related to those same things, even if there is not in them a similar or proportionate foundation of a corresponding relation.

9. From this the solution to the fifth difficulty[15] is easily clear, because in this instance measure is not taken as it entails a disposition to our knowledge, that is, insofar as it is a medium which we can use in order to know the quantity of something else, either a mass or a perfection, in the way that we have said above that the character of measure does not add any real nature (*rationem*)[16] to things. But measure is taken for a real terminus or an object, to which some thing expresses a disposition insofar as it is adapted or is commensurate with it, in the way that knowledge is compared to the knowable, and judgment to a thing known, and it is the same regarding other things. Therefore, this commensuration is nothing real besides a transcendental disposition of such things to their objects, but that is a sufficient foundation for a categorical relation. Nor does it matter that the terminus or the object that is said to have the character of a measure, can sometimes not exist. For then a categorical relation will not arise. But we say only that in such a thing there is sufficient foundation for a

---

debate.

14 See Section 15, below.

15 Cf. Section 10, n. 10, above.

16 Here Rábade *et al.* translate "rationem" as "relación." Even if I were to agree with the sense of that, I cannot find it in the Latin of any edition that I have seen.

special relation, which will be real, if the extremes exist and if whatever else is necessary concurs.

Section XIV.
Is the Stated Division Sufficient and Does It Include All Relations?

1. This is the second principal doubt proposed above in regard to this division, in which we must explain what was asked in the sixth difficulty raised in Section 10:[1] how all real relations are reduced to these three modes.

About the Relation of Appetite to the Appetible And of Love to the Lovable.

2. But first of all it was asked of what sort is the relation of appetite to the appetible and /col. b/ of love to the lovable. For although Aristotle has given examples in the cases of sense and intellect, he has said nothing about appetite and love. St. Thomas, however, touching on this point in [his *Sentences* commentary], Book 1, Distinction 30, Article 3, in reply to Objection 3, says that the nature of the relations of knowledge to the knowable and of love to the beloved is diverse.[2] *"For"* (he says) *"the former is real in only one extreme, but the latter [is real] in both."*[3] And he gives the reason: because the former has a foundation in knowledge, but not in the knowable, by the fact that that relation is founded in the apprehension of the thing according to the spiritual being that it has in the knower, not in the thing known. But the relation of love is founded upon the appetite of the good. The good, however, is not only in the soul but also in things, [according to] *Metaphysics*, Book 7 [sic], Text 8,[4] and thus this relation has a real foundation in both extremes and, therefore, the relation also is real in both. In this opinion, St. Thomas has followed Avicenna, in Book 3 of his *Metaphysics*, Chapter 10.[5]

3. However, St. Thomas does not explain in which of the members posited by Aristotle this foundation of the relation of love to its object, and *vice versa*, should be placed. For it cannot be placed in this third class, because about this whole class Aristotle universally says its relation is only in one extreme, while the other [extreme] is said in a relative way only because something else is related

1 See Section 10, n. 11, above.
2 Cf. S. Thomae Aquinatis, *Scriptum in lib. Sent.*, I, d. 30, q. 1, a. 3, ad 3, ed. Mandonnet, tomus I, pp. 708-709.
3 I cannot find these exact words in the text of St. Thomas. Yet, Suárez here, and in the rest of this paragraph, is accurately reporting Thomas's opinion.
4 Cf. *Metaphysics* 6.4.1027b26-7.
5 Cf. *Avicenna Latinus: Liber de philosophia prima sive scientia divina, I-IV*, Tr. 3, c. 10, éd. S. Van Riet (1977), p. 175, ll. 51-55.

to it. Neither, again, could it belong to the second class, because an object is not related (*comparatur*) to love or to an appetite, as a passive potency, nor as the effect of some action, but only as an object or a subject matter (*materia circa quam*), in which it is similar to knowable and sensible objects. Perhaps, therefore, it will be said to be reduced to the first mode, because love is founded upon some agreement and proportion. However, as I said above,[6] while treating of active and passive potency, that is not the way of agreement or of unity that founds the first class of relations. Then, also, the same manner of proportion is found between knowledge or sensation and an object—indeed much more, insofar as knowledge is said to come about through a kind of assimilation.

4. Moreover, it is not apparent why knowledge or sensation are said to be measured from an object, and not also love. For the perfection of love is not less measured from an object, in a certain way for an even greater reason, since love tends toward things as they are in themselves. Nor is it enough to say that the foundation of this third class is the measure of truth, because this is not an adequate foundation, since in sensation there is not a formal truth of cognition. Nor is the intellect /p. 838/ itself, insofar as it is a potency, measured with regard to truth by an intelligible object, but insofar as it is an entitative perfection. Then, if the measure of truth is a sufficient foundation, why not the measure of the honesty or the goodness of love? Therefore, I see no sufficient reason why the relation of love should not be placed in this third class, nor why it should be denied that, according to this class of foundation and relation, there is among all those that have a relation (*habitudo*) to objects and are specified by those [objects] a special agreement by reason of which they constitute a subalternate kind of relations, with the presupposition that it is said of certain ones, namely, sensation, understanding, and knowledge.

5. About the relation of the lovable or the loved, although Avicenna's opinion is probable, nevertheless, the opposite [opinion] seems more conformed to the doctrine of Aristotle. First, because either it will be necessary to exclude the relation of love from this third class, which is contrary to what has been said, or to admit in that class mutual relations, which is contrary to Aristotle. Second, because the difference set up between knowledge and love is not satisfactory. For if a knowable and a lovable object are compared with respect to foundations (so to speak), each is something intrinsic and real in the object itself. For just as a thing is good in itself, so also it is, according to its being, true and apt to be understood. For, in this way, Aristotle has said, in *Metaphysics*, Book, 2, Text 4, "*Each thing is true and intelligible insofar as it is being.*" And

6 Cf. Section 12, nn. 10-11, above.
7 Cf. "ὥσθ' ἕκαστον ὡς ἔχει τοῦ εἶναι, οὕτω καὶ τῆς ἀληθείας." *Metaphysics* 2.1.993b 30-31. While Suárez's version may catch Aristotle's intent, it is not exact.

in *Metaphysics*, Book 9, Chapter 7, [sic] he has said that act is more knowable than potency.[8] Indeed, these remarks can be true of intelligibility only insofar as it is founded in things themselves.

However, if sometimes the reason for apprehending a knowable object can be extrinsic, also the reason for loving is often extrinsic to the object itself, as is evident in the love of a means on account of an extrinsic end—therefore, in regard to both there is the same proportion. But if we are talking about the knowable and the appetible, or about the known and the loved, insofar as they are such, both are completed through an extrinsic denomination from a potency or an act, which can easily be evident from what we have said above, in the Tenth Disputation, about goodness.[9]

Finally, if we consider transcendental relations (*habitudines*), neither object as it really is in itself entails a transcendental relation to potencies or acts of understanding or loving, but, contrariwise, only the potencies or the acts entail relations to their objects. Thus we should speak of them with the same proportion. Therefore, just as /col. b/ the knowable is said to be related only because something else is related to it, so also is the lovable.

Whether between Every Effect and Cause There Is a Relation of Measure.

6. Therefore, according to this opinion, which seems more probable, it must be said to the sixth difficulty[10] that those relations that pertain to acts, habits, and potencies of desiring (*appetendi*) with respect to objects belong to this

---

Here, he is not following Fonseca whose translation reads: "As each thing is, so also it is true." (... ut unumquodque est, ita etiam verum est.), *In Metaphys*. II, c. 1, tomus II, col. 386.

8 Cf. *Metaphysics* 9.8.1049b16-17.

9 In Disputation 10, Suárez treats of goodness, like truth, as a property of being. There is the added nuance that in goodness a double extrinsic denomination is involved, since beings, in order to be good, must be true. But, like truth, the property of goodness does not consist only in an extrinsic denomination. Primarily, what goodness signifies is the intrinsic perfection of being, and what it further denominates is a certain "suitability" (*convenientia*) or "appetibility" (*appetibilitas*) in a being, either for itself or to another. By the identification of being and goodness *in re*, the reality of goodness is secured: by the connotation of suitability or appetibility the distinction of goodness and being *in ratione* is preserved. For some of this, cf. *DM* 10, 1, n. 14, vol. 25, p. 333; *ibid.*, n. 20, p. 335; ibid. 3, n. 10, pp. 349-50; also *DM* 3, 2, n. 9, pp. 109-110; *ibid.*, n. 14, p. 111; and *DM* 8, prol., p. 274. Again, on all of this, cf. Rolf Darge, *Suárez' transzendentale Seinsauslegung* ..., esp. pp. 313-85.

10 Cf. Section 10, n. 11, above.

third class, which can be founded not only in the measure of truth, but also of perfection, or in the commensuration and proportion of some thing to an object.

However, to the reply that is made there,[11] that all effects could be located in this class, insofar as they can be measured through their principles or causes, it can first be answered by conceding the consequence, if in those things the character of measure and measured is precisely considered, even if otherwise they are related by a relation of dependence belonging to the second class, or of similarity belonging to the first. For it is not unreasonable that between two things under diverse aspects diverse relations arise, which everyone seems to say especially about the relation of something exemplified to an exemplar.

Nevertheless, because besides the dependence of an effect on a cause, or the similarity between them, I think that the character of measure does not add any real relation, but rather a denomination from an order to cognition, therefore, I do not think that there can be in that case a special real relation that is distinct from that which is founded in causality, or dependence, or similarity. And therefore a second answer lies in denying the consequence. For in this third class there are located only relations of certain things that have a peculiar mode of specification from a tendency, and a quasi-commensuration, to another, as to an object, or a terminus, or an intrinsic end to which they are essentially, immediately, and intrinsically ordered, as they are potencies, habits, acts, and the like. For that objective termination, as such, is not some proper similarity, as is self-evident, and also it is not a proper causality, as we mentioned above, in Disputation 12, Section 3, [Paragraph] Number 17;[12] therefore, relations which are founded on this commensuration with an object do not belong to the second class of relations. Conversely, the commensuration or proportion that is between an efficient cause and its effect belongs to this third class, because it is either causality or effective dependence alone, or it is /p. 839/ only a similarity that can be present between a cause and an effect.

About the Relation of Union.

7. To the second part of that [sixth] difficulty,[13] about the relation of union, and similar cases, it is possible to answer in two ways. First, it can be said that this relation and similar ones belong to the first class of these relatives, inasmuch as a union is in fact a kind of unity, or it is like a way to unity. Indeed, specific or generic identity itself is also like a certain union of several things in

---

11 Ibid.
12 Cf. Suárez, *Opera omnia*, vol. 25, p. 393.
13 Cf. Section 10, n. 11, above.

a same essence or formal character. Therefore, much more could a proper and real union between extremes that are real, and really distinct, found a relation belonging to another class. Therefore, even though the numerical unity of some simple thing with respect to itself, or of a composite thing with respect to the whole composite, cannot found a real relation, nevertheless, the numerical unity of the whole composite, insofar as in it there are united parts that would be otherwise really distinct, is a sufficient foundation for a real relation belonging to the same class. And for the same reason a relation of contact pertains to the same class, and also a relation of nearness, inasmuch as it is as it were a certain imperfect likeness in place. So also co-existence belongs to that class, inasmuch as it is a certain likeness in existing; and the same is true in similar cases. And, according to this way of speaking, relations of causes can be so distributed that only the relation of an efficient cause belongs to the second class. But relations of material and formal cause belong to the first [class], because the proximate reason of founding them is a union, since those causes cause only by means of a union, as we have seen in their places.[14] But the relation of final cause belongs to the third class, for the reason that of its special nature it is a non-mutual relation, as we have said with probability above, in Disputation 23, and because it causes only insofar as it is the reason that an effect is ordered to itself and it is commensurate with that.[15]

8. Or, secondly, it could be said that all relations of causes belong to the second class. For even though Aristotle explained that especially in the case of active potency and causality, which is more evident, still, with proportion observed, it can be applied to the particular causes insofar as there is in each an aptitude to its own effect and a proper causality, by which in its own way it exerts influence on its effect, and the effect depends upon that [causality]. And in regard to material cause, this opinion seems consonant with Aristotle, who puts in that class the relation of a passive potency, whose causality is material. Moreover, the same /col. b/ reasoning seems to hold about the relation of a (so to speak) informative potency and about its causality and about the relation that is founded in that. And consequently, the same will also be true about the relation of effects to these causes. And the same could be said about the relation of an effect of a final cause as such to its cause; for from the side of the cause I think it is more probable that, as I have said, that relation is not real. And in line with this way of answering, a relation of union that presupposes causality or some imitation of that, would be reduced to the second class of

---

14 That is, in those Disputations which earlier have treated of material and formal causes.

15 Cf. Suárez, *DM* 23, 1, n. 13, vol. 25, p. 846a. For the counterpart question about how a relation may have an element of final causality, cf. ibid., 6, n. 20, p. 874a.

relations. But other relations, of nearness, co-existence, and the like, belong without doubt to the first class. Therefore, I think, no relation can be found that is not easily reduced to these classes.

Section XV.
Whether Relations of the Third Class Are Non-Mutual And Differ in This from Relations of the Other Classes.

1. Relations can be said to be non-mutual in two ways: first, according to the specific natures of the relations; second, in a highest and most general nature. In the first way, a relation will be called non-mutual that is not of the same specific nature in both extremes. However, in the second way that will be called non-mutual which is a true and real relation in one extreme, but not in the other. The first meaning is unusual and improper; for if each extreme is related through its own relation to the other, they are truly and properly related mutually, even if they are related by relations of diverse natures. Hence these relatives are rather called of diverse natures, or, as others say, "relatives of non-equiparence."[1]

The Division of Relations of the Same or of Dissimilar Nature.

2. And thus, mutual relations are usually divided into relations of equiparence and disequiparence.[2] For all relations of the second class are [relations] of non-equiparence, because the reason of founding is in some way diverse in the extremes, since in one it is an active potency while in the other it is a passive potency or dependence on its cause—from which it also comes about that the termini of such relations are of diverse characters, inasmuch as they

---

1 For Duns Scotus earlier using this terminology, cf. *Ordinatio* II, d. 1, qq. 4-5; ed. Vat. vol. 7 (1973), n. 205, p. 104. For its attribution to "recentiores" (i.e. more recent authors), cf. P. Fonseca, *Institutiones dialecticae* II, c. 13; ed. Coimbricae, 1575, re-edited in Pedro da Fonseca, *Instituições dialécticas: Institutionum dialecticarum libri octo*, introdução, estabelecimento do texto, tradução e notas por Joaquim Ferreira Gomes (Coimbra: Universidade de Coimbra, 1964), I, p. 120. For Suárez in a different context using "disquiparent" and attributing it to others, cf. *DM* 29, 3, n. 16, vol. 26, p. 53a. For him using it himself, cf. Section 17, n. 5, below.

2 Rábade *et al.* translate these as "reciprocal and non-reciprocal." In a number of places, St. Thomas has spoken of relations of equiparence. For example, cf.: "Moreover, marriage is a relation of equiparence, since it is, as has been said, a conjunction. Therefore husband and wife are equals in the marriage act." (*Praeterea, matrimonium est relatio aequiparentiae, cum sit conjunctio, ut dictum est. Ergo vir et uxor sunt aequales in actu matrimonio.*) *In Sent.* III, d. 32, q. 1, a. 3, *Sed contra*. While in the body of his reply St. Thomas has qualified this equality between husband and wife, he basically accepts the argument here. However, I have not found him speaking explicitly of relations of non-equiparence.

proportionately correspond to foundations, as was mentioned above[3] and will be said more extensively below.

But relations of the first class are sometimes of the same and sometimes of diverse natures in both extremes. For relations of unity are of equiparence /p. 840/, as Alexander of Hales correctly noted [in commenting on] *Metaphysics*, Book 5, Text 20, and is clear about a relation of equality, similarity, or identity. But relations founded upon number or diversity according to their proper and specific natures are non-equiparent, as is clear with regard to the double and the sub-double, as well as other proportions, which in one extreme express an excess and in the other a defect.[4]

I say, however, "according to proper and specific natures," because they can agree in a generic character and according to that can be said in a similar way about both extremes. Thus, indeed, each extreme, both the greater and the lesser, is said to be unequal to the other. And, likewise, whiteness is said to be dissimilar to blackness, and *vice versa*, although, however, it is probable that the proper relations are distinct according to their own specific natures, because both the foundation and the terminus are much more diverse in one than in the other. But relations of the third class are thought to be more than non-equiparent, from the fact that equiparence or non-equiparence are properly said between real extremes. However, in this third class, Aristotle does not think that there is a real relation in both extremes, and therefore they are called non-mutual.

A Difficulty Is Proposed with regard to Non-Mutual Relations.

3. Therefore, the present question is understood to be about these non-mutual relations properly taken, in which question Aristotle's opinion is difficult for a double reason. The first is that it does not seem true that relations of the third class are non-mutual, for if it would be true, that would be especially in cases of the knowable and the sensible, but in these there is as much a true real relation as there is in knowledge and sensation; therefore, [they do not seem to be non-mutual]. The minor [premiss] is proven, because a denomination of knowable, or sensible, is relative, and, indeed, essentially (*per se*) "toward something," as Aristotle himself says in the same place[5] and is clear from reciprocation; for as knowledge is knowledge of the knowable, so the knowable is knowable by knowledge. But this reciprocation and correlative denomination is not manufactured by the intellect, but rather has arisen from

---

3 Cf. Section 12, nn. 10-11.

4 Cf. [Pseudo] Alexandri de Ales, O.M. *In duodecim Aristotelis Metaphysicae libros dilucidissima expositio*, V, t. 20 (Venetiis, 1572), f. 139vab.

5 *Metaphysics* 5.15.1021a30.

things themselves. Therefore, in each extreme it is from a proper form and a real relation.

4. Secondly, because if for some cause this relation is not real in the knowable object, it is either because there is no real foundation in the object itself or because to be known in such an object is not something in it, nor is it known through a change of itself, but through a denomination from a form existing in something else; for besides these no other probable reason occurs.

But neither /col. b/ of these is satisfactory. The first certainly assumes something false; for an object's being intelligible or sensible has a foundation in things themselves and in their real properties. For light is visible because it is of such a nature according to which it has the power to change a potency in a certain way; and an immaterial thing, because it is spiritual, is said to be actually intelligible. But the second reason concludes badly. Otherwise, also the relation of an agent in act would not be real in that [agent] itself, because without a change of itself it becomes an actual agent, and without the addition of any absolute form that is in itself.

But if you say that the potency of acting itself is intrinsic, although the condition that is action is extrinsic, the same can be said about an object. For the aptitude that it be known is intrinsic, and that can be a foundation, even though the condition that is actually to be known, is something extrinsic. [It can be said of an object] especially because the act itself of knowing or sensing has a real dependence on an object just as an action [depends] on an agent, although not in the same class of cause.

You will say that an object insofar as of itself it is apt to be known or seen does not have reference (*habitudo*) to knowledge. But if this is understood about a relative categorical disposition, the question is begged—for we asking the reason for this. But if it is understood about a transcendental disposition, it was already shown above[6] that this [disposition] is not always a necessary prerequisite for a categorical relation. For even in an agent the principle of acting does not always have a transcendental disposition to an effect, as is clear from those things that we treated above about potency and act.[7]

5. Third is the principal difficulty: because the terminus of a relation is another relation existing in the other extreme; therefore, it is impossible that a relation be real in one extreme and not in the other. The consequence is evident, because there cannot be a real relation without a real formal terminus. But the antecedent is clear, because relations are said to be simultaneous in

6 Cf. Section 12, n. 12, above.
7 Cf. *DM* 43, 5, n. 7, vol. 26, p. 654.

nature, definition, and cognition,[8] because one is without doubt the terminus of another.

6. On a second score there arise no lesser difficulties. For if non-mutual relations must be admitted, they will be found not only in the third, but also in the other classes. The antecedent is clear. For, first of all, the relation that is between God and a creature in the character of efficient cause and effect belongs to the second class, and yet it is not mutual, according to the opinion that is more accepted by theologians. Similarly, in the first class there are found many relations between God and creatures, such as the relation of real distinction /p. 841/, or of likeness in being, or in the character of substance, or intellectual degree. For, even though it is an analogous likeness, it is still true and real and, as I have said above,[9] sufficient for founding a real relation. And, nevertheless, although such a relation is real in a creature, it cannot be in God. Again, an argument can be taken from the relation of union between the [divine] Word and humanity, which is non-mutual, and still belongs to the first or the second class. Moreover, among creatures there is a peculiar difficulty about the relation between a final cause and its effect, which [relation] we say is non-mutual, and still it belongs to the second class. Finally, the relation of right and left between a man and a column is thought, in the opinion of all, to be non-mutual, and yet it does not belong to the third class, for no character of measure is present in that case.

7. Therefore, on account of these and similar arguments, Gregory [of Rimini], whom some Nominalists follow, in [his *Sentences* commentary], Book 1, Distinction 28, Question 1[10] thinks that there are no non-mutual relations.

Assertions about Non-Mutual Relations.

8. Nevertheless, two things must be said briefly. The first is that there are some non-mutual relations, that is, [relations that are] real in one extreme and not in the other. This is the opinion of Aristotle, which all interpreters admit and almost all theologians, especially St. Thomas, in [*Summa Theologiae*], Part 1, Question 13, Article 7,[11] as well as other [theologians] to be cited very soon. And this is an opinion that is received with so much consensus that philosophers should not call it into doubt. Its reason, however, will be clear from the following assertion and more from the solution of difficulties.

---

8 On this threefold simultaneity, see Section 16, n. 3, note 4, below.

9 Cf. Section 11, n. 18.

10 Cf. Gregorii Ariminensis, *Lectura ... In I Sent.* dist. 28-32, qu.1, tomus III (1984), p. 108, and qu. 3, pp. 169-170, 177-180.

11 Cf. S. Thomae Aquinatis, *Summa Theologiae* I, q. 13, a. 7, in *Opera omnia*, tomus I (Romae, 1888), esp. p. 153a.

The second thing to say[12] is that these non-mutual relations essentially (*per se*) and as if from the proper nature of their foundation are found in the second class, but not at all in the other classes, except as in a material way from the peculiar condition of some subject or extreme. I think that the opinion of Aristotle should be interpreted in this way. And the reason of the first part should be taken from the peculiar mode of specification and commensuration that potency, habit, and the like, have to their objects. For formally it consists only in the disposition that they have of their nature to objects, according to which [disposition] they are commensurate to those.[13] But in this the object does not have a proper causality but rather the character of a specifying terminus. For, even though otherwise it can be moving either actively or finally, still, as an extreme of this relation it is considered under none of these characters, but it is solely that to which such a thing is commensurate. /col. b/ But under this aspect it itself does not concur as able to be ordered to another but only as that to which another is ordered. And, therefore, by virtue of such a reason of founding there does not arise a relation in both extremes, but only in that which is commensurate to the other.

Because of this, therefore, relations of the third class from the proper formal nature of their foundation are non-mutual. But in the other classes this is not found, as is clear from what has been said. For more frequently or almost always relations of those classes are mutual. But if sometimes they are non-mutual, that is only because of the peculiar nature or condition of some thing, as will be more clearly evident from the solutions of the arguments.[14]

Whether in Non-Mutual Relatives Both Extremes Are Really Related.

9. Therefore, to the arguments proposed at the beginning,[15] which proceed against the first assertion and against the first part of the second assertion, an answer must be given. And, indeed, Cajetan [in commenting on *Summa Theologiae*], Part 1, Question 13, Article 7, answers by conceding that even in non-mutual relatives both correlatives are real, and that the knowable, for example, is really related to knowledge. However, he puts a difference between these and mutual relatives in the fact that in mutuals both [extremes] are related by an intrinsic relation, but non-mutuals are not this way, but [in their case] one extreme is really related by a relation which exists in the one and is extrinsically denominating the other.[16]

---

12 Here Suárez has "dictum"—i.e. "thing said."
13 Actually, Suarez has "ei" which is "to that" instead of "eis" which is "to those."
14 That is, the arguments in nn. 3-6, this Section.
15 Cf. n. 3, this Section.
16 Cf. Cajetan, *Commentaria*, in I, 13, 7, n. 10; tomus IV, 155ab.

This answer seems to have a basis in Aristotle, first because among those things which are simply "toward another," he numbers the knowable as it is related to knowledge and the sensible as it is related to sensation.[17] But, as we said above, only those things that are really related are without qualification "toward something." Therefore, these[18] also are from Aristotle's opinion real relatives. Also, second, because below, in the same chapter, he says that these are "toward something," because other things are said toward them, where he does not say that these are "toward something," because [our] reason fashions or considers that, but because other things are said to be toward them, which is [something] found in reality itself.[19] Moreover, third, because a little later, embracing the three classes treated in Sections above, he says that all these are said to be "toward something" through themselves. Things, however, that are only related by reason are not related through themselves but rather through reason.

Finally, because a metaphysician does not consider relations (*respectus*) of reason,[20] but, according to Aristotle, those three classes essentially (*per se*) belong to the category, "toward something," and they also essentially (*per se*) fall under metaphysical consideration;[21] therefore, [the conclusion follows].[22] And before Cajetan, /p. 842/ Gregory also in [his *Sentences* commentary], Book 1, Distinction 28, Question 3,[23] seems to have taught this opinion.

---

17 Cf. *Metaphysics* 5.15.1020b31-32.

18 That is, "the knowable" and "the sensible."

19 This very important point should not be missed. When Cajetan and other medievals speak, for example, of our real relation to God in contrast to God's relation only of reason to us, they never mean to reduce the latter relation to a mere consideration of ours. Instead, they aim to base the latter relation on a real foundation, while respecting the non-reciprocity in reality between creatures and God. I believe that Suárez's reaction to this is somewhat ambiguous.

20 Suárez himself considers them in a last addendum to his *Disputationes metaphysicae* in Disputation 54, Section 6, vol. 26, pp. 1039-41. For translation, cf. Francisco Suárez, S.J., *On Beings of Reason (De Entibus Rationis): Metaphysical Disputation LIV*, translated from the Latin with an introduction and notes by John P. Doyle (Milwaukee: Marquette University Press, 1995), pp. 116-22.

21 While Aristotle certainly does distinguish and treat these three classes of relation in *Metaphysics*, Book 5, Chapter 15, I can find no precise justification there for Suárez's stress on "essentially." Or even translating "per se" as "through themselves," "directly," or "as such," I cannot find its exact basis in Aristotle's text.

22 Suárez here and in other places does not bother to explicitly state his obvious conclusion.

23 Cf. Gregorii Ariminensis, *Lectura ... In I Sent.* dist. 28-32, qu. 3, tomus III (1984), p. 180.

10. But this answer of Cajetan is peculiar[24] and it contradicts St. Thomas, in *Contra Gentiles*, Book 2, Chapter 13, where he[25] explicitly proves that the relations of God to creatures are not some things existing outside God from which he is extrinsically denominated in a relative way.[26] But since between God and creatures the relation is non-mutual, if Cajetan's opinion were true, God also would be really related to creatures, not indeed by a real relation existing in God himself, but by a relation existing in a creature. Hence, in the second argument St. Thomas explicitly takes up a principle that is contrary to Cajetan's interpretation, namely, *"from a relation there is not denominated something else existing as it were outside, but rather inhering."*[27] Here, Ferrara interprets well that this must be understood to be about a respective denomination, by which something is said to be related to something else, for, by another kind of denomination, it is not unreasonable that something be denominated by an extrinsic relation,[28] as we will say later.

11. Moreover, if the knowable is really related to knowledge by a relation existing in the knowledge, I ask whether this should be understood about the relation by which knowledge itself is related to the knowable, or about some other distinct relation.

The first cannot be said, because one and the same relation cannot give to diverse subjects denominations of diverse characters, such as are knowledge and the knowable. Nor can it relate them to opposite formal termini. Otherwise, for an equal reason, the same sonship existing in a son could intrinsically denominate the son and refer [him] to the father, and extrinsically denominate the father himself and refer him to the son. Finally, a form that is one in species has one formal effect. But relation is a form whose formal effect is to relate one thing to another; therefore, one and the same relation cannot have two modes of relating that are of diverse characters.

Also the second cannot be said, namely, that there are in knowledge two distinct real relations, one by which the knowledge itself is related to a knowable and another by which it relates a knowable to itself. For up to now this has been said by no one, and it does not have a basis in Aristotle, but rather it contradicts him. For he says that a knowable is said to be such from the fact

---

24 That is, "idiosyncratic."

25 That is, Thomas.

26 Cf. *Summa contra Gentiles*, II, c. 13, in *Opera omnia*, tomus xiii (Romae: R. Garrone, 1918), p. 293a.

27 Cf. St. Thomas, *Summa Contra Gentiles* II, c. 13, in *Opera omnia*, tomus XIII, p. 293a.

28 Cf. Ferrara, *Commentaria in Contra Gentiles* II, c. 13, n. 2, in S. Thomae Aquinatis, *Opera omnia*, tomus XIII, pp. 293b-94a.

that knowledge is related to it.[29] Therefore, he does not recognize between these another real relation apart from that by which knowledge is related to the knowable. Also, neither is it consonant with reason, because that plurality of relations is neither necessary nor does it have a foundation in that knowledge itself, since in /col. b/ that there is only a unique adaptation and transcendental disposition toward the knowable.

12. It is possible to say that there are two relations that are distinct only by reason. For, this multiplication can be easily admitted, since it is not a property of things nor truly in reality. And it suffices for the aforementioned relative denominations even of diverse characters, just as the same mode or the same dependence, because of only a distinction of reason between action and passion, gives the diverse denominations of agent and patient, one intrinsically and the other extrinsically.[30]

However, this distinction of relations should not be admitted in the present case. For even for a distinction of reason of this kind some foundation in reality is needed, which is not in the present case. Hence, the example of action and passion is not similar. For in change there is a true transcendental relation (*habitudo*) to a principle from which the change flows and to a patient that it changes; and, therefore, there is in that change a great foundation for rationally distinguishing action and passion in the manner of two accidental forms. However, in knowledge there is no foundation for distinguishing, even according to reason, relations of diverse characters.

Add the general reason on which is founded that principle of St. Thomas that a relation does not denominate extrinsically,[31] because without doubt since its denomination is through a disposition toward another it is unreasonable that a form that so denominates be in that to which there is the disposition. But if it is not in that, it is necessary that it be in that which is related, since in a relation other extremes do not essentially occur.

Finally, it can scarcely be conceived by the mind what there may be in knowledge by reason of which it would cause the knowable to be really related

---

29 Cf. *Metaphysics* 5.15.1021a29-31.

30 As I have suggested previously, in Aristotelean philosophy there is one reality between agent and patient. It resides intrinsically in the patient and is extrinsically from the agent. The one reality, for example, of *motion* is intrinsically in the thing that is moved and only extrinsically derived from the mover. This will ultimately permit Aristotle and his followers to attain the highest point of their metaphysics in an "unmoved mover" that moves, as extrinsically causing motion, without itself being in motion. For more of what is involved here, cf. my article: "'Prolegomena' to a Study ...," esp. pp. 138-40.

31 Cf. *Contra Gentiles* II, c. 13, as cited above in notes 22 and 23, this Section.

to itself, since the whole nature of knowledge is to be turned toward the knowable, and from this it does not, essentially speaking, order that [knowable] to itself.

The First Difficulty Proposed in the Beginning Is Resolved.

13. Therefore, to the first argument put at the beginning[32] it must be said that the knowable can be denominated in two ways: first, merely terminatively and as it were passively, and second, correlatively with knowledge. In the first way it is denominated extrinsically from the real knowledge, and in this way such a denomination can be said to be in things themselves and not to be fashioned by the intellect.[33] Indeed, this denomination itself is not taken only from the categorical relation that is in knowledge, but also from an absolute form as this includes a transcendental disposition toward an object. Aristotle suggested this well enough /p. 843/ when he said that the intelligible is said from the fact that the intellect is occupied with it.[34] For it is so occupied not only through a categorical relation, but also through its own act on which the relation follows.

The second denomination of the knowable is relative (*respectiva*), and this is only through a relation of reason, because our mind, in order to explain the relation that knowledge has to that knowable, conceives that [knowable] as correlative to the knowledge. The argument, therefore, proceeds only with regard to the first denomination.

When, however, Aristotle places the knowable, the sensible, and the like, among those things that are "toward something,"[35] it can be first explained that through these he does not understand only those extremes, but also the relation that intervenes between these and their correlatives, in whichever of them there is that relation. Or secondly he can be said to posit these extremes among those things that are "toward something," insofar as they have denominations of this kind from certain real relations. And in the same sense, it can be understood that he says that these are "toward something," because other things are related to them. They are (I say) toward something, not as correlatives, but as termini that are passively denominated from these relations. And in a similar way these will be said to be essentially (*per se*) "toward something" as termini essentially connected with real relations from which they receive such denominations. Or it can be said in another way, when Aristotle says that these are called "toward something" because other things are said to be toward

---

32 Cf. n. 3, this Section.
33 Read again note 19, in paragraph 9, this Section.
34 Cf. *Metaphysics* 5.15.1021a31.
35 Ibid., 1020b31-32.

them,[36] this is understood causally. For if the knowable, the sensible, and the like, are taken and conceived by us in a correlative way, it is then because other things are related to them and not because they themselves are truly and really related.

But Gregory [of Rimini] says that the same interpretation is valid, even if the relation of the knowable is real, because it belongs to that [knowable] only because knowledge is concerned with it. But this is not correctly said, because if the foundation of that relation is only the relation (*habitudo*) of another thing, namely, of knowledge to the knowable, the relation founded on that cannot be real.

14. An answer to the second argument[37] is that the cause on account of which this non-mutual relation is not real in one of the two extremes in this third class [of relations] is that in one extreme, for example, in the knowable object, there is not a real foundation for such a relation. And it is not enough that in the intelligible or sensible thing itself there is some foundation on account of which it is apt to be understood or to be sensed, because that foundation, considered precisely in the character of measure, is not taken as something that can be ordered to another, but only as the terminus or the object with which something is commensurate. And, therefore, it is said that in it there is no foundation of a relation, not because /col. b/ there is nothing in that thing itself, but because in that thing there is no reason of founding a relation, which is required for the foundation of a relation, speaking formally of such, as was explained above in Section 7.[38] The third argument[39] asks a serious question about the terminus of a relation, which we will treat in the following Section.

With Regard to the Second Difficulty We Treat
Of the Relations of God to Creatures.

15. In the second part of the arguments,[40] first of all, the question is asked: whether between a creature and God there is always a non-mutual relation, even if it seems to belong to the first and second class of relations. This is a theological question, and it is usually proposed in other words: whether the names that are given to God through a temporal relation to a creature express a real relation in God or one of reason only. For some names (*nomina*)[41] that seem

---

36 Ibid., 1021a30.
37 Cf. n. 4, this Section.
38 Cf. Section 7, nn. 12-14.
39 Cf. n. 5, this Section.
40 Cf. n. 6, this Section.
41 "Names" or simply "terms."

to imply a relation to a creature are said from eternity of God, which names are sometimes said to imply a free relation (*respectus*) but sometimes one that is simply necessary or natural. For example, knowledge, power, and the like, express a natural and necessary relation, but predestination, providence, and knowledge of vision,[42] express a free or not natural relation, because, absolutely speaking, they could not belong to God. And about these latter relations there is no doubt that they are not real in God, because from eternity they do not have real termini.

It is true that some theologians think that the relations of knowledge and power, even in God, are real and transcendental, and, therefore, that they can be independent of the existence of a terminus and not be variable nor accidental, but belonging to the intrinsic substance of God. However, I think more truly (something that must be treated more at length elsewhere[43]) that these do not entail in God a true transcendental relation,[44] but are signified only "accord-

---

42 "Knowledge of Vision" is the total knowledge that God has of things that exist or will exist in some moment of time; cf. *DM* 30, 15, n. 40, vol. 26, p. 182.

43 Cf. Suárez, *De SS. Trin. Myst.*, V, c. 2, n. 2, in *Opera*, vol. 1, p. 655. It may be noted that Rodrigo de Arriaga, S.J. (1592-1667), who was broadly a follower of Suárez, thought that Suárez, in contrast to their fellow Jesuit, Gabriel Vásquez (1549-1604), did posit transcendental relations in God toward possible creatures; cf. "You will ask, whether there is given this transcendental relation to an effect not only in created causes, but also in God with respect to possible creatures. Father Vasquez denies it, because he thinks that God does not depend upon the possibility of a monkey or of an ant. Father Suárez, to whom I subscribe, affirms it, because of the argument that was made, namely, that for God to be able to produce creatures is something essential to God, which would be lacking if creatures were impossible; therefore, God essentially relates to those creatures as they are possible." (*Rogabis, utrum non solum in causis creatis detur haec relatio transcendentalis ad effectum, sed etiam in Deo ad creaturas possibiles. Negat P. Vasquez, quia censet non dependere Deum a possibilitate simiae vel formicae. Affirmat P. Suarez, cui subscribo, propter rationem factam, scilicet hoc, quod est Deum posse producere creaturas, est essentiale Deo; quod deficeret, si repugnarent creaturae: ergo Deus essentialiter illas respicit ut possibiles.*) Arriaga, *Physica*, d. 7, s. 2, n. 19, in *Cursus philosophicus* (Parisiis: Apud Martinum Durand, 1637), p. 287. For Vásquez, see *Commentariorum ac disputationum in primam partem Summae Theologiae Sancti Thomae Aquinatis*, Tomus primus. Editio novissima (Lugduni: Sumptibus Iacobi Cardon, 1631), In Qu. 25, a. 3, d. 104, c. 6, n. 25; pp. 512-3.

44 At times, Suarez does seems to admit a transcendental relation to possible creatures on the part of God (cf. e.g.: "I answer that that possibility on the part of creatures cannot not be taken away without taking away from God the positive perfection of omnipotence, and immediately thereafter [the perfection] of knowledge and of

ing to being said" (*secundum dici*) in the manner of relative things, from the fact that they are conceived by us in the manner of those things that include similar transcendental relations. For, in other respects, God is with regard to his essence a totally absolute thing, and since his knowledge and his power are his very essence, they also are absolute apart from every transcendental relation, which also we mentioned above when we had to explain the attributes of God.[45]

And we further gave the reason: because the power of God is not such that it is essentially and immediately (*per se primo*) ordered to a task outside itself, but it has that efficacy as it were concomitantly, speaking according to reason, and without any ordering. And similarly, /p. 844/ the knowledge and the will of God essentially and immediately are concerned only with his own essence,

---

the whole divine reality." [*Respondeo, ... non posse tolli illam possibilitatem ex parte craturarum, quin tollatur a Deo positiva perfectio omnipotentiae, ac subinde scientiae, et totius divini esse.*] *De Trinitate*, IX, c. 6, no. 20, vol. 1, p. 740 and *DM* 30, 16, n. 42, vol. 26, p. 197). Generally at other times, Suarez is more orthodox, denying all transcendental (and, of course, all categorical) relations in God (cf. e.g. above *DM* 47, s. 4, n. 4). Suarez's ambivalence on this has been noted by Diego de Alarcon, S.J. (1585-1634): "Of these authors, some teach that the Divine Omnipotence is really related by a transcendental relation to any creature, so much that if even the smallest creature were to be lacking, God himself would also be lacking ... and sometimes Father Suárez thinks this way, for in Book 9 of the *De Trinitate*, Chapter 6, number 20, he says that if the possibility of any creature is lacking, there would necessarily be lacking in God the positive perfection of omnipotence and of the whole divine reality. However, he seems to have taught the opposite in *Metaphysics*, Disputation 30, Section 15, number 26, and in places cited above, where with many others he teaches that there is in God no real intrinsic relation to creatures." (*Ex quibus Auctoribus nonnulli docent omnipotentiam divinam realiter referri per relationem transcendentalem ad quamlibet creaturam; adeo ut qualibet minima deficiente, etiam ipse Deus deficieret ... et aliquando ita sensit P. Suarez: nam lib. 9 de Trinitate, c. 6, n. 20, fatetur deficiente possibilitate alicuius creaturae necessario defecturam in Deo perfectionem positivam omnipotentiae, et totius esse divini: oppositum tamen videtur docuisse in Metaphys. d. 30, sec. 15, n. 26 et locis supra citatis, ubi cum multis aliis docet nullam esse in Deo relationem realem intrinsecam ad creaturas.*) Prima Pars Theologicae Scholasticae* (Lugduni, 1633), Tract. II, disp. 2, cap. 2 (p. 96a), cited by N. J. Wells, "Suarez on the Eternal Truths," Part II, in: *The Modern Schoolman*, LVIII (1981), 171, n. 1 20. Prof. Wells has raised the question of Suarez having changed his mind on this point. But for another resolution, cf. above *DM* 47, 3, n. 8, where, as here, the divine omnipotence is said to be relative *secundum dici* because we cannot conceive it or explain it otherwise; also: ibid., n. 9.

45 On the Attributes of God in relation to His Essence, cf. *DM* 30, s. 6, vol. 26, pp. 89-95.

but from that they consequently reach or can reach other things without a transcendental relation. Therefore, these relations are only "according to being said," or, if they are conceived as relations "according to being," they are only relations of reason, at least as long as their termini do not exist in reality (*in re*). Nor does the argument proposed above proceed in their regard, but rather about certain relations that include the co-existence of a terminus, which therefore belong to God from time, inasmuch as the creatures that are the termini of such relations exist only in time, for example, the relations of creator, lord, and the like.

The Opinion of the Nominalists about Real Relations in God from Time.

16. Regarding these, therefore, many theologians think that they are real relations. Ockham holds this in [his *Sentences* commentary], Book 1, Distinction 30,[46] as does Gabriel [Biel] in the same place,[47] Question 5, and Durandus, Question 3,[48] as well as Gregory [of Rimini], [Book 1], Distinction 28, Question 3, Article 4, and Marsilius [of Inghen], in Book 1, Question 32, Article 1.[49] The basis for these authors is that a real relation adds nothing to a subject or to the other thing that is said to be related through that [relation], but it is either a denomination from the concomitance of the extremes, or it is an absolute thing itself that, when another co-exists, through itself respects that [other], on account of some link or some connection found between them. Hence, it happens that a real relation can without any imperfection come anew to something, because it comes without any real and intrinsic addition, and without composition, and consequently also without any dependence upon some extrinsic thing but, at most, in a certain mode of denomination. But these are the only imperfections that can be imagined here; therefore, every imperfection is excluded. And, in every other respect, in God all things necessary for a relation concur. For he is the true efficient cause of a creature, and he has true power and action with regard to that creature. Therefore, when

---

46 Cf. Guillelmi de Ockham, *Scriptum in librum primum ...*, d. 30, q. 5, in *Opera theologica*, vol. 4, p. 394.

47 Cf. Gabriel Biel, *In I Sent.*, d. 30, q. 5, a. 2, concl. 2, in *Collectorium circa quattuor libros Sententiarum, Prologus et Liber primus*, collaborantibus Martino Elze et Renata Steiger, ediderunt Wilfredus Werbeck et Udo Hofmann (Tübingen: J.C.B. Mohr [Paul Siebeck], 1973), vol. 1, p. 605.

48 Cf. D. Durandi, a Sancto Porciano, O.P., *In Petri Lombardi Sententias*, I, d. 30, q. 3 (ed. Venetiis, 1571), vol. 1, f. 85ra-86ra.

49 Cf. *Questiones Marsilii super quattuor libros Sententiarum*, I, q. 32, a. 1 (Argentinum: Ex Officina Martini Flach, 1501), fol. 132ra-vb.

the other extreme [i.e. the creature] is posited, there will be in God a true real relation.

And in favor of this opinion is the common way of denominating God from these relations. For he is as truly and really the maker and creator of a creature as one man is the father of another. And the same is true about the relation of "distinct" and "similar," etc. Therefore, either all of these relations are real in God, or there is no basis for admitting real relations in creatures.

Finally, St. Anselm favors this opinion in the *Monologium*, Chapter 24 [sic],[50] when after he has said that in God nothing can occur accidentally because he is invariable, objects to himself: "*How is he not receptive of an accident, since even this very fact that he is greater than all other natures and that he is dissimilar to them seems to be accidental to him?*" And he answers: "*But why are [God's] natural immutability and the receptability of certain things that are called accidents incompatible, if from their assumption no variability of substance follows?*" And further on he adds that there are relations of this kind. And lest he be thought to speak about relations of reason, he adds an example in the case of created relations. "*For I*" (he says) "*am neither greater nor smaller, neither equal nor similar to a man who will be born a year from now. But once he has been born I will be able to have all these relations without any change in myself.*" But he adds later that these things that are said to happen to a thing without any mutation, are *improperly* called accidents, and therefore it is *simply* true that no accident comes anew to God.

The Opposite Opinion Is Proven.

17. But nevertheless, many and more weighty theologians deny that names of this kind signify in God real relations to creatures that belong to him from time. This is the opinion of St. Thomas, [in *Summa Theologiae*], Part 1, Question 13, Article 7,[51] and in *Contra Gentiles*, Book 2, Chapter 12.[52] And in these places, Cajetan[53] and Ferrara[54] teach the same thing, as well as other Thomists, Capreolus, in [*Defensiones*], Book 1, Distinction 30, Question 1, Article 1,

---

50 Cf. *Monologium*, Chapter 25, in *Obras Completas de San Anselmo*, vol. 1, p. 258.

51 Cf. S. Thomae Aquinatis, *Summa Theologiae* I, q. 13, a. 7, in *Opera omnia*, tomus I (Romae, 1888), esp. p. 153a, and ad 4, p. 153b.

52 Cf. S. Thomae Aquinatis, *Summa contra Gentiles* II, c. 12, in *Opera omnia*, tomus xiii, pp. 290-91.

53 Cf. Cajetan, *Commentaria*, in I, 13, 7, nn. 14-18; tomus IV, 156a-157b.

54 *Commentaria in Contra Gentiles*, II, c. 12, in S. Thomae Aquinatis, *Opera*, tomus XIII, pp. 291-92.

Conclusion 3,[55] and Article 2, Conclusions 2 and 3,[56] and in the same place Hispalensis [i.e. Diego Deza], Article 1;[57] [St.] Bonaventure, Article 1, Question 3;[58] Richard [of Middleton], Article 1, Question 4;[59] Scotus, Question 1;[60] Giles [of Rome][60bis], Question 2; Henry [of Ghent], *Quodlibet* 9, Question 1;[61] and [Alexander] of Hales, in [*Summa*], Part 1, Question 35 [sic].[62] And the Master [of the *Sentences*, i.e. Peter the Lombard], in that thirtieth Distinction seems to be of the same opinion.[63]

And there are those who think that this opinion is so certain that the opposite is contradictory of sacred doctrine. However, it is one thing to speak supposing that a relation is a thing or a mode that is really (*ex natura rei*) distinct from a foundation or a related subject, and consequently added anew to that when it is newly related or begins to be relatively denominated, but it is something else to speak of a relation, supposing that it is not something distinct from absolute things. With the first supposition having been made, it would without doubt be most absurd and generally erroneous, to say that real relations to creatures in time result in God when creatures are produced or are lost when creatures are changed. For according to this kind of opinion, a true accident is posited in God, because a mode that is really (*ex natura rei*) distinct from a substance,

---

55 Cf. *Defensiones, In I Sent.*, d. 30, q. 1, a. 1, ed. Paban-Pègues, tom. II, pp. 283b-284a.

56 Ibid., a. 2, pp. 312-313.

57 See *Nouarum deffensionum doctrine ... Beati Thome de Aquino ...*, I, d. 31, q. 1, a. 1, fol. 214ra.

58 S. Bonaventurae, *Commentarius in I. librum Sententiarum*, d. 30, a. un., q. 3, in *Opera omnia*, tomus I (Quaracchi: Ex Typographia Collegii S. Bonaventurae, 1882), pp. 524-26, esp. 525b-26a.

59 Cf. Ricardi de Mediavilla, O.M. Conv., *Super quatuor libros Sententiarum Petri Lombardi quaestiones subtillissimae*, I, d. 30, a. 1, q. 4 (Brixiae, 1591; reprint: Frankfurt am Main: Minerva, 1963), tomus 1, pp. 268-270.

60 Cf. *Ordinatio* I, d. 30, q. 1-2, in *Opera omnia*, tomus vi (ed. Vat, 1963), pp. 169-202.

60bis Cf. *In Sent.* I, d. 30, q. 2 (Venetiis, 1521), f.157rb.

61 Cf. Henrici de Gandavo, *Quodlibet* IX, qu. 1, ed. Macken, pp. 3-25.

62 For this, cf. Alexandri de Hales, O.M., *Summa theologica*, I, Pars secunda, Inquisitio secunda, Tractatus primus, Qu. V, membrum 1, c. 4, aa. 1-2 (Quaracchi: Ex typographia Collegii S. Bonaventurae, 1924), tomus 1, pp. 554-5. According to the "Index of Questions" in this tome, the reference here was designated under "Question 53" in the Cologne, 1622 edition of Alexander's *Summa*.

63 For this, cf. Magistri Petri Lombardi, Parisiensis Episcopi, *Sententiae in IV libris distinctae*, Lib. I, Dist. XXX, Cap. 1, in Tom. 1, Pars II (Grottaferrata [Romae]: Editiones Collegii S. Bonaventurae ad Claras Aquas, 1971), p. 220.

which can be in that [substance] and can depart [from that substance], is an accident. And, consequently, it is necessary to posit in God a composition of substance and such a distinct mode, and finally change, potentiality, and the like. /p. 845/

18. For neither can it be said that such a relation is real and is not in a creature and that it really relates God himself to a creature and nevertheless is not in God but rather stands near (*assistere*) him, as Gilbert de la Porrée thought, as [Alexander] of Hales and others report.[63bis] For this is easily refuted inasmuch as if that relation is real it needs be in some subject. Since, then, it is not in a creature, it will be in God, unless someone imagines it to be subsistent, which cannot be said, since otherwise it follows that there is a certain created substance standing near (*assistentem*) God in time, since it is a temporal and consequently a created relation. But that is clearly false and unintelligible. For how could such a substance cause God to be related? Again, there would also be another relation in God to that substance, because he would be its maker, and in this way we would proceed to infinity.

But if it be said that that relation is subsistent, but still not with another subsistence than the divine, I will ask whether it is in that by a hypostatic union[64]—to say which is so absurd that it does not need to be refuted. Or [is it that] by identity? And then again let me ask whether this is by an identity in every way, which excludes even a modal distinction, and thus we are receding from the hypothesis that we put forward earlier, namely, that every real relation that comes anew is a distinct mode. But if we are talking about a real identity with a modal distinction, we fall into all the problems that were deduced, and we do not avoid such a relation being in God not through a distinct inherence but by itself, just as in created substances accidental modes also affect them and inhere in them.

19. However, the whole certitude of this opinion in this sense is more conditioned, or [a matter] of the consequence rather than of the consequent. That is to say, that if the relation is real, such as it is supposed to be in that opinion, it cannot be in God. But because that antecedent is uncertain and perhaps false, therefore it is not enough for the conclusion to be certain insofar as it absolutely denies real relations of God to creatures. Neither have the authors

---

63bis Cf. Alexandri de Hales, O.M., *Summa theologica*, I, Pars secunda, Inquisitio secunda, Tractatus primus, Qu. V, membrum 1, c. 3 (Quaracchi, 1924), tomus 1, pp. 552-4. For Gilbert, see *Gilberti Porretae Commentaria in librum [Boethii] De Trinitate*, in *Patrologia Latina*, vol. 64, col. 1292.

64 See Section 4, note 4, above.

of the first opinion[65] spoken in that sense, nor do they admit the aforesaid supposition.

20. But if we suppose that these relations are not something real and actually distinct from all absolute things, neither can it be certain that these relations cannot be attributed to God nor is it a question of great importance, but almost about the way we speak. And certainly those who think that these relative denominations, which can come anew by just a change of another extreme without any change of that thing that is said to be referred, are /col. b/ only extrinsic denominations from the co-existence of the extremes, speak logically enough in giving these relations to God, because there is no problem with God being denominated in time from some real form that exists in a creature, as is evident in [his] creative action, and in other things that God does "toward the outside" (*ad extra*). And, certainly, St. Anselm, in the place cited,[66] seems to lean very much toward this opinion, although at the end of the chapter he puts that way of speaking aside as uncertain. But, nevertheless, we abandoned that opinion above as less probable and less agreeable with Aristotle.

We can now confirm this from the fact that according to that [opinion] there will be no non-mutual relations. And what Aristotle says will be false, namely, that certain things are called relative because others are related to them, while other things [are called relative] because they have in themselves that from which they are related.[67]

21. But further, even supposing that a relation is something intrinsic, but not something distinct in reality (*in re*) and consequently making neither a change nor a composition, the difficulties deduced above do not follow, even if God is said to be temporally related to creatures, and therefore the opinion in that sense is not worthy of any censure. Hence, even among the Thomists, Soncinas, in *Metaphysics*, Book 5, Question 25, in reply to Objection 4,[68] admits that the relation of dominion that God has with respect to creatures is real, because it is founded on true real power. This also is in part what Hervaeus thinks, in [his *Sentences* commentary], Book 1, Distinction 30, the Single Question, Article 3 [sic],[69] although in his way of speaking he tries to accomodate himself to the common opinion, which he explains with difficulty. And this is not strange, because in fact, supposing this opinion, it is not easy to give a reason why this

---

65 Cf. n. 16, this Section.
66 *Monologium*, Chapter 25.
67 Cf. *Metaphysics* 5.15.1021a26-30.
68 *Quaestiones metaphysicales* ..., V, q. 25, ad 4, p. 85b.
69 For this, see Hervei Natalis Britonis, *In I Sent.*, d. 29, q. 1, resp. ad 3, et ad 1, 2, 3 (Parisiis, 1647), p. 127ab.

should be denied, since no imperfection follows in God, as is clear from what has been said.

22. But I do not, nevertheless, think one should abandon the way of speaking of St. Thomas and the more weighty theologians, because, even if those problems deduced above do not follow when we attribute to God a real relation in the stated sense, God can, nonetheless, in no way be related to creatures through his intrinsic form and entity. For this is proper to beings of the same order, but God and a creature are of entirely diverse orders, as is self-evident.

23. But those things are said to be of the same order, which are either outside every genus and outside every dependence, such as the divine persons, or are under the same genus, such as created substances or quantities and the like, or at least /p. 846/ those things that are under diverse genera, of which one can be perfected by another, and *vice versa*, such as are the genus of created substance and the genera of accidents compared among themselves.

And for this reason, all created beings, as regards the present matter, are said to be of the same order (for uncreated persons, as they are related among themselves, do not belong to the present discussion), because, if they are of the same genus, they both have a univocal agreement among themselves, and they mutually help one another in some way for the perfection or the complement of their nature, either in an individual, or in a species, or at least in a genus. Hence, it is the case that the causality that is found among beings of this kind also redounds to the perfection not only of effects but in some way also of the causes, either because they are ordered to acting or because they are preserved in the effects, at least according to species or certainly because according to genus they are perfected by a variety of differences or species. But if created beings are of diverse genera, they all have among themselves some connection, either according to generic or according to specific natures, if we compare them with proportion. Therefore, in this sense, in the present case, we are saying that all created beings are of the same order.

24. This can be explained in a different way from Cajetan [commenting on *Summa Theologiae*], Part 1, Question 4, Article 3, in Reply to Objection 4, where he says that those things are of diverse orders that have among themselves an essential dependence in the character of cause and effect.[70] In this way, all creatures are related (*comparantur*) to God, but not among themselves, because, even though sometimes they are caused by one another, it is not according to a proper essential dependence.

But although this explanation is probable and satisfactory with respect to extrinsic causes, still, in the case of intrinsic ones, namely, material and formal,

---

70 Cf. Cajetan, *Commentaria*, in I, 4, 3, n. 5; tomus IV, 54b-55a.

it does not seem to have any place. But in their case there is a special reason, because they are related (*comparantur*) to an effect as parts that are ordered to composing a whole, and in this regard they are of the same order with that [effect]. Hervaeus, [in the place cited] above,[71] has another explanation, but one that is more obscure and less satisfactory, and therefore, I am omitting it. Therefore, we assert that, in the stated sense, nothing is related to something else truly and really through an intrinsic form unless it is of the same order with that thing. But the reason is because a real relation consists in an order of one thing to another. It is, therefore, rightly required for such a relation that it be between extremes of the same order.

25. And this can be confirmed from what was said about knowledge and the knowable. For, under that aspect, they are thought to belong to diverse orders, insofar as /col. b/ knowledge is ordered to the knowable, but the knowable as such is not ordered to knowledge. However, God is much more of another order from every creature. Therefore, through himself he is much less able to be really related to creatures than the knowable [is able to be related] to knowledge. And St. Thomas uses almost all this reasoning in the cited places and more extensively in *De Potentia*, Question 7, Article 11.[72]

Accordingly, the divine nature, power, and other attributes are so absolute in themselves and so abstract and independent from every order of creatures, that whether creatures exist or not, they relate God to creatures neither according to reality (*secundum rem*) nor according to some true real formality. Hence, neither can they be truly conceived as so denominating or relating God, but every denomination that is conceived as relative (*respectiva*) in God is only according to our reason and mode of conceiving.

26. Neither is it an obstacle that God is really denominated creator or lord. For he is really denominated at least extrinsically from a real action and in this way he is called a creator, but intrinsically from the real power which he has in himself over a created thing and in this way he is called a lord, or from knowledge or real love and in this way he is said to be knowing and loving that which he makes. Finally, these denominations are real only insofar as they are taken from some absolute forms or quasi-forms. But insofar as they are formally relative, they are founded only in our way of conceiving.

27. Therefore, in answer to the principal difficulty[73] posited at the beginning, we concede that between God and creatures there are given non-mutual relations, which not only belong to the third class or foundation of relations, but also to the first or the second [class or foundation]. Nor is that a problem

---

71 Cf. *In I Sent.*, d. 29, q. 1, resp. ad 3, et ad 1, 2, 3 (Parisiis, 1647), p. 127ab.
72 Cf. *Quaestiones disputatae de potentia Dei*, q. 7, a. 11, ed. Bazzi et al., p. 212b.
73 Cf. n. 6, this Section.

that it is not necessary that relatives of the third class be distinguished from other [relatives] insofar as all relations in that [class] are non-mutual, while in the others they are never so, but insofar as in the third class they are always non-mutual, while in the others not always, but rather rarely.

Hence Aristotle is correctly explained, as I said—that in the third class by virtue of a formal foundation or a reason of founding, the relations are non-mutual. But in the first and second class, if sometimes they are non-mutual, this results as if from a material thing or subject or quasi-subject of the relation. For example, in the relation of cause and effect between God and creatures, if we formally consider only the feature of potency and action, it can be enough for a mutual relation, but nevertheless in God, because of the eminence of his entity, that relation is non-mutual, and the same can be said /p. 847/ about a relation of similar or distinct, and the like.

28. However, a relation between a final cause and an effect,[74] if it is non-mutual, can rightly be reduced to the third class. For means are adapted to an end, and thus they take their species from that, and in their own way they are measured through that.

29. About the relation of right and left between a man and a column, it is quite doubtful whether it is real from the side of any extreme. For although the form or the aptitude (*virtus*) from which the denomination has been taken is real and existing intrinsically in an animal, but only extrinsically in the column, it is still not very apparent why a real relation arises from this, even in the animal, since that denomination is not founded upon some unity or quantity, as is self-evident. Nor also [is it founded] in the character of active potency as such. Otherwise, the relation would be mutual, since a passive potency corresponds to that in the column, or sometimes also active [potency], is lacking because it is not necessary that the motive power (*virtus*) of the right side be so great that it suffices for moving the column. And that relation is also not founded in some commensuration, because the right [hand] power of the animal entails no transcendental disposition toward the column, nor is it commensurate with that in any way. Therefore, a true reason for founding a real relation does not seem to be present, but that denomination seems to have arisen soley from a comparison of the intellect through a certain proportion or proportionality[75] to the right and the left parts of the same man or animal. For between these parts there is a real mutual relation taken from a diversity of positions together with a diversity of real powers existing in both parts. And from this a similar denomination has been transferred to an inanimate thing that occupies the

---

74 Cf. n. 6, this Section.
75 On this, cf. Section 11, n. 6, above.

left or the right place. This [relation] is as regards the denomination likened in this to non-mutual relations, because the foundation of that denomination is only in one extreme, and from this it redounds to the other. Therefore, non-mutual relations are usually explained by this example, although a true and proper relation does not seem to be necessary in that case. For a mere diversity of positions as such does not suffice for the denomination of right and left, as is self-evident. But the diversity of power in that case is only privative, since in the animal the power is proper, but in the column there is only a privation of that, and, therefore, in neither extreme does it seem to be enough for a real relation. But if someone really wishes to defend the position that this is a real non-mutual relation, he may use the general response given above. /col. b/

Section XVI.
Whether the Formal Terminus of a Relation Is Another Relation Or Some Absolute Nature (*ratio*).

1. This question has arisen from the preceding Section, and it is very necessary in order to explain the nature of a relation, which in its own way depends both on a foundation and on a terminus. And for this reason it falls very well into this place; since in the two immediately preceding Sections we have explained the formal foundations of relations, it now remains in sequence that we explain the formal terminus.

The Title of the Question Is Explained, and What It Is "To Actually Terminate."

2. But it must be noted that here we are not treating of the formal denomination of a terminus as it is actually terminating but of the character or form that is required in that thing itself that is a terminus in order that it be apt for terminating. For under the first aspect the being of a terminus, or terminating, is not something in a terminating thing, but it is an extrinsic denomination taken from the fact that something else tends toward that [terminating thing]. In this way, that a wall is *seen* is not something in the wall, but is rather a denomination from [an act of] vision relating to that [wall]. For, although the words are different, to be seen is the same as to actually terminate vision.

But nevertheless, there is as a prerequisite in the wall some form, by which it is constituted apt to terminate vision. In this way, then, it should be understood about the terminus of a relation; for it is said actually to terminate only because it is respected by another, which denomination is not a prerequisite for the relation, but follows on that, as all agree. But there is necessarily supposed in the terminus some character and as it were formal cause, on account of which it is terminative (so to speak) of the relation. For not every being can terminate any relation whatever. Therefore, in each thing there is required some character on account of which it is apt to terminate this or that relation.

At present, then, we are asking about this formal character [that is necessary] for terminating. And since it was said above[1] that the terminus of a relation must be a real being, and, in order that it terminate, it necessarily requires actual existence; therefore we are further inquiring whether it must be a formally relative or an absolute being. From this it will easily be evident in each relation

---

1 Cf. Section 8, n. 4, above.

whether the proportionate terminus must be such or such, an absolute or a relative being. /p. 848/

Various Opinions.

3. *First.*—On this matter there are three opinions. The first says that in all relations, both mutual and non-mutual, the formal terminus must be relative. Cajetan taught this [in his commentary on *Summa Theologiae*], Part 1, Question 13, Article 7;[2] and Hispalensis [Diego Deza], in [his *Sentences* commentary], Book 1, Distinction 30, Question 1, Note 3,[3] seems to have spoken in line with the same opinion, although he does not discuss the question, nor does he speak explicitly about the formal character of terminating.

To be sure, some modern Thomists have followed this opinion. And it can be proven first because every relative is formally terminated at its correlative; therefore, the formal character of terminating one relation is the corresponding opposite relation in the other extreme. The consequence is evident, and the antecedent is proven, because relatives are simultaneous in nature, in knowledge and in definition, as is clear from Aristotle, in the Chapter, "Toward Something,"[4] and as will be

---

2 Cf. *Commentaria*, in I, q. 13, a. 7, n. 11, tomus IV, p. 155b.

3 See *Nouarum deffensionum doctrine ... Beati Thome de Aquino ...*, I, d. 30, q. 1, a. 3, not. 3, fol. 222vab.

4 On simultaneity in nature, cf. *Categories* 7.7b15 and ibid., 13.14b27-32. On simultaneity in knowledge, ibid., 7.8b13. On simultaneity in definition, ibid., 7.8a35-37. For the derivation and understanding of this last simultaneity, cf. esp. D. Soto: "In the eighth text, Aristotle infers from this second definition [of relation] the following corollary, namely, that if someone were to definitively know one relative he would also definitively know the other. This can be established as a fifth property of relatives 'according to being.' The reason of the corollary is manifest: for if the whole quiddity of a relative is to be toward another, the quidditative definition [of that relative] cannot be unless it make explicit the terminus of that relation. For since a relation is between two extremes, it cannot be quidditatively known unless the extremes are known." (*In textu octavo infert Arist. hoc corollarium ex hac secunda definitione, videlicet quod si quis definite noverit unum relativorum, definite etiam novit et reliquum. Quae potest constitui quinta proprietas relativorum secundum esse. Ratio corollarii est manifesta: Nam si tota quidditas relativi est esse ad aliud, definitio quidditativa esse non potest nisi explicet terminum illius habitudinis: nam cum habitudo sit inter duo extrema, quidditative cognosci non potest, nisi extremis cognitis: ...*) *In Porphyrii Isagogen, Aristotelis Categorias, librosque de Demonstratione commentaria* (Venice, 1587), p. 202b.

said below.[5] But they would not have any of these unless one relative were formally terminated at another. Therefore, [the conclusion follows].

The minor [premiss][6] is proven as regards its first part:[7] for if a father, for example, as a father is not terminated at a son insofar as the son is relative, but insofar as he is this man who has been begotten by that man, then the father as father is not simultaneous in nature with the son as son, but with this man as begotten. But this man is begotten by the other prior in nature to his having a relation of sonship to that other, because sonship is a property resulting in a begotten man. Therefore, a father as a father will be prior in nature to a son as son.

And this part[8] is confirmed because a relation as a relation depends only on a foundation and a terminus; therefore, if the formal terminus is not another relation, it does not essentially depend on that [first relation], nor does it require it; therefore, of itself it is by nature prior to that. And by a similar argument the other two parts[9] are proven. For a relation is perfectly known when the foundation and the terminus are known, and it does not need anything else. Therefore, if the terminus of one relation is not another relation, the one does not depend in knowledge on the other. Therefore, they are not necessarily known simultaneously.

Again, for the same reason, in the definition of a relation there is posited only a formal terminus, because the whole being of a relation is toward its own terminus. Therefore, if the terminus of one relative is not another relative, but something absolute, one relative will not be defined by another, and *vice versa*, which is to be simultaneous in definition. And this is especially confirmed in the case of non-mutual relatives, in which there seems to be greater difficulty, since otherwise, in order to know the relation of a creature, it would be /col. b/ necessary to know the absolute entity of God and his nature; and, similarly, in order to know the relation of knowledge or of sensation, it would be necessary

---

5 Cf. nn. 20, 24, 25, 26, 28, 29, 30, 33, and 34, this Section. In these paragraphs, Suárez will raise and answer most questions about the threefold simultaneity in Aristotle's text.

6 That is: "But they would not have any of these unless one relative were formally terminated at another."

7 That is: "Relatives would not be simultaneous in nature unless one were formally terminated at another."

8 That is, the first part of the minor premiss: again: "Relatives would not be simultaneous in nature unless one were formally terminated at another."

9 "Relatives would not be simultaneous in knowledge unless one were formally terminated at another" and "Relatives would not be simultaneous in definition unless one were formally terminated at another."

to know the absolute nature of a knowable or a sensible object, which seems plainly false.

4. *The Second Opinion.*—The second opinion uses a distinction. For it thinks the same thing about mutual relations as does the preceding opinion and for the same reasons, but about non-mutual relations, it says that they are terminated at something absolute and not relative, because relations of this kind are formally terminated at something real. But in their termini there does not correspond some real relative thing, but only something absolute.

Ferrara, [commenting on] *Contra Gentiles*, Book 2, Chapter 14, holds this opinion,[10] and Hispalensis, as cited above,[11] inclines more toward it, as regards its second part, for he often says that some absolute divine attribute, namely, strength, power, or something of this kind, is the reason that God terminates the relation of a creature to himself. Also, Nifo, in *Metaphysics*, Book 5, Disputation 14, follows this opinion.[12] And we will afterwards confirm it with regard to non-mutual relatives, but with regard to mutual ones it has the same basis as the preceding opinion has. And there is usually added an argument taken from the divine relations, which are mutual, and still are terminated one in another.

5. The third opinion teaches that universally all relations, both mutual and non-mutual, are formally terminated in an absolute. Scotus holds this, in [his *Sentences* commentary], Book 1, Distinction 30, Question 1,[13] in which place Lychetus and other Scotists think the same.[14] And Capreolus, [in his *Defensiones*], Question 1, Article 2, in answer to Objection 3,[15] clearly follows it, whom Soncinas, in *Metaphysics*, Book 5, Question 30, in reply to Objection 2,[16] imitates. For they say that the character of terminating (*rationem termi-*

10 Cf. Ferrara, *Commentaria in Contra Gentiles*, II, cc. 13-14, n. 4, in S. Thomae Aquinatis, *Opera*, tomus XIII, p. 294ab.

11 Cf. this Section, n. 3.

12 Cf. *Dilucidarium Metaphysicarum disputationum, in Libros Metaphysicorum*, L. V, disp. 14 (Venetiis, 1559) pp. 152-4. Note that Nifo holds the general position of an absolute terminus but says nothing about the particular refinement of Hispalensis.

13 Cf. *Ordinatio* I, d. 30, q. 1-2., in *Opera omnia*, tomus vi (ed. Vat., 1963), pp. 182-85, nn. 31-38; idem, *Quaestiones in lib. I Sententiarum*, d. 30, q. 1 (ed. 1639), tomus v, pars secunda, pp. 1193-4.

14 Cf. Lychetus, *Commentarius in J. Duns Scoti, In lib. I. Sententiarum*, d. 30, q. 1 (Lugduni, 1639), tomus v, pars secunda, p. 1195-96. Up to now, I have not found other Scotists commenting directly in this vein.

15 For this, cf. *Defensiones, In I Sent.*, d. 30, q. 1, a. 1, ed. Paban-Pègues, tom. II, p. 315a.

16 Cf. *Quaestiones metaphysicales ...*, V, q. 30, ad 2, p. 93b.

nandi) is absolute, but it requires a relation or a concomitant correlation when it actually terminates. This is without qualification true in the case of mutual relatives, but in the case of non-mutual ones it is only according to our way of conceiving, as we will explain. And I think that this opinion is true, when it is formally and essentially understood. But why I am adding this will be clear from what is to be said. For it is necessary to distinctly propose and prove this opinion in the cases of both mutual and non-mutual, because it is not equally certain in both, although from non-mutual to mutual a solid argument may be taken.

The Third Opinion Is Confirmed by Two Proposed Assertions.

6. *The First Assertion.—The Reason for the Assertion.*—Therefore, I say first that in non-mutual relatives /p. 849/ the character that is in one extreme in order to terminate the relation of the other [extreme] is not some relation that is opposite to the relation of the other, but it is the very entity or some property of the terminus in question. This is proven by an argument made in the second opinion, which seems to me to be most efficacious. For this relation has a terminus that is real and really existing. But in that terminus there does not exist any real corresponding relation that is opposite to the other relation. Therefore, that terminus is not rendered apt for terminating by a relation but by some absolute thing. The consequence is evident from a sufficient enumeration of the parts; while the major and minor [premises] have been proven above.

7. *Cajetan's Evasion.—It Is Disproven.*—In order to escape the force of this reasoning, Cajetan thought up an opinion that we have refuted above,[17] namely, that even non-mutual relatives are really related to one another, although the relation is not in both. And in this way he tries to defend [the view that] even an extreme in which there is no relation does not terminate the relation of another [extreme], except insofar as it is in turn related to that. But this opinion is both false, as we have shown, and it can contribute nothing toward explaining the present matter. For even if we grant that the knowable is really related to knowledge by a relation that exists in the knowledge itself, nevertheless, what Aristotle says is true, namely, that one of these extremes is not related to the other except inasmuch as the other is related to it.[18] Therefore, according to reason it is first necessary to understand that the relation of knowledge is terminated at the knowable rather than, conversely, that the knowable is related to knowledge, since that former is as it were the cause and the foundation of this

---

17 Cf. Section 15, nn. 10-12.
18 Cf. *Metaphysics* 5.15.1021a30.

latter. Therefore, the character of terminating (*ratio terminandi*) from the side of the knowable cannot be a relation by which it is related to knowledge.

Moreover, although to actually terminate is, as we have said above,[19] an extrinsic denomination, the aptitude, nevertheless, for terminating a categorical relation cannot be an extrinsic denomination from the opposite relative, because the character of terminating is presupposed in a thing before every extrinsic denomination from another. For an actual termination is included in the extrinsic denomination itself. Therefore, the aptitude for such a denomination is presupposed, especially when the terminus must be a thing that is real and really existing. Therefore, it can in no way be understood that one extreme is rendered proximately apt for terminating the relation of the other through that real relation itself that is in that other extreme, since every categorical relation arises, presupposing /col. b/ a foundation and a terminus, not indeed actually terminating but rather as apt to terminate. For as actually terminating it is not presupposed but rather is constituted from the relation (*habitudine*) of the other to it itself.

8. *An Opinion of Others Is Disproven.*—Others usually answer that although in the knowable, for example, or in the creator there corresponds only a relation of reason, nevertheless, the relation of knowledge or of a creature is formally terminated only at its correlative as such, and, consequently, a relation of reason is a real character of terminating.

But this answer is easily refuted from what was said above[20] about the terminus of a real categorical relation. For we have shown that it must be a true and really existing thing. This certainly is true for equal or greater reason about that form that is the reason of terminating and about the quasi material subject of the denomination in question. For if the terminus must be real, therefore it must be in reality apt for terminating in the same way; otherwise, it will not be a terminus, either actually or in aptitude. Therefore, this aptitude must belong to it through some real character existing in it.

9. This is confirmed, because a real relation exists only when the foundation and the terminus exist. But the relation of a creature exists, and indeed it is terminated in God, without any relation of reason existing in God, not only because a relation of reason never truly exists, but also because, in the way in which it can be, namely, objectively in an intellect, it is not necessary that it actually be, that is, that it be considered as the relation of a creature is terminated at the creator. For even if no intellect fashions or considers such

---

19 Cf. this Section, n. 2.
20 Cf. Section 8, n. 4, above.

a relation, nevertheless, the relation of a creature will be truly terminated at God.

You will say: it is impossible that that relation not be objectively in some intellect, at least in a divine [intellect], whether that [divine intellect] itself immediately effects it or knows it as able to be produced in its own way by a human intellect. In answer: whatever of these things is true, it is irrelevant to the matter that we are treating. For, even though that may be necessary because of the infinite knowledge of God, nevertheless, essentially (*per se*) and formally, the relation of a creature does not demand that. For it does not relate to God as looking at (so to speak) a relation of reason, but as pouring being into it.[21] Hence, if it has this, it is enough that such a relation be terminated in him. However, a relation of reason, as it is known by the divine intellect, is irrelevant. And the same is true about sensation and the sensible, as well as knowledge and the knowable. For if, by some impossibility, no intellect would be concerned with them, the relation of sensation would be terminated at the sensible and that of knowledge at the knowable. /p. 850/

10. But some reply that this argument proceeds correctly regarding a relation of reason as actually existing in its own way, but nevertheless, that relation of reason, insofar as it is in proximate potency to a certain terminus is the character of terminating a real relation of the other extreme. But this also is of no importance; for I ask: what do they understand by a relation of reason in proximate potency?

For either they understand that real foundation itself, which gives an occasion to the intellect that it conceive in the way of a relative that which is not so much a true foundation for a relation as it is the proximate cause or the occasion inducing the human intellect to such a way of conceiving, and in this sense a relation of reason in proximate potency is only an absolute thing existing in such a terminus, as, for example, in God there is a potency by which He actually exerts influence on creatures, and so it is with regard to other things. Therefore, that the relation of a creature is terminated at a relation of reason, as it is only in a proximate foundation from the side of God, is indeed to be terminated in something absolute that is in God.

Or by a relation of reason in potency there is understood a relation of reason itself according to its own being of essence (*esse essentiae*), such as it can be or, better, be imagined in that [relation of reason]. And in this sense, that answer seems improbable to me, because that relation can only be, and there can be imagined some being of essence (*esse essentiae*) in that in which the human intellect, for example, can conceive an absolute thing in the manner of some-

---

21 That is, in a quasi-practical rather than theoretical way.

thing relative. But this is irrelevant and extrinsic to the nature and the essence of the real relation of creature and also as that is terminated at its terminus. Therefore, it cannot be the character of terminating. And this is confirmed and explained, because God as creator cannot terminate the real relation of a creature in this way because he can be conceived by us in the manner of a correlative, but because truly and really he pours being into the creature by his omnipotence.

Finally, in other cases of real termini, a being of essence in the terminus itself is not enough for the relation to arise, unless it is reduced to existence, because otherwise it is something potential, and simply nothing.[22] Therefore, much less could the being of essence or the potential being of a relation of reason be enough to be the character of terminating a real relation.

11. *How Fonseca Answers the Argument.*—Finally, Fonseca, [in commenting on *Metaphysics*], Book 5, Chapter 15, Question 5 [sic], Section 4, has found another argument, in which he says that a relation of reason, even if it does not actually exist, can actually belong to, for example, the creator, that is, [belong] in its own way, objectively in the intellect, and /col. b/ that this is enough in order that a real relation be terminated at it. For by the very fact that there is a real relation in a creature, a relation of reason belongs to God, even if it does not actually exist. But he proves that these two things are separable because to be an animal actually belongs to a man even if he does not exist.[23]

But this answer is not any more probable than the rest. For, first of all, what it assumes, namely, that a form can actually belong even when it does not actually exist, either contains a great equivocation, or it is plainly false. For, actually to belong, if it is taken properly and really, is to actually be in [something] in that way in which a form can be in [something], namely, either by inhering, or by denominating, or by relating (*referendo*), or in another similar respect. However, in order that it belong actually in this way, it is necessary that it actually exist in the way in which it can exist. But if actually to belong only means the truth of a proposition through the connection of its extremes, abstracting from their existence, that indeed is not actually to belong, but rather [to belong] in potency, and in that way in which in those propositions an actual truth can be understood, they do not have that [truth] except insofar as they are actually in some intellect, as was mentioned above.[24]

Moreover, when *actually to belong* has been taken in this sense, a relation of reason cannot truly be said to actually belong to God by the very fact that a

---

22 That is, nothing actual.
23 Cf. Fonseca, *Commentaria in Metaph.*, V, c. 15, q. 4, s. 4, vol. 2, cols. 832-3.
24 On this being of truth in propositions, cf. *DM* 31, 1, n. 2, vol. 26, p. 225; ibid., 12, nn. 45-47, vol. 26, pp. 297-8.

creature exists. For, as the same author well argues such a relation belongs to God contingently and from the outside, even after the making of the creature. Contingent predicates, however, belong in act only when they exist, but that [belonging in act] is proper to predicates that necessarily belong to subjects. Yet the answer that he employs, by limiting the subsumed proposition and by excepting these relations of reason, first seems arbitrary and then against reason. For setting aside the actual existence that is proportionate to each predicate, the predicate cannot be said to actually belong to the subject, unless either because it is of its essence or, indeed, because it flows from that [essence], so that it has a necessary and essential (*per se*) connection with that. Therefore, as often as a predicate is not of this kind, but merely contingent and resulting from an extrinsic cause, whether it is a real predicate or one of reason, it can in no true sense be said to actually belong when it does not exist.

And this is confirmed, for this very thing, namely, *actually to belong*, requires at least the truth of a proposition. But these propositions are false: *God has a relation*, or, *He is actually related to a creature*, as long as that relation in no way actually exists. Indeed, according to the principles of /p. 851/ Dialectic, such propositions cannot be truly abstracted from time, since they are simply contingent.

12. I add, finally, even if we grant all that is assumed in that answer, it is not satisfactory, because that mode of actually belonging is not enough for the terminus of a real relation. Otherwise, an actually existing Peter could have a real relation of specific identity with an only potentially existing Paul. For it actually belongs to Paul that he be a man, even if he does not exist, because he is intrinsically a man. Therefore, a relation of real specific identity with Peter actually belongs to him, even if that relation does not actually exist. Therefore, conversely, in order that a real relation exist in Peter, it will be enough that another similar one and its foundation actually belong to Paul, even though he does not exist.

13. Therefore, there is no room for a subterfuge, but admitting the common doctrine about non-mutual relatives, it evidently follows that the terminus of that relation is something absolute, speaking formally and essentially (*per se*).

However, I am adding these last words, because sometimes it can happen that the terminus of some non-mutual relation is some real relation, but not one opposite to the other relation or reciprocal with it. So, for example, knowledge of some relation, or a love that directly, essentially, and immediately, tends to some relation, is really related to that relation as to an object or a measure.

Hence, it is clear that, just as the object of such a knowledge is a relation, so also the terminus of the relation of such knowledge will be a relation, but not formally as a relation that is opposite to the relation of that knowledge, but rather as the [subject] matter about which the knowledge in question is employed, and which is presupposed for its relation, and therefore, it is, as it were, something material that the thing known is a relation. And in this way we say that an absolute thing, or what appears to be[25] an absolute thing, terminates a relation of this kind. [This is] finally the known or loved thing itself, of whatever sort that is.

You will say: what if the object known is some relation of reason? The answer is: the transcendental relation of that knowledge will also be terminated at that [relation of reason], but that knowledge will be incapable of a categorical relation to its own object, because of the lack of a real terminus.

A Second Assertion.

14. *Mutual Relations Are Terminated at an Absolute.*—I say, secondly, even in mutual relations the formal character of terminating is not an opposite relation, but rather some absolute /col. b/ character, which is the formal foundation of the opposite relation. I understand this assertion essentially and formally, just as I have explained the preceding one. For the general rule is that that thing or formal character that is in one relative the proximate reason for founding a relation to the other [relative], is also the proximate and formal reason for terminating the relation of the other to it itself.

So, for example, if in Peter the proximate foundation for having in himself the relation of sonship is his whole substance insofar as it was produced through a certain generation by Paul, this same is the reason why Peter can terminate the relation of Paul's paternity to him. And, conversely, because the potency of generating in Paul, on the presupposition of such a generation as a necessary condition, is the proximate foundation of the relation of paternity, it is also therefore the proximate reason why Paul can terminate the sonship of Peter toward him.

It is the same in relations of the first class. For the whiteness, which in this white thing is the foundation of its similarity with another, on account of a formal unity with itself, is also the proximate reason for terminating the relation of similarity of the other to it itself.

Therefore, if this is true, sometimes one relation can be the proximate reason for founding another relation, as, for example, paternity [can be the reason for founding] similarity, then that paternity that in one father founds a similarity

---

25 Literally, "what carries itself in the manner of."

with another [father] will be in that [first father] the reason for terminating the relation of the other [father] to him. In that, however, it does not behave formally as a relation, nor is it relatively opposed to that relation that it terminates through itself, but it is opposed through another relation, which it founds in itself. And therefore it then behave just as if it were an absolute form, and in this sense we say that the formal terminus is, essentially speaking, something absolute.

15. This assertion is usually proven from the fact that when relation is defined as an accident whose whole being is toward another, by that "other" there cannot be understood another relation, since otherwise either there would not be one supreme genus of relation, but rather two, or the same thing would be put in its own definition.

And a similar argument is that similarity in general cannot be related to some relation, because otherwise it would be related to another similarity, since it is a relation of equiparence. But besides similarity in general there cannot be another similarity.

However, I am putting these arguments aside, both because they are derived through extrinsic means and do not explain the matter and also because they touch on a difficulty that is to be treated in the following Section. Indeed, these /p. 852/ [arguments] are more easily and fittingly explained according to our present opinion, although perhaps for that reason alone it[26] is not absolutely necessary.

16. *The First Reason for the Conclusion.*—Therefore, this conclusion is proven first from the preceding one. For from the fact that in non-mutual relatives we see that the relation of one extreme is not formally terminated in the relation of the other, we can infer that, although in mutual relatives there is a real relation in both extremes, one does not formally tend to the other, but simultaneously and concomitantly one tends toward the subject or the foundation of the other, and vice versa.

This inference is proven: for if by some impossibility in one extreme the relation were to be impeded, but with its whole foundation preserved, nevertheless, the relation of the other extreme could be terminated at that [first extreme]. Therefore, this is a sign that those two relations are simultaneous by concomitance and not by a formal termination of one at the other. The consequence is evident and the antecedent is clear. For, as was seen above, not only in relations of the third class, but also [in those] of the first and second [classes], when one extreme is such that it cannot found a relation, it is, nev-

---

26 The antecedent here seems to be "opinion."

ertheless, apt for terminating the relation of the other, as is clear in the case of God as terminating the relation of a creature as such.

Accordingly, for whatever reason it would happen that one extreme should remain with a foundation and without a relation, it will, nevertheless, still be sufficient for terminating the relation of the other extreme. For the argument is the same, because the fact that one foundation or extreme is apt, or not apt, for founding its own relation is accidental with respect to the termination of the other [relation]. Hence, if through a precision of the intellect a relation is separated from such an extreme, it is understood to remain equally sufficient for terminating another relation as that extreme that is not capable of a relation. Therefore, this is a sign that mutual relations are simultaneous on account of concomitance and on account of the condition of the extremes, which are apt for founding a relation, not on account of a formal termination of one in the other which corresponds to it.

17. *The Second Reason for the Conclusion.*—Secondly, I argue that the common axiom is that, when a foundation and a terminus are posited, a categorical relation results, and not otherwise. Therefore, the terminus of one relation cannot be an opposite relation.

The antecedent is certain with the agreement of all, and it is clear from what was said above[27] about the nature of this relation. Hence,, /col. b/ although he excepts the relations that he terms "extrinsically advenient" (*extrinsecus advenientes*), Scotus, nonetheless, also logically denies that they belong to this category. And we will show below, in the following Disputation, that those [extrinsically advenient relations] are either non-existent or are merely other than transcendental ones.[28]

However, it is necessary that that axiom be understood about a formal and proximate terminus, and one that is (so to speak) as if in first act, about which we also are debating in the present question, as we have said. For it cannot be understood about a terminus that is terminating as if in second act (so to speak). For about that terminus as such, it is not true that, when it is posited together with a foundation, a relation follows. For it itself is rather constituted in the character of a terminus actually terminating through the relation that actually tends toward it and extrinsically denominates it with a terminative denomination.

Again, neither can it be understood about a material and remote terminus, since when that alone is posited together with the foundation of another extreme, it is not necessary that a relation result, as is self-evident and can easily

---

27 Cf. Section 4, n. 2.
28 Cf. *DM* 48, 1, nn. 5-8, vol. 26, pp. 869-70.

be shown by examples. Therefore, that axiom (*principium*) must be understood about a terminus that is formal and as if in proximate first act.

And from this the first consequence is easily proven. For one relation does not arise from the positing of another. For that word, "from" (*ex*), expresses some antecedence of nature or origin. However, one categorical relation is not antecedent to another relation that corresponds to it, nor does one express an origin from the other, as is self-evident in all created [relations], about which we are now speaking. Otherwise, they would not be simultaneous. But when a relation is said to result once a foundation and a terminus are posited, the undoubted sense is that the positing of the foundation and the terminus are antecedent or are presupposed by an order of nature, and immediately the relation results from this. This is obvious from the proper character of this utterance itself, since in the case of mutual relatives both relations result when the foundations and termini are posited.

18. *A Third Reason for the Assertion.*—Thirdly, I argue by confirming and explaining that principle, namely, *"That which in one extreme is the reason of founding a proper relation is the reason for terminating another correlation."* For, just as the reason for founding is that through which there is given a proximate cause on account of which such a thing has a relation to another, so the reason for terminating is that through which there is given a proximate cause on account of which the thing is such that another can be related to it. But in cases of mutual relatives this cause is taken from the same form or character; therefore.

The major [premiss] seems self- /p. 853/ evident from its terms. The minor is made clear by induction. For, just as a white thing is apt for founding a relation of similarity, because it has whiteness, and that whiteness itself is an apt foundation, because it has a certain formal unity, so also the same white thing is apt for terminating the relation of another, because it has a whiteness of the same character or unity with the whiteness of the other. For another white thing is not related to this one because there is a relation of similarity in this one, but because there is whiteness in this one, just as there is in the other. Were it otherwise, there would not be a similarity in whiteness, but rather there would be a similarity in similarity. And from this an *a priori* argument can be perceived; for the similarity as such is in the whiteness, for example, and therefore, it has place between the white things as such, and it relates them as similar. Therefore, just as from the side of one it is founded in whiteness, so from the side of the other it is terminated in whiteness.

19. The same is easily evident in relations of non-equiparence. For, distinguishing relation formally from generation, Peter, for instance, is related to Paul as to a father, precisely because he has generated him, and not because

Paul is related to him. For staying precisely with that reason, we understand that there is sufficient cause from the side of the one generating that the son be related to him. Moreover, the cause is the same on his part why there results a relation of paternity in him. And the same is true about paternity itself, if we assign its character from the side of its terminus. For thus the relation of paternity that is in Paul is terminated at Peter, because he has been generated by him [i.e. Paul], and in this we precisely conceive a sufficient cause from the side of the terminus. And thus, universally, since a relation essentially requires two things, namely, a foundation and a terminus, a reason for any relation can be given from the side of each. And that which truly and proximately is given from the side of the terminus is the reason for terminating, just as that which is given from the side of the subject is the foundation or the reason for founding.

20. However, the reason that can be given from the side of the terminus is never another relation, if we are speaking formally and not just concomitantly or identically. For although a father is related to a son only when the son is related to him, this is still not the reason that can be given from the side of the terminus for why the father is related to the son, namely, because the son is related to him, but rather it is precisely because [the son] was generated by him. For one relation is in no way the reason of another, neither from the side of the terminus, nor from the side of the foundation; otherwise, they would not be simultaneous in nature. For that which would be the reason of another as such would be /col. b/ in some way first, especially since we are talking about a real and, in its way, formal character from the side of the terminus. This character, then, is always something else, distinct from the relation, and consequently something absolute, which in mutual relatives is not anything else but that very thing that in each founds its relation; for that is the reason of terminating the relation of the other. For, when the relation is removed, no other character is nearer or more necessary, as was clear enough in the induction that was made.

21. *An Objection Is Met.*—You will say: in non mutual relatives this rule cannot be observed. For in the terminus of one relative there is no real foundation of any relation. The answer is that there is always understood something proportionable.

So, for example, if the non-mutual relatives belong to the second class, as is the case between the creator and the creature, the reason of terminating the relation of the creature from the side of God is the very power of creating as it is actually influencing [the creature]. For if God were otherwise not incapable of a relation, that would have to be the foundation of a relation of the creator to the creature. [This is so] further because if we want to give a reason from the side of the terminus of the relation of the creature, it is no other than that God through his omnipotence has created that [creature]. And the same is easily understood in mutual relations that can be in the first class, as is the relation of similarity or of distinction between a creature and God.

However, in the third class, the reason of terminating from the side, for example, of the knowable and of similar objects, is the entity of each one insofar as in that [entity] there is a certain objective aptitude, inasmuch as a certain act, habit, or potency, can be employed in its regard, which [objective aptitude] can be named truth, or goodness, or something similar. For that aptitude is the reason that can be given from the side of the object or the terminus of such a relation. For knowledge therefore is employed with regard to such an object because it has such truth or intelligibility, and the same is so with regard to other things.

22. *Why a Character That Cannot Found a Relation Can Terminate [One].*—But if you ask why an aptitude or a character of this kind, which is not a sufficient reason in itself for founding a proper relation, is a sufficient reason for terminating the relation of another, the answer is that this is because, for the task of founding a relation, there is necessary an ordinability to another (so to speak) from the side of the foundation itself, and thus it is necessary that they be of the same order. However, for terminating a relation, it is not necessary that a terminus be ordinable to another, but that the other be /p. 854/ ordinable to it. And therefore a terminus can have a real aptitude for terminating even if it is not of the same order with the other extreme that is ordered to it.

The Bases of the Other Opinions Are Met.

23. It remains to answer the bases of the other opinions. And, first of all, it is denied that a relative is formally terminated at a correlative as such, which is clearly evident in the case of non-mutual relatives. For where there is no correlative, another relative cannot be terminated at a correlative. But from this we understand that even in the case of mutual [relatives], although a relative is terminated at a correlative, it is still not formally such in a way that those relations tend between themselves and to themselves, but one tends to the foundation of the other, and *vice versa*, as has been stated.

24. *How Relatives Are Simultaneous in Nature.*—But to the first objection, about a simultaneity of nature, the answer is that the opposite is rather inferred from this. For a relation is posterior in nature to its terminus, as that [terminus] in its first or formal act has been sufficiently constituted for terminating, because, as we have said, a relation arises from a foundation and a terminus. Indeed, some authors, who think that a relation is something distinct, think that it is effectively produced by a terminus. If, therefore, one relation were the

terminus of another, from the positing of the one the other would result, and thus they could not be simultaneous in nature. Therefore, they are said to be simultaneous in nature when they are mutual, because when one results from a foundation and a terminus, the other results in an altogether concomitant way, without any order of prior and posterior between them, and this is to be simultaneous in nature.

But this simultaneity is founded not in their formal relation (*habitudo*) among themselves, but in a necessary connection that they have in a foundation and a terminus, inasmuch as neither can arise unless its foundation and terminus is already posited, and when these are posited, both necessarily and immediately arise. Otherwise, the formal foundation of one is the formal terminus of the other, and vice versa. From this it comes about that the foundation and the terminus of both are necessarily posited in reality (*in re*), for, as I have explained, they are the same, with the proportion changed.

And finally, in this way, it is brought about that those relations themselves necessarily arise with simultaneity in duration, for, with equal necessity, both result from the terminus and the foundation as soon as these are posited, and also by nature, because they have no order between themselves. Therefore, in this way, those correlatives, formally taken as they are correlatives, if they are mutual, are simultaneous in nature. But if they are non-mutual /col. b/ since they are not simultaneous in duration, neither can they be so in nature.

25. *Reply Is Made to an Objection.*—But if indeed this comparison is made between one relative and its terminus in second act, or as it is actually terminating, they can in this way be called in a formal sense simultaneous in nature. For, as was said above,[29] a terminus as so terminating is formally constituted by an extrinsic denomination from the relation that tends toward it. Hence, when that [relation] is posited [the terminus] is so denominated, and when that is taken away the terminus in that way ceases to be, while losing nothing intrinsic, as is self-evident. However, a relation is not prior in nature to being terminated at another; therefore, it is simultaneous in nature with the terminus as it is terminating.

You will say: the relation itself is a kind of formal cause of that denomination of an actual terminus; therefore, it is prior in nature. I answer: it is not properly a formal cause, even though on account of the denomination it is conceived by us in that way. And therefore, a true priority of nature is not present in this instance, because, without any other causality and only because from its intrinsic essence the relation respects a terminus it denominates that [terminus] as terminating. This is just as vision denominates a thing as seen without a true

---

29 Cf. this Section, n. 2, above.

causality, but from the fact only that it exists with such an intrinsic disposition (*habitudo*); hence, just as it is not prior in nature to having this disposition, so it is not prior in nature to denominating the object as seen.

26. This is most of all true when we are speaking of these forms in the concrete, that is, about [something] relative, or [someone] seeing. For, speaking about abstract things, a relation can in some way be conceived as prior in nature to a relative—in that way in which between a form, especially one that is inhering, and its formal effect there can be a priority of nature. For a relation is the form of a relative. For a relation, as abstractly conceived, is properly not itself related to a terminus, but it is that by which a subject is related, and therefore as long as it itself is conceived as prior to actually affecting the subject, it is not yet conceived as relating to a terminus. Therefore, it is not strange that as such that relation itself is also prior to the denomination of the terminus as terminating.

And perhaps here can be applied the distinction that Cajetan uses elsewhere, about relation as designated (*signata*) or exercised (*exercita*).[30] For in this case a relation is conceived as not yet exercising the act of relating, but according to its own abstract nature. Yet, as so conceived, it is, in the case of mutual relations, simultaneous in nature with another opposite relation. For even relations taken in the abstract arise in a completely simultaneous way when both foundations are posited.

/p. 855/

27. Finally, in order to omit nothing, it could be added that even a relation that is abstractly conceived tends to a terminus, although not as a "which" (*quod*) but only as a "by which" (*quo*). For it is a form by which a relative thing respects a terminus and as much as you may want that it be conceived in the abstract, its essence always consists in a formal disposition toward a terminus. And under this consideration, although it is understood in some way prior to [something] relative, even under that aspect it tends in its own way to a terminus, and consequently denominates that [terminus] as actually terminating not the whole relative thing but the relation itself.

From these [remarks], therefore, it is evident enough how opposite relations are simultaneous in nature, and also a relation and a terminus as actually terminating, but not a relation and a terminus in first act or with respect to the character of terminating. For in that way it can also precede in time, when the foundation in the other extreme has not been posited, and even when the

---

30 Cf. Thomas de Vio Cardinalis Caietanus (1469-1534), *Scripta philosophica, Commentaria in Praedicamenta Aristotelis*, ed. M.-H. Laurent (Romae: Apud Institutum "Angelicum," 1939), p. 111.

other extreme has been posited, it always precedes by an order of nature,[31] since from that foundation the relation results, as was stated.

28. Therefore, to the argument of the first opinion[32] the reply in form is to deny the sequence, that is, the father as father is not simultaneous with the son as he is a son, but as he is this begotten man. Indeed, just as this man, as begotten, is prior in nature than he is as son, so also he is prior to the father as father, although he is posterior in nature to this man as begetting. And, therefore, although the father as such is terminated at this man as he is begotten by him, he is, nevertheless, not in nature terminated at him before there is sonship (*filiatio*) in him, not on account of a formal termination at that sonship itself, but on account of an altogether necessary simultaneous concomitance, as was stated. Therefore, even though this man, as begotten, is prior in nature than he is as son, nevertheless, in that priority as such, paternity is not yet understood to be in the father. Indeed, it is also most truly said that this man, as begotten, is prior in nature to a paternity being in the father; for from the positing of this terminus, with a foundation that is in the begetter, the paternity results.

29. In answer to the confirmation,[33] I concede that formally speaking one relation does not depend upon another. However, I deny that from this it follows that they are not simultaneous in nature, naturally speaking.

And the first of these, in addition to all that has been said, I confirm with a theological example, according to one opinion of St. Thomas. For in Christ, the Lord, according to St. Thomas, there is not a real sonship in relation to his mother, but in the Virgin there is a real relation of /col. b/ maternity to Christ. This is a sign, therefore, that one of these relations does not depend essentially and formally on the other. Otherwise, one could not remain without the other, even by the absolute power [of God]. And, likewise, it is a sign that one is not the formal terminus of the other, since a relation also cannot be conserved without its own terminus. All these principles are certain in the doctrine of St. Thomas, and therefore I think that this is a very effective *ad hominem* argument against Cajetan and the Thomists who follow him.

However, I say that one relation does not depend on the other "formally." For they can be said in some way to depend on one another "concomitantly." For one cannot be without the other from the nature of the thing (*ex natura rei*), not even by the absolute power, at least unless the foundation of the other extreme is changed in some way and it becomes incapable of the relation, in

---

31 On priority of nature as opposed to priority of time, cf. *DM* 14, 3, n. 42, vol. 25, p. 486.

32 Cf. n. 3, this Section.

33 Ibid.

order that we may abstract from the opinions about the relation of sonship in Christ.

And from this the other part is easily made clear, namely, from the aforesaid mode of independence it does not follow that relations are not simultaneous in nature. For, if one were to properly and formally depend upon the other, the one would rather have to be prior in nature to the other, since that dependence itself is a certain posteriority of nature. But since they have a necessary concomitance, by which one cannot be without the other, apart from any order between themselves, they are, therefore, simultaneous in nature.

30. *How Relatives Are Simultaneous in Knowledge.*—Moreover, from what has been said, it is clear what must be said about the simultaneity of knowledge, which was demanded in the second argument of the confirmation of the opposite position (*contrarii fundamenti*).[34] For by the same proportion it must be said that formally and immediately a relation does not depend on knowledge, except from its terminus according to its proper character of terminating, and not according to an opposite relation, which the argument correctly proves. And this is obvious in non-mutual relatives. For in order that I know the relation of servitude of a creature in regard to God, it is not necessary to know a real relation of Lord in God, since there is none. And it is also not necessary to fashion a relation of reason in God; for this does not essentially (*per se*) pertain to the knowledge of another relation, but if it comes to be in us, it results from our imperfect way of knowing. For an angel, as well as God Himself, comprehends the relation of servitude in a creature, without imagining any relation of reason in God.

You will say: is it not necessary to know God as Lord in order to know a creature as servant? The answer is that it is necessary to know God as being really Lord, not relatively according to reason. But God is really /p. 856/ the Lord, without qualification, as St. Thomas has noted in *De Potentia*, Question 7, Article 10, In reply to the Fourth Objection,[35] and often in other places. This is first through his real power to coerce subjects; second, because the real relation of servitude that is in a creature is terminated at him; and in both ways it is necessary to know God as a Lord in order to know the creature's relation of servitude.

For the first, that is, the power to coerce subjects, is from the side of God the reason of terminating the relation of servitude, and, therefore, knowledge of it is as it were antecedently and causally the reason of knowing the relation of servitude. For, just as that relation arises by virtue of that terminus and foun-

---

34 Cf. n. 3, this Section.
35 *Quaestiones disputatae de potentia Dei*, q. 7, a. 10, ad 4, ed. Bazzi, p. 211a.

dation, so it cannot be known, except when such a terminus and foundation are known.

But the second belongs to God, only by extrinsic denomination, through an actual respective tendency of a creature toward him. And because a relative as such can be known only as terminated at its terminus, therefore under that aspect God is known as Lord not antecedently but concomitantly. And what has been explained in the present example has a place in the relation of a creature and in all non-mutual relations.

31. Neither is the argument made [just] above[36] against this of any importance. For we concede that the relation of servitude cannot be known without knowing some absolute character in its terminus, not only as entirely simultaneous but also antecedently or causally, as I have said.[37] However, it is not necessary that that absolute character be known exactly or insofar as it is in itself. For it is enough that it be apprehended abstractly or under some confused concept, although the more perfectly it will have been known, so much the more perfect will be the knowledge of the relation.

All these things are easily explained in the mentioned example. For in order to know the relation of servitude that a creature has toward God, it is necessary to know at least in a common way that God has a certain superior power over a creature, by reason of which he can either command that [creature] or dispose of it by his choice. And the more the extent of this power will have been known, the more perfectly will it be known of what kind that servitude is. Neither can it happen that an angel or God himself know this servitude, without knowing such power in himself. However, it is not necessary that an angel, for example, who naturally intuits the relation of servitude in a creature, also naturally intuit the power of God in himself. But it is enough that he know such power of God abstractly and from its effects. And much less is it necessary to /col. b/ know the whole nature of God, or his other attributes, formally and essentially (*per se*) speaking, because those [attributes] as such are not the reason of terminating such a relation. And in this way it is easy to understand the same thing in the relation of a creature as it is an effect of God, or [in relations] of knowledge, or sensation, and in other non-mutual [relations].

32. However in mutual relatives, the argument is partly the same and partly diverse. For the argument is the same with regard to the formal dependence of knowledge on a terminus as such, and not on a correlative as such; for this also is true in mutual relatives. For in order that I may know in some man the

---

36 Cf. n. 30, immediately preceding.
37 Ibid.

relation of father, it is enough that I know that there is in the world another man who has been begotten by him, even if I stop there and do not know the relation of sonship in the other extreme.

And according to the opinion of St. Thomas, an angel, even a bad one, through its natural power saw (if it was not impeded) in the Blessed Virgin the relation of maternity to this man, Christ, and still did not see in Christ the relation of sonship. Therefore, [the angel] had knowledge of one relative with an intrinsic dependence on its terminus without knowledge of the correlative as such. For neither is it probable that it was necessary for the angel to imagine another relation of reason in one extreme in order that he might be able to know the other [relation]. Therefore, the same is true in every other mutual relation, for in this regard the argument is the same for all.

33. But as regards concomitance there is some diversity. For from the nature of the thing, when one mutual relation is known, the other is necessarily known simultaneously, at least concomitantly. For just as a relation exists through a certain resultance when the foundation and the terminus are posited, so it is known when these are known with their comparison between themselves. Because, therefore, these mutual relations simultaneously result at least through concomitance when a foundation and a terminus are posited, then for a similar reason they are simultaneously known when the foundation and the terminus are known and compared between themselves. And because this is necessary for the knowledge of individual relations, therefore, consequently it happens that when one is known the other is concomitantly known simultaneously.

In us this is necessary for a special reason, because we do not know these relations insofar as they are in themselves, but only by knowing and comparing between themselves foundations and termini. From this, moreover, it happens that we know even those extremes that do not have a mutual relation in the way of mutual correlatives. And from this also it happens that where to one relation there does not correspond another real relation, we conceive a /p. 857/ relation of reason, so that in this way we know concomitantly both extremes in the mode of correlatives.[38]

But in a perfect knowledge of things as they are in themselves, that is not necessary as regards non-mutual relatives, as was said. But as regards mutual relatives, there is the same or greater necessity, either because the relations are not actually distinguished in reality (*a parte rei*) from their own foundations, or if perhaps they are in reality (*ex natura rei*) distinguished, they are so conjoined and connected with foundations simultaneously existing and compared between themselves that the relation (*respectus*) of one to the other cannot be known

---

38 Literally: "by way of a correlative."

without there also being known in turn the relation of the other to the one. In these ways, therefore, we must understand that a correlative is simultaneous in knowledge with its terminus, or with its correlative.

34. *How Relatives Are Simultaneous in Definition.*—But to the third part of that basis,[39] that concerned simultaneity of definition, we must respond in entirely the same manner. For a definition is only some knowledge, if it is in the mind, or a sign of knowledge, and consequently of a thing known, if it is in the [spoken] word. And, therefore, relatives can be simultaneous in definition only insofar as they are simultaneous in knowledge. It therefore must be said in a proportional way that one relative is not defined by another correlative but by its own terminus, that it essentially respects.

Indeed, Scotus [as cited] above, thinks that this is necessary lest a circle or a nonsense utterance (*nugatio*) be fallen into (*committatur*), if in place of a word posited in the definition there is put its definition, or lest the same thing be prior and posterior to itself, since what is posited in a definition is in some way prior to what is defined. But these [arguments] are not very cogent, if those things are considered with regard to these definitions, which Aristotle mentioned in an addition at *Metaphysics*, Book 7, Chapter 5,[40] and which we have noted in that place.[41] And those difficulties in the case of transcendental relatives, such as matter and form, are easily insisted upon, about which there can also be seen what was said above, in Disputation 43,[42] the Last Section, at the end.[43] Not, therefore, in order to avoid these difficulties, but because of the matter itself, since each thing is defined formally and precisely through that to which it has a relation (*habitudo*), it is true that in the definition of one relative the other extreme is not posited, except under that aspect that is necessary in it in order to terminate such a relation (*relatio*). But concomitantly, just as relatives are simultaneous in cognition so [they are] also in definition, and because we more easily conceive and explain them in this way, it is, therefore, usually said without qualification that one relative is defined by another, and *vice versa*. And when it is commonly said that correlatives are simultaneous in definition, it must be taken in this sense.

---

39 Cf. n. 3, this Section.

40 Cf. 1030b14-31a14.

41 Cf. Suárez, *DM, Index locupletissimus*, VII, c. 5, vol. 25, pp. xxxii-xxxiii; translation in Francisco Suárez, *A Commentary on Aristotle's Metaphysics (Index locupletissimus in Metaphysicam Aristotelis)*, translated from the Latin with an introduction and notes by John P. Doyle (Milwaukee: Marquette University Press, 2004), pp. 124-5.

42 "On Potency and Act."

43 Cf. *DM* 43, 6, nn. 25-6, vol. 26, pp. 662-3.

About the Termini of Divine Relations.

35. In reply to the ultimate argument, which was added in the second opinion,[44] and was taken from divine relations, which are terminated at one another, the answer is first of all that the argument is not parallel. For those relations do not have a foundation besides themselves, because they are substantial and subsisting from their own proper characters. And therefore it is not strange that just as they are founded in themselves (so to speak), and in this way each one terminates its own correlative by itself. For in this there is rather observed a proportional argument. For we have said that the foundation of one relation is the reason of termination of its correlation. So, therefore, the foundation of divine paternity is the reason of terminating divine filiation. However, just as the foundation of that paternity is nothing else than that paternity itself, so the reason of terminating filiation is nothing other than that same [paternity].

36. Add that although all of this is true in reality (*secundum rem*), if, however, these things are, according to reason and our imperfect concepts, thought as distinct, in the way in which someone might conceive relations and foundations as distinct, he should also conceive that the reason of terminating one relation is not another relation as such, but rather the foundation of that. So, for example, if someone distinguishes by reason relations and origins, and with Bonaventure thinks that the persons are constituted by their origins, whereas the relations come to them and are founded in them,[45] he will consequently say that the formal terminus of paternity, for example, is a passive origin in the Son.[46]

But, on the contrary, the terminus of filiation is the active generation in the Father. For the Father relates to (*respicit*) him whom he has generated as such, and the Son indeed [relates to him] by whom he has been generated. Similarly, he who, with Cajetan, would distinguish paternity as conceived or as exercised, and under the first aspect would think to constitute a person, but under the second to relate that [person], and then that the second aspect is founded in the first, may say it is consequently necessary that one relation as exercised be terminated in another as conceived, and *vice versa*.

And, indeed, whether we use those words, or others, a relation does not have the character of a terminus as it relates to (*respicit*) another, but as it is in itself

---

44 Cf. n. 4, this Section.

45 Cf. St. Bonaventure, *In Sent.* I, d. 26, a. un., q. 3, in *Opera*, tomus I, p. 458a. On this, cf. Suárez, *Tractatus de SS. Trinitate*, VII, c. 6, nn. 4, 5, and 8, in *Opera omnia*, vol. 1, pp. 703-704; and A. Michel, "Trinité," *Dictionnaire de théologie* catholique, tome 15, deuxième partie (Paris: Letouzey et Ané, 1950), cols. 1735-38.

46 Cf. St. Bonaventure, *In Sent.* I, d. 26, a. un., q. 3, ad 1, in *Opera*, tomus I, p. 458ab; ibid., d. 27, a. un., q. 2, 469b.

something that is apt to be related to (*respici*) by another. And in this way also according to our way of conceiving, by whatever reason there is distinguished there a foundation from a relation or a person /p. 858/ constituted by a relation (respectus), there is also distinguished a reason of terminating from a relation.

37. This appears more clearly in passive spiration with respect to active [spiration]. For the Father and the Son, besides active spiration, have their own proper relations by which they are constituted in their own personal reality (*esse*), and as so constituted they are one principle breathing forth (*spirans*) the Holy Spirit. From this production (speaking in our way) there results in them a relation of active spiration, to which, therefore, it can more properly be attributed that it has a foundation and a reason of founding according to reason, because it neither constitutes a person, nor perhaps does it have a proper subsistence. And thus it is easily understood in that case that the passive relation of spiration, which is in the Holy Spirit, is terminated not formally at the active spiration, but at the Father and the Son, as they are one spirating principle, to which by our mode of conceiving there comes the relation of active spiration. For the proper and formal reason on account of which the Father and the Son terminate, or can terminate, the relation of the Holy Spirit, is not because they are related to the Holy Spirit, but because they produce the Holy Spirit and they are its one principle, from which they have it concomitantly that they are related to that [Holy Spirit]. If, however, through something possible or impossible, we were to understand that that relation did not result in the Father and the Son, as long as they would produce the Holy Spirit, that would be enough in order that they could terminate its relation.

38. From this a theologian will incidentally understand how *de facto* the Son is distinguished from the Holy Spirit, not first through the relation of active spiration, but through the filiation by which he is completely constituted in personal reality (*esse*) and is, consequently, distinguished from every other person. And nevertheless, it is true that if the Son were not to produce the Holy Spirit, he would not be distinguished from that, because in that case, given this hypothesis, filiation would not be a foundation of active spiration nor a reason of terminating a passive procession. And, consequently, neither would it have with that an opposition of origin. Now, however, it truly has all these things, and therefore it is a sufficient principle of distinction. But let us leave all this to the theologians.

About Relative Opposition.

39. Finally, from what we have said in this Section, it may be understood in what proper relative opposition consists and of what kind it is. For we left this

above[47] for this place. However, this opposition can be understood as either between a relation /col. b/ and its terminus, or between one relation of one extreme and another corresponding to that in the other extreme, or between one relative and its correlative.

The first opposition is general to all relations, even non-mutual ones, as is clear from what has been said, and therefore, it most formally belongs to a relation as such. But it consists in the fact that a relative thing as such and a terminus have between themselves such a disposition (*habitudo*) and conditions so distant, that they necessarily require a distinction between themselves. For a relative is that which respects (*respicit*) [another], while a terminus is that which is respected by another, and thus from their proper concepts they require (so to speak) "otherness."

40. However, the second opposition is not truly and really universal to all real relations. For it does not belong to non-mutual relations, although by our way of conceiving it can be imagined as if it did belong, which matters nothing at the moment.

However, among real and mutual relatives and the relations themselves, there is present a relative opposition, which does not consist in the fact that one respects the other as a terminus, but in the fact that one respects as a terminus that which is the foundation of the other, and *vice versa*. Or (what is the same) that they have opposite characters, inasmuch as one relates its subject to the other; the second, on the contrary, relates that other to that which was the subject of the first. From this they have between themselves such incompatibility that both relations cannot be simultaneously in one and the same thing, because one and the same thing cannot be the foundation and the terminus with respect to the same thing. Although this mode of opposition more clearly appears in relations of dissimilar characters, as for example between paternity and sonship, it, nevertheless, in its own way also belongs to relations of equiparence. For although these are of the same species, they can in an individual be in some way relatively opposite, because they affect their subjects according to opposite dispositions, from which they have an incompatibility in the same subject. But even though this opposition is in some way of a diverse nature, with respect to a terminus and with respect to a co-relation, still, because they are related (*se habent*) concomitantly wherever they are found, they are, therefore, named and judged in the manner of a unit. But a relation can be said to be opposed to one terminus terminatively, but to another relation relatively. And this latter is as it were a formal opposition, for it is between proper forms insofar as they mutually exclude one another from the same subject. But the

---

47 Possibly, Section 9, n. 3, above.

Francisco Suárez: *Metaphysical Disputation 47, On Real Relation*

prior [opposition] is an incompatibility of relatives, because they demand /p. 859/ a distinction of extremes, which St. Thomas also has indicated, in *De Potentia*, Question 7, Article 8, in reply to Objection 4.[48]

---

48 Cf. *Quaestiones disputatae de potentia Dei*, q. 7, a. 8, ad 4, ed. Bazzi, p. 206b.

Section XVII.
How the Category, "Toward Something," Can Be Set Up Under One Supreme Genus through Diverse Subalternate Genera and Species down to Individuals.

1. We have explained almost all things that have seemed necessary for understanding the essence of relation as well as its causes and formal effect (for it does not have any other). It remains for the completion of this matter that we say a few things about the subordination, agreement, and distinction of those things themselves in order that the constitution of the whole category be held, as it were, before our eyes. But now in the title of the question three points are suggested, which are treated by others very extensively and which should be explained very briefly by us.

About the Supreme Genus of the Category, Toward Something."
2. Therefore, the first difficulty is: how can all relatives be reduced to one highest genus? And the reason for the question is that the essence of a relation is that its being is toward something else. Therefore, a relative cannot be so abstracted that something else does not adequately correspond to it. Therefore, there cannot be one highest genus, but at least there must be two, which respect one another.

The consequence is evident: because that which relates (*respicit*) cannot be one and the same, both because in its definition it is contained that its being must be other, and also because the same thing cannot be really related to itself. And then, finally, [this is true] because, if the essence of a relative in general were to be related to itself, this very feature would be of the nature and essence of any particular relation, since the essence of the superior is included in the inferior.[1] This difficulty is common in this matter and would occasion a serious obstacle, especially for those who think that one relative is formally related to another correlative as such. For according to this opinion, when a relative is said in general to be that whose being is to be toward another, it is necessary to understand in that definition, "to another that is correlative." Therefore, since the same thing cannot be related to itself by a real relation (about which we are now treating), it will be necessary that there is not one supreme genus, but rather two, which respect each other adequately and are in reality (*in re ipsa*) distinct.

---

1 For example, "man" which is inferior to, in the sense of less extensive than, "animal" includes in its essence, i.e. "rational animal," what is essential to animal.

3. *There Is Given One Supreme Genus of Relation.*—Yet it is, nevertheless, certain that there can be given one supreme genus of all relatives. For it matters not whether we speak about abstract rather /col. b/ than concrete things, since one can be inferred from the other. Thus if there is a most general concept of real and categorical relation[2] in common, there could also be one of relative[3] in common, both because of a proportional argument, and also because to every abstract form there can correspond something composed or concrete that is adequate to it. But that there can be one supreme genus of relations is clear, first, from the very way of speaking about relation in common as such. For this term is common to all relations and is distributed over all, because it is said univocally and essentially (*in quid*) of all. Also, second, because the definition of relation in common is unique, and it belongs to all categorical relations. Finally, third, if someone imagines those two supreme genera of relatives, he will find an essential agreement between them in the character of being toward something else. Therefore, he could abstract from them a univocal and essential concept that would be common to both, in which he will also easily find differences outside the nature of that [concept], which are not complete relations. Therefore, [the conclusion follows].

4. *How Some Answer the Question.*—But some reply to the stated difficulty[4] that in the definition of a relative in general, when it is said, "toward another," through that word, "another," a correlative is indeed understood, and that cannot be the very thing that is being defined as such, on account of the reason given, namely, that the same thing cannot be really related to itself. And there is also not any other relative that is equally common and not contained under that which is defined, on account of the difficulty mentioned with regard to one supreme genus. Therefore, they say that through that word, "another," there is meant individual specific correlatives or particulars of individual relations.

This is the answer of Albert, in *Metaphysics*, Book 5, Tractate 3, Chapter 7,[5] and *On the Categories*, [the Treatise] "Toward something,"[6] and in the same

---

2 Which is abstract.

3 Which is concrete.

4[4] Cf. n. 2, this Section.

5 Cf. Alberti Magni, O.P., *Metaphysica* V, tr. 3, c. 7, ed. B. Geyer, in *Opera omnia Alberti Magni*, tomus xvi, pars i (Monasterium Westfalorum in Aedibus Aschendorff, 1960), p. 267b.

6 Cf. B. Alberti Magni, *Liber de praedicamentis*, Tr. IV, c. 2, in *Opera omnia*, ed. A. Borgnet (Parisiis: Vivès, 1890), vol. 1, p. 226.

place [the answer] of Simplicius[7] and Boethius[8]. And it can be explained in this way, because, even though a relation in common is defined through being toward another, it, nevertheless, exercises this being toward another only in determinate relations. And, therefore, it is not necessary that, insofar as it is most abstractly conceived, it be understood to exercise the task of a relation in an order to another correlative that is adequate to itself, because as such the essence of a relation is conceived as if in designated act (*in actu signato*), or as designating that in which it consists, rather than in exercised act (*in actu exercito*), that is, as exercising that disposition "toward something" in that whole community. Therefore, it must rather be understood that that nature so abstractly conceived exercises its disposition toward another only in its inferiors. /p. 860/

5. This is also understood in a different way in the cases of relatives of equiparence and disquiparence. For in relatives of disquiparence, at least in their common specific natures, it can be understood that one common relative is related to another that is equal and opposite to itself, as for example, a father to a son, or more to less. And the reason is that since these relations are of different characters, they are not conceived with one common specific concept, and therefore there can be abstracted two common and equal concepts that are opposite and corresponding to each other.

This is otherwise in the case of relations of equiparence. For since they are of the same nature, they have the same common concept of species, and therefore there cannot correspond to such a concept another objective concept that is common and correlatively opposite, in such way that *similar* is not said in relation to another similar in general (*in communi*), nor *equal* to another equal in general (*in communi*), but only by reason of individuals in which there is given one equal that is distinct from another.

And about these, it is true what Augustine said in the book, *On the Categories*, Chapter 11: "*In special cases and as a rule, in order that this category be*

---

7 For this, see Simplicii, *In Aristotelis Categorias commentaria*, c. 7, ed. Carolus Kalbfleisch, in *Commentaria in Aristotelem Graeca*, vol viii (Berolini: Typis et Impensis Georgii Reimeri, 1907), p. 160, ll. 15-34. For an English translation, cf. *Simplicius on Aristotle's "Categories 7-8,"* translated by Barrie Fleet (Ithaca: Cornell University Press, 2002), p. 14. For a Latin version of which Suárez would have known, cf. William of Moerbeke, in: Simplicius, *Commentaire sur les Catégories d'Aristote*, traduction de Guillaume de Moerbeke, édition critique, par A. Pattin en collaboration avec W. Stuyven, tome i (Louvain: Publications Universitaires de Louvain, 1971), p. 218, ll. 71-92.

8 Cf. An. Manlii Severini Boetii, *In Categorias Aristotelis*, lib. 2, in *Patrologia Latina*, tomus 64 (Parisiis: Apud J.-P., Migne, 1847), col. 217.

more evidently known, "toward something" is rightly said only when a singular is related to a singular."[9] It is true that Augustine immediately gives examples not only in cases of relatives of equiparence, but also in those that are of diverse names and concepts. However, in this there is no obstacle, as I have said, that one, even in common, be understood to be related to another common correlative. And Scotus and others noted the same thing in this way, in [*Sentences* commentary], Book 1, Distinction 21.[10]

6. This doctrine is probable. And even though it supposes a false basis, namely, that one relative is formally terminated at its correlative, it can, nevertheless, be useful for explaining how correlatives can be assigned, when they are abstracted by our concepts and conceived in common. For in this way it is correctly and without doubt said that only in relations of dissimilar names and concepts can one common relative correspond to another common one. But in the case of relatives of equiparence, or in the case of a relative in general (*in communi*), this is not possible. For, since these are abstracted either from relatives of the same nature or simply from all relatives, both relatives are conceived together in the way of one according to that in which they agree, and therefore to a common relative of this kind another equal one cannot correspond. And, therefore, it is also rightly said about a relative of this kind when it is conceived in general (*in communi*) that it is not of its essence that there corresponds to it, as immediately so conceived, an equal correlative. But it is enough /col. b/ that when it is contracted by its inferiors, this reciprocation of relatives be found in those [inferiors].

Moreover, speaking of a relative in general, I add that it is not of its essence that even mediately and in its inferiors it exercise the mentioned relative reciprocation. For the common concept of a categorical relation as such does not demand that another relation in another extreme correspond to it, at least as it is contracted to its inferiors. For if this were of the essence of relation in general, it would have to belong to all specific relations. But this is false; for in no way does it belong to non-mutual relations. Neither is it relevant that a relation of reason can correspond to them in the other extreme; for this does not pertain to the essence of a real relation, since it is merely extrinsic, [resulting] from our imperfection.

---

9 Cf. [Pseudo-] Augustine, *Categoriae decem ex Aristotele decerptae*, c. 11, in *Patrologia Latina*, tomus 32 (Parisiis, 1841), col. 1430; on the provenance of this work, cf. ibid., cols. 1419-20. Suárez's quotation is substantially accurate but not exactly so.

10 Cf. *Ordinatio* I, d. 21, q. un., in *Opera omnia*, tomus v (ed. Vat., 1959), pp. 335-6, nn. 25-6.

7. *A Relative in General Is Not toward Something Else as toward a Correlative.*—And from this I further conclude that when a relative in general is defined as being toward an other, that "other" cannot be taken as a correlative, since there is given through that definition something that is essential to a relative as such. But it is not essential to a relative that a correlative correspond to it, neither immediately in a common concept, nor in all its particulars, as has been shown.

Moreover, this is confirmed because if the "other" is the correlative itself, I ask whether it is a real correlative or one of reason or indifferently either one, that is, according to the requirement of the inferior relations. However, none of these can be admitted. For the first two members are easily excluded, since neither of them can be universal for all relations, as is clear enough from what has been said. The third [member] also is not probable: first, because otherwise that "other" would be taken in an extremely equivocal sense, inasmuch as a relative of reason is a relative in almost an equivocal way. Then also, second, because (as I said) the correspondence of a relation of reason is not from the natures of things, and therefore it cannot belong to the essence of relation.

8. I say, therefore, that the "other" in the stated definition expresses the terminus of a relation as such, which does not entail a correlative, as it is such, but another extreme, insofar as it has in itself a sufficient reason of terminating—which reason is almost always absolute. And if it is sometimes a relation, it is not as it is exercising the function of an opposite relation to the first relation, but insofar as it has some unity or common character similar to absolute things.

9. *A Relative in General Has a Terminus in General That Corresponds to it.*—Hence, I further conclude that a relation in general can be conceived /p. 861/ as having an other to which it entails a disposition, not only in its inferiors, but also as conceived by that most common concept. For to a relation in general there corresponds also a terminus in general. Nor does it follow from this that there are two supreme genera, because a terminus in general is not something relative as such, and therefore it does not constitute some genus in the category, "toward something."

10. *Why the Common Nature of a Terminus Does Not Constitute a Special Category.*—You will say: therefore, at least it will constitute some common genus of another category, which is plainly false, because that character of terminus is found (*vagatur*)[11] throughout all categories; indeed, it is outside [any] category, because it belongs to God himself.

---

11 Literally: "wanders".

The answer is to deny the consequence. For the character of terminus is not some real character or property in things, which is in some way distinct from those things or accidental to them. Rather it is the very entity of each thing, insofar as it is apt for terminating the relation of another. This character is quasi-transcendental, and it is incidentally not univocal, especially since it belongs to God and creatures. Hence, under that aspect it is essentially placed in no category, but it can be reduced to the category of relatives, as something added, as it is posited in their definition.

And this can be shown from a parallel (*a simili*) [argument]. For just as it belongs to relation in general to have a terminus, so also [it belongs to it] to have a foundation. Nor does there seem to be any doubt that this character of the foundation of relations can in some way be conceived in general as adequately corresponding to relation as also conceived in general. For it is included in the proper nature of a categorical relation as such that it supposes a foundation, and in that [foundation] some character on account of which it arises or results. However, it is not necessary that this common character of a foundation be some category (*genus*), but it a quasi-transcendental character that is found in all the categories. Hence, Aristotle attributes it to quantity, by way of a property, that it is a sufficient foundation of equality or inequality, and to quality that it be the foundation of similarity and dissimilarity[12] (for we have explained those properties in this way in that place). This character of a foundation as such is not some relative character in those things, and it is also not some absolute character that is distinct from them, but it is the very entity of each one, inasmuch as it essentially has a certain aptitude. And, therefore, it is reduced by way of a property to the category of each form, and indirectly it could be reduced under that aspect to the category /col. b/ of relation as its foundation. Therefore, I believe we must think about the terminus of a relation in this way. And this is enough about the first point.[13]

How the Supreme Genus of Relatives Descends to Inferiors.

11. The second point of this Section[14] is how this highest genus of relation descends, or is divided, through various genera down to the lowest species. This matter has in great part been explained above where we have mentioned and explained various divisions of relation. The first and principal one of these [divisions] was into three members through various, generically

---

12 Cf. *Metaphysics* 5.15.1021a11-12.
13 See n. 1, this Section.
14 Ibid.

diverse foundations, which are usually considered under the terms, *unity, action*, and *measure*.

From this it is easily understood that it is possible to proceed further under any one of these members. For example, in the first [we can proceed] through various modes of unities. And because under unity multitude is understood, first, relations of unity will have to be divided from relations of multitude or diversity, and afterwards, according to various modes of unity or of real multitude, relations will be divided under both genera. And the same thing proportionally must be said about action, and consequently also about passion, and of active and passive potency, or more broadly even about cause and effect, if all of these are comprehended under that word. Finally, the same is true about the character of measure. For also in that class relations are varied, according to diverse proportions of measures and measurables.

12. Of What Sort Is the Division of Relation into Mutual and Non-Mutual.—But from this division others arise that were also mentioned above, [and] without doubt, the division of relation into mutual and non-mutual, which has been explained extensively enough.

However, from what has been said it is clear that this is not a subdivision of any member of the preceding division.[15] But it is rather another adequate division of relation in general, embracing under one member, that is, under non-mutual relation, the third member of the prior division and some other relations contained under the first two members, while under the other member [i.e. mutual relation] it almost comprehends the first two classes of the preceding division.

However, these two divisions could be so subordinated that relation is first divided into that which by virtue of its formal foundation is non-mutual and that which by virtue of its foundation or from its own genus is not such,[16] and this in turn may be subdivided into relation founded upon action or unity. /p. 862/ And thus we may proceed until we arrive in those two classes at relations between God and creatures, which are[17] non-mutual not so much from the formal character or the reason of founding as from the peculiar nature and condition of God. And in this way it will be easy to constitute this category through subordinate divisions of this kind.

13. A Dictum of St. [John] Damascene Is Explained.—But it is worthy of notice that St. Damascene, in his *Dialectica*, Chapter 50, while positing many other divisions of relations, has omitted this one. Indeed, he indicates that this divi-

---

15 That is: unity, action, and measure.
16 Literally: "does not have that."
17 Literally: "have it that they are."

sion does not correctly harmonize with the nature of relatives. *"For,"* he says, *"a mutual disposition causes those things that are 'toward something.'"*[18]

However, either these words should not be understood about single relatives, but about the complex of both; for that truly consists in a mutual disposition, but it is not necessary that such, at least real, reciprocation be present in all relatives. Or, if those words are applied to single relatives, the mutual disposition must be understood with proportion, because from the side of a relation it is necessary that it tend toward something else, but from the side of a terminus [it is necessary] that it be that to which something else tends.

But that Damascene has omitted that division is not strange. For he has not said everything that can be said about relations, and perhaps the reason was because by our way of conceiving they are all apprehended as mutual.

14. *A Division of Relation into Those of the Same or of Diverse Name.*—A second division mentioned above[19] is into a relation of the same or of a diverse name, or of equiparence or disquiparence. And Damascene treats this extensively in the cited Chapter 50, which he subdivides into a relation of preeminence, such as to be master, to be greater, to be a cause; and a relation of inferiority, such as to be a slave, an effect, or less, etc.[20] These subdivisions pertain to relations of disquiparence; for in relations of equiparence there cannot be that diversity since they are of the same nature.

And perhaps there is never found among created things a relation of disquiparence apart from that diversity. However, among divine persons it is found without pre-eminence, or inequality, unless one wants, with the Greek Fathers, to call the order of origin a dignity [of origin], which [I treat] elsewhere. But this division, taken properly and with rigor, is not a division of relation in general, but of mutual [relation]. For since non-mutual [relation] is not reciprocal, it is not of the same nor of a diverse character in both extremes. [That is] unless one wants to extend what he says to that /col. b/ correlative denomination that is taken from a relation of reason. For in this way all correlatives will be of the same or of a diverse denomination.

Finally, as can be evident from what has been said, this division is not given through that which essentially and formally pertains to a relation of reason, because, as we have said, one relation does not formally terminate another. Hence, neither does it give species or essential diversity to that [other]. But when to one relation there corresponds another of the same or of a diverse character, it is an indication of the diversity of the foundation and the formal

---

18 Cf. St. John Damascene, *Dialectica*, Chapter 50, in *Patrologia Graeca*, vol. 94, col. 630 A.
19 Cf. Section 15, nn. 1-2, above.
20 Cf. *Dialectica*, c. 50, 630 A.

terminus. And thus, as regards the constitution of this category, this division must be reduced to the preceding ones.

Whence Is the Essential and Specific Difference of Relations Derived.

15. But there could remain one question about this second point,[21] namely, whence should be derived the specific and essential distinction of relations down to their ultimate species, namely, whether it is from a foundation or from a terminus? For some so divide tasks between these two, that they say that a relation has entity from its foundation, but from its terminus it has its species or essence and essential distinction. But others attribute both functions to both, to each in its own genus. This is not displeasing to me, but I think that both ways of speaking contain truth when they are correctly explained. Therefore, relations are formally and intrinsically constituted by their proper differences in their proper species, and they are essentially distinguished through those [species], for this is common to all things.

However, because a relation has its whole essence in an order to a terminus, it, therefore, takes its specification from that [terminus], as if from an ultimate extrinsic form, it, and therefore, through that [terminus] it is distinguished and defined, as was said above in Section 8.[22] But because the formal foundation is also essentially and intrinsically required for a relation, it can further be said to concur for the essence of a relation, as if by way of an extrinsic material cause. And in this way St. Thomas sometimes attributes this to the foundation and sometimes to the terminus, as is clear from [the *Summa Theologiae*], Part 3, Question 35, Article 5,[23] and Part 1, Question 32, Article 2,[24] where he simply attributes it to the terminus, because that is, as it were, ultimate and more formal with respect to a relation. See Soncinas, in *Metaphysics*, Book 5, Question 32,[25] and the above mentioned Section 8, Number 9 [sic],[26] and Section 10, Number 14.

Are There Simultaneously in the Same Subject Several Relations That Are Diverse only in Number?

16. As regards the third point, at this place there is usually raised /p. 863/ a question about the individuation of relations. For it is certain that, just as

---

21 Cf. n. 11, this Section.

22 Cf. Section 8, n. 11, above.

23 Cf. S. Thomae Aquinatis, *Opera omnia*, tomus XI (Romae: Ex Typographia Polyglotta, 1903), p. 356b.

24 Ibid., tomus IV (1888), p. 352.

25 Cf. *Quaestiones metaphysicales ...*, V, q. 32, p. 95.

26 Cf. Section 8, n. 11.

in the other categories the constitution of the categorical line descends from a supreme genus down to individuals, so is it also in this [category]. But it is controverted whether, just as for the constitution and specification of relations a terminus concurs in its own way, so also [does it do so] for individuation. From this depends also the answer to that common question: whether the same subject, under the same specific aspect, is related to several termini by a relation that is the same in number, or [is related] by diverse [relations]? I have touched on the question, enough I think (for it is a matter not of great importance), above in Disputation 5, Section 8, where I have generally treated the individuation of accidents and whether they can be several in number in the same subject.[27]

17. And according to the principles posited there, it can be without any difficulty conceded that several relations, differing only in number, respecting diverse termini can be simultaneously in the same subject, as, for example, two paternities in the same man with respect to two sons. For the formal effect of one is not entirely similar to the formal effect of another, as I declared in the cited place.

Again, [this is so] because when one terminus is posited, there results some relation that entirely depends on that terminus, but when another terminus is added, there is added a new respect, which will remain even if the other terminus is destroyed. Likewise, [this is so] because each terminus is the total terminus of some relation, when indeed, when that alone has been posited, some relation arises. And similar arguments can easily be multiplied, because of which Scotus, and others, whom I have cited in that place, embrace this opinion. Nor is there a difficulty of any importance in that, apart from the general one that accidents are individuated by a subject, about which in the cited place we have spoken extensively enough.

18. *What Consequently Must Be Said about This Matter, If a Relation Is Distinct in Reality from its Foundation.*—But since in this matter there can be great dissension in the way of speaking, it must be noted that we would have to proceed in one way if we hold that a relation is a thing or a real mode that is really distinct from its foundation, but in another way if it is distinguished only by reason.

For according to the first opinion, it cannot be denied that when the termini are multiplied, the respects are really increased, and that, when some new terminus is added, something real is added to a pre-existing relative. For

---

27 For this, cf. *DM* 5, 8 ("Whether, because of their individuation, it is impossible for two accidents which are only numerically diverse to be in the same subject" [*An repugnet duo accidentia solum numero diversa, esse simul in eodem subjecto ob eorum individuationem*])., vol. 25, pp. 189-97.

example, when a father generates a second son, he acquires something relative (*respectivum*) that he did not have before, something equally distinct from himself as was the paternity that he had before, for, speaking logically, the arguments that were made prove this. And because it is completely the same argument, for if when Peter generated his first son, he needed a new thing or a new mode that is real and distinct, in order that he mght be really related to that [son], why not also when he begins anew to be related to the second one? Neither indeed can it be said that the prior entity or mode is sufficient, both because a formal effect cannot increase unless the form really increases, and also because the prior relation was adequately related to the first son and it depends on him in being and in definition and knowledge. For this relation as singular in number[28] is not known, except as it relates to this singular in number terminus,[29] as Aristotle plainly stated in the *Categories*, the Chapter, "Toward Something."[30]

19. But now if it is once admitted that a real addition is made in a relative, when the addition of a new terminus has been made, it is perhaps only a verbal question whether that thing added is a distinct relation or composes one with the pre-existing relation, just as a second degree [of heat] composes one heat with a first [degree]. For in this way some explain the unity of this relation, lest they seem to multiply relations to infinity, and in order to universally defend that axiom that in one subject there is only one accident of one species.

However, those who speak in this way cannot sufficiently explain that unity, except only denominatively by reason of one subject or supposite. For if they are speaking logically, it is necessary that they say that the distinction between a paternity to a first son and that which is added when the second is begotten is as great as that which exists between that paternity itself and its foundation. Therefore, if the latter are distinguished really or modally, so also are the former. This is proven, because the relation of paternity to the first son is so compared to that which is added with respect to the second son, that that first paternity can be without this one added, and conversely, this added one can remain and constitute a father, without that first paternity. Therefore, if paternity is a real and distinct mode, because it is separable from its foundation, these two modes will also be actually distinct in reality between themselves, because one is separable from the other, and *vice versa.*

Likewise, if paternity is a proper entity really distinct from a foundation, those two respects also will be really distinct between themselves, as Scotus logically and correctly teaches, because they are mutually and in turn separable.

---

28 Literally: "as this in number."
29 Literally: "as this in number terminus."
30 Cf. *Categories* 7.8a37-b15.

But it was shown above, in Disputation 7, that whenever two things are so distinguished in reality that they can in turn both remain, one without the other, and they are not otherwise the modes of some subject with which they have a real identity, then that is a sufficient sign of a real distinction between them.[31] But the relations according to that opinion are not modes, but proper entities really distinct from their subjects, and between themselves, the respects of the father to the first son and to the second [son] are related (*comparantur*) so that the former can exist without the latter and the latter [can exist] without the former. Therefore, they are distinguished between themselves with a true real distinction.

20. But with this distinction posited, no reason can be given as to why those [respects] are not distinguished as two relations, or why they are said to be two degrees or two parts of one relation instead of two relations. For, first, they are not correctly equated with degrees of intension.[32] For between these latter degrees there is an essential subordination and in them there is a proper composition and a union through a proper extension, or proper indivisibles, as was explained in the preceding Disputation.[33] But those two relations do not have an essential subordination. For one does not suppose the other nor does it depend upon the other, nor does each of them have some extension in itself, but it is indivisible only in an order to its own terminus. Hence, they do not properly compose some quasi-continuous extension, because this [extension] is not composed of indivisibles. Then, no other kind of union can be imagined between those two entities, on account of which they may be said to be two parts of one relation, because they are not related between themselves as potency and act, nor do they have between themselves another relation (*habitudo*) besides that which is to be in the same subject. And this can be *a fortiori* confirmed from what we have said above about a similar unity or physical composition of habits.[34] Nay rather, that artificial unity or composition that is considered

---

31 Cf. *DM* 7, 2, nn. 2-3, in vol. 25, pp. 261-2.

32 Cf. degrees of heat in n. 19, this Section.

33 That is, *DM* 46, "On the Intension of Qualities" (*De intensione qualitatum*), vol. 26, pp. 753-781. In this forty-sixth Disputation, see esp. Section 1, "Whether among qualities there is an intensive range? And what is that?" (*An sit latitudo intensiva in qualitatibus, et quid illa sit.*), pp. 753-66 and Section 3, "Whether this range is achieved by change or by continuous succession?" (*An haec latitudo acquiratur mutatione, seu successione continua.*), pp. 794-99.

34 For this, cf. *DM* 44, esp.: Section 9, "Whether a habit is generated by one or by several acts?" (*An habitus uno, vel pluribus actibus generetur.*), vol. 26, pp. 686-90; Section 10, "Whether and how a habit is increased by acts?" (*Utrum habitus per actus augeatur, et quomodo.*), ibid., pp. 690-94; and Section 11, "Of what kind is

in the case of habits[35] can scarcely have place [here], and, therefore, nothing will be said of it.

21. But someone could imagine the unity of this relation to several termini in another way: not through an addition or a real composition, but through a change of relations, in such way that each in itself is indivisible, but they differ among themselves, because one has for its adequate terminus one thing, for example, one son, while a second has two [sons], and a third three [sons], etc.

Hence, according to this opinion, when a father begets a second son, a new relation is indeed acquired by that father, but it is not added to the pre-existing one. Rather the first one perishes and a second /col. b/ results anew, which [second] indivisibly and adequately relates that man to two sons, and not to more or to fewer. And if he begets a third [son], he loses that [relation], and acquires another that relates to three [sons] in the same way. For it seems certain that one relation can adequately relate indivisibly to several termini. For in this way in real categorical relatives a whole is related to several parts, or unity is related to a couple (*binarium*) by a subduple relation.[36] And in transcendental [relations] the same intellect respects several intelligibles inadequately, and in relatives [of reason] the same relation of genus respects several species. So it can, therefore, be understood that in any genus or species of relations there are some in individual cases (*in individuo*) that indivisibly and adequately respect several termini, which with respect to them will be partial, but from those there arises an adequate terminus, which is one by a certain collection. And, therefore, such a relation arises only when an adequate terminus is posited, but not when one or another partial [terminus] is posited. But, on the contrary, it is taken away or changed when a partial terminus is taken away or added, because by this very fact the whole terminus is changed.

22. Finally, many think in this way about the relation of one son to a father and a mother. For that this relation, essentially speaking, is an indivisible one, is probable from the fact that a father and a mother concur as one cause, and by an essentially necessary and unique action (especially if the mother concurs actively).[37] Hence, when either one of the parents has died, it is necessary that that relation perish. For if it indivisibly respects two parents, it cannot be di-

---

the extensive increase of a habit?—where there is also [discussion] about the unity of a habit." (*Quale sit augmentum extensivum habitus, ubi etiam de unitate habitus*), pp. 694-716.

35 For some of this, see my article: "Suárez on the Unity of a Scientific Habit," *The American Catholic Philosophical Quarterly*, 65 (1991), pp. 309-31.

36 That is, by a relation of one to two.

37 See nn. 24-28, below.

vided into parts, nor can the whole [relation] remain, since then it would not have an adequate terminus, nor would it relate to two [parents]. Therefore, the whole [relation] perishes. Therefore, it will be necessary that another arise, which relates to only one parent, if there is a survivor. For the son is truly and really related to that [parent].

23. But although this way of speaking seems to be carefully thought out in order to speak logically within that opinion, nevertheless, it is in fact arbitrary and without basis. For what necessity is there to introduce that frequent changing of relations? Otherwise, as often as a new thing would become white, all other white things that previously existed would change their relations of similarity with respect to all and would acquire new ones. Then, why will a father lose his relation to a first son, when a second is begotten, since none of those things is taken away that were necessary for the being of that first relation? For, notwithstanding the second son, the first is always a sufficient terminus of that /p. 865/ relation. Again, even though it is true that one relation can adequately respect several things, when essentially (*per se*) and by virtue of its species it requires those things in order that it result or be conserved or that it exercise its own formal effect, as is the case in the relation of the whole or of the subduple, nevertheless when a relation does not demand this of its nature, and the termini are multiplied only by accident, as happens in paternity, filiation, similarity, etc, it is said merely *gratis* that there arises one indivisible relation that adequately respects the collection of several termini, from the fact that or especially because the several sons are produced by distinct acts of generation. Why, therefore, will there result one indivisible relation which embraces both termini?

About the Relation of a Son to a Father and a Mother.

24. *An Opinion of Ferrara Is Disproved.*—But what was said about the relation of a son to two parents is also uncertain. For some think that in a son there are two relations, different not only in number but also in species, since they think that the relations of a father and a mother are different in species, by the fact that the former actively concurs while the latter [concurs] only passively. This is what Ferrara holds, *In Contra Gentiles*, Book 2, Chapter 11 [sic], § *Ex istis*, although he adds that those relations are formally two, but really and materially one.[38] I do not see how this is said logically, supposing that a relation is something distinct in reality from its foundation, as he supposes.

---

38 For this, see Ferrara, *Commentaria in Contra Gentiles*, II, c. 12, V., n. 3, in S. Thomae Aquinatis, *Opera omnia*, tomus XIII, p. 292ab.

25. *Fonseca's Opinion Is Not Proven.*—But others say that there is one relation to both parents, even if the father actively and the mother only passively concur. And at the same time they say that the relation remains completely identical and unchanged, even if one parent dies. Fonseca says this in *Metaphysics*, Book 5, Chapter 15, Question 5, Section 3.[39]

But both points are hard for me to believe. First, indeed, because if a mother concurs only passively, then the relations of father and mother will be specifically diverse, since they have such distinct foundations. Therefore, it cannot happen that a single relation in a correlative corresponds to them, which St. Thomas teaches in [*Summa Theologiae*], Part 1, Question 32, Article 2.[40] For specifically diverse correlatives are either formally diverse termini, or they indicate these; but relations have diversity from their formal termini. Again, the relation of an effect to a cause of diverse genus is also diverse, whether that [cause] is material, formal, or efficient. If, therefore, the causalities of father and mother differ as efficient and material, the relations in the effect will be diverse. Hence, supposing that opinion, /col. b/ a father and a mother do not so much compose one total cause, since they are not causing in the same genus, as [they compose] a collection of several diverse causes, such as are matter and the efficient [cause].

Secondly, it is difficult to believe in this opinion that a relation is indivisibly one with regard to a father and a mother, such that they make up one total cause, and nevertheless that the same total relation remains when that adequate terminus is removed from one side, because a relation depends upon its adequate terminus. This, I explain as follows: for when one parent is removed, then that relation of son cannot have its adequate formal effect, since it cannot relate the son to both parents. Therefore, it cannot simply have its own formal effect, for, since it indivisibly causes that [effect], it cannot contribute a part of that and not the whole, nor can the whole [cause] remain without contributing the whole effect, since it remains only in a subject and as inhering.

---

39 Cf. *Commentaria in Metaph.*, V, c. 15, q. 5, s. 3, vol. 2, col. 851.
40 Cf. S. Thomae Aquinatis, *Opera omnia*, tomus IV, p. 352.

26. *The Opinion of Others.*—Others, therefore, who with Galen,[41] Scotus,[42] and still others, figure that it is probable enough that a mother concurs actively, think that a son is related to his father and mother by two relations of the same species, and that the diversity in paternal and maternal concurrence is only accidental. And even though a father and a mother at once compose one total efficient cause, according to this opinion, nevertheless, just as they are one cause only by a collection of several partial ones, so it is enough that there correspond to them one correlative by a collection of several relations. Although here it could be said with some probability that those relations compose one, not properly by a physical unity, but as it were artificially and as fitted to the unity of the terminus. But by whichever of these modes one thinks about the relation of a son, it matters nothing for the mentioned opinion, which we are impugning. For I find no author who has said that when a son loses one parent, he loses the relation that he has to both and acquires a new one by which he is related only to the survivor, nor does that have any probability.

27. In this way, therefore, it seems we should think about the multiplication of relations that differ only in number in the same subject with respect to several adequate termini of the same nature. This indeed is easily explained according to the opinion that we think to be true, namely, that a relation is not a thing or a mode of a thing that is really distinct from its foundation. For it cannot be doubted that respects to really distinct termini, of which one can be without /p. 866/ the other, and conversely, are distinguished "by reasoned reason" (*ratione ratiocinata*), which has a basis in reality. Hence, just as this distinction suffices in order that relation constitute a special category (*genus*),[43] and be thought as another form [differing] from its foundation, so also it suf-

---

41 For a possible source of this, cf. Galen, *De Semine*, II, 5, translated by Phillip de Lacy in: *Galen On Semen*, edition, translation and commentary (Berlin: Akademie Verlag, 1992), p. 183-5: "... there are manifestly two kinds of similarities of offspring to parents; first is the similarity in kind of the /p. 185/ entire substance, when human being is produced from human being, horse from horse; and here the mother appeared to contribute the greater share. The second is the difference between animals of the same kind, between human being and human being, between horse and horse; and here the dominant semen was shown to make the greater contribution." At least in the first kind of similarity here there is an active contribution by the mother. Also, cf. de Lacy's note, ibid., p. 233, P. 154, 9-10.

42 Cf. *Quodlibet* XV, a. 1, n. 10, in *Obras del Doctor Sutil Juan Duns Escoto*, edicion bilingüe, ed. Alluntis, pp. 553-4. For an English translation, cf. *John Duns Scotus, God and Creatures, The Quodlibetal Questions*, translated with an Introduction, Notes, and Glossary by Felix Alluntis, O.F.M. and Allan B. Wolter, O.F.M. (Washington: The Catholic University of America Press, 1981), p. 353.

43 Cf. Section 2, n. 22, above.

fices in order that those respects to diverse termini be called several relations, distinct in number by that kind of distinction that has place in relations of this kind, namely, "of reasoned reason." And thus there is easily removed any wonder about the multiplication of relations; and all the arguments which are usually put forward to the contrary have no difficulty, especially, when those things are presupposed that we have said about the principle of individuation. Nor in order to further this opinion in this sense is it also necessary to multiply arguments. For apart from the fact that it is by itself probable, what [arguments] have been suggested are enough.

28. Finally, in this sense, St. Thomas is not much opposed to this opinion. For in [*Summa Theologiae*], Part 3, Question 35, Article 5, in reply to Objection 3, he says that in one son there is one relation to two parents, and two [relations] according to reason, and conversely he says, in several men rowing a boat there is one relation, which cannot be understood about the unity of a thing, since the subjects are really distinguished.[44] And in other places, although he says that in one father there is one relation to several sons, he, nevertheless, says that there are in that [father] several respects. Also Hispalensis speaks in the same way, in [his *Sentences* commentary], Book 3, Distinction 8, Note 3,[45] as does Capreolus in the same place, in his Solution of Arguments.[46] But these respects are not called several except on account of a distinction of reason. Therefore, in the same way, there can be said to be several relations. And finally, it is explained by a parallel (*a simili*): for the theologians call paternity and active spiration in the Trinity two relations on account of a distinction of termini even though in themselves they are distinguished only by reason. Why then is it strange that in the present case also there be said to be several relations to several really distinct termini?

---

44 Cf. S. Thomae Aquinatis, *Opera omnia*, tomus XI (Romae: Ex Typographia Polyglotta, 1903), p. 356b.

45 I have not had access to Book 3 of Hispalensis' *Commentary on the Sentences*. Therefore, I have been unable to verify this reference of Suárez.

46 Cf. *Defensiones, In 3 Sent.*, d. 8, q. 1, a. 3, ed. Paban-Pègues, tom. V, p. 130.

Section XVIII.
Which Properties Are Common to All Relatives.

1. About this matter Aristotle says nothing in the *Metaphysics*. But in his Logic[1] he has posited some properties of relatives, which it is necessary briefly to explain, even though some of them have already been explained. However, we could extend the discussion to the common attributes of being, especially, one and good; for they have a special difficulty in the way in which they agree with /col. b/ relations. But about unity many things have sufficiently been said. But concerning goodness, the question usually occurs: whether a relation expresses a perfection. This [question] we have treated above, in Disputation 10, and we have shown that it entails perfection just as it has entity.[2] Hence, if it is a thing distinct from its foundation or even a real mode that is really distinct, it is necessary that it add some perfection to that [foundation]. But if it adds nothing real, but is distinguished only by reason, it will indeed express a real perfection, but not one that is distinct in reality. And consequently, speaking in an absolute way, it will not add a perfection to its foundation, but it will express the same [perfection as its foundation] under a different aspect. Other remaining things have been sufficiently treated in the mentioned place.

Whether a Relation Has a Contrary.

2. Going on, therefore, to the properties of relatives designated by the Philosopher, the first is that a relation has a contrary.[3] For virtue is contrary to vice.[4] But this is not designated by Aristotle from his own opinion, but as a consequent of the first definition of relatives, which embraced all relatives "according to being said." Rather a contrary can, therefore, be numbered among the properties of a relation, because nothing is contrary to that, insofar as it is such, as the Philosopher himself said in the Chapter, On Quality.[5] But relation has its own proper kind of opposition, which was already explained.

Whether a Relation Receives More or Less.

3. The second property is that a relation receives more and less, which Aristotle says belongs to certain relations, but not to all. For the double is not

---

1 That is, in *Categories*, Chapter 7.
2 On this, cf. *DM* 10, 3, nn. 11-18, vol. 25, pp. 350-52.
3 Cf. *Categories* 7.6b15.
4 Ibid., 6b16.
5 Cf. *Categories* 8.10b22.

more and less double, but the similar or the equal are said to be more and less.[6] But it must be noted that this property is attributed to a relation in another way than to a quality. For it belongs to this latter, because it is truly capable of intension and remission, as was treated in the preceding Disputation.[7] But a relation is not in this way capable of intension. For it is not so by itself, since it not produced by itself, nor may it be [so] increased. Neither is it [capable of intension] by reason of its foundation. For even though a foundation is intensified, it is not necessary that a relation be intensified. For two white things intensified as eight are not more similar than they were earlier as four. But on the contrary, sometimes they become more similar through the remission of a foundation or of a terminus, but sometimes their similarity is diminished.

4. But this more or less is not on account of their intension, but on account of their variation, as Fonseca noted well /p. 867/ in his [Commentary on] *Metaphysics*, Book 5, Chapter 15, Question 5, Section 2.[8] For the relation of equality, for example, properly stated (and the same is true about perfect similarity) does not receive more and less, because it consists in something indivisible. For if one of two equals increases, they do not become less equal, but rather the equality perishes. But an inequality can be greater and lesser, on account of greater and lesser recession from perfect equality. And in the same way, equality or similarity said broadly and in a common way is said to be greater and lesser. However, those relations of greater or lesser inequality are indeed diverse and not the same thing that may be increased or diminished, because their termini and foundations are diverse, and the proportions in which they consist are also diverse, and thus each one in its own grade of inequality consists in something indivisible. So, therefore, certain relatives are said to receive more and less, that is, to be denominated more and less such, through approaching or receding from a perfect terminus, not through intension or remission.

How Relatives Are Said with Respect to Convertibility.

5. The third property is that relatives are said with respect to convertibility,[9] which some explain in this way that it is the same as being mutually related or that to one relation there always corresponds another. But, as it evident from what has been said, in this sense this property does not belong to all

---

6 Cf. *Categories* 7.6b19-27. On more or less equality, cf. n. 4, this Section, immediately following.

7 For this, see the whole of Disputation 46 ("About the Intension of Qualities" [*De intensione qualitatum*]), vol. 26, pp. 753-81.

8 Cf. *Commentaria in Metaph.*, V, c. 15, q. 5, s. 2, vol. 2, cols. 848-9.

9 Cf. *Categories* 7.6b27.

relations, unless it be extended to a relation of reason. Hence, this is not the sense of Aristotle, but rather only that according to some denomination one is denominated in conjunction with the other, and vice versa.

For example, knowledge is said to be knowledge of the knowable, and the knowable is said to be knowable by knowledge.[10] And therefore, Aristotle says that this convertibility is sometimes realized in the same and sometimes in a diverse case.[11] Hence, this property belongs more to the mode of speaking about relations than to the reality, although that mode of speaking has a basis in reality. But this is not a peculiar property of categorical relations. For it also belongs to transcendental relatives and even to relatives of reason.

6. The fourth property is that relatives are simultaneous in nature.[12] Fifth, that they are simultaneous in knowledge[13] and in definition,[14] which have already been explained by us;[15] and, therefore, with regard to the present Disputation, let these things suffice.

---

10 Ibid., 6b33-35.
11 Ibid., 6b36-38.
12 Ibid., 7b15.
13 Ibid., 8b13.
14 Ibid., 8a35-37.
15 See Section 16, esp. nn. 20, 24, 25, 26, 28, 29, 30, 33, and 34, above.

DISPUTATIO XLVII

The Latin Text

DISPUTATIO XLVII.
DE RELATIONE REALI IN COMMUNI.

Post duo praecedentia genera quantitatis et qualitatis, tractat Aristoteles de ad aliquid, in V Metaph., c. 15, non quia perfectius sit in entitate sua quam omnia sex ultima praedicamenta, cum Commentator, XII Metaph., com. 19, dicat relationem inter omnia genera esse minimae entitatis; quod quam verum sit, ex dicendis constabit. Non ergo perfectionis ordinem, sed ordinem doctrinae videtur Aristoteles observasse, tum quia doctrina ad hoc praedicamentum pertinens universalior est; tum etiam quia est quodammodo necessaria ad caeterorum praedicamentorum cognitionem, eo quod magna ex parte videntur in relatione consistere. Accedit etiam quod quamplurimae relationes ad quantitatem et qualitatem proxime consequuntur. De relatione igitur prius in communi videbimus an sit, quid sit, et quotuplex, et quas proprietates vel causas habeat, et deinde de praecipuis relationum generibus earumque fundamentis ac terminis magis in particulari disseremus.
/p. 782/

SECTIO PRIMA.
AN RELATIO SIT VERUM GENUS ENTIS REALIS, DISTINCTUM A RELIQUIS.
Variae rationes quibus tota fere difficultas hujus praedicamenti proponitur.

1. *Prima.*—Prima ratio dubitandi esse potest quia relatio ut relatio nihil rei ponit in re quae referri dicitur; ergo non potest constituere reale genus entis. Consequentia est evidens, quia reale genus fundatur in ente reali, quod in rerum natura sit seu ponat aliquid; relatio autem, prout rebus creatis tribuitur (sic enim nunc de illa agimus), non potest aliquid rei esse in rerum natura, si illud non ponit in re ipsa relata, quia neque in termino aliquid ponit, ut per se notum est, licet forte supponat, de quo postea; neque in sese manet, cum non sit substantia; ergo, si in re ipsa relata nihil ponit, absolute nihil rei est. Probatur autem antecedens, primo, quia ad, ut ad, non dicit realem rationem, tum quia univoce et secundum totam proprietatem suam convenit relationibus rationis; tum etiam quia ad, ut ad, praescindit ab esse in; ergo ut sic nihil rei ponit in aliquo. Alioqui secundum propriam et ultimam rationem suam includeret inesse, quod repugnat; ergo relatio nihil rei ponit in re quam refert.

Patet consequentia, quia relatio ut relatio nihil aliud dicit quam esse ad, dicente Aristotele relativa illa esse quorum totum esse est ad aliud se habere.

2. *Secunda.*—Secundo, quia haec denominatio relativa adveniens alicui de novo, non immutat illud nec in re ipsa facit illud aliter se habere quam antea, dicente Arist. V Phys., text. 10, relationem advenire sine rei mutatione; ergo relatio nihil ponit in tali re. Patet consequentia, quia impossibile est intelligere aliquid rei de novo adjungi alicui subjecto, et illud non se habere in re ipsa aliter quam antea, quia, si ei aliquid est additum, aliquid habet quod antea non habebat: hoc autem ipsum est aliter se habere. Quod autem quidam respondent non habere aliquid, sed ad aliquid, ludus quidem verborum esse videtur; nam interrogo an illud ad aliquid sit aliquid; nam, si est, ergo qui habet ad aliquid de novo, aliquid etiam de novo habet; ergo aliter se habet, et mutatum est; si vero ad aliquid non est aliquid, ergo nihil est, et hoc intendimus.

/col. b/

3. *Tertia.* Tertio declaratur hoc amplius, quia relatio, ut relatio, nihil est praeter absoluta; ergo simpliciter nihil est. Patet consequentia, quia, cum quaerimus an relatio sit aliquid rei, de illa agimus ut distinguitur vel praescinditur a rebus absolutis; alioqui quomodo erit distinctum genus entis? Antecedens vero probatur, quia si ponamus, verbi gratia, duo alba in rerum natura, illa, ex vi qualitatum absolutarum quas habent, sunt inter se similia; ergo habent illam denominationem relativam ex vi absolutorum simul existentium seu simul sumptorum, absque aliqua alia additione reali; ergo relatio nihil rei addit rebus absolutis. Utraque consequentia est manifesta, quia, si relatio aliquid est, solum est propter illam denominationem relativam quae intercedere videtur inter illa absoluta; si ergo haec ipsa denominatio ex solis absolutis sumitur, quidquid aliud adjungitur, fictitium est. Probatur autem antecedens, quia, positis duobus albis in rerum natura, sive mente separes omne aliud reale eis additum, sive per potentiam Dei absolutam ponamus illud separari aut impediri, nihilominus illa duo manebunt inter se similia, nec mens potest aliud concipere, quia necessario retinent unitatem formalem, et nihil aliud est esse similes quam habere qualitates ejusdem rationis. Quod si quis respondeat hoc vere dici de rebus similibus fundamentaliter, non formaliter, petet sane principium; nam hoc est quod intendimus, scilicet, ibi non esse aliam denominationem nisi hanc quae appellatur fundamentalis; nam haec satis est ut illae res vere sint similes, et illa alia formalis denominatio aut nihil est, aut ad summum est consideratio rationis.

4. Et confirmatur, nam hoc modo salvantur multae denominationes similes absque additione aliqua quae intrinsece fiat in re denominata; sic enim dicitur Deus creator vel dominus ex tempore; sic columna dicitur dextra vel sinistra; sic paries dicitur visus, etc.; ergo, eadem ratione, potest sufficienter salvari omnis

similis denominatio sine additione relationis quae sit aliquid rei. Quod si quis dicat in exemplis positis deesse fundamentum ex parte rerum denominatarum, respondebimus et fortasse hoc non esse in universum verum, quod postea tractabimus, et non satisfacere, quia, si res quae non habet fundamentum denominari potest relative ex positione alterius, etiamsi nihil rei ipsi addatur, ergo multo magis, res quae habet /p. 783/ aliquod fundamentum poterit ex vi ejus et coexistentiae alterius praecise, sic denominari, absque additione alicujus rei respectivae; ergo hujusmodi respectus nihil rei est praeter absolutum.

5. *Quarta.*—Quarto argumentari possumus (et est altera ratio principalis dubitandi), quia, licet demus relationem esse aliquid rei, non tamen potest novum genus entis constituere, diversum a reliquis. Probatur: quoniam ordo ad aliud, intrinsece includitur in omni reali conceptu entis creati. Nam imprimis omne ens creatum, quatenus tale est, etiam ipsa substantia, dicit habitudinem essentialis dependentiae ad ens increatum, et ideo est analogice ens, vel substantia, comparatione illius. Omne item accidens dicit essentialem habitudinem ad subjectum, ob quam dicitur esse entis ens, potius quam ens. Rursus, in singulis generibus accidentium invenire est singulas habitudines; nam quantitas quatenus continua est, dicit essentialem habitudinem ad terminos quibus continuatur, et e converso punctus, et alii similes termini, dicunt essentialem habitudinem ad partes quarum sunt termini. Et inter qualitates potentia dicit essentialem habitudinem ad objectum, et de scientia, et consequenter de habitus ac dispositione, Aristot., in cap. de Qualit., fatetur esse ad aliquid.

6. Addit vero, esse ad aliquid secundum rationes genericas, scientiae, verbi gratia, non vero secundum specificas, *nam scientia* (inquit) *est ad scibile, grammatica vero ut sic non est ad aliud.* Sed hoc imprimis est falsum; nam, licet forte nomina non sint tam clare imposita, tamen secundum rem, sicut scientia in communi, dicit habitudinem ad objectum scibile in communi, ita haec scientia ad hoc objectum. Deinde nihil refert ad praesentem difficultatem; nam genus et species ad idem praedicamentum pertinent; ergo, si haec scientia in specie est qualitas, ergo scientia in communi est genus de praedicamento qualitatis; ergo cum sit etiam ad aliquid, impossibile erit ut ea, quae sunt ad aliquid, in speciali praedicamento collocentur. Multo vero minus satisfacere videtur, quod statim subdit Aristoteles, non esse absurdum idem collocari sub qualitate, et ad aliquid, si utrumque ei convenit. Quia idem non potest essentialiter constitui in diversis praedicamentis; scientia autem, verbi gratia, non accidentaliter tantum, sed essentialiter est ad aliquid, tum quia tota ejus entitas intrinsece /col. b/ ordinatur ad scibile, ut in cap. de Ad aliquid, Aristoteles fatetur; tum etiam quia alias, si tantum accidentaliter scientia referretur ad scibile, non constitueretur ipsa scientia sub genere Ad aliquid, sed illa relatio, quae illi accidentaliter advenit, quod est contra Aristotelem in eodem c. de Qualitate.

Eademque difficultas urget de sex ultimis praedicamentis, quae ex omnium sententia relationem aliquam includunt, et sic de situ id expresse fatetur Aristoteles in Praedicam., et de caeteris suis locis dicemus. Ergo haec ratio Ad aliquid, transcendens est, et inclusa in omni entitate, praesertim creata; non ergo constituit peculiare genus.

7. Duae vero responsiones dari solent ad hanc ultimam difficultatem. Prior est, haec omnia, quae enumeravimus in caeteris praedicamentis, solum esse relativa secundum dici; ea vero, quae constituunt speciale praedicamentum, solum esse relativa secundum esse. Sed haec responsio refutabitur facile, si interrogemus quid significetur per relativa secundum dici; aut enim sic appellantur res illae, de quibus ita loquimur, ac si essent relativae, cum nullam in re habeant inter se habitudinem, aut ita appellantur quaedam res, quae habent quidem in re aliquam habitudinem, alterius tamen rationis a relatione reali. Primum dici non potest, tum quia scientia non solum in modo loquendi, sed in re habet suum esse ordinatum ad scibile, et potentia ad objectum suum, et sic de aliis; tum etiam quia si hae denominationes vel locutiones respectivae, dicuntur esse in nostro modo loquendi et non in re, idem dicetur de omni simili denominatione, nec relinquetur probabilis via ad ponendas hujusmodi relationes reales, nam maxime colliguntur ex hujusmodi denominationibus. Si vero alterum membrum eligatur, explicandum est quaenam sint hujusmodi habitudines, aut in quo distinguantur a relationibus, vel ad quid sint necessariae relationes diversae rationis ab hujusmodi habitudinibus. Et in hoc indicatur alia responsio, et difficultas ejus. Dici enim solet, in praedictis rebus aliorum praedicamentorum includi respectus transcendentales, non vero proprias relationes praedicamentales, quae peculiare genus constituunt. Statim vero circa hujusmodi partitionem interrogandum occurrit, quid necesse sit multiplicare hos diversos modos respectuum; nam si respectus transcendens est verus et realis, ille sufficit ad omnes denominationes relativas, quae non /p. 784/ sunt pure denominationes extrinsecae; ergo supervacaneum est fingere alias relationes. Deinde oportebit explicare quidnam discriminis sit inter hujusmodi respectus, vel cur unus constituat peculiare genus, et non alius.

Variae sententiae proponuntur.

8. *Prima.*—Hae videntur esse principuae difficultates quae circa relationem realem in communi occurrunt. Aliae vero, quae circa singula genera relationum offerri poterant, inferius proponentur. Ob has ergo difficultates possunt esse duo dicendi modi. Prior est, nullas esse veras relationes reales, sed denominationes omnes quae ad modum relationum explicantur, desumi ab ipsis absolutis, vel ex eorum coexistentia. Hanc opinionem referunt Averroes, 12 Metaph., com-

ment. 19; et Avicen., lib. 3 suae Metaph., c. 10; eamque secutus est Aureolos apud Capreol., in 1, dist. 30, quaest. 1.

9. *Secunda.*—Alia sententia esse potest, esse quidem in rebus relationes reales, illas vero non constituere peculiare genus entis, sed esse conditionem quamdam transcendentem, quae in omnibus entibus includi potest. Hanc sententiam Zenoni et antiquioribus philosophis ante Platonem tribuit Soto in principio praedicamenti Ad aliquid, ex Albert. et Alexand., ibidem.

10. *Tertia.*—Jam vero recepta sententia, et quasi philosophicum et commune axioma est, dari in rebus creatis relationes reales, proprium ac speciale praedicamentum constituentes. Haec fuit sententia Platonis, eumque secutus est Aristoteles, et hunc omnes ejus interpretes, Averroes, Simplicius, et caeteri omnes Graeci et Latini, quos imitati sunt Theologi, D. Thomas, 1 p., q. 13, art. 7, quaest. 28, art. 1 et 2, et saepe alias; Capreol. et alii, in 1, d. 33; Gregor., late, d. 28, q. 1; Henric., Quodl. 3, q. 4, et Quodl. 9, quaest. 3. Non solum propter rationes philosophicas, sed etiam quod illa sententia aptior sit ad mysterium Trinitatis declarandum, et ex illo plurimum confirmari videatur.

11. Docet enim fides Catholica esse in Deo tres relationes reales, constituentes et distinguentes divinas personas: ex quo fit evidens argumentum, conceptum relationis ut sic, non addendo quod creata sit vel increata, non esse fictitium, et rem aliquam referri non esse denominationem extrinsecam provenientem ex sola comparatione mentis, sed /col. b/ esse aliquid rei, quandoquidem in Deo aliquid rei est. Et hinc ulterius magna verisimilitudine colligitur, etiam in rebus creatis esse posse aliquid rei. Quia vel repugnaret rebus creatis ob perfectionem earum, vel repugnaret ob imperfectionem. Primum dici non potest, quia si relatio non repugnat summae perfectioni Dei, cur repugnabit perfectioni creaturae? Dices: quia illa relatio Dei substantialis est, in creatura vero esse debet accidentalis. Sed contra, quia relationi ut sic non magis repugnat quod sit accidentalis, quam quod sit substantialis, quia sicut accidens dicit esse in alio, ita substantia dicit esse in se; si ergo cum hac ratione conjungi potest esse ad aliud, multo magis cum illa; et alioqui creaturae ut sic non repugnat accidens reale; ergo nec repugnabit illi talis relatio, quae, etsi sit accidentalis, aliquid rei sit. Nec vero repugnare potest ob imperfectionem, quia relatio ut relatio non dicit imperfectionem; quod si aliquid imperfectionis ei adjungitur ex eo quod accidentalis sit, talis imperfectio non est extra latitudinem rei creatae. Hoc ergo argumento Theologico efficaciter probari videtur dari posse in rebus creatis, et de facto dari respectus reales.

12. Argumentis autem ex sola naturali ratione desumptis probari hoc solet, praecipue ex locutionibus et denominationibus relativis quae in rebus ipsis existunt, absque ulla fictione intellectus, quas proinde necesse est in aliquo ente reali fundari; non fundantur autem in absoluto; ergo in relativo; datur

ergo in rebus ens reale relativum. Antecedens patet in his denominationibus, *majus, minus, aequale, simile, propinquum, remotum, pater, filius,* et similibus. Hae namque omnes habitudinem plane dicunt ad aliud, sine quo nec esse, nec intelligi possunt, et in rebus ipsis existunt, ut per se notum videtur.

13. Quanta vero sit vis harum probationum, videbimus in sequentibus; nam posterior naturalis ratio magna ex parte pendet ex solutionibus argumentorum, quas tradere non possumus, nisi prius multa de distinctione et divisione relationum explicemus. Argumentum autem Theologicum aliquibus non videtur satis efficax ad ostendendas relationes praedicamentales, quia relationes divinae extra omne praedicamentum sunt; quod si Deus esset in praedicamento substantiae, ad illud idem pertinerent vel reducerentur illae relationes, eo quod sint personalitates divinae naturae. Sicut personalitates vel substantiae /p. 785/ creatae ad illud ipsum praedicamentum pertinent. Unde neque argumentum a simili, a paternitate, verbi gratia, divina ad creatam, est multum efficax, quia paternitas divina non est resultans, neque consequens generationem, sed potius constituit personam, quae est generationis principium. Et ideo illa paternitas increata, sicut substantialis est, ita existimari potest quasi transcendentalis, id est, intime inclusa in conceptu adaequato talis entis, seu substantiae personalis. Ex illis ergo relationibus non videntur posse colligi relationes praedicamentales, sed ad summum respectus reales transcendentales intime inclusi in aliquibus entibus.

14. Alia vero ostensio dictarum relationum specialiter sumi solet ex ordine universi, qui est accidentarium quid rebus ipsis absolutis, quibus constat universum; nam etsi elementa et coeli alio ordine constituerentur, res ipsae absolutae eaedem essent; est ergo ordo, quem nunc habent, aliquid accidentarium ipsis. Et non est aliquid per rationem confictum, nam per se constat in rebus ipsis esse, et ad magnam universi perfectionem spectare, ut testis est Aristot., 12 Metaphys., text. 52; et non est nisi relatio, quam necesse est per se ad proprium praedicamentum pertinere, quia non est de intrinseca ratione alicujus rei absolutae, nec etiam signari potest ad quod aliorum praedicamentorum pertineat vel revocetur. Verumtamen haec probatio eas patitur difficultates quae inter argumentandum tactae sunt, quia ordo pertinens ad perfectionem universi tantum est, ut singula corpora in suis naturalibus locis sint constituta, quod quidem absolutum est in singulis, et in omnibus simul dicit coexistentiam eorum; quod vero ad hoc consequitur peculiare accidens, quod sit relatio realis, nihil videtur referre ad universi perfectionem.

Quaestionis resolutio.

15. Nihilominus tertiam et communem sententiam, ut veram et in philosophia certam supponimus, quam nunc maxime auctoritate confirmamus.

Ratio vero ejus et ostensio potissimum sumenda est ex illis denominationibus relativis, addendo duo. Primum est, illas esse tales ut accidant rebus creatis absolutis, possintque variari in aliquo subjecto sine amissione formae absolutae, quod satis constat in omnibus fere exemplis supra adductis. Secundum est, has non esse denomin- /col. b/ nationes mere extrinsecas, et in hoc est difficultas, pendet tamen ex infra dicendis; oportet enim prius modum entitatis talium relationum et denominationum declarare.

SECTIO II.
Utrum relatio realis praedicamentalis distinguatur realiter, vel modaliter ac ex natura rei, a substantia, et omnibus accidentibus absolutis.

1. Haec quaestio maxime necessaria est ad explicandum quo sensu relationes creatae sint aliquid reale, et quid etiam sint, quamve entitatem habeant. In eaque variae sunt opiniones.

Prima opinio ponens distinctionem realem rejicitur.

2. Prima docet relationem realem semper esse rem distinctam realiter a suo subjecto et fundamento. Haec est opinio veterum Thomistarum, Capreoli, in 1, dist. 30, quaest. 1; Cajetan, 1 part., quaest. 28, art. 2; Ferrar., 4 cont. Gent., cap. 14. Qui fundantur in verbis D. Thomae eisdem locis, et quaest. 8 de Potent., art. 1, et in 1, dist. 33, quaest. 1, art. 1, quibus locis constituit differentiam inter relationem creatam et increatam, quod prior non identificatur cum substantia, *sed est alia res et facit compositionem cum illa*, quod secus est in relatione increata. Haec tamen sententia intellecta de propria et rigorosa distinctione reali, qualis est inter entitates omnino condistinctas, nullum habet fundamentum satis probabile. Nam quae ab his auctoribus afferuntur de separabilitate relationis a fundamento, aut diversis mutationibus quae in eis fieri possunt, ad summum probant distinctionem ex natura rei, si tamen aliquid probant; nam probabilius fortasse est etiam illud non ostendere, ut videbimus tractando sequentes opiniones. Ex quarum etiam argumentis, et ex probationibus nostrae sententiae haec opinio sufficienter refutabitur. Quanquam ad eam rejiciendam sufficere possint ea, quae in principio sectionis praecedentis proposita sunt; illa enim, ut opinor, sufficienter demonstrant, relationem non esse rem in se habentem propriam entitatem realiter distinctam ab omnibus entitatibus absolutis.

Rejicitur opinio Scoti, quatenus superiori concordat.

3. Atque idem judicium ferendum est de /p. 786/ opinione Scoti, in 2, dist. 1, quaest. 3, et in 3, dist. 8, quaest. 1, quantum ad eam partem qua cum praecedenti convenit. Distinguit enim ille quasdam relationes quae separari nullo modo possunt a suis fundamentis, ut est relatio creaturae, ab aliis quae separari possunt, ut est, verbi gratia, relatio similitudinis, et has posteriores ait distingui realiter a fundamentis, propter ipsammet separationem; illas vero negat distingui, quia cum inseparabiles sint, nullum relinquitur signum distinctionis realis, neque aliunde apparet necessitas ejus. Verumtamen, quod attinet ad priorem partem, jam supra ostensum est, illud signum non indicare distinctionem realem, sed ad summum modalem, maxime quando separatio non est convertibilis (ut sic dicam), sicut accidit in praesenti; nam, licet fundamentum possit manere sine relatione, relatio tamen non potest ullo modo manere sine fundamento. Ex quo potest non leve argumentum sumi contra hanc partem, et contra totam superiorem sententiam. Addo praeterea, hoc signum in praesenti non esse sufficiens ad indicandam distinctionem modalem, quae sit actualis et ex natura rei, quia, licet denominatio relativa tollatur manente fundamento, et ablato termino, tamen utroque manente auferri non potest, et ideo ex illo signo non concluditur efficaciter relationem esse aliquid distinctum a fundamento, quod ab illo aufertur quando cessat illa denominatio, quia potest denominatio illa includere vel connotare concomitantiam, aut coexistentiam alterius extremi, et ideo cessare, non quia aufertur aliquid a fundamento, sed quia aufertur aliquid a termino. Unde, si aliquae relationes sunt inseparabiles a fundamentis, ideo est quia termini earum non possunt non existere, et ideo positis fundamentis necesse est ut denominationes relativae insurgant. Ut, si per impossibile manere posset essentia creata non existente Deo, cessaret relatio creaturae ad ipsum; quod ergo nunc separari non possit, non solum est propter identitatem cum fundamento, sed etiam propter intrinsecam termini necessitatem. Ergo, e converso, ex eo quod aliae relationes cessent ablatis terminis, non recte infertur distinctio ex natura rei, nisi aliunde ostendatur solam destructionem ipsius termini ad id non sufficere.

Durandi in hoc sententia non probatur.

4. Quapropter Durandus, in 1, dist. 30, /col. b/ quaest. 2, alia distinctione utitur, scilicet, quasdam esse relationes quae sunt verae habitudines et respectus reales, consequentes ad sua fundamenta, per se, vel accidentaliter, ut inhaerentia per se sequitur ad naturam accidentis, et tangere aut tangi consequitur per accidens ad corpora quanta; alias vero esse, quae solum sunt denominationes relativae, ut esse aequale et simile. Dicit igitur has posteriores non distingui in re a fundamentis, neque addere aliquid rei ultra existentiam et concomitantiam

utriusque extremi absoluti, ex qua mutua coexistentia ait sumi denominationes illas, quas nihilominus dicit pertinere ad praedicamentum relationis, et sufficere ad illud constituendum. Et de hac parte posterius videbimus. De prioribus autem respectibus ait distingui realiter a suis fundamentis, in quo convenit cum praecedentibus opinionibus, et eodem utitur fundamento, scilicet, illo signo separabilitatis fundamenti a tali respectu. De quo signo jam dictum est, ad summum posse ostendere distinctionem modalem; neque Durandus amplius intendit, ut legenti facile patebit; solumque differt in usu vocis, appellans eam realem, quia in rebus ipsis invenitur.

5. Quod vero attinet ad hanc partem sententiae Durandi, advertenda est quaedam subdivisio prioris membri, seu realis habitudinis, quam in eadem parte breviter attigit, et consideranda etiam sunt exempla quibus utrumque membrum declarat. Nam quidam respectus (inquit) consequitur per accidens ad fundamentum, ut tactus ad quantitatem; alius sequitur per se, ut inesse consequitur etiam ad quantitatem, et utrumque respectum ait distingui in re a suo fundamento. Sed in priori membro et exemplo, non videtur Durandus constanter loqui; nam qua ratione ait res dici similes vel aequales, non per additionem alicujus respectus ex natura rei distincti, sed per solam coexistentiam utriusque extremi, et denominationem inde ortam, consequenter dicere deberet, duo corpora sese tangere per denominationem ortam ex coexistentia utriusque extremi in tali loco, absque aliquo alio respectu ex natura rei distincto. Suppono enim sermonem esse de tactu pure quantitativo; nam tactus physicus aliquid aliud addit, quamvis non solam relationem, sed actionem physicam unius in aliud. Tactus ergo quantitativus nihil aliud est quam propinquitas quaedam inter duas quantitates et terminos earum, ita /p. 787/ ut nulla alia quantitas interposita sit. Sed hoc convenit duobus corporibus, hoc ipso quod in talibus locis seu spatiis existunt, absque additione alicujus modi, vel respectus ex natura rei distincti, saltem juxta doctrinam ipsius Durandi, quia eadem argumenta, quae hoc probare possunt de similitudine, probant de tactu, et de quacumque propinquitate vel distantia, nimirum, quia positis duobus corporibus in talibus locis, et praecisa omni alia re vel modo reali vel per intellectum, vel per divinam potentiam, impossibile est quin illa corpora se tangant; ergo est eadem ratio de hac denominatione. Et in universum idem est de omni respectu, qui dicitur per accidens consequi ad fundamentum; nam ille ideo per accidens erit, quia est talis denominatio, quae requirit coexistentiam alterius extremi, quam tamen ipsum fundamentum secundum se non requirit, ut aperte constat in dicto exemplo de tactu. Ergo semper potest illa denominatio sumi ex coexistentia extremorum, absque alio respectu in re ipsa distincto ab extremis; vel si illa non est sola denominatio, sed intrinseca habitudo, idem erit in omnibus illis quas Durandus ponit in secundo membro suae principalis distinctionis.

6. Quod vero spectat ad aliud membrum de respectu, qui per se consequitur ad fundamentum, et de exemplo inhaesionis, nomine respectus potest significari ipsemet modus inhaesionis, seu unionis, vel relatio aliqua praedicamentalis inde exorta. In priori sensu, verum est illum respectum distingui ex natura rei a forma seu re cujus est modus, quae appellatur fundamentum talis respectus, quod a nobis in superioribus saepe traditum est, et eodem argumento confirmatum. Quanquam illud, quod Durandus ait, scilicet, hunc respectum nullam compositionem facere cum suo fundamento, falsum sit, ut in superioribus saepe dictum est, tractando de distinctionibus rerum, et de compositione naturae et suppositi, et aliis locis. Hic vero respectus non est praedicamentalis, sed transcendentalis, quia ille modus unionis vel inhaerentiae non est aliquid resultans ex fundamento et termino, sed est modus absolutus, qui per se fieri potest per actionem aliquam, quamvis intime et essentialiter includat respectum transcendentalem ad unibilia, quod etiam est in superioribus tactum, et infra ex professo declarabitur, partim in hac disputatione, partim disputando de actione. Con- /col. b/ sideratio ergo illius respectus in praedicto sensu nihil refert ad praesentem quaestionem. Si autem sit sermo de respectu praedicamentali, qui resultare censetur inter formam inhaerentem et subjectum ejus, et in universum inter ea quae sunt unita, eadem erit ratio de tali respectu, quae de contactu, similitudine et omnibus similibus, quod nimirum ille, nulla res vel modus realis sit ex natura rei distinctus ab extremis, sed solum mutua denominatio orta in extremis ex coexistenita eorum sub tali modo existendi. Quod facile ostendi potest applicando rationem superius factam. Igitur proprie loquendo de respectu praedicamentali, haec etiam distinctio Durandi necessaria non est, sed vel dicendum est omnem relationem praedicamentalem esse aliquid distinctum, vel non esse.

Quarta opinio de distinctione modali vel formali relationis a fundamento exponitur.

7. Est igitur quarta sententia, quae in universum affirmat relationem realem distingui actualiter a suo subjecto et fundamento, non tamen omnino realiter ut rem a re, sed modaliter tanquam modum realem ab ipsa re. Hanc opinionem videntur tenere Javell., 5 Metaph., quaest. 22; et Sotus, circa praedicamentum Ad aliquid, quaest. 2. Illi tamen non appellant hanc distinctionem modalem, sed formalem, sentiunt tamen esse actualiter in rebus ante omnem considerationem intellectus. At vero Fonseca, lib. 5 Metaph., cap. 15, quaest. 2, sect. 5, affirmat quidem relationem praedicamentalem distingui a fundamento, formali distinctione, ita ut habeat proprium esse essentiae et existentiae distinctum ab esse fundamenti; negat tamen illam distinctionem esse realem, aut esse modalem, aut rationis tantum, sed quamdam aliam mediam, quam significat

esse minorem reali distinctione, majorem modali. Diversitatem autem in hoc
constituere videtur, quod in distinctione modali modus non habet proprium
esse distinctum ab esse rei, cujus est modus; in hac vero distinctione formali
utrumque extremum habet proprium esse. Item in hac utrumque extremum
est propria entitas; in distinctione autem modali modus non est entitas. Unde
in hoc maxime fundat sententiam suam, quod relatio habet proprium esse
distinctum ab esse fundamenti; nam esse fundamenti est absolutum, et in se
tantum; esse vero relationis est esse consis- /p. 788/ tens in habitudine ad aliud,
ut ex Aristotelis definitione constat.

8. Ego tamen imprimis non percipio distinctionem hanc mediam inter realem et modalem, quae sit vera distinctio actualis in re, et multo major quam
distinctio rationis, cum dicatur etiam esse major quam modalis. Primo, quia
in distinctione modali, sicut modus in re ipsa distinguitur ab ipsa re cujus est
modus, ita habet aliquod esse proprium, aeque et proportionaliter distinctum
ab esse ipsius rei, ut tractando de existentia declaratum est. Rursus sicut modus
est aliquid in rebus existens, ita dici potest habere entitatem aliquam, prout
hac voce significatur quidquid non est nihil; quia vero talis entitas ejus est naturae et conditionis, ut per se non valeat ens reale primo ac per se constituere,
sed necessario debet esse conjuncta et identificata alicui enti, quod afficiat et
modificet, ideo non res, sed modus rei appellatur.

9. Hinc ergo constat nullum posse esse medium, in distinctionibus ex natura
rei, inter realem, et modalem, ut in genere supra tractatum est in disputatione
septima. Et in particulari declaratur in re de qua agimus. Nam relatio realis, ex
eo praecise quod habeat proprium esse, et sit aliquid in re distinctum a fundamento, non habet quod sit entitas, aut modus realis; nam illud commune
est utrique; ergo praecise ex illo principio non concluditur sufficienter major
distinctio quam modalis, neque aliud genus entitatis, praeter illud quod in
modis realibus reperitur. Deinde vel relatio realis talem habet entitatem, quae
possit intelligi primo ac per se et essentialiter constituta per solam rationem
respectivam, ita ut ex hoc capite non repugnet talem entitatem solam esse
sine entitate fundamenti: aut vero talem habet entitatis modum, ut intrinsece
postulet esse conjunctum fundamento, et suo modo afficiens illud, ita ut per
nullam potentiam aliter esse possit. Si primum dicatur, aperte concluditur
esse veram ac propriam rem, omnino realiter distinctam a fundamento, quod
haec sententia non admittit. Si vero dicatur secundum, non erit illa distinctio
alia quam modalis, supposito quod actu sit in re. Ergo sicut inter illa duo non
potest cogitari medium, ita neque inter illas duas distinctiones ex natura rei
potest medium excogitari. Aut enim extrema distinctionis possunt in re mutuo
separari, et unum sine alio vicissim conservari, et sic est distinctio realis omnino
propria et rigo- /col. b/ rosa; aut unum tantum extremum potest separari, et

manere sine alio, non vero e converso, et hanc distinctionem nos vocamus modalem; praeter hos autem duos modos non est alius, quia si utrumque extremum sit inseparabile in re ab alio, erit distinctio rationis, non vero ex natura rei. Cum ergo in praesenti fundamentum et relatio non sint mutuo separabilia, ut est per se notum apud omnes, quia nullo modo potest intelligi relatio praedicamentalis sine fundamento, non potest major aut alia distinctio, quae in re actu sit, intervenire inter relationem et fundamentum, praeterquam modalis. Quamvis ergo dicti auctores aliis vocibus utantur, appellantes hanc distinctionem formalem, tamen necesse est ut de modali loquantur, si tamen de actuali distinctione, quae in rebus ipsis existat, suam sententiam intelligant: nam aliqui eorum non satis hoc ipsum explicant, ut inferius dicemus.

Suadetur dicta opinio.

10. Praecipuum autem fundamentum hujus sententiae sic expositae de modali distinctione est illud, quod ex signo separationis sumitur. Nam fundamentum est ita separabile a relatione, ut possit in re manere sine illa; ergo necesse est ut in re ipsa distinguantur, saltem modaliter, juxta principia superius posita, disputat. 7. Secundo, hoc satis apparenter confirmat illa ratio, quod relatio habet proprium esse, intrinsece consistens in habitudine ad aliud: ergo oportet ut in re ipsa distinguatur ab esse absoluto. Tertio id declaro in hunc modum, quia quando, existente uno tantum albo, verbi gratia, quod antea nulli erat simile, fit aliud album, vel illud prius habet aliquod esse reale respectivum, quod antea non habebat, vel nihil habet de novo. Hoc secundum dici non potest, alias relatio nihil rei est, quia si antea nihil erat, et postea nullum esse reale recipit, nunquam est aliquid; ergo illud esse respectivum, quod additur, necessario debet esse distinctum ab eo cui additur, saltem modali distinctione. Nam si unum erat, et aliud nondum erat, et postea additur seu consurgit, non possunt esse unum et idem in re.

11. Quarto, nam cum una res dicitur similis alteri, vel unus homo pater alterius, vel istae sunt denominationes mere extrinsecae, aut sunt intrinsecae. Primum dici non /p. 789/ potest; ergo necessario dicendum est secundum; ergo necessaria est aliqua forma intrinsece denominans; ergo illa necessario esse debet distincta ex natura rei, saltem modaliter, a re denominata. Minor probatur primo, quia si esset denominatio extrinseca, ut sic non esset respectiva, quia potius esset veluti applicatio formae extrinsecae ad subjectum denominatum, quam habitudo ipsius subjecti ad terminum extrinsecum. Secundo, quia ob hanc causam denominatio vestiti, aut loco circumdati, aut etiam agentis, non est respectiva proprio respectu praedicamentali. Tertio est difficilius, quia alias non minus esset relatio realis creatoris ad creaturam, quam cujuslibet agentis creati ad suum effectum; nam extrinseca denominatio aeque potest intercedere.

Secunda item consequentia clara est, quia denominatio intrinseca dicitur, quae ab intrinseca forma sumitur. Ultima vero consequentia nititur in fundamento saepe repetito, quod haec denominatio amitti potest, et acquiri de novo, conservando omnem formam absolutam; ergo forma intrinseca et respectiva, a qua sumitur, est in re aliquo modo distincta ab omnibus formis absolutis, saltem modali distinctione. Atque haec sententia ita explicata et confirmata est probabilior caeteris, quae in re ponunt distinctionem aliquam actualem inter relationem et fundamentum. Quae si semel asseritur in aliquibus relationibus, consequenti ratione ponenda est in omnibus creatis et praedicamentalibus, quia nulla est sufficiens ratio ad utendum aliqua distinctione, ut ex dictis contra Scot. et Durandum intelligi potest.

Quinta opinio negans in re actualem distinctionem relationis a fundamento.

12. Nihilominus est alia sententia extreme his opposita, quae negat relationem distingui in re aliqua distinctione actuali a suo fundamento absoluto, sed tantum aliqua distinctione rationis habente in rebus aliquod fundamentum. Hanc sententiam docent multi Theologi, praesertim Nominales, in 1, dist. 30; Ocham, quaest. 1, et dist. 31, quaest. 1; Gregorius, dist. 29, quaest. 2, art. 2; et in eadem sententia aperte est Aegidius in 1, dist. 26, quaest. 4, dum ait, relationem nullum esse proprium habere ultra esse fundamenti, neque aliquam compositionem ei adjunctam, quod non potest esse verum, nisi ratione omnimodae identitatis in re ipsa. Eamdem plane /col. b/ tenet Sylvester, in Conflato, quaest. 28, dubio 1, ubi ait, relationem esse eamdem rem cum suo fundamento proximo. Et quamvis addat distingui formaliter, tamen statim satis declarat, eam distinctionem solum esse rationis ex diversitate conceptuum, quatenus eadem res solitarie sumpta absolute concipitur, posita vero alia, concipitur relative, nihil penitus in ea addito vel variato quoad rem ipsam. Expressius vero et melius hanc sententiam docet et tractat Hervaeus, in 1, dist. 30, a. 1, et Quodlib. 7, q. 15, et Quodlib. 10, q. 1; quia etiam declaravit, has denominationes relativas sumi ex consortio plurium rerum absolutarum, et non ex peculiaribus entitatibus, aut modis ex natura rei distinctis, quos addant ipsis rebus absolutis.

13. Habetque haec sententia fundamentum in D. Thoma, opusculo 48, cap. 2, de Ad aliquid, ubi sic ait: *Cum autem dico, quod similitudo Socratis habet albedinem ejus ut fundamentum, non est intelligendum quod similitudo Socratis sit aliqua res in Socrate, alia ab ipsa albedine, sed solum est ipsa albedo, ut se habet ad albedinem Platonis, ut ad terminum.* Idque statim confirmat ratione supra facta, scilicet, quia alias non posset similitudo alicui advenire sine ejus mutatione, quae ratio tam probat de modo reali ex natura rei dis-

tincto, quam de propria realitate. Unde etiam fundatur haec sententia in illo dicto Philosophi, 5 Physic., textu 10, quod relatio advenit rei, ipsa immutata manente. Et simili modo sumitur eadem sententia ex Anselmo, in Monolog., cap. 24, quem locum inferius referemus latius tractando de relationibus non mutuis; et similis fere est apud Augustinum, lib. 5 de Civitate Dei, cap. 16. Favent denique huic sententiae verba Damasceni in sua Dialectica, cap. 52: *Oportet ea, quae ad aliquid dicuntur, prius ad aliud praedicamentum reduci tanquam separatim considerata, et tunc demum ut habitudinem et affectionem ad alterum habentia, ad ea quae ad aliquid sunt referri; quippe prius aliquid sine habitudine ac relatione esse necesse est, ac tunc habitudinem in ipso considerare;* quam Damasceni sententiam de relationibus non subsistentibus intelligendam existimo; nam alia est de subsistentibus ratio.

14. Rationes pro hac sententia praecipuae sunt illa, quibus aliae opiniones, quae distinctionem in re ponunt, improbantur; nam illis seclusis, a sufficienti partium enumeratione haec sententia concluditur. Deinde ex re ipsa, /p. 790/ quia haec distinctio rationis, et hic modus denominationis sufficit ad omnia, quae de rebus absolutis relative dicuntur, ut videntur etiam convincere rationes primo loco positae in principio sectionis praecedentis. Si autem hoc sufficit, superfluum est quippiam addere; nam distinctio ac multiplicatio rerum ac modorum realium fingenda aut asserenda non est absque necessitate, vel ratione sufficiente.

15. Tertio, possumus retorquere argumentum illud de separabilitate; nam positis, verbi gratia, duobus albis, impossibile est etiam de potentia absoluta facere, ut non sint similia; ergo haec denominatio non sumitur ex aliqua re, aut modo reali distincto ex natura rei ab utroque albo, simul sumpto. Alioqui cur repugnaret Deum auferre modum illum, si in re ipsa distinctus est, aut cur non posset impedire resultantiam talis modi? Nam si haec est circa rem distinctam, aliqualis efficientia est, quae sine influxu Dei esse non potest; poterit ergo Deus suum influxum suspendere, et illam resultantiam impedire. Quod aliqui argumento convicti concedunt, ut Mairon., in 1, dist. 29, q. 2. At tunc interrogo an illa duo alba maneant similia, necne; hoc posterius non potest mente concipi, cum retineant eamdem unitatem in albedine; si vero dicatur primum, convincitur modum illum distinctum, et resultantiam quae nunc fingitur, esse sine fundamento adinventa, cum sine illis maneat vera similitudo. Signum ergo est hanc denominationem non sumi, nisi ab his absolutis coexistentibus, et eodem modo se habentibus. Unde, ut supra dicebam, quod per ablationem termini cesset illa denominatio, nullum argumentum est, quod similitudo sit aliquis modus realis ex natura rei distinctus ab albedine, sed solum est argumentum quod ipse terminus est in re distinctus a fundamento, et aliquo modo concurrit, vel necessarius est ad complendam talem

denominationem; hoc enim sufficit ut illo ablato cesset denominatio, etiamsi nihil rei auferatur a re denominata. Ergo ex inseparabilitate relationis posito fundamento et termino, potius infertur omnimoda identitas in re, seu (quod idem est) infertur relativam denominationem nihil rei addere supra omnes res absolutas.

16. *Quomodo aliqui negent mutari fundamentum per acquisitionem relationis.*—Quarto urget argumentum illud, quod res fit similis vel aequalis alteri, sine ulla sui mutatione, per positionem alterius; nam sive similitudo sit res /col. b/ omnino distincta, sive modus realis ex natura rei distinctus, non potest de novo advenire alicui absque illius mutatione. Aliqui respondent, modum respectivum non sufficere, ut ratione illius solius res dicatur mutari, quia non est aliquid, sed ad aliquid, et quia totum fundamentum, a quo illa relatio habet suam entitatem, jam praeexistit in re. Hoc vero non satisfacit, quia illa verba, scilicet, relationem non esse aliquid, sed ad aliquid, vel involvunt repugnantiam, vel sunt valde aequivoca, et minime ad rem. Nam si non esse aliquid, absolute et transcendenter sumatur, sequitur plane relationem esse nihil, et esse ad aliquid, nihil rei esse, ut supra argumentabar. Si vero contractius sumatur esse aliquid, ut idem sit quod esse rem vel modum absolutum, petitur principium, et non solvitur, sed eluditur argumentum. Nam quamvis relatio non sit aliquid absolutum, si tamen est aliquid rei, novum, et ex natura rei distinctum ab omni eo quod antea erat, ergo ratione illius vere ac proprie intrinsece aliter se habet res, quam autem se habebat; ergo vere mutata est. Neque etiam sufficit ad vitandam mutationem, quod totum relationis fundamentum praeexistat, quia non diximus rem mutari propter fundamentum, sed propter id quod additur fundamento, quod dicitur esse aliquid rei, et ex natura rei distinctum ab ipso. Unde juxta hanc sententiam non potest consequenter dici, quod relatio habeat suam propriam seu modalem entitatem ab ipso fundamento formaliter, sed ad summum radicaliter, quatenus ab ipso fundamento pullulat relatio posito termino; hoc autem non excludit veram mutationem, quandoquidem aliquid novum et distinctum fit in re, etiamsi ab intrinseco manet.

17. *Admittentes mutari fundamentum per resultantiam relationis, ut explicent Aristotelem.*—Unde aliqui tandem fatentur, per adventum novae relationis seu denominationis relativae fieri in re ipsa relata veram mutationem realem, non quidem per propriam actionem, sed per intrinsecam dimanationem; Aristotelem autem non esse locutum universe de quacunque mutatione communissime sumpta, sed de illa quae per propriam actionem et passionem fit. Verumtamen, quamvis haec responsio consequenter procedat, supposita dicta sententia, possitque facile defendi ad effugiendum testimonium Aristotelis in citato loco 5 Phys., tamen per sese considerata quippiam dicit creditu difficilli-/p. 791/ mum, et nullo sufficienti signo aut experimento fundatum, nimirum,

quoties aliquis de novo fit albus aut calidus, pullulare in omnibus aliis rebus calidis aut albis, quae sunt in mundo, aliquid novum et reale, vere ac proprie unicuique inhaerens. Ut enim in superioribus videtur satis probatum, ad solas illas denominationes, similis, aequalis, et hujusmodi, non est necessaria illa resultantia novi realis modi et entitatis; secluso autem hoc signo, nullum est aliud unde colligi potest; gratis ergo et sine probabilitate fingitur. Accedit quod illa qualiscunque mutatio vel acquisitio illius novi realis modi vel entitatis, non potest esse sine efficientia, saltem per modum resultantiae, quia omnis mutatio, eo modo quo talis est, includit actionem proportionatam. Inquiro ergo an illa efficientia sit ab ipso termino in fundamentum, vel ab ipso fundamento in se ipsum per naturalem resultantiam. Primum a nemine asseritur; neque est probabile; quomodo enim terminus ageret simul in res pene infinitas, et quantumcunque distantes? Item, quia si ita fieret relatio, nihil ei deesset, quominus per propriam actionem et per se fieret ab extrinseco agente. Denique quia relatio intrinsece convenit rei posito fundamento et termino; non ergo pendet ex efficientia extrinseci agentis. Secundum etiam improbari potest, quia talis efficientia, etiamsi sit ab intrinseco principio, erit per propriam actionem, et consequenter per propriam mutationem, quia licet talis resultantia non sit nisi posito termino, id solum erit, quia terminus est aut necessaria conditio ut relatio resultet, aut quasi objectum specificans, sine quo esse non potest; hoc autem non obstat quominus resultantia, quae fit ex fundamento, sit per propriam actionem, quae in tali subjecto fit absque alia actione, quae tunc in illo interveniat. Sicut descensus deorsum naturaliter resultat ex gravitate lapidis ablato impedimento, et nihilominus fit per propriam actionem et mutationem. Ac denique hic habet locum argumentum saepe tactum, quod talis resultantia, et qualiscunque efficientia non potest esse sine concursu Dei, quem ipse potest suspendere. Et quamvis ponamus illum suspendere, et consequenter nullam intervenire resultantiam realem, adhuc intelligimus res esse similes, vel aequales, positis talibus extremis; ergo nullum signum est talem resultantiam vel mutationem intervenire.

/col. b/

Tractatur opinio distinguens inter esse in, et esse ad relationis.

18. Quapropter alii, ut huic difficultati respondeant, quadam distinctione utuntur; et posset haec referri ut sexta opinio in praesenti quaestione, quam tractamus de distinctione relationis et fundamenti. Distinguunt ergo in relatione *esse in* et *esse ad*, et dicunt relationem, secundum esse in, non resultare proprie, nec pullulare a fundamento, sed resultare tantum secundum esse ad ut ad, et idcirco non mutari fundamentum per talem resultantiam, quia res non mutatur nisi per id quod de novo ei inest, atque adeo secundum esse in.

Ex qua distinctione plane efficitur, relationem, secundum esse in, non distingui ex natura rei a fundamento, quia necessario convenit illi, etiam antequam terminus existat, seu independenter a termino; at vero esse ad, distingui ex natura rei, ideoque posse resultare ex fundamento, posito termino.

19. *Quot inconvenientia ex allata opinione oriantur.—Primum.*—Quapropter haec sententia multa involvit impossibilia, et quae non satis intelligi possunt. Primum, quia ex illa sequitur, in una et eadem relatione distinguenda esse actualiter et ex natura rei, esse in, et esse ad; nam esse in, dicitur esse in re idem et indistinctum a fundamento, esse autem ad, dicitur actu distinctum in re a fundamento; ergo esse in, et esse ad, erunt inter se actu distincta, nam quae ita comparantur ad unum tertium, ut unum sit idem cum illo, aliud vero minime, neque etiam inter se possunt esse idem. Consequens autem est impossibile, quia esse in, et esse ad, comparantur tanquam superius et inferius, seu tanquam commune vel transcendens, et modus determinans seu modificans illum, quae impossibile est esse in re distincta, ut in superioribus traditum est.

20. *Secundum.*—Secundum inconveniens est, quia sequitur, esse ad, relationis realis creatae ut sic, non esse accidens alicujus, et consequenter non constituere verum accidens reale, quod est contra rationem hujus praedicamenti. Sequela patet, quia illud esse ad, non includit essentialiter esse in, cum ab illo ex natura rei distinguatur et praescindatur. Item, quia si illud esse ad, esset accidens alicujus, illud afficeret, et de novo ei adveniret, et ita redit difficultas quam tractamus, quod, nimirum, ex resultantia ipsius esse ad, /p. 792/ mutaretur res seu fundamentum ex quo resultat. Sed aiunt, esse ad ut ad, non esse aliquid reale, et ideo mirum non esse quod neque sit accidens, neque insit, neque immutet relativum quod denominat. Sed hoc neque est vere, neque consequenter dictum, si univoce terminis utamur, et praesertim juxta dictam sententiam, quae supponit relationem realem esse aliquid in re ipsa, quod in rebus sit, et secundum aliquid sui in re ipsa a fundamento distinguatur. Quamvis enim loquendo de esse ad, ut attribuitur relationibus rationis, illud non sit aliquid reale, tamen, ut infra ostendam, illud solum aequivoce, vel ad summum secundum analogiam quamdam proportionalitatis, appellatur esse ad, de quo nunc non est sermo, sed de vero esse ad, quod reale praedicamentum accidentis constituit; illud autem non potest non esse aliquid reale, alias quomodo posset verum accidens reale constituere? Aut quomodo posset relatio esse intrinseca forma referens suum subjectum ad terminum, si non afficeret illud secundum propriam rationem suam et consequenter etiam secundum ipsum esse ad?

21. Et confirmatur, nam quoad hoc eadem est fere ratio de ipso esse in; potest enim aequivoce vel analogice sumi, ut attribuitur entibus rationis; sic enim dicitur caecitas esse in oculo; ergo ut sic, esse in, non dicit aliquid reale; nihilominus tamen, verum esse in reale est, quod accidens reale constituit.

Simili ergo modo philosophandum est de vero esse ad, quod nimirum sit quippiam reale, unde fit ut necessario esse debeat aut intrinsece subsistens, quod dici non potest de relatione accidentali, aut intrinsece inhaerens, quod intendimus. Igitur, si esse ad, relationis realis est quid distinctum ex natura rei a fundamento talis relationis, etiam esse in, proprium et intrinsecum talis relationis, erit distinctum, vel e converso, si nullum esse in relationis distinguitur ex natura rei[1] a fundamento, neque esse ad distinguetur. Unde tandem argumentor, quia impossibile est ut relatio secundum esse ad, resultet a fundamento, tanquam quid reale ex natura rei distinctum ab ipso, quin illud ipsum reale, quidquid est, alicubi insit; nam vel in se existit, et sic erit subsistens, vel ab aliquo sustentatur, et ita illi inerit; ergo, vel inest in termino, quod dici non potest, ut per se notum est, vel inest in proprio subjecto seu fundamento, et ita ab illo distin- /col. b/ guetur tale esse ad, etiam secundum proprium esse in, quod intrinsece includit. Est ergo vana illa distinctio ad praesentem rem explicandam, nec per illam vitatur difficultas tacta, quod per relationem resultantem mutetur aliquo modo res relata, si relatio secundum proprium esse reale est aliquid ex natura rei actualiter distinctum a suo fundamento.

Quinta sententia convenienter exposita approbatur.

22. Inter has ergo sententias mihi maxime probatur quinta, quam Hervaeus et nonnulli alii Thomistae docuere, a quorum sensu fere nihil discrepant Nominales, et Aristoteles et D. Thom. multum favent, ut vidimus. Haec tamen sententia ita est interpretanda, ut non intelligatur, rationem formalem relationis nihil esse, aut denominationem relativam esse mere extrinsecam, sumptam ab aliqua forma absoluta; juxta hunc enim sensum omnino everteretur, et e medio tolleretur reale praedicamentum Ad aliquid. Sed intelligendum est, relationem quidem dicere formam aliquam realem, et intrinsece denominantem proprium relativum, quod constituit; illam vero non esse rem aliquam aut modum, ex natura rei distinctum ab omni forma absoluta, sed esse in re formam aliquam absolutam, non tamen absolute sumptam, sed ut respicientem aliam, quam denominatio relativa includit seu connotat. Ita ut similitudo, verbi gratia, aliqua forma realis sit existens in re, quae denominatur similis; illa tamen non sit in re distincta ab albedine, quantum ad id, quod ponit in re, quae dicitur similis, sed solum quantum ad terminum quem connotat; et ita similitudo in re non est aliud quam ipsamet albedo, ut respiciens aliam albedinem, tanquam ejusdem seu similis rationis. Atque haec distinctio rationis sufficit, tum ad diversas loquendi formas, tum etiam ad praedicamentorum distinctionem; nam, ut supra diximus, praedicamentalis distinctio interdum est sola distinctio

---

1 The Vivès edition omits "rei".

rationis cum aliquo fundamento in re, ut de actione etiam et passione, et de aliis praedicamentis inferius dicemus. Atque haec sententia magis declarabitur, tum ex solutionibus argumentorum, tum etiam ex sequentibus sectionibus.

Fundamentis aliarum opinionum satisfit.

23. Fundamenta ergo primae, secundae, tertiae, et sextae opinionis, inter eas referendas et impugnandas tacta sunt et soluta; ne- /p. 793/ que aliquod aliud argumentum occurrit, quod in favorem earum difficultatem aliquam ingerere possit, cui satisfacere necesse sit. Solum ergo supersunt solvenda argumenta quartae opinionis. Et primum quidem de separabilitate relationis a fundamento jam solutum est; negamus enim relationem separari unquam a fundamento secundum aliquid reale quod ei intrinsecum sit. Sed solum contingit, separari aut destitui terminum, quo ablato cessat etiam relativa denominatio, non quia aliquid rei vel realis modi auferatur ab ipso relativo, sed quia denominatio relativa includit aliquo modo terminum, sine quo non manet actualiter, sed fundamentaliter tantum, seu in proxima aptitudine. Ad secundum respondetur, esse relationis in re non esse aliud ab esse fundamenti, ratione tamen distingui, quatenus illudmet esse concipitur ut includens aliquo modo, seu connotans terminum quem respicit. Ad tertium respondeo, quando unum album de novo fit, nihil rei de novo addi altero albo, ut declaratum et probatum est. Neque inde sequitur relationem similitudinis nihil esse, sed solum sequitur non esse aliquid distinctum ab albedine, quae antea inerat tali rei albae. Cum autem instatur, quia prius in tali re alba non erat similitudo, et postea est similitudo; ergo vel similitudo nihil rei est, vel aliquid rei de novo est in illa re alba: respondetur negando consequentiam quoad utramque partem; nam praeter illa duo membra est aliud tertium, nimirum aliquid rei esse de novo, non in re, quae prius erat alba, sed in termino, qui de novo factus est albus, quem terminum aliquo modo includit seu connotat illa res, quae est similitudo, sub ratione et conceptu similitudinis, et non sub ratione albedinis. Ad quartum respondetur, has denominationes respectivas, non esse mere extrinsecas, ut recte ibi probatur. Unde consequenter concedimus, hujusmodi denominationem esse ab aliqua forma intrinseca, includendo tamen seu connotando aliquam aliam extrinsecam in extrinseco termino. Ac propterea negatur ultima consequentia, nimirum, hanc formam sic denominantem intrinsece cum habitudine ad extrinsecum, debere esse ex natura rei distinctam, saltem modaliter, ab omni forma absoluta; nam supposito termino extrinseco, ipsamet forma absoluta secundum rem sufficit ad talem denominationem tribuendam, quae auferri vel cessare potest per solam ablationem extrinseci termini, ut dictum est.
/col. b/

Satisfit argumentis ex sectione prima relictis.

24. *Primo.—Secundo.—Tertio.*—Ex his etiam quae in hac sectione dicta sunt, soluta manent multa ex argumentis propositis in principio sectionis praecedentis. Nam quod ad primum attinet; jam explicatum est quomodo ipsum *esse ad* relationis realis et accidentalis, sit aliquid in re ipsa quae referri dicitur. Falsumque est, esse ad, univoce dici de relationibus rationis et realibus. Falsum item est, verum esse ad, posse ita praescindi ab esse in, ut illud intrinsece non includat; ad eum modum quo in superioribus diximus, modos entis non posse ita praescindi ab ente, quin illud in se claudant. De secundo item argumento, nimirum, quod relatio adveniat sine mutatione fundamenti, satis multa dicta sunt; concedimus enim inde recte concludi, relationem non esse aliquid in re distinctum a fundamento, non tamen non esse aliquid rei. Unde ad tertium negatur prima consequentia (scilicet, relatio nihil est praeter absoluta; ergo simpliciter nihil est), si in antecedente, illa particula, *praeter*, indicet actualem distinctionem ex natura rei. Nam licet relatio non sit aliquid in re distinctum ab absolutis, potest esse aliquid ratione distinctum; et ideo non sequitur, quod sit simpliciter nihil. Neque refert quod relatio ut relatio praescinditur ab absolutis, quia neque praescinditur ut aliquid per rationem confictum, neque etiam ut aliquid in re ipsa praecisum et distinctum, sed ut aliquid verum et reale, ratione sola praecisum: saepe enim distinctio est rationis inter extrema vera et realia, quae ad praedicamenta constituenda sufficiunt; unde probationes omnes, quae in illo tertio argumento afferuntur, utiles sunt ad declarandum quomodo relatio realis non addat rebus absolutis rem, vel realem modum, ex natura rei distinctum ab ipsis, non tamen quicquam valent ad concludendum hujusmodi relationem nihil omnino esse.

25. *Notabile.*—Duo tamen in illis argumentis cavenda sunt. Primum est, cum dicitur denominatio respectiva consurgere ex coexistentia plurium absolutorum absque ulla reali additione, non esse intelligendum, illam denominationem aeque ac simul sumi ex pluribus formis absolutis, una intrinseca, et altera extrinseca. Sed intelligendum est, illam denominationem requirere quidem consortium, seu coexistentiam talium rerum seu /p. 794/ formarum; tamen in unoquoque extremo sumi a propria forma ut respiciente aliam, quae ut sic habet rationem relationis, quamvis in re non sit alia ab ipsa forma absoluta. Secundo (propter exemplum quod ibi adducitur de Deo quatenus denominatur dominus, vel creator, etc.), cavendum est ne quis existimet hujusmodi denominationes esse ejusdem modi et rationis in omnibus; id enim verum esse non potest, juxta communem doctrinam, quae distinguit relationes in mutuas et non mutuas, quae distinctio nulla esset, si praedictae denominationes omnes essent ejusdem modi in omnibus extremis. Quae autem sit haec diversitas, non est facile ad explicandum, juxta doctrinam ac sententiam quam defendimus. Quapropter

de hac re erit inferius specialis sectio instituenda; nunc solum dicimus, quando in re denominata est aliquod proprium et proportionatum fundamentum talis denominationis, tunc provenire ex propria relatione reali; quando vero attribuitur rei sine tali fundamento, tunc denominationem esse extrinsecam seu rationis.

SECTIO III.
Quotuplex sit relatio, et quae sit vere praedicamentalis.

1. Haec dubitatio proponitur propter difficultatem tactam in quarto argumento in prima sectione proposito. Ad quam expediendam nonnullae distinctiones relativorum praemittendae sunt ac declarandae, ut seclusis iis quae ad hoc praedicamentum non pertinent, concludamus quale possit esse genus accidentis realis ab aliis diversum, et proprium praedicamentum ad aliquid, constituens.

Prima divisio relationis in realem et rationis.

2. Primo ergo dividi solet relatio in eam quae realis est, vel tantum rationis, quam aliqui ita interpretantur, ut doceant, genus praedicamenti Ad aliquid, utramque relationem sub se continere, ac propterea illam divisionem esse univocam, imo et generis in species. Cui sententiae videtur favere divus Thom. 1 p., quaest. 28, art. 1, ubi sic inquit: *Considerandum est, quod solum in iis quae dicuntur ad aliquid, inveniuntur aliqua secundum rationem tantum, et non secundum rem.* Sentit ergo ea, quae secundum rationem tantum referuntur, vere ac univoce esse ad ali- /col. b/ quid: nam si tantum esset sermo de denominatione aequivoca vel analoga, non tantum in his quae sunt ad aliquid, sed etiam in aliis generibus invenirentur aliqua secundum rationem tantum, ut caecitas in qualitate, et sic de aliis. Idem sumi potest ex art. 2 ejusdem quaestionis, et ex quaest. 13, art. 7, et Quodlib. 1, art. 2, Quodlib. 9, art 5, et quaest. 2 de Potent., art. 5, et saepe alibi. Unde Cajetanus dictis locis primae partis, aperte sentit ipsum esse ad, univoce dici de relatione reali, vel rationis; quod antea videtur docuisse Capreol., in primo, dist. 33, quaest. 1; et sequi videtur ibi Deça, quaest. 1, notab. 4; et Ferrara, 4 contra Gent., c. 14; et expressius Soncin., 5 Metaph., quaest. 26, concl. 2, qui afferunt alia testimonia D. Thomae. Fundamentum eorum est, quia definitio relativorum, quam Aristoteles tradit, et proprietates omnes quae ad illam consequuntur, aeque conveniunt relationibus rationis, ac realibus. Patet, nam relativa esse dicuntur, quorum totum esse est ad aliud se habere; hoc autem omnino et propriissime convenit respectibus rationis; nam licet esse eorum sit magis imperfectum ac diminutum, quam esse relativorum realium, tamen illud esse qualecunque est, tam proprie consistit totum in

habitudine ad aliud, sicut esse relationis realis. Unde fit ut relatio rationis nec cognosci possit, nec definiri sine habitudine ad aliud, aeque ac relatio realis.

Sola relatio realis praedicamentum Ad aliquid constituit.

3. Nihilominus dicendum est, solas relationes reales pertinere ad constitutionem praedicamenti Ad aliquid, quod est satis evidens ex iis quae in superioribus tradita sunt de conceptu entis, et de divisione ejus in novem genera summa. Ostendimus enim ens non solum non esse univocum ad ens reale et rationis, verum etiam non habere unum conceptum communem illis, etiam analogum, sed vel esse aequivocum, vel ad summum, analogum analogia proportionalitatis. Et hac ratione etiam diximus, objectum adaequatum et directum metaphysicae non esse ens commune ad reale et rationis, sed ad reale tantum; et hoc etiam ostendimus dividi in decem suprema genera. Cum ergo relationes rationis non sint entia realia, et consequenter nec vera entia, non possunt ad praedicamentum Ad aliquid, quod reale est, pertinere. Addo praeterea, non posse habere uni- /p. 795/ vocam convenientiam cum relationibus realibus, si supponamus illas esse vera entia realia, ut supra ex communi sententia suppositum est, et in discursu hujus materiae paulatim declarabitur et probabitur. Ratio autem est, quia cum ens rationis nihil sit, non potest habere veram similitudinem ac convenientiam cum ente reali, in qua convenientia fundari solet univocatio et unitas conceptus; ergo non potest aliquis verus conceptus et essentialis esse communis enti reali et rationis. Et ideo merito Soncin., 4 Metaph., q. 5 et 6, approbat dictum Hervaei (quamquam errore typographi tribuatur Henrico), Quodl. 3, q. 1, articulo primo, in fine, non magis posse ens esse univocum ad ens reale et rationis, quam sit homo ad hominem vivum et mortuum. Habet autem hoc dictum eamdem rationem veritatis in ente in communi, et in tali ente, scilicet, relatione, quia sicut ens rationis non est verum ens, sed fictum, sic relatio rationis non est vera relatio, sed ficta, vel quasi per intellectum.

4. *Objectioni satisfit.* Dicet fortasse aliquis, hoc verum esse de integro et completo conceptu relationis, de quo procedit ratio facta, quia in hujusmodi conceptu relationis realis includitur, quod sit verum ens, et accidens reale; non tamen ita procedit de praeciso conceptu ipsius modi seu constitutivi relationis, qui per hanc vocem significatur, *esse ad*, quia talis conceptus per se praescindit a ratione entis et accidentis. Quo sensu videntur locuti citati auctores, cum quibus videtur sentire Henricus, Quodl. 9, q. 3, ubi de hac materia obscurissime disputat; inter alia vero ait: *Esse ad aliud ex se nullam recipit distinctionem, aut diversitatem, sive fuerit in divinis, sive in creaturis, sive in relationibus secundum rem, sive in relationibus secundum rationem.* Verumtamen contra hanc evasionem eamdem vim habet ratio facta; nam vel illud esse ad, prout est modus constituens relationem realem, est etiam realis modus, vel est tantum ens rationis;

hoc secundum dici non potest, alioqui relatio realis non habebit proprium et formale constitutivum reale, quae est implicatio in adjecto; quomodo enim potest ens reale ut sic, per id quod reale non est, constitui? De qua re diximus multa superius disputatione 2, tractando de modis contrahentibus ens. Si autem illud esse ad, in relatione reali est modus realis, rursus interrogo an in relatione rationis sit etiam verus et realis modus, vel tantum per intel- /col. b/ lectum confictus. Primum dici non potest, quia repugnat relationi rationis, de cujus essentia est, ut non dicat habitudinem in re existentem, sed in mentis comparatione seu denominatione. Item, quia contradictionem implicat, quod ens fictum existens tantum objective in intellectu, per modum realem et in re ipsa existentem constituatur; est ergo illud esse ad, in relatione rationis, purum ens rationis. Ergo sicut non potest dari conceptus communis vel univocus ad ens reale et rationis, vel ad relationem realem et rationis, ita neque esse ad, ut sic praecise conceptum, potest dicere unum communem conceptum et uni-vocum ad esse ad relationis realis et rationis, quia non magis potest esse inter haec vera similitudo et convenientia, quam inter quaelibet alia entia realia et rationis. Nec magis potest in his quam in caeteris intelligi qualis sit ille con-ceptus abstrahens ab ente reali et rationis, aut qualis esse possit contractio vel determinatio talis conceptus ad ens reale per modum realem, et ad ens rationis per modum rationis.

5. *Sola relatio realis est proprie ad aliquid.—D. Thomae locus explicatur.*—Di-cendum ergo est solam relationem realem esse vere et proprie ad aliquid; rela-tionem autem rationis non esse, sed concipi ac si esset ad aliquid, ideoque solas relationes reales ad proprium praedicamentum Ad aliquid pertinere; relationes autem rationis non constitui in reali praedicamento, sed per analogiam et proportionem ad veras relationes declarari, ut magis in particulari dicemus in disputatione ultima hujus operis. Neque D. Thomas in citatis locis oppositum intendit; nunquam enim dixit aut relationem rationis esse univoce relationem cum reali, aut esse ad aliud non esse aliquid reale in relatione reali, sed solum dixit naturam relationis realis talem esse, ut per similitudinem et proportionem ad illam possint entia rationis per modum relationum ab intellectu confingi cum aliquo fundamento in re, potius quam per modum quantitatis vel qualitatis, etc. Quod ait, ex eo provenire, quod relatio ut relatio solum significat respectum ad aliud. Ubi particula *solum* non excludit concomitantia; unde neque excludere potest transcendentalem rationem entis, vel accidentis, si relatio accidentalis sit. Quia vero relatio quatenus praecise concipitur aut significatur ut est ad aliud, non concipitur nec significatur /p. 796/ expresse ut inhaerens, ideo ait D. Thomas, ut sic solum dicere respectum ad aliud, non quia in re ipsa non sit aliquid in se, vel in subjecto existens, sed quia in tali modo concipiendi et significandi nihil aliud exprimitur. Et inde etiam fit ut facilius possint entia

292 Francisco Suárez: *Metaphysical Disputation 47, On Real Relation*

rationis secundum illum modum habitudinis concipi, non quod in tali relatione sit vera habitudo, seu verum esse ad, tale quale est in relatione reali, sed quid ad instar seu proportionem ejus concipitur. Unde idem D. Thomas postquam dixit relationem secundum propriam rationem solum significare respectum ad aliud, subdit hunc respectum aliquando esse in ipsa natura rerum, aliquando vero esse solum *in apprehensione rationis conferentis unum alteri*. Ad rationem autem illius sententiae facile respondetur, negando propriam rationem relationis vere reperiri in relatione rationis, quia in tali relatione nec est vera habitudo, nec verum esse ad aliquid, sed solum apprehenditur ac si esset ad aliquid.

Secunda divisio relationis, secundum dici, et secundum esse.

6. Secunda divisio relationis est in relationem secundum esse, et secundum dici. Quae divisio fundamentum habet in Aristotele, cap. de Ad aliquid, ubi prius tradit definitionem communem relativis secundum dici, postea vero tradit propriam definitionem relativorum secundum esse. Relatio ergo secundum dici, definiri solet, quod sit res quae concipitur et explicatur, seu dicitur per modum respectus, cum in re ipsa verum respectum non habeat; relatio autem secundum esse dicitur, quae revera habet proprium esse cum habitudine ad aliud.

7. *Relatio* secundum dici *ut explicetur ab aliquibus.*—Ex quo aliqui, et non sine verisimilitudine, opinati sunt, relationem secundum dici, esse eamdem cum relatione rationis. Quod significat Henric., Quodl. 3, q. 4, ex Avicenna, l. 3, suae Metaph., dicente relationem secundum dici, esse illam quae solum habet esse in intellectu, et convenit rebus quae non sunt simpliciter et absolute ad aliquid, sed solum secundum quod ab intellectu concipiuntur. Et videtur hoc consentaneum rationi; nam sicut concipimus, ita loquimur; relationes autem secundum dici, non alia de causa sic appellantur, nisi quia ita a nobis dicuntur aut explicantur, ac si relationes essent, cum tamen non sint; ergo ille /col. b/ modus loquendi de his relationibus supponit modum concipiendi nostrum, ex quo nascitur, nimirum, quod hae res concipiuntur a nobis cum relatione et habitudine, seu per modum relationis et habitudinis, cum vere et in re habitudinem non habeant; sed in hoc consistit ratio et essentia relationis rationis; ergo relatio secundum dici, idem est quod relatio rationis.

8. *Vera essentia relationis secundum dici.*—Sed nihilominus communiter non ita intelligitur haec divisio; nam relatio rationis, eo modo quo est, censetur esse relatio secundum esse sibi proportionatum, ut patet de relatione generis et speciei, et similibus, quia eo modo quo haec cogitantur, non solum dicuntur, sed etiam sunt ad aliquid. Et e converso relatio secundum dici non limitatur ad relationem rationis, sed dicitur de quacunque reali re, cujus esse sit absolutum, et a nobis non nisi per modum habitudinis seu relationis relativae

explicatur. Sic enim divinam omnipotentiam dicimus esse relativam secundum dici, non propter relationem rationis quam in illa fingamus, sed quia illam non concipimus, nec explicamus, nisi cum concomitantia alterius, ad quod est potentia, et per modum habentis habitudinem ad illud. Unde, licet verum sit, hunc dicendi modum seu loquendi de relatione secundum dici, supponere modum concipiendi, tamen ille modus concipiendi non est talis, ut ex illo necessario resultet vel apprehendatur relatio rationis, quia non est conceptus reflexivus, aut comparativus, sed est conceptus directus rei absolutae, imperfecte tamen conceptae ad modum earum rerum quae habent habitudinem ad alia; in quo modo concipiendi non attribuitur ipsi objecto cognito habitudo ulla nec realis, nec rationis, sed solum ex parte concipientis fit conceptus per quamdam imitationem et analogiam ad conceptus rerum respectivarum. Sicut quando a nobis concipitur res spiritualis instar corporeae, non attribuimus objecto corporeitatem realem, alias falsa esset conceptio, neque etiam fingimus aut cogitamus in illo objecto aliquod ens rationis; quale enim illud esset? Solum ergo concipimus unam rem per analogiam ad aliam. Sic igitur interdum concipimus rem absolutam instar respectivae, et de illa ita loquimur ac si respectiva esset, et ideo dicitur esse relativa secundum dici tantum. Unde constat, relationes tantum secundum dici, extra genus relationis esse, nec per se posse /p. 797/ pertinere ad praedicamentum Ad aliquid, imo sub ea ratione ad nullum praedicamentum pertinere, nam, ex eo quod res a nobis imperfecte concipiatur aut dicatur, non accipit peculiarem naturam, ratione cujus debeat in peculiari praedicamento collocari. Et ideo Aristoteles, in praedicamento Ad aliquid, ut ibi Boetius et alii notarunt, exclusa priori definitione relativorum, quae relativis etiam secundum dici communis erat, posteriorem addidit, quae propria est relativorum secundum esse.

9. *Relationes secundum dici diversae sunt a praedicamentalibus et transcendentalibus.*—Sunt vere qui existiment divisionem hanc relationis secundum dici et secundum esse coincidere cum alia partitione relationis in transcendentalem et praedicamentalem, ita ut relatio transcendentalis tantum sit relatio secundum dici; omnis vero relatio secundum esse, praedicamentalis sit (de creatis loquimur). Haec vero sententia licet in ore fere omnium circumferri videatur, mihi non probatur. Opinor enim relationes transcendentales includere in re ipsa et in suo esse veras et reales habitudines, quod paulo inferius ostendam; relationes autem quae tantum sunt secundum dici, proprie et in rigore sumptas, distingui ab omnibus relationibus secundum esse, sive transcendentales sint, sive praedicamentales. Non enim requirunt in re sic concepta, seu relative denominata, veram aliquam habitudinem, quae ratione sui esse illi conveniat, sed tantum denominationem ex modo nostro concipiendi et loquendi, ut a nobis explicata est. Ut in exemplo posito de potentia Dei, probabilius est non

includere respectum etiam transcendentalem, etiamsi relativa secundum dici appelletur. Igitur relatio secundum dici tantum, non est idem quod relatio transcendentalis; imo ab illa etiam condistinguitur, si cum praecisione sumatur prout sumi debet. Quod ideo addo, quia etiam relatio transcendentalis potest dici relatio secundum dici, quia etiam de ea loquimur ad modum relativorum; imo et relatio praedicamentalis erit relatio secundum dici, quia etiam ipsa dicitur cum habitudine ad aliud. Ut ergo proprie fiat divisio, sumi debet relatio secundum dici, cum exclusione et praecisione, ita ut solum in ipso dici, habitudinem habere videatur, in esse tamen nullam habeat, nec transcendentalem, nec praedicamentalem. Dices: si res sit tam absoluta, ut in esse /col. b/ nullam habeat habitudinem, etiam transcendentalem, cur necesse erit concipi vel dici cum habitudine, cum unaquaeque res possit concipi eo modo quo est, absque omni eo quod est extra essentiam, ejus? Respondetur, id saepe provenire ex nostro modo imperfecto concipiendi, quia non valemus concipere res prout ipsae sunt. Addo praeterea interdum contingere, ut res etiam perfecte concepta cognosci non possit sine concomitantia aliarum, etiam si sint extra essentiam ejus, non propter habitudinem aut dependentiam, sed propter aliam altiorem connexionem in ratione causae eminenter continentis suos effectus, quo modo aiunt Theologi non posse Deum perfecte videri aut comprehendi, quin in eo cognoscantur creaturae: de quo alias.

Tertia divisio inter relationem transcendentalem et praedicamentalem.

10. Tertio ac praecipue dividitur relatio realis et secundum esse, in transcendentalem et praedicamentalem, quae divisio maxime necessaria est ad concludendum et declarandum id quod in praesenti sectione intendimus. Hactenus enim solum constat, relationem pertinentem ad hoc praedicamentum, Ad aliquid, debere esse realem et secundum esse; nunc autem videndum superest an omnis relatio hujusmodi ad hoc praedicamentum pertineat. Ex quarto vero argumento in prima sectione proposito constat, non omnem habitudinem realem et secundum esse, posse ad unum definitum praedicamentum spectare. Et ideo proponitur haec divisio, qua significatur esse certum quemdam modum realis habitudinis habentem particularem ac definitum essendi modum, qui peculiare genus entis constituit, et hujusmodi esse relationes praedicamentales. Praeter has vero esse alias habitudines veras etiam et reales, essentialiter pertinentes ad varia et fere ad omnia genera entium, quae propterea transcendentales dicuntur, et a praedicamentalibus distinguuntur, quia ad certum aliquod praedicamentum non pertinent, sed per omnia vagantur.

11. Imprimis ergo divisio sic explicata quoad singula membra probanda est. Quod enim dentur quaedam relationes praedicamentales, ex recepta divisione praedicamentorum supponimus, et ex communi omnium sententia,

ut in prima sectione dictum est; quod vero praeter has dentur relationes /p. 798/ transcendentales, quae non sint tantum secundum dici, sed verae et reales habitudines secundum esse, satis probatur inductione et discursu facto in illo quarto argumento sectione prima proposito. Et potest confirmari, nam in genere substantiae materia et forma habent inter se veram et realem habitudinem essentialiter inclusam in proprio esse illarum, et ideo una definitur per habitudinem ad aliam, et inde accipiunt specificationem suam. Eademque ratio est de potentiis accidentalibus per se primo institutis et ordinatis ad suos actus; et de habitibus operativis, de quibus supra ostensum est, natura sua specificari per habitudinem ad actus vel objecta, quia, nimirum, in suo esse includunt veram habitudinem ad actus, et illis mediantibus ad objecta; ergo hi respectus transcendentales sunt veri et secundum esse reale earum rerum quibus conveniunt. Quocirca, sicut inductio facta nititur in communioribus, magisque receptis sententiis, ita haec doctrina communiter a Doctoribus approbata censenda est. Praesertim vero in favorem ejus notanda sunt verba D. Thomae, 1 p., quaest. 28, art. 1, ubi sic scribit: *Ea quae dicuntur ad aliquid significant secundum propriam rationem solum respectum ad aliud, qui quidem respectus aliquando est in ipsa natura rei, utpote quando aliquae duae res secundum naturam suam ad invicem ordinata sunt, et invicem inclinationem habet, et hujusmodi relationes oportet esse reales, sicut in corpore gravi est inclinatio et ordo ad locum medium; unde respectus quidam est in ipso gravi respectu loci medii, et similiter est de aliis hujusmodi.* Haec enim ratio D. Thomae aeque aut maxime procedit de respectu transcendentali; nam secundum illum praecipue inveniuntur res ad invicem ordinatae. Et quidem exemplum D. Thomae optime intelligitur ac verificatur de respectu transcendentali; nam gravitatis inclinatio et propensio ad locum medium non pertinet ad praedicamentum relationis, sed qualitatis; nam est propria essentia talis qualitatis.

12. *Objectio.—Prima responsio.—Verior responsio.*—Dices: nullus realis respectus includitur in conceptu rei absolutae; sed hic respectus transcendentalis includitur in conceptu rei absolutae; ergo non est verus respectus secundum esse, sed tantum secundum modum loquendi et concipiendi nostrum; hoc enim potissimum argumento nituntur, qui ita sentiunt de his respectibus /col. b/ transcendentalibus, ut solum in verbis consistere arbitrentur. Aliqui vero respondent, et sumi potest ex Scoto, in 4, d. 12, q. unica, hujusmodi respectus consequi ad res absolutas, non vero esse de intrinseca ratione illarum. Hac enim de causa negat Scotus, inhaerentiam aptitudinalem esse de essentia accidentis, quia est verus respectus. Juxta quam responsionem hi respectus non essent extra latitudinem praedicamenti Ad aliquid, unde nec possent dici proprie transcendentales, neque a praedicamentalibus condistingui, quia non est contra rationem determinati praedicamenti, ut res in illo contentae consequantur ex

rebus aliorum praedicamentorum, si non sunt de essentia earum, sed proprietates consequentes illas. Melius tamen respondetur cum Cajetano, de Ente et essent., c. 7, q. 15, non esse contra rationem rei absolutae, ut in sua essentiali ratione includat respectum transcendentalem, suae naturae proportionatum; nam revera inhaerentia aptitudinalis non est proprietas consequens naturam accidentis, sed est intrinseca essentia ejus, ut in superioribus ostensum. Quinimo verisimile est, in entibus creatis nullum esse ita absolutum, quin in sua essentia intime includat aliquem transcendentalem respectum, saltem quatenus est ens per participationem, per se essentialiter pendens ab ente per essentiam. Nam, licet ipsa actualis dependentia sit aliquid ex natura rei distinctum ab ipso ente creato, tamen ipsa aptitudo et necessitas dependendi est intrinseca et essentialis illi; non videtur autem posse concipi, aut esse sine transcendentali respectu et habitudine ad illud a quo pendet, in quo respectu maxime consistere videtur potentialitas et imperfectio entis creati ut tale est.

13. Quidquid vero sit de completis entibus, ut sunt integrae substantiae, praesertim simplices et immateriales, quae inter creata entia videntur maxime absoluta, ex reliquis omnibus, quae incompleta dicuntur, nullum est ita absolutum, ut non includat essentialiter aliquem transcendentalem respectum. Et ratio est, quia omnia illa ex natura sua sunt instituta ad aliud, seu propter aliud; nam materia est propter formam, forma vero est ad actuandam materiam et complendum compositum, et accidens est ad substantiam, potentia ad actum, et actus propter objectum, et sic de reliquis. Unaquaeque autem res accipit modum entitatis accommodatum /p. 799/ suo primario fini et institutioni; quia ergo omnes hae res per se primo ordinantur ad alias, ideo talem modum entitatis accipiunt, ut intime includant habitudinem ad aliud, et haec est propria habitudo seu respectus transcendentalis; sunt ergo inter reales habitudines veras et secundum esse, aliquae transcendentales, quae ad speciale praedicamentum revocari non possunt, et ideo a praedicamentalibus distinguuntur.

SECTIO IV.
Quomodo differat praedicamentalis respectus a transcendentali.

1. Sed jam occurrit magna difficultas in explicanda differentia inter hos duos ordines respectuum, et consequenter in explicanda ratione ob quam necesse sit praeter transcendentales respectus, praedicamentales admittere.

Proponuntur nonnulla discrimina inter dictos respectus.

2. Variae igitur possunt excogitari differentiae inter hujusmodi respectus. Prima, et quae plures includit, est, quia relatio transcendentalis non requirit

eas conditiones quas postulat praedicamentalis relatio, quae praecipue sunt tres, ut infra videbimus. Prima, quod relatio praedicamentalis requirit aliquod fundamentum reale absolutum, ut similitudo albedinem, paternitas vim generandi seu generationem; secunda, quod requirit terminum realem et realiter existentem; tertia, quia petit distinctionem realem, vel saltem ex natura rei, inter fundamentum et terminum. At vero respectus transcendentalis nullam harum conditionum per se requirit. Nam divina scientia, verbi gratia, habitudinem transcendentalem dicit ad divinam essentiam, ut ad proprium objectum, et divinus amor ad divinam bonitatem, et tamen inter ea nulla est distinctio ex natura rei, sed rationis tantum. Rursum transcendentalis respectus non semper requirit realem terminum, sed interdum esse potest ad ens fictum, seu rationis, vel ad extrinsecam aliquam denominationem; ut conceptus seu cogitatio de ente rationis, seu privatione, ut sic, transcendentalem habitudinem dicit ad illud objectum, quod tamen ens reale non est. Saepe etiam hic transcendentalis respectus, licet sit ad terminum realem, non tamen requirit realem existentiam ejus, ut scientia de futura eclipsi /col. b/ dicit habitudinem realem transcendentalem ad illam, quamvis non existat; et idem est in qualibet scientia de objecto possibili, et de potentia respectu actus non existentis. Denique hic respectus transcendentalis nullum requirit fundamentum, respectus enim transcendentalis materiae ad formam nullum habet fundamentum, sed intime includitur in ipsa materia. Et idem est de respectu formae ad materiam, scientiae ad objectum, et similium. Et ratio est manifesta, quia hic transcendentalis respectus non advenit alicui rei jam constitutae in suo esse essentiali, sed est quasi differentia constituens et complens essentiam illius rei, cujus respectus esse dicitur. Et ideo, sicut illa res, cum sit absoluta, non requirit aliud fundamentum ut sit, praeter proprium subjectum, si fortasse sit accidentalis entitas, ita etiam hic respectus transcendentalis non praerequirit fundamentum aliud, sed constituit potius ipsam rem, quae potest esse fundamentum aliarum relationum praedicamentalium.

3. Atque hinc colligi potest aliud discrimen: nam relatio praedicamentalis est quaedam forma accidentalis, adveniens fundamento plene constituto in suo esse essentiali et absoluto, ad quod comparatur ut completa forma in suo accidentali genere, afficiens ipsum, et referens ad aliud. Respectus vero transcendentalis nec comparatur ut accidens, neque ut completa forma ad illam rem quam proxime actuat, et ejus est respectus; sed comparatur ut essentialis differentia, et consequenter ut ens incompletum in illo genere ad quod pertinet illa res quam actuat vel constituit, eamque non proprie refert ad aliud per modum physicae formae, sed illam constituit per modum metaphysicae differentiae, ut ordinatam vel relatam ad aliud.

Objectiones contra positas differentias.

4. Sed hae differentiae partim verae non sunt, partim non videntur satisfacere. Nam quod in prima differentia dicitur inveniri transcendentalem respectum ejusdem rei ad seipsam propter solam distinctionem rationis, verum non est; alias dici etiam posset identitatem rei ad seipsam esse transcendentalem respectum, et ad illum sufficere distinctionem rationis. Quod si dicas requiri distinctionem rationis ratiocinatae, et fundatam in re, saltem sequitur, inter rationem genericam et specificam esse respectum rea- /p. 800/ lem transcendentalem actus et potentiae, quia genus et differentia distinguuntur ratione cum fundamento in re. Item exempla adducta falsa sunt; nam scientia vel amor Dei non dicit respectum realem etiam transcendentalem ad ipsum Deum, ut ad primarium objectum, sed potius illa scientia et amor sunt absolutissima ab omni respectu reali, quia per se primo non respiciunt aliquod objectum extra se. Unde, sicut ibi non distinguuntur actus et objectum nisi ratione, ita nullus intervenit respectus actus ad objectum, nisi rationis. Et ratio universalis est, quia cum respectus et habitudo sit veluti tendentia quaedam ad aliud, non potest inveniri verus et realis respectus ejusdem ad seipsum, nulla in re interveniente distinctione, saltem ex natura rei.

5. *Respectus transcendentalis quo modo ad ens rationis possit terminari.—Respectus aliqui transcendentales requirunt existentiam terminorum.*—Quod vero ulterius dicitur, transcendentalem respectum interdum esse posse ad ens rationis, est quidem verum, quando ille respectus est ad aliquid, quod se habet per modum objecti, in quo sufficit esse objectivum, ut possit habere rationem termini transcendentalis habitudinis. Et eadem ratione vera est etiam alia pars, nimirum, posse interdum transcendentalem respectum tendere in rem seu essentiam realem, nondum actu existentem, quia etiam ad rationem objecti sufficit saepe esse essentiae, absque esse existentiae. Verumtamen non est in universum verum, quod nullus respectus transcendentalis requirat terminum realem et realiter existentem; nam imprimis actus visionis vel intellectionis creatae intuitivae et naturalis, dicit transcendentalem habitudinem ad rem actu existentem, neque sine illa potest naturaliter esse aut conservari. Deinde, modus actualis unionis dicit transcendentalem respectum ad terminum seu extremum unionis, in quo requirit et realitatem, et actualem existentiam, ita ut neque esse, nec intelligi possit actualis unio realis, nisi actu existat res ad quam sit unio, ut in superioribus saepe tactum est. Actio etiam ut actio, et passio ut passio, dicunt transcendentales respectus ad reale agens, vel patiens actu existens, sine quibus neque esse, neque intelligi possent. Ac denique creatura, praecisa relatione praedicamentali, ex hoc solum quod est ens participatum et dependens, dicit essentialem habitudinem transcendentalem ad /col. b/ primum efficiens, et ad ens per essentiam actu existens. Non est ergo de ratione transcendentalis

respectus, ut non requirat in termino realem et actualem existentiam. Ergo ex illo discrimine solum habetur, inter transcendentales respectus quosdam esse qui terminum realem vel actu existentem non requirunt, etiam si sint alii, qui hujusmodi terminum habeant et postulent, in quibus non habet locum illa secunda differentia.

6. Quod si dicas differentiam consistere in hoc, quia respectus transcendentalis ex se non requirit talem terminum, licet ex peculiari aliqua ratione possit illum habere, respectum autem praedicamentalem ex adaequata ratione sua postulare hujusmodi terminum, instari contra hoc potest, quia haec doctrina supponit, inter respectus ad terminos realiter existentes, quosdam esse transcendentales, et alios praedicamentales, qui differunt in ratione ob quam requirunt talem terminum. At vero hoc ipsum est quod inquirimus, quodque non satis videtur explicari, scilicet, quaenam sit haec diversa ratio in his respectibus postulantibus similem terminum, et quaenam sit necessitas multiplicandi illos. Quandoquidem distinctio illa respectuum transcendentalium habentium terminos reales vel non reales, existentes vel non existentes, sufficiens videatur ad quascunque rerum habitudines declarandas.

7. Praeterea quod de fundamento reali asserebatur, non minus obscurum et incertum est. Primo quidem, quia non omnis relatio praedicamentalis requirit fundamentum reale ex natura rei distinctum a suo subjecto, sed solum illa quae medio aliquo accidente substantiae convenit, ut patet de relatione identitatis specificae inter duos homines, vel animas, verbi gratia, quae censetur relatio praedicamentalis, et immediate fundatur in ipsa natura substantiali, de quo infra latius. Deinde relatio praedicamentalis, quae convenit substantiae medio accidente, quamvis comparata ad substantiam dicatur habere aliud fundamentum proximum, nempe illud accidens, quo mediante convenit substantiae, tamen respectu ipsiusmet accidentis immediate et sine alio fundamento illi convenit, ut similitudo albedini; alioqui procedendum esset in infinitum. At vero idem proportionaliter reperitur in relationibus transcendentalibus; nullum ergo est illud discrimen. Declaratur minor, nam si quae sunt relationes transcendentales in ipsismet substantiis inclusae, illae /p. 801/ non requirunt aliud fundamentum; tamen multae aliae sunt quae non conveniunt substantiae, nisi mediis accidentibus, et illae respectu substantiae etiam habent fundamentum, quamvis respectu accidentis illud non habeant, sed immediate talibus accidentibus conveniant. Ut relatio scientiae ad scibile convenit scienti mediante scientia, ipsi autem scientiae immediate inest. Ergo in necessitate fundamenti nullum videtur esse discrimen inter respectus transcendentales et praedicamentales.

8. *Contra ultimam allatam differentiam objectio.*—Ultima denique differentia etiam est difficilis ad explicandum, nam vel respectus comparatur ad formam, vel essentiam proxime constitutam per ipsam, vel ad subjectum talis formae. Si

priori modo fiat comparatio, tam respectus praedicamentalis quam transcendentalis, est essentialis formae, vel essentiae per ipsum constitutae, et comparatur ad illam ad modum differentiae constituentis ipsam. Unde etiam loquendo de ipso summo genere relationis praedicamentalis, constitui dicitur per ipsum esse ad, tanquam per essentialem modum determinantem communem rationem accidentis, et formaliter ac essentialiter constituentem talem essentiam; ergo in hoc non est differentia inter respectum transcendentalem et praedicamentalem. Si vero posteriori modo fiat comparatio, sicut respectus praedicamentalis est accidentalis alicui subjecto, etiam potest esse respectus transcendentalis; ut respectus scientiae ad objectum, licet sit essentialis scientiae, est tamen accidentalis scienti. Unde, licet ille respectus, metaphysice consideratus, non sit forma physica referens subjectum ad aliud, sed differentia constituens aliquam formam, tamen illa forma, constituta per talem respectum, est forma physica respectiva, referens subjectum ad suum terminum. Neque enim potest forma respectiva informare aliquod subjectum secundum ultimam rationem suam, quin illud referat ad terminum quem ipsa suo modo respicit. Ut in exemplo de gravitate, quod supra ex D. Thoma afferebamus, sicut gravitas est inclinatio ad infimum locum, in quo includit respectum transcendentalem ad illum, ita afficiendo seu informando ipsum grave, inclinat illud, et hoc ipsum est referre illud in centrum. Et idem est de quacunque potentia et scientia, et similibus. Valde ergo obscurum et difficile est, ex his differentiis proprias rationes relationis transcendentalis et praedicamentalis, et ea- /col. b/ rum discrimen, et veram necessitatem admittendi relationes praedicamentales praeter transcendentales colligere.

Alia differentia inter dictos respectus a Cajetano tradita expenditur.

9. Aliter ergo Cajetanus, in opusc. de Ente et essent., cap. 7, quaest. 15, attingens hanc divisionem respectuum realium in transcendentales et praedicamentales, differentiam inter illos declarat ex parte terminorum; nam respectus praedicamentalis (inquit) est, qui respicit terminum pure sub ratione termini; transcendentalis autem respicit aliud, non ut pure terminum, sed sub aliqua alia determinata ratione, vel subjecti, vel objecti, vel efficientis, aut finis. Quae differentia aptior videtur ad hanc rem declarandam, quia omnis respectus sumit speciem suam a termino, seu ab ea re ad quam tendit; et ideo, si quod est discrimen inter hos duos ordines respectuum, ex terminis desumendum videtur. Non est tamen facile ad explicandum quomodo assignata differentia generalis sit, et in quo proprie consistat, seu quid per eam importetur. Ratio difficultatis circa priorem partem est, quia motus, actio et passio dicunt transcendentalem respectum ad terminum, et tamen non respiciunt illum, nisi sub pura ratione termini. Item unio, verbi gratia, hypostatica dicit transcendentalem habitudinem

ad Verbum divinum, et tamen non respicit illud, nisi sub pura ratione termini. Ratio vero difficultatis circa posteriorem partem est, quia omnis respectus, si abstracte et in communi sumatur, solum dicit habitudinem ad aliud sub ratione termini, abstrahendo ab aliis rationibus; si vero sumatur contracte, ut est talis vel talis respectus, sive transcendentalis ille sit, sive praedicamentalis, dicit habitudinem ad talem terminum, qui sit vel causa, vel effectus, vel objectum, vel aliam particularem rationem termini habeat. Ut respectus paternitatis, etiamsi praedicamentalis dicatur, respicit talem terminum, qui sit effectus vel productus a patre, et sic de aliis.

Positum discrimen defenditur et probatur.

10. Respondetur tamen ad priorem rationem, laborare in aequivoco. Nam relatio praedicamentalis dicitur respicere aliud, ut pure terminum, quia circa illud nullum aliud munus exercet, nisi respiciendi tantum. Hoc autem modo non potest dici motus, aut actio, vel passio esse purus respectus ad terminum; /p. 802/ nam habitudo motus ad terminum est habitudo viae, per quam ipse terminus in esse constituitur; unde non dicit habitudinem ad terminum, ut respiciendum tantum, sed ut constituendum per ipsum, et ita non respicit ut pure terminum in praedicto sensu: atque idem est proportionaliter de actione et passione; unio vero hypostatica dicitur a Theologis attingere Verbum ut purum terminum, ut per illam particulam, *purum*, excludant omnem causalitatem propriam quam Verbum ut sic habet circa talem unionem; non est tamen Verbum pure terminus illius unionis in eo sensu in quo hic dicitur de termino relationis praedicamentalis, quia illa unio, ut est realis modus humanae naturae, non utcunque respicit Verbum, sed realiter illi conjungit humanam naturam, et realiter attingit Verbum ipsum tanquam alterum extremum illius unionis, a quo intime et realiter pendet, quamvis sine propria causalitate. Sic igitur universaliter convenit formae, vel modo absoluto includenti respectum transcendentalem, aliquod reale munus exercere circa illum, ad quem dicit respectum, vel causando, vel uniendo, vel repraesentando illum, vel aliquid aliud simile efficiendo, et hac ratione dicitur non respicere illum ut pure terminum. At vero relatio praedicamentalis ita respicit terminum, ut circa illum nullum aliud munus exerceat, nisi pure respicere, ut patet in similitudine unius albi ad aliud: et hoc modo dicitur esse proprium talis relationis respicere aliud ut pure terminum.

11. Unde etiam patet responsio ad alteram rationem, in qua etiam laboratur in aequivoco. Nam respicere aliud ut pure terminum, non est respicere terminum abstracte et in communi, ut videtur in argumento supponi; constat enim praedicamentales relationes specificas et diversarum rationum, tendere etiam in terminos particulares et diversarum rationum. Omnibus tamen illis

commune est, ut circa illos terminos, etiam ut tales sunt, nullum aliud munus exerceant, nisi respiciendi illos; et ideo semper eos respiciunt ut pure terminos, etiamsi sub propriis eorum rationibus eos respiciant. Quod secus est in respectu transcendentali, ut declaratum est.

Sic ergo explicata illa differentia, vera et universalis esse videtur, recteque explicare proprium munus relationis praedicamentalis, quod est referre formaliter seu respicere aliud, a munere et officio respectus transcendentalis, quod est constituere formam vel naturam, /col. b/ aliquid causantem, vel operantem aliquo modo circa rem ad quam dicit habitudinem, vel e converso.

Aliud discrimen ex praecedenti colligitur.

12. Atque hinc oritur alia differentia communiter recepta, quae licet a posteriori esse videatur, confert tamen ad explicandam naturam horum respectuum. Respectus ergo praedicamentalis talis est, ut a natura non sit per se intentus, et ideo nunquam per se fit ex vi actionis alicujus agentis, sed consequitur posito fundamento et termino, teste Aristotele, 5 Physicorum, cui in hoc caeteri consentiunt. At vero respectus transcendentalis saepe est per sese maxime intentus a natura, et ideo forma essentialiter includens talem respectum saepe fit formaliter ac per se primo per actionem propriam; per calefactionem, verbi gratia, fit calor, ut inhaerens, in quo intime includitur transcendentalis respectus; et per actionem videndi fit actus includens transcendentalem habitudinem ad objectum; et per actionem unitivam fit modus unionis, qui includit transcendentalem habitudinem ad unibilia; idemque in multis aliis videre licet. Et hoc ipsum fortasse est quod Scotus distinxit de relationibus extrinsecus et intrinsecus advenientibus, dicens, ad priores posse terminari per se actionem, non vero ad posteriores, quae solae sunt praedicamentales. De qua divisione sub illis vocibus dicemus disputatione sequenti, quae erit prima de sex ultimis praedicamentis, propter quae videtur Scotus potissimum invenisse distinctionem illam. Quae sub illis vocibus non est nobis necessaria, et res ipsa non limitatur ad sex ultima praedicamenta, sed in aliis etiam invenitur, ut ibi videbimus.

13. Ratio ergo hujus discriminis inter relationes praedicamentales et transcendentales est, quia relatio praedicamentalis non est in rerum natura instituta ad aliquod peculiare munus obeundum, sed ad hoc solum res alias comitari dicitur, ut aliquae res sese respiciant ex vi alicujus rationis, seu fundamenti realis, quod in ipsis supponitur, et ideo talis relatio nihil aliud est quam respectus consurgens posito fundamento et termino, nunquam autem per se fit. Respectus autem transcendentalis convenit alicui formae vel entitati, aut modo entis, quatenus a natura per se est institutus et ordinatus ad aliquod peculiare munus, quod potest per se intendi per aliquam actionem; et ideo ille etiam respectus /p. 803/ potest per se fieri per actionem, ut inclusus in forma dicente

talem respectum. Cum enim talis forma in proprio et specifico conceptu illum respectum includat, non potest ille respectus minus esse per se intentus, aut minus per se fieri, quam ipsa forma, cum actio et intentio agentis per se tendat ad totam formam, usque ad specificam rationem ejus.

Aliud discrimen inter dictos respectus.

14. Et hinc etiam fit ut relatio pura et praedicamentalis nunquam sit principium agendi, tum quia sicut nunquam per se fit, ita etiam nunquam per se agit; tum etiam quia, ut diximus, non est instituta a natura ob aliquod peculiare munus per se necessarium ad esse, vel fieri rei, sed solum est quidam respectus ex consequenti resultans; principia autem agendi sunt per se instituta, et ad peculiare munus ordinata. At vero forma dicens respectum transcendentalem, secundum propriam etiam rationem respectivam, saepe est principium per se agendi, ut patet de scientia, potentia, et similibus.

Quarta differentia, et aliarum explicatio.

15. Tandem ex his intelligitur, respectum praedicamentalem concipiendum esse tanquam formam quamdam minimam et accidentalem, quae non dat subjecto aliquod esse, nisi respicere aliud, neque ad aliquid aliud in natura deservit. Respectus autem transcendentalis non est concipiendus tanquam integra forma, cujus munus sit tantum referre, sed est essentialis modus, seu differentia alicujus formae seu entitatis, quatenus ad causandum aliquo modo, vel operandum circa alia, per se primo instituta est, vel e converso, quatenus ab alia essentialiter pendet. Et juxta hanc rationem explicandi hos respectus, potest ad eumdem sensum reduci differentia superius tacta, quod respectus transcendentalis semper est intrinsecus et essentialis alicui entitati, sub entitate modos etiam reales comprehendendo; relatio autem praedicamentalis habet propriam et peculiarem rationem accidentis. Et ita etiam possunt ad convenientem sensum reduci duae aliae differentiae sumptae ex parte fundamenti, et realitatis, seu existentiae termini.

Quae relationes sint praedicamenti Ad aliquid.

16. Tandem ex his differentiis concluditur, respectus transcendentales, etiamsi vere sint /col. b/ in rebus secundum proprium esse eorum non pertinere ad unum aliquod speciale praedicamentum, quia res illae, seu naturae, vel essentiae quibus conveniunt, ad varia munera, et interdum primo diversa ordinantur, ideoque ad varia praedicamenta revocantur, juxta diversas eorum conditiones et naturas. Et ideo praedicamentum Ad aliquid solas illas relationes complectitur, quae proprie ac peculiariter praedicamentales appellantur, nam omnes illae inter se conveniunt, et ab aliis distinguuntur in peculiari modo pure referendi

rem quam afficiunt. Et ideo generatim etiam conveniunt in modo quo esse incipiunt per coexistentiam extremorum, seu fundamenti et termini, et in aliis conditionibus quas requirunt, ut ex discursu sequentis sectionis magis constabit.

Responsio ad quartam difficultatem, ex sectione prima relictam.

17. *Scientia, an secundum Aristotelem sit de genere relationis.—Singulas scientias ad singula objecta referri oportet.*—Ex his etiam soluta relinquitur difficultas tacta in argumento quarto primae sectionis. Nam respectus illi, in quibus ibi fit inductio, omnes sunt transcendentales, et ut sic fatemur non pertinere ad speciale praedicamentum. Unde in illo speciali exemplo, quod ibi tangitur de scientia, quatenus dicit respectum ad scibile, fateor responsiones ibi tactas ex Aristotele, capit. de Qualitate, magnam habere difficultatem. Nam prima videtur satis improbata objectionibus ibi factis, quae confirmari possunt testimoniis ejusdem Aristotelis, 4 Topicorum, cap. 1, loco 4, ubi generatim ait,[2] genus et speciem in eadem divisione, scilicet praedicamentali, esse oportere, et in particulari adhibet exemplum de Ad aliquid: *Nam genera* (inquit) *eorum quae sunt ad aliquid, oportet habere species quae sint etiam ad aliquid, et e converso*; et idem ait de qualitate; idemque repetit 5 Topicorum, cap. 4, loco 39, ubi sic ait: *Amplius in his quae ad aliquid sunt, considerandum, si ad quod genus assignatur, et species ad illud quoddam assignatur, ut si opinio et opinatum, et quaedam opinio ad quoddam opinatum; si autem non sic assignatur, manifestum, quoniam peccatur.* Idemque patet ex regulis positis ab Aristotele in Antepraedicament., c. 3, praesertim illa: *Genera non subalternatim posita, non habent easdem differentias.* Et in praesenti satis constat ex re ipsa; nam quaelibet /p. 804/ scientia secundum propriam et specificam rationem suam dicit propriam habitudinem ad suum proprium objectum. Quod enim Soto ait in praedicamento qualitatis, exponens illum locum Aristotelis, licet scientia ut sic dicat habitudinem ad scibile, ut mensurabile ad mensuram, tamen scientias particulares non dicere proprias relationes mensurabilis ad propria objecta, hoc (inquam) falsum est, et contra expressa verba Aristotelis in dicto loco sexto Topicorum, et contra manifestam rationem. Nam, sicut veritas scientiae in communi mensuratur ex objecto scibili in communi, ita veritas hujus scientiae ex hoc objecto scibili. Item, quia determinata scientia sumit suam speciem ex habitudine ad suum objectum; ergo non solum ut scientia, sed etiam ut talis scientia, dicit respectum ad tale scibile.

---

2   Here I am following the reading of Salamanca, 1597, vol. 2, p. 554, which is "ait" rather than the Vivès "agit."

18. Quare dicendum est, Aristotelem non approbasse illam primam responsionem, et ideo addidisse secundam, nimirum, eamdem rem quae est scientia, in diversis praedicamentis collocari, scilicet, qualitatis, et Ad aliquid, utique sub diversis rationibus, nam sub una et eadem non potest una res in diversis praedicamentis constitui.

Sed contra hanc etiam responsionem non parum urgent objectiones superius appositae, et ideo aliqui sentiunt Aristotelem ibi non ex propria sententia esse locutum, sed juxta opinionem eorum qui amplectebantur primam definitionem relativorum, quam in cap. de Ad aliquid, tradiderat, scilicet omnia, quae ad aliquid aliquo modo dicuntur, esse de praedicamento Ad aliquid. Nam juxta illam ibidem subjunxerat, habitum, dispositionem et scientiam esse ad aliquid; postea vero illam definitionem non approbat, et ideo neque censendus est approbare omnia quae ex illa consequuntur, quamvis insinuet quomodo juxta illam consequenter loquendum sit. Nec vero satisfacit alia responsio, quod haec sint tantum relativa secundum dici, nam sufficienter ostenditur, in proprio esse harum rerum includi respectum. Vera ergo responsio est illa quae ultimo loco, in eodem argumento quarto, proposita est, nimirum, scientiam, et alia hujusmodi entia secundum essentialem suam rationem non dicere respectum praedicamentalem, sed transcendentalem tantum, et ideo ut sic non pertinere ad praedicamentum Ad aliquid. Quatenus vero scientiae adjungi potest aliquis purus respectus accidentalis, et extra essentiam ejus, ut sic non pertinere ad /col. b/ praedicamentum qualitatis, sed Ad aliquid. Juxta quem sensum posset etiam explicari secunda Aristotelis responsio.

19. *Quae sit ratio asserendi relationes praedicamentales.* ——Erat vero ultima replica, quae per interrogationem fiebat in illo quarto argumento, scilicet, quid necesse sit hujusmodi respectus accidentales et praedicamentales adjungere et admittere, praeter transcendentales. Si enim attente considerentur rationes quibus a doctoribus probari solet, dari relationes reales, illae certe maxime probant dari in rebus hujusmodi respectus reales secundum esse, ut maxime videre licet apud D. Thomam, in 1 p., quaest. 13, art. 7, et quaestione vigesima octava, articulo 1, et 2; et Scotum, in 2, dist. 1, et alios supra citatos. Quod vero praeter relationes transcendentales dentur praedicamentales ab illis distinctae, non videtur posse demonstrari. Nihilominus tamen sufficit communis philosophorum consensus, ut ab ea sententia nullo modo recedendum sit. Ratio autem introducendi et admittendi hujusmodi respectus fuit, quia invenimus multas praedicationes respectivas accidentales, quae non desumuntur ex solis transcendentalibus respectibus, ut esse patrem, similem, aequalem, etc.; neque etiam ortae sunt ex aliqua apprehensione aut fictione intellectus, sed ex rebus ipsis, in quibus existunt formae, a quibus tales denominationes et praedicationes oriuntur. Neque etiam tales denominationes sunt extrinsecae, id est ab extrinsecis rebus aut formis desumptae, nam res non dicitur similis

alteri per quod in altera est, sed per id quod in se habet, et sic de caeteris.
Hinc ergo intellectum est, hujusmodi denominationes desumi a quibusdam
respectibus resultantibus ex coexistentia plurium rerum habentium ad id sufficiens fundamentum, quorum munus solum est referre et ordinare unam rem
ad aliam, ita ut una alteram respiciat ratione alicujus fundamenti quod in ea
supponitur. Et hi respectus, quoniam peculiarem modum habent efficiendi,
in proprio praedicamento collocati sunt.

20. Addo vero, hanc communem sententiam, et rationem ejus, faciliorem et
verisimiliorem fieri, si dicamus has relationes praedicamentales non esse novas
res, aut modos reales ex natura rei distinctos ab illis rebus in quibus fundari
dicuntur, sed illasmet res duplicem habere modum denominandi: unum per
se, et (ut ita dicam) ex primaria /p. 805/ institutione sua; alium quasi resultantem ex coexistentia unius rei cum alia. Prior modus denominationis vel est
omnino absolutus, vel, si includat respectum, erit transcendentalis, qui saepissime non postulat coexistentiam alterius extremi ad quem tendit, et quando
illum requirit, non ideo est quia talis respectus consurgat quasi per accidens
ex coexistentia talium extremorum, sed quia talis res est per se instituta ad
actualiter exercendum aliquod munus circa aliam, quod exercere non potest
nisi circa rem existentem, et hoc modo explicata, quaedam differentia relationum transcendentalium supra tacta, optima est. Posterior vero denominatio
est peculiari modo respectiva, et ex suo genere accidentalis, quia quod una res
coexistat alteri, praecise spectando conceptum et rationem coexistentiae, est
extra rationem uniuscujusque rei, et ideo denominatio etiam quae requirit hanc
coexistentiam, non ob aliam causam, nisi ut ex ea resultet talis denominatio,
accidentaria est. Et ideo, licet in re sumatur ab eadem entitate, tamen quia
accidentaria est, habet sufficiens fundamentum distinctionis, ut intellectus
concipiat illam entitatem ad modum duarum formarum. Ac denique quia
denominatio illa ex rebus ipsis sumitur, sufficit etiam ut ratione illius speciale
praedicamentum accidentis realis et respectivi constituatur. Hoc ergo modo
videtur sufficens ratio reddi et praedictae divisionis, et constitutionis praedicamenti Ad aliquid.

21. *Relationes in divinis quales.*—Hic vero occurrebat difficultas theologica de
relationibus divinis, quomodo ad illas applicari possit doctrina data, et ad quod
membrum dictae divisionis revocandae sint. Sed haec disputatio ad nos non
spectat, neque oportet ut praedicta omnia in illis relationibus locum habeant,
quia illae relationes non sunt accidentales, sed substantiales. Certum est tamen
non esse relationes tantum secundum dici, sed secundum esse, neque esse proprie
in rigore relationes praedicamentales, quia substantiae sunt infinitae, et altioris
ordinis, ideoque in nullo praedicamento collocantur; unde neque etiam habent
illam imperfectionem seu modum essendi per resultantiam ex fundamento

et termino, sed sunt, vel ex se, ut relatio producentis, verbi gratia, paternitas, vel per se producuntur per propriam productionem, aut (ut juxta nostrum modum concipiendi loquamur) comproducuntur, et, formaliter loquendo, per se attinguntur per /col. b/ ipsas origines, ut filiatio, et processio passiva. Sunt ergo illae relationes altioris ordinis, eminenter complectentes quidquid perfectionis et proprietatis necessariae ad verum respectum realem reperitur in respectu transcendentali, et praedicamentali, seclusis imperfectionibus.

SECTIO V.
Quaenam sit essentia propriaque definitio ipsius ad aliquid, seu relationis praedicamentalis.

1. Quae hactenus disputavimus, fere pertinent ad explicandam et definiendam quaestionem, an sit relatio realis praedicamentalis, de qua hic agimus; obiter tamen multa attigimus, ex quibus facilius nobis erit essentiam hujus relationis, et definitionem quam Aristoteles in hac re approbat, explicare.

Relationis praedicamentalis definitio.
2. Dicendum ergo est, relationem (de sola praedicamentali jam est sermo) esse accidens, cujus totum esse est ad aliud esse, seu ad aliud se habere, seu aliud respicere. Haec definitio sumitur ex Aristotele, in lib. Praedicamentor., c. de Ad aliquid, ubi duas designat definitiones eorum quae sunt ad aliquid, quae solum in uno verbo differunt. Prior est, *ea esse ad aliquid, quae id quod sunt, aliorum esse aut ad aliquid aliquo alio modo dicuntur.* Posterior est, *ea esse ad aliquid, quorum esse est ad aliquid sese habere.* Tota ergo differentia est in verbo illo, *dicuntur.* Quod quidem praesertim in usu philosophorum frequenter usurpari solet pro verbo essendi, ut ipsemet Aristoteles dixit, *qualitatem esse, qua quales quidam dicuntur,* et ideo multi volunt non esse admodum curandum de discrimine aut diversitate inter illas descriptiones. Nihilominus tamen juxta mentem Aristotelis constat illas esse diversas, et in priori verbum, *dicuntur,* sumptum esse cum rigore et proprietate, ac praeterea sub disjunctione in illa definitione positum esse, ea esse ad aliquid, *quae id quod sunt aliorum sunt, vel aliquo modo aliorum esse dicuntur,* ut indicetur non esse de ratione relationis ut sit ad aliud, sed ut sit vel dicatur; et hoc voluit Aristoteles in secunda definitione, corrigere, ut in propria definitione praedicamenti Ad aliquid solum relationes secundum esse, et non relativa secundum dici comprehendantur. Ex illa ergo posteriori definitione, nostra desumpta est, vel potius eadem est cum illa; solum enim majoris claritatis gra- /p. 806/ tia per quamdam proportionem generis et differentiae constituta et composita est.

3. *Quod genus in definitione relationis.*—*Accidens* ergo positum est in illa definitione loco generis. Per quod imprimis excluduntur divinae relationes, quae non sunt accidentia, sed substantiae. Excluduntur deinde omnes substantiae creatae, quae relationes praedicamentales esse non possunt, ut ex dictis in praecedenti sectione constat. Excluduntur praeterea relationes rationis, quae proprie et simpliciter non possunt dici accidentia, cum accidens simplicter dictum sub ente reali contineatur. Nec probo quod Cajetanus, 1 p., 13, a. 7, significat, definitionem relativorum datam in praedicamentis communem esse relativis rationis et realibus, *quia data est* (inquit) *de eis secundum quod important ad, et ita ut abstrahunt ab ente reali.* Repugnat enim hoc Aristoteli, qui prius divisit ens reale, et unum ejus membrum posuit Ad aliquid, et postea hoc definivit. Deinde ex illa sententia sequitur, aut relationes rationis constitui in praedicamento Ad aliquid, aut definitionem illam latius patere quam suum definitum. Quamvis ergo Aristoteles non posuerit expresse in illa definitione nomen accidentis, illud tamen tacite subintelligit ex priori divisione entis in novem genera. Eo vel maxime quod etiam illa posterior particula, scilicet *esse ad*, proprie et in rigore sumpta, non convenit relationibus rationis, sed tantum per quamdam analogam imitationem seu proportionem, ut superius declaratum est. Et ideo per illam etiam particulam cum proprietate sumptam possent relationes rationis excludi, quae non tam sunt quam apprehenduntur esse ad aliquid.

4. *Differentia in definitione relationis quae.*—Altera pars illius definitionis, quae locum differentiae habet, separat praedicamentum hoc a reliquis praedicamentis accidentium, nam illa cum sint absoluta, habent suum esse in alio, non vero ad aliud; quod proprium relationis. Statim vero insurgunt duae difficultates.

Prima difficultas circa definitionem.

5. Prima est, quia tota illa definitio competit relativis transcendentalibus, nam etiam scientia habet totum suum esse ad aliud. Ad quam difficultatem communiter responderi solet, hujusmodi entia exclusa esse ab Aristotele in secunda definitione, auferendo verbum illud *dicuntur*, quod erat in prima. Sed /col. b/ haec responsio non est consentanea doctrinae a nobis traditae in superiori sectione, nam hujusmodi entia, concepta etiam prout in se sunt, includunt in suis rationibus essentialibus habitudinem ad aliud; non ergo tantum dicuntur, sed vere sunt ad aliud; ergo etiam ablato a definitione verbo illo, *dicuntur*, vere illis competit definitio. Denique illud verbum solum est ablatum ad excludenda relativa secundum dici; ostendimus autem haec non esse relativa tantum secundum dici, sed etiam secundum suum esse; ergo non satis exclusa sunt. Existimo ergo hujusmodi transcendentales respectus excludendos esse per illam particulam, *cujus totum esse est esse ad aliud*, si in ea proprietate

intelligatur, quam in fine praecedentis sectionis declaravimus. Nam illa entia, quae transcendentalem respectum includunt, non sunt ita ad aliud, ut totum suum esse positum habeant in puro respectu ad aliud, et ideo non respiciunt aliud sub pura ratione termini, sed sub aliqua alia ratione, et exercendo circa illud aliquod munus, ad quod hujusmodi res sunt per se institutae. At vero relatio quae hic definitur, habet totam suam essentiam in puro respectu ad aliud, et ideo illi specialiter convenit, ut totum illius esse ad aliud sit, tanquam ad purum terminum talis respectus, seu habitudinis.

Si relatio habet esse in, quomodo sit tota ad aliud.

6. Sed tunc insurgit secunda difficultas, quae praecedentem auget, nam haec posterior definitionis pars videtur repugnare priori; nam si relatio est accidens, ergo non potest totum esse illius consistere in habitudine ad aliud; necesse est enim ut aliquid ejus in subjecto sit, ut ea ratione accidens esse possit, cum accidentis esse sit inesse. Ad quam difficultatem respondent aliqui, cum dicitur relatio habere totum suum esse ad aliud, intelligendum esse de esse proprio relationis, ut sic, quod est esse ad, non de esse, quod habet commune cum caeteris accidentibus, quod est esse in. Et hinc ortum habuit opinio supra tractata de distinctione inter esse ad, et esse in relationis, et quod esse ad, ut sic, abstrahat ab omni esse reali, et de se commune sit univoce relationibus rationis, et realibus. Verumtamen haec responsio ex superius dictis contra praedictam sententiam satis refutata est. Primo, quia de ratione accidentis, prout in re ipsa existit, non solum /p. 807/ est quod insit secundum aliquam rationem genericam vel communem, sed etiam secundum propriam, et prout est talis forma in rerum natura; imo impossibile est quod forma informet vel afficiat secundum communem rationem, et non secundum aliquam propriam, cum hae rationes a parte rei non distinguantur. Secundo, quia alias relatio non tribueret subjecto proprium effectum formalem relativum, quia accidens non dat effectum formalem, nisi inhaerendo et afficiendo; si ergo relatio non inest secundum propriam rationem, non confert proprium et specificum effectum formalem. Tertio, quia si illud esse proprium relationis, quod dicitur esse ad, non inesset, nihil reale esset in rerum natura, et consequenter relatio praedicamentalis secundum proprium constitutivum ejus non esset reale quid. Unde merito D. Thomas, in 1, dist. 25, quaest. 1, art. 4, ad tertium, dicit, quod relatio realis secundum propriam quidditativam rationem ponit aliquid in eo cujus est relatio, quamvis illud quod ponit, non sit absolutum. Quod latius docuit in alio opere super primum Sentent. Ad Annibaldum, dist. 25, art. 4, ad 3, dicens: *Quamvis relatio non ponat ex illo respectu aliquid absolutum, ponit tamen aliquid relativum, et ideo relatio est quaedam res; si enim secundum rationem relationis sive respectus non poneret aliquid, cum secundum suum esse,*

ratione cujus ponit aliquid inhaerens, non cadat in genere relationis, non esse aliquod genus entis.

7. Igitur ad difficultatem positam concedendum est, relationem secundum se totam esse accidens; haec enim ratio, ut in superioribus diximus, est quasi transcendentalis respectu novem praedicamentorum. Unde, cum dicitur totum esse relationis esse ad aliud, particula exclusiva ibi virtualiter contenta non excludit concomitantia, seu extrinsecas et transcendentales rationes; quare, sicut non excludit rationem entis realis, ita nec rationem accidentis et inhaerentis. Solum ergo excludit esse absolutum, et indicat, esse relationis ut sic non sistere in subjecto, quod suo modo afficit seu denominat, sed illud ordinare ad terminum, et in hoc positam esse totam formalem rationem relationis. Itaque, licet similitudo, verbi gratia, secundum totam rationem suam etiam relativam conci- /col. b/ pienda sit ut forma afficiens rem quam denominat similem, tamen tota illius affectio in hoc posita est, quod illam rem ordinat seu refert ad aliam, et in hoc sensu dicitur totum esse relationis esse ad aliud se habere.

8. *Objectio.—Dissolvitur.*—Dices, hoc commune esse formis illis seu modis realibus et absolutis includentibus respectum transcendentalem; scientia enim ita inest et afficit scientem, ut illum suo proprio modo ordinet ad objectum scibile, neque aliter possit suum formalem effectum exercere; et idem est de potentia, unione, et similibus. Respondetur concedendo in hoc esse aliquam similitudinem et proportionem, propter quam hae formae dicuntur includere aliquem respectum secundum esse, licet transcendentalem. Differentia vero est illa eadem saepe tacta, quod relationes praedicamentales consistunt in puro respectu; aliae vero formae vel qualitates dant proprium aliquod esse absolutum, exercendo aliquod munus, ad quod natura sua ordinantur, in quo propterea includunt alquam habitudinem, et ideo non ita habent totum suum esse ad aliud, sicut relationes praedicamentales.

Essentia relationis sitne apta actu vel aptitudine referre.

9. Ultimo vero objici potest, quia si relatio in abstracto consideretur, ut est forma quaedam referens subjectum vel fundamentum ad terminum, sic non est de ratione ejus ut actu referat, sed ut sit apta referre; ergo non consistit totum esse ejus in esse ad terminum. Patet consequentia, quia esse ad terminum importat actuale exercitium (ut sic dicam) talis habitudinis ad terminum. Antecedens vero patet, tum quia communis ratio accidentis non est actu efficere, sed aptitudine; tum etiam quia potest mens concipere relationem integram, afficientem subjectum, et ut nondum referentem. Quomodo etiam Theologi aiunt, in divinis concipi paternitatem ut constituentem primam personam et quasi adhaerentem illi, prius quam referentem; ergo non consistit ratio relationis in actuali respectu.

10. Respondetur falsum esse antecedens; nam res non constituitur apta referri per relationem ut sic, sed per fundamentum proximum relationis; proprius autem effectus formalis relationis est actu referre. Alias nec distingueretur, etiam secundum rationem formalem, a fundamento, nec requireret coexis- /p. 808/ tentiam termini, nec vere diceretur totum esse ejus positum esse in respectu ad aliud.

11. Ad primam ergo probationem antecedentis respondetur primo, aliud esse considerare an effectus formalis accidentis sit constituere actu tale, aliud vero an de essentia accidentis sit actu exercere suum effectum formalem; haec enim duo distincta sunt. Vere enim dicimus, effectum formalem albedinis esse constituere actu album, et non tantum aptitudine, quanquam absolute non sit de essentiali ratione albedinis, ut actu conferat talem effectum formalem. Unde etiam dici potest quod, licet de ratione albedinis, simpliciter loquendo, non sit constituere actu album, tamen de ratione albedinis ut afficientis et informantis subjectum, est constituere actu album. Sic igitur in praesenti in hoc posteriori sensu dicimus, formalem effectum relationis esse actu referre, quia hoc est quod ipsa per se primo confert formaliter subjecto, quod suo modo afficit.

12. *Relationis essentia sita est in actuali affectione subjecti.*—Addo vero deinde, non omni accidenti commune esse aptitudine tantum afficere, sed quaedam esse de quorum essentiali conceptu est, ut non possint in rerum natura esse quin afficiant, ut de modis accidentalibus in superioribus diximus. Relationes ergo in hoc posteriori ordine continentur, quia non possunt esse in rerum natura, quin actu referant, eo quod non possint ab omni subjecto separatae conservari, quia in re non distinguuntur a suis proximis subjectis, ut ostensum est. Quanquam non desint qui contrarium doceant, ut Major, in 4, dist. 12, quaest. 3; Ledesm., 1 p. quarti, quaest. 28, a. 2, dub. 4; qui aiunt posse Deum conservare paternitatem, verbi gratia, creatam sine proprio subjecto, vel per se separatam, vel in alio subjecto. Putant enim paternitatem esse rem omnino distinctam a caeteris, et ideo consequenter loquuntur, praesertim quoad priorem partem. Nam quoad posteriorem impossibile apparet quod haec paternitas ponatur in eo qui non genuit hunc filium; alias vel constitueret patrem eum qui non genuit, vel inhaereret alicui cui non daret suum effectum formalem; utrumque autem impossibile est. Sicut autem verius est, relationem non esse rem distinctam a fundamento, ita etiam verius esse non posse ab illo separatam, vel per se conservari. Quod si interdum distinguitur realiter relatio a subjecto remoto, eatenus id est, quatenus /col. b/ fundamentum proximum relationis est aliqua res distincta a subjecto remoto. Unde eatenus etiam potest talis relatio conservari separata a tali subjecto, quatenus illa res, quae est fundamentum ejus, potest sine illo subjecto conservari. Tunc autem relatio sic conservata af-

ficit suum fundamentum per modum subjecti, et illud actu refert, quo modo quantitas consecrata est aequalis alteri, et albedo separata, esset similis alteri, et ita nunquam potest esse actu relatio, quin actu referat ad aliud.

13. Ad alteram probationem respondetur, impossibile esse concipere relationem cum suo effectu formali plene ac proprie concepto, quin concipiatur ut actu referens; sicut impossibile est concipere albedinem cum suo effectu formali integre concepto, quin concipiatur ut constituens actu album, quia non potest res integre concipi sine eo quod est de essentiali ratione ejus. Contingit tamen aliquando ut intellectus noster, concipiens aliquam formam ut afficientem, non concipiat distincte, proprie ac integre effectum formalem ejus, sed tantum confuse, sistendo in hac communi ratione afficendi, vel inhaerendi; nam quia haec ratio est quasi transcendens, et inclusa in quolibet modo seu differentia formae, ideo potest tota forma, ut afficiens, confuse tantum concipi quoad effectum suum; ut si quis concipiat albedinem secundum se totam esse formam adhaerentem subjecto, et informantem illud, non quidem concipiet illam ut constituentem actu album, non quia ille non sit effectus formalis albedinis, sed quia diminute et confuse concipit effectum ejus. Ad hunc ergo modum potest concipi relatio secundum se totam ut afficiens vel adhaerens, aut constituens quidpiam, etiamsi non intelligatur ut actu referens, non quia effectus formalis relationis non sit actu referre, sed quia tunc non concipitur effectus formalis relationis proprio et adaequato conceptu, sed confuso et communi. Atque ita nobis contingit, quando in divinis concipimus paternitatem ut priorem actu referendi ad Filium; de qua re latius Theologi disputant.

SECTIO VI.
De subjecto, fundamento ac termino
ad praedicamentalem relationem requisitis.

1. *An sit aliqua causa finalis relationis.—An habeat causam efficentem.—Quae sit relationis causa materialis.*—Explicui- /p. 809/ mus an sit, et quid sit praedicamentalis relatio; nunc oportet exponere causas vel principia ejus, qualiacunque sint, et quatenus ei convenire possunt. Cum enim haec relatio non sit per se intenta in rebus, non habet proprie causam finalem, quamvis eo modo quo est, dici possit esse propter suum formalem effectum, vel propter suum terminum. Et simili ratione, cum per se non fiat, sed resultet, vel formaliter consequatur positis fundamento et termino, nullam habet vel requirit efficientem causam, praeter eas quae fundamentum et terminum efficiunt. Nisi quis velit ipsi fundamento aut termino efficientiam aliquam circa relationem tribuere, saltem per resultantiam naturalem, quod esset probabile respectu fundamenti, si relatio esset modus ex natura rei distinctus ab illo; tamen, quia contrarium ut

verum supponimus, ideo non putamus ibi intervenire resultantiam effectivam, sed quasi formalem. Rursus, cum ipsa relatio sit forma quaedam, non habet aliam causam formalem propriam et physicam, sed habet suam quidditatem, et rationem formalem metaphysicam, quam jam explicuimus. Habet etiam terminum, qui, quatenus specificans est, rationem quamdam formae participat. Fundamentum vero et subjectum causam materialem complere videntur, et ideo in his tribus, subjecto, fundamento et termino, omnia principia et causae relationum positae sunt; ideoque de illis sigillatim dicendum est, et inde postea constabit quomodo ex horum varietate diversa genera aut species relationum distingui possint.

De subjecto relationum accidentalium.

2. Primo igitur dicendum est, omnem relationem praedicamentalem requirere aliquod subjectum reale. Haec assertio in communi sumpta clara est, nam relatio est accidens, ut dictum est; omne autem accidens requirit aliquod subjectum; ergo. Item, relatio est quaedam forma; omnis autem forma aliquid informat; id autem quod informat, dicitur subjectum ejus, praesertim si ei inhaereat, et ab eo pendeat, quod de relatione, etiam ut relatio est, ostendimus. Oportet autem advertere, posse nos loqui de relatione in abstracto, vel in concreto, sicut de aliis accidentibus; ut in communi hoc ipsum nomen relationis abstractum est, et in particulari nomen paternitatis, similitudinis, etc; et similiter relativum in communi est /col. b/ quoddam concretum, in particulari vero pater, simile, et similia. Cum ergo dicimus relationem requirere subjectum, de relatione in abstracto id intelligere oportet, nam relativum in concreto non habet proprie subjectum, sed potius ipsum est quid constans ex subjecto et relatione, si formaliter sumatur ut relativum est, seu ut compostium quoddam ex relatione et subjecto ejus. Nam interdum ipsum subjectum relationis dici solet relativum, denominative potius quam formaliter, id est, tanquam affectum, non tanquam constitutum relatione, et ideo proprius ac formalius dicitur de ipso constituto. Nam id quod relatione afficitur, non dicitur proprie ipsum relativum, sed subjectum relationis, et saepe etiam vocatur extremum relationis, quia habitudo relativa veluti clauditur inter duo subjecta relationum, ut inter duo extrema.

Unam relationem, etiam secundum esse ad, in uno tantum subjecto esse posse, contra Henricum ostenditur.

3. Quaeri vero hic potest an una relatio unum habeat subjectum, et quodnam illud sit. Quod praecipue interrogo propter Henricum, qui Quodlib. 9, q. 3, sentit relationem secundum proprium esse ad, unam et eamdem esse inter duo extrema quae referuntur. Nam relatio secundum propriam rationem est veluti medium quoddam inter extrema relata, et ideo, sicut Aristoteles dixit eamdem

esse viam ab Athenis ad Thebas et a Thebis ad Athenas, ita dicit Henricus unam et eamdem esse habitudinem quorumcunque duorum extremorum ad invicem se habentium, scilicet, patris ad filium, et filii ad patrem, vel duorum fratrum, aut similium inter se. Quod si objicias, quia relatio patris, verbi gratia, est paternitas, et filii filiatio, et quod in universum necesse est distingui ex fundamentis, quia non potest unum et idem accidens esse in diversis subjectis, respondet, relationes consideratas ut existentes in fundamentis, et ut inseparabiles ab illis, multiplicari secundum distinctionem et pluralitatem eorum; nihilominus tamen, quatenus relatio est quoddam medium et quasi intervallum duorum habentium inter se habitudinem, sic esse unam et eamdem utriusque.

4. Verumtamen aut haec distinctio et tota opinio in solis verbis consistit, aut intelligibilis non est. Quomodo enim fieri potest, ut unum et idem numero accidens sit in sub- /p. 810/ jectis reipsa distinctis, et inter se non unitis, sed omnino disjunctis, et loco etiam separatis? Nam vel relatio haec dicitur una, vera et propria unitate, tanquam simplex forma, et in hoc sensu procedit ratio facta, quae convincit non posse unam et eamdem relationem simul esse in utroque extremo; vel dicitur illa relatio una, solum collectione quadam, quia nimirum ex utraque relatione existente in utroque extremo coalescit integra habitudo et veluti connexio in utroque extremo, et hoc modo solo nomine vocatur illa relatio una, qui est inusitatus modus loquendi, et ideo vitandus est. Et praeterea juxta illum, consequenter loquendo, dicendum esset talem habitudinem, eo modo quo una est, habere unum subjectum, non simpliciter, sed collectione utriusque extremi invicem ordinati. Quod si quis dicat illam mutuam habitudinem esse unam simpliciter utriusque extremi, non tamen esse in illis ut in subjectis, sed tantum esse inter illa, quod magis significat Henricus, hoc sane evidentius falsum est, minusque intelligibile; nam vel intervallum illud seu mutua habitudo est aliquid rationis tantum, et sic est impertinens ad relationem realem, ut recte contra Aureolum ostendit. Gregor., in 1, dist. 28, q. 1; vel est aliquid rei, et sic vel est aliquid in se subsistens, quod dici non potest; vel necesse est ut sit in aliquo subjecto; non potest autem esse nisi in extremis inter se relatis, vel in aliquo eorum. Vel denique est aliquid abstrahens ab ente reali et rationis, ut indicat Henricus, et hoc et simpliciter falsum est, ut supra est ostensum; et licet daremus, ut est in conceptu nostro, posse abstrahi, nihilominus in singulis relationibus non posset abstrahere; ergo necesse est ut in relationibus realibus et accidentalibus sit aliquid reale et accidentale, et ita redit argumentum factum, quod debet esse in uno aliquo subjecto.

Quomodo unius relationis possint esse plura
subjecta subordinata.

5. *Relationes in denominatione subjecti quem ordinem servent.*—Aliter ergo dicendum est, et distinguendum de subjectis. Possunt enim esse plura subjecta diversarum rationum, et subordinata inter se, vel ejusdem rationis, et aeque immediate affecta relatione. Hoc igitur posteriori modo, fieri non potest ut una relatio sit in pluribus subjectis, ut probat ratio contra Henricum facta, quae universalis est de quolibet accidenti habente in re /col. b/ veram ac propriam unitatem. Priori[3] autem modo distingui possunt plura subjecta unius relationis, unum proximum, et aliud remotum; ut relatio aequalitatis proxime est in quantitate, remote vero in substantia, et relatio similitudinis proxime est in qualitate, et remote in quantitate, et adhuc remotius in substantia. Verumtamen hujusmodi relatio per se ac proprie solum afficit proximum subjectum, in quo suo modo inest; ad subjectum autem remotum solum comparatur medio proximo, in quantum hoc in illo inest et sustentatur. Jam enim in superioribus, disputat. 14, ostendimus posse unum accidens proxime inesse alteri, et non attingere substantiam in se, sed solum quatenus illud accidens, cui aliud inest, in substantia sustentatur. Sic igitur potest una relatio immediate esse in aliquo subjecto accidentali, et remote in alio, vel in substantia. An vero hoc sit universale in omnibus relationibus, statim videbimus.

6. Est tamen quoad denominationem relationis consideranda quaedam varietas inter relationes: nam interdum relatio aeque vel in eodem modo denominat subjectum proximum et remotum, ut quantitas dicitur aequalis, et similiter substantia materialis; et albedo dicitur similis, et ipsum album, vel etiam subjectum, ut homo, vel paries. Aliquando vero relatio denominat subjectum proximum, et non remotum, ut intellectus dicitur referri relatione potentiae ad suum actum, anima vero non item, et sic de aliis. Aliquando vero, e converso, relatio denominat subjectum remotum, vel suppositum ipsum, et non proximum, ut filiatio denominat suppositum filium, non vero humanitatem, quamvis probabile sit proxime inesse humanitati; et paternitas proxime dicitur esse in potentia, et tamen non denominat patrem, nisi ipsum suppositum. Ratio autem hujus varietatis provenit ex diversitate fundamentorum, quae aliquando secundum eamdem proportionem comparantur ad terminos relationum, aliquando vero secundum diversam, ut inferius magis constabit explicando diversa genera relationum. Aliquando etiam provenit ex eo quod relatio consequitur suum proximum fundamentum, et illud denominat, non prout afficit vel denominat aliud subjectum, sed secundum suam praecisam et abstractam rationem, quomodo accidenti convenit relatio inhaerendi; interdum

---

3 This reading is from Salamanca, 1597. The Vivès edition reads "Posteriori".

vero relatio consequitur fundamentum, solum prout afficit vel denominat /p. 811/ tale subjectum aut suppositum, interdum vero indifferenter sub utraque ratione. Et haec de subjecto relationis.

SECTIO VII.
De fundamento relationis praedicamentalis.

1. *Relatio realis eget reali fundamento.*—Circa fundamentum autem relationis principio statuendum in communi est, omnem relationem realem indigere aliquo reali fundamento. Ita supponitur fere sine probatione aut disputatione ab omnibus scribentibus in hac materia. Et ratio esse videtur, quia relatio ex se non habet propriam entitatem, cum ostensum sit non esse rem distinctam ab absolutis; ergo necesse est ut habeat illam saltem identice et secundum rem ab aliquo alio; non habet autem illam a termino, nam terminus est quid extrinsecum et distinctum, entitas vero rei est intrinseca; ergo habet relatio realis suam entitatem a fundamento reali; ergo semper illud requirit. Et confirmatur ac declaratur amplius, nam relatio talis est naturae, ut nec per se fiat, nec sit per se intenta in natura; ergo consequitur et quasi resultat in subjecto, posito termino; ergo requirit in subjecto aliquam realem rationem vel cauam ob quam in illo resultat talis relatio, posito tali termino; illa ergo causa vocatur fundamentum reale relationis.

De distinctione fundamenti a subjecto relationis.

2. Sed ut haec assertio amplius explicetur, inquiri potest imprimis, an oporteat hoc fundamentum esse in re ipsa distinctum a subjecto relationis. Potest autem hoc intelligi aut de proximo subjecto inhaesionis, aut de remoto et quasi fundamentali subjecto, quod est ipsa substantia. Et quidem de priori subjecto certum est non oportere ut praeter illud sit aliud fundamentum relationis ex natura rei ab illo distinctum, alioqui esse abeundum in infinitum. Unde certum est relationem aequalitatis, quae inest quantitati, etiam separatae a substantia, non habere aliud fundamentum praeter ipsam quantitatem, quia nec fingi potest quale illud sit, nec sisteretur in illo alio fundamento, nam illud etiam esset subjectum proximum, et ita respectu illius quaerendum esset aliud fundamentum; vel si in eo sistitur, majori ratione sistendum erit in ipsa quantitate. Difficultas ergo est de /col. b/ subjecto principali et fundamentali, quod est quaerere an respectu substantiae, omnis relatio realis requirat aliquod fundamentum accidentale distinctum in re ipsa, saltem ex natura rei, ab ipsa substantia. Multi enim ita sentire videntur. Et ratio esse potest, quia relatio est accidens; ergo debet convenire substantiae medio accidente in quo fundetur. Patet consequentia, quia relatio, ut supra dictum est, non distinguitur a parte

rei a suo fundamento proximo; ergo ut sit accidens, oportet ut proxime fundetur in accidente; nam si immediate conveniret substantiae, esset in re idem cum illa, et ita non esset accidens, sed substantia.

3. Et ideo D. Thomas, quaest. 8 de Potent., art. 2, ad primum, ait, nullam relationem posse esse idem cum substantia, quae est in genere, id est, cum substantia creata; et in 4 cont. Gent., c. 14, versus finem, ait, in creaturis relationes habere esse dependens, quia earum esse est aliud ab esse substantiae, et inferius ait: *Relatio realiter substantiae adveniens, et postremum, et imperfectissimum esse habet; postremum quidem, quia non solum praeexigit esse substantiae, sed etiam esse aliorum accidentium, ex quibus causatur relatio.* Ergo ex D. Thomae sententia, semper relatio supponit in substantia aliud accidens in quo fundetur. Unde 1 p., q. 28, art. 2, ad 2, ait, in creaturis semper relationi supponi aliquid absolutum, quod est alia res ab ipsa relatione. Quod juxta superius dicta non potest verificari ratione solius fundamenti proximi; ergo saltem ratione substantiae, quod ibi praecipue D. Thomas intendit; ergo inter substantiam et relationem semper intercedit aliquod aliud fundamentum, ratione cujus possit esse relatio alia res ab ipsa substantia. Et confirmatur ex Aristotele, 5 Metaph., ubi enumerans fundamenta relationum, semper ponit aliquid a substantia distinctum, nempe qualitatem, actionem, vel aliquid hujusmodi. Confirmatur secundo, quia alias in sola materia possent fundari et inniti relationes, quod esse falsum constat, praecipue juxta communem sententiam, negantem posse in sola materia prima esse aliquod accidens.

Aliquae relationes possunt immediate in substantia fundari in re ipsa.
4. Nihilominus dicendum est, necessarium non esse ut fundamentum proximum relationis sit aliquod accidens, vel res aliqua, /p. 812/ aut modus realis, ex natura rei distinctus a primo subjecto relationis. Haec est communis sententia, ut statim referam. Eam vero probo primo, quia nulla est causa aut ratio hujus necessitatis. Rationes enim quibus supra probatum est, relationem realem requirere fundamentum reale, non probant necessarium esse ut illud fundamenlum sit in re distinctum a subjecto. Quia, licet in subjecto requiratur realis causa, vel ratio ob quam, posito termino, consequatur relatio, tamen illa ratio vel causa esse potest ipsa intrinseca natura talis subjecti, et non res aliqua, vel modus ei superadditus. Cur enim, sicut quantitas ex sua naturali conditione et natura habet sufficientem rationem ob quam ad illam consequantur quaedam relationes, et similiter qualitas, non poterit etiam substantia simile quippiam habere per seipsam?

5. Unde argumentor secundo inductione, nam, sicut duae quantitates aut albedines referuntur realiter relatione similitudinis vel aequalitatis, ita duae substantiae, relatione identitatis specificae; ergo haec relatio inest substantiae

absque accidentali fundamento, ex natura rei ab illa distincto. Patet consequentia, tum quia una substantia non est ejusdem speciei cum alia, ratione alicujus accidentis, sed ratione suaemet entitatis et propriae naturae; tum etiam quia sicut inter albedinem et similitudinem nihil mediat, ita neque inter substantialem naturam et relationem identitatis specificae. Antecedens vero sumitur ex D. Thoma, 1 p., quaest. 28, a. 1, ad 2; et est expresse Aristotelis, 5 Metaph., text. 15, ubi eodem modo censet de identitate in substantia, quo de similitudine in qualitate, et aequalitate in quantitate. Ex quo etiam sumitur argumentum a paritate rationis; nam tanta est convenientia inter duas substantias, sicut inter duas albedines vel quantitates; item tanta est proportio, quia aeque sunt ejusdem ordinis; ergo tam est relatio realis identitas specifica in substantia, sicut similitudo et aequalitas in quantitate et qualitate. Et ita docent frequenter Thomistae, Sonci., 5 Metaphys., q. 35; Javell.; 5 Metaph., q. 21.

6. *Relatio creaturae in quo fundetur.*—Aliud exemplum est de relatione creationis, nam haec (ex sententia omnium) realis est, et praedicamentalis, et tamen immediate fundatur in substantia. Quod docet expresse D. Thomas, quaest. 7 de Potent., art. 9, ad quartum, ubi sic ait: *Creatura refertur ad Deum secundum suam substantiam, sicut secundum causam re-* /col. b/ *lationis; secundum vero relationem ipsam formaliter; sicut aliquid dicitur simile secundum qualitatem causaliter, secundum similitudinem formaliter.* Et idem sumitur ex quaest. 3 de Potent., art. 3; et ex Cajet., 1 part., q. 45, art. 3; Ferrar., 4 cont. Gent., cap. 14; Soncin., 5 Metaphys., q. 31; et Javell., q. 21. Et patet ratione, quia substantia secundum seipsam immediate terminat creationem Dei; ergo per seipsam immediate refertur ad Deum relatione creaturae. Dices, creationem passivam esse modum quemdam ex natura rei distinctum a termino, in quo potest proxime fundari illa relatio, et non immediate in substantia. Respondeo primum, licet totum concedatur, nihilominus non dari aliquod accidens quod sit fundamentum illius relationis, quia illa dependentia creativa non est accidens, ut supra diximus. Deinde, licet verum sit in illa dependentia posse fundari propriam quamdam relationem, tamen ideo non excluditur quin ipsamet substantia per seipsam referatur causaliter seu fundamentaliter in Deum, quatenus illa ipsa, ratione sui esse, essentialiter postulat illam dependentiam, et illam per seipsam terminat.

7. Et confirmatur in relatione filiationis, quae non potest ita fundari in generatione activa vel passiva, ut illi proxime insit, nam transacta actuali generatione permanet relatio filiationis. Nec potest fundari in alio accidente, quia nullum est quod sit causa ejus; fundatur ergo in ipsamet substantia. Ratio autem est, quia substantia ipsa creaturae, quatenus creabilis est, vel generabilis ab alia causa, est sufficiens ut in ea possit fundari relatio, si a tali causa, creata vel genita sit.

8. *Quodnam accidens possit esse idem cum substantia.*—Ad argumenta in contrarium respondetur, ex superius dictis de divisione entis in substantiam et accidens, proprium et physicum accidens non posse esse in re omnino idem cum substantia; accidens vero praedicamentale interdum posse sola ratione ratiocinata distingui, ut patet de duratione.

Sic ergo dicendum est, relationes, quae proxime in substantia fundantur, non esse accidentia physica, et quoad entitatem suam, sed solum esse accidentia praedicamentalia, quoad figuram et modum praedicationis, quia secundum rationem formalem suam sunt extra rationem substantiae, et ideo non est inconveniens quod tales relationes non distinguantur in re a substantia.

9. Testimonia vero ibi citata ex D. Thom. /p. 813/ probabiliter suadent, illum sensisse relationem realem distingui aliquo modo ex natura rei a fundamento, quae est probabilis sententia. Quia vero, in quarto contra Gentes, dicit talem relationem convenire substantiae, medio alio accidente, quod non potest universaliter esse verum, etiam supposita illa sententia, ideo probabile mihi est ipsum loqui de relationibus, quae physice et realiter accidentia sunt, et ideo fortasse eam vocat, relationem, quae realiter substantiae advenit; sic enim ibi loquitur, et ideo etiam exempla ponit in similitudine et aequalitate, non in aliis. Aliter Ferrar. exponit, cum D. Thomas ait relationem praeexigere in substantia esse aliorum accidentium, intelligi vel secundum rem, vel secundum modum. Sed hoc violentum est, et non potest omnibus his relationibus accommodari, ut patet de relatione actus et potentiae inter materiam et formam, de relatione unionis substantialis, et similibus. Ad testimonium Aristotelis respondetur, potius esse in contrarium; quomodo autem intelligenda sit divisio fundamentorum relationis ab ipso tradita, in sequenti sectione declarabimus. Ad ultimam vero confirmationem concedimus plures relationes posse esse proxime in materia, ut relatio potentiae, relatio causae materialis, relatio unionis, creaturae, et similes. Et quidquid sit de accidentibus physicis, de his praedicamentalibus, et sola ratione distinctis, nullum est inconveniens esse proxime in materia, ut per se notum videtur.

De ratione fundandi, et comparatione illius ad fundamentum.

10. *Rationes probantes fundamentum et rationem fundandi idem esse.*—Ulterius vero inquiri potest circa relationis fundamentum, an idem sit cum ratione fundandi, vel si haec sint diversa, quae sit utriusque ratio et necessitas. Est autem causa dubitandi, quia fundamentum relationis nihil aliud esse videtur quam id quo mediante relatio convenit subjecto; sed hoc ipsum fundamentum est ratio fundandi seu recipiendi relationem; ergo haec non distinguuntur. Item quia si praeter fundamentum oporteret aliam rationem fundandi intervenire, nullus esset terminus in his fundamentis vel rationibus assignandis; nulla est

enim ratio cur magis sit duplex quam triplex, vel quaduplex; ergo sistendum est in unico fundamento, quod ipsum sit ratio fundandi. Imo, ut diximus, neque fundamentum hoc oportet semper esse re dis- /col. b/ tinctum a subjecto relationis, sed ratione sufficit aliquando, nam subjectum dicitur quatenus est id cui inest relatio; fundamentum vero in quantum habet talem rationem, ad quam relatio consequitur posito termino, vel in quantum ab illo habet relatio entitatem suam.

11. *Rationes oppositum suadentes.*—In contrarium vero est, quia saepissime auctores de his ut de distinctis loquuntur, et indicant rationem fundandi esse aliquid requisitum in ipso fundamento, vel ultra fundamentum et terminum, ut relatio resultet. Ut ad relationem paternitatis necessaria est actio generandi, quae non est fundamentum, quia paternitas non habet ab illa entitatem suam, cum actio generandi sit in filio genito, paternitas vero sit in patre; est ergo ratio fundandi. Similiter, licet inter duo alba albedo sit fundamentum similitudinis, proxima tamen ratio fundandi dicitur esse unitas formalis utriusque albedinis. Unde, cum fundamenta relationum possint esse innumera, rationes tamen fundandi ad tria capita ab Aristotele revocantur, ut sequenti sectione videbimus; est ergo ratio fundandi aliquid aliud a fundamento.

12. *Mens auctoris.*—In hac re potest nonnulla diversitas in usu vocum, nam apud auctores interdum hae voces confundi videntur, et pro eadem sumi, interdum diversis rebus tribuuntur; explicabimus ergo prius quo modo res se habeat, et deinde usum vocum accommodabimus. In omni ergo relatione reali requiritur ex parte subjecti res aliqua, natura sua apta et accommodata ut fundare possit respectum ad aliud, ut ab illa proxime habeat relatio realitatem suam, eo modo quo declaravimus. Hujusmodi ergo res proprie appellatur fundamentum relationis in quocunque relationum genere. Contingit vero in aliquibus relationibus, ut praeter totam entitatem subjecti et fundamenti requiratur aliqua alia conditio medians inter fundamentum et terminum, et in re ipsa aliquo modo distincta ab ipsis, ut possit inter ea consurgere relatio. Atque hoc modo est necessaria actio vel generatio, ad relationem agentis, seu patris, et fortasse eodem modo materia supponit modum unionis ad[4] relationem unionis. Quod enim hujusmodi conditio sit simpliciter necessaria, explicari facile potest in actione, nam si Petrus et Paulus (qui nunc sunt pater et filius) essent immediate creati a Deo cum omnibus proprietatibus absolutis /p. 814/ quas nunc habent, si inter eos non intervenisset actio generationis et processionis unius ab alio, non fuisset inter eos exorta relatio, nec de potentia absoluta fieri posset ut oriretur; nunc vero, adjuncta sola illa conditione, statim resultat relatio; ergo est illa conditio simpliciter necessaria. Et tamen

---

4 Here I am following the reading of Salamanca, 1597, vol. 2, p. 560. The Vivès edition here reads "ac".

non est fundamentum, per hanc vocem intelligendo illud in quo, et a quo relatio proxime habet entitatem suam. Unde factum est ut talis conditio, ratio fundandi appellata sit, vel quia non est aliud speciale nomen quo nominetur, praeter illud commune quo vocatur conditio necessaria, vel quia illa conditio est quasi ultimo seu proxime requisita, ut relatio pullulet. Re tamen vera non tam proprie dicitur ratio fundandi quam conditio necessaria, quia ratio alicujus rei proprie dicitur, quae habet aliquem influxum per se in talem rem, praesertim formalem, aut effectivum secundum rem vel rationem; haec vero conditio in presenti non habet talem influxum in relationem paternitatis, cum sit extra ipsum patrem, et nullam habeat in illum propriam causalitatem; est ergo magis proprie necessaria conditio.

13. Non est autem hoc generale in omnibus relationibus, ut requirant similes conditiones ex natura rei distinctas a fundamentis, et terminis actu existentibus, ut consurgant. Nam inter duo alba statim consurgit relatio similitudinis, a quocunque facta sint, et ubicunque existant, aut quascunque alias conditiones habeant, et idem est de relatione scientiae ad scibile, et similibus. Et ita hujusmodi ratio fundandi, etiamsi hac voce illam conditionem appellemus, non est necessaria in omnibus relationibus. Omnibus autem fundamentis relationis commune est ut habeant aliquam naturalem proprietatem, vel conditionem, ratione cujus apta sint ad fundandam relationem, quae proprietas respectu talis fundamenti potest appellari ratio fundandi relationem. Ut, verbi gratia, scientiae creatae naturale est ut sit mensurabilis ab objecto scibili, ratione cujus potest fundare relationem ad illud. Similiter tali formae, verbi gratia, albedini, naturale est ut habeat talem unitatem formalem, qualem habere etiam potest alia forma ejusdem speciei; haec ergo est ratio ob quam talis forma potest fundare relationem similitudinis. Atque hoc modo etiam in relatione paternitatis, vel cujuslibet agentis creati, praeter actionem ipsam, consideranda necessario, est aliqua /col. b/ ratio fundandi per se conveniens ipsi fundamento. Ponamus enim tale fundamentum esse ipsum principium efficiendi, sive proximum, sive principale; in hoc ipso principio aliqua ratio consideranda est, ob quam esse possit relationis fundamentum, nam in divina actione ad extra, quamvis in Deo sit verum principium efficiendi, non tamen resultat in ipso Deo relatio realis, quia illud principium non est aptum fundamentum illius relationis, ut infra dicemus. Ergo, si principium efficiens creatum est aptum fundamentum, oportet ut in eo assignetur aliqua ratio intrinseca connaturalis, ob quam natura sua aptum fundamentum relationis realis, ut, verbi gratia, quod est principium per se ordinatum ad actionem, vel aliquid hujusmodi, de quo infra videbimus.

14. Sic igitur, quantum ad rem ipsam constat in omni fundamento intervenire rationem fundandi per se et intrinsecam; constat item haec duo physice et in

re ipsa non esse distincta, metaphysice vero seu ratione distingui ad explicandas rerum rationes, et hoc modo posse etiam diversis vocibus denominari. Nos vero ne videamur res multiplicare, rationes has fundandi in fundamentis includimus. Unde quidam ita loquuntur, ut dicant fundamentum, formaliter loquendo, non esse, verbi gratia, qualitatem absolute, sed qualitatem ut unam. Vide Hispalens., in 1, dist. 13, q. 1, art. 3, notab. 4. At vero conditionem necessariam (quando intercedit), hoc communi nomine appellamus. Jam vero, occurrebat hic quaestio de distinctione fundamentorum, aut rationum fundandi, ab Aristotele tradita in 5 Metaph., c. 15; tamen, quia prolixiorem sermonem postulat, de illa instituemus propriam sectionem, post sequentem.

SECTIO VIII.
De termino praedicamentalis relationis.

1. *Relatio realis terminum exigit realem.*—Dicendum imprimis est, ad relationem praedicamentalem necessarium esse aliquem terminum realem. Haec assertio in communi sumpta fere est communis omnium, et facile colligi potest ex intrinseca ratione relationis. Cum enim essentia ejus sit ad aliud se habere secundum suum esse essentiale, in hoc ipso includitur terminus; cumque relatio haec praedicamentalis et realis sit, terminum ejus realem esse necesse est. Sed in expli- /p. 815/ candis conditionibus requisitis ex parte termini ad esse relationis, et quomodo huiusmodi terminus ad essentiam relationis concurrat, multa tractari solent, quae a nobis breviter indicanda et expedienda sunt.

An requiratur terminus actu existens.

2. *Dubitandi ratio.*—Primum est, an terminus relationis realis praedicamentalis requirat terminum realem actu existentem. Et ratio difficultatis est, quia ordo realis transcendentalis potest esse ad rem quae non existit, imo et ad id quod non est verum ens, sed ens rationis, ut supra dictum est; quid ergo habet relatio praedicamentalis, cur non possit similem terminum respicere? Et confirmatur ac declaratur, nam scientia perinde respicit scibile, quando illud non existit, ac quando existit, quia scientia abstrahit a singularibus et ab existentia. Item productivum refertur ad producibile, teste Aristotele, 5 Metaph; producibile autem ut sic non requirit existentiam. Item imago, et phantasma, et similia, aeque repraesentant rem existentem, et non existentem, et albedo existens tam est similis in essentia alteri albedini possibili, sicut existenti, nam eamdem convenientiam habet cum illa, in natura et essentia. Similiter effectus causae finalis aeque pendet a fine existente et non existente. Ratio denique a priori esse potest, quia nec ex parte relationis, nec ex parte termini, seu ex munere terminandi, videtur necessaria haec actualis existentia termini. Primum patet,

quia relatio habet entitatem suam a fundamento; ergo ex parte ejus illud sufficit ad existentiam relationis. Secundum patet, quia terminare actu, solum dicit denominationem extrinsecam ex habitudine alterius ad rem quae terminare dicitur; ergo talis denominatio potest cadere in rem non existentem, quantum est ex parte ejus.

3. *Aliquorum opinio.*—Atque hanc opinionem sequitur Gregor., in 1, dist. 28, quaest. 23, qui etiam addit, etiam e converso non ens posse referri realiter ad ens; putat enim relativa realia semper esse mutua, quod fundamentum falsum est, ut infra videbimus. Et ipsum consequens, quod infert, valde est improbabile; qui enim intelligi potest, ut quod nihil est actu, referatur relatione reali, aut quomodo potest accidens existere sine subjecto reali? Denique nihil est reale actu , nisi actu existat; ergo nec relatio potest esse realis actu, nisi sit rei actu exis- /col. b/ tentis, quia non potest aliter existere, nisi etiam subsistat. Itaque de correlativo reali, quod possit esse non ens, improbabilis est illa opinio, ut patet etiam ex duabus sectionibus praecedentibus; de termino vero minus improbabilis est.

Terminum actu existentem requiri ostenditur.
4. Nihilominus dicendum est, ad relationem praedicamentalem necessarium esse terminum realem et realiter existentem. Haec est sententia communis, tam philosophorum, et interpretum Aristotelis in Praedicamentis, c. Ad aliquid, et in 5 Metaph., c. 15, quam Theologorum, ut patet ex D. Thoma, 1 p., quaest. 13,, art. 7, ubi ait, relationes omnes, quae sunt inter ens et non ens, esse rationis, quia eas format ratio apprehendens non ens tanquam quoddam extremum. Idem q. 28, art. 1, ad 2, et 2 contra Gent., c. 12, rat. 3, et quaest. 3 de Potentia, art. 3, ad 5, ubi adducit Avicennam, 3 suae Metaph., cap. ult. Et idem sentiunt omnes Thomistae, Cajet. et Ferrar., citatis locis; Soncin., 5 Metaph., q. 27; Capreol., in 1, d. 7, quaest. 2, et latius d. 13 et 20; Scot. et alii, in 1 d. 13; et Mairon., d. 29, q. 6, et 8, qui tamen quadam distinctione utitur; ait enim relationem fundamentalem posse esse ad non ens, non vero relationem formalem. Per hanc vero posteriorem intelligit relationem praedicamentalem, atque ita ipse se explicat, in quo aperte consentit assertioni positae. Quid vero per relationem fundamentalem intelligat, non declarat; si autem (ut apparet) respectum aliquem transcendentalem intelligit, mihi non displicet ejus sententia. Jam enim supra ostendimus, relationes reales transcendentales, esse posse ad terminos non solum non existentes, verum etiam qui non sint entia realia secundum essentiam. Et hoc etiam satis probant argumenta Gregorii, nam potentia, quae per se primo ordinata est ad actum, sine dubio habet transcendentalem ordinem ad illum, etiam possibilem et nondum existentem. Scientia etiam habet relationem ad scibile, quod, per se loquendo, non solum

non necessario existit, verum etiam est quid universale abstrahens a singularibus, quod eo modo existere non potest.

5. *Nonnullae rationes, quibus probari solet assertio, expenduntur.*—Quapropter non est facile rationes convincentes adducere, quae /p. 816/ assertionem positam probent in relationibus praedicamentalibus; nam quae communiter afferri solent, videntur aeque procedere de transcendentalibus, ut, videlicet, quod nullum ens reale potest esse ordinatum ad non ens. Item quia alias etiam posset esse ordinatum ad ens rationis, quod repugnat, cum ens rationis pendeat ex fictione intellectus. Item quia relatio est quasi nexus inter extrema; ergo non potest esse realis nisi inter extrema realia. Quae rationes, et similes, si efficaces sunt, locum habent in respectibus transcendentalibus. Constat autem in eis non habere vim, quia non repugnat ens reale habere transcendentalem ordinem ad non ens actu. Primum, quia potentia potest habere ordinem ad ens possibile, quamvis non respiciat illud secundum solam possibilatem ejus, sed in ordine ad actum, ita tamen ut habitudo ipsa potentiae prior sit et independens ab actuali existentia actus vel objecti. Similiter non ens, quatenus cogitari potest, terminare etiam potest habitudinem transcendentalem cogitationis, vel scientiae ad ipsum; atque ita non ens, quamvis ex se videatur ineptum, ut sit terminus realis habitudinis, tamen quatenus aliqua actio circa illum exerceri potest, etiam actio ipsa, vel habitus aut potentia, quae sunt principia ordinata ad illam actionem, possunt dicere habitudinem transcendentalem ad rem quae non est. Atque ob similem rationem potest actus aliquis intellectus respectum transcendentalem dicere ad aliquod ens rationis, quia, nimirum, illud potest esse sufficiens objectum talis actus. Et ideo ad hujusmodi habitudinem non solum non obstat quod ens rationis sit quid fictum ab intellectu, verum etiam in hoc ipso fundatur illa transcendentalis habitudo.

6. Recte vero probatur illa ratione, nullas alias res posse habere transcendentales habitudines ad entia rationis, praeter ipsosmet actus mentis, quibus ipsa entia rationis cogitantur aut finguntur, sub quibus comprehendo actus aliquos imaginationis quatenus per illos fingi possunt et repraesentari entia imaginaria et impossibilia. Et idem erit de actibus voluntatis, quatenus versari possunt circa entia rationis; aut, si vera est opinio Scoti, quod per eos fieri possunt entia rationis. Denique id etiam suo modo extendi potest ad habitus proportionatos his actibus quatenus dicunt per se ordinem ad eadem objecta. In his ergo omnibus reperitur haec /col. b/ habitudo, propter transcendentalem ordinem ad objectum; aliae vero res, quae non possunt habere pro objectis entia rationis, non possunt habere habitudinem realem et transcendentalem ad illa. Quia, ut supra ostendimus, habitudo transcendentalis semper est secundum aliquod munus reale, quod active vel passive ad aliquod genus causae reducatur; circa ens autem rationis nullum munus reale exerceri potest, nisi in

quantum sumitur in ratione objecti. Denique relatio praedicamentalis non est proprie nexus aut unio, sed solum velut tendentia quaedam, quae potest solum extrinsece terminari ad aliud, et ideo ex hac parte non repugnat esse entis ad non ens. Sicut ergo hae rationes solvantur in relationibus transcendentalibus, ita videntur solvi posse in praedicamentalibus.

7. Ratio assertionem convincens.—Quaerenda est ergo aliqua propria ratio, quae specialiter procedat de relationibus praedicamentalibus. Et primo quidem argumentari possumus ex principiis receptis de his relationibus, nimirum, quod relatio et terminus sunt simul tempore, et quod ablato correlativo seu termino aufertur relatio, et quod posito termino, si jam supponitur fundamentum, consurgit relatio; haec enim omnia sumpta sunt ex Aristotele et communi sententia; omnia vero illa supponunt realem existentiam termini, nam includunt coexistentiam extremorum, quae supponit utriusque existentiam. Ratio vero propria sumenda est ex iis quae superius dicta sunt de esse, et essentia hujus relationis, nimirum, quod consistit in puro respectu, neque aliud munus habet in natura, et ideo non est per se intenta, sed mere resultans, tanquam quid accidens rebus praeter omne id quod ex se est, et ex intentione naturae illis convenit. Ex natura enim hujus relationis sic explicata, plane colligitur illum ut sic non esse, nisi supponatur fundamenti et termini coexistentia, ex qua ipsa resultat: tum quia non habet rerum naturalium modum productionis; tum etiam quia solum hac ratione potest habere rationem accidentis, nam alii respectus qui possunt esse ad non entia, sunt essentiales, et pertinent ad praedicamenta earum rerum quarum sunt essentiales differentiae. Quae ratio habet aliquam efficaciam, etiam in eorum sententia, qui putant hanc relationem esse aliquem modum in re distinctum a fundamento et termino; hi enim facile sibi accommodant hanc discursum factum; solum illis difficile est ratio- /p. 817/ nem talis entitatis aut modi distincti reddere. In nostra vero sententia magis urgeri potest, quia si relatio praedicamentalis in re non est aliud nisi ipsummet fundamentum, ut accidentaliter dans denominationem relativam, ergo non potest in re ipsa dare illam, nisi coexistente termino; nam omnis alia denominatio aut erit omnino absoluta et essentialis, et consequenter ad summum erit respectiva transcendentaliter, aut non erit denominatio ex solis ipsis rebus sumpta, sed ex comparatione nostrae rationis. Ob hanc ergo causam, ad relationem praedicamentalem necessarius semper est terminus realis, et realiter existens.

Rationes contrariae sententiae dissolvuntur.

8. Argumenta vero oppositae sententiae, si attente considerentur, solum procedunt de respectu transcendentali; jam vero est sufficienter declarata differentia inter illum et relationem praedicamentalem. Unde ad ultimam ratio-

nem respondetur, terminum realem requiri ad relationem praedicamentalem ex natura et modo talis relationis, quae solum consistit in puro respectu orto ex coexistentia extremorum. Unde, licet verum sit ipsam actualem terminationem nihil ponere in termino, tamen necessario supponet entitatem in illo, accommodatam ut ex positione ejus cum termino possit insurgere relatio, et ut ipsa relatio habeat quasi objectum in quod possit respicere. Unde, sicut de fundamento diximus posse in eo secundum rationem distingui rem quae fundat relationem et rationem seu aptitudinem fundandi, ita ex parte termini distingui potest res seu forma termini, et ratio terminandi, quae est in tali forma. Jam vero sese hoc loco insinuabat quaestio, qualisnam esse debet haec forma et ratio terminandi, et praesertim an sit absoluta vel respectiva. Sed quia haec quaestio prolixior est, et multa supponit tractanda sectione sequenti, ideo post illam disputabitur.

Quomodo terminus sit de essentia relationis, ex dictis educitur.

9. *Aliquorum opinio.—Aliorum sententia.—*Ex praedicta vero resolutione et ejus ratione intelligi potest primo, hujusmodi terminum realem esse aliquo modo de essentia relationis, quanquam in hoc sit nonnulla diversitas inter auctores, quae magis est in modo loquendi, quam in re. Quidam enim absolute negant terminum esse de essentia re- /col. b/ lationis, ut Francisc. Maironis, in 1, dist. 49, q. 5; quod ex parte etiam sentit Soncin., 5 Metaph., q. 33; et Cajet., in Praedicabil., c. de Specie. Et ratio esse potest, quia terminus est omnino extra ipsam relationem, et res ab illa condistincta; ergo non potest esse de essentia ejus, nam quod est de essentia, est omnino intrinsecum, et idem cum re, de cujus essentia existit. Alii vero dicunt terminum esse de essentia relationis. Quae est communis Peripateticorum sententia, ut supra Cajetanus refert, et Niphus, lib. 5 Metaph., disputat. 16. Et ratio est, quia totum esse relationis est esse ad terminum; ergo terminus est de essentia relationis.

10. *Sententia auctoris.-* Verumtamen vix potest esse dissensio in re, ut dixi, nam terminus non est intrinseca pars, nec genus aut differentia intrinseca relationis; unde non potest esse de essentia ejus in dicto sensu, et in hoc omnes conveniunt. Certum deinde est relationem praedicamentalem, ut talis est, non esse nisi respiciendo et tendendo ad terminum, et in hoc consistere essentiam ejus. Unde sub ea ratione dici potest includere aliquo modo terminum in sua essentia, quia non potest absolvi ab illo, neque secundum propriam rationem concipi, quin in tali conceptu terminus includatur. Et hoc sensu locuti sunt omnes antiqui, qui propterea non tam dicunt terminum esse de essentia, quam esse de conceptu quidditativo relationis; quod etiam admittunt Cajetanus et Soncinas.

11. *Relativum praedicamentale nequit nisi per ordinem ad terminum definiri.*— Qui merito inferunt relationem secundum propriam rationem definiri non posse, quin terminus relationis in definitione ponatur, nam res sicut esse essentialiter, ita definiri debet; sed essentia relationis talis est ut non possit absolvi a termino; ergo nec definitio potest a termino absolvi; ergo debet necessario includere in se terminum. Et in hoc non recte sentit Maironis supra, nam videtur dicere posse relationem definiri sine additione termini, in quo etiam ab Scoto dissentit, ut patet ex eodem, in primo, distinctione trigesima. Sed est attente observandum, semper nos esse locutos de termino relationis, non de correlativo, ut abstrahamus ab illa quaestione, an ipsum correlativum sit terminus, quam infra tractabimus, et ibi etiam videbimus an hoc possit etiam extendi ad correlativum, ut sic, etiamsi non sit formalis termi- /p. 818/ nus; et ibi etiam solvemus difficultatem hic occurrentem, an terminus sit prius cognitione quam relatio, et quomodo correlativa possint esse simul cognitione et definitione non committendo circulum.

12. *Transcendentales respectus, ut respiciant terminum.*—Ultimo observandum est, doctrinam hanc aliquo modo generalem esse ad respectus etiam transcendentales; nam etiam illi, et formae vel entitates de quarum essentia sunt, non possunt adaequate et essentialiter definiri absque additione illius rei, quam respiciunt, quae sub ea ratione terminus dici potest. Differentia vero est, quod relatio praedicamentalis ex peculiari et propria ratione sua requirit terminum actu existentem, tum ut ex illo in suo genere resultet, tum ut illum respiciat sub praecisa ratione termini; relatio vero transcendentalis nec resultat ex termino, proprie loquendo, nec illum respicit sub praecisa ratione termini, sed adjuncta semper aliqua alia ratione objecti, aut causae, vel alterius similis. Atque ita est aliquo modo magis intrinseca et formalis habitudo ad terminum, praesertim existentem, in relatione praedicamentali quam in respectu transcendentali.

Etiam de potentia absoluta non posse relationem manere sine termino.
13. Secundo resolvitur quaestio, an tanta sit dependentia relationis ab existentia sui termini, ut non solum ex natura rei illam requirat, verum etiam de potentia absoluta non possit conservari sine illa. Videtur enim hoc creditu difficile, nam cum illae sint res distinctae, ut supponimus, et fundamentum non componat intrinsece relationem, neque habeat realem influxum in illam, nulla reddi potest sufficiens ratio ob quam non possit Deus sine termino relationem conservare. Nihilominus tamen dicendum est non posse per ullam potentiam conservari relationem praedicamentalem ut sic sine suo actuali termino. Ita docent fere omnes scriptores. Ratio autem est, quia in ipso effectu formali relationis involvitur aliquo modo terminus realis et actualis. Ostensum est autem supra, non posse relationem conservari in rerum natura, quin actu

exerceat suum effectum formalem; ergo non potest relatio actu conservari sine suo termino actuali. Patet consequentia, quia non potest effectus formalis conservari sine omnibus per se et essentialiter requisitis ad illum. /col. b/ Major vero patet, quia formalis effectus relationis est actu referre ad terminum; in hoc autem effectu includitur ipse terminus. Sicut motus aut actio non potest esse sine termino proprio, eo quod sit actualis via ad illum.

14. Estque hoc longe facilius ad intelligendum in nostra sententia, scilicet, quod relatio non sit res, aut modus realis distinctus a fundamento, et ei additus, sed sit ipsamet entitas fundamenti, ut sic denominans subjectum. Nam cum illa denominatio sit pure respectiva, tantum consistit in quadam habitudine orta ex coexistentia termini; ideo mirum non est quod talis entitas fundamenti conferre nullo modo possit denominationem illam, nisi posita coexistentia termini. Et ita facile solvitur ratio dubitandi in contrarium. Nulla enim hic intervenit entitas, quam Deus non possit conservare sine alia realiter distincta; nam totam entitatem fundamenti potest conservare sine termino; non tamen potest conservare illam entitatem sub tali ratione et denominatione quia secundum illam involvit ipsum terminum; non tamen potest conservare illam entitatem sub tali ratione et denominatione quia secundum illam involvit ipsum terminum; imo in re ipsa nihil distinctum addit praeter coexistentiam termini.

SECTIO IX.
Quae distinctio necessaria sit inter fundamentum et terminum.

1. Haec quaestio etiam expeditur facile ex hactenus dictis. Quidam enim existimant necessariam esse inter illa distinctionem realem, ut Soncin., 5 Metaph., q. 29, et significat debere esse omnimodam distinctionem, ita ut non sufficiat distingui tanquam totum et partem. Fundatur praecipue, quia alias totum continuum referretur infinitis relationibus realibus diversarum proportionum majoris inaequalitatis ad infinitas partes proportionales, quod est inconveniens. Unde simili argumento probat D. Thomas, 2 cont. Gent. c. 12, rat. 3, non posse unam quantitatem referri relatione reali ad quantitatem majorem possibilem, quia alias haberet simul relationes infinitas, cum numeri vel quantitates majores possint in infinitum multiplicari.

2. Alii vero putant nullam distinctionem in re esse necessariam, quod maxime videri potest in relatione identitatis ejusdem ad seipsum. Quia tam proprie et a parte rei sine fictione intellectus est aliquod ens idem sibi sicut est diversum ab alio, vel simile alteri; ergo tam est illa relatio realis, sicut alia. At /p. 819/ que hoc maxime opinantur aliqui, si contingat idem fundamentum esse in diversis subjectis; ut, verbi gratia, si eadem albedo esset in duobus hominibus, aiunt

referri inter se similitudine reali, quia fundamentum distinguitur a termino qui terminat, etiamsi non distinguatur ab ipsa ratione terminandi. Et hoc sentit Scot., in 1, dist. 31, et in Quodl., quaest. 6.

Resolutio.

3. Dicendum vero est, ad relationem realem necessarium esse ut fundamentum, et terminus formaliter sumptus, in re ipsa distinguantur. Haec est sententia D. Thomae, 1 part., quaest. 42, art. 1, ad 3, ubi propter hanc causam negat aequalitatem inter divinas personas esse relationem realem; negat etiam idem referri ad seipsum relatione reali. Et hoc sequuntur omnes Thomistae. Et quod requiratur aliqua distinctio in re inter correlativa realia est fere principium per se notum in metaphysica. Nam correlativa censentur realiter opposita; non opponitur autem idem sibi ipsi; oportet ergo ut correlativa in re aliquo modo distinguantur. Unde necesse etiam est relationes reales oppositas, esse in re aliquo modo distinctas, tum propter oppositionem, tum etiam quia unaquaeque relatio in re est idem cum suo extremo, ut supra ostensum est; ergo si extrema sint distincta, etiam relationes. Quocirca si relationis terminus est relatio opposita, hinc satis concluditur relationem et terminum debere in re esse distincta. Si vero formalis terminus relationis est aliqua forma absoluta, etiam concluditur debere in re distingui. Quia talis formalis terminus non potest esse nisi fundamentum oppositae relationis, ut infra dicam; sed non minus necesse est fundamentum unius relationis distingui a relatione opposita, quam relationes ipsas oppositas; ergo. Probatur minor, quia relatio et fundamentum sunt in re idem; ergo quantum relatio distinguitur a relatione opposita, tantum in re distinguitur fundamentum unius relationis ab ejus opposita; ergo aeque etiam, distinguitur a fundamento relationis oppositae. Item, quia non solum relationes , sed etiam extrema seu subjecta relationum debent esse in re distincta, quia non potest intelligi realis et vera habitudo inter ea quae in re non distinguuntur, quia omnis habitudo, ut ex termino ipso constat, postulat extrema; extrema vero includunt pluralitatem, et consequenter ali- /col. b/ quam distinctionem rei. Denique in ipsa definitione relativorum hoc continetur, quia debent esse ad aliud. Si autem, subjecta relationum oppositarum debent esse inter se distincta, maxime. id verum habet de subjectis, seu fundamentis proximis, quibus relationes proxime insunt; nam illis proxime per se conferunt suas proprias et formales habitudines; ergo distinctio haec maxime requiritur inter ipsa fundamenta oppositarum relationum, et consequenter etiam inter relationes ipsas, ac denique relationem et terminum.

Quantum oporteat esse distinctionem praedictam.

4. Quanta vero debeat esse haec distinctio dubitari potest. Breviter tamen censeo non esse necessariam aequalem in omnibus, sed juxta naturam fundamentorum et modum relationum pensandum id esse. Saepe enim haec distinctio debet esse realis et suppositalis, ut in relatione patris et filii; nam quia tales relationes fundantur in reali processione unius suppositi, et non potest unum suppositum realiter procedere, nisi ab alio supposito, ideo talis relatio requirit distinctionem realium suppositorum. Et similiter relatio specificae identitatis requirit realem distinctionem naturarum substantialium, et consequenter etiam suppositorum, seclusis miraculis. Et idem est, proportione servata, de relatione aequalitatis vel similitudinis; requirunt enim distinctionem realem talium formarum, et consequenter etiam subjectorum, ex natura rei. Ad aliquas vero relationes existimo sufficere distinctionem modalem; nam, sicut est vera efficientia aut emanatio inter rem et modum, ita etiam potest esse vera relatio. Item quia distinctio modalis, vera distinctio est, et sufficit ad oppositionem vel habitudinem, propter quam necessaria est distinctio inter relationem et terminum.

5. An vero sufficiat distinctio inter totum et partes, dubitari potest, propter argumentum Soncinatis de infinitate relationum. Unde dici posset quod, licet distinctio inter totum et partem, quatenus aliquo modo realis est, sit major quam modalis distinctio, tamen quatenus extrema non sunt ita condistincta, sed in uno aliud includitur, minus sufficere ad fundandam relationem realem. Sed difficile hoc creditu est, primo, quia simpliciter illa distinctio est vere in re, et est /p. 820/ major quam modalis. Item quia causa materialis vel formalis videntur realiter referri ad suum effectum, qui est compositum ipsum, a quo tamen non distinguuntur, nisi sicut pars a toto. Item quia duae medietates ejusdem continui videntur inter se referri relatione reali aequalitatis; nam in re vere distinguuntur, et non ut includens et inclusum, sed ut condistinctae, et si essent contiguae tantum, referrentur relatione reali; unio autem, per continuationem non potest hanc relationem impedire; major enim est unio inter rem et modum, aut inter materiam et formam, quia unio non tollit omnem distinctionem. Quod si illae medietates inter se referuntur relatione reali, idem erit de earum medietatibus inter se comparatis, et ita etiam sequitur infinitas relationum. Neque videtur esse ullum inconveniens, quod in continuo ita sint infinitae relationes, sicut sunt infinita puncta vel partes, cum relationes nihil rei addant ipsis fundamentis.

Solutio argumentorum.

6. *Idem ad seipsum rationis tantum relatione refertur.—Duo alba eadem albedine, an relativa per relationem realem similitudinis.*—Per haec ergo satis responsum

est priori sententiae. Ad posteriorem vero negatur identitatem ejusdem ad seipsum esse relationem realem, sed rationis tantum. Quod autem res dicatur eadem sibi sine relatione rationis, vel falsum est, quia necessaria est comparatio intellectus, qua eadem ad seipsam ita comparatur, ac si essent duo extrema; vel certe si secludatur haec comparatio, in re solum est res ipsa, et negatio distinctionis, quam solam potest addere haec identitas ipsa rei, ut supra, disput. 8, visum est. Atque idem censeo de propria similitudine inter duo subjecta alba, si eamdem numero haberent albedinem, quia convenientìa illa, quam in albedine haberent, potius esset identitas in eadem numerica forma. Quod ut magis intelligatur, distinguere ibi possumus convenientiam in forma albedínìs, vel in unione ad eamdem formam; prior convenientia est identitas quaedam, et ideo non est relatio realis; posterior vero potest esse similitudo et relatio, quia, licet forma sit eadem, unio ad diversa subjecta necessario est diversa, et ideo quantum ad illam est sufficiens distinctio, ut similitudo vel relatio realis fundari possit. Ut si duae humanitates essent unita Verbo divino, non videtur du- /col. b/ bium quin essent vere similes in unione hypostatica, quae non esset in eis eadem numero, sed distincta, ideoque possent sub ea ratione referri relatione reali. Non potest vero hinc argumentum sumi ad relationes divinas prout terminantes (ut nostro modo loquamur) eamdem essentiam Dei, quia non terminant per unionem, sed per simplicissimam identitatem.

SECTIO X.
An tria relationum genera triplici fundamento recte fuerint ab Aristotele distincta.

1. In hac sectione examinanda est doctrina Aristotelis, lib. 5 Metaph., c. 15, ubi agens de Ad aliquid, ad tria genera relativorum omnia refert, quas distinguit ex triplici fundamento seu ratione fundandi relationem.

Partitio et doctrina Aristotelis proponitur.

2. *Quas relationes in primo genere collocet Aristoteles.*—In primo genere constituit eas relationes quas dicit fundari in unitate vel multitudine, quod postea subdividit in varias species; nam in unitate ait fundari aequalitatem, similitudinem, et in universum identitatem eorum quorum una est substantia. Nam similia dicuntur, quae habent unam qualitatem; aequalia, quae habent unam quantitatem; eadem vero, quae habent unam substantiam, quod potest intelligi vel proprie et in rigore de substantia, vel generatim de essentia, quod infra videbimus. In numero vero ait fundari omnes relationes quae aliquo modo secundum quantitatem dicantur, et ab unitate recedunt, ut sunt omnes proportiones inter numeros inaequales, sive illae indefinite seu generatim

significentur, ut excedens. multiplex, etc.; sive definite, ut duplum, triplum, etc. Unde, licet hae relationes inveniri etiam possint inter quantitates continuas, tamen dicuntur fundari in numero, quatenus requirunt diversitatem in quantitate. Atque eadem ratione ad idem fundamentum pertinent relationes omnes dissimilitudinis, distinctionis, et similes, quia in numero aliquo modo fundantur; hic enim non sumuntur in rigore unitas et numerus pro quantitate, sed generalius. Illud enim est considerandum , Aristotelem semper loqui de his relativis in plurali, quia, propriissime loquendo, ambae relationes oppositae hujus generis sunt quae requirunt in fundamento, aut numerum aut /p. 821/ aliquam unitatem plurium (ita enim est haec unitas intelligenda). Unde si de singulis relationibus loquamur, unaquaeque requirit fundamentum, non quod simpliciter sit numerus, sed quod cum alio componat numerum, vel habeat unitatem.

  3. *Quae relationes sint in secundo genere.* -In secundo genere ponit Aristoteles ea relativa quae fundantur in potentia agendi et patiendi, vel in actionibus earum, quod subinde distinguit in varias species, quas partim sumit, vel ex eo quod relationes fundantur in sola potentia abstrahendo ab actione, vel ut subest actioni. Et adhibet exempla, ut calefactivum et calefactibile, calefaciens et calefactum. In quibus oportet duo advertere: unum est, cum Aristoteles ponit relationem realem inter potentiam et possibile, nunquam loqui de effectu possibili objective sumpto, ut videtur intellexisse Gregorius in superioribus citatus, qui ex hoc exemplo Aristotelis colligebat, dari relationes reales ad terminos non existentes, sed possibiles; Aristoteles autem aperte loquitur de potentia passiva seu subjecto calefactibili, ut declarat his verbis: *Et uno nomine, activum ad passivum;* et infra: *Activa autem et passiva, ex potentia activa et passiva potentiarumque actionibus dicuntur, ut calefactivum ad calefactibile.* Hinc secundo considerandum est alium esse terminum realem relationis potentiae activae ut sic abstrahendo ab actione, a termino potentiae activae, ut subest actioni, seu ut facientis; nam prior terminus est potentia passiva, et alioqui non potest esse terminus realis; posterior vero est ipse effectus, ut jam fluens a potentia agente. Rursus vero addit Aristoteles, hanc relationem, quae fundatur in potentia sub actione, variari juxta varias temporis differentias; alia enim fundatur in praesenti actione, ut relatio aedificantis, calefacientis, etc.; alia in actione praeterita, ut relatio patris; et alia in actione futura, *ut quod facturum est* (inquit) *ad id quod faciendum,* quod habet difficultatem infra tractandam.

  4. *Quae relationes sint in tertio genere.* _- In tertio genere ponit Aristoteles relationes quas vocat mensurabilis ad mensuram, ut sunt (inquit) relatio scientiae ad scibile, intellectus ad intelligibile, aspectus ad spectabile. Assignat autem notandum discrimen (quod gravibus quaestionibus occasionem praebet) inter hoc genus et duo priora, quia in prioribus (inquit) utrumque relativum dicitur ad /col. b/ aliquid, quia idipsum, ad quod unumquodque est, aliud dicitur,

et non quia, aliud ad ipsum; at vero in tertio genere, licet unum relativorum dicatur ad aliquid, quia vere est ad aliud, alterum vero, quod illi correspondet, non dicitur ad aliud quia vere sit ad aliud, sed quia aliud est ad ipsum. Ut scientia et scibile, quamvis ad aliud dicantur, tamen diverso modo; nam scientia sic dicitur, quia vere est ad aliud; scibile vero minime, sed solum quia scientia est ad ipsum; idemque est de intellectu, intelligibili et similibus. Quam differentiam nulla ratione probat Aristoteles, sed ut manifestam tradit.

Sitne divisio convenienter data.
5. *Quae rationes ingerunt difficultatem.—Prima.*—Haec est Aristotelis divisio et doctrina. Circa quam duo praecipue declaranda occurrunt, in quibus variae difficultates attingentur. Primum, an singula membra illius divisionis convenienter assignata sint. Secundum, an illa divisio sit adaequata relationi praedicamentali, ita ut sufficienter totam ejus latitudinem comprehendat. Ratio dubitandi circa priorem partem est primo, quia relationes primi generis non videntur reales; ergo. Probatur antecedens primo quoad relationes unitatis, quia unitas illa in qua fundantur, non est realis, sed rationis tantum; ergo nec relatio in ea fundata potest esse realis. Antecedens patet, quia illa non est unitas numeralis; nam haec fundat identitatem ejusdem ad seipsum, quae est relatio rationis, ut supra diximus; ergo est unitas specifica, vel alia superior; omnis autem alia unitas praeter numeralem est unitas rationis. Nec refert si quis dicat unitatem formalem esse realem, nam haec etiam non est realis, nisi in quantum in re est eadem cum numerica, licet ratione distinguantur; unde ita multiplicatur in rebus, sicut ipsa unitas numerica, ut in superioribus visum est; ergo non magis potest esse fundamentum relationis realis, quam unitas numerica. Et confirmatur ac declaratur; nam unitas quae sit fundamentum relationis, debet esse unitas plurium; nam unitas uniuscujusque ut sic non fundat relationem ad aliud; debet ergo esse unitas plurium; sed omnis unitas plurium re distinctorum est unitas rationis; ergo. Dices hoc esse verum de unitate quasi positiva et universali, tamen unitatem negativam, qua una res non se habet aliter quam alia in aliqua forma vel proprietate, in rebus ipsis esse; ita enim /p. 822/ respondent aliqui Thomistae, Capreolus, in 1, dist. 30, quaest. 1; Soncin., 5 Metaphys., q. 34; et Cajetan., q. 7 de Ente et essentia. Sed contra, quia non magis potest negatio aut privatio fundare relationem realem, quam ens rationis , quia etiam privatio secundum se sumpta ens rationis est, nihilque reale in rebus ponit; ergo non potest fundare relationem realem. Atque haec ratio videtur etiam probare, relationem fundatam in numero non posse esse realem, quia proxima ratio fundandi ejus est aliqua negatio, nam numerus vel multitudo distinctione constituitur; distinctio autem seu divisio in negatione formaliter consistit, ut in superioribus visum est. Et declaratur

exemplis, nam inaequalitas, verbi gratia, in hoc proxime fundatur, quod haec quantitas aliquid non habet quod habet alia; haec autem negatio est; similiter dissimilitudo proxime fundatur in hoc, quod haec qualitas non habet essentiam quam alia, et e converso.

6. *Secunda.*—Secundo principaliter argumentor, nam si unitas specifica est sufficiens fundamentum relationis, sequuntur multa absurda. Primum est, inter res singulorum praedicamentorum, quatenus sunt ejusdem speciei, consurgere relationem identitatis seu similitudinis; quod ipsemet Aristoteles concessisse videtur, cum dixit, *eadem esse, quorum una est substantia,* id est, essentia, et illa omnia collocat in hoc genere. Nec refert si quis nomine substantiae, non essentiam, sed propriam substantiam intelligat, quod est probabile, quia saltem a paritate rationis sumitur sufficiens argumentum, quia tam similes sunt duae actiones, vel duo Ubi, sicut duae albedines. Falsitas autem consequentis probatur, quia inde fieret, etiam duas relationes ejusdem speciei, ut duas paternitates, referri relatione reali similitudinis; est enim omnino eadem ratio. Consequens autem est falsum, quia relatio non potest fundari in relatione; alioquin in qualibet relatione essent infinitae relationes, nam sicut prima fundat secundam, ita et secunda poterit fundare tertiam; nam erit similis, vel dissimilis, seu distincta ab aliis, et idem erit de tertia respectu quartae, et sic in infinitum. Secundo sequitur, inter duas quantitates bipedales esse duas relationes reales, alteram identitatis, quatenus sunt ejusdem essentiae, alteram aequalitatis, quatenus sunt ejusdem magnitudinis; poteritque amitti prior manente posteriore, nam inter quantitatem bipedalem et tripedalem est si- /col. b/ militudo essentiae, quanquam non sit aequalitas. Similiter dicendum erit, calorem intensum et remissum referri una relatione reali identitatis in essentia, et altera dissimilitudinis intensione, et similia, quae videntur absurda.

7. Tertio sequitur, non tantum similitudinem specificam, sed etiam genericam vel analogam fundare propriam relationem realem; est enim proportionalis ratio; nam, licet similitudo generica non sit tanta quanta specifica, tamen est vera similitudo et unitas; ergo fundabit relationem realem, quamvis non ejusdom rationis, nec fortasse tam perfectam. Item, quia si unitas generica non sufficiat ad hanc relationem, propter varias differentias specificas, neque unitas specifica sufficeret, propter varias differentias individuales; nam eamdem proportionem servant in identitate reali et distinctione rationis; est ergo eadem ratio; ergo, sicut specifica unitas fundat relationem rationis, ita generica. Consequens est falsum, tum quia res specie distinctae, quamvis conveniant in genere, simpliciter sunt dissimiles, potius quam similes, ut albedo et nigredo; tum etiam quia alias, cum rerum convenientiae et differentiae possint in infinitum, multiplicari per intellectus abstractiones, etiam relationes similitudinis vel dissimilitudinis infinitae essent in una re, vel respectu alterius, cum qua

convenit in differentia specifica, et in omnibus superioribus praedicatis, vel respectu diversarum, quatenus uni est similis in specie, alteri in genere proximo vel remoto. Eademque difficultas, proportione servata, invenitur in relationibus quae dicuntur fundatae in numero vel disconvenientia; nam una relatio erit ad rem distinctam in specie ultima, aliae ad varias res in uno vel alio genere diversas, quae fere in infinitum multiplicari possunt. Addo etiam, incredibile videri, quod proportiones omnes, quas arithmetici inter numeros speculantur, sint reales, tum quia non potest assignari unum subjectum adaequatum talis relationis, cum totus numerus non habeat in re veram et realem unitatem; tum etiam quia illae potius videntur comparationes et considerationes intellectus, quam reales habitudines; at vero Aristoteles aeque numerat omnes illas ut species sub hoc genere contentas.

8. *Tertia difficultas contra primum genus relationum.*- Tertia principalis difficultas est circa idem genus, quia vel hujusmodi relatio- /p. 823/ nes sunt aliquae res vel modi reales additi ipsis formis absolutis, vel non. Primum dici non potest, ut superius de toto hoc praedicamento generaliter dictum est, et specialiter de hoc genere videntur satis probare duae primae difficultates hic propositae, quia multiplicantur in eadem re infiniti modi, qui non solum necessarii non sunt, verum nec intelligi possunt, nec ad certam aliquam rationem reduci. Item, quia unitas inter hujusmodi res non est aliquid aliud ab ipsis rebus; cur ergo erit ratio ut aliquid distinctum inde resultet? Si vero non sunt modi in re distincti, non possunt esse habitudines reales, sed mera coexistentia plurium rerum absolutarum talium conditionum. Probatur, quia habitudo realis non potest rei convenire, nisi vel sit ei intrinseca, et ex se, vel sit ei addita; in praesenti autem, quando una albedo fit similis alteri, non additur ei intrinseca habitudo realis: nam si adderetur, esset ex natura rei distincta; neque enim potest intelligi additio in re sine distinctione inter id quod additur, et id cui additur. Rursus neque illa habitudo est intrinseca et essentialis albedini, tum quia simpliciter potest esse sine illa, tum etiam quia omnis habitudo intrinseca et essentialis rei absolutae est transcendentalis; una autem albedo nullam habet habitudinem transcendentalem ad aliam. Ac propterea est major ratio dubitandi in his formis absolutis, quam in his quae includunt transcendentalem respectum; nam in his posterioribus intelligi aliquo modo potest, ut sine additione reali idem respectus sub diversis rationibus sit transcendentalis et praedicamentalis; tamen in prioribus rebus absolutis nullo modo videtur posse intelligi habitudo realis, si eis nihil intrinsecum additur, ut revera non additur. Hoc igitur primum genus relationum videtur saltem magis continere relationes rationis, aut denominationes extrinsecas, et modos loquendi ortos ex comparationibus variis nostri intellectus inter res diversas, quam veras et reales habitudines.

9. *Quarta.*—Quarta difficultas est circa secundum genus, in quo, ut a difficilioribus inchoemus, falsum plane videtur quod Aristoteles ait, relationem causae effecturae ad effectum futurum, esse sub hoc genere; nam illa non potest esse relatio realis, tum quia terminus non est actu existens; nam quod futurum est, nondum est; imo nondum fit; alias non esset relatio causae operaturae, sed operantis. Tum etiam quia ratio fundandi, /col. b/ vel conditio necessaria, scilicet actio, nondum est; quod autem illa conditio necessaria sit, patet, quia alias nullo modo esset relatio agentis, seu acturi, sed solum potentis agere. Deinde, est etiam difficile, quo modo relatio fundata in actione praeterita, sit realis, tum quia illa actio jam non est; ergo nec potest esse fundamentum aut ratio alicujus relationis; tum etiam quia Petrum, verbi gratia, genuisse Paulum, est solum denominatio extrinseca ab actione praeterita; quomodo ergo potest in eo fundari intrinsecus respectus realis? Maxime quia ea denominatio aeque dicitur, sive filius genitus vivat, sive non; semper enim verum est dicere, Petrum genuisse Paulum; imo, si modum loquendi attendamus, eodem modo dicitur pater ejus. Atque hinc rursus etiam est difficile, quod relatio agentis, etiam de praesenti, sit realis in ipso agente, cum ipsa actio non sit in agente, et consequenter extrinsece denominet agens. Et confirmatur, nam Aristoteles ait in tertio genere, relationem scibilis non esse realem, eo quod res dicatur scibilis per habitudinem scientiae ad ipsam; at vero etiam agens sic denominatur per habitudinem actionis quae est in passo ad ipsum principium agendi; ergo, pari ratione, non resultabit in ipso principio agendi aliqua relatio intrinseca ipsi agenti. Ultimo de relatione agentis in potentia, ut sic, etiam dubitari potest, saltem quando principium agendi non est per se institutum ad illud munus; tunc enim non habet habitudinem transcendentalem ad rem in potentia, vel effectum possibilem; ergo neque habebit praedicamentalem. Consequentia fundatur in tertia difficultate supra proposita.

10. *Quinta.*—Quinta difficultas est circa tertium genus. In quo primum dubitari potest de discrimine assignato ab Aristotele inter hoc genus et alia; sed hoc peculiarem sectionem requirit, quam infra tractabimus. Nunc propriam difficultatem habet, quomodo ratio mensurae possit esse fundamentum relationis realis, cum ipsa ratio mensurae realis non sit, sed rationis tantum, ut supra ostensum est, tractando de quantitate. Quod si dicas ibi fuisse sermonem de mensura quantitatis, hic autem de mensura veritatis, hoc potius auget difficultatem, quia multo minus potest haec ratio mensurae esse realis, ut patet, quia scientia vel judicium intellectus aeque mensuratur ab objecto existente vel non existente. Item illa mensuratio non est /p. 824/ actio aliqua, nec est aliquid rei, ut patebit discurrendo per singula praedicamenta.

Sitne sufficiens dicta divisio.

11. *Sexta.*—Sexta et ultima difficultas est, quia non videntur sub his tribus membris sufficienter comprehensae omnes relationes; sunt enim aliae, quae non minus reales videntur, quam quae in praedictis generibus continentur. Assumptum patet primo de relatione appetitus ad appetibile, et omnium quae sub hoc genere continentur, ut amoris ad amabile, desiderii ad desiderabile, etc. Hae namque relationes non fundantur in unitate, vel actione, ut constat; neque etiam in ratione mensurae, quia in amore non est veritas, quae mensuratur per objectum amabile. Quod si dicas, non veritatem, sed perfectionem vel honestatem amoris mensurari ex objecto amabili, certe hoc modo, intercedet relatio mensurae inter omnem effectum et causam, vel formalem, quae est mensura intrinseca perfectionis rei, vel efficientem, exemplarem, aut finalem, quae possunt esse mensurae extrinsecae. Et imperfectiores species unius generis referentur relatione mensurati ad supremam speciem, tanquam ad mensuram earum. Praeterea relatio unionis ad nullum genus ex praedictis videtur pertinere, quia maxime ad primum (nam de aliis non videtur posse esse dubium); sed neque ad illud pertinet, quia aliud est convenientia et unitas, de qua ibi est sermo, aliud vero unio, seu conjunctio, quae potest esse rerum omnino distinctarum, ut est relatio unionis, verbi gratia, humanitatis ad Verbum, et aliae similes. Similis fere est difficultas de relatione contactus, propinquitatis et distantiae, ac denique de relatione causae finalis, formalis et materialis; nam hae omnes non habent illa fundamenta.

Defenditur divisio ab Aristotele tradita.

12. Hae sunt potissimae difficultates quae circa dictam divisionem occurrunt, quibus non obstantibus, amplectenda est et convenienter explicanda Aristotelis doctrina aut divisio, quam omnes ejus interpretes, et scriptores metaphysicarum quaestionum sequuntur, et Theologi etiam, ut patet ex D. Thoma, 1 part., quaest. 13, art. 7, et quaest. 28, a. 1, et 2 cont. Gent., cap. 11 et 12; quibus locis Cajetan. et Ferraries. de his relationibus multa disputant; Capreol. et Hispalens., in 1, partim d. 19, quaest. 2, et 3, partim d. 30 et /col. b/ 31, ubi etiam Scot. et alii Theologi, et aliis locis supra citatis. Fundamentum praeter auctoritatem Aristotelis est, quia relationes pertinentes ad singula ex his generibus sunt reales, ut patet ex communi omnium philosophorum consensu, et ex dictis supra de entitate harum relationum. Nam si quae sunt relationes reales, maxime similitudo aut paternitas, aut relatio scientiae ad scibile, quae sunt relationes ad tria genera dicta pertinentes, quia si hae relationes non sunt reales et praedicamentales, quaenam esse possent, quae rationabiliter possint tales existimari? Hoc ergo satis est ut illa tria genera in praedicamento Ad aliud constituantur, sive sint aliquae relationes rationis, quae habeant proportionem

cum his generibus, sive non. Nam si non sunt, satis constabit esse haec genera omnino realia; si vero sunt, non pertinebunt directe ad haec genera, ut dividunt praedicamentum Ad aliquid, sed habebunt in illis analogiam quamdam seu proportionalitatem.

13. Quod autem haec genera inter se distincta sint in ratione relativa, primum videtur satis notum ex ipsis denominationibus quas tribuunt, sunt enim valde diversae. Deinde optime explicatur res ipsa ab Aristotele ex ipsis fundamentis, seu rationibus fundandi; nam cum una ex potissimis causis relationis sit fundamentum ejus, imo cum ab eo habeat entitatem suam, nullum potest esse majus indicium distinctionis relationum, quam distinctio fundamentorum formalium ac proximorum, de his enim sermo esse debet. Nam fundamentum remotum vel potius subjectum non ita per se concurrit ad relationem, et ideo distinctio ejus non est ita sufficiens fundamentum ad distinguendas relationes. Quod vero fundamenta illorum trium generum sint omnino distincta, etiam per se manifestum est; recte ergo ex eorum distinctione distinctio illa relationum sumpta est.

14. Dices, potius fuisse sumendam distinctionem relationum ex terminis; nam quae dicunt essentialem habitudinem ad aliud, ab illo sumunt specificationem, et consequenter distinctionem, ut motus a terminis, potentiae et habitus ab objectis. Respondetur primo, id esse verum de distinctione specifica et ultima; distinctionem vero genericam, seu subalternam, posse interdum aliunde sumi. Secundo respondetur, in illa distinctione non esse praetermissos terminos formales, sed vel expresse, vel saltem implicite significatos esse in illis tribus generibus. Nam cum relatio /p. 825/ primi generis dicitur fundari in unitate, ibi includitur, quod terminatur etiam ad aliud, quatenus aliquo modo unum est; nam, ut infra ostendam, quod in uno relativo est fundamentum relationis ad aliud, est etiam ratio terminandi relationem alterius. Et simili ratione, cum in secundo genere dicitur relationem fundari in potentia, hoc ipso indicatur terminari etiam ad potentiam vel effectum, si relatio non in nuda potentia, sed ut est sub actione fundetur; sic enim relatio potentiae activae terminatur ad passivam, et e converso; relatio vero potentiae agentis terminatur ad suum effectum. In tertio autem genere clarius constat, relationem mensurabilis ad mensuram terminari. Non est ergo illa distinctio ita sumpta ex fundamentis, quin termini etiam includantur. Cum enim haec sint duo principia suo modo intrinseca relationum, neutrum potest excludi ab earum constitutione et distinctione; sed fundamentum est quasi materiale, terminus vero quasi formale, quia est ultimum in quod tendit relatio.

De sufficientia dictae divisionis.

15. *Prima ratio sufficientiae.—Quot subjecta sit difficultatibus ratio sufficientiae allata.*—Tandem, quod illa divisio sufficiens sit, et complectens omnes relationum species quae ad praedicamentum Ad aliquid, pertinere possunt, omnes citati auctores docent. Rationem autem sufficientiae ejus tradit D. Thomas, 5 Metaph., lect. 17, quia tribus tantum modis contingit unam rem ordinari ad aliam, scilicet , vel secundum esse, secundum quod una res pendet in esse ab alia, et sic est tertius modus, vel secundum unitatem activam et passivam, secundum quod una res ab alia recipit, vel alteri confert aliquid, et sic est secundus modus, vel secundum quod quantitas unius rei potest mensurari per aliam: et sic est primus modus. Difficilis vero est haec ratio; nam habitudo ad aliud secundum dependentiam in esse, si generatim sumatur, magis videtur pertinere ad secundum genus, cum effectus pendeat in esse a sua causa; si vero sumatur secundum peculiarem modum dependentiae, quae est scientiae vel potentiae ab objecto, sic tot essent distinguendi modi relativorum, quot sunt modi dependentiarum. Cur enim potius ille modus dependentiae constituit peculiare genus relativorum, quam alii? Item falsum videtur quod quantitas, ut habet rationem mensurae, fundet primum /col. b/ modum, tum quia Aristoteles non assignat ibi rationem mensurae, sed unitatis vel numeri, quae est longe diversa ratio; nam quando duae quantitates dicuntur aequales, non est una mensura alterius, nec e converso, nec inter eas hoc attenditur, sed ratio unitatis, et idem a fortiori est de similitudine, vel identitate, et ideo, ut diximus, unitas ibi non sumitur quantitative, sed generalius. Tum etiam quia ratio mensurae quantitativae non est per se apta ad fundandam relationom realem, cum solum sit extrinseca denominatio rationis, ut supra tactum est.

16. *Secunda ratio sufficientiae.—Quot in ea difficultates.*—Aliam rationem hujus differentiae indicat eodem loco Alexander Alensis, dicens illam divisionem sumptam esse ex tribus modis universalibus entis, qui sunt, idem et diversum, quoad primum; potentia vel actus, quoad secundum; et perfectum (inquit) vel imperfectum, quoad tertium, eo modo quo imperfectum a perfecto mensuratur, et diminutum a completo; et quia isti modi sufficienter variant naturam fundamentorum, ideo sunt tres species relationis. Sed difficile est quod ait, tertium membrum sumi ex modo entis secundum perfectum vel imperfectum; nam, licet sensus referatur ad sensibile secundum illud genus, non mensuratur ab illo ut imperfectum a perfecto, sed solum dicitur mensurari tanquam a termino specificante, qui interdum potest esse perfectior, interdum aequalis, interdum minus perfectus, ut videre etiam est in intellectu et intelligibili. Deinde, quamvis asserat illos tres modos sufficienter dividere fundamenta relationum, non tamen rationem sufficientiae reddit, neque ex vi illius explicationis declarat distinctionem eorum inter se. Nam etiam potentia

et actus comparantur ut perfectum et imperfectum, et potentia dici potest mensurari per actum, quatenus illi proportionatur et commensuratur, propter quod etiam dicuntur potentiae per actus specificari. Existimo ergo nullam aliam rationem sufficientiae Aristotelem habuisse, praeter inductionem quamdam, qua intellexit nullam inveniri relationem, quae ad aliquod ex dictis capitibus revocari non possit, quod non potest melius constare, quam respondendo difficultatibus tactis. Nam si nullam invenimus relationem quae non habeat aliquod ex his fundamentis, sufficiens signum nobis erit, divisionem illam sufficientem esse.
/p. 826/

SECTIO XI.
De primo genere relationum, in numero vel unitate fundato.

1. Ad singulas difficultates sectione superiori propositas, majoris claritatis gratia fere singulis sectionibus respondebimus.

2. Ad primam igitur respondetur, aliud esse loqui de duabus relationibus duorum extremorum, quae dicuntur in unitate fundari, aliud vero de singulis earum. Unaquaeque enim duarum relationum similitudinis, verbi gratia, fundatur in una qualitate in quantum in se est una unitate formali, non quidem quantum ad id quod addit unitas supra ens, nam illud est negatio, et ideo non potest fundare relationem realem, ut recte argumentum probat, sed quantum ad illam positivam rationem entis, quae substernitur illi negationi. At vero loquendo de ambabus relationibus duorum extremorum, illae dicuntur fundari in unitate eorum, quia ratio cur simul consurgant illae duae relationes, positis illis duobus extremis, non est solum quia singula extrema habent inter se talem unitatem, sed etiam quia illa unitas est ejusdem rationis in utroque, quod idem est ac si diceretur, ideo illa referri inter se, quia habent convenientiam realem. Et quamvis haec convenientia non sit aliqua unitas realis illorum duorum extremorum inter se, ut bene etiam in argumento sumitur, loquendo de propria et formali unitate, datur tamen in re fundamentum illius unitatis, sive quoad negationem, sive quoad unitatem rationis, et illud fundamentum sufficit ut in illis extremis tales relationes consurgant.

3. Et simili modo respondendum est ad alteram partem de relationibus fundatis in multitudine, distinctione vel diversitate. Nam, licet multis propter illud argumentum probabiliter visum sit, illas relationes non esse reales, sed rationis, quia non habent reale fundamentum proximum, vel formalem terminum, nihilominus, loquendo cum communi sententia et consequenter, verius dicitur eamdem esse rationem de his relationibus, et de illis quae fundantur

in unitate. Nam, sicut distinctio includit negationem, ita etiam unitas; et e converso, sicut negatio, quam dicit unitas, supponit entitatem, quae potest esse fundamentum relationis, ita etiam distinctio realis est inter extrema realia, in quibus fundatur negatio ibi inclusa; in eis /col. b/ ergo ut talia sunt, poterit etiam fundari relatio realis.

Unde in exemplis ibi adductis, quamvis verum sit in relatione inaequalitatis alterum extremum carere parte aliqua magnitudinis alterius extremi, tamen relatio non fundatur formaliter in ea carentia, sed in hoc quod haec quantitas tanta est, illa vero tanta. Et idem est de dissimilitudine; supponit enim duas essentias, quarum una non est alia, non tamen fundatur proxime in illa negatione, sed in ipsismet essentiis, quatenus secundum unitates formales plures essentialiter sunt. Quod declaratur exemplo; nam lucidum et tenebrosum etiam habent dissimilitudinem quoad illam negationem, quia in uno non est forma lucis quae est in alio, et tamen non est inter ea relatio realis dissimilitudinis, quia ex parte alterius extremi, nec est fundamentum, nec formalis terminus positivus talis relationis.

Relatio unitatis in rebus omnium praedicamentorum fundari potest.

4. In secunda difficultate multa tanguntur, quae singulas possent quaestiones postulare; ea tamen breviter transigemus, ne in explicandis minutissimis entibus nimium morosi simus. Primo itaque petitur an relatio similitudinis et aliae huius generis fundari possint in sola quantitate, et qualitate, vel etiam in rebus aliorum praedicamentorum. Et quidem de substantia jam vidimus, sectione praecedenti, eamdem esse rationem, quoad hanc partem, de quantitate et qualitate. Et ratio ibi facta videtur mihi concludere de quacumque re vel modo seu entitate, praesertim absoluta, ut interim relationes omittamus; cur enim duo calores sunt realiter similes, et ut sic realiter referuntur, et non duae calefactiones, vel, duo Ubi, et quaecumque alia similia? Item inter duas actiones est vera et positiva contrarietas; haec est autem relatio, quae ad hoc genus pertinet; fundatur enim in peculiari quodam modo distinctionis. Itaque quantum ad caetera praedicamenta, extra Ad aliquid, facile concedimus illationem ibi factam. Neque contra hoc consequens, quantum ad hanc partem, aliquid ibi objicitur. Verum est, D. Thomam, 5 Met., lect. 17, omnino excludere quatuor ultima praedicamenta, ut non possint esse fundamenta relationum, *quia magis* (inquit) *consequuntur relationem, quam possint relationem causare.* Sed exponi potest, ut intelligatur de his praedicamentis secundum pro- /p. 827/ prias rationes eorum, non vero secundum quod habent proportionem aut convenientiam cum aliis in ratione unitatis vel distinctionis.

Una relatio quomodo aliam fundare possit.

5. *Prima sententia.*—Major vero difficultas est de ipsismet relationibus, in qua insinuatur secunda et generalis difficultas, an relatio possit fundari in relatione. Est enim multorum sententia, relationem nunquam posse in relatione fundari. Ita sentit D. Thomas, 1 p., quaest. 42, art. 4, et 2 cont. Gent., c. 13, et q. 7 de Potent., art. 11, et in 1, d. 3, q. 1, art. 1, idque sequuntur frequentius Thomistae, Sonc., 5 Met, q. 29, ad 1; Ferrar., 4 cont. Gent., c, 1l. Fundamentum praecipuum est illud de processu in infinitum, qui inde sequeretur. Sicut ob rationem similem, ad actionem non potest esse actio, nec ad motum motus, et in universum procedendo ab effectu formali ad formam, si forma ipsa aliquo modo participat effectum vel denominationem ejus, sistendum est in illa, ut per seipsam talis sit, quod aliter dici solet, procedendo a quod in quo, sistendum esse in quo. Ergo cum relatio sit, qua relativum refertur, sistendum est in illa, ut non per aliam relationem referatur. Et confirmari potest haec sententia Theologico argumento, quia alias inter divinas relationes plures essent relationes reales, nimirum realis distinctionis et dissimilitudinis quasi specificae in ratione relativa, et similitudinis genericae in eadem, et aliae hujusmodi, quod est contra communem Theologorum doctrinam, qui tantum quatuor relationes reales in divinis agnoscunt.

6. *Secunda sententia.*—Contrariam sententiam tenet Scot., in 2, d. 4, quaest. 4 et 5, et in 4, d. 6, quaest. 10, quem sequuntur Lychet. et Mairon. his locis; item Mairon., in 4, dist. 29, quaest. 6; Ant. Andr., 5 Met., quaest. 13, et lib. de Sex princip., quaest. 10. Fundamentum est tactum a nobis in praedicta difficultate, quia non apparet sufficiens ratio ob quam similitudo inter duas paternitates non sit tam vera relatio, sicut inter duas albedines, cum in re ipsa habeant eumdem modum convenientiae et unitatis formalis, et eodem etiam modo a parte rei denominentur similes. Nam si quis velit dicere duas paternitates denominari similes tantum fundamentaliter, vel negative, scilicet, quia non habent diversam rationem, qui sic respon- /col. b/ det, occasionem praebet ut de quibuscumque rebus similibus idem dici possit, vel oportet ut sufficientem rationem differentiae reddat, quae nulla certe apparet. Idem argumentum est de relatione dissimilitudinis quae esse potest inter paternitatem, et relationem scientiae, verbi gratia. Item arithmetici ponunt proportionalitatem fundatam in duobus proportionibus, quia sicut quatuor ad octo, ita tria ad sex; proportio autem non est nisi relatio; proportionalitas ergo nihil aliud esse videtur quam similitudo proportionum, quae est relatio relationis. Atque haec argumenta videntur sane convincere, consequenter loquendo, quod una relatio possit referri realiter ad aliam per relationes spectantes ad hoc primum genus. Quocirca, sicut unum et multa transcendunt omnia praedicamenta, ita et relationes hujus

primi modi in rebus omnium praedicamentorum inveniri possunt, non ut de essentia illorum, sed ut fundatae in ipsis.

7. *Tertia sententia utrumque praecedentem concilians.*—Nonnulli vero conantur has sententias in concordiam redigere, tum propter auctoritatem D. Thomae, tum propter vim rationum. Aiunt enim unam relationem posse referri realiter ad aliam, non tamen alia relatione, sed seipsa, ut vitetur processus in infinitum, et eadem sit simul quo et quod. Atque ita proprie relatio non fundat relationem, cum non sit alia relatio quae refertur, et qua refertur; secundum rationem, autem potest dici fundare, in quantum ipsa secundum rationem distinguitur in id quod refertur, et quo refertur. Cui sententiae favet Cajet., 1 p., quaest. 42, art. 1, fundatus in verbis D. Thomae, in solution. ad 4, quae sunt haec: Una relatio non refertur ad aliam per aliquam aliam relationem. Circa quae Cajetanus addit, ex hac conditione relationis, scilicet, ut non fundetur supra aliam relationem, non sequi relationes relationum non esse reales, sed eas non esse alias a fundamentis. Unde subdit, quod si relationes divinae alioqui non haberent identitatem in natura, referri possent relatione reali aequalitatis; tunc vero aequalitas Filii ad Patrem esset ipsa filiatio, et Patris ad Filium, ipsa paternitas.

8. *Sententia auctoris.*—Verumtamen haec sententia non videtur posse in universam sustineri; nam, ut forma quoad aliquam denominationem susci-piendam per se ipsam sufficiens sit, vel (sicut aiunt) ut se habeat ut quo et quod, necesse est quod illa denomi- /p. 828/ natio sit et ejusdem rationis cum tali forma, et intrinseca et inseparabilis ab ipsa, ut patet in actione quae seipsa fit, quia ratio actionis est ut fiat, cum per eam fit aliquid, et in quantitate qua seipsa est quanta intrinsece. At vero si una relatio refertur realiter ad aliam, saepe ille respectus est longe diversae rationis a propria ratione et effectu for-mali talis relationis, et est illi extrinsecus et accidentalis; ergo non potest illa relatio per seipsam ita referri, sed per aliam relationem. Probatur minor, quia formalis ratio, et effectus paternitatis est referre ad filium; cum vero ipsa dicitur similis alteri paternitati, si ad illam refertur realiter, ille est effectus formalis valde diversae rationis, cum tendat ad terminum, diversae rationis, et habeat rationem fundandi diversae etiam rationis. Rursus haec denominatio, *similis,* est accidentaria paternitati; nam si in mundo non esset alia paternitas, non denominaretur similis, nec referretur illo modo; ergo quando sic refertur, non per seipsam, sed per aliam relationem refertur.

9. Et confirmatur, nam quando dicitur una relatio referri ad aliam realiter, non vero per aliam relationem, aut intelligitur non per aliam, nec re, nec ratione distinctam, et hoc manifeste probatur esse falsum argumento facto; nam quae potest esse major distinctio rationis, quam quae est ex terminis di-versarum rationum, et quae satis est ut una relatio sit accidentaria alteri? Aut

est sensus, quod non refertur per aliam relationem re distinctam, sed ratione tantum, et hoc non est peculiare in relatione; nam supra etiam a nobis dictum est, relationes, quibus referuntur res absolutae, non distingui nisi ratione a fundamentis absolutis. Vel si quis contendat fundamentum absolutum referri relatione reali et in re distincta, unam vero relationem posse referri relatione reali, non tamen in re distincta, primo supponit falsum, deinde oportet ut aliquam rationem hujus discriminis reddat, quam hactenus nullus reddidit. Nam, quod quidam aiunt, relationem esse minutissimam entitatem, et ideo non posse fundare aliam in re distinctam, non satisfacit, tum quia etiam relatio, quae fundatur, est minutissimae entitatis, tum etiam quia jam supponitur prima relatio fundata in absoluto, et ideo mirum non est quod possit fundare aliam proportionatam, sicut etiam motus vel tempus est satis diminutae entitatis, et tamen potest fundare relationem.

10. Distinguendum ergo videtur: nam quidam sunt respectus intime inclusi in ipsis relationibus, et inseparabiles ab ipsis secundum proprias rationes earum; alii vero sunt accidentarii. Priores tantum sunt ad proprios terminos vel ad relationes oppositas; posteriores vero sunt ad alios terminos, qui simpliciter sunt per accidens ad esse talis relationis. Exemplum sit in paternitate, quae, hoc ipso quod refert patrem ad filium, includit intrinsece et inseparabiliter oppositionem cum filiatione, et consequenter etiam distinctionem; est enim distinctio veluti quid superius inclusum in oppositione; oppositio autem est quid inclusum in correlatione. At vero respectus unius paternitatis ad aliam in ratione similis, non est ita inclusus in propria ratione paternitatis, et alia paternitas est terminus accidentarius et extrinsecus respectu alterius paternitatis.

11. De prioribus ergo respectibus, satis consentaneum est quod Cajetanus ait, etsi secundum omnes illos eadem relatio referatur, non tamen alia relatione, sed seipsa referri, cum in sua adaequata ratione omnes illos includat. At vero in respectibus posterioris generis non video quomodo possit consequenter negari, quin una relatio possit per aliam referri, et ita aliam in se fundare, quia nec videtur posse negari quin illo etiam modo relatio realiter referatur, ut argumenta facta probant; nec etiam potest dici quod illo modo referatur per seipsam, ut persuadent ea quae contra ultimam sententiam diximus. Hinc vero ulterius addo, sicut supra exponebam D. Thomam negantem relationes fundari in quatuor ultimis praedicamentis, ita etiam exponi posse de relationibus; nam relationes secundum propriam et intrinsecam rationem non referuntur relatione a se distincta, nec fundant illam; at vero prout aliquo modo participant vel conveniunt cum quantitate in unitate vel multitudine, sic non repugnat referri relatione similitudinis, et aliis similibus, et hoc solum videntur probare fundamenta secundae sententiae.

12. *Si fundet una relatio aliam, an in infinitum necessario abeundum sit.*—Ad argumentum autem de processu in infinitum, primo responderi potest non esse magnum inconveniens illum admittere in relationibus, ut supra dicebamus de relationibus partium vel punctorum. Quanquam hic videatur habere nonnullam majorem difficultatem, quia inter fundamentum et relationem est ordo /p. 829/ per se; at in per se ordinatis non videtur posse procedi in infinitum, ut in lib. 2 ab Aristotele traditur. Responderi vero potest id esse verum in iis quae in re distincta sunt, non vero in iis quae ratione distinguuntur. Secundo responderi potest negando processum in infinitum, quia sistendum est in ea relatione quae eamdem denominationem suscipit, quam praebet fundamentum, et necessario ac intrinsece illam secum affert. Ut, verbi gratia, quamvis paternitas referatur similitudine, et illa similitudo sit similis alteri ejusdem speciei, non oportet ut sit similis per aliam relationem, sed se ipsa, quia illa denominatio est ejusdem rationis, et intrinsece illam secum affert, quia non potest referre unam paternitatem ad aliam similem, quin illi respondeat alia relatio cui ipsa sit similis; et hoc ad summum probant exempla de actione et motu, et similibus.

13. Quod si instetur, quia quaelibet relatio est capax alterius denominationis relativae diversae rationis, nam relatio similitudimis potest esse dissimilis alteri, et e converso, respondeo, relationes fundatas in eodem fundamento absoluto, cum sola ratione distinguantur, posse mutuo sese ita referre et denominare; unde, cum illae denominationes diversarum rationum finitae sint, necessarium non est propter illas admittere infinitas relationes, vel processum in infinitum. De relationibus autem divinis alia est ratio, quia seclusa identitate essentiae, in qua non fundatur relatio realis, sed rationis, non habent inter se veram et realem similitudinem, sed potius distinctionem et dissimilitudinem, quam in propriis relationibus includant; ideo non referuntur inter se alia relatione, sed seipsis; sed haec disputatio alterius est loci.

De relationibus identitatis, similitudinis et aequalitatis.

14. Tertio petitur in illa difficultate, quae sit propria relatio identitatis, similitudinis et aequalitatis, et an possint eidem rei convenire diversis respectibus. Ad quod breviter dicendum est, relationem identitatis proprie esse identitatem essentialem, minorem numerica, ut abstrahamus nunc ab specifica, et superioribus omnibus, de quibus statim. Hoc patet ex Aristotele dicente illa esse eadem, quorum substantia, id est, essentia, est una. Quocirea ad argumentum ibi factum concedendum est duas qualitates, ut sunt ejusdem speciei es- /col. b/ sentialis, proprie referri relatione identitatis; nam est eadem ratio in eis quae in caeteris entibus ejusdem speciei. Unde consequenter etiam dicendum est, propriam relationem similitudinis (ad rem ipsam attendendo, quidquid sit de

usu vocum) esse illam quae convenit qualitatibus ratione intensionis; relationem vero aequalitatis esse illam quae convenit quantitatibus ratione actualis
extensionis. Denique (quod rem ipsam magis explicat) admittendum est, in
eadem qualitate aliam esse relationem identitatis, seu fundatam in essentia ejus,
ut sic; aliam vero, relationem similitudinis, fundatam in unitate intensionis,
adeo ut haec sit separabilis ab illa, quia potest manere unitas essentiae sine
intensione. Imo, et e converso, quamvis respectu alterius albedinis non possit
alia albedo esse similis in intensione, quin sit etiam una in essentia, tamen
respectu nigredinis possunt albedo et nigredo ut octo dici similes in modo
seu gradu intensionis, etiamsi sint dissimiles, vel potius diversae in essentia.
Neque est inconveniens hujusmodi relationes multiplicari, praesertim si verum
est non propterea multiplicari res aut modos reales ex natura rei distinctos.

15. Atque eodem modo sentiendum est de relationibus aequalitatis et identitatis specificae in quantitate continua; est enim eadem proportionalis ratio, ut
in dicto argumento satis declaratur. Dico autem in quantitate continua, quia
in numeris non videtur esse diversa relatio aequalitatis et identitatis specificae,
quia duo binarii, verbi gratia, ex propriis rationibus essentialibus habent aequalitatem, nec potest, non solum in re, verum etiam ratione separari inter eos
relatio specificae identitatis a relatione aequalitatis. Et ratio esse videtur, quia
quantitas discreta non habet aliam propriam essentiam vel speciem, praeter
talem actualem extensionem, seu numerabilitatem, neque ibi est separabilis
talis species a tali multitudine, quod secus est in quantitate continua; nam,
retinendo propriam extensionem essentialem, potest esse in majori vel minori
magnitudine.

An unitas generica fundet relationem realem.

16. *Affirmative respondetur.*—Quarto quaeritur in illo argumento, an relationes
hujus primi modi pertinentes ad unitatem fundentur in sola unitate specifica,
vel etiam /p. 830/ in generica. Et quamvis utraque pars possit facile disputari,
ut ibi insinuatum est, et possent facile conjecturae in utramque partem multiplicari, nihilominus breviter dicendum censeo non solum unitatem specificam,
sed etiam genericam sufficere ad aliquam relationem similitudinis. Quae est
expressa sententia D. Thomae, 1 p., q. 26, art. 1, ad 2, ubi ait: *Relatio, quae
importatur per hoc nomen, idem, est relatio rationis tantum, si accipiatur simpliciter idem; secus autem est cum dicuntur aliqua eadem esse non in numero, sed
in natura generis sive speciei.* Hoc etiam sequitur Ant. Andreas, lib. 5 Metaph.,
quaest. 13, ad 3. Et rationes inter argumentandum tactae satis probabiliter hoc
persuadent. Neque obstat quod res differentes specie potius dicantur dissimiles
simpliciter, quam similes; nam hinc solum sequitur relationem similitudinis
genericae praecise

sumptae non esse (ut ita dicam) tam potentem ad denominandum, sicut relationem similitudinis vel dissimilitudinis specificae; nihilominus suam confert denominationem, nempe talis similitudinis, scilicet, genericae.

17. Videtur autem satis probabile, has relationes similitudinis in specie vel genere non esse proprie diversas nisi respectu diversorum, seu quando unaquaeque est adaequata suo termino, et proprio ac formali fundamento. Ut, verbi gratia, licet duo homìnes sint similes in specie et genere, non est necessarium ut duplici relatione reali referantur, quia in una relatione adaequata uterque respectus includitur,[5] scilicet, in relatione specificae similitudinis, quia illa relatio prout est in re, non fundatur in sola differentia ultima, sed fundatur in tali forma dante tale esse specificum. Relatio tamen qua homo est similis equo in ratione animalis, diversa est in specie ab illa qua unus homo est similis alteri; tamen illa etiam includit omnem aliam relationem similitudinis, quae inter hominem et equum excogitari potest in gradibus superioribus inclusis in ratione animalis, et sic est proportionaliter philosophandum in caeteris. Atque ita evitatur facile non solum infinitas, sed etiam nimia multitudo relationum; solum enim multiplicantur juxta multitudinem et formalem distinctionem terminorum seu unitatum.

18. *Unitas analogica an fundet relationem praedicamentalem.*—Quaeri vero non immerito potest an hujusmodi relatio possit interdum fundari in unitate analoga, in ea prae- /col. b/ sertim quae dicit unum conceptum objectivum, intrinsece convenientem utrique analogatorum. Nam de aliis modis analogiae certum est non sufficere ad relationem realem, quia non fundatur in aliqua propria similitudine, aut convenientia reali, sed in metaphorica, quae praecipue fit per comparationem intellectus nostri. In priori vero genere analogiae, non est improbabile posse inter analogata intervenire relationem realem fundatam in tali unitate, quia inter illa extrema est aliqua realis convenientia. Unde interdum D. Thomas significat effectus Dei referri ad Deum aliqua relatione realis similitudinis vel imaginis, ut sumi potest ex 1 p., quaest. 4, art. 3, ad 4, cum his quae ibi acute notat Cajetan.; item ex eodem D. Thoma, 1 part., quaest. 93, art. 1, ad ult., et de Potent., quaest. 7, art. 6, ubi ait esse in creaturis relationes varias ad Deum, prout ipse illas producit a seipso diversas, aliqualiter tamen sibi adsimilatas. Idem sentit Ant. Adr. supra.

19. Ultimo petitur in illa difficultate, an hae relationes, ut fundantur proprie in multitudine, et inter varios numeros versantur, sint reales relationes vel solum denominationes ex comparationibus quas noster intellectus facit. Et quidem si attendamus communem modum loquendi Aristotelis et aliorum

---

5 Here I am following Salamanca, 1597, vol. 2, p. 575, over the "inducitur" of the Vivès edition.

philosophorum, non est dubium quin ita censeant de his relationibus, sicut de aliis realibus quae ad hoc primum genus spectant; nam denominationes aequalitatis vel inaequalitatis eodem modo ex rebus ipsis sumuntur. Si autem relatio est res vel modus ex natura rei distinctus a fundamento, difficile est explicare talem relationem realem in binario vel ternario fundatam, quia non potest esse vere una et simplex in toto binario; in quo enim subjecto esset? Neque enim potest esse in una unitate potius quam in alia, cum nulla sit disparitatis ratio, neque in omnibus simul, quia non potest unum accidens esse simul totum in multis subjectis, et in singulis eorum, ut per se constat. Maxime quia nulla unitas est dupla aut tripla, ut possit in sola illa esse tota relatio dupli aut tripli. Nec vero potest esse partim in uno subjecto, partim in alio, alias non esset vere una et simplex, sed composita, eodem modo quo numerus. Non potest autem esse illo modo composita, si relatio est res aut modus distinctus; alias in qualibet unitate consurgeret specialis entitas, aut modus, qui, per se sumptus, esset una relatio, et cum aliis componeret unam tantum /p. 831/ secundum quid, ad eum modum quo numerus est unus. Id autem esse non potest, quia in nulla unitate per se sumpta est ratio aut fundamentum unde talis modus resultet. At vero si relatio non est aliquis modus realiter additus suo fundamento, facile intelligitur, numerum, eo modo quo in rebus est, et secundam illam imperfectam unitatem quam habet, posse per modum unius extremi comparari et referri ad alium numerum ut aequalem aut duplum, vel alio simili modo. Quia fundamentum illius relationis in singulis numeris nihil aliud est, quam ipsamet quantitas discreta, ut habet talem unitatem, vel diversitatem ab alia, et illamet quantitas in re est ipsa relatio, quatenus potest illam, denominationem tribuere subjecto in ordine ad similem vel dissimilem terminum.

Quales sint relationes ad primum fundamentum pertinentes.
20. Ad tertiam difficultatem dicendum est, non esse necessariam ut relatio hujus primi modi sit aut realiter addita ipsi fundamento, tanquam ex natura rei distincta ab ipso, aut mera denominatio extrinseca ex coexistentìa alterius extremi; nam inter haec duo potest medium inveniri, nimirum, quod sit denominatio intrinseca includens coexistentiam alterius extremi ad quod dicit habitudinem. Cum autem quaeritur de hac habitudine, an praesupponatur intrinsece in fundamento, etiam quando terminus non existit, licet tunc non habeat rationem praedicamentalis relationis, sed transcendentalis, an vero de novo addatur posito termino, dicendum est non praesupponi proprie sub ratione habitudinis vel relationis, vel praedicamentalis, vel transcendentalis; nam, ut recte in tertia illa difficultate probatur, fundamentum hujus primi generis per se non includit habitudinem transcendentalem; nulla ergo formalis

habitudo praesupponitur intrinsece in tali fundamento, neque etiam realiter et intrinsece additur, posito termino.

21. Dicendum ergo est habitudinem illam fundamentaliter et quasi inchoative praesupponi ex vi fundamenti, compleri autem per positionem termini; compleri (inquam) non per extrinsecam additionem, sed solum per extrinsecam positionem termini. Nam fundamentum ipsum aptum est de se ad tribuendam hujusmodi denominationem relativam, et hac ratione dicitur continere habitudinem /col. b/ relativam quasi inchoatam; ut tamen actu tribuat illam denominationem, requirit terminum actu existentem, et ideo posito termino completur statim illa denominatio absque alia additione intrinseca et reali. Habitudo autem relativa in praesenti non est aliud quam haec eadem denominatio relativa, seu forma ipsa quatenus actu tribuens illam. Quae autem conditio sit in fundamento necessaria, ut ex parte sua sit aptum tribuere hanc denominationem, dicemus commodius in sectione sequenti; et hactenus de primo membro illius divisionis.

SECTIO XII.
De secundo genere relationum in potentia vel actione fundato.

1. Circa secundum genus relationum multa attinguntur in quarta difficultate superius posita. De quibus relationibus in communi loquendo, certum est esse reales et praedicamentales; ita enim sentiunt Doctores omnes, et ita exponunt Aristotelem. Nam si inter aliqua extrema concurrunt omnia necessaria ad hujusmodi relationem, maxime inter haec, ut ex dictis constare potest, et magis patebit ex dicendis. In particulari vero duo sunt quae hic habent difficultatem. Primum est, an omnes relationes, quas Aristoteles gratia exempli numerat in illo genere, sint vere reales et praedicamentales. Secundum est, quodnam sit proprium fundamentum talium relationum.

An omnes relationes secundi generis sint reales.

2. Circa priorem partem difficilis sane est prima objectio, quae in quarta difficultate fit contra membrum illud de relationibus fundatis in futura actione, quae dicuntur esse, *inter id quod facturum est, et illud quod faciendum est*; haec enim sunt Aristotelis verba; objectio tamen facta, ut existimo, concludit talem relationem non posse esse realem, ex defectu termini, et proximae conditionis requisitae. Unde dicendum existimo, non omnia exempla, quae Aristoteles ibi posuit, esse in rigore de relationibus realibus et praedicamentalibus. Ipse enim non intendit illo loco tradere propriam et rigorosam coordinationem praedicamenti Ad aliquid, sed explicare omnes modos relativorum, et ad certa quaedam

capita eos revocare, sive sint propria relativa realia, sive solum ea imitentur secundum nos- /p. 832/ trum loquendi modum. Et potest hoc confimari; nam ibidem ait, ad hoc secundum genus pertinere quaedam relativa, quae dicuntur secundum privationem potentiae, ut impossibile, et similia; constat autem haec non esse vera relativa realia, cum privatio potentiae non sit reale fundamentum. Solum ergo ponuntur in hoc genere per quamdam reductionem; idem ergo dicendum censeo de relationibus quae dicuntur fundari in actione futura.

3. At vero de relatione exorta ex praeterita actione, quae terminum actu existentem reliquit, aliter censendum est. Illa enim relatio realis est et praedicamentalis, duratque quamdiu effectus et causa actu existunt, ut habet communis sententia. Nam ibi interveniunt extrema realia, et apta ut inter sese habere possint realem ordinem (agimus enim nunc de causis creatis), et fuere jam in re posita omnia, quae ad illum ordinem seu relationem necessaria sunt, ut patebit solvendo difficultatem propositam.

4. In qua imprimis petitur quomodo relatio, quae manet, possit fundari in actione praeterita, quae jam non est. Dicendum vero est non fundari in illa ut in proprio fundamento in quo insit, aut a quo habeat suam entitatem, sed illam esse rationem fundandi talem relationem, vel, ut supra dicebamus, conditionem requisitam ut talis relatio resultet. Non est autem talis, ut ab illa relatio pendeat quasi in fieri et in esse, et ideo nihil mirum est quod, transacta actione, maneat relatio. Est autem illa conditio requisita, non solum quia per eam positus est terminus necessarius ad talem relationem, quantum ad solam ejus entitatem absolutam; potuit enim poni in rerum natura per aliam actionem, quod non satis fuisset ut insurgeret dicta relatio. Est ergo necessaria, quia per illam influit causa in talem effectum; ex quo influxu manet ordinata ad illum effectum, et respective denominata a relatione insurgente, vel a suamet potentia seu virtute agendi, quatenus peculiariter influxit in illum effectum.

De fundamento proximo paternitatis.

5. Unde controverti solet in quo principio proxime insit, et cum quo identificetur talis relatio, an, scilicet, in potentia proxima et accidentali, vel in principali et substantiali. Nam multi censent esse in principio proximo, seu in potentia generandi, quod posset apparentibus argumentis fieri verisimile. Alii /col. b/ vero existimant ipsummet principale principium et substantiale identificare sibi hanc relationem. Fortasse tamen verum est, ad unumquodque principium sequi relationem illi accommodatam, quia est par ratio de utroque; nam relatio potentiae absolute sumptae, et abstrahendo ab actu, utrique inest; ergo etiam in utroque, ut est sub actu suo, aliqua relatio consequitur. Relationem autem propriam paternitatis existimo esse illam quae proxime inest ipsi substantiae medio principio principali; nam in supposito genito, filiationis relatio sine dubio

afficit immediate ipsam substantiam, vel etiam ipsum suppositum, ut multi volunt, de quo late tractavi in 2 tom. tertiae partis. Ergo cum hae relationes sibi proportionate respondeant, etiam relatio paternitatis proxime afficit substantiale principium, eique identificatur. Item, quia separato quolibet accidente realiter distincto, etiam per potentiam Dei, si maneat substantiale suppositum, quod genuit, et quod genitum est, durat relatio paternitatis, alioqui nulla superest ratio ad ponendam illam; nam ille homo vere ac propriissime dicetur pater; ergo signum est hanc relationem esse intime in ipsa substantia. Tandem est hoc maxime consentaneum modo denominandi ejus, nam solum denominat ipsum suppositum principaliter operans.

6. *Qui genuit, si privetur filio, non remanet pater.*—Non manebit autem haec relatio paternitatis mortuo filio, ut falso in illa quarta difficultate assumitur. Neque vere ac proprie dicetur pater esse, ille qui orbatus est filiis, sed fuisse, quod non solum in philosophico rigore verum est, sed etiam vulgari sermone observari videtur. Quapropter non est idem esse patrem, quod genuisse; nam haec est denominatio extrinseca ab actione praeterita, et ideo durat, etiamsi mortuum sit genitum; altera vero est denominatio relativa, quae includit co-existentiam extremorum.

An relatio agentis illi insit.

7. Atque hinc a fortiori constat (quod ulterius in ea quarta difficultate tangitur), relationem actualiter agentis seu generantis esse etiam realem; nam si hoc verum est post actionem praeteritam, cur non magis praesente et durante actione? Duo vero hic inquiri possunt. Unum est, an haec relatio sit intrinsece inhaerens ipsi agenti, vel solum extrinsece denominans, sicut ipsa actio. Videtur enim /p. 833/ hoc posterius sufficere ad relationem realem, et esse magis, consentaneum denominationi talis relationis. Actio enim ipsa realis est, et realiter denominat agens, et in hac ipsa denominatione includitur transcendentalis quaedam habitudo ad effectum, quia actio ut actio terminum respicit, sicut infra dicemus; ergo similiter poterit relatio esse realis, quamvis solum extrinsece, et media actione denominet ipsum agens, tanquam relatum ad terminum seu effectum suum.

8. Nihilominus dicendum est propriam relationem, quae per se refert causam agentem vel generantem, ab eo instanti in quo actu generat, esse intrinsecam, et immediate inhaerentem illi. Primo quidem , quia si post actionem praeteritam manet in causa agente relatio intrinsece adhaerens illi, multo magis talis relatio resultabit et inhaerebit, etiam durante ipsa actione. Deinde, quia, ut D. Thomas docet, 2 cont. Gent., c. 13, licet in aliis formis inveniantur extrinsecae denominationes, *a relatione vero non invenitur aliquid denominari quasi exterius existente, sed inhaerente,* ait D. Thomas; unde subdit: *Non enim denominatur*

aliquis pater, nisi a paternitate quae ei inest. Cujus ratio esse videtur, quia quod extrinsece denominat, potius refertur ad ipsum quod denominat, quam referat ipsum; atque ita actio potius refertur ad agens, quam ipsum referat, quamvis sit occasio vel conditio ut in agente resultet relatio. Quare, licet, verum sit actionem ipsam referri ad terminum, tamen non proprie refert ipsummet suppositum agens, quia non denominat illud ut id in quo est, sed ut a quo est; atque ita solum dici potest quod manat ab agente cum respectu ad terminum; ille autem non est respectus ipsius agentis nisi remote, ut magis ex sequenti dubitatione patebit.

Sitne eadem relatio in agente dum actio durat, et illa transacta.

9. *Affirmative respondetur.*—Rursus enim inquiri potest an haec relatio agentis in actu, vel de praesenti, sit eadem et specie et numero cum relatione agentis de praeterito, verbi gratia, cum paternitate. Quidam enim putant esse diversam, et videtur favere Aristoteles, dum ait has relationes variari secundum tempora. Potestque fundari in diverso modo denominandi; nam altera denominat ut actu agentem, altera vero ut illum qui egit. Quare videtur una relatio solum durare /col. b/ quamdiu durat actio, et ad desitionem ejus alteram consurgere. Verius tamen existimo, in patre, verbi gratia, (et idem est in similibus) eamdem numero esse relationem, quae in ipsomet instanti, quo generat, consurgit, et permanet quamdiu talis pater cum filio durat. Ut enim Theologice argumentemur, quis dicat Beatissimam Virginem, in primo instanti quo Christum concepit, habuisse unam relationem matris, et immediate post amisisse illam et acquisivisse aliam? Deinde actio generandi est ratio vel conditio, qua posita resultat relatio paternitatis; interrogo ergo an sit talis ratio vel conditio ut ab illa pendeat relatio paternitatis in fieri et conservari, necne. Nam si non pendet in conservari, ergo transacta illa actione generandi, manebit eadem paternitas, quia non est unde varietur; si autem pendet, ergo, transacta actione, transibit cum illa dicta relatio; ergo non est unde resultet alia relatio. Quia cessatio actionis, cum sit privatio quaedam, non est sufficiens ratio ut resultet nova relatio realis; neque actio praeterita potest esse ratio talis relationis novae, quia illa actio, ut existens, jam habuit suam relationem proportionatam, ut praeterita vero nihil addit nisi dictam privationem. Melius ergo et facilius dicitur illam relationem esse unam et eamdem, manere vero postea, quia non pendet in conservari ab ipsa actione, sed a fundamente, et termino, quae in praecedenti puncto explicata sunt. Quocirca paternitas ut sic nec includit denominationem de praeterito, nec de praesenti, sed absolute refert ad eum qui habet esse ab illo qui pater denominatur, abstrahendo ab hoc, quod actio, per quam habet esse, existat vel non existat; hae namque denominationes includentes hos temporales respectus, potius sunt ab ipsa actione ut praesente vel praeterita.

De relatione agentis in potentia.

10. Ultimo petitur in eadem quarta difficultate, ut explicemus qualis sit relatio agentis in potentia, de qua jam diximus non posse esse realem et praedicamentalem in ordine ad solum effectum possibilem ut sic, sed in ordine ad aliquam potentiam realem passivam, et actu existentem, quia non potest habere alium terminum realem; hoc autem modo interveniunt omnia ad realem relationem necessaria. Dicunt vero aliqui, hanc relationem non pertinere ad hoc secundum genus relationum, sed ad primum, quia non fundatur /p. 834/ in actione, sed praecise in proportione, quae est inter duas facultates, ut una possit in alteram agere, et altera ab alia pati; quae proportio est quaedam unitas, et ideo ad primam rationem fundandi pertinere videtur.

11. Haec vero sententia non est consentanea Aristoteli, qui in hoc secundo membro nunquam dixit, ad illud pertinere relationes in actione fundatas, sed potius in principio capitis dixit: *Alia* (scilicet dicuntur ad aliquid) *ut calefactivum ad calefactibile, sectivum ad sectabile, et uno nomine activum ad passivum*; ubi nullam fecit mentionem actionis et passionis, sed potentiarum tantum; postea vero utrumque conjunxit, dicens: *Activa autem et passiva ex potentia activa et passiva potentiarumque actionibus dicuntur.* Deinde, relatio quae est potentiae agentis ad patientem, non fundatur in unitate, quae ad fundamentum primum pertinet, sed in virtute ad agendum; illa enim unitas, quae est ratio fundandi in priori modo, consistit in aliqua reali et formali convenientia inter ea quae similia vel eadem dicuntur; at vero inter potentiam agentem et patientem non intercedit talis unitas et convenientia, nisi fortasse quatenus conveniunt in generica ratione potentiae, sub qua ratione non referuntur propria relatione potentiae agentis et patientis, sed relatione similitudinis quoad rationem genericam. Illa ergo proportio non est vera unitas; quod si per analogiam ita nominetur, est longe alterius rationis ab unitate, quae fundat primum modum relativorum. Quapropter haec relatio non ad primum, sed ad secundum modum pertinet, differtque ab alia superius explicata, quia haec sequitur rationem potentiae praecise sumptam, illa vero quatenus est sub actu; unde haec terminatur ad potentiam passivam ut sic, illa vero ad effectum.

12. *Quaenam potentiae referantur reali relatione in actione vel passione fundata.*—Petitur vero ulterius an haec relatio inveniatur in quacumque virtute activa et passiva, sive sit propriae potentiae de genere qualitatis, sive cujuscumque alterius generis seu transcendentalis rationis. Et sane, de potentiis praedicamentalibus per se primo ordinatis, ut una agat in aliam, vel altera patiatur ab altera, non est difficile ad intelligendum, quod sint aptissimae ad fundandam relationem inter se, dummodo sint in re ipsa, distinctae, quia, hoc ipso quod existunt, sese mutuo respiciunt, ratione transcendentalis ordinis quem inter /col. b/ se habent, ratione (inquam) ejus ut proximi fundamenti. Dixi autem,

dummodo in re sint distinctae, nam potentia, quae simul est activa in seipsam, et passiva a seipsa, etiamsi propria potentia ac praedicamentalis sit, et utramque rationem per se primo habeat ex institutione sua, non potest secundum illas habere relationem realem, ex defectu distinctionis quae ad hanc relationem necessaria est. Unde neque illas rationes habet talis potentia per habitudines transcendentales ejusdem ad seipsam, sed per quamdam eminentem habitudinem ad suum actum, quem respicit sub utraque ratione. Quod si talis potentia, ut activa, indiget alio comprincipio ad agendum in se, ut intellectus indiget specie, secundum illud poterit referri realiter ad seipsam solam, in ratione activi ad passivum, non tamen ratione suae propriae et intrinsecae activitatis, propter rationem dictam de identitate. At vero ubi intervenit sufficiens distinctio, et alioqui est intrinseca et naturalis coordinatio potentiarum, non est dubium quin concurrant omnia necessaria ad realem respectum praedicamentalem, si extrema coexistant.

13. *Quaevis virtus activa vel passiva potest referri relatione secundi generis.*— Addendum vero ulterius est, relationem hanc non esse coarctandam ad hoc potentiarum genus, sed intercedere inter omnes res creatas (nam de Deo infra dicam) quae quacumqne ratione habent realem virtutem agendi et patiendi inter se. Hoc constat, tum ex generali locutione Aristotelis, tum ex exemplis ejus, quae alia etiam genera potentiarum comprehendunt; tum etiam ex communi sententia interpretum et philosophorum. Tum denique quia ut intercedat praedicamentalis relatio, non semper necesse est supponi in fundamento transcendentalem relationem, ut in solutione tertiae difficultatis dictum est. Satis ergo in proposito est, quod una virtus sit ejusdem ordinis cum alia potentia, et quod natura sua habeat vim agendi, quod est habere veluti physicum quoddam dominium in illam, ut inde possit oriri respectus praedicamentalis, seu relativa denominatio.

14. Atque hinc tandem intelligitur non debere in hoc secundo fundamento nomen potentiae stricte sumi, ut distinguitur ab habitu, nam etiam habitus, quatenus vim habet agendi suos actus, solet ab Aristotele sub nomine potentiae activae comprehendi, ut saepe in superioribus notatum est, et ut sic potest /p. 835/ esse fundamentum relationis realis non quidem ad objectum, nam haec pertinet ad tertium modum, sed vel ad actum quem efficit, vel ad potentiam in quam efficere potest; quae ratio ad hoc secundum genus pertinet, ut ex dictis a paritate rationis constat.

SECTIO XIII.
De tertio genere relationis in ratione mensurae fundato.

1. Superest ut explicemus quod in quinta difficultate petitur, quomodo , scilicet, relationes tertii generis dicantur fundari in ratione mensurae; ita enim fere omnes auctores loquuntur, et sumunt ex Aristotele in hoc loco.

Difficultas circa Philosophi mentem proponitur.

2. Si tamen Aristoteles attente legatur, non videtur dicere has relationes fundari in ratione mensurae, sed inter alia exempla quibus hunc modum explicat, unum esse mensurabilis ad mensuram; verba enim ejus sunt: *Alia ut mensurabile ad mensuram, et scibile ad scientiam, et sensibile ad sensum*; ubi nullum fundamentum harum relationum declarat, sed solum adhibitis illis tribus exemplis, proponit hoc tertium relationis genus. Nec potest dici, in illis primis verbis, *ut mensurabile ad mensuram*, explicare communem, rationem harum relationum, alia vero esse exempla et species hujus generis; hoc enim non potest accommodari contextui, tum quia Aristoteles non dixit, Ut scibile ad scientiam, sed tantum copulative, *et scibile ad scientiam*; tum, etiam quia si haec posteriora verba adhibuisset in exemplum priorum, non debuisset dicere, Ut scibile ad scientiam, sed potius, Ut scientia ad scibile; at vero non ita dixit, sed, quod attente considerandum est, eodem modo dicit referri mensurabile ad mensuram, et scibile ad scientiam, et sensibile ad sensum; at vero scibile non refertur ad scientiam, ut mensurabile ad mensuram; nam, eo modo quo inter haec ratio mensurae intervenire potest, potius scientia mensuratur per scibile, quam e converso. Adde, quod in hoc tertio genere nullam mentionem videtur facere Aristoteles, relationum scientiae ad scibile, vel sensus ad sensibile, sed solum oppositarum relationum (ut sic dicam), scilicet, scibilis ad scientiam, et sensibilis ad sensum, quibus adjungit relationem mensurabilis ad /col. b/ mensuram tanquam eis similem; ergo non constituit communem rationem hujus tertii generis, in hoc quod fundetur in ratione mensurae, sed in aliqua alia ratione communi mensurabili, scibili, et aliis hujusmodi.

3. Quae omnia confirmari possunt ex modo quo inferius Aristoteles declarat hoc tertium genus relationum; nullam, enim aliam communem rationem ejus ponit, nisi quia alia relativa, per relationes quas in se habent, relativa dicuntur, haec vero solum suscipiunt denominationem relativam, quia alia ad ipsa dicuntur repetitque eadem exempla, scilicet, mensurabile, scibile, intelligibile, quamvis solum ultimum declaret dicens: *Nam et intelligibile significat, quod in eo versetur intellectus*. Unde simpliciter interpretando hanc litteram Aristotelis, non videtur ipse in hoc tertio genere ponere novam aliquam relationem realem, quae intrinsece insit, et referat suum subjectum, sed solum denominationes

quasdam relativas, sumptas ex relationibus existentibus in oppositis extremis. Quocirca, cum scientia ad scibile, et scibile ad scientiam relative dicantur, ad hunc tertium modum relativorum, juxta mentem Aristotelis sic expositam, solum pertinet relatio vel denominatio ipsius scibilis, qualiscumque illa sit; relatio autem scientiae ad scibile non videtur ab Aristotele collocari in hoc tertio genere, quia scientia non dicitur relative, eo quod aliud referatur ad ipsam, sed quia ipsa in se vere habet respectum ad aliud. Aristoteles autem solum ponit in tertio modo ea quae dicuntur relativa, quia alia referuntur ad ipsa.

4. Quod si inquiras, juxta hanc expositionem, ad quod genus relationis pertineat ipsa relatio scientiae ad scibile, et sensus ad sensibile, etc., responderi poterit, illam esse relationem cujusdam effectus ad suam causam in aliquo genere, et ita reduci ad secundum genus, ut statim in simili dicemus, solvendo sextam difficultatem. Vel, si cui placuerit omnem relationem in proportione fundatam ad primum modum revocare, dicere poterit ad illum pertinere relationem scientiae; consistit enim in quadam coaptatione et proportione ad objectum suum.

5. Sed adhuc potest objici, nam juxta hanc interpretationem relatio inter mensuram et mensurabile erit intrinseca et realis in mensura; in mensurabili autem solum erit rationis, aut per denominationem, ad ipsam mensuram, quod est contra communem senten- /p. 836/ tiam, et contra rationem; nam id quod mensuratur est inferius, et sic potius ipsum ordinatur ad mensuram, quam e converso. Quod etiam patet inductione, nam scientia mensuratur a scibili, et ideo in ipsa est relatio, et cognitio mensuratur in veritate ab objecto, et creatura in suo esse seu veritate essendi ab idea divina, et omnes hae relationes sunt in ipsis mensuratis. Respondeo, Aristotelem idem judicium ferre de mensurabili ac de scibili et intelligibili, et de omnibus ait, dici ad aliquid, *quia aliud ad ipsa dicitur.* Videtur autem loqui Aristoteles de mensurabili, per extrinsecam et superadditam mensuram, non per intrinsecam coaptationem vel proportionem, qualis invenitur in exemplis quae in contrarium afferuntur; illa enim intrinseca commensuratio non consistit nisi in quadam similitudine vel coaptatione (ut sic dicam), vel in dependentia aut specificatione, et sic reducitur ad primum vel secundum modum relationum. Sicut etiam imago est commensurata exemplari ratione similitudinis, et effectus causae, ratione dependentiae, vel etiam similitudinis. At vero extrinsece dicitur res mensurabilis, sicut et cognoscibilis, vel visibilis, quia per applicationem extrinsecae mensurae potest ejus quantitas manifestari. Et hoc modo ait Aristoteles rem dici mensurabilem per relationem alterius ad ipsam, quia, nimirum, per mensuram potest ejus quantitas notificari.

6. Nec refert quod mensura sit quasi naturalis, vel ex institutione humana. Quia utroque modo res non est mensurabilis formaliter, nisi per extrinsecam

potentiam et denominationem, quamvis fundamentum, vel proportio quae ad talem mensurabilitatem supponitur, saepe sit quid intrinsecum, et possit esse fundamentum alicujus relationis realis alterius generis. Sicut etiam visibile supponit aliquod fundamentum reale et intrinsecum in objecto visibili, imo et vim activam specierum, ratione cujus refertur realiter ad visum relatione pertinente ad secundum genus. Et in mensuris etiam quantitativis, quae designantur per institutionem humanam, supponitur aliquod fundamentum extensionis et alicujus proportionis realis, quae aliquam veram relationem habet conjunctam, pertinentem tamen ad primum modum, quia non est alia a relatione aequalitatis vel inaequalitatis. Sic ergo rem esse mensurabilem formaliter, solum dicit relationem alterius ad ipsam, quatenus per applicationem mensurae potest no- /col. b/ tificari ejus quantitas, licet fundamentaliter aliquid intrinsecum in ipsa re mensurabili supponatur.

7. Ultimo objici potest, quia ex dicta expositione sequitur quoddam membrum ex illis tribus numeratis ab Aristotele, non continere relationes reales, sed tantum rationis, atque ita sine causa recenseri inter ea quae vere sunt ad aliquid. Sequela patet, quia juxta dictam expositionem, in tertio genere tantum sunt illae relationes quae non conveniunt relativis, eo quod ipsa referantur, sed eo quod alia referantur ad ipsa; illae autem relationes rationis tantum sunt. Respondetur, quidquid sit de his relationibus rationis, an tales sint necessariae in hujusmodi extremis, quod infra videbimus, Aristotelem hic non agere de his relationibus, sed de variis modis, quibus res denominantur relativae ex rebus ipsis. Et ita distinguit duos generales modos, scilicet, quod quaedam denominantur, quia ipsa referuntur; alia vero quia alia referuntur ad ipsa. Et rursus primum membrum distinguit ex duplici fundamento quantitatis, seu unitatis, vel potentiae, et ita constituuntur tres modi relativorum. Atque ita fit ut juxta hanc interpretationem, illi tres modi relativormn non sint tria genera relativorum realium, nam tertius modus non addit novum genus relationis, sed declarat solum specialem modum denominationis, quae ex aliquibus relationibus aliorum generum in terminos earum redundat.

Resolutio.

8. Haec tota sententia et hujus textus interpretatio solum disputationis gratia proposita sit, quoniam in littera Aristotelis simpliciter inspecta, videtur habere non parvum fundamentum, et in ratione stando non improbabiliter defendi posset. Nihilominus tamen nolumus discedere a communi sententia, quae habet, hunc tertium modum relativorum constituere tertium genus relationum realium quae in uno extremo realiter insunt, illudque per se primo referunt ad aliud, quod non iterum refertur per propriam relationem realem quam in se habeat, sed terminat tantum relationem alterius, et inde denominatur. Quod

enim aliquae sint hujusmodi relationes, et inductione constat in scientia et scibili, et similibus, et in sequenti sectione id latius tractabitur. Quod vero hae constituant diversum genus a reliquis, et requirant fundamentum diversae rationis, ex eo videtur /p. 837/ per se probabile, quod habent modum habitudinis valde diversum. Sicut enim ex effectibus cognoscimus causas, ita intelligere possumus fundamentum, ex quo oritur in utroque extremo intrinseca relatio esse diversae rationis ab eo quod in uno tantum extremo relationem fundare potest. Denique appellatum est hoc fundamentum, mensura et mensurabile, quia hae relationes potissimum fundantur in quibusdam rebus quae perfectionem suam habent aliis commensuratam, et ut sic referuntur ad ipsas, etiamsi in eis non sit simile aut proportionale fundamentum correspondentis relationis.

9. Ex quo patet facile solutio ad quintam difficultatem, quia hic non sumitur mensura ut dicit habitudinem ad nostram cognitionem, scilicet, quatenus est medium quo nos uti possumus ad cognoscendam alterius quantitatem, aut molis aut perfectionis; quomodo diximus supra, rationem mensurae non addere rebus aliquam rationem realem. Sed sumitur mensura pro reali termino vel objecto ad quod res aliqua dicit habitudinem, secundum quam illi coaptatur seu commensuratur; quomodo scientia comparatur ad objectum scibile, et judicium ad rem cognitam, et sic de aliis. Quapropter haec commensuratio nihil rei est praeter habitudinem transcendentalem talium rerum ad sua objecta, illa vero est sufficiens fundamentum relationis praedicamentalis. Nec refert quod terminus vel objectum quod dicitur habere rationem mensurae, possit interdum non existere, nam tunc non consurget relatio praedicamentalis; nos autem solum dicimus in tali re esse sufficiens fundamentum peculiaris relationis, quae erit realis, si extrema existant, et reliqua necessaria concurrant.

SECTIO XIV.
Sitne sufficiens dicta divisio, omnesque relationes comprehendat.

1. Haec est secunda principalis dubitatio superius proposita circa hanc divisionem, in qua explicandum est quod in sexta difficultate posita in sectione 10 petebatur, quomodo relationes reales omnes ad hos tres modos reducantur.

De relatione appetitus ad appetibile, et amoris ad amabile.

2. Primum autem omnium inquirebatur, qualis sit relatio appetitus ad appetibile, et /col. b/ amoris ad amabile; Aristoteles enim, quamvis in sensu et intellectu exempla posuerit, de appetitu et amore nihil dixit. At vero D. Thomas, hunc punctum attingens in 1, dist. 30, q. 1, art. 3, ad 3, dicit, diversam esse rationem de relatione scientiae ad scibile, et amoris ad amatum. *Nam* (inquit)

illa est realis in uno extremo tantum; haec vero in utroque. Et reddit rationem, quia illa habet fundamentum in scientia, non in scibili, eo quod illa relatio fundatur in apprehensione rei secundum esse spirituale, quod habet in sciente, non in re scita; relatio vero amoris fundatur super appetitum boni; bonum autem non est tantum in anima, sed etiam in rebus, 7 Metaph., text. 8, atque ita, haec relatio habet fundamentum reale in utroque extremo, ideoque relatio etiam in utroque realis est. In qua sententia secutus est D. Thomas Avicennam, lib. 3 suae Metaph., c. 10.

3. Non explicat autem D. Thomas in quo ex membris positis ab Aristotele ponendum sit hoc fundamentum relationis amoris ad objectum suum, et e converso. Nam in hoc tertio genere collocari non potest, quoniam de toto illo in universum ait Aristoteles, relationem ejus solum esse in uno extremo, alterum vero relative dici solum quia aliud refertur ad ipsum. Neque etiam pertinere poterit ad secundum genus, quia objectum non comparatur ad amorem vel ad appetitum, ut potentia passiva, neque ut effectus alicujus actionis, sed solum ut objectum seu materia circa quam, in quo convenit cum objecto scibili et sensibili. Unde forte dicetur reduci ad primum modum, quia amor fundatur in aliqua convenientia et proportione. Verumtamen, ut supra dicebam tractando de potentia activa et passiva, non est ille modus convenientiae vel unitatis, qui fundat primum genus relationum. Et deinde idem modus proportionis invenitur inter scientiam aut sensum et objectum, imo tanto major, quanto cognitio per assimilationem quamdam fieri dicitur.

4. Ac praeterea non apparet cur scientia aut sensus dicantur mensurari ex objecto, et non etiam amor, quia non minus perfectio amoris mensuratur ex objecto, imo quodammodo majori ratione, quia amor tendit ad res prout sunt in se. Nec satis est dicere fundamentum hujus tertii generis esse mensuram veritatis, quia hoc non est fundamentum adaequatum, nam in sensu non est formalis veritas cognitionis, nec intellectus /p. 838/ ipse, quatenus est potentia, mensuratur quoad veritatem ab objecto intelligibili, sed quoad perfectionem entitativam. Deinde si mensura veritatis est sufficiens fundamentum relationis, cur non mensura honestatis, vel bonitatis amoris? Itaque non video sufficientem rationem, cur relatio amoris non sit in hoc tertio genere constituenda; neque cur negandum sit, secundum hoc genus fundamenti et relationis, esse inter omnia ea quae habent habitudinem ad objecta, et ab eis specificantur, specialem convenientiam ratione cujus constituant unum genus subalternum relationum, supposito quod de quibusdam, scilicet, de sensu, intellectu et scientia id affirmatur.

5. De relatione autem amabilis seu amati, quamvis probabilis sit sententia Avicennae, tamen opposita videtur conformior doctrinae Aristotelis. Primo, quia vel oportebit relationem amoris excludere ab hoc tertio genere, quod est

contra dicta, vel in eo admittere relationes mutuas, quod est contra Aristotelem. Secundo, quia differentia constituta inter scientiam et amorem non satisfacit; nam si objectum scibile et amabile comparentur quoad fundamenta (ut sic dicam), utrumque est aliquid intrinsecum et reale in ipso objecto; nam sicut res est in se bona, ita etiam, est vera secundum esse, et apta ut intelligatur; nam hoc modo dixit Aristoteles, 2 Metaph., text. 4: *Unumquodque ita est verum et intelligibile, sicut est ens.* Et 9 Met., c. 7, dixit actum esse magis agnoscibilem, quam potentiam; haec enim non possunt esse vera nisi de intelligibilitate, quatenus in rebus ipsis fundatur. Quod si interdum ratio attingendi objectum scibile potest esse extrinseca, etiam ratio amandi saepe est extrinseca ipsi objecto, ut patet in amore medii propter finem extrinsecum; ergo quoad haec est eadem proportio. Si vero sermo sit de scibili et appetibili, aut de scito et amato formaliter quatenus talia sunt, utrumque completur per extrinsecam denominationem a potentia vel actu, quod facile constare potest ex iis quae supra diximus de bonitate, disputatione decima. Denique si consideremus transcendentales habitudines, neutrum objectum secundum id quod realiter est, dicit habitudinem transcendentalem ad potentias vel actus intelligendi aut amandi, sed solum e converso potentiae vel actus dicunt habitudines ad objecta; est ergo de illis eadem proportione loquendum; sicut ergo /col. b/ scibile non dicitur referri nisi quia aliud refertur ad ipsum, ita neque amabile.

An inter omnem effectum et causam relatio mensurae intercedat.

6. Juxta hanc ergo sententiam, quae probabilior apparet, dicendum est ad sextam difficultatem, relationes illas pertinentes ad actus, habitus et potentias appetendi respectu objectorum pertinere ad hoc tertium genus, quod non tantum in mensura veritatis, sed etiam perfectionis, seu in commensuratione et proportione alicujus rei ad objectum fundari potest. Ad replicam autem, quae ibi fit, quia omnes effectus possent in hoc genere collocari, quatenus per sua principia vel causas mensurari possunt, primo responderi potest concedendo sequelam, si praecise in eis consideretur ratio mensurae et mensurati, etiamsi alioqui referantur relatione dependentiae pertinente ad secundum genus, aut similitudinis pertinente ad primum. Quia non est inconveniens, inter duas res sub diversis rationibus diversas relationes consurgere, quod praesertim de relatione exemplati ad exemplar omnes videntur fateri. Verumtamen, quia praeter dependentiam effectus a causa, aut similitudinem inter illa, existimo rationem, mensurae non addere aliquam rationem realem, sed denominationem ex ordine ad cognitionem, ideo non opinor posse ibi intervenire specialem relationem realem distinctam ab illa quae fundatur in causalitate, vel dependentia, vel in similitudine. Et ideo respondetur secundo negando sequelam, quia in hoc tertio genere solum collocantur relationes quarumdam rerum, quae habent

peculiarem modum specificationis ex tendentia, et quasi commensuratione ad aliud ut ad objectum, vel terminum, vel intrinsecum finem ad quem per se primo et intrinsece ordinantur, ut sunt potentiae, habitus, actus, et similia. Illa enim terminatio objectiva ut sic non est propria aliqua similitudo, ut per se constat, neque etiam est propria causalitas, ut supra attigimus, disp. 12, sect. 3, num. 17, et ideo relationes, quae in hac commensuratione ad objectum fundantur, non pertinent ad secundum genus relationum; neque e converso commensuratio vel proportio, quae est inter causam efficientem ut sic ad suum effectum, pertinet ad hunc tertium modum, quia illa vel est sola causalitas seu dependentia effectiva, vel est /p. 839/ tantum similitudo, quae inter causam et effectum intervenire potest.

De relatione unionis.

7. Ad alteram partem illius difficultatis de relatione unionis, et similibus, duobus modis responderi potest. Primo, hanc relationem et similes pertinere ad primum genus horum relativorum, nam unio revera est aliqua unitas, vel est quasi via ad unitatem; imo ipsa identitas specifica vel generica, est etiam veluti unio quaedam plurium in eadem essentia seu ratione formali; ergo multo magis propria et realis unio inter extrema realia, et distincta in re, poterit fundare relationem ad aliud genus pertinentem. Quapropter, licet unitas numerica alicujus rei simplicis respectu suiipsius, vel compositae etiam respectu totius compositi, non possit fundare relationem realem, tamen unitas numerica totius compositi, quatenus in eo uniuntur partes alioqui realiter distinctae, est sufficiens fundamentum relationis realis ad idem genus pertinentis. Atque eadem ratione relatio contactus ad idem genus spectat, et relatio etiam propinquitatis, quia est veluti quaedam similitudo imperfecta in loco; sicut etiam coexistentia ad illud genus pertinet, quia est similitudo quaedam in existendo, et idem est in similibus. Et juxta hunc dicendi modum, relationes causarum ita distribui possunt, ut sola relatio efficientis causae ad secundum genus spectet; relatio vero causae materialis et formalis pertineant ad primum, quia proxima ratio fundandi illas est unio, quia illae causae non causant nisi media unione, ut suis locis vidimus; relatio vero causae finalis ad tertium genus pertinet, eo quod ex speciali ratione sua sit relatio non mutua, ut supra probabiliter diximus, disput. 23, et quia non causat nisi quatenus est ratio ut effectus ordinetur ad ipsam, eique commensuretur.

8. Vel secundo dici posset omnes relationes causarum pertinere ad secundum modum, nam, licet Aristoteles illum praesertim explicuerit in potentia et causalitate activa, quae notior est, tamen, servata proportione, applicari potest ad singulas causas, quatenus in unaquaque est aptitudo ad suum effectum, et propria causalitas, qua suo modo influit in effectum, et effectus pendet ab

ipsa. Et quantum ad causam materialem, videtur haec sententia consentanea Aristoteli, qui in illo genere ponit relationem potentiae passivae, cujus causalitas materialis est. Eadem autem /col. b/ ratio esse videtur de relatione potentiae informativae (ut sic dicam) et de causalitate ejus, et de relatione in ea fundata. Et consequenter idem etiam erit de relatione effectuum ad has causas; idemque dici poterit de relatione effectus causae finalis ut sic ad causam suam, nam ex parte causae probabilis existimo illam relationem non esse realem, ut dixi. Et juxta hunc respondendi modum, relatio unionis, quae supponit causalitatem vel aliquam imitationem ejus, reduceretur ad secundum genus relationum; aliae vero relationes propinquitatis, coexistentiae, et similes, ad primum genus sine dubio pertinent. Nulla ergo (ut opinor) inveniri poterit relatio, quae ad haec genera non facile reducatur.

SECTIO XV.

Utrum relationes tertii generis sint non mutuae, et in hoc differant a relationibus aliorum generum.

1. Duobus modis possunt relationes dici non mutuae: primo, secundum specificas rationes relationum; secundo in suprema et generalissima. Priori modo dicetur relatio non mutua, quae non est ejusdem rationis specificae in utroque extremo; posteriori autem modo dicetur non mutua, quae in uno extremo est vera et realis relatio, non vero in alio. Prior significatio inusitata est et impropria; nam si utrumque extremum per propriam suam relationem refertur ad alterum, vere ac proprie referuntur mutuo, etiamsi relationibus diversarum rationum referantur. Unde haec relativa potius vocantur diversaram rationum, vel, ut alii loquuntur, relativa disquiparantiae.

Divisio relationum ejusdem vel dissimilis rationis.

2. Sicque relationes mutuae distingui solent in relationes aequiparantiae et disquiparantiae. Nam relationes omnes secundi generis, disquiparantiae sunt, quia ratio fundandi est aliquo modo diversa in extremis, nam in altero est potentia activa, in alia vero potentia passiva seu dependentia a sua causa, ex quo etiam fit ut termini talium relationum sint diversarum rationum, nam illi proportionate respondent fundamentis, ut superius tactum est, et infra latius dicetur. Relationes vero primi generis interdum sunt ejusdem, interdum diversarum rationum in utroque extremo; relationes enim unitatis, aequipa- /p. 840/ rantiae sunt, ut recte notavit Alexander Alensis, lib. 5 Metaphys., text. 20, et patet de relatione aequalitatis, similitudinis, identitatis; relationes vero fundatae in numero seu diversitate secundum proprias et specificas rationes sunt disquiparantiae, ut patet de duplo et subduplo, et aliis proportionibus,

quae in uno extremo dicunt excessum, in alio defectum. Dico autem, *secundum proprias et specificas rationes*, quia in generica ratione convenire possunt, et secundum eam similiter dici de utroque extremo; sic enim utrumque extremum, tam majus quam minus, dicitur inaequale alteri. Et similiter albedo dicitur dissimilis nigredini, et e converso, cum tamen verisimile sit proprias relationes secundum specificas rationes earum esse distinctas, quia et fundamentum et terminus longe diversa sunt in una quam in alia. At vero relationes tertii generis plus quam disquiparantiae censentur, eo quod aequiparantia vel disquiparantia dicatur proprie inter extrema realia; in hoc autem tertio genere non censet Aristoteles esse in utroque extremo relationem realem, et ideo non mutuae dicuntur.

Proponitur difficultas circa relationes non mutuas.

3. De his ergo relationibus non mutuis proprie sumptis intelligitur praesens quaestio, in qua duplici ex capite difficilis est sententia Aristotelis. Primum est, quia non videtur verum relationes tertii generis esse non mutuas, nam si in aliquibus verum esset, maxime in scibili et sensibili; at in his tam est vera relatio realis, sicut in scientia et sensu; ergo. Probatur minor, quia denominatio scibilis et sensibilis, relativa est; imo, et per se ad aliquid, ut Aristoteles ipse in eodem loco fatetur, et patet ex reciprocatione, quia sicut scientia est scibilis scientia, ita scibile est scientia scibile; haec autem reciprocatio et correlativa denominatio non est per intellectum conficta, sed ex rebus ipsis orta; ergo in utroque extremo est a propria forma et relatione reali.

4. Secundo, quia si ob aliquam causam haec relatio non est realis in objecto scibili, aut est quia in ipso objecto non est fundamentum reale, aut quia esse scitum in tali objecto non est aliquid in ipso, nec scitur per sui mutationem, sed per denominationem e forma existente in alio; nam praeter has nulla alia probabilis ratio occurrit. Neutra /col. b/ autem ex his satisfacit. Prima enim falsum sumit, nam quod objectum sit intelligibile, aut sensibile, habet fundamentum in ipsis rebus, et in realibus proprietatibus earum; lux enim visibilis est, quia est talis naturie secundum quam habet vim sic immutandi potentiam; et res immaterialis, quia spiritualis est, dicitur actu intelligibilis. Secunda vero ratio male colligit, alias etiam relatio agentis in actu non esset realis in ipso, quia sine sui mutatione fit agens actu, et sine additione alicuius formae absolutae, quae in ipso sit. Quod si dicas ipsam potentiam agendi esse intrinsecam, licet conditio quae est actio, sit extrinseca, idem dici poterit de objecto, nam aptitudo ut sciatur est intrinseca, et illa potest esse fundamentum, quamvis conditio, quae est actu sciri, sit quid extrinsecum. Eo vel maxime quod ipse actus sciendi aut sentiendi habet realem dependentiam ab objecto, sicut actio ab agente, quamvis non in eodem genere causae. Dices, objectum quatenus de

se est aptum sciri aut videri, non habere habitudinem ad scientiam. Sed si hoc intelligatur de habitudine relativa praedicamentali, petitur principium, nam hujus rei rationem inquirimus. Si vero intelligatur de habitudine transcendentali, jam supra ostensum est hanc non semper esse necessario praerequisitam ad relationem praedicamentalem; nam etiam in agente principium agendi non semper habet transcendentalem habitudinem ad effectum, ut patet ex iis quae supra de potentia et actu tractavimus.

5. Tertio est praecipua difficultas, quia terminus relationis est altera relatio existens in alio extremo; ergo impossibile est relationem esse realem in uno extremo, et non in alio. Patet consequentia, quia non potest relatio esse realis sine formali termino reali. Antecedens vero patet, quia relationes dicuntur[6] esse simul natura, definitione et cognitione, quia nimirum unum est terminus alterius.

6. Ex secundo vero capite oriuntur non minores difficultates: nam si relationes non mutuae admittendse sunt, non tantum in tertio, sed et in aliis generibus invenientur. Antecedens patet, nam imprimis relatio, quae est inter Deum et creaturam in ratione causae efficientis et effectus, est secundi generis, et tamen est non mutua, juxta sententiam magis receptam a Theologis. Similiter in primo genere reperiuntur multae relationes inter Deum et creaturas, ut relatio distinctionis /p. 841/ realis, vel similitudinis in esse, aut in ratione substantiae, aut intellectuali gradu; nam, licet sit analoga similitudo, vera tamen et realis est, et sufficiens ad fundandam relationem realem, ut supra dixi. Et tamen talis relatio, licet in creatura sit realis, in Deo esse non potest. Item sumi potest argumentum de relatione unionis inter Verbum et humanitatem, quae est non mutua, et tamen pertinet ad primum vel secundum modum. Praeterea inter creaturas est peculiaris difficultas de relatione inter causam finalem et effectum, quam diximus esse non mutuam, et tamen pertinet ad secundum genus. Denique relatio dextri et sinistri inter hominem et columnam censetur non mutua, ex sententia omnium, et tamen non pertinet ad tertium genus: nulla enim ratio mensurae ibi intervenit.

7. Propter haec ergo et similia, Greg., in 1, d. 18, quaest. 1, sentit nullas esse relationes non mutuas, quem sequuntur aliqui Nominales.

Assertiones de relationibus non mutuis.

8. Duo nihilominus breviter dicenda sunt. Primum est, aliquas esse relationes non mutuas, id est, reales in uno extremo, et non in alio. Haec est sententia Aristotelis hoc loco, quam omnes expositores admittunt, et fere Theologi, praesertim D. Thom., 1 p., q. 13, a. 17, et alii statim citandi. Estque sententia

---

6 Vivès reads: "discuntur."

tanta consensione recepta, ut non liceat philosophis eam in dubium revocare. Ratio autem ejus constabit ex sequenti assertione, et magis ex solutionibus difficultatum. Secundum dictum est, has relationes non mutuas per se et quasi ex propria ratione sui fundamenti inveniri in tertio genere, in aliis vero minime, nisi veluti materialiter ex peculiari conditione alicuius subjecti seu extremi. Ita censeo esse interpretandam Aristotelis sententiam. Et ratio prioris partis sumenda est ex peculiari modo specificationis et commensurationis quam habent potentia, habitus, et res similes, ad objecta sua. Nam formaliter solum consistit; in habitudine quam ex natura sua habent ad objecta, secundum quam ei commensurantur; objectum vero in hoc nullam habet propriam causalitatem, sed rationem termini specificantis. Nam, licet alioqui possit esse movens aut active, aut finaliter, tamen ut extremum hujus relationis, sub nulla harum rationum consideratur, sed solum est id cui talis res commensuratur. /col. b/ Sub hac autem ratione ipsum non concurrit, ut ordinabile ad aliud, sed solum ut id ad quod aliud ordinatur; et ideo ex vi talis rationis fundandi non oritur relatio in utroque extremo, sed in solo illo quod alteri commensuratur. Hac ergo de causa relationes tertii generis ex propria ratione formali sui fundamenti non mutuae sunt. In aliis vero hoc non reperitur, ut ex dictis constat, quia frequentius ac fere semper relationes illorum generum mutuae sunt. Quod si aliquando sunt non mutuae, id solum est ob peculiarem naturam vel conditionem alicujus rei, ut ex solutionibus argumentorum clarius patebit.

An in relativis non mutuis utrumque extremum realiter referatur.
9. Ad argumenta ergo in primo capite proposita, quae contra priorem assertionem, et contra primam partem secundae assertionis procedunt, respondendum est. Et quidem ad primum respondet Cajet., 1 p., q. 13, art. 7, concedendo, etiam in relativis non mutuis utrumque correlativum esse reale, et scibile, verbi gratia, referri realiter ad scientiam. Differentiam tamen inter haec et relativa mutua ponit in hoc, quod in mutuis utrumque refertur per intrinsecam relationem, non mutua vero, non ita, sed alterum extremum refertur realiter per relationem existentem in alio, et extrinsece denominantem alterum. Quae responsio videtur habere fundamentum in Aristotele, tum quia inter ea, quae sunt simpliciter ad aliquid, numerat scibile ut refertur ad scientiam, et sensibile ut refertur ad sensum; non sunt autem ad aliquid simpliciter, nisi quae realiter referuntur, ut supra diximus; ergo haec etiam sunt relativa realia ex sententia Aristotelis. Tum etiam quia inferius, in eodem capite, dicit haec esse ad aliquid, quia alia ad ipsa dicuntur, ubi non ait haec esse ad aliquid, quia ratio id fingit aut considerat, sed quia alia ad ipsa dicuntur, quod in re ipsa invenitur. Tum praeterea quia paulo inferius ait, haec omnia per seipsa ad aliquid dici, complectens tria genera superioribus sectionibus tractata; quae

autem sola ratione referuntur, non per seipsa, sed per rationem referuntur. Tandem quia metaphysicus non considerat respectus rationis; sed illa tria genera per se pertinent ad praedicamentum ad aliquid, teste Aristotele, et per se etiam cadunt sub metaphysicam considerationem; ergo. Et hanc sententiam /p. 842/ ante Cajet. videtur docuisse Greg., in 4, d. 23, q. 3.

10. Sed haec responsio Cajetani singularis est, et contradicit D. Thom., 2 cont. Gent:, c. 13, ubi ex professo probat, relationes Dei ad creaturas non esse res aliquas extra Deum existentes, a quibus extrinsece denominetur relative. Cum autem inter Deum et Creaturas sit relatio non mutua, si vera esset Cajetani sententia, etiam Deus referretur realiter ad creaturas, non quidem per relationem realem in ipso Deo existentem, sed per relationem existentem in creatura. Unde in ratione secunda expresse sumit D. Thomas, principium contrarium interpretationi Cajetani, scilicet, *a relatione non denominari aliud quasi exterius existente, sed inhaerente.* Ubi bene Ferrariensis interpretatur, id intelligendum esse de denominatione respectiva, qua dicitur aliquid referri ad aliud, nam alio genere denominationis non est inconveniens aliquid denominari relatione extrinseca, ut postea dicemus.

11. Praeterea, si scibile refertur realiter ad scientiam per relationem existentem in scientia, interrogo an hoc intelligendum sit de relatione, qua ipsamet scientia refertur ad scibile, vel de aliqua alia relatione distincta. Primum dici non potest, quia una et eadem relatio non potest dare diversis subjectis donominationes diversarum rationum, quales sunt scientiae et scibilis; nec potest referre eas ad oppositos terminos formales; alias pari ratione eadem filiatio existens in filio posset filium denominare intrinsece et referre ad patrem, et patrem ipsum extrinsece denominare patrem, et referre illum ad filium. Denique una forma specie unum habet formalem effectum; sed relatio est forma, cujus effectus formalis est referre unum ad aliud; ergo una et eadem relatio non potest habere duos modos referendi diversarum rationum. Neque etiam dici potest secundum, nempe esse in scientia duas relationes reales distinctas, aliam, qua ipsa scientia refertur ad scibile, aliam, qua refert scibile ad se; hoc enim a nemine hactenus dictum est, et non habet fundamentum in Aristotele, sed potius ei repugnat; dicit enim scibile dici ex eo quod scientia refertur ad ipsum; non ergo agnoscit inter haec aliam relationem realem, nisi qua scientia refertur ad scibile. Nec etiam est consonum rationi, quia illa pluralitas relationum neque est necessaria, neque habet fundamentum in ipsa scientia, cum in /col. b/ ea tantum sit unica coaptatio et habitudo transcendentalis ad scibile.

12. Dici potest esse duas relationes solum ratione distinctas; haec enim multiplicatio cum non sit rerum, nec proprie in re, facile admitti potest, et sufficit ad praedictas denominationes respectivas etiam diversarum rationum; sicut idem modus seu eadem dependentia propter solam distinctionem rationis

inter actionem et passionem tribuit denominationes diversas agentis et patientis, unam intrinsece, et aliam extrinsece. Verumtamen neque haec distinctio relationum admitti debet in praesenti, nam etiam ad hujusmodi distinctionem rationis oportet esse aliquod fundamentum in re, quod in praesenti nullum est. Unde non est simile exemplum de actione et passione, nam in mutatione est vera et transcendentalis habitudo ad principium, a quo manat, et ad passum, quod immutat, et ideo est in ea magnum fundamentum ad distinguendum ratione actionem et passionem, ad modum duarum formarum accidentalium; Accedit universalis ratio, in qua fundatur illud principium D. Thomae, quod relatio non denominat extrinsece, quia nimirum cum denominatio ejus sit per habitudinem ad aliud, repugnat formam sic denominantem esse in eo ad quod est habitudo; quod si in eo non est, oportet ut sit in eo quod refertur, quia in relatione non concurrunt per se alia extrema. Denique vix potest mente concipi quidnam sit in scientia, ratione cujus faciat scibile ad se realiter referri, cum tota ratio scientiae sit versari circa scibile, et inde non habeat, per se loquendo, illud ad se ordinare.

Solvitur prima difficultas in principio proposita.

13. Ad primum ergo argumentum in principio positum dicendum est, scibile dupliciter posse denominari: primo, mere terminative et quasi passive; secundo, correlative ad scientiam. Primo modo denominatur extrinsece ab ipsamet scientia reali, atque ita talis denominatio dici potest esse in rebus ipsis, et non esse per intellectum conficta. Imo haec ipsa denominatio non sumitur solum ex relatione praedicamentali, quae est in scientia, sed etiam ex ipsamet forma absoluta, ut includente transcendentalem habitudinem ad objectum; quod satis insinuavit Aristoteles /p. 843/ cum dixit, intelligibile dici eo quod in eo versetur intellectus; versatur enim non per solam relationem praedicamentalem, sed per proprium actum ad quem consequitur relatio. Secunda denominatio scibilis est respectiva, et haec solum est per relationem rationis, quia mens nostra ad explicandam illam relationem, quam scientia habet ad ipsum scibile, concipit illud ut correlativum scientiae. Argumentum ergo solum procedit de priori denominatione. Cum autem Aristoteles, scibile, sensibile et similia ponit inter ea quae sunt ad aliquid, primo exponi potest, quod per haec non intelligat tantum haec extrema, sed relationem intervenientem inter haec, et sua correlativa, in quocumque eorum sit illa relatio; vel secundo dici potest, ponere haec extrema inter ea quae sunt ad aliquid, quatenus hujusmodi denominationes habent a quibusdam relationibus realibus. Et eodem sensu intelligi potest quod ait, haec esse ad aliquid, quia alia referuntur ad ipsa; esse (inquam) ad aliquid, non tanquam correlativa, sed tanquam termini passive denominati ab his relationibus. Et simili modo dicentur haec esse per se ad

aliquid tanquam termini per se connexi cum relationibus realibus, a quibus tales denominationes recipiunt. Vel aliter etiam dici potest, cum ait Aristoteles haec dici ad aliquid, quia alia dicuntur ad ipsa, intelligi causaliter, nam si scibile, sensibile, et similia, correlative sumantur et concipiantur a nobis, ideo est quia alia referuntur ad ipsa, non quia ipsa vere ac realiter referantur. Sed dicit Gregorius eamdem interpretationem habere locum, etiamsi relatio scibilis sit realis, quia ei non convenit, nisi quia scientia versatur circa illud; sed hoc non recte dicitur, quia si fundamentum illius relationis est tantum habitudo alterius, scilicet scientiae ad scibile, non potest relatio in ea fundata esse realis.

14. Ad secundum argumentum respondetur, causam, ob quam haec relatio non mutua in altero extremo non est realis in hoc tertio genere, esse quia in uno extremo, verbi gratia, in objecto scibili non est fundamentum reale talis relationis. Neque satis est quod in ipsa re intelligibili aut sensibili sit aliquod fundamentum, ob quod apta sit intelligi aut sentiri, quia illud fundamentum praecise consideratum in ratione mensurae, non accipitur ut aliquid ordinabile ad aliud, sed solum ut terminus vel objectum cui aliquid commensuratur; et ideo dicitur in illo non esse fundamentum relationis, non quia /col. b/ nihil rei sit in ipso, sed quia in illa re nulla est ratio fundandi relationem, quod requiritur ad fundamentum relationis, formaliter de illo loquendo, prout explicatum est supra, sect. 7. Tertium argumentum petit difficultatem gravem de termino relationis, quam tractabimus sectione sequenti.

Circa secundam difficultatem tractatur de relationibus Dei ad creaturas.

15. In secunda parte argumentorum petitur imprimis difficultas, an inter creaturam ad Deum sit semper relatio non mutua, etiamsi ad primum et secundum genus relationum pertinere videantur. Quae est quaestio Theologica, et aliis verbis proponi solet, an nomina, quae Deo tribuntur ex tempore per relationem ad creaturam, dicant in Deo relationem realem, vel rationis tantum. Aliqua enim nomina, quae videntur importare relationem ad creaturam, dicuntur de Deo ex aeternitate, quae interdum dicuntur importare respectum liberum, interdum vero simpliciter necessarium, seu naturalem; ut scientia, potentia, et similes, dicunt respectum naturalem et necessarium; praedestinatio autem, providentia, et scientia visionis dicunt respectum liberum seu non naturalem, quia, absolute loquendo, possent Deo non convenire. Et de his relationibus non dubium est quin non sint reales in Deo, quia ex aeternitate non habent reales terminos. Verum est aliquos Theologos existimare, respectum scientiae et potentiae, etiam in Deo, esse reales transcendentales, ideoque posse esse independentes ab existentia termini, et non esse variabiles, neque accidentales, sed de intrinseca substantia Dei. Verius tamen existimo (quod alibi latius tractandam est) haec non dicere in Deo verum respectum transcendentalem, sed tantum

secundum dici, significari ad modum rerum respectivarum, eo quod a nobis concipiantur ad modum earum rerum quae similes respectus transcendentales includunt. Alioqui enim Deus, quantum ad essentiam suam, est res omnino absoluta, cumque ejus scientia et potentia sit ipsamet essentia ejus, absolutae etiam sunt ab omni respectu transcendentali, quod etiam, supra tetigimus inter explicanda altributa Dei. Et rationem etiam reddidimus, quia potentia Dei non est talis, ut sit per se primo ordinata ad opus extra se, sed eam efficacitatem habet quasi concomitanter, secundum rationem loquendo, et absque ulla ordinatione. Et simi- /p. 844/ liter scientia Dei et voluntas per se primo non versantur nisi circa suam essentiam, inde vero consequenter attingunt vel attingere possunt reliqua sine trancendentali respectu. Sunt ergo hi respectus aut secundum dici tantum; aut, si concipiantur ut relationes secundum esse, sunt tantum relationes rationis, saltem quamdiu termini in re non existunt. Neque de his procedit argumentum supra propositum, sed de quibusdam respectibus qui includunt coexistentiam termini, qui propterea conveniunt Deo ex tempore, quia creaturae, quae sunt termini talium respectuum, non existunt nisi ex tempore, ut sunt relationes creatoris, domini, et similes.

Opinio Nominalium de relationibus realibus Dei ex tempore.

16. De his ergo multi Theologi existimant esse relationes reales. Ita tenet Ocham, in 1, d. 30; et ibi Gabr., quaest. 5; Durand., q. 3; Gregor., dist. 28, q. 3, art. 4; Marsil., in 1, q. 32, art. 1. Fundamentum horum auctorum est, quia relatio realis nihil rei addit subjecto seu alteri rei quae per eam referri dicitur, sed vel est denominatio ex concomitantia extremorum, vel est ipsamet res absoluta quae, coexistente alia, per seipsam illam respicit, propter aliquod vinculum, vel aliquam connexionem inter eas inventam. Unde fit ut relatio realis possit absque ulla imperfectione advenire alicui de novo, quia advenit sine additione ulla reali et intrinseca, et sine compositione, et consequenter etiam sine ulla dependentia in aliqua re extrinseca, sed ad summum in tali modo denominationis; solum autem hae imperfectiones possunt hic excogitari; ergo excluditur omnis imperfectio; et alioqui in Deo concurrunt omnia necessaria ad relationem; nam est vera causa efficiens creaturae, et habet veram potentiam et actionem circa illam; ergo, posito altero extremo, erit in Deo vera relatio realis. Favetque huic sententiae communis modus denominandi Deum ex his relationibus; tam enim vere ac realiter est effector aut creator creaturae, sicut unus homo est pater alterius, et idem est de relatione distincti, similis, etc.; ergo vel omnes istae relationes sunt in Deo reales, aut nullum est fundamentum ad admittendas relationes reales in creataris. Favet denique huic sententim D. Anselmus, in Monolog., cap. 24, ubi cum dixisset Deo nihil posse accidere, quia est invariabilís, objicit sibi: *Quomodo non est par-* /col. b/ *ticeps accidentis, cum*

et hoc ipsum quod maior est omnibus aliis naturis, et quod illis dissimilis est, illi videatur accidere? Et respondet: *Sed quid repugnant quorumdam quae accidentia dicuntur, susceptibilitas, et naturalis incommutabilitas, si ex eorum assumptione nulla substantiae consequitur variabilitas?* Et subdit inferius hujusmodi esse relationes. Et ne existimetur loqui de relationibus rationis, exemplum addit in relationibus creatis. *Nam ego* (inquit) *nec major, vel minor, nec aequalis vel similis sum homini post annum nascituro; omnes autem relationes has illo nato habere potero sine omni mei mutatione.* Addit vero inferius, haec quae sine mutatione rei accidere dicuntur, improprie dici accidentia, et ideo simpliciter verum esse, Deo nullum accidens de novo advenire.

Contraria sententia probatur.

17. Nihilominus tamen plures et graviores Theologi negant hujusmodi nomina significare in Deo relationes reales ad creaturas, quae ex tempore ei conveniunt. Haec est sententia D. Thomae, 1 p., q. 13, art. 7, et 2 cont. Gent., cap. 12; et idem docent his locis Cajet. et Ferrar., et reliqui Thomistae; Capreolus, in 1, d. 30, q. 1, art. 1, concl. 3, et art. 2, concl. 2 et 3, et ibidem Hispalens., art. 1; Bonav., art. 1, quaest. 3; Richard., art, 1, q. 4; Scotus, q. 1; Aegid., quaest. 2; Henric., Quodlib. 9, quaest. 1; et Alens., 1 p., q. 35; et in eadem sententia videtur esse Magister, in illa distinctione trigesima. Et sunt qui existiment hanc sententiam tam certam esse, ut altera repugnet sacrae doctrinae. Verumtamen aliud est loqui supponendo relationem esse rem vel modum ex natura rei distinctum a fundamento, seu subjecto relato, et consequenter ei de novo additum, quando de novo refertur, seu relative denominari incipit; aliud vero est loqui de relatione, supponendo non esse aliquid distinctum a rebus absolutis. Facta priori suppositione, sine dubio esset absurdissimum, ac fere erroneum dicere, resultare in Deo relationes reales ad creaturas ex tempore, quando creaturae producantur, vel amitti, cum creaturae mutantur. Quia juxta hujusmodi sententiam et ponitur in Deo verum accidens, quia modus ex natura rei distinctus a substantia, qui potest inesse illi, et abesse, accidens est; et consequenter necesse est ponere in Deo compositionem ex substantia et tali modo distincto, ac denique mutationem et potentialitatem, ac similia. /p. 845/

18. Neque enim dici potest talem relationem esse realem, et non esse in creatura, et referre realiter ipsum Deum ad creaturam, et nihilominus non inesse Deo, sed assistere illi, ut Gilbert. Porret. cogitavit, ut Alensis et alii referunt. Refutatur enim hoc facile, nam si illa relatio realis est, in aliquo subjecto esse necesse est; cum ergo non sit in creatura, erit in Deo. Nisi quis fingat esse subsistentem, quod dici non potest, alias sequitur esse quamdam substantiam creatam assistentem Deo ex tempore, cum, sit relatio temporalis et consequenter

creata; at illud est plane falsum et inintelligibile; quomodo enim talis substantia referre posset Deum? Item etiam ad illam substantiam esset alia relatio in Deo, quia esset factor ejus, et sic procederetur in infinitum. Quod si dicatur illam relationem esse subsistentem, non tamen alia subsistentia nisi divina, interrogabo an in ea sit per unionem hypostaticam: quod dicere tam absurdum esset, ut impugnandum non sit; vel per identitatem: et tunc rursus quaeram an id sit per omnimodam identitatem, quae excludat etiam distinctionem modalem, et sic receditur ab hypothesi quam praemisimus, quod, nimirum, omnis relatio, realis de novo adveniens sit modus distinctus. Si vero sit sermo de identitate reali cum distinctione modali, inciditur in omnia inconvenientia illata, et non evitatur quin talis relatio insit Deo non per inhaerentiam distinctam, sed per seipsam, sicut etiam in substantiis creatis modi accidentales ipsas afficiunt, eisque inhaerent.

19. Verumtamen tota certitudo hujus sententiae in hoc sensu magis est conditionata, seu consequentiae, quam consequentis, videlicet quod si relatio realis sit, qualis in ea sententia supponitur, non potest esse in Deo; quia vero antecedens illud incertum est et fortasse falsum, ideo non satis est ut illa conclusio sit certa, prout absolute negat relationes reales Dei ad creaturas. Neque auctores primae sententiae in eo sensu locuti sunt, nec praedictam suppositionem admittunt.

20. Si vero supponamus has relationes non esse aliquid rei actu distinctum ab omnibus absolutis, nec potest esse certum has relationes non posse tribui Deo, nec est quaestio magni momenti, sed fere de modo loquendi. Et sane qui putant has denominationes relativas, quae possunt de novo advenire per solam mutationem alterius extremi sine ulla mutatione ejus rei quae referri dicitur, esse /col. b/ tantum denominationes extrinsecas ex coexistentia extremorum, satis consequenter loquuntur tribuendo has relationes Deo, quia nullum inconveniens Deum ex tempore denominari ab aliqua forma reali existente in creatura, ut patet in actione creativa, et in aliis quas Deus ad extra operatur. Et certe D. Anselmus, citato loco, in hanc sententiam multum propendere videtur, quanquam in fine capitis modum illum loquendi ut incertum praetermittat. Nihilominus tamen eam sententiam supra reliquimus ut minus probabilem, minusque consentaneam Aristoteli; quod nunc ex eo confirmare possumus, quod juxta illam nullae erunt relationes non mutuae; falsumque erit quod Aristoteles ait, quaedam dici relative, quia alia referuntur ad ipsa, alia vero quia ipsa in se habent unde referantur.

21. Ulterius vero etiam supponendo relationem esse quid intrinsecum, non tamen quid distinctum in re, et consequenter nec mutationem nec compositionem faciens, non sequuntur inconvenientia prius illata, etiamsi dicatur Deus ex tempore referri ad creaturas, et ideo illa opinio in eo sensu non est digna

aliqua censura. Unde etiam inter Thomistas, Soncinas, 5 Metaph., quaest, 25, ad 4, admittit, relationem dominii, quam Deus habet ad creaturas, esse realem, quia fundatur in vera potentia reali; quod etiam ex parte opinatur Hervaeus, 1, dist. 30, quaest. unica, art. 3, licet in modo loquendi conetur sese accommodare communi sententiae, quod difficile explicat; nec id est mirum, quia revera non est facile rationem reddere cur hoc negandum sit, supposita illa sententia, cum nulla imperfectio sequatur in Deo, ut ex dictis constat.

22. Nihilominus tamen non censeo esse recedendum a modo loquendi D. Thomae et graviorum Theologorum, quia, etiamsi illa incommoda supra illata non sequantur attribuendo Deo relationem realem in dicto sensu, nihilominus tamen malo modo per intrinsecam formam et entitatem suam referri possit ad creaturas. Hoc enim est proprium entium ejusdem ordinis; Deus autem et creatura omnino sunt diversorum ordinum, ut per se satis constat.

23. Dicuntur autem esse ejusdem ordinis ea, quae vel sunt extra omne genus, et extra omnem dependentiam, ut divinae personae, vel sunt sub eodem genere, ut substantiae creatae, vel quantitates, et similia; vel certe /p. 846/ quae sunt sub diversis generibus, quorum unum potest perfici per aliud, et, e converso, ut sunt genus substantiae creatae, et genera accidentium inter se comparata. Et hac ratione, omnia entia creata, quantum ad praesens spectat, dicuntur esse ejusdem ordinis (personae enim increatae, ut inter se referuntur, non pertinent ad praesentem disputationem), quia, si sint ejusdem generis, et habent inter se univocam convenientiam, et mutuo se aliquo modo juvant ad perfectionem vel complementum suae naturae, vel in individuo, vel in specie, vel saltem in genere. Unde fit ut etiam causalitas, quae inter hujusmodi entia intercedit, redundet in perfectionem non solum effectuum, sed aliquo modo etiam causarum, vel quia ad agendum ordinantur, vel quia in effectibus conservantur saltem secundum speciem, vel certe quia secundum genus perficiuntur varietate differentiarum aut specierum. Si vero entia creata sint diversorum generum, omnia habent inter se aliquam connexionem, aut secundum rationes genericas, aut secundum specificas, cum proportione eas comparando. In hoc ergo sensu dicimus in praesenti, omnia entia creata esse ejusdem ordinis.

24. Aliter id exponi potest ex Cajetano, 1 parte, quaest. 4, art. 3, ad 4, ubi ait, ea esse diversorum ordinum, quae habent inter se essentialem dependentiam in ratione causae et causati; quo modo comparantur omnes creaturae ad Deum, non tamen inter se, quia, licet interdum ad invicem causentur, non tamen secundum propriam dependentiam essentialem. Sed haec expositio, licet sit probabilis, et quoad causas extrinsecas satisfaciat, tamen in intrinsecis, scilicet, materiali et formali, non videtur habere locum; sed in eis est specialis ratio, quia comparantur ad effectum, ut partes quae ad componendum totum ordinantur, et quoad hoc sunt ejusdem ordinis cum illo. Aliam expositionem

habet Hervaeus supra, sed obscuriorem, minusque satisfacientem, et ideo eam omitto. In dicto ergo sensu asserimus nihil referri ad aliud vere ac realiter per intrinsecam formam, nisi sit ejusdem ordinis cum eo. Ratio autem est, quia relatio realis consistit in ordine unius rei ad aliam; merito ergo ad talem relationem requiritur, ut sit inter extrema ejusdem ordinis.

25. Potestque hoc confirmari ex dictis de scientia et scibili, nam, sub ea ratione censentur esse diversorum ordinum, quatenus /col. b/ scientia ordinatur ad scibile, scibile autem ut sic non ordinatur ad scientiam; multo autem magis est Deus alterius ordinis ab omni creatura; ergo multo minus est per seipsum realiter referibilis ad creaturas, quam scibile ad scientiam. Et hoc fere discursu utitur D. Thom. citatis locis, et latius in quaest. 7 de Potentia, art, 11. Divina, ergo natura, potentia, et reliqua attributa, tam sunt absoluta in se, tamque abstracta et independentia ab omni ordine creaturarum, ut sive creaturae existant, sive non, nec secundum rem, nec secundum aliquam veram formalitatem realem referant Deum ad creaturas. Unde nec vere possunt concipi ut sic denominantes vel referentes Deum, sed omnis denominatio quae ut respectiva concipitur in Deo ad creaturam, est tantum secundum rationem et modum concipiendi nostrum.

26. Neque obstat quod Deus denominetur realiter creator aut Dominus; denominatur enim realiter, extrinsece quidem ab actione reali, et sic dicitur creator; intrinsece vero a potestate reali quam in se habet super rem creatam, et sic dicitur Dominus, vel a scientia, aut amore reali, et sic dicitur sciens vel amans id quod facit. Denique hae denominationes non sunt reales, nisi prout sumuntur ab aliquibus formis, vel quasi formis absolutis; prout vero relativae formaliter sunt, tantum fundantur in modo concipiendi nostro.

27. Ad principalem ergo difficultatem in principio positam, concedimus inter Deum et creaturas dari relationes non mutuas, quae non solum pertinent ad tertium genus seu fundamentum relationum, sed etiam ad primum vel secundum. Neque id est inconveniens, quia non oportet relativa tertii generis in hoc distingui ab aliis, quod in eo omnes relationes sint non mutuae, et in aliis nunquam, sed in hoc quod in tertio genere semper sint non mutuae, in aliis vero non semper, sed potius raro. Unde etiam recte exponitur Aristoteles, ut dicebam, quod in tertio genere ex vi formalis fundamenti seu rationis fundandi, relationes sunt non mutuae; in primo vero et secundo genere, si aliquando sunt non mutuae, provenit quasi ex materiali re aut subjecto, vel quasi subjecto relationis; verbi gratia, in relatione causae et effectus inter Deum et creaturas, si formaliter solum consideremus rationem potentiae et actionis, potest esse sufficiens ad relationem mutuam; tamen in Deo, propter eminentiam suae entitatis, relatio illa est non mutua; et idem dici /p. 847/ potest de relatione similis aut distincti, et similibus.

28. Relatio autem inter causam finalem et effectum, si non mutua est, reduci merito potest ad tertium genus; coaptantur enim media fini, et sic ab eo speciem sumunt, et suo modo per illum mensurantur.

29. De relatione autem dextri et sinistri inter hominem et columnam, satis dubium est an sit realis ex parte alicujus extremi. Nam, licet forma seu virtus a qua illa denominatio sumpta est, realis sit, et intrinsece existens in animali, columna vero tantum extrinsece, tamen non satis apparet cur inde oriatur relatio realis, etiam in animali, cum illa denominatio non fundetur in unitate aliqua seu quantitate, ut per se constat. Neque etiam in ratione potentiae activae ut sic; alias relatio esset mutua, quia illi correspondet in columna potentia passiva, vel interdum etiam activa deficit, quia non oportet ut virtus motiva partis dextrae tanta sit, ut ad movendam columnam sufficiat. Neque etiam fundatur illa relatio in aliqua commensuratione, quia virtus dextra animalis nullam habitudinem transcendentalem dicit ad columnam, neque illi commensuratur ullo modo. Non ergo videtur intervenire vera ratio ad fundandam relationem realem, sed videtur illa denominatio orta ex sola comparatione intellectus per quamdam proportionem seu proportionalitatem ad dextram et sinistram partem ejusdem hominis vel animalis. Nam inter has partes est relatio realis mutua sumpta ex diversitate situum, cum diversitate virtutum realium in utraque parte existentium; et hinc similis denominatio translata est ad rem inanimatam, locum sinistrum vel dextrum occupantem. Quae quoad denominationem in hoc assimilatur relationibus non mutuis, quia fundamentum illius denominationis solum est in uno extremo, et inde redundat in aliud; ideo solent hoc exemplo declarari relationes non mutuae, quamvis vera ac propria relatio realis non videatur ibi necessaria. Quia sola diversitas situum ut sic non sufficit ad donominationem dextri et sinistri, ut per se constat; diversitas autem virtutis ibi, non est nisi privativa, quia in animali est propria virtus, in columna vero tantum est privatio illius, et ideo in neutro extremo videtur sufficere ad relationem realem. Quod si quis omnino velit defendere illam esse relationem realem non mutuam, utatur generali responsione superius posita. /col. b/

SECTIO XVI.
Utrum formalis terminus relationis sit altera relatio, vel aliqua ratio absoluta.

1. Haec quaestio suborta est ex sectione praecedente, et est per se valde necessaria ad explicandam naturam relationis, quae tum ex fundamento, tum ex termino, suo modo pendet; et ob hoc etiam optime in hunc locum cadit, nam in duabus sectionibus proxime praecedentibus explicuimus formalia fundamenta relationum; superest ergo ut consequenter formalem terminum declaremus.

Exponitur quaestionis titulus, et quid sit actu terminare.

2. Est autem advertendum, hic nos non agere de formali denominatione termini ut actu terminantis, sed de ratione seu forma, quae in ipsa re, quae est terminus, requiritur ut sit apta ad terminandum. Nam sub priori ratione esse termini seu terminare, non est aliquid in re terminante, sed est denominatio extrinseca, sumpta ex eo quod aliud tendat in ipsam. Sicut, parietem esse visum, non est aliquid in pariete, sed est denominatio a visione respiciente ipsum; nam idem est videri, quod actu terminare visionem, licet voces diversae sint; nihilominus tamen praerequiritur in pariete aliqua forma, qua constituitur aptus ad terminandam visionem. Sic ergo intelligendum est de termino relationis; dicitur enim actu terminare, solum quia respicitur ab alio, quae denominatio non est praerequisita ad relationem, sed, consequens ad illam, in quo omnes conveniunt. Necessario vero supponitur in termino aliqua ratio et quasi causa formalis, ob quam est terminativus (ut sic dicam) relationis, quia non omne ens potest terminare quamcunque relationem; ergo in unoquoque requiritur aliqua ratio, ob quam est natum terminare hanc vel illam relationem; hanc ergo rationem formalem terminandi in praesenti inquirimus. Et quoniam in superioribus dictum est, terminum relationis debere esse ens reale, et, ut actu terminet, requirere actualem existentiam, ideo ulterius inquirimus an debeat esse ens formaliter relativum vel absolutum; ex quo facile constabit in unaquaque relatione, an proportionatus terminus debeat esse tale ens absolutum, vel tale relativum. /p. 848/

Variae Sententiae.

3. *Prima.*—Sunt ergo in hac re tres sententiae. Prima affirmat in omnibus relationibus, tam mutuis quam non mutuis, formalem terminum debere esse relativum. Ita docuit Cajet., 1 part., quaest. 13, art. 7; et Hispalens., in 1, dist. 30, quaest. 1 , notab. 3, videtur secundum eamdem sententiam loqui, quamvis nec quaestionem disputet, neque de formali ratione terminandi expresse loquatur. Nonnulli vero ex modernis Thomistis hanc sententiam secuti sunt. Et potest probari primo, quia quodlibet relativum formaliter terminatur ad suum correlativum; ergo formalis ratio terminandi unam relationem est relatio opposita correspondens in altero extremo. Consequentia evidens est; et antecedens probatur, quia relativa sunt simul natura, cognitione et definitione, ut constat ex Aristotele, c. de Ad aliquid, et inferius dicetur; sed nihil horum haberent nisi unum relativum ad aliud formaliter terminaretur; ergo. Probatur minor quoad primam partem, quia si pater, verbi gratia, ut pater non terminatur ad filium, ut filius est relativus, sed ut est hic homo genitus ab illo, ergo pater ut pater non est simul natura cum filio ut filio, sed cum hoc homine ut genito; at vero hic homo prius natura est genitus ab alio, quam habeat relationem filiationis

ad ipsum, quia filiatio est proprietas resultans in homine genito; ergo pater, ut pater, erit prius natura quam sit filius ut filius. Et confirmatur haec pars, quia relatio, ut relatio, non pendet nisi ex fundamento et termino; ergo, si formalis terminus non est altera relatio, per se non pendet ab illa, nec requirit illam; ergo ex se est prior natura quam illa. Similique argumento probantur aliae duae partes, quia relatio perfecte cognoscitur cognito fundamento et termino, et aliud non requirit; ergo si terminus unius relationis non est alia relatio, non pendet una in cognitione ab alia; non ergo simul necessario cognoscuntur. Rursus ob eamdem causam in definitione relationis solum ponitur terminus formalis, quia totum esse relationis est ad suum terminum; ergo si terminus unius relativi non est aliud relativum, sed aliquid absolutum, non definietur unum relativum per aliud, et e converso, quod est esse simul definitione. Et confirmatur hoc specialiter in relativis non mutuis, in quibus videtur esse major difficultas, quia alias ad cognoscendam relationem creaturae, opor- /col. b/ teret cognoscere entitatem Dei absolutam et naturam eius, et similiter ad cognoscendam relationem scientiae, vel sensus, oporteret cognoscere naturam absolutam objecti scibilis vel sensibilis, quod videtur plane falsum.

4. *Secunda opinio.*—Secunda sententia distinctione utitur, nam de relationibus mutuis idem sentit quod praecedens sententia, propter easdem rationes. De non mutuis autem affirmat terminari ad absolutum, et non relativum, quia hujusmodi relationes terminantur formaliter ad aliquid reale; in terminis autem earum non correspondet aliquid reale relativum, sed absolutum tantum. Hanc sententiain tenet Ferrar., 2 cont. Gent., c. 14, et in ea, magis inclinat, quoad posteriorem partem ejus, Hispalensis supra, nam saepe ait, aliquod divinum attributum absolutum, scilicet, virtutem, potentiam vel aliquid hujusmodi, esse rationem, quod Deus terminet relationem creaturae ad ipsum. Hanc etiam sententiam sequitur Niphus, 5 Metaph., disp. 14. Eamque quoad relativa non mutua nos postea confirmabimus; quoad mutua vero eadem habet fundamenta, quae praecedens sententia. Et addi solet argumentum sumptum ex relationibus divinis, quae mutuae sunt, et tamen una ad aliam terminatur.

5. Tertia sententia universaliter docet omnes relationes, tam mutuas quam non mutuas, terminari ad absolutum formaliter. Hanc tenet Scot., in 1, dist. 36, q. 1, ubi Lychetus et alii Scotistae idem sentiunt. Et eam plane sequitur Capreol., quaest. 1, art. 2, ad 3, quem imitatur Soncin., 5 Metaph., quaest. 30, ad 2. Aiunt enim absolutum esse rationem terminandi, requirere tamen relationem seu correlationem concomitantem quando actu terminat, quod est simpliciter verum in relativis mutuis; in non mutuis autem solum secundum nostrum modum concipiendi, ut explicabimus. Atque hanc sententiam censeo esse veram, formaliter ac per se intellectam; cur autem hoc addam, ex dicendis constabit; oportet enim sententiam hanc distincte proponere et probare

in relationibus mutuis, et non mutuis, quia non est aeque certa in utrisque,
quamvis ex non mutuis ad mutuas non leve argumentum sumatur.

Tertia Sententia duobus assertionibus propositis confirmatur.
6. *Prima assertio.—Ratio pro assertione.*—Dico ergo primo, in relativis non
mutuis /p. 849/ ratio quae est in uno extremo ad terminandam relationem
alterius, non est aliqua relatio opposita relationi alterius, sed est ipsa entitas, vel
proprietas aliqua absoluta talis termini. Probatur argumento facto in secunda
sententia, quod mihi videtur efficacissimum, nam haec relatio habet terminum
realem et realiter existentem; sed in illo termino nulla existit relatio realis correspondens opposita alteri relationi; ergo, ille terminus non per relationem, sed
per aliquam rem absolutam constituitur aptus ad terminandum. Consequentia
est evidens a sufficienti partium enumeratione; major autem et minor probatae
sunt in superioribus.

7. *Effugium Cajetani.—Improbatur.*—Ut Cajetanus effugeret vim hujus
rationis, excogitavit sententiam quam supra refutavimus, quod, nimirum,
etiam relativa non mutua realiter invicem referantur, quamvis relatio non
utrique insit, atque ita conatur defendere, etiam illud extremum, in quo non
est relatio, non terminare relationem alterius, nisi quatenus ad illud vicissim,
refertur. Sed ea sententia et falsa est, ut ostendimus, et ad praesentem rem
explicandam nihil conferre potest. Nam etsi demus scibile referri realiter ad
scientiam per relationem in ipsa scientia existentem, nihilominus verum est,
quod Aristoteles dixit, unum ex his extremis non referri ad aliud, nisi quia
aliud refertur ad ipsum; ergo prius secundum rationem necesse est intelligere
relationem scientiae terminari ad scibile, quam vicissim scibile referri ad scientiam, cum illud prius sit veluti causa, seu fundamentum, hujus posterioris;
ergo ratio terminandi ex parte scibilis non potest esse illa relatio qua refertur ad
scientiam. Praeterea licet terminare actu, ut supra dicebamus, sit denominatio
extrinseca, tamen aptitudo terminandi relationem praedicamentalem non
potest esse denominatio extrinseca ab opposito relativo, quia ratio terminandi
supponitur in re ante omnem denominationem ab alio extrinseco; nam in ipsamet denominatione extrinseca includitur actualis terminatio; ergo aptitudo
supponitur ad talem denominationem, maxime quando terminus esse debet
res realis, et realiter existens. Quocirca intelligi nullo modo potest, quod unum
extremum constituatur proxime aptum ad terminandam relationem alterius,
per ipsammet relationem realem, quae est in altero extremo, cum omnis relatio
praedicamentalis consurgat, praesuppositis /col. b/ fundamento, et termino,
non quidem actu terminante, sed apto ad terminandum, nam ut actu terminans
non supponitur, sed constituitur ex alterius habitudine ad ipsam.

8. *Improbatur aliorum sententia.*—Alii respondere solent, quamvis in scibili, verbi gratia, vel creatore non respondeat nisi relatio rationis, nihilominus relationem scientiae aut creaturae non terminari formaliter nisi ad suum correlativum ut sic, et consequenter relationem rationis esse rationem terminandi realem. Sed haec responsio facile refutatur ex dictis supra de termino relationis realis praedicamentalis; ostendimus enim debere esse rem, veram, et realiter existentem. Quod sane aequali vel majori ratione, verum est de forma illa quae est ratio terminandi, ac de subjecto quasi materiali talis denominationis; nam si terminus debet esse realis, ergo eodem modo debet esse in re ipsa aptus ad terminandam, alioqui non erit terminus, neque actu, neque aptitudine; ergo haec aptitudo debet ei convenire per rationem aliquam realem in ipso existentem.

9. Et confirmatur, quia relatio realis non existit nisi existentibus fundamento et termino; sed relatio creaturae existit, et revera terminatur ad Deum, nulla existente in Deo relatione rationis, non solum quia relatio rationis nunquam vere existit, sed etiam, quia, eo modo quo esse potest, nimirum objective in intellectu, non est necesse illam actu esse, id est, considerari, ut relatio creaturae terminetur ad creatorem; nam etiamsi nullus intellectus talem relationem fingat aut consideret, nihilominus relatio creaturae vere terminabitur ad Deum. Dices, impossibile esse quin illa relatio sit objective in aliquo intellectu, saltem divino, sive ipse illam immediate efficiat, sive cognoscat ut factibilem suo modo ab intellectu humano. Respondetur, quidquid horum verum sit, esse impertinens ad rem de qua agimus, quia, licet id sit necessarium ex infinita scientia Dei, tamen per se ac formaliter id non postulat relatio creaturae, quia non respicit Deum ut speculantem (ut sic loquar) relationem rationis, sed ut influentem esse in ipsam; unde si hoc habeat, hoc sufficit ut talis relatio terminetur ad ipsum; relatio autem rationis ut scita ab intellectu divino, est impertinens. Et idem est de sensu et sensibili, et scientia et scibili, nam si per impossibile nullus intellectus de illis consideraret, relatio sensus terminaretur ad sensibile et scientiae ad scibile. /p. 850/

10. Sed respondent aliqui, argumentum hoc recte procedere de relatione rationis ut actu existente suo modo, nihilominus tamen ipsam relationem rationis, quatenus est in proxima potentia talis termini, esse rationem terminandi relationem realem alterius extremi. Sed hoc etiam nullius momenti est; interrogo enim, quid intelligant per relationem rationis in potentia proxima. Aut enim intelligunt ipsum fundamentum reale, quod praebet occasionem intellectui, ut per modum relativi illud concipiat, quod non tam est verum fundamentum relationis, quam proxima causa vel occasio inducens humanum intellectum, ad talem modum concipiendi, et in hoc sensu relatio rationis in potentia proxima non est nisi res absoluta in tali termino existens, ut, verbi

gratia, in Deo est potentia, qua actu influit in creaturam, et sic de aliis; igitur quod relatio creaturae terminetur ad relationem rationis, ut tantum est in fundamento proximo ex parte Dei, revera est terminari ad aliquid absolutum, quod est in Deo. Aut per relationem rationis in potentia intelligitur ipsamet relatio rationis secundum suum esse essentiae, quale in ea esse, vel potius fingi potest, et hoc sensu improbabilis mihi videtur illa responsio, quia illa relatio in tantum esse potest, et in ea fingi potest aliquod esse essentiae, in qua intellectus, verbi gratia, humanus potest concipere rem absolutam per modum relativae; sed hoc est impertinens et extrinsecum ad naturam et essentiam relationis realis creaturae, et ut ipsa terminetur ad suum terminum; ergo non potest esse illa ratio terminandi. Et confirmatur ac declaratur, nam Deus ut creator non ideo potest terminare relationem realem creaturae, quia potest a nobis concipi per modum correlativi, sed quia vere ac realiter influit esse[7] in creaturam per omnipotentiam suam. Denique in aliis terminis realibus, et in relationibus mutuis, non sufficit esse essentiae in ipso termino ut relatio consurgat, nisi sit redactum ad existentiam, quia alias est potentiale quid, et simpliciter nihil; ergo multo minus poterit sufficere esse essentiae vel potentiale relationis rationis, ut sit ratio terminandi relationem realem.

11. *Fonseca ut solvat argumentum.* — Aliam denique responsionem adinvenit Fonseca , lib. 5, c. 15, quaest. 5, sect. 4, ubi dicit, posse relationem rationis actu convenire, verbi gratia, creatori, etiamsi actu non existat, suo modo, id est, objective in intellectu, atque /col. b/ hoc satis esse ut ad illam possit terminari relatio realis; nam, hoc ipso quod relatio realis est in creatura, relatio rationis creatoris actu convenit Deo, etiamsi actu non existat. Quod autem haec duo separabilia sint, probat, quia homini actu convenit esse animal, etiamsi non existat. Sed haec responsio non est probabilior caeteris. Nam imprimis, quod assumit, posse formam actu convenire, quando actu non existit, aut magnam continet aequivocationem, aut est plane falsum. Nam actu convenire, si proprio et realiter sumatur, est actu inesse eo modo quo forma inesse potest, scilicet aut inhaerendo, aut denominando, aut referendo, vel alia simili ratione; quod autem hoc modo actu convenit, necesse est quod actu existat, eo modo quo existere potest. Quod si actu convenire solum dicit veritatem propositionis per connexionem extremorum abstrahentium ab existentia, illud revera non est actu convenire, sed potius in potentia, et eo modo quo in illis propositionibus intelligi potest actualis veritas, illam non habent, nisi prout sunt actu in aliquo intellectu, ut in superioribus tactum est. Et praeterea, sumpto hoc modo, *actu convenire*, non potest vere dici relatio rationis actu convenire Deo, hoc ipso

---

7 Here I am following Salamanca, 1597, vol. 2, p. 588, to introduce "esse" which is lacking in the Vives edition.

quod creatura existit, quia, ut bene idem auctor argumentatur, talis relatio contingenter et ab extrinseco convenit Deo, etiam post effectionem creaturae; at praedicata contingentia non conveniunt actu nisi quando existunt, sed illud est proprium praedicatorum, quae necessario conveniunt subjectis. Responsio vero quam adhibet, limitando subsumptam propositionem, et excipiendo has relationes rationis, primum videtur voluntaria, deinde contra rationem; nam, seclusa actuali existentia unicuique praedicato proportionata, non potest dici praedicatum actu convenire subjecto, nisi vel quia est de ejus essentia, vel certe quia ab illa manat, ut necessariam connexionem et per se cum illa habeat; ergo quotiescunque praedicatum non est hujusmodi, sed mere contingens, et ab extrinseca causa proveniens, sive, sit praedicatum reale, sive rationis, in nullo vero sensu potest dici actu convenire, quando actu non existit. Et confirmatur, nam hoc ipsum, scilicet, *actu convenire*, requirit saltem veritatem propositionis; sed hae propositiones sunt falsae, Deus habet relationem, vel, actu refertur ad creaturam, quamdiu illa relatio nullo modo actu existit; imo, juxta principia dia- /p. 851/ lecticae tales propositiones non possunt vere abstrahi a tempore, cum simpliciter contingentes sint.

12 Addo denique, etiamsi demus totum id quod in illa responsione sumitur, non satisfacere, quia ille modus actu conveniendi non sufficit ad terminum relationis realis. Alias Petrus actu existens posset habere relationem realem identitatis specificae ad Paulum potentia tantum existentem, quia actu convenit Paulo quod sit homo, etiamsi non existat, quia ab intrinseco est homo; ergo etiam actu conveniet illi relatio realis identitatis specificae cum Petro, etiamsi illa relatio actu non existat; ergo, e converso, ut relatio realis existat in Petro, satis erit quod alia similis et fundamentum ejus actu conveniat Paulo, licet non existat.

13. Nullus est ergo tergiversationi locus, sed, admissa communi doctrina de relativis non mutuis, evidenter sequitur terminum illius relationis esse aliquid absolutum, formaliter ac per se loquendo. Addo autem haec ultima verba, quia interdum potest contingere, ut terminus alicuius relationis non mutuae sit aliqua relatio realis, non tamen opposita alteri relationi, nec reciproca illi. Ut, verbi gratia, scientia de aliqua relatione, aut amor qui directe ac per se primo tendat in aliquam relationem, refertur realiter ad illam relationem ut ad objectum seu mensuram; unde constat quod, sicut objectum talis scientiae est relatio, ita etiam terminus relationis talis scientiae erit relatio, non tamen formaliter ut relatio opposita relationi illius scientiae, sed potius ut materia circa quam talis scientia versatur, et quae supponitur ad relationem ejus, et ideo veluti materiale quid est, quod illa res scita sit relatio. Et hoc modo dicimus, rem absolutam terminare hujusmodi relationem, seu quae per modum absolutae se gerat; denique res ipsa scita vel amata, qualiscunque illa sit. Dices: quid si objectum

scitum sit aliqua relatio rationis? Respondetur: etiam relatio transcendentalis illius scientiae terminabitur ad illam, erit tamen incapax illa scientia relationis praedicamentalis ad suum objectum, propter defectum termini realis.

Assertio secunda.

14. *Relationes mutuae ad absolutum terminantur.*—Dico secundo:, etiam in relationibus mutuis formalis ratio terminandi est non relatio opposita, sed aliqua ratio abso- /col. b/ luta, quae est fundamentum formale relationis oppositae. Hanc assertionem intelligo per se ac formaliter, sicut praecedentem explicavi: generalis enim regula est illam rem seu rationem formalem, quae in uno relativo mutuo est proxima ratio fundandi relationem ad aliud, esse etiam proximam et formalem rationem terminandi relationem alterius ad se. Ut, verbi gralia, si in Petro proximum fundamentum habendi in se relationem filiationis est tota substantia ejus quatenus producta per talem generationem a Paulo, haec eadem est ratio ob quam Petrus potest terminare relationem paternitatis Pauli ad ipsum; et e converso, quia in Paulo potentia generandi, supposita tali generatione ut conditione necessaria, est proximum fundamentum relationis paternitatis, ideo etiam est proxima ratio, ob quam Paulus potest terminare filiationem Petri ad ipsum. Idem est in relationibus primi generis, nam albedo, quae in hoc albo est fundamentum similitudinis ad aliud, ob unitatem formalem cum ipso, est etiam proxima ratio terminandi relationem similitudinis alterius ad ipsum. Quocirca si verum est, interdum posse unam relationem esse proximam rationem fundandi aliam relationem, ut, verbi gratia, paternitas similitudinem, tunc illa paternitas quae in uno patre fundat similitudinem ad aliud, erit in illo ratio terminandi relationem alterius ad se; in eo tamen non se gerit formaliter ut relatio, neque opponitur relative illi relationi, quam terminat per seipsam, sed opponitur per aliam relationem, quam in se fundat, et ideo tunc perinde se gerit ac si esset forma absoluta, et in hoc sensu dicimus formalem terminum esse aliquid absolutum, per se loquendo.

15. Solet autem haec assertio probari ex eo quod, cum relatio definitur esse accidens cujus totum esse est ad aliud, per illud aliud non potest intelligi altera relatio, quia alias vel non daretur unum supremum genus relationis, sed duo, vel idem poneretur in definitione sui ipsius. Et simile argumentum est quia similitudo in communi non potest referri ad aliquam relationem, quia alias referretur ad aliam similitudinem, cum sit relatio aequiparantiae; at praeter similitudinem in communi non potest esse alia similitudo. Verumtamen haec argumenta praetermitto, tum quia per extrinseca desumuntur, et rem non declarant; tum etiam quia attingunt difficultatem tractandam sectione sequenti; quae /p. 852/ quidem facilius et commodius expedientur juxta hanc nostram

sententiam, quamvis fortasse ob eam solam causam non sit simpliciter neces-saria.

16. *Prima ratio conclusionis.*—Primo ergo probatur haec conclusio ex prae-cedenti, nam ex eo quod in relativis non mutuis videmus relationem unius extremi non terminari formaliter ad relationem alterius, colligere possumus, quod, licet in relativis mutuis sit relatio realis in utroque extremo, una non tendit in aliam formaliter, sed simul et concomitanter una tendit in subjectum seu fundamentum alterius, et e converso. Probatur haec illatio, nam si per impossibile in altero extremo impediretur relatio, conservato toto fundamento ejus, nihilominus relatio alterius extremi posset ad illud terminari; ergo signum est illas duas relationes esse simul per concomitantiam, et non per formalem terminationem unius ad aliam. Consequentia est evidens, et antecedens patet, quia, ut in superioribus visum est, non solum in relationibus tertii generis, sed etiam secundi et primi, quando unum extremum tale est, ut non possit fundare relationem, nihilominus est aptum ad terminandam relationem alterius, ut patet in Deo ut terminante relationem creaturae ut sic; ergo quacumque ra-tione contigerit, alterum extremum manere cum fundamento et sine relatione, nihilominus manebit sufficiens ad terminandam relationem alterius extremi; est enim eadem ratio, nam quod unum fundamentum, seu extremum sit aptum necne ad fundandam propriam relationem, est per accidens ad terminationem alterius. Unde, si per intellectus praecisionem separetur relatio a tali extremo, intelligitur manere aeque sufficiens ad terminandam aliam relationem, ac illud extremum, quod non est capax relationis. Ergo signum est relationes mutuas esse simul propter concomitantiam, et propter conditionem extremorum, quae apta sunt ad fundandam relationem, non propter formalem terminationein unius relationis ad aliam sibi correspondentem.

17. *Secunda ratio conclusionis.*—Secundo argumentor, quia commune axioma est, posito fundamento et termino, resultare relationem praedicamentalem, et non alias; ergo terminus unius relationis non potest esse relatio opposita. Antecedens certum est omnium consensu, et constat ex supra dictis de natura hujus relationis. Unde etiam Scotus, /col. b/ licet excipiat relationes quas vo-cat extrinsecus advenientes, tamen consequenter negat illas pertinere ad hoc praedicamentum, et nos infra ostendemus, illas vel nullas esse, vel non nisi alias a transcendentalibus, disputatione sequenti. Necesse est autem axioma illud intelligi de termino formali et proximo, et quasi in actu primo (ut sic dicam), de quo etiam nos in praesenti quaestione disputamus, ut diximus. Non enim potest intelligi de termino terminante quasi in actu secundo (ut ita loquar). Nam de illo termino ut sic, non est verum quod illo posito cum fundamento sequatur relatio, nam potius ipse constituitur in ratione termini actu termi-nantis per ipsammet relationem ut actu tendentem in ipsum, et extrinsece

denominantem ipsum denominatione terminativa. Rursus nec potest intelligi de termino materiali et remoto, quia illo tantum posito cum fundamento alterius extremi non est necesse resultare relationem, ut per se constat, et facile potest exemplis ostendi; ergo intelligendum est illud principium de termino formali, et quasi in actu primo proximo. Et hinc facile probatur prima consequentia, quia una relatio non consurgit ex positione alterius, quia illa particula *ex* dicit antecessionem aliquam naturae vel originis; una autem relatio praedicamentalis non antecedit alteram relationem sibi correspondentem, neque una dicit ex altera originem, ut per se constat in omnibus creatis, de quibus loquimur; alias non essent simul. Cum autem relatio dicitur resultare positis fundamento et termino, sensus indubitatus est, positionem fundamenti et termini antecedere, seu praesupponi ordine naturae, et inde statim resultare relationem, quod ex proprietate ipsius locutionis manifestum est, et ex re ipsa, quia in relativis mutuis utraque relatio simul resultat, positis fundamentis et terminis.

18. *Tertia assertionis ratio.*—Tertio argumentor confirmando et declarando illud principium, scilicet: *Id quod in unoquoque extremo est ratio fundandi propriam relationem, est ratio terminandi alteram correlationem.* Nam, sicut ratio fundandi est illa, per quam convenienter redditur proxima causa, ob quam talis res habet relationem ad aliud, ita ratio terminandi est illa, per quam redditur proxima causa, ob quam res est talis, ut ad ipsam altera referri possit; haec autem causa ex eadem forma vel ratione sumitur in relativis mutuis; ergo. Major videtur per /p. 853/ se nota ex terminis. Minor declaratur inductione; nam, sicut album aptum est ad fundandam relationem similitudinis, quia habet albedinem, et ipsa albedo est aptum fundamentum, quia habet talem unitatem formalem, ita etiam idem album est aptum ad terminandam relationem alterius, quia habet albedinem ejusdem rationis vel unitatis cum albedine alterius. Non enim aliud album refertur ad hoc, quia in hoc est relatio similitudinis, sed quia in hoc est albedo, sicut est in alio, alioqui non esset similitudo in albedine, sed esset similitudo in similitudine. Et hinc potest percipi ratio a priori, nam similitudo ut sic est in albedine, verbi gratia; versatur ergo inter alba ut sic, et ea refert ut similia; ergo sicut ex parte unius fundatur in albedine, ita ex parte alterius terminatur ad albedinem.

19. Idem facile constat in relationibus disquiparantiae; nam Petrus, verbi gratia, ideo refertur ad Paulum ut ad patrem, quia genuit ipsum, et non quia Paulus refertur ad ipsum, formaliter distinguendo relationem a generatione; nam praecise in ea ratione sistendo intelligimus esse sufficientem causam ex parte generantis ut filius referatur ad ipsum. Eadem est autem causa ex parte ejus, ob quam in ipso resultat relatio paternitatis. Et idem est de ipsa paternitate, si rationem ejus ex parte termini reddamus; ideo enim relatio paternitatis, quae est in Paulo, terminatur ad Petrum, quia genitus est ab ipso, et in hoc praecise

concipimus sufficientem causam ex parte termini. Atque ita in universum, cum relatio essentialiter requirat duo, scilicet fundamentum et terminum, ex parte utriusque potest reddi ratio cujuscunque relationis, et illa, quae vere et proxime redditur ex parte termini ut sic, est ratio terminandi, sicut quae redditur ex parte subjecti, est fundamentam, seu ratio fundandi.

20. Ratio autem, quae ex parte termini reddi potest, nunquam est altera relatio, si formaliter loquamur, et non tantum concomitanter vel identice. Quanquam enim pater non referatur ad filium, nisi cum filius refertur ad ipsum, non tamen haec est ratio quae ex parte termini reddi possit, cur pater referatur ad filium, scilicet, quia filius refertur ad ipsum, sed praecise quia genitus est ab ipso; nam una relatio nullo modo est ratio alterius, nec ex parte termini, nec ex parte fandamenti, alias non essent simul natura; illa enim, quae esset ratio alterius, ut sic es- /col. b/ set aliquo modo prima, maxime cum sit sermo de ratione reali et formali suo modo ex parte termini. Ratio ergo haec semper est aliquid aliud distinctum a relatione, et consequenter aliquid absolutum, quod non est aliud in relativis mutuis nisi illud ipsum quod in unoquoque fundat relationem ejus, nam illud est ratio terminandi relationem alterius. Quia praecisa relatione, nulla alia ratio est propinquior, neque magis necessaria, ut in inductione facta satis declaratum est.

21. *Objectioni satisfit.*—Dices: in relativis non mutuis non potest haec regula servari, quia in termino unius relativi non est fundamentum reale alicujus relationis. Respondetur, semper intelligi aliquid proportionabile. Ut, verbi gratia, si relativa non mutua sint secundi generis, ut est inter creatorem et creaturam, ratio terminandi relationem creaturae ex parte Dei, est ipsa potentia creandi ut actu influens. Quia si alioqui Deus non esset incapax relationis, illamet deberet esse fundamentum relationis creatoris ad creaturam. Et quia si velimus rationem reddere ex parte termini relationis creaturae, non est alia, nisi quia Deus per suam omnipotentiam creavit illam. Et idem facile intelligitur in relationibus mutuis, quae esse possunt in primo genere, ut est relatio similitudinis, aut distinctionis inter creaturam et Deum. In tertio autem genere, ratio terminandi ex parte scibilis, verbi gratia, et similium objectorum, est uniuscujusque entitas, prout in ea est quaedam aptitudo objectiva, ut circa illam possit talis actus, vel habitus, aut potentia versari, quae potest nominari veritas aut bonitas, vel quid simile; illa enim aptitudo est ratio quae reddi potest ex parte objecti, seu termini talis relationis; ideo enim scientia versatur cirea tale objectum, quia talem habet veritatem, seu intelligibilitatem, et sic de aliis.

22. *Ratio quae nequit fundare relationem cur terminare possit.*—Quod si inquiras cur hujusmodi aptitudo vel ratio, quae non est sufficiens ad fundandam in se propriam relationem, sit sufficiens ratio ad terminandam relationem alterius, respondetur causam esse, quia ad fundandam relationem necessaria

est ordinabilitas ad aliud (ut sic dicam) ex parte ipsius fundamenti, atque ita requirit quod sint ejusdem ordinis. Ad terminandam autem relationem, non est necesse ut terminus sit ordinabilis ad aliud, sed ut aliud sit /p. 854/ ordinabile ad ipsum, et ideo potest terminus habere realem aptitudinem ad terminandum, etiamsi non sit ejusdem. ordinis cum alio extremo, quod ad ipsum ordinatur.

Aliarum opinionum fundamentis satisfit.

23. Ad fundamenta aliarum opinionum respondendum superest. Et imprimis negatur relativum formaliter terminari ad correlativum ut sic, quod manifeste constat in relativis non mutuis, quia ubi non est correlativum, non potest alterum relativum ad correlativum terminari. Inde vero intelligimus, etiam in mutuis, quamvis relativum ad correlativum terminetur, non tamen formaliter, ita ut relationes ipsae inter se et ad se tendant, sed una tendit ad fundamentum alterius, et e converso, ut declaratum est.

24. *Relativa quomodo sint simul natura.*— Ad primam vero objectionem, de simultate naturae respondetur, potius inde inferri oppositum, quia relatio est posterior natura quam terminus ejus, ut in actu primo seu formali ad terminandum sufficienter constitutus est, quia ex fundamento et termino consurgit relatio, ut diximus. Imo aliqui auctores, qui opinantur relationem esse quid distinctum, putant effective fieri a termino. Si ergo una relatio esset terminus alterius, ex positione unius resultaret alia, et ita non possent esse simul natura. Dicuntur ergo simul natura, quando mutuae sunt, quia cum resultat una ex fundamento et termino, resultat alia omnino concomitanter absque ullo ordine prioris et posterioris inter se, et hoc est esse simul natura. Fundatur autem haec simultas, non in formali habitudine earum inter se, sed in necessaria connexione quam habent in fundamento et termino, quia neutra insurgere potest, nisi jam positis suo fundamento et termino, et illis positis ambae statim necessario consurgunt. Et alioqui formale fundamentum unius est formalis terminus alterius, et e converso; ex quo fit ut necessario simul sint posita in re fundamentum et terminas utriusque, nam sunt eadem, commutata proportione, ut explicui; atque ita tandem efficitur ut ipsae relationes necessario simul consurgant, et duratione, quia utraque aequali necessitate resultat ex termino et fundamento quamprimum ponuntur, et natura, quia nullam inter se habent ordinem. Hoc igitur modo correlativa ipsa formaliter sumpta, ut correlativa sunt, si sint mutua, sunt simul natura; si vero sint non mu- /col. b/ tua, cum neque duratione sint simul, nec natura esse possunt.

25. *Occurritur objectioni.*—At vero si haec comparatio fiat inter unum relativum et terminum ejus in actu secundo, seu ut actu terminantem, sic dici possunt simul natura formaliter, quia, ut supra dictum est, terminus ut sic terminans

formaliter constituitur per extrinsecam denominationem a relatione, quae in illum tendit; unde illa posita sic denominatur, et illa ablata desinit esse hoc modo terminus, nihil intrinsecum amittendo, ut per se notum est. Relatio autem non prius natura est, quam terminetur ad aliud; est ergo simul natura cum termino ut terminante. Dices: ipsa relatio est veluti causa formalis illius denominationis termini actualis; ergo est prior natura. Respondeo, non esse proprie causam formalem, licet propter denominationem ad eum modum a nobis concipiatur, et ideo non intercedere ibi veram prioritatem naturae, quia relatio sine alia causalitate, solum quia ex intrinseca sua essentia respicit terminum, illum denominat terminantem. Sicut visio denominat rem visam sine vera causalitate, sed ex eo solum, quod est cum tali intrinseca habitudine; unde sicut non prius natura est quam habeat illam habitudinem, ita non prius natura est quam denominet objectum visum.

26. Quod maxime verum est loquendo de his formis in concreto, id est, de relativo, aut vidente; nam, loquendo de abstractis, potest aliquo modo concipi relatio, ut prior natura quam relativum, eo modo quo inter formam praesertim inhaerentem, et effectum ejus formalem, potest esse prioritas naturae. Nam relatio est forma relativi; relatio enim abstracte concepta proprie non refertur ipsa ad terminum, sed est qua subjectum refertur, et ideo quamdiu ipsa concipitur ut prior quam afficiens actu subjectum, nondum concipitur ut referens ad terminum, et ideo mirum non est quod ut sic sit etiam prior ipsa relatio, quam denominatio termini terminantis. Et fortasse hic potest applicari distinctio, qua utitur alias Cajetanus, de relatione signata vel exercita, nam tunc concipitur relatio, ut nondum exercens actum referendi, sed secundum suam abstractam rationem. Adhuc tamen sic concepta, est simul natura cum altera relatione opposita, in relationibus mutuis, quia etiam relationes in abstracto sumptae omnino simul consurgunt, posito utroque fundamento.
/p. 855/

27. Denique ut nihil omittamus, addi posset, etiam relationem abstracte conceptam, licet non ut quod, saltem ut quo, tendere in terminum, nam est forma qua relativum respicit terminum, et quia quantumvis in abstracto consideretur, semper ejus essentia consistit in formali habitudine ad terminum. Et sub hac consideratione, quamvis intelligitur aliquo modo prior quam relativum, etiam sub ea ratione tendit suo modo in terminum, et consequenter denominat illum actu terminantem, non integrum relativum, sed relationem ipsam. Ex his ergo satis constat quomodo relationes oppositae sint simul natura, et relatio etiam et terminus ut actu terminans, non vero relatio, et terminus in actu primo, seu quantum ad rationem terminandi; sic enim etiam tempore antecedere potest, quando fundamentum in alio extremo non est positum, et posito etiam alio

extremo semper antecedit ordine naturae, quia ex illo fundamento resultat relatio, ut declaratum est.

28. Ad argumentum ergo primae sententiae respondetur in forma negando sequelam, nimirum, patrem ut patrem non esse simul natura cum filio ut filius est, sed ut est hic homo genitus; imo sicut hic homo, ut genitus, est prius natura quam ut filius, ita etiam est prius natura quam pater ut pater, quamvis sit posterius natura quam hic homo ut generans. Et ideo, quamvis pater ut sic terminetur ad hunc hominem ut a se genitum, nihilominus non prius natura terminatur ad ipsum quam in ipso sit filiatio, non propter terminationem formalem ad ipsam filiationem, sed propter simultaneam concomitantiam omnino necessariam, ut declaratum est. Quapropter, licet hic homo, ut genitus, sit prius natura quam ut filius, tamen in illo priori ut sic nondum intelligitur in patre paternitas; imo verissime etiam dicitur, prius natura esse hunc hominem ut genitum, quam in patre sit paternitas, nam ex positione hujus termini cum fandamento, quod est in generante, resultat paternitas.

29. Ad confirmationem concedo, formaliter loquendo, unam relationem non pendere ab alia, nego tamen inde sequi non esse simul natura, naturaliter loquendo. Et horum primum, praeter omnia dicta, confirmo Theologico exemplo, juxta quamdam opinionem D. Thomae, nam in Christo Domino, secundum D. Thomam, non est realis filiatio ad matrem, in Virgine vero est realis relatio ma- /col. b/ ternitatis ad Christum; signum est ergo unam ex his relationibus non pendere essentialiter et formaliter ab alia; alias non posset una manere sine alia, etiam de potentia absoluta; et similiter est signum unam non esse formalem terminum alterius, quia etiam non potest relatio sine suo termino conservari. Quae omnia principia sunt certa in doctrina D. Thomae, et ideo censeo hoc argumentum valde efficax ad hominem contra Cajetanum, et Thomistas qui eum sequuntur. Dico autem formaliter non pendere unam relationem ex alia; nam concomitanter possunt dici aliquo modo invicem pendere, quia non potest esse una sine alia ex natura rei, imo nec de potentia absoluta, saltem nisi aliquo modo mutetur fundamentum alterius extremi, et fiat incapax relationis, ut ab opinionibus de relatione filiationis in Christo abstrahamus. Atque hinc facile declaratur altera pars, nimirum, ex praedicto modo independentiae non sequi, relationes non esse simul natura. Nam potius si proprie ac formaliter una ab alia penderet, non posset non esse una prior natura alia, quia ipsamet dependentia est quaedam posterioritas naturae; quia vero habent necessariam concomitantiam, qua non potest esse una sine alia, absque ullo ordine inter se, ideo sunt simul natura.

30. *Relativa ut sint cognitione simul.* --Ex his praeterea constat quid dicendum sit de simultate cognitionis, quod in secundo argumento contrarii fundamenti petebatur. Nam eadem proportione dicendum est, formaliter et immediate

relationem non pendere in cognitione, nisi a suo termino secundum propriam rationem terminandi, et non secundum relationem oppositam, quod recte probat argumentum. Et in relativis non mutuis est manifestum, nam ut cognoscam relationem servitutis creaturae ad Deum, non oportet cognoscere relationem realem domini in Deo, quia nulla est; necque etiam necesse est fingere relationem rationis in Deo; hoc enim non pertinet per se ad cognitionem alterius relationis, sed si in nobis fit, provenit ex imperfecto modo cognoscendi nostro; Angelus enim, et Deus ipse comprehendit in creatura relationem servitutis, nullam fingentes in Deo relationem rationis. Dices: nonne necesse est cognoscere Deum ut dominum, ad cognoscendam creaturam ut servam? Respondetur necessarium esse cognoscere Deum ut dominum realiter, non relative secundum rationem. Est autem Deus realiter /p. 856/ dominus simpliciter, ut quaest. 7 de Potent., art. 10, ad 4, et saepe alias, D. Thomas notavit: primo per potestatem realem coercendi subditos; secundo, quia ad ipsum terminatur relatio realis servitutis, quae est in creatura; et utroque modo necesse est cognoscere Deum ut dominum ad cognoscendam relationem servitutis creaturae. Nam primum, id est, potestas coercendi subditos, est ex parte Dei ratio terminandi relationem servitutis, et ideo cognitio ejus quasi antecedenter et causaliter est ratio cognoscendi relationem servitutis; nam, sicut illa relatio consurgit ex vi illius termini et fundamenti, ita cognosci non potest, nisi cognito tali termino et fundamento. At vero secundum convenit Deo per actualem tendentiam respectivam creaturae in ipsum, denominatione tantum extrinseca, et quia non potest cognosci relativum ut sic, nisi ut terminatum ad suum terminum, ideo sub ea ratione non antecedenter, sed concomitanter cognoscitur Deus ut dominus. Atque hoc, quod in hoc exemplo declaratum est, habet locum in relatione creaturae, et omnibus non mutuis.

31. Neque ratio superius facta contra hoc est alicujus momenti; concedimus enim non posse cognosci relationem servitutis non cognita in termino aliqua ratione absoluta, non tantum omnino simul, sed etiam antecedenter seu causaliter, ut dixi; non est tamen necesse ut illa ratio absoluta exacte, aut prout in se est, cognoscatur, nam satis est quod abstractive, vel sub aliqua confusa ratione apprehendatur, quanquam quo terminus perfectius fuerit cognitus, eo perfectior erit cognitio relationis. Quae omnia facile declarantur in dicto exemplo, nam ad cognoscendam relationem servitutis quam creatura habet ad Deum, necesse est saltem in communi cognoscere Deum habere superiorem quamdam potestatem in creaturam, ratione cujus potest aut illi praecipere, aut de illa disponere suo arbitrio, et quanto amplitudo hujus potentiae magis fuerit cognita tanto perfectius cognoscetur qualis sit illa servitus; nec fieri potest ut Angelus vel Deus ipse cognoscat hanc servitutem, nisi cognoscendo in ipso talem potentiam. Non oportet autem ut Angelus, verbi gratia, qui in creatura

naturaliter intuetur relationem servitutis, naturaliter etiam intueatur potentiam Dei in seipso, sed satis est quod abstractive et ex effectibus cognoscat talem Dei potentiam. Multoque minus necesse est co- /col. b/ gnoscere totam Dei naturam, vel alia attributa, formaliter ac per se loquendo, quia illa ut sic non sunt ratio terminandi talem relationem. Atque ad hunc modum facile est idem intelligere in relatione creaturae, ut est effectus Dei, vel scientiae, aut sensus, et in aliis non mutuis.

32. At vero in relativis mutuis partim eadem est ratio, partim diversa. Est enim eadem ratio quantum ad formalem dependentiam cognitionis a termino ut sic, et non a correlativo ut sic; hoc enim etiam in relativis mutuis verum est. Nam ut cognoscam in aliquo homine relationem patris, satis est ut cognoscam esse in mundo alium hominem ab illo genitum, etiamsi ibi sistam, et non cognoscam in alio extremo relationem filiationis; et juxta opinionem D. Thomae, Angelus, etiam malus, per virtutem naturalem (si non impediebatur) intuebatur in beata Virgine relationem maternitatis ad hunc hominem Christum, et tamen non intuebatur in Christo relationem filiationis; ergo habebat cognitionem unius relativi cum intrinseca dependentia ab ejus termino, sine cognitione corelativi ut sic. Nec enim probabile est, necessarium fuisse Angelo fingere aliam relationem rationis in uno extremo, ut alteram valeret cognoscere; idem ergo est in qualibet alia relatione mutua, nam quoad hoc eadem est omnium ratio.

33. Quoad concomitantiam vero est nonnulla diversitas, quia ex natura rei, cognita una relatione mutua, necessario simul cognoscitur alia, saltem concomitanter. Nam sicut relatio est per quamdam resultantiam, posito fundamento et termino, ita cognoscitur cognitis illis, cum comparatione eorum inter se. Quia ergo hae relationes mutuae saltem per concomitantiam simul resultant positis fundamento et termino, ideo consimili ratione simul cognoscuntur cognitis et inter se collatis fundamento et termino; et quia hoc necesse est ad singularum relationum cognitionem, ideo consequenter fit ut, una cognita, simul concomitanter cognoscatur alia. Quod in nobis speciali ratione necessarium est, quia non cognoscimus has relationes prout in se sunt, sed solum cognoscendo et inter se conferendo fundamenta et terminos; ex quo praeterea oritur ut etiam illa extrema, quae non habent mutuam relationem, per modum correlativorum mutuorum cognoscamus; et inde etiam fit ut ubi uni relationi non correspondet altera relatio realis, nos concipiamus re- /p. 857/ lationem rationis, ut ita concomitanter cognoscamus utrumque extremum per modum correlativi. In cognitione autem perfecta rerum, prout in se sunt, id non est necessarium quoad relativa non mutua, ut dictum est. Quoad relativa vero mutua, est eadem vel major necessitas, aut quia relationes non distinguuntur actu a parte rei a suis fundamentis, aut si fortasse distinguuntur ex natura rei, sunt ita conjunctae et connexae cum fundamentis simul existentibus, et inter

se collatis, ut non possit cognosci respectus unius ad aliud, quin cognoscatur etiam vicissim respectus alterius ad alterum. His ergo modis intelligendum est correlativum esse simul cognitione cum suo termino, vel cum suo correlativo.

34. *Relativa quomodo sint simul definitione.*—Ad tertiam autem partem illius fundamenti, quae erat de simultate definitionis, eodem prorsus modo respondendum est. Nam definitio non est nisi cognitio quaedam, si in mente sit, vel signum cognitionis, et consequenter rei cognitae, si sit in voce; et ideo in tantum possunt relativa esse simul definitione, in quantum sunt simul cognitione. Est igitur proportionali modo dicendum, unum relativum, formaliter loquendo, non definiri per aliud correlativum, sed per suum terminum, quem essentialiter respicit. Imo Scotus supra existimat hoc esse necessarium ne committatur circulus aut nugatio, si loco nominis positi in definitione ponatur ejus definitio, aut ne idem sit prius et posterius seipso, quia quod ponitur in definitione, est aliquo modo prius definito. Sed haec non admodum cogunt, si considerentur quae de his definitionibus per additum attigit Aristoteles, 7 Metaph., c. 5, et quae ibi notavimus; instanturque facile illa incommoda in relativis transcendentalibus, ut sunt materia et forma, de quo videri etiam possunt supra dicta, disput. 43, sect. ult., in fine. Non ergo propter vitanda haec incommoda, sed propter rem ipsam, quia unumquodque definitur formaliter ac praecise per id ad quod habet habitudinem, verum est in definitione unius relativi per se non poni aliud extremum, nisi sub ea ratione quae in illo necessaria est ad terminandam talem relationem. Concomitanter vero, sicut relativa sunt simul cognitione, ita etiam definitione, et quia nos facilius ita illa concipimus et explicamus, ideo simpliciter dici solet unum relativum definiri per aliud, et e converso. Atque in hoc sensu accipiendam est cum communiter dicitur correlativa esse simul definitione.

De terminis divinarum relationum.

35. Ad ultimam rationem, quae in secunda sententia addebatur, sumptam ex relationibus divinis, quae invicem terminantur, respondetur imprimis esse disparem rationem, quia illae relationes non habent fundamentum praeter seipsas, eo quod sint substantiales et subsistentes ex propriis rationibus, et ideo mirum non est quod, sicut seipsis fundantur (ut ita loquar), ita unaquaeque seipsa terminet suum correlativum. Quia potius in hoc servatur proportionalis ratio; diximus enim fundamentum unius relationis esse rationem terminandi correlationem ejus; ita ergo fundamentum paternitatis divinae est ratio terminandi divinam filiationem; tamen sicut fundamentum illius paternitatis nihil est praeter paternitatem ipsam, ita ratio terminandi filiationem nihil etiam est praeter ipsam.

36. Adde, quamvis haec vera sint secundum rem, si tamen secundum rationem vel imperfectos conceptus nostros cogitentur haec ut distincta, eo modo quo quis conceperit relationes et fundamenta ut distincta, debere etiam concipere rationem terminandi unam relationem, non esse aliam relationem ut sic, sed fundamentum illius.

Ut, verbi gratia, si quis ratione distinguat relationes et origines, et cum Bonaventura sentiat personas originibus constitui, relationes autem eis advenire, et in eis fundari, consequenter dicet formalem terminum paternitatis, verbi gratia, esse passivam originem in Filio; e contrario vero terminum filiationis esse generationem activam in Patre; respicit enim Pater eum quem genuit ut sic, et Filius enim a quo genitus est. Similiter qui cum Cajetano distinxerit paternitatem ut conceptam, vel ut exercitam, et sub priori ratione senserit constituere personam, sub posteriori vero referre illam, et ita hanc posteriorem rationem fundari in priori, dicat necesse est consequenter, unam relationem ut exercitam, terminari ad aliam ut conceptam, et e converso. Et quidem sive utamur illis vocibus, sive aliis, relatio non habet rationem termini, ut aliud respicit, sed ut in se est aliquid, quod ab alio aptum est respici; atque ita etiam secundum modum concipiendi nostrum, quacunque ratione distinguatur ibi fundamentum a relatione, vel persona cons- /p. 858/ tituta, a respectu, distinguitur etiam ratio terminandi a relatione.

37. Quod clarius apparet in spiratione passiva respectu activae, nam Pater et Filius praeter spirationem activam habent proprias relationes quibus in suo esse personali constituuntur, et sic constituti, sunt unum principium spirans Spiritum sanctum; ex qua productione (loquendo more nostro) resultat in eis relatio spirationis activae, cui propterea magis proprie attribui potest, quod habeat fundamentum et rationem fundandi secundum rationem, quia neque constituit personam, nec fortasse habet propriam subsistentiam. Atque ita ibi facile intelligitur relationem passivam spirationis, quae est in Spiritu Sancto, terminari non ad spirationem activam formaliter, sed ad Patrem et Filium, ut sunt unum principium spirans, cui nostro modo concipiendi advenit relatio spirationis activae. Quia propria ac formalis ratio ob quam Pater et Filius terminant, vel terminare possunt relationem Spiritus sancti, non est quia referuntur ad Spiritum sanctum, sed quia producunt Spiritum sanctum et sunt unum principium ejus, unde concomitanter habent ut ad ipsum referantur. Si tamen, per possibile vel impossibile, intelligeremus non resultare in Patre et Filio illam relationem, dummodo producerent Spiritum sanctum, id satis esset ut possent terminare relationem ejus.

38. Ex quo obiter intelliget Theologus quomodo de facto Filius distinguitur ab Spiritu sancto, non primo per relationem spirationis activae, sed per filiationem per quam complete constituitur in esse personali, et consequenter distinguitur a qualibet alia persona. Et nihilominus verum est, quod si Filius

non produceret Spiritum sanctum, non distingueretur ab illo, quia tunc, posita illa hypothesi, filiatio non esset fundamentum spirationis activae, nec ratio terminandi processionem passivam; et consequenter neque haberet cum illa oppositionem originis; nunc autem vere habet haec omnia, et ideo est sufficiens principium distinctionis; sed haec Theologis relinquamus.

De oppositione relativa.

39. Tandem ex his quae in hac sectione diximus, intelligere licet in quo consistat, et qualis sit propria oppositio relativa; hoc enim supra in hunc locum remisimus. Potest autem intelligi haec oppositio aut inter rela- /col. b/ tionem et terminum ejus, aut inter relationem unam unius extremi, et alteram correspondentem illi in alio extremo, seu inter unum relativum, et correlativum ejus. Prior oppositio est generalis omnibus relationibus, etiam non mutuis, ut constat ex dictis, et ideo formalissime convenit relationi ut sic. Consistit autem in hoc, quod relativum ut sic et terminus, habent inter se talem habitudinem, et conditiones ita distantes, ut necessario requirant inter se distinctionem, nam relativum est id quod respicit, terminus autem est id quod respicitur ab alio, atque ita ex propriis rationibus requirunt alietatem (ut sic dicam).

40. At vero posterior oppositio non est universalis omnibus relationibus realibus vere ac secundum rem; nam[8] relationibus non mutuis non convenit, quamvis modo nostro concipiendi fingi posset ac si conveniret, quod ad praesens nihil refert. Inter relativa autem realia et mutua, ac relationes ipsas, intercedit relativa oppositio, quae non consistit in hoc quod una respiciat aliam ut terminum, sed in hoc quod unum respiciat ut terminum id, quod est fundamentum alterius, et e converso, seu (quod idem est), quia habent oppositas rationes, nam una refert suum subjectum ad aliud, alia vero, e contrario, refert illud aliud ad id quod erat subjectum alterius. Ex quo talem inter se habent repugnantiam, ut non possint ambae relationes uni et eidem simul inesse, quia non potest unum et idem esse fundamentum et terminus respectu ejusdem. Qui modus oppositionis licet clarius appareat in relationibus dissimilium rationum, ut inter paternitatem et filiationem, tamen etiam suo modo convenit relationibus aequiparantiae, quia licet sint ejusdem speciei, possunt in individuo esse aliquo modo oppositae relative, quia afficiunt sua subjecta secundum oppositas habitudines, ex quo repugnantiam habent in eodem subjecto. Quamvis autem haec oppositio aliquo modo sit diversae rationis, respectu termini, et respectu correlationis, tamen quia concomitanter se habent ubicunque inveniuntur,

---

8   Here the Vivès edition inserts "quid," which is lacking in Salamanca, 1597, vol. 2, p. 594.

ideo per modum unius nominantur et judicantur. Dici vero potest relatio opponi termino terminative, alteri vero relationi relative. Et haec posterior est quasi formalis oppositio, nam est inter proprias formas quatenus se mutuo excludunt ab eodem subjecto; prior vero proprie est repugnantia relativorum, quia postulant dis- /p. 859/ tinctionem extremorum, quod significavit etiam D. Thomas, q. 7 de Potentia, art. 8, ad 4.

SECTIO XVII.
Quomodo praedicamentum Ad aliquid sub uno supremo genere, per diversa genera subalterna et species usque ad individua constitui possit.

1. Explicuimus fere omnia quae ad intelligendam essentiam relationis, et causas ejus, et formalem effectum (non enim habet alium), necessaria visa sunt; superest ad hujus rei complementum, ut de subordinatione, convenientia, et distinctione ipsarum pauca dicamus ut ita totius praedicamenti constitutio quasi prae oculis habeatur. Tria autem puncta in titulo quaestionis insinuantur, quae ab aliis latissime tractantur, et a nobis brevissime expedienda sunt.

De supremo genere praedicamenti Ad aliquid.

2. Prima ergo difficultas est, quomodo possint omnia relativa ad unum genus summum reduci. Et ratio dubitandi est, quia essentia relationis est, ut ejus esse sit ad aliud; ergo non potest ita relativum abstrahi, quin ei aliud adaequate correspondeat; ergo non potest dari unum genus summum, sed ut minimum debent esse duo, quae se invicem respiciunt. Patet consequentia, quia non potest esse unum et idem id quod respicit, tum quia in ipsa definitione continetur, quod debet esse aliud, tum etiam quia non potest idem realiter referri ad seipsum. Tum denique quia si essentia relativi in communi esset referri ad se, hoc ipsum esset de ratione et essentia cujusvis relationis particularis, cum essentia superioris in inferiori includatur. Quae difficultas vulgaris est in hac materia, et magnum facessit negotium, iis praesertim qui putant unum relativum formaliter referri ad alterum correlativum ut sic; nam juxta hanc sententiam, cum dicitur relativum in communi esse id cujus esse est esse ad aliud, necesse est subintelligi in definitione, ad aliud correlativum; unde cum non possit idem referri ad se relatione reali, de qua agimus, necessarium erit ut non sit unum supremum genus, sed duo, quae se invicem et adaequate respiciant, sintque in re ipsa distincta.

3. *Unum supremum genus relationis datur.*—Nihilominus tamen certum est posse dari unum supremum genus omnium relativorum; nil enim refert de abstractis po- /col. b/ tius quam de concretis loqui, et ex uno potest inferri

aliud. Nam, si datur generalissimus conceptus relationis realis et praedicamentalis in communi, poterit etiam dari relativi in communi, tum ob rationem proportionalem, tum etiam quia omni formae abstractae potest respondere constitutum, seu concretum illi adaequatum. Quod vero possit dari unum supremum genus relationum, patet, tum ex ipso modo loquendi de relatione in communi, ut sic, nam hic terminus communis est omnibus relationibus, et pro omnibus distribuitur, quia de omnibus univoce dicitur, et in quid. Tum etiam quia definitio relationis in communi unica est, et omnibus relationibus praedicamentalibus convenit. Tum denique quia si quis fingat duo illa genera suprema relativorum, inter illa inveniet convenientiam essentialem in ratione essendi ad aliud; ergo ab eis abstrahere poterit conceptum univocum et essentialem utrique communem, in quo etiam facile inveniet differentias extra illius rationem, quae non sint completae relationes; erqo.

4. *Ut solvant aliqui rationem dubitandi.*—Ad difficultatem autem positam respondent aliqui, in definitione relativi in communi cum dicitur esse ad aliud, per illud *aliud*, intelligi quidem correlativum, et illud non posse esse ipsummet, quod definitur, ut sic, propter rationem factam, quod non potest idem realiter ad se referri. Nec etiam esse aliquod aliud relativum aeque commune, et non contentum sub eo quod definitur, propter difficultatem tactam de uno supremo genere. Aiunt ergo per illud *aliud*, importari singula correlativa specifica, vel particularia singularum relationum. Quae est responsio Alberti, 5 Metaph., tractat. 3, cap. 7, et in praedic. Ad aliquid, ibique, Simplicii et Boetii. Potestque ita exponi, quia, licet relatio in communi definiatur per esse ad aliud, tamen non exercet hoc esse ad aliud nisi in determinatis relationibus, et ideo non est necesse ut, quatenus abstractissime concipitur, intelligatur exercere munus relationis in ordine ad aliud correlativum sibi adaequatum, quia ut sic potius concipitur essentia relationis quasi in actu signato, seu designando id in quo consistit, quam in actu exercito, id est, exercendo illam habitudinem ad aliquid, in tota illa communitate. Potius ergo intelligendum est illam rationem sic abstracte conceptam non exercere suam habitudinem ad aliud, nisi in suis inferioribus. /p. 860/

5. Quod etiam diverso modo intelligitur in relativis aequiparantiae et disquiparantiae, nam in relativis disquiparantiae, saltem in communibus rationibus specificis, potest intelligi, unum relativum commune referri ad aliud sibi aequale et oppositum, ut patrem ad filium, majus ad minus. Et ratio est, quia cum hae relationes sint diversarum rationum, non concipiuntur uno conceptu communi specifico, et ideo possunt abstrahi duo conceptus communes aequales, et sibi oppositi ac correspondentes. Quod secus est in relationibus aequiparantiae; nam cum sint ejusdem rationis, habent eumdem communem conceptum specierum, et ideo non potest tali conceptui respondere alius conceptus objec-

tivus communis et oppositus correlative, ut simile non dicitur ad aliud simile
in communi, nec aequale ad aliud aequale in communi, sed solum ratione
individuorum, in quibus datur unum aequale distinctum ab alio. Et de his
verum habet quod dixit Augustinus in lib. Categoriar., cap. 11, *specialiter ac
regulariter, ut haec categoria manifestius dignoscatur, non recte dici ad aliquid,
nisi cum singulare ad singulare refertur.* Verum est statim ponere Augustinum
exempla non solum in relativis aequiparantiae, sed etiam in eis quae diversorum
sunt nominum et rationum; tamen in his nihil impedit, ut dixi, quominus
unum etiam in communi ad aliud commune correlativum referri intelligatur.
Et in hunc modum hoc notavit Scotus, in 1, d. 21, et alii.

6. Haec doctrina probabilis est, et licet supponat unum fundamentum falsum,
nimirum, unum relativum terminari formaliter ad suum correlativum, nihilominus potest esse utilis ad explicandum quomodo possint correlativa assignari,
quando nostris conceptibus abstrahantur, et in communi concipiuntur; sic
enim recte sine dubio dicitur, non nisi in relationibus dissimilium nominum
et rationum posse unum relativum commune alteri communi respondere; in
relativis autem aequiparantiae, aut in relativo in communi non posse, quia cum
haec abstrahantur vel a relativis ejusdem rationis, vel simpliciter ab omnibus
relativis, unite concipitur utrumque relativum per modum unius secundum
id in quo conveniunt, et ideo non potest hujusmodi relativo communi aliud
aequale correspondere. Et ideo etiam de hujusmodi relativo in communi
concepto recte dicitur non esse de essentia ejus, ut immediate illi sic concepto
respondeat aequale correlativum, sed satis /col. b/ esse ut dum contrahitur ab
inferiora, in eis inveniatur haec relativorum reciprocatio. Imo addo, loquendo
de relativo in communi, non esse de essentia ejus ut etiam mediate et in inferioribus exerceat dictam reciprocationem relativam, quia communis ratio
relationis praedicamentalis ut sic non postulat ut ei saltem ut contractae ad
inferiora respondeat altera relatio in alio extremo; nam si hoc esset de essentia
relationis in communi, omnibus relationibus specificis deberet convenire; at hoc
falsum est, nam relationibus non mutuis minime convenit. Nec refert quod eis
possit respondere relatio rationis in alio extremo, quia hoc non spectat ad essentiam relationis realis, cum sit mere extrinsecum ex imperfectione nostra.

7. *Relativum in communi non est ad aliud tamquam ad correlativum.*—Atque
hinc ulterius colligo, cum relativum in communi definitur esse ad aliud, illud
aliud non posse accipi pro correlativo, quia per illam definitionem traditur
aliquid essentiale relativo, ut sic , non est autem essentiale relativo ut ei respondeat correlativum, neque immediate et in communi concepto, neque in suis
particularibus omnibus, ut ostensum est. Quod praeterea confirmatur, quia
si *aliud* est ipsum correlativum, quaero an sit correlativum reale, aut rationis,
vel alterutrum indifferenter, seu juxta exigentiam inferiorum relationum; nihil

autem horum dici potest. Nam duo prima membra facile excluduntur, quia neutrum eorum potest esse universale omnibus relationibus, ut satis constat ex dictis. Tertium etiam non est verisimile, tum quia alias illud aliud valde aequivoce sumeretur, cum relativum rationis fere aequivoce relativum sit; tum etiam quia (ut dicebam) correspondentia relationis rationis non est ex naturis rerum, et ideo non potest ad essentiam relationis pertinere.

8. Dico igitur, illud aliud in dicta definitione dicere terminum relationis ut sic, qui non dicit correlativum, ut tale est, sed aliud extremum, prout in se habet sufficientem rationem terminandi, quae ratio fere semper est absoluta; et si interdum est aliqua relatio, non tamen ut exercet munus relationis oppositae alteri relationi, sed prout in se habet aliquam unitatem, vel similem rationem communem rebus absolutis.

9. *Relativum in communi habet terminum in communi sibi respondentem.*—Unde infero ulterius, relationem in communi posse conci- /p. 861/ pi ut habentem aliud ad quod dicat habitudinem, non solum in suis inferioribus, sed etiam ut conceptam illo communissimo conceptu, nam relationi in communi correspondet etiam terminus in communi. Neque inde sequitur dari duo genera suprema, quia terminus in communi non est aliquod relativum ut sic, et ideo non constituit, in praedicamento Ad aliquid, aliquod genus.

10. *Ratio communis termini cur proprium non constituat praedicamentum.* —Dices: ergo saltem constituet commune aliquod genus alterius praedicamenti, quod est plane falsum, quia illa ratio termini vagatur per omnia praedicamenta, imo et extra praedicamentum, quia ipsi Deo convenit. Respondetur negando consequentiam, quia ratio termini non est in rebus aliqua ratio vel proprietas realis aliquo modo distincta ab ipsis, vel accidens ipsis, sed est ipsamet entitas uniuscujusque rei, quatenus apta est ad terminandam relationem alterius. Quae ratio est quasi transcendentalis, et forte non est univoca, praesertim cum in Deum et creaturam conveniat. Unde sub ea ratione in nullo praedicamento per se ponitur, sed reduci potest ad praedicamentum relativorum, tanquam quoddam additum, sicut ponitur in definitione eorum. Potestque hoc a simili declarari, quia sicut convenit relationi in communi habere terminum, ita et habere fundamentum; nec videtur dubium quin haec ratio fundamenti relationum possit aliquo modo in communi concipi tanquam adaequate respondens relationi etiam in communi conceptae, quia in propria natura relationis praedicamentalis ut sic includitur, quod supponat fundamentum, et in eo rationem aliquam ob quam consurgat seu resultet. Non est autem necesse ut haec communis ratio fundamenti sit aliquod genus, sed est ratio quasi transcendentalis, quae vagatur per omnia praedicamenta. Unde Aristoteles quantitati attribuit per modum proprietatis, quod sit sufficiens fundamentum aequalitatis vel in aequalitatis, qualitati vero, quod sit fundamentum similitudinis, vel dissimilitudinis (ita

enim has proprietates ibi declaravimus). Quae ratio fundamenti ut sic non est in eis aliqua ratio respectiva, neque etiam est aliqua ratio absoluta distincta ab ipsis, sed est ipsamet entitas uniuscujusque, quatenus per se habet talem aptitudinem, et ideo ad praedicamentum uniuscujusque formae reducitur per modum proprietatis, et indirecte posset reduci sub ea ratione ad praedica-/col. b/ mentum relationis tanquam fundamentum ejus; ita ergo de relationis termino existimandum censeo. Atque haec sint satis de primo puncto.

Quomodo supremum genus relativorum ad inferiora descendat.

11. Secundus punctus hujus sectionis est, quomodo hoc summum genus relationis per varia genera usque ad infimas species descendat, seu dividatur. Quae res magna ex parte declarata est in superioribus, in quibus varias divisiones relationis attigimus et explicavimus. Quarum prima ac praecipua fuit trimembris, per varia fundamenta genere diversa, quae sub his nominibus unitatis, actionis et mensurae recenseri solent. Ex quo facile intelligitur, sub quolibet horum membrorum ulterius procedi posse, verbi gratia, in primo per varios modos unitatum, et quia sub unitate multitudo subintelligitur, primo dividendae erunt relationes unitatis a relationibus multitudinis seu diversitatis, et postea, juxta varios modos unitatis aut multitudinis realis, dividentur etiam sub utroque genere relationes. Idemque proportionaliter dicendum est de actione, et consequenter etiam de passione, et de potentia activa et passiva, vel latius etiam de causa et effectu, si haec omnia sub illa voce comprehenduntur. Ac denique idem est de ratione mensurae, nam etiam in eo genere variantur relationes, juxta diversas proportiones mensurarum et mensurabilium.

12. *Divisio relationis in mutuam et non mutuam, qualis.*—Ex hac autem divisione insurgunt aliae, quae in superioribus etiam tactae sunt, nimirum, divisio relationis in mutuam et non mutuam, quae satis late declarata est. Ex dictis tamen constat hanc non esse subdivisionem alicujus membri praecedentis divisionis, sed potius esse aliam adaequatam divisionem relationis in communi, complectentem sub uno membro, scilicet, sub relatione non mutua, tertium membrum prioris divisionis, et nonnullas alias relationes contentas sub prioribus membris; sub altero autem membro comprehendentem fere prima duo genera praecedentis divisionis. Possent autem hae duo divisiones ita subordinari, ut prius dividatur relatio in eam, quae ex vi fundamenti formalis est non mutua, et eam quae ex vi fundamenti seu ex genero suo id non habet, et haec rursus subdividatur in relationem fundatam in actione, vel unitate, /p. 862/ et sic procedatur, donec in illis duobus generibus perveniatur ad relationes inter Deum et creaturam, quae non tam ex formali ratione fundamenti seu rationis fundandi, quam ex peculiari natura et conditione Dei habent quod sint non

mutuae, et ita facile erit per subordinatas divisiones hujusmodi praedicamentum constituere.

13. *D. Damasceni dictum explicatur.*—Illud enim animadversione dignum est, Divum Damascenum, in sua Dialectica, c. 50, cum alias plures relationum divisiones ponat, hanc praetermisisse, imo significare, non recte consentire hanc divisionem cum relativorum natura, *siquidem* (ait) *mutua habitudo ea quae ad aliquid sunt efficit.* Verumtamen haec verba vel non sunt intelligenda de singulis relativis, sed de complexu utriusque; ille enim vere consistit in mutua habitudine; non est autem necesse ut talis reciprocatio saltem realis in omnibus relativis interveniat; vel, si illa verba applicentur ad singula relativa, mutua habitudo intelligenda est cum proportione, quia ex parte relationis necesse est ut ad aliud tendat, ex parte vero termini ut sit id ad quod aliud tendit. Quod vero Damascenus illam divisionem praetermiserit, mirum non est, quia non omnia dixit, quae de relationibus dici possunt, et fortasse causa fuit, quia, nostro modo concipiendi, omnes apprehenduntur ut mutuae.

14. *Divisio relationis in ejusdem vel diversae appellationis.*—- Altera divisio supra tacta est in relationem ejusdem vel diversae appellationis, seu aequiparantiae vel disquiparantiae, et hanc late tractat Damasc., dicto cap. 50, quam subdividit in relationem praecellentiae, ut esse dominum, esse majus, esse causam; et relationem inferioritatis, ut esse servum, effectum, aut minus, etc., quae subdivisiones ad relationes disquiparantiae pertinent, nam in relationibus aequiparentiae, cum sint ejusdem rationis, non potest esse illa diversitas. Et fortasse inter res creatas nunquam reperitur relatio disquiparentiae, absque illa diversitate; tamen inter personas divinas invenitur sine praecellentia, vel inaequalitate, nisi quis velit cum Patribus Graecis ipsum ordinem originis dignitatem appellare; de quo alias. Haec autem divisio, in rigore et proprietate sumpta, non est divisio relationis in communi, sed mutuae; nam non mutua cum non sit reciproca, non est ejusdem nec diversae rationis in utroque extremo. Nisi quis velit sermonem extendere ad eam denomi- /col. b/ nationem correlativam, quae ex relatione rationis sumitur; sic enim omnia correlativa erunt ejusdem vel diversae denominationis. Denique haec divisio, ut ex dictis constare potest, non datur per id quod per se ac formaliter pertinet ad rationem relationis, quia, ut diximus, una relatio formaliter non terminat alteram; unde neque dat illi speciem aut essentialem diversitatem: quando autem uni relationi altera respondet ejusdem vel diversae rationis, est indicium diversitatis fundamenti ac termini formalis, et ita, quod attinet ad constitutionem hujus praedicamenti, haec divisio ad praecedentes revocanda est.

Differentia essentialis et specifica relationum unde sumenda.

15. Una tamen poterat superesse quaestio circa hunc secundum punctum, videlicet, unde sit sumenda distinctio specifica et essentialis relationum usque ad ultimas species, an, scilicet, ex fundamento vel ex termino. Aliqui enim ita distribuunt inter haec duo munera, ut dicant a fundamento habere relationem entitatem, a termino autem speciem seu essentiam et distinctionem essentialem. Alii vero utrumque munus utrique attribuunt, unicuique in suo genere. Quod mihi non displicet; existimo tamen utrumque dicendi modum recte explicatum continere veritatem. Itaque formaliter et intrinsece relationes constituuntur suis propriis differentiis in propriis speciebus, et per eas essentialiter distinguuntur, hoc enim commune est omnibus rebus. Tamen, quia totam suam essentiam habet relatio in ordine ad terminum, ideo ab illo quasi ab ultima forma extrinseca sumit suam specificationem, et ideo per illum distinguitur et definitur, ut supra dictum est, sect. 8. Quia vero etiam fundamentum formale est per se et intrinsece requisitum ad relationem, potest dici etiam concurrere ad essentiam relationis, quasi per modum causae materialis extrinsecae. Et ita D. Thomas interdum hoc tribuit fundamento, interdum termino, ut patet ex 3 parte , quaest. 35, art. 5, et 1 parte, q. 32, art. 2, ubi simpliciter id tribuit termino, quia ille est quasi ultimum et magis formale respectu relationis. Vide Soncin., 5 Metaph., quaest. 32, et supra dicta, sectione 8, num. 9, et sect. 10, n. 14.

Sintne plures relationes solo numero diversae simul in eodem subjecto.

16. Circa tertium punctum occurrebat hoc /p. 863/ loco quaestio de individuatione relationum; certum est enim quod, sicut in caeteris praedicamentis constitutio lineae praedicamentalis descendit a supremo genere usque ad individua, ita etiam in hoc; controversum autem est an, sicut ad essentialem constitutionem et specificationem relationum concurrit suo modo terminus, ita etiam ad individuationem. Ex quo pendet etiam decisio illius vulgaris quaestionis, an idem subjectum sub eadem ratione specifica referatur ad plures terminos eadem numero relatione, vel diversis. Quaestionem sufficienter, ut existimo (est enim res non magni momenti) attigi supra, disp. 5, sect. 8, ubi de individuatione accidentium, et an possint esse plura numero in eodem subjecto, generatim tractavi.

17. Et juxta principia ibi posita, sine ulla difficultate concedi potest, plures relationes solo numero differentes, respicientes diversos terminos, esse simul in eodem subjecto, ut, verbi gratia, duas paternitates in eodem homine respectu duorum filiorum. Quia effectus formalis unius non est omnino similis effectui formali alterius, ut citato loco declaravi. Item quia , posito uno termino, resultat aliqua relatio, quae omnino pendet ab illo; addito vero alio termino,

additur novus respectus, qui manebit etiamsi alter terminus destruatur. Item quia unusquisque terminus est totalis terminus alicujus relationis, quando quidem illo solo posito consurgit aliqua relatio. Et similes rationes possunt facile multiplicari, propter quas Scotus, et alii, quos ibi citavi, hanc opinionem amplectuntur. Neque in ea est difficultas alicujus momenti, praeter eam generalem, quod accidentia individuantur ex subjecto, de qua citato loco satis fuse dictum est.

18. *Quid consequenter dicendum hac super re, si relatio est distincta in re a fundamento.*—Quoniam vero in hac re potest magna ex parte dissensio esse in modo loquendi, advertendum est, aliter procedendum esse si teneamus relationem esse rem, vel modum realem ex natura rei distinctum a fundamento, aliter vero si solum ratione distinguitur. Nam juxta priorem sententiam, non potest consequenter negari quin, multiplicatis terminis, realiter augeantur respectus, et quin, addito novo termino, aliquid reale addatur praeexistenti relativo. Ut cum pater generat secundum filium, aliquid respectivum acquirit quod antea non habebat, aeque distinctum ab ipso, ac erat Paternitas quam antea ha- /col. b/ bebat, quia hoc convincunt, consequenter loquendo, rationes factae. Et quia est omnino eadem ratio, nam si Petrus cum genuit primum filium, indiguit nova re, aut novo modo reali distincto, ut ad illum realiter referretur, cur non etiam quando de novo incipit referri ad secundum? Neque enim dici potest priorem entitatem aut modum sufficere, tum quia non potest effectus formalis crescere, nisi realiter crescat forma; tum etiam quia prior relatio adaequate referebat ad primum filium, et ab illo pendet in esse, et in definitione et cognitione; non enim cognoscitur haec relatio ut haec numero, nisi ut referens ad hunc numero terminum, ut aperte Aristoteles declaravit in Praedicam., c. de Ad aliquid.

19. Jam vero si semel admittatur fieri additionem realem in relativo, facta additione novi termini, fortasse est solum de nomine quaestio, an illud additum sit distincta relatio, vel componat unam cum praexistente, sicut secundus gradus cum primo componit unum calorem; ita enim aliqui explicant unitatem hujus relationis, ne videantur in infinitum relationem multiplicare, et ut universe defendant illud axioma, in uno subjecto tantum esse unum accidens unius speciei. Verumtamen qui sic loquuntur, non possunt satis illam unitatem explicare, nisi tantum denominative, ratione unius subjecti seu suppositi. Nam si consequenter loquantur, necesse est ut dicant, tantam esse distinctionem inter paternitatem ad primam filium, et id quod additur patri, genito secundo, quanta est inter paternitatem ipsam et fundamentam ejus; itaque si haec distinguuntur realiter vel modaliter, etiam illa. Probatur, quia relatio paternitatis ad primum filium ita comparatur ad id quod additur respectu secundi filii, ut possit illa paternitas esse sine hoc addito, et e converso possit manere hoc additum, et constituere patrem, sine illa prima paternitate; ergo si paternitas

est modus realis distinctus, quia est separabilis a fundamento, etiam isti duo modi erunt inter se actu distincti ex natura rei, quia unus est separabilis ab alio, et e converso. Et similiter, si paternitas est propria entitas realiter distincta a fundamento, etiam illi duo respectus erunt inter se realiter distincti, ut recte et consequenter docet Scot., quia sunt mutuo et vicissim separabiles. Ostensum est autem supra, disp. 7, quandocumque duo ita distinguuntur in re, ut vicissim /p. 864/ et unum sine alio, et alterum sine altero manere possit, et alioqui non sunt modi alicujus subjecti, cum quo habeant identitatem realem, tunc illud esse sufficiens signum distinctionis realis inter illa. Sed relationes, juxta illam sententiam, non sunt modi, sed propriae entitates realiter distinctae a subjectis, et inter se ita comparantur respectus patris ad primum filium, et ad secundam, ut et prior sine posteriori et posterior sine priori existere possit; ergo distinguuntur inter se vera distinctione reali.

20. Posita autem hac distinctione, nulla ratio reddi potest cur illae non distinguantur ut duae relationes, vel cur dicantur esse duo gradus, vel duae partes unius relationis, et non potius relationes duae. Primum enim non recte aequiparantur gradibus intensionis; nam inter hos gradus est subordinatio per se et in eis est propria compositio et unio per propriam latitudinem, vel propria indivisibilia, ut praecedenti disputatione declaratum est; illae autem duae relationes non habent subordinationem per se; neque enim una per se supponit alteram, vel ab illa pendet, neque habet unaquaeque earum latitudinem aliquam in se, sed est mere indivisibilis in ordine ad suum terminum; unde neque proprie componunt aliquam latitudinom quasi continuam, quia haec non componitur ex indivisibilibus. Deinde, nullum aliud genus unionis inter illas duas entitates excogitari potest, ob quam dicantur esse duae partes unius relationis, quia neque inter se comparantur ut potentia et actus, neque habent inter se aliam habitudinem, praeter eam quae est esse in eodem subjecto. Et hoc a fortiori confirmari potest ex his quae supra diximus de simili habituum unitate vel compositione physica. Imo illa unitas vel compositio artificiosa, quae in habitibus consideratur, vix potest habere locum, in relationibus, et ideo de illa nihil tractatur.

21. Alio vero modo posset quis excogitare unitatem hujus relationis ad plures terminos, non per additionem aut compositionem realem, sed per mutationem relationum, ita ut unaquaeque in se sit indivisibilis; differunt tamen inter se, quia una habet pro adaequato termino unam rem, verbi gratia, unum filium, alia vero duos, alia tres, etc. Unde juxta hanc sententiam, quando pater secundum filium generat, nova quidem relatio ei acquiritur, non tamen praeexistenti additur, sed prior perit, et alia de /col. b/ novo resultat, quae indivisibiliter et adaequate refert illum hominem ad duos filios, et non ad plures nec pauciores: et si generet tertium, amittet illam, et acquiret aliam referentem ad tres eodem

modo. Quod enim una relatio possit adaequate respicere plures terminos indivisibiliter, certum videtur; sic enim in relativis realibus praedicamentalibus
totum refertur ad plures partes, vel unitas ad binarium relatione subdupli; et
in transcendentalibus idem intellectus respicit plura intelligibilia inadaequate,
et in relativis eadem relatio generis respicit plures species. Sic ergo intelligi
potest in quocunque genere vel specie relationum dari aliquas in individuo,
indivisibiliter, et adaequate respicientes plures terminos, qui respectu illarum
erunt partiales, ex illis vero consurget terminus adaequatus, qui sit unus collectione quadam; et ideo talis relatio non consurgit nisi posito adaequato
termino, non vero posito uno vel altero partiali; e contrario vero aufertur seu
mutatur ablato vel addito quocunque termino partiali, quia hoc ipso mutatur
terminus totalis.

22. Tandem hoc modo opinantur multi de relatione unius filii ad patrem et
matrem. Nam quod illa relatio, per se loquendo, sit una indivisibilis, inde fit
probabile, quod pater et mater concurrunt ut una causa, et per se necessaria
et unica actione (praesertim si mater concurrit active). Unde alterutro parente
mortuo, necesse est illam relationem perire, quia si indivisibiliter respiciebat
duos, nec potest dividi in partes, nec tota manere, cum jam non habeat adaequatum terminum, nec referat ad duos; perit ergo tota; necessarium ergo erit
ut oriatur alia, quae ad unum tantum parentem referat, si superstes sit; nam
vere ac realiter ad illum refertur filius.

23. Sed licet hic modus dicendi ad consequenter loquendum in illa sententia
videatur acute excogitatus, tamen revera est voluntarius et sine fundamento. Quae
est enim necessitas introducendi illam frequentem mutationem relationum.
Alias quoties nova res alba fieret, mutarent caetera omnia alba, quae antea erant,
suas relationes similitudinis respectu omnium, et novas acquirerent. Deinde
cur pater amittet relationem ad primum filium, genito secundo, cum nihil eorum tollatur, quae ad esse illius relationis necessaria erant? Quia, non obstante
secundo filio, prior semper est sufficiens terminus illius /p. 865/ relationis
Item quamvis verum sit, posse unam relationem respicere plura adaequate
quando per se et ex vi suae speciei illa requirit ut resultet vel conservetur, seu
ut exerceat suum effectum formalem, ut est in relatione totius aut subdupli,
tamen quando relatio non postulat hoc ex sua ratione, et termini solum per
accidens multiplicantur, ut contingit in paternitate, filiatione, similitudine, etc.
mere gratis dicitur consurgere unam indivisibilem relationem, quae adaequate
respiciat collectionem plurium terminorum, eo vel maxime quod plures filii
distinctis generationibus producuntur; cur ergo resultabit una indivisibilis
relatio complectens utrumque terminum?

De relatione filii ad patrem et matrem.

24. *Ferrariensis opinio improbatur.*—Quod vero dicebatur de relatione filii ad duos parentes, etiam est incertum. Nam aliqui putant in filio esse duas relationes, non solum numero, sed etiam specie differentes, quia existimant relationem patris et matris etiam specie differre, eo quod ille active, haec tantum passive concurrat. Ita tenet Ferrar., 2 contra Gent., c. 11, § Ex istis, quanquam addat, illas relationes esse duas formaliter, unam vero realiter seu materialiter; quod non video quomodo consequenter dicatur, supponendo relationem esse quid distinctum in re a fundamento, ut ille supponit.

25. *Fonsecae opinio non probatur.*—Alii vero dicunt esse unam relationem ad utrumque parentem, etiamsi pater active et mater solum passive concurrat; et simul aiunt, eamdem omnino relationem, et immutatam manere, etiamsi alter parens moriatur. Ita Fons., lib. 5 Metaph., cap. 15, quaest. 5, sect. 3. Sed utrumque est mihi difficile creditu. Primum quidem, quia si mater solum passive concurrit, ergo relationes patris et matris ad filium erunt specie diversae, cum habeant fundamenta adeo distincta; ergo fieri non potest ut eis respondeat unica relatio in correlativo, quod docet D. Thomas, 1 parte, q. 32, art. 2. Quia correlativa specie diversa vel sunt termini formaliter diversi, vel eos indicant; relationes autem habent diversitatem ex terminis formalibus. Item relatio effectus ad causam diversi generis etiam est diversa, sive illa materialis sit, sive formalis, sive efficiens; si ergo causalitates patris et matris differant, ut efficiens et materialis, relationes in effectu erunt diversae. Unde, illa sententia supposita, /col. b/ pater et mater non tam componunt unam causam totalem, cum non causent in eodem genere, quam collectionem plurium causarum diversorum generum, qualia sunt materia et efficiens. Secundo, est difficile creditu in illa sententia, quod relatio sit una indivisibiliter ad patrem et matrem, ut complent unam causam totalem, et tamen quod eadem relatione integra maneat, ablato illo adaequato termino ex altera parte, quia relatio pendet ex termino adaequato. Quod ita declaro, quia, ablato uno parente, jam illa filii relatio non potest habere suum adaequatum effectum formalem, cum non possit referre filium ad utrumque parentem; ergo absolute non potest habere effectum formalem suum, quia, cum indivisibiliter illum causet, non potest conferre partem ejus, et non totum, nec potest tota manere quin conferat totum effectum, cum non maneat nisi in subjecto, et inhaerens.

26. *Aliorum opinio.*—Alii ergo, qui cum Galeno, Scoto, et aliis, satis probabiliter censent matrem active concurrere, existimant filium referri ad patrem et matrem duabus relationibus ejusdem speciei, et quia diversitas in concursu paterno et materno accidentalis tantum est. Et quamvis pater et mater simul componant unam causam totalem efficientem, juxta hanc sententiam, tamen sicut non sunt una causa, nisi collectione plurium partialium, ita satis est

ut illis correspondeat unum correlativum collectione plurium relationum. Quanquam hic posset cum aliqua probabilitate dici illas relationes componere unam, non proprie physica unitate, sed quasi artificiali, et accommodata unitati termini. Quocunque vero ex his modis de relatione filii sentiatur, nihil refert ad dictam sententiam, quam impugnamus; nullum enim auctorem invenio qui dixerit, filium cum orbatur altero parente, amittere relationem quam habet ad utrumque, et novam acquirere, qua ad solum superstitem referatur, neque id habet ullam verisimilitudinem.

27. Ita ergo sentiendum videtur de multiplicatione relationum solo numero differentium in eodem subjecto respectu plurium terminorum adaequatorum et ejusdem rationis. Quod quidem juxta sententiam, quam veram existimamus, scilicet, relationem non esse rem aut modum ex natura rei distinctum a fundamento, facilius expeditur. Quia dubitari non potest quin respectus ad terminos distinctos realiter, quorum unus potest sine /p. 866/ alio esse, et e converso , distinguantur ratione ratiocinata, quae habet fundamentum in re. Unde, sicut haec distinctio sufficit, ut relatio constituat peculiare genus, et censeatur quasi alia forma a fundamento, ita etiam sufficit ut illi respectus ad diversos terminos dicantur plures relationes numero distinctae eo genere distinctionis, quod in hujusmodi relationibus locum habet, scilicet rationis ratiocinatae. Et ita facile tollitur admiratio de multiplicatione relationum, et omnia argumenta, quae in contrarium objici solent, difficultatem non habent, praesertim his suppositis, quae de principio individuationis diximus; neque etiam ad persuadendam hanc sententiam in hoc sensu oportet rationes multiplicare, nam praeterquam quod per se satis est verisimilis, quae insinuatae sunt, sufficiunt.

28. Denique in hoc sensu non multum repugnat D. Thomas huic sententiae; nam 3 parte, quaest. 35, art. 5, ad 3, ait in uno filio esse unum relationem ad duos parentes, et duas secundum rationem, et e converso ait, in pluribus hominibus trahentibus navim, esse unam relationem, quod non potest intelligi de unitate rei, cum subjecta realiter distinguantur; et aliis locis, licet dicat in uno patre esse unam relationem ad plures filios, dicit tamen in eo esse plures respectus. Et eodem modo loquitur Hispalens., in 3, dist. 8, notab. 3, et Capreol., ibidem, in solut. argument. Non vocantur autem illi respectus plures nisi ob distinctionem rationis; ergo eodem modo, dici possunt plures relationes. Et tandem declaratur a simili; nam Theologi simpliciter vocant paternitatem et spirationem activam in divinis duas relationes propter distinctionem terminorum, etiamsi in se ratione tantum distinguantur; quid ergo mirum quod in praesenti dicantur etiam plures relationes ad plures terminos realiter distinctos?

SECTIO XVIII.
Quaenam proprietates communes sint omnibus relativis.

1. De hac re nihil Aristoteles dicit in Metaphysica; in Dialectica vero nonnullas posuit relativorum proprietates, quas breviter exponere oportet, quanquam earum aliquae jam explicatae sint. Possemus autem sermonem extendere ad communia entis attributa, praesertim unum et bonum; nam peculiarem habent difficultatem in modo quo relationi- /col. b/ bus conveniunt. Sed de unitate jam satis multa dicta sunt. Circa bonitatem vero occurrebat illa quaestio, an relatio dicat perfectionem, quam supra tractavimus, disp. l0, et ostendimus ita dicere perfectionem, sicut habet entitatem. Unde si est res distincta a fundamento, vel etiam modus realis ex natura rei distinctus, necesse est ut perfectionem aliquam realem illi addat; si vero nihil rei addit, sed sola ratione distinguitur, perfectionem quidem realem dicet, non tamen in re distinctam; et consequenter, simpliciter loquendo, non addet perfectionem suo fundamento, sed dicet eamdem, sub diversa ratione. Caetera in dicto loco satis tractata sunt.

An relatio contrarium habeat.

2. Deveniendo ergo ad proprietates relativorum a Philosopho assignatas, prima est, quod relatio habeat contrarium; nam virtus vitio contraria est. Sed haec non assignatur ab Aristotele ex propria sententia, sed tanquam consequens ex prima definitione relativorum, quae omnia relativa secundum dici complectebatur. Potius ergo contrarium numerari potest inter proprietates relationis, quod illi, quatenus talis est, nihil est contrarium, ut idem Philosophus dixerat in c. de Qualit. Sed habet relatio suum proprium oppositionis genus, quod jam explicatum est.

An relatio magis aut minus suscipiat.

3. Secunda proprietas est, quod relatio suscipit magis et minus, quam dicit Aristoteles convenire quibusdam relationibus, non omnibus; nam duplum non est magis et minus duplum, simile autem vel aequale dicitur magis et minus. Sed est advertendum, aliter tribui hanc proprietatem relationi quam qualitati; huic enim convenit, quia vere est intensibilis et remissibilis, ut praecedenti disputatione tractatum est. Relatio vero non est ita intensibilis, quia nec per se, cum per se non fiat, nec augeatur; nec ratione fundamenti; nam, licet fundamentum intendatur, non necesse est intendi relationem; non sunt enim magis similia duo alba intensa ut octo, quam antea cum erant ut quatuor; e contrario vero interdum fiunt magis similia per remissionem fundamenti, aut termini, aliquando vero minuitur similitudo.

4. Hoc vero magis aut minus in relationibus non est propter intensionem earum, sed propter variationem, ut bene notavit Fonsec., /p. 867/ lib. 5 Met., c. 15, q, 5, sect. 2. Relatio enim aequalitatis, verbi , gratia, proprie dictae (et idem est de perfecta similitudine) non suscipit magis et minus, quia in indivisibili consistit; nam si ex duobus aequalibus alterum crescat, non fiunt minus aaqualia, sed perit aequalitas; inaequalitas vero esse potest major et minor, propter majorem et minorem recessum a perfecta aequalitate; et eodem modo aequalitas vel similitudo late et vulgari modo dicta dicitur major et minor; tamen illae relationes majoris vel minoris inaequalitatis revera sunt diversae, et non eadem, quae augeatur vel minuatur, quia termini et fundamenta earum sunt diversa, et proportiones in quibus consistunt sunt etiam diversae, atque ita unaquaeque in suo gradu inaequalitatis in indivisibili consistit. Sic ergo dicuntur quaedam relativa suscipere magis et minus, id est, denominari magis et minus talia per accessum vel recessum ab uno perfecto termino, non per intensionem aut remissionem.

Quomodo relativa ad convertentiam dicantur.

5. Tertia proprietas est, quod relativa dicuntur ad convertentiam, quam aliqui ita exponunt, ut idem sit quod mutuo referri, seu quod uni relationi semper correspondeat alia. Sed, ut constat ex dictis, in hoc sensu non conveniet haec proprietas omnibus relationibus, nisi extendatur ad relationem rationis. Unde non est hic sensus Aristotelis, sed solum quod secundum aliquam denominationem unum denominetur cum adjunctione alterius, et e converso, ut scientia dicitur scibilis scientia, et scibile dicitur scientia scibile; et ideo ait Aristoteles, hanc convertentiam interdum in eodem, interdum in diverso casu fieri. Unde haec proprietas magis pertinet ad modum loquendi de relationibus quam ad rem, quanquam ille modus loquendi in re habeat fundamentum. Non est autem haec proprietas peculiaris relationum praedicamentalium; nam etiam convenit relativìs transcendentalibus, imo et relativis rationis.

6. Quarta proprietas est, quod relativa sunt simul natura. Quinta, quod sint simul cognitione et definitione, quae jam sunt a nobis expositae; et ideo de praesenti disputatione haec sufficiant.

PERSONS MENTIONED BY SUÁREZ

Albert the Great, St., O.P. (ca. 1200-1280)—Dominican theologian, Bishop of Regensburg, and teacher of St. Thomas Aquinas.

Alexander of Aphrodisias (fl. ca. 200)—Commentator on the works of Aristotle.

Alexander of Hales, O.F.M. (ca. 1186-1245)—Franciscan theologian at the University of Paris.

Anselm, St. (1033-1109)—Theologian, Archbishop of Canterbury, author of *Proslogion* and *Monologium*.

Antonio Andreas (d. ca. 1320)—A disciple of Duns Scotus whose own writings were mingled with those of his master. Among other works, Antonio authored "Questions on the 12 Books of the *Metaphysics*" and was the probable author of the "Exposition of the 12 Books of the *Metaphysics*," which was attributed to Duns Scotus in the 1639 Wadding edition of Scotus's *Opera omnia*.

Aquinas, St. Thomas (1225-1274)—Dominican and foremost philosopher-theologian of the Middle Ages.

Aristotle (384-322 BC)—Greek philosopher, disciple of Plato, called "The Philosopher" (*Philosophus*) by the Latins

Augustine of Hippo, Saint (354-430)—Bishop of Hippo, most important Latin theologian and Church Father.

Averroes (*aka* Ibn Rushd [1126-1198])—Arabic philosopher, commented on Aristotle's works for which he was called by the Latins as "the Commentator" (*Commentator*).

Avicenna (*aka* Ibn Sina [980-1037]—Arabic philosopher, renowned for learning and medical skill; author of numerous scientific, religious, and philosophical works, including an original presentation of Aristotelian metaphysics.

Biel, Gabriel (1410?-95)—Philosopher and theologian at Tübingen, follower of Ockham's nominalism.

Boethius, Anicius Manlius Severinus (ca. 480-524/5)—Christian Latin philosopher and theologian, translated and commented on logical writings of Aristotle, author of "On the Consolation of Philosophy" (*De consolatione philosophiae*).

Cajetan (*aka* Thomas de Vio, O.P. [1469-1534])—Cardinal, theologian, Master General of the Dominicans, and principal commentator on the *Summa Theologiae* of St. Thomas Aquinas

Capreolus, Joannes, O.P. (1380-1444)—Thomistic commentator, known as the "Prince of Thomists" (*Princeps thomistarum*).

Damascene, St. John (d. 780)—Christian archbishop of Damascus, theologian, author of "On the Orthodox Faith" (*De fide orthodoxa*) and "Dialectic" (*Dialectica*).

Durandus of Saint Pourçain, O.P. (ca. 1275-1334)—Dominican theologian, Bishop of Meaux, important figure in early 14th century theology at Paris.

Ferrara, [Francis Sylvester of] Ferrara, O.P. (1474-1528)—Theologian, Master General of the Dominicans, and principal commentator on the *Summa contra Gentiles* of St. Thomas Aquinas.

Fonseca, Pedro da, S.J. (1548-1599)—Jesuit philosopher, edited and translated the *Metaphysics* of Aristotle. He was himself known as "the Portuguese Aristotle."

Francis of Mayronnes, O.F.M. (ca. 1280-1325)—Fransciscan theologian, a pupil of Duns Scotus, whom he interpreted in an often independent way.

Giles of Rome *(aka* Aegidius Romanus, O.S.A. [ca. 1244/7-1316])—Philosopher and theologian, a pupil of St. Thomas Aquinas, and later Archbishop of Bourges. Commented on Aristotle at the University of Paris before 1300.

Gregory of Rimini, O.S.A. (d. 1358)—Theologian, Minister General of the Augustinians, influenced by nominalism.

Henry of Ghent (1217?-1293)—Belgian, secular master of theology at Paris, influenced by St. Augustine and Avicenna, opposed on many points by Duns Scotus.

Hervaeus Natalis, O.P. *(aka* Hervé Nédélec [d. 1323])—Dominican theologian, Master General of his Order, author of various works including a "Treatise on Second Intentions" *(Tractatus de secundis intentionibus)*.

Hispalensis (aka Diego Deza O.P. [1444-1523]—Professor of Theology at Salamanca, Archbishop of Seville (1505), patron of Christopher Columbus. His chief work was *Defensiones Doctoris Angelici, S. Th. Aquinatis* (Seville, 1491).

Javelli, Chrysostom, O.P. (d. ca. 1538)—Philosopher and theologian. He often followed the opinions of Hervaeus Natalis.

Lychetus, Francis, O.F.M. (d. 1512)—Franciscan philosopher and theologian, principal commentator on the works of Duns Scotus.

Marsilius of Inghen (ca. 1340-1396)—Philosopher and theologian at Paris and then at Heidelberg. He was the first to receive a Magister's degree in Theology at Heidelberg.

Nifo, Agostino, (ca. 1470-1538)—Italian professor of Philosophy. Taught at Padua, Naples, and Pisa. Commented on Averroes and Aristotle, especially the *Metaphysics*.

Ockham, William of (ca. 1285 -1349)—Most important philosopher of the 14th century. Principal medieval nominalist.

Petrus Aureoli (ca. 1280-1322)—Franciscan, Archbishop of Aix, regarded as nominalist precursor of Ockham.

Plato (428-348 BC)—Greek philosopher, disciple of Socrates, and teacher of Aristotle.

Pseudo-Alexander of Hales (Alessandro Bonini, O.F.M. [ca. 1270-1314])—Author of a commentary on Aristotle's *Metaphysics* which was published at Venice in 1572 erroneously under the name of Alexander of Hales.

Peter the Lombard (ca. 1095-1160)—Bishop of Paris, author of the "*Sentences*," which became the standard text for theological instruction at medieval universities. As a condition for graduation all Masters of Theology were required to write commentaries on the *Sentences* of Peter the Lombard.

Richard of Middleton, O.F.M. (ca. 1249-1300/8)—Franciscan theologian.

Scotus, John Duns (1266-1308)—"The Subtle Doctor," the most important Franciscan philosopher and theologian.

Silvester [Mazzolini a.k.a. Prierias, O.P. (ca. 1456-1523)]—Dominican theologian. Taught at Rome. Was opponent of Martin Luther. His theological works include a famous *Summa Summarum quae Silvestrina dicitur, Compendium Capreoli,* and *Conflatum ex sancto Thoma,* which last was cited in Section 2 of Disputation 47.

Simplicius (ca. 490-560)—Neoplatonist philosopher. The last head of the Platonic Academy in Athens. Author of important commentaries on Aristotle.

Soncinas, Paul, O.P. (d. 1494)—Dominican philosopher, author of a much cited "Metaphysical Questions" (*Quaestiones metaphysicales*).

Soto, Domingo de, O.P. (1494-1560)—Dominican philosopher and theologian. Among other works, he authored commentaries on the *Isagoge* of Porphyry, as well as the *Categories* and the *Posterior Analytics* of Aristotle.

Bibliography
General Bibliographies

Iturrioz, J., "Bibliografía suareciana," *Pensamiento*, numero extraordinario (Madrid, 1948), 603ff.

Santos-Escudero, C., "Bibliografía suareciana de 1948 a 1980," *Cuadernos Salmantinos de Filosofía*, 7 (1980), 337-75.

Schmutz, Jacob, avec la collaboration de Salvador Castellote Cubells, *Francisco Suárez, S.J. (1548-1617: Bibliographie Generale*, Madrid, Dernière actualisation : 21 juillet 2003: at ⟨http://www.ulb.ac.be/philo/scholasticon/bibsuarez.htm⟩.

Latin Edition Principally Used in this Work

Suarez, Franciscus, S.J., *Opera omnia*, 26 vols., Paris: L. Vivès, 1856-1866; plus two volumes of indices, 1878.

Disputationes Metaphysicae (originally: 1597), Vols. 25-26 of *Opera omnia* (Vivès), reprinted: Hildesheim: G. Olms, 1965.

Spanish Translation of the Disputationes Metaphysicae

Francisco Suárez, *Disputaciones metafísicas*, 7 vols., edición y traducción de Sergio Rábade Romeo, Salvador Caballero Sánchez y Antonio Puicerver Zanón, Madrid: Editorial Gredos, 1960-1966.

Various English Translations
from the Disputationes Metaphysicae

Suárez, Francisco, *On the Various Kinds of Distinctions (Disputatio VII)*, tr. Cyril Vollert, Milwaukee: Marquette University Press, 1947.

_____, *On Formal and Universal Unity (Disputatio VI)*, tr. James F. Ross, Milwaukee: Marquette University Press, 1964.

_____, *Disputatio V: Individual Unity and its Principle*, tr. Jorge J.E. Gracia, in *Suárez on Individuation*, Milwaukee: Marquette University Press, 1982.

_____, *On the Essence of Finite Being as Such, on the Existence of that Essence and their Distinction (Disputatio XXXI)*, translated from the Latin with an Introduction by Norman J. Wells, Milwaukee: Marquette University Press, 1983.

_____, *The Metaphysics of Good and Evil according to Suárez: Metaphysical Disputations X and XI and Selected Passages from Disputation XXII and Other Works*, Translation with Introduction, Notes, and Glossary, by Jorge J.E. Gracia and Douglas Davis, München: Philosophia Verlag, 1989.

_____, *On Efficient Causality: Metaphysical Disputations 17, 18, and 19*, translated by Alfred J. Freddoso, New Haven: Yale University Press, 1994.

_____, *On Beings of Reason (De Entibus Rationis): Metaphysical Disputation LIV*, translated from the Latin with an Introduction and Notes by John P. Doyle, Milwaukee: Marquette University Press, 1995.

_____, *On Creation, Conservation, and Concurrence: Metaphysical Disputations 20, 21, and 22*, Translation, Notes, and Introduction by Alfred J. Freddoso, South Bend, Indiana: St. Augustine's Press, 2000.

_____, *The Metaphysical Demonstration of the Existence of God (Metaphysical Disputations 28-29)*, translated and edited by John P. Doyle, South Bend, Indiana: St. Augustine's Press, 2004.

_____, *A Commentary of Aristotle's Metaphysics (Index locupletissimus in Metaphysicam Aristotelis)*, translated from the Latin with an Introduction and Notes by John P. Doyle, Milwaukee: Marquette University Press, 2004.

Further Reading

Alcorta, J.I., *La Téoría de los modos en Suárez*, Madrid: CSIC—Instituto Luis Vives, 1949.

Bannach, Klaus, "Relationen: Ihre Theorie in der spätmittelalterlichen Theologie und bei Luther," *Freiburger Zeitschrift für Philosophie und Theologie*, 47 (2000): 101-126.

Baum, M., "Relation. III Neuzeit," in *Historisches Wörterbuch der Philosophie*, Band 8 (Basel: Schwabe, 1971), cols. 595-602.

Bos, Egbert P., "Francis of Meyronnes on Relation and Transcendentals," in *Miscellanea Mediaevalia*, Band 30: *Die Logik des Transcendentalen (Festschrift für Jan A. Aertsen zum 65. Geburtstag)*, ed. M. Pickave, pp. 32–36.

Burns, J. Patout, "Action in Suarez," *The New Scholasticism*, 38 (1964): 453-72.

Copleston, Frederick, S.J., *A History of Philosophy*, vol. 3: *Ockham to Suarez*, Westminster, MD: Newman Press, 1953.

Courtine, Jean-François, *Suarez et le système de la métaphysique*, Paris: Presses Universitaires de France, 1990.

_____, "La doctrine cartésienne de l'idée et ses sources scolastiques," in *Les catégories de l'être: Études de philosophie ancienne et médiévale* (Paris: PUF, 2003), pp. 241-65.

Cronin, Timothy, S.J., *Objective Being in Descartes and in Suarez*, Rome: Gregorian University Press, 1966.

Darge, Rolf, *Suárez' transzendentale Seinsauslegung und die Metaphysiktradition*, Leiden/Boston: Brill, 2004.

Decorte, Jos, "Relatio as Modus Essendi: The Origins of Henry of Ghent's Definition of Relation," *International Journal of Philosophical Studies*, 10 (2002): 309-336.

_____, "Giles of Rome and Henry of Ghent on the Reality of a Real Relation," in *Documenti e Studi sulla Tradizione filosofica medievale*, 7 (1996): 183-211.

Deely, John, *Tractatus de Signis: The Semiotic of John Poinsot*. Interpretive Arrangement in consultation with Ralph Austin Powell, Berkeley: University of California Press, 1985.

_____, *Introducing Semiotic: its History and Doctrine*, Bloomington: Indiana University Press, 1982.

_____, *Four Ages of Understanding: The First Postmodern Survey of Philosophy from Ancient Times to the Turn of the Twenty-first Century*, Toronto/Buffalo/London: University of Toronto Press, 2001.

De Libera, Alain, *La querelle des universaux de Platon à la fin du Moyen Age*, Paris: Éditions du Seuil, 1996.

Denzinger, Henricus, and Adolfus Schönmetzer, S.J., *Enchiridion symbolorum definitionum et declarationum de rebus fidei et morum*, editio xxxii, Barcinone/Friburgi/Romae/ Neo-Eboraci: Herder, 1963.

Dibon, Paul, *La philosophie néerlandaise au siècle d'or, tome I: L'enseignment philosophique dans les universités à l'époque précartésienne (1575-1650)*, Paris/Amsterdam/Londres/New York, 1954.

Doig, James C., "Suarez, Descartes, and the Objective Reality of Ideas," *The New Scholasticism*, 51 (1977), pp. 350-71.

Doyle, John P., *The Metaphysical Nature of the Proof for God's Existence according to Francis Suarez, S.J.*, unpublished Ph.D. dissertation, University of Toronto, 1966.

_____, "Suarez on the Reality of the Possibles," *The Modern Schoolman*, 44 (1967): 29-40.

_____, "Suarez on the Analogy of Being," *The Modern Schoolman*, 46 (1969): 219-249; 323-341.

_____, "Heidegger and Scholastic Metaphysics," *The Modern Schoolman*, 49 (1972): 201-220.

_____, "*Prolegomena* to a Study of Extrinsic Denomination in the Work of Francis Suarez, S.J.," *Vivarium*, 22, 2 (1984): 121-160.

_____, "Suarez on Beings of Reason and Truth," *Vivarium*, 25, 1 (1987): 47-75; 26, 1 (1988): 51-72.

_____, "Suárez on the Unity of a Scientific Habit," *The American Catholic Philosophical Quarterly*, 65 (1991): 309-31.

_____, "Suárez, Francisco," *Routledge Encyclopedia of Philosophy* (London/New York: Routledge, 1998), vol. 9, pp. 189-196.

_____, "Gedankendinge bei den Jesuiten des 17. Jh.," in *Imagination—Fiktion—Kreation: Das kulturschaffende Vermögen der Phantasie*, hrsg. von Thomas Dewender und Thomas Welt (München/Leipzig: K.G. Saur, 2003), pp. 213-228.

Erler, M., "Relation. I Antike," in *Historisches Wörterbuch der Philosophie*, Band 8 (Basel: Schwabe, 1971), cols. 578-86.

Eschweiler, Karl, "Die Philosophie der spanischen Spätscholastik auf der Universitäten des 17 Jahrhunderts," in *Spanische Forschungen der Gorresgesellschaft*, Münster i.W.: Aschendorff, 1928, 251-325

Ferrater Mora, José, "Suárez and Modern Philosophy," *Journal of the History of Ideas*, 14 (1953): 528-43.

Fichter, Joseph, *Man of Spain: Francis Suarez*, New York: Macmillan, 1940 (A readable biography in English).

Francisco Suárez: *Metaphysical Disputation 47, On Real Relation*

Fitzpatrick, Edward A., *St. Ignatius and the* <u>Ratio Studiorum</u> (New York and London: McGraw-Hill, 1933

Giacon, C., "Suárez, Francisco," *Enciclopedia Filosofica*, IV (Venezia/Roma: Instituto per la Collaborazione Culturale, 1957), cols. 1025-30.

Gilson, Etienne, *Being and Some Philosophers*, 2nd edition, Toronto: Pontifical Institute of Mediaeval Studies, 1952, especially pp. 96-120.

Goudriaan, Asa, *Philosophische Gotteserkenntnis bei Suárez und Descartes in Zusammenhang mit der niederländischen reformierten Theologie und Philosophie des 17. Jahrhunderts*, Leiden/Boston/Köln: Brill, 1999.

Grabmann, Martin, "Die 'Disputationes Metaphysicae' des Franz Suarez in ihrer methodischen Eigenwart und Fortwirkung," in *Mittelalterisches Geistesleben*, Vol. I, München: Hueber, 1926.

Gracia, Jorge J.E., editor, *Francisco Suárez*, special issue, *American Catholic Philosophical Quarterly*, 65, 3 (1991). (Contains articles on various aspects of Suárez's work.)

Guy, Alain, "L'analogie de l'être selon Suarez," *Archives de Philosophie*, 42 (1979): 275-294.

Heidegger, Martin, *The Fundamental Concepts of Metaphysics: World, Finitude, Solitude*, translated by William McNeill and Nicholas Walker, Bloomington and Indianapolis: Indiana University Press, 1995.

_____, *Die Grundbegriffe der Metaphysik: Welt—Endlichkeit—Einsamkeit*, in *Gesamtausgabe, II. Abteilung: Vorlesungen 1923-1944*, Band 29/30, Frankfurt am Main: Vittorio Klostermann, 1976.

Hellin, José, S.J., *La analogia del ser y el conocimiento de Dios en Suárez*, Madrid: Gráficas Uguina, 1947.

_____, "Sobre el transito de la potentia activa al acto segun Suárez," *Razón y fe*, 138 (1948): 353-407.

_____, "El ente real y los posibles en Suárez," *Espiritu*, X (1961): 146-163.

_____, "Obtenación del concepto del ente, objeto de la metafísica," *ibid.*, 17 (1961): 135-154.

_____, "El concepto formal según Suárez," *Pensamiento*, 18 (1962): 407-432.

_____, "Esencia de la relación predicamental según Suárez," *Las Ciencias*, 23 (1958): 648-96.

_____, "Principio de identidad comparada," *Espiritu*, 24 (1975): pp. 135-42.

Henninger, Mark G., S.J., *Relations, Medieval Theories 1250-1325*, Oxford: Clarendon Press, 1989.

Hoeres, W., "Francis Suarez and the Teaching of John Duns Scotus on *Univocatio entis*," in *John Duns Scotus (1265-1965)*, ed. J.K. Ryan and B.M. Bonansea, Washington, DC: Catholic University of America Press, 1965.

Hoffmann, Philippe, "Les Analyses de l'enoncé catégories et parties du discours selon les commentateurs néoplatoniciens," in *Théories de la phrase et de la proposition de Platon à Averroès*, éd. P. Büttgen et al. (Paris: Éditions Rue d'Ulm, 1999), pp. 209-48.

Honnefelder, Ludger, *Scientia transcendens: Die formale Bestimmung der Seiendheit und Realität in der Metaphysik des Mittelalters und der Neuzeit*, Hamburg: Felix Meiner Verlag, 1990.

Iriarte, Joaquín, S.J., "La proyección sobre Europa de una gran metafísica, o Suárez en la filosofía de los dias del barocco," *Razón y fe*, 138 (1948): 229-65.

Iturrioz, Jesús, S.J., *Estudios sobre la metafísica de Francisco Suárez*, Madrid: Ediciones Fax, 1949.

_____, "Fuentes de la metafísica de Suárez," *Pensamiento*, numero extraordinario (Madrid, 1948): 31-89

Jansen, Bernhard, S.J., "Die Wesenart der Metaphysik des Suarez," *Scholastik*, 15 (1940): 161-85.

Jansen, F., "Eucharistiques (Accidents)," in *Dictionnaire de théologie catholique*, 5, 2ᵉ partie (Paris: Letouzey et Ané, 1939, cols. 1368-1452

Junk, Nikolaus, *Die Bewegungslehre des Franz Suarez*, Innsbruck/Leipzig: F. Rauch, 1938.

Klima, Gyula, "Ockham's Semantics and the Ontology of the Categories," in *The Cambridge Companion to Ockham*, ed. Paul Vincent Spade (Cambridge: Cambridge University Press, 1999), pp. 118-42.

Kobusch, Theo, *Sein und Sprache: Historische Grundlegung einer Ontologie der Sprache*, Leiden/New York: E.J. Brill, 1987.

_____, "Ens inquantum ens und ens rationis: ein aristotelisches Problem in der Philosophie des Duns Scotus und Wilhelm von Ockham," in *Aristotle in Britain during the Middle Ages: Proceedings of the International Conference at Cambridge, 8-11 April 1994 organized by the Société internationale pour l'étude de la philosophie médiévale*, edited by John Marenbon (Turnhout: Brepols, 1996), pp. 157-175

Krempel, A., *La doctrine de la relation chez saint Thomas*, Paris: Librarie Philosophique J. Vrin, 1952.

Lewalter, Ernst, *Spanische-jesuitische und deutschlutherische Metaphysik des 17 Jahrhunderts*, Darmstadt: Wissenschaftliche Buchgesellschaft, 1967 (reprint of Hamburg, 1935).

Marion, J.-L., "Entre analogie et principe de raison: la *causa sui*," in J.-M. Beyssade and J.-L. Marion (eds), *Descartes. Objecter et répondre* (Paris: Presses Universitaires de France, 1994), pp. 305-334.

Mathieu, V., "Relazione," *Enciclopedia Filosofica*, IV (Venezia/Roma: Instituto per la Collaborazione Culturale, 1957), cols. 26-38.

Mesnard, P., S.J., "Comment Leibniz se trouva placé dans le sillage de Suarez," *Archives de Philosophie*, XVIII (1949): 7-32.

Michel, A., "Relations divines," *Dictionnaire de Théologie Catholique*, tome XIII, deuxième partie (Paris: Letouzey et Ané, 1937), cols. 2135-56.

_____, "Hypostatique (Union)," in *Dictionnaire de théologie catholique*, tome septième (Paris: Letouzey et Ané, 1927), cols. 437-568.

_____, "Trinité, La théologie latine du VIe au XXe siècle," *Dictionnaire de Théologie Catholique*, tome XV, deuxième partie (Paris: Letouzey et Ané, 1950), cols. 1702-1830.

Mojsisch, B., "Relation. II Spätantike, Mittelalter und Renaissance," in *Historisches Wörterbuch der Philosophie*, Band 8 (Basel: Schwabe, 1971), cols. 586-95.

Monnot, P., "Suarez, François. I. Vie et oeuvres," in *Dictionnaire de Théologie Catholique*, XIV, 2$_0$ partie (Paris, 1941) cols. 2638-2649.

Morison, Samuel Eliot, *Harvard College in the Seventeenth Century* (Cambridge: MA, Harvard University Press, 1936.

Negro, Paola, "Intorno alle fonti scolastiche in Hugo Grotius," in *Dalla prima alla seconda Scolastica*, a cura di A. Ghisalberti (Bologna: Edizioni Studio Domenicano, 2000), pp. 200-251

Neidl, Walter M., *Der Realitätsbegriff des Franz Suarez nach den Disputationes Metaphysicae*, München, 1966.

Noreña, Carlos G., "Ockham and Suárez on the Ontological Status of Universal Concepts," *The New Scholasticism*, LV (1981): 348-62.

_____, "Suárez on the Externality and Internality of Relations," *Cuadernos Salmantinos de Filosofía*, X (1983): 183-95.

_____, "Heidegger on Suárez: The 1927 Marburg Lectures," *International Philosophical Quarterly*, 23:92 (1983): 407-24.

_____, "Suárez and Spinoza: the Metaphysics of Moral Being," *Cuadernos Salmantinos de Filosofía*, 12 (1985): 163-82.

_____, "Suárez and the Jesuits," *ibid.*: 267-86.

Owens, Joseph, C.Ss.R., *The Doctrine of Being in the Aristotelian Metaphysics*, third edition (Toronto: Pontifical Institute of Mediaeval Studies, 1978).

_____, "The Real Distinction of a Relation from its Immediate Basis," in *Summaries of Panel Discussions, American Catholic Philosophical Association, 39th Annual Meeting, April 20-21, 1965, Denver Colorado*, pp. 14-20.

Pavur, Claude N., S.J., *Ratio atque Institutio Studiorum Societatis Jesu: The Official Plan for Jesuit Education*, St. Louis: Institute for Jesuit Sources, 2005.

Pernoud, Mary Anne, "The Theory of the Potentia Dei according to Aquinas, Scotus and Ockham, *Antonianum*, 47 (1972): 69-95.

Rast, Max, S.J., "Die Possibilienlehre des Franz Suarez," *Scholastik*, 10 (1935): 340-68.

Robinet, A., "Suarez dans l'oeuvre de Leibniz," *Cuadernos Salmantinos de Filosofía*, VII (1980): 269-84.

_____, "Suarez im Werk von Leibniz," *Studia Leibnitiana*, XIII (1981): 76-96.

Roig Gironella, Juan, S.J., "La analogía del ser en Suárez," *Espíritu* (Barcelona), 36: 95 (1987): 5-47.

Schmutz, Jacob, "La doctrine médiévale des causes et la théologie de la nature pure," *Revue Thomiste*, 101 (2001): 217-264.

Schneider, Marius, O.F.M., "Der angebliche philosophische Essentialismus des Suarez," *Wissenschaft und Weisheit*, 24 (1961): 40-68.

Scorraille, Raoul de, S.J., *François Suarez de la Compagnie de Jesus*, 2 vols., Paris: Lethielleux, 1912-13. (still the definitive biography of Suárez).

Seigfried, Hans, *Wahrheit und Metaphysik bei Suarez*, Bonn, 1967.

South, J.B., "Francisco Suárez on Imagination," *Vivarium*, 39 (2001): 119-158.

Spade, Paul Vincent, "Ockham's Distinction between Absolute and Connotative Terms," *Vivarium*, 13 (1975): 55-76.

Varii, *Suárez en el cuarto centenario de su nacimiento (1548-1617)*, *Pensamiento*, 4, numéro extraordinario, Madrid, 1948.

Vezzosi, Giovanni, "Sulla relazione in San Tommaso: In dialogo con Krempel," *Sapienza*, 54 (2001): 489-96.

Wells, Norman J., "Suarez, Historian and Critic of the Modal Distinction between Essential Being and Existential Being," *The New Scholasticism*, 36 (1962): 419-444.

_____, "Old Bottles and New Wine: A Rejoinder to J.C. Doig," *The New Scholasticism*, LIII (1979-80): 515-23.

_____. , "Suarez on the Eternal Truths, I and II," *The Modern Schoolman*, 58 (1980-81): 73-104 and 159-174.

_____., "Material Falsity in Descartes, Arnauld, and Suárez," *Journal of the History of Philosophy*, 22 (1984): 25-50.

Werner, Karl, *Franz Suarez und die Scholastik der letzten Jahrhunderts*, 2 vols., Regensburg, 1889.

Max Wundt, *Die deutsche Schulmetaphysik des 17 Jahrhunderts*, Tubingen: J.C. Mohr, 1939

Zabalza Goicoecheandía, Miguel Angel, *"Relación" en Leibniz: significado y usos*, Pamplona: EUNATE, 1995.

Index of Names

Abraham de Balmes, 101
Albert the Great, 25, 407
Albert of Saxony, 67
Alcorta, J., 100, 412
Alluntis, F. 25, 98, 143, 259–260
Annibaldus Annibaldensis, 111
Anselm, St., 47, 63, 210
Antonio Andreas, 166, 174, 407
Aquinas, St. Thomas, 10–11, 16, 20,
    24, 25, 27, 42, 46, 51, 62, 66–67,
    73–74, 79–80, 83, 88, 95, 103, 110,
    124–128, 134, 143–144, 157, 159,
    164–165, 167–168, 170, 172–174,
    180, 185, 191, 197, 200, 203–204,
    210, 213, 215, 236–237, 239, 244,
    253, 259–260, 407–408, 416
Argyropolos, J., 18
Arias, L. 63
Ariew, R., 14
Aristotle, 78, 11, 15–22, 24–26, 30–31,
    3941, 43–44, 46, 49, 58, 63, 6566,
    6870, 7374, 80, 84–85, 98, 100–
    103, 107–109, 118, 125–126, 128,
    131, 133–134, 137, 149–152, 154–
    158, 160–161, 170–171, 174, 177,
    181–182, 184–189, 191–192, 195,
    198, 200–205, 213, 216, 220–221,
    223, 240, 247, 250, 255, 263, 265,
    407–409, 412, 415
Arriaga, R., 12, 207
Aubenque, P., 23
Augustine, St. 63, 247–248, 407–408,
    412
Averroes (aka Commentator), 16,
    22–23, 39, 45–46, 269, 272–273,
    407–408, 414
Avicenna, 11, 45, 49, 84, 135, 191–192,
    292, 407–408

Bazzi, P. 51, 79, 124, 126, 135, 165,
    174, 215, 237, 244
Bellarmine, R., 10
Bessarion, N., 18
Boehner, Ph., 24

Boethius, 23, 247, 407
Brentano, F., 15
Brown, S., 24
Buridan, J., 67
Büttgen, P., 23

Caballero, S., 28
Cajetan (aka Tommaso de Vio), 51, 80,
    89, 96, 108, 126, 135, 139–140,
    152, 168, 170, 174, 201–203, 210,
    214, 220, 223, 235–236, 241, 275,
    333, 337, 347, 407
Capreolus, J., 46, 51, 80, 135, 152,
    157–158, 210, 222, 261, 333, 370,
    407
Castellote, S., 18, 411
Cathala, M.D., 24
Cavellus (aka Hugh MacCaugwell), 166
Celluprica, V., 23
Chiaradonna, R., 23
Clement of Alexandria, St., 23
Cottingham, J., 14
Cratylus, 19

Damascene, St. John, 63, 251–252, 407
D'Ancona, C., 23
Darge, R., 45, 74, 163, 193, 412
De Haas, F., 23
De Libera, A., 23, 413
Denzinger, H., 47, 96, 413
Descartes, R., 1214, 412–415, 417
Descoqs, P., 71
Dewender, T., 136, 413
Diaz Diaz, G., 114
Dibon, P., 13, 413
Doyle, J., 3, 9, 18, 63, 72, 88, 202, 240,
    412413
Duhr, B., 12
Duns Scotus, John, 25–26, 33, 67, 89,
    98, 103, 135, 137, 143, 197, 259,
    407–409, 414–415
Durandus de SaintPourçain, 53–56, 61,
    209, 276–278, 407

Échard, J., 62
Eschweiler, K., 12, 413
Etzkorn, G., 61

Ferrara (aka Franciscus de Sylvestris
    Ferrariensis), 51, 80, 126, 128, 135,
    165, 203, 222, 258, 289, 408
Fichter, J., 9, 413
Fiering, N., 14
Fitzpatrick, E., 1617, 414
Fonseca, Pedro da, 18, 57–58, 150, 182,
    185187, 193, 197, 226, 258, 264,
    278, 379, 408
Francis of Mayronnes, 64, 135, 139,
    166, 408

Gabriel Biel, 209, 407
Gál, G., 24
Galen, 259
George, R.,15
Ghisalberti, A., 13, 416
Gilen, L., 14
Giles of Rome, 25, 61, 211, 408, 412
Gilson, E., 11, 14–15, 166, 414
Goudriaan, A., 13–14, 16, 414
Gracia, J., 9, 411, 414
Gregory of Rimini, 30, 46, 61, 67, 119,
    134, 150, 200, 206, 209, 408
Grotius, H., 13, 416

Heidegger, M., 1516, 413–414, 416
Hellin, J., 71, 414
Henry of Ghent, 47, 81, 84, 118, 211,
    408, 412
Heraclitus, 19
Hervaeus Natalis, 23, 62, 75, 81, 408
Hispalensis (aka Diego Deza), 80, 131,
    157158, 211, 220, 222, 261, 376,
    408
Hoffmann, P., 23, 414
Hurtado de Mendoza, P., 12

Ignatius of Loyola, St., 9, 12, 16–17,
    414
Iriarte, J., 12–13, 415
Iturrioz, J., 11, 411, 415
Javellus, Chrysostomus, 57

John Major, 113
Junk, N., 15, 415

Kalbfleisch, K., 23–24
Keckermann, B., 13
Kelley, F., 61
Klima, G., 24, 415
Kobusch, T., 22, 26, 415
Krempel, A., 2425, 33–34, 415, 417

Lampe, E., 12
Laurent, P. M.H., 89, 96, 152, 235
Ledesma, Martin de, 114
Ledesma, Pedro de, 114
Leibniz, G., 1415, 415–417
Lequien, M., 63
Lewalter, E., 13, 415
Lossada, L. de, 12
Lychetus, F., 166, 222, 376, 408
Luther, M., 42, 409, 412

Macken, R., 47, 82, 118–119, 211
Maggiolo, P., 66
Malou, J.B., 10
Mancio, J., 9
Mandonnet, P., 51, 62, 110–111, 165,
    191
Marcolino, V., 47, 61
Marega, M., 139–140
Marenbon, J., 26, 415
Marsilius of Inghen, 209, 408
Martini, J., 13, 209
Maurer, A., 25, 64
Mauro, S., 12
McNeill, W., 16, 414
McQuarrie, J., 16
Melanchthon, P., 12, 114
Michel, A., 71, 96, 241, 415
Miller, P.,14
Moerbeke, William of, 18, 23, 247
Molina, L., 10
Monnot, P., 9, 416
Morison, S., 14, 416

Negro, P., 13, 416
Nifo, A., 139, 222, 408
Noreña, C., 1, 416

Norton, A., 14
Oviedo, F., 12
Owens, J., 20, 416

Paban, C., 46
Parmenides, 19
Pattin, A. 23, 247
Paul V, Pope, 10
Pavur, C., 16, 416
Pègues, T. 46
Pépin, J., 23
Perler, D., 23
Pernoud, M. 42, 416
Peter the Lombard, 17
Petrus Aureoli, 119, 408
Philip II, King, 9
Plato, 46, 62, 407–408
Poinsot, J. (aka John of St. Thomas), 12, 39, 80, 412
Porphyry, 409
Puigcerver, A., 28

Quétif, J., 62

Rábade Romeo, S., 28, 101, 188–189, 197, 411
Reiser, B., 12, 39
Richard of Campsall, 25
Robinson, E., 16

Scheibler, C., 1314
Schmitt, F. 47, 63
Schmutz, J., 9, 411, 416
Schönmetzer, A., 47, 96, 413
Schopenhauer, A., 15
Scorraille, R. de, 9, 417
Seidl, H., 185
Silvester (Mazzolini aka Prierias, O.P.), 61, 409
Simplicius, 2224, 46, 247, 273, 409
Soncinas, 8081, 126, 135, 139140, 143, 152, 165, 213, 222, 253, 327, 371, 409
Sorell, T., 14
Soto, D., 46, 57, 102, 220, 273, 304, 409
South, J., 137, 412, 417

Spade, P., 24, 73, 415, 417
Spiazzi, R., 24

Timpler, C., 13
Toletus, Franciscus (Francisco de Toledo), 71
Trapp, A., 47, 61
Trombetta, A., 33

Van Riet, S., 45, 49, 84, 135, 191
Vásquez, G., 207
Vollert, C., 56, 411

Walker, N., 16, 414
Walter Chatton, 25
Welt, T., 15, 136, 413
Wells, N., 58, 208, 411, 417
William of Ockham, 2425, 74, 408
Wolff, C., 1415
Wolter, A., 25, 260
Wright, T., 14
Wundt, M., 13, 417

Zannata. M., 43

Index of Subjects

Absolute and relative, 7, 19–21, 29, 32

Absolute Accidents, 29, 51,

Absolute Power of God, 30, 42, 64, 129, 141, 179, 236

Abstract and Concrete Speaking of Relation, 118

Accident, 11, 20, 22, 30, 43, 47, 49, 53–55, 71–72, 79, 81–83, 89–90, 92, 94–95, 100, 104, 107–113, 117–121, 124–125, 127, 134, 138, 174, 179, 210–212, 229, 255, 258

Action, 8, 21–22, 24–25, 44, 55–56, 66–70, 74, 76, 93, 96–99, 125, 129–131, 136, 141, 150–151, 155–156, 159, 164–165, 168, 171, 177–183, 192, 199, 204, 209, 213, 215–216, 250–251, 257, 412

Active and Passive, 150, 159, 182–183, 192, 251

Active and Passive Potency, 150, 182, 192, 251

Actual Existence, 93, 133, 136, 219, 227

Agent, 25, 31, 60, 68–69, 93, 98–99, 129–130, 155–156, 180–183, 199, 204

Analogical Unity as founding a Relation, 173

Analogy, 43, 72, 81, 83, 85, 158, 173–174, 183, 413

Antepredicaments, 101

Appetite, 156, 191–192

Appetible, 156, 191, 193

Aptitudinal Inherence, 89

Aristotle's Divisions of Being, 22, 39,

Arithmeticians, 154, 167

Being of Reason, 7, 11, 21, 26, 81–83, 85, 91, 93, 119, 133, 136–137, 152

Being in and being toward, 29, 70–71, 110

Blessed Virgin Mary, 5, 27–28, 42, 181, 239, 416

Categorical versus Transcendental Relation, 7, 29,

Categorical Relation, 7, 21, 28–30, 51, 55–57, 59–60, 86–87, 91–95, 97–100, 107, 110, 117, 123, 133–135, 137–138, 140–141, 151, 173, 175, 184, 190, 199, 205, 224, 228, 230–231, 248, 250

Categories, 7, 11, 19–26, 31, 39–41, 43–45, 49, 58, 74, 76, 79, 81, 84, 86–87, 89, 99–102, 107–109, 111, 134, 138, 152, 156, 164–165, 167, 170, 183–184, 220, 246–247, 249–250, 253, 255, 263–264, 409, 412, 414–415

Causes of a Relation, 158

Change or Mutation and relation, 19–20, 63, 65–73, 76

Christ, 2728, 96, 181, 236237, 239

Classes of Relatives, 149

Coexistence of Absolutes, 154, 195–196

Conditions for Categorical Relation, 91, 129–131, 133, 155, 228

Connotation, 26, 193

Continuum, 143, 145–146, 328

Contrary, 30, 32, 44, 102, 127–128, 142, 166, 187, 192, 203, 241, 243, 257, 260, 263–264

Convertibility, 264–265

Coordination, Constitution, or Genus of the Category of Relation, 177, 245–253

Correlatives, 140, 144, 201, 205, 234, 239–240, 246, 248, 252, 259

Creator, 42, 60, 77, 209–210, 215, 224, 226, 232, 270, 288, 369, 373, 379

Creatures, relation to God, 63, 174, 200, 214, 224–225

Definitions (first and second) of Relation, 7, 28–29,

Dependence in Being, 160

Desiring, 193

Disposition toward, 33, 58, 60, 80, 84–93, 96, 98, 102, 109–110, 112, 137, 144, 154–156, 159, 175, 180, 204–205, 216, 235, 247

Disquiparence, 247, 252

Distance, 55, 157

Distinction between a Foundation and a Subject of a Relation, 30

Distinction between a Relation and its Foundation, 29, 52, 61

Distinction of the Reasoned Reason, 29,

Distinction of Reason, 29, 58–59, 61, 64, 74, 76, 92, 153, 169, 204, 261

Distinction of Categories, 74

Divine Action ad extra, 130

Divine Concurrence, 70, 412

Divine Word, 96, 146, 157, 200

Divine Persons, 63, 144, 214, 252

Divine Relations, 104–105

Division of Categorical Relation, 7, 28, 30,

Dominion of God, 213

Efficient Cause, 107, 157, 194, 200, 209

Equality, 27, 31, 66, 120, 123, 125–126, 128, 144–145, 149, 153, 168, 171–172, 174, 188, 197–198, 250, 264

Equiparence, 197–198, 229, 243, 247–248, 252

Essential Being, 9293, 133

Eucharist, 114

Existential Being, 57, 93, 417

Extremes of a Relation, 32, 118, 177–179, 184, 197–201, 204–206, 209–210, 213, 215, 216–217

Extrinsic Denomination, 41, 4748, 60, 77, 91, 134, 155, 160, 175, 179–180, 193, 219, 224, 234, 238, 413

Extrinsically Occurring (or Arriving) Relations, 98, 230

Father, 27, 32, 48, 60, 97, 103, 111, 115, 118, 121, 129–130, 145, 150, 155, 166, 168–169, 179–182, 203, 207–208, 210, 221, 228–229,

231–232, 236, 239, 241–242, 247, 254–261, 407

Filiation or Sonship, 105, 118, 120, 168–169, 221, 228, 236–237, 239, 242, 258

Final Cause, 107, 117, 133, 157, 195, 200, 216

First Class of Relations (founded in number or unity), 154, 163

Formal Cause, 117, 145, 157, 195, 219, 234

Formal Distinction, 56–9, 91, 158–159, 173

Formal Effect of a Relation, 112–113, 116, 141

Formal Unity, 42, 130, 152, 163, 167, 228, 231

Foundation of a Relation, 8, 28–32, 112, 123, 125, 128, 130, 152, 159, 163, 206, 232

Future Action, 151, 177–178

General and Particular Relation, 118, 245–254

Generic Similarity, 153, 166, 173

Generic Unity as Founding a Relation, 172–173

Genus and Species, 85, 101, 173

Genus of Relation, 85, 229, 246, 250, 257

Goatstag, 135, 177,

God's relation to creatures, 8, 209–211

God's Knowledge and Love, 215

Goodness, 18, 26, 91, 157, 192–193, 233, 263

Grammar, 41, 43

Gravity, 6768, 70, 88, 95

Greater or lesser, 48, 198, 210, 252

Hypostatic Union, 9697, 146

Identity, 31, 53, 61, 65, 71, 92, 94, 125–126, 143, 145–147, 149, 151–153, 160, 168, 171–172, 183, 195, 198, 212, 227, 255

Imagination, 136–137, 417

Impossible Objects, 136, 174, 177

Incarnation, 77
Infinity, 143, 145
Inherence, 53–56, 89, 98, 212
Intellect and the Intelligible, 151, 161
Intelligible Species, 183
Intension and/or Remission, 153, 171–172, 256, 264
Intrinsic Denomination, 60, 175

Knowable, 4344, 95, 100, 102, 112, 130, 133, 135, 151, 155, 158, 185–187, 189, 191–193, 198–199, 201–206, 215, 222–225, 233, 265
Knower, 21, 26, 95, 111, 191
Knowledge (or Science), 13, 21, 24, 32, 39, 43–44, 91–93, 95, 99–103, 109, 111, 130, 133, 135–136, 151, 155–156, 158, 160, 185–187, 189, 191–192, 198–199, 201–208, 215, 220–221, 223–225, 227–228, 233, 237–240, 255, 265
Knowledge and the Knowable, 43–44, 100, 130, 135, 151, 185–187, 189, 191, 193, 198–199, 201–206, 215, 223–225, 233, 265
Knowledge of Vision, 207

Last Six Categories, 7, 21–22, 24–25, 44, 74, 99
Light, 12, 24–26, 67, 164, 199
Likeness, 52, 55–56, 62–65, 72, 75, 81–83, 91, 94, 143, 145–146, 167, 171, 174, 195, 200
Lord, 42, 77, 209, 215, 236–238
Love, 91, 93, 156–157, 166, 191–193, 215, 227
Lovable, 156157, 191–193

Master and Slave, 252
Maternity, 2728, 236, 239
Material Cause, 117, 128, 157, 195, 253, 259
Matter and Form, 87, 128, 146, 240
Measurable, 102, 130, 151, 159, 185–189

Measure, 8, 21, 27, 31, 81, 102, 151, 156–157, 159–160, 185–190, 192–194, 200, 206, 227, 250–251
Measuring, 156
Middle Distinction, 58
Modal Distinction, 53–54, 57–61, 145, 212, 417
Mode, 28, 49, 55–59, 62–65, 69, 71, 73, 75–77, 82–83, 87–88, 90, 93, 95, 97–99, 104–105, 115, 117, 120, 125, 127–129, 138, 141, 145–146, 155, 160, 164, 172, 174–175, 179, 188–189, 192, 194, 201, 204, 209, 211–212, 215, 227, 237, 239, 242–243, 254–255, 260, 263, 265
More or Less, 32, 263–264
Mother, 5, 28, 32, 181, 236, 257–260
Motion, 19–20, 25, 67–68, 96–97, 141, 165, 169, 171, 204
Mutual and non–Mutual Relations, 32, 54, 56, 77, 119, 166, 192, 197, 200–201, 216, 220, 222–223, 228–235, 238–239, 243, 251–252

Nearness, 48, 55, 157, 195–196
Negative Unity, 152
Nominalists, 31, 61, 73, 200, 209
Number, 8, 17, 77, 103, 149, 152, 154, 160, 163, 172–175, 181, 194, 197–198, 208, 253–255, 258, 260

Objects, existing and non existing, 91–92
Objective Being, 93, 412
Objective Termination, 194
One Relation founded upon another, 31
Operative Habits, 88
Order of Doctrine, 39
Order of the Universe, 48
Order to a Terminus, 253
Ordinable, 233

Passion, 21–22, 24–25, 44, 68, 74, 76, 93, 96–97, 182–183, 204, 251
Past Action, 150, 155, 178–181
Paternity, 27, 31, 48, 91, 97, 105, 112, 114–116, 118, 121, 129–130, 158,

166–170, 178–181, 228, 232, 236, 241, 243, 254–255, 258, 261
Patient, 93, 156, 182–183, 204
Potency and Act, 92, 128, 161, 199, 240, 256
Potency and Habit, 184, 201
Power, 207
Predestination, 207
Privation, 91, 152, 177–178, 181, 217
Providence, 207
Process to Infinity, 94, 143, 146, 165, 167, 170–171, 173, 212
Productive and Producible, 133
Properties of Relatives, 263
Proximate Foundation of a Relation, 112, 125

Quantity, continuous and discrete, 172, 175

Real and Rational Relation, 29,
Real Relations, 7, 24, 27–29, 31, 45–49, 76, 80–81, 83, 103, 110, 135, 143–144, 150, 153, 158, 166, 174, 188–189, 191, 203, 205, 209–212, 243, 251
Real Distinction, 11, 21, 30, 51–54, 57–59, 76–77, 91, 143–145, 163, 166, 200, 255–256, 416
Reason of Founding, 30, 128–131, 152, 155, 168, 178, 182, 195, 197, 201, 206, 216, 231, 242, 251
Relation as Least in Being or Entity, 39
Relations as Principles of Acting, 99, 156, 199, 204
Relations founded in Multitude, Distinction, or Diversity, 149, 152, 158, 163, 174, 251
Relations in God, 8, 27, 31, 166, 207–209
Relations of Reason, 21, 40, 72, 76, 80–81, 83, 108–110, 134, 155, 158, 163, 188, 204, 209–210, 227
Relative "according to being", 44, 85–86
Relative Denomination, 41, 53, 65–66, 73, 75, 77, 138, 171, 176, 179, 184, 186

Relative "according to being said," 44, 85–86
Relatives as distinguished from Relations, 118
Remote Subject of a Relation, 115, 120,
Resultance, 64, 66–67, 69–70, 105, 117, 239
Right and Left, 200, 216–217

Science, 100, 102, 130, 133, 167, 187
Second Class of Relations (founded in action and passion), 31, 177, 182, 187, 194, 196, 206
Semiotic, 80
Sense and Sensible, 198
Separability of a Relation, 52, 75
Sight and the Seeable, 151, 188
Similarity, 31, 52, 65, 73–74, 111–112, 118, 120, 125–126, 128, 130, 149, 152–153, 158, 160, 164, 166, 170–173, 183, 187, 194, 198, 228–229, 231, 233, 250, 258–259, 264
Simultaneity in Definition, 32, 220–221, 240
Simultaneity in Nature, 32, 220, 233–234
Simultaneity in Knowledge, 32, 220, 237–240
Son, 12, 32, 48, 96, 111, 115–116, 118, 121, 129, 145, 151, 155, 166, 168–169, 179, 181, 203, 221, 232, 236, 241–242, 247, 254–260
Species, 11, 43, 79, 85, 88, 96, 101–102, 117, 125, 130, 139, 149–150, 152–154, 157, 159–160, 170–173, 181, 183, 185, 188, 203, 214, 216, 243, 245, 247, 250, 252–253, 255, 257–258, 260, 271, 289, 304, 313, 331–332, 335, 337, 339, 346, 355, 393, 397, 399, 402
Species Intelligibilis, 183
Specific Similarity, 153, 173,
Spiration, 166, 242, 261
Subject Matter, 11, 192, 228
Subject of a Relation, 30, 118, 121, 123
Subordinated Subjects of a Relation, 120

Subsisting Relations, 63, 241
Substance, 11, 20–24, 29–30, 40, 43,
    47–48, 51, 56, 67, 87, 90, 94, 120,
    123–128, 149, 153, 164, 171, 179,
    200, 207, 210–212, 214, 228, 259
Supposit, 120–121, 145, 179
Summa totius logicae Aristotelis, 62, 73

Terminology of Relation, 7, 33, 55
Terminus of a Relation, 8, 140, 144,
    150, 199, 206, 219, 249–250
Third Class of Relations (between the
    measurable and the measure), 31,
    186–187, 206
Touching, 56, 96, 191
"Toward Something," 8, 19, 29, 32 33,
    39, 41, 43–44, 46, 57–58, 62–63,
    65, 71, 79–81, 83–89, 93, 100–104,
    107–109, 111, 134, 149, 151, 158–
    159, 164, 177, 182, 186–188, 198,
    202, 205, 220, 245–249, 251–252,
    255
Trinity, 7, 27 28, 47, 111, 261
Truth, measure of, 81, 102, 156, 192–
    193

Union, 55–56, 77, 93, 96–98, 112,
    128–129, 137, 146–147, 157, 194–
    195, 200, 256, 415
Unity of a Composite, 174, 195,
    256–257
Univocity and Relations, 79–83, 250

Whiteness, 24, 52, 62, 64–65, 74–75,
    91, 94, 112–113, 115, 120, 125,
    130, 133, 143, 146, 153–154, 172,
    198, 228, 231
Will and Beings of Reason, 137

Mediæval Philosophical Texts in Translation
Complete List
Under the Editorship of Gerard Smith, S.J.

Grosseteste: *On Light.* Clare Riedl, Tr. ISBN 0-87462-201-8 (Translation No. 1, 1942). 28 pp. $5.

St. Augustine: *Against the Academicians.* Mary Patricia Garvey, R.S.M., Tr. ISBN 0-87462-202-6. (Translation No. 2, 1942). 94 pp. $10

Pico Della Mirandola: *Of Being and Unity.* Victor M. Hamm, Tr. ISBN 0-87462-203-4. (Translation No. 3, 1943). 40 pp. $10

Francis Suarez: *On the Various Kinds of Distinctions.* Cyril Vollert, S.J., Tr. ISBN 0-87462-204-2. (Translation No. 4, 1947). 72 pp. $10

St. Thomas Aquinas: *On Spiritual Creatures.* Mary C. Fitzpatrick, Tr. ISBN 0-87462-205-0. (Translation No. 5, 1949). 144 pp. $15

Guigo: *Meditations of Guigo.* John J. Jolin, S.J., Tr. ISBN 0-87462-206-9. (Translation No. 6, 1951). 96 pp. $10

Giles of Rome: *Theorems on Existence and Essence.* Michael V. Murray, S.J., Tr. ISBN 0-87462-207-7. (Translation No. 7, 1953). 128 pp. $15

John of St. Thomas: *Outlines of Formal Logic.* Francis C. Wade, S.J., Tr. ISBN 0-87462-208-5. (Translation No. 8, 1955). 144 pp. $15

Hugh of St. Victor: *Soliloquy in the Earnest Money of the Soul.* Kevin Herbert, Tr. ISBN 0-87462-209-3. (Translation No. 9, 1956). 48 pp. $5

Under the Editorship of James H. Robb

St. Thomas Aquinas: *On Charity.* Lottie Kendzierski, Tr. ISBN 0-87462-210-7. (Translation No. 10, 1960). 120 pp. $15

Aristotle: *On Interpretation: Commentary by St. Thomas and Cajetan.* Jean T. Oesterle, Tr. ISBN 0-87462-211-5. (Translation No. 11, 1962). 288 pp. $20

Desiderius Erasmus of Rotterdam: *On Copia of Words and Ideas.* Donald B. King and H. David Rix, Tr. ISBN 0-87462-212-3. (Translation No. 12, 1963). 124 pp. $15

Peter of Spain: *Tractatus Syncategorematum and Selected Anonymous Treatises.* Joseph P. Mullally and Roland Houde, Tr. ISBN 0-87462-213-1. (Translation No. 13, 1964). 168 pp. $15

Cajetan: *Commentary on St. Thomas Aquinas' On Being and Essence.* Lottie Kendzierski and Francis C. Wade, S.J., Tr. ISBN 0-87462-214-X. (Translation No. 14, 1965). 366 pp. $20

Suárez: *Disputation VI, On Formal and Universal Unity.* James F. Ross, Tr. ISBN 0-87462-215-8. (Translation. No. 15, 1965). 132 pp. $15

St. Thomas, Siger de Brabant, St. Bonaventure: *On the Eternity of the World.* Cyril Vollert, S.J., Lottie Kendzierski, and Paul Byrne, Tr. ISBN 0-87462-216-6. (Translation No. 16, 1965). 132 pp. $15

Geoffrey of Vinsauf: *Instruction in the Method and Art of Speaking and Versifying.* Roger P. Parr, Tr. ISBN 0-87462-217-4. (Translation No. 17, 1968). 128 pp. $15

Liber De Pomo: *The Apple, or Aristotle's Death.* Mary F. Rousseau, Tr. ISBN 0-87462-218-2. (Translation No. 18, 1968). 96 pp. $5

St. Thomas Aquinas: *On the Unity of the Intellect against the Averroists.* Beatrice H. Zedler, Tr. ISBN 0-87462-219-0. (Translation No. 19, 1969). 96 pp. $10

Nicholas of Autrecourt. *The Universal Treatise.* Leonard L. Kennedy, C.S.B., Tr. ISBN 0-87462-220-4. (Translation No. 20, 1971). 174 pp. $15

Pseudo-Dionysius Areopagite: *The Divine Names and Mystical Theology.* John D. Jones, Tr. ISBN 0-87462-221-2. (Translation No. 21, 1980). 320 pp. $25

Matthew of Vendome: *Ars Versificatoria.* Roger P. Parr, Tr. ISBN 0-87462-222-0. (Translation No. 22, 1981). 150 pp. $15

Francis Suárez. *On Individuation.* Jorge J.E. Gracia, Tr. ISBN 0-87462-223-9. (Translation No. 23, 1982). 304 pp. $35

Francis Suárez: *On the Essence of Finite Being as Such, on the Existence of That Essence and Their Distinction.* Norman J. Wells, Tr. ISBN 0-87462-224-7. (Translation No. 24, 1983). 248 pp. $20

The Book of Causes (Liber De Causis). Dennis J. Brand, Tr. ISBN 0-87462-225-5. (Translation No. 25, 1984). 56 pp. $5

Giles of Rome: *Errores Philosophorum.* John O. Riedl, Tr. Intro. by Josef Koch. ISBN 0-87462-429-0. (Translation No. 26, 1944). 136 pp. $10

St. Thomas Aquinas: *Questions on the Soul.* James H. Robb, Tr. ISBN 0-87462-226-3. (Translation No. 27, 1984). 285 pp. $25

Under the Editorship of Richard C. Taylor

William of Auvergne. *The Trinity.* Roland J. Teske, S.J. and Francis C. Wade, S.J. ISBN 0-87462-231-X (Translation No. 28, 1989) 286 pp. $20

Under the Editorship of Roland J. Teske, S.J.

Hugh of St. Victor. *Practical Geometry.* Frederick A. Homann, S.J., Tr. ISBN 0-87462-232-8 (Translation No. 29, 1991) 92 pp. $10

William of Auvergne. *The Immortality of the Soul.* Roland J. Teske, S.J., Tr. ISBN 0-87462-233-6 (Translation No. 30, 1992) 72 pp. $10

Dietrich of Freiberg. *Treatise of the Intellect and the Intelligible.* M. L. Führer, Tr. ISBN 0-87462-234-4 (Translation No. 31, 1992) 135 pp. $15

Henry of Ghent. *Quodlibetal Questions on Free Will.* Roland J. Teske, S.J., Tr. ISBN 0-87462-234-4 (Translation No. 32, 1993) 135 pp. $15

Francisco Suárez, S.J. *On Beings of Reason. Metaphysical Disputation LIV.* John P. Doyle, Tr. ISBN 0-87462-236-0 (Translation No. 33, 1995) 170 pp. $20

Francisco De Vitoria, O.P. *On Homicide,* and *Commentary on Thomas Aquinas: Summa theologiae IIaIIae, 64.* Edited and Translated by John Doyle. ISBN 0-87462-237-9. (Translation No. 34, 1997) 280 pp. $30

William of Auvergne. *The Universe of Creatures.* Edited, Translated, and with an Introduction by Roland J. Teske, S.J. ISBN 0-87462-238-7 (Translation No. 35, 1998) 235 pp. $25

Francis Suarez, S.J. *On the Formal Cause of Substance. Metaphysical Disputation XV.* Translated by John Kronen & Jeremiah Reedy. Introduction & Explanatory Notes by John Kronen. ISBN 0-87462-239-5 (Translation No. 36, 2000) 218 pp. $25

William of Auvergne. *The Soul.* Translated from the Latin with an Introduction and Notes by Roland J. Teske, S.J. ISBN 0-87462-240-9 (Translation No. 37, 2000) 516 pp. $50

The Conimbricenses: Some Questions on Signs. Translated with Introduction and Notes by John P. Doyle.ISBN 0-87462-241-7 (Translation No. 38, 2001) 217 pp. $25

Dominicus Gundissalinus.*The Procession of the World (De processione mundi).* Translated from the Latin with an Introduction & Notes by John A. Laumakis. ISBN 0-87462-242-5 (Translation No. 39, 2002) 87 pp. $10

Francisco Suárez. *A Commentary on Aristotle's Metaphysics or "A Most Ample Index to the Metaphysics of Aristotle" (Index locupletissimus in Metaphysicam Aristotelis).* Translated with an Introduction & Notes by John P. Doyle. ISBN 0-87462-243-3 (Translation No. 40, 2003) 430 pp. $45

Henry of Ghent. *Quodlibetal Question on Moral Problems.* Translated from the Latin with an Introduction and Notes by Roland J. Teske, S.J. ISBN 0-87462-244-1 (Translation No. 41, 2005) 82 pp. $10

Francisco Suárez. *On Real Relation (Disputatio Metaphysica XLVII)* A Translation from the Latin, with an Introduction and Notes by John P. Doyle. ISBN-13: 978-0-87462-244-1. ISBN-10: 0-87462-244-1 (Translation No. 42, 2006) 430 pp. $45

Mediæval Philosophical Texts in Translation
Roland J. Teske, S.J., Editor

This series originated at Marquette University in 1942, and with revived interest in Mediæval studies is read internationally with steadily increasing popularity. Available in attractive, durable, colored soft covers. Volumes priced from $5 to $50 each. Complete Set [0-87462-200-X] receives a 40% discount. John Riedl's *A Catalogue of Renaissance Philosophers*, hardbound with red cloth, is an ideal reference companion title (sent free with purchase of complete set). New standing orders receive a 20% discount and a free copy of the Riedl volume. Regular reprinting keeps all volumes available. Recent volumes are also available as ebooks.

Order online from our web page: http://www.marquette.edu/mupress/
Order by phone from:
Marquette University Press
30 Amberwood Parkway
Ashland OH 44805
  Tel. 800-247-6553 Fax: 419-281-6883

Editorial Address for **Mediæval Philosophical Texts in Translation**:
Roland J. Teske, S.J., Editor MPTT
Department of Philosophy
Marquette University
Box 1881
Milwaukee WI 53201-1881

Marquette University Press office:
Marquette University Press
Dr. Andrew Tallon, Director
Box 3141
Milwaukee WI 53201-1881
  Tel: (414) 288-1564 FAX: (414) 288-7813
    email: andrew.tallon@marquette.edu.

http://www.marquette.edu/mupress/